M000231534

INSIDERS' GUIDE® TO

WASHINGTON, D.C.

SEVENTH EDITION

**MARY JANE SOLOMON AND BARBARA RUBEN
REVISED BY REBECCA ALOISI**

INSIDERS' GUIDE®

GUILFORD, CONNECTICUT
AN IMPRINT OF THE GLOBE PEQUOT PRESS

The prices and rates in this guidebook were confirmed at press time. We recommend, however, that you call establishments before traveling to obtain current information.

INSIDERS' GUIDE®

Text design by Nancy Freeborn
Maps by XNR Productions Inc. © Morris Book Publishing, LLC

Metro System map courtesy of the Washington Metropolitan Area Transit Authority

ISSN: 1538-8174
ISBN: 978-0-7627-4410-7

Manufactured in the United States of America
Seventh Edition/First Printing

CONTENTS

Preface ix

Acknowledgments xi

How to Use This Book 1

Metro Washington Overview 3

History 20

Getting around the Metro Area 31

Accommodations 50

Restaurants 76

Nightlife 122

Shopping 140

Annual Events 167

Attractions 189

The Arts 221

Kidstuff 249

Spectator Sports 276

Parks and Recreation 289

Day Trips and Weekend Getaways 317

International Washington 342

Relocation 352

Child Care 368

Health Care 375

Education 394

Senior Scene 417

Worship 432

Media 441

Index 455

About the Authors 482

CONTENTS

Directory of Maps

Washington, D.C. and Surrounding Counties v

Metro Washington, D.C. vi

The Mall and Vicinity vii

Metro System viii

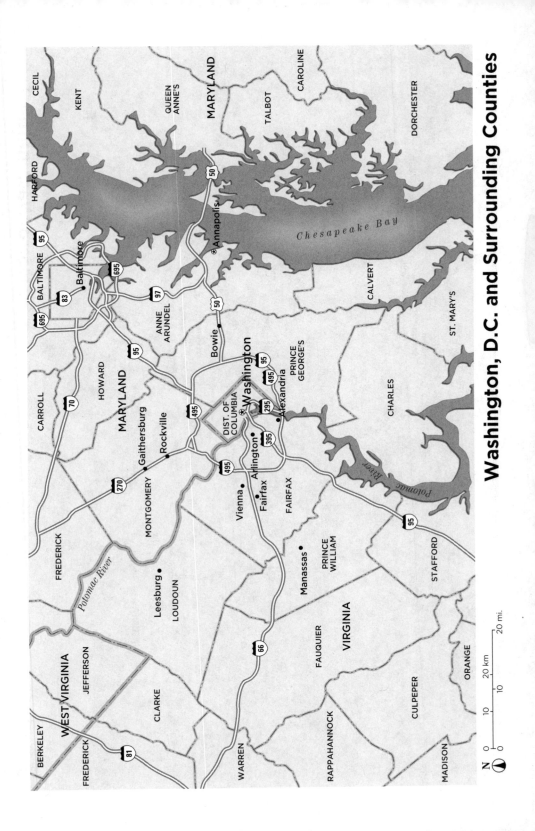

Washington, D.C. and Surrounding Counties

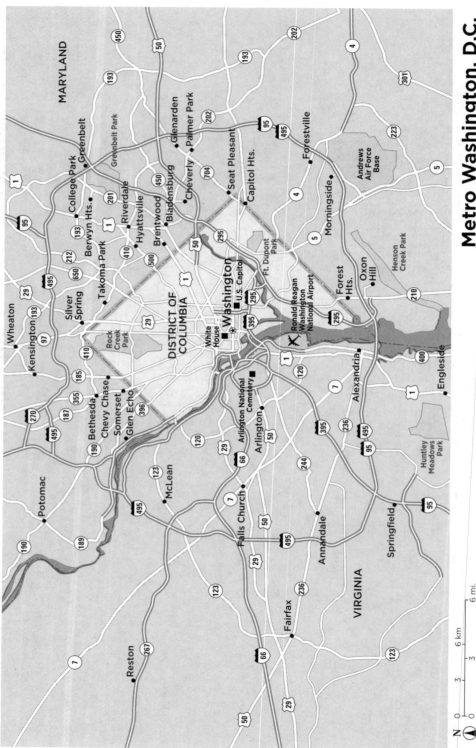

Metro Washington, D.C.

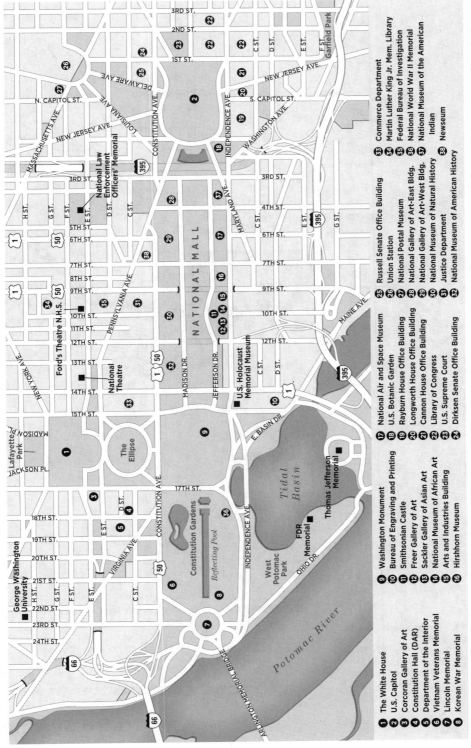

The Mall and Vicinity

1. The White House
2. U.S. Capitol
3. Corcoran Gallery of Art
4. Constitution Hall (DAR)
5. Department of the Interior
6. Vietnam Veterans Memorial
7. Lincoln Memorial
8. Korean War Memorial
9. Washington Monument
10. Bureau of Engraving and Printing
11. Smithsonian Castle
12. Freer Gallery of Art
13. Sackler Gallery of Asian Art
14. National Museum of African Art
15. Arts and Industries Building
16. Hirshhorn Museum
17. National Air and Space Museum
18. U.S. Botanic Garden
19. Rayburn House Office Building
20. Longworth House Office Building
21. Cannon House Office Building
22. Library of Congress
23. U.S. Supreme Court
24. Dirksen Senate Office Building
25. Russell Senate Office Building
26. Union Station
27. National Postal Museum
28. National Gallery of Art–East Bldg.
29. National Gallery of Art–West Bldg.
30. National Museum of Natural History
31. Justice Department
32. National Museum of American History
33. Commerce Department
34. Martin Luther King Jr. Mem. Library
35. Federal Bureau of Investigation
36. National World War II Memorial
37. National Museum of the American Indian
38. Newseum

N

0   0.25   0.5 km

0   0.25   0.5 mi.

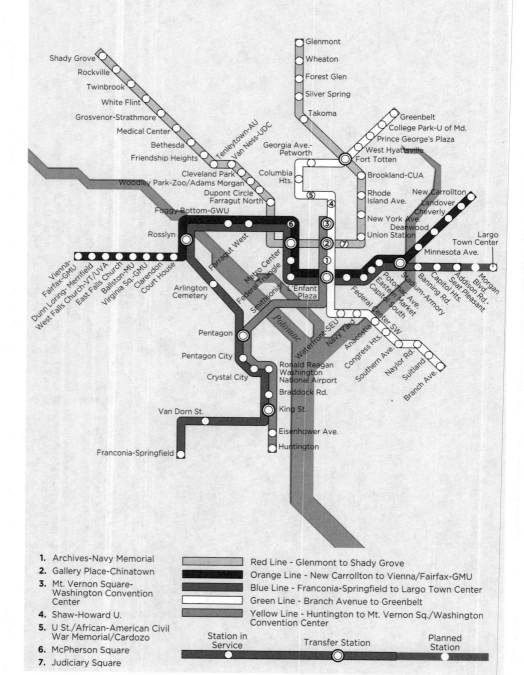

Metro System

1. Archives-Navy Memorial
2. Gallery Place-Chinatown
3. Mt. Vernon Square-Washington Convention Center
4. Shaw-Howard U.
5. U St./African-American Civil War Memorial/Cardozo
6. McPherson Square
7. Judiciary Square

Red Line - Glenmont to Shady Grove
Orange Line - New Carrollton to Vienna/Fairfax-GMU
Blue Line - Franconia-Springfield to Largo Town Center
Green Line - Branch Avenue to Greenbelt
Yellow Line - Huntington to Mt. Vernon Sq./Washington Convention Center

Station in Service   Transfer Station   Planned Station

N

PREFACE

Setting about the task of writing *Insiders' Guide to Washington, D.C.* is every bit as daunting as it is exciting. Perhaps no other region in the country is as diverse, dynamic, intriguing and, for that matter, misunderstood as the Nation's Capital.

All of us, no doubt, have strong perceptions of Washington. It is, after all, a city that lives and breathes under an international microscope. The idealist in us views Washington as a great shrine to the American heritage, a beacon reinforcing the beliefs in freedom and democracy for all nations. We are awed by the inspiring landmarks, monuments, and memorials; the broad avenues; sprawling parks; world-class museums and galleries; and stately embassies. The cynic in us, however, takes another view, one that frames the Nation's Capital as a maze of long-standing problems, and new ones brought in the wake of the September 11, 2001 terrorist attacks. Beyond terrorism's impact, we are dismayed by the contrast between downtown's new prosperity and the sight of homeless people sleeping on steam grates and park benches. Horrific traffic on the Beltway and elsewhere is the second worst in the nation, just after Los Angeles.

In fact Washington must claim these realities, but those of us who are troubled by all of this will be heartened to know that problems are being addressed. Perhaps this is why a new optimism has taken hold in Washington. Under former mayor Anthony A. Williams, the city enjoyed an economic turnaround, witnessing a boom of development, particularly in its downtown district.

In the last decade or so, we all have come to view Washington in a dramatically new light. This once largely one-dimensional government town has blossomed into a premier national and global business center; it is in Washington where the rules are made for the complex game of international trade and commerce. The decision-makers are here. The information is here. The communication channels are here. It might surprise you to learn that only about 11 percent of the area's residents are employed by the federal government. The rest have jobs in Washington's burgeoning service industries, including tourism, and in law, banking, medical research, telecommunications, publishing, and higher education. Indeed, these factors might be why you are, or are soon to be, headed here.

And you're not alone.

Metro Washington's population now stands at some 6 million, an increase of nearly 750,000 since 1990, and its annual visitor count tops 15 million.

Despite the area's growth, Washington doesn't have the sprawling metropolitan feel of other large cities. There are no skyscrapers, the streets are clean, and flowers and trees abound. The city is alive with outdoor cafes, colorful neighborhoods, and inviting parks. Visitors are more likely to compare it to Paris than New York.

The neighborhood feeling isn't limited to just the 63-square-mile stretch of federal land bounded by the Potomac River, Virginia, and Maryland. "Washington" has come to mean much of Northern Virginia, including Fairfax, Arlington, Loudoun, and Prince William Counties as well as the city of Alexandria. "Washington" also is the fast-growing Suburban Maryland counties of Prince George's, Montgomery, and Anne Arundel. Residents of each area can be fervent advocates of their own stomping grounds, but what holds the vast array together is the District of Columbia.

For practical purposes, this book concentrates primarily on the District and the aforementioned core counties of Northern Virginia and Suburban Maryland. They encompass what we view as Metro Washington, D.C., or the Nation's Capital.

In the pages that follow, you will find what we hope is a fresh, insightful, and comprehensive guide to our region. It is our goal that *Insiders' Guide to Washington, D.C.*, proves to be an invaluable source for newcomers, as it sketches the nuts and bolts of touring the area or even relocating here.

ACKNOWLEDGMENTS

I'm delighted to collaborate on another edition with longtime friend Barbara Ruben, whose skills, dedication, and good humor prove invaluable.

Thanks to all the folks who promptly and cheerfully provided facts and photographs for this update. Laura Bergheim's The *Washington Historical Atlas: Who Did What When* and *Where in the Nation's Capital* and Suzanne Hilton's *A Capital Capital City, 1790–1814* served as helpful and entertaining references regarding Washington history.

As always, special thanks to my English teachers and professors, without whom I wouldn't have a career; and to the many editors—especially those at *Weekend* and *Northern Virginia Parent*—whose great assignments contribute to my "Insider's" knowledge.

I'm blessed with wonderful friends and relatives who provide unlimited encouragement and support, not to mention lots of wonderful ideas. You know who you are. Thank you, all!

Finally, I'm eternally grateful to my loving, understanding family for putting up with wacky hours, overlapping deadlines, and unwashed dishes and laundry. My heartfelt thanks especially go to Donald and Johanna Hoak; Sheldon and Sharon Solomon; Susan Hoak and Terry Layne; Jeff, Rachael, Julianna, and Adam Solomon; and, most of all, my treasures, Steve, Rachel, Anna, and Macaroon.

—Mary Jane Solomon

My thanks go to my co-author, friend, and long-ago college roommate Mary Jane Solomon for her invaluable assistance in updating this book. I'm also indebted to the many helpful organizations that offered information and photos, including the Washington, D.C. Convention and Tourism Corporation, the Greater Washington Board of Trade, the Metropolitan Washington Council of Governments, Metropolitan Regional Information Systems, and the U.S. Census Bureau. The tireless efforts of Google were also indispensable in researching this book.

Thanks also to my seven-year-old daughter Sarah, adventuress extraordinaire, for her unbridled enthusiasm for visiting sites in this book and her patience during my umpteen phone calls.

—Barbara Ruben

Capitol Hill, the city's largest residential district, features abundant rowhouses of varying architectural styles.

HOW TO USE THIS BOOK ?

Whether you're visiting the Nation's Capital for a business trip or family vacation, relocating to the Washington Metro area, or just looking for new ways to spend your leisure time, you'll find something of interest in this book. As longtime local residents, the authors are well acquainted with the area, from its awe-inspiring landmarks to its diverse educational and cultural opportunities. We know firsthand the joy of hearing the National Symphony perform at the Kennedy Center, and the frustration of almost being late for the concert because of a Beltway traffic tie-up! We relish dining at Bethesda's intriguing restaurants—when we're not gazing at Monets and Whistlers at the National Gallery of Art or bagging bargains at Potomac Mills.

We've designed this book as a portable, accessible guide to Washington, D.C. and its surrounding suburbs: Northern Virginia and Suburban Maryland. The paperback is small enough to stuff in a suitcase or backpack, yet detailed enough to give you an overview of this vast region's best cultural, historical, and recreational attractions, as well as tips on how to get around and where to dine and sleep. If you're planning to stay awhile, check out the chapters on relocation, education, retirement, child care, and health care. We also describe a variety of weekend getaways, ideal for travelers extending their vacations or residents in need of quick escapes.

In most chapters you'll find information organized in a listing format under the three regional headers. Northern Virginia listings encompass the cities of Alexandria and Fairfax and the counties of Arlington, Fairfax, Loudoun, and Prince William. Suburban Maryland includes Montgomery and Prince George's Counties, as well as occasional notable attractions in nearby Anne Arundel and Howard Counties.

Wherever possible, we include an address, phone number, and Web address followed by a description of the attraction, event, or organization, often including fees and hours of operation. We also list Web sites for many popular attractions. For restaurants, accommodations, bed-and-breakfasts, country inns, and attractions we include a price code with each listing. Check the price-code keys for explanations. Please be aware that prices and hours are subject to change. You'll find some attractions mentioned in more than one chapter, and cross-referenced accordingly. For instance, we describe Smithsonian Institution museums in Attractions, but detail their family programs in Kidstuff and highlight their collections of paintings and sculpture in The Arts.

Throughout the book, you'll also find Insiders' tips—look for the ℹ—that let you in on local secrets. We've also included occasional Close-ups, informative profiles of special events and attractions.

We hope you'll find this guide to be a handy reference book. We also appreciate hearing from our readers. Tell us what you find helpful and let us know if something is missing. We update the book regularly and find your comments invaluable.

The Capitol Dome symbolizes Washington, D.C. to many people. COURTESY WASHINGTON, D.C. CONVENTION AND TOURISM CORPORATION

METRO WASHINGTON OVERVIEW

Like the elected officials that come and go, Washington is in perpetual transition. It's a markedly different creature today than it was just 10 years ago—let alone in 1800, the year it became the Nation's Capital. It is fitting that Washington's growing pains reflect America's. It was almost destroyed in the War of 1812, and in the Civil War it reflected the nation's hotly divided sentiments. It celebrated the arrival of the Second Industrial Revolution and the success of the great barons who transformed the nation's economic landscape. It teemed with energy and a sense of sacrifice during World Wars I and II. It grew wary and then outright divided over the Korean and Vietnam Wars. It became cynical in the wake of Watergate; hopeful, then pessimistic during the Carter years; and a bit overconfident during the Reagan/Bush tenure. Clinton found himself right at home for eight years in the heavily Democratic region, while George W. Bush's two terms have been plagued with divisive issues of national security.

The downtown area and many of the surrounding suburbs are in the midst of a building boom, even a cultural renaissance. Trendsetting restaurants and designer boutiques, which in past years eschewed Washington as too stodgy, now compete for hot metro area locations.

To really understand where the District and its surrounding suburbs are today and where they're headed in the twenty-first century, it's helpful to go back a few decades, to at least the beginning of the post–World War II years. As the 1940s gave way to the '50s, Washington's population soared. In the nearby countryside of Maryland and Virginia, forests of oak and pastures of bluegrass yielded to subdivisions and shopping centers. Business was booming. The future looked bright. As the federal government continued to grow dramatically during the '60s, so did the physical size (and, some may say, the ego) of the region.

Then came a bombshell, a watershed event that changed the face of Washington and impacted the entire country: the 1968 assassination of the Rev. Martin Luther King Jr. Parts of Washington erupted into a riot zone. Many residents who could afford to do so fled to suburban enclaves. The city became a ghost town by night. The suburbs ballooned farther out, and the resulting polarization was both psychological and physical. On the one hand were the commuters, a daily influx who increased traffic problems exponentially but paid no taxes that might have helped the D.C. infrastructure meet new demands placed on it. Remaining in Washington were the riot survivors, who lived in burned-out neighborhoods a few blocks from the White House. Amidst the downtown chaos were pockets of extreme affluence: Georgetown, Foxhall Road, Embassy Row. The lines of demarcation were clear and rarely crossed.

The Vietnam War and the Watergate era, culminating in President Richard Nixon's resignation in 1973, only added to the divisiveness in Washington. But those events also indirectly revitalized D.C. because they brought about a new era of grassroots activism. The activism resulted in closer interaction between government and industry as consumer advocates and environmental groups demanded that Washington investigate and regulate U.S. business. No large company or industry in America could afford to be without a presence in the Nation's Capital. Some opened government relations offices, some funded industry coalitions, and some even moved their companies' headquarters to the area. Big government started to get

Washington, D.C.'s Vital Statistics

Founded: The city received its charter in 1802; it entered the union as a municipal corporation in 1871.

Mayor: Adrian M. Fenty

Maryland governor: Martin O'Malley

Virginia governor: Timothy M. Kaine

Population: Washington, D.C.: 572,000; Washington, D.C. metropolitan statistical area: 5.4 million

Area: Washington, D.C.: 67 square miles. Highest elevation is 420 feet.

Counties and cities in the Washington, D.C. Metropolitan Area:
Maryland counties: Anne Arundel, Calvert, Charles, Frederick, Howard, Montgomery, Prince George's
Virginia cities: Alexandria, Fairfax, Falls Church, Manassas, Manassas Park, Vienna
Virginia counties: Arlington, Fairfax, Loudoun, Prince William, Stafford

Time zone: Eastern Standard Time

Washington, D.C. motto: *Justitia omnibus* (Justice to all)

Bird: Wood thrush

Tree: Scarlet oak

Flower: American beauty rose

Major airports: Baltimore-Washington International Thurgood Marshall Airport, Ronald Reagan Washington National Airport, Washington Dulles International Airport

Major roadways: Interstates 66, 95, 395, 495 (the Beltway), and 270

Average temperatures: Winter: High 45°F, Low 30°F
Summer: High 85°F, Low 67°F

Average annual precipitation: 34.8 inches

Major colleges and universities: American University, George Mason University (Virginia), George Washington University, Georgetown University, Howard University, University of Maryland

Major area employers: AES, Amtrak, AOL, AT&T, Capital One Financial, COMSAT, Corporate Executive Board, Exxon Mobil, Fannie Mae, Federal Government, Freddie Mac, Gannett Corporation, General Dynamics, Lockheed Martin, Marriott International Corporation, Maximus Inc., Med Immune, Inc., Sprint-NEXTEL Communications Inc.

Famous sons and daughters: Edward Albee, Warren Beatty, Carl Bernstein, Sandra Bullock, Connie Chung, Dominique Dawes, Frederick Douglass, Duke Ellington, Mia Hamm, Goldie Hawn, Helen Hayes, Grant Hill, J. Edgar Hoover, Samuel L. Jackson, Shirley MacLaine, Maury Povich, Leonard Rose, Pete Sampras, John Philip Sousa, Ben Stein

Public transportation: Washington Metropolitan Area Transit Authority (Metro) operates a Metrorail subway system and bus system.

Military bases: Andrews Air Force Base, Bolling Air Force Base, Davison Army Airfield, Fort Belvoir

Driving laws: Speed limits in residential and business areas throughout the metropolitan region range from 25 to 45 mph; the speed limit on most interstate highways is 55 mph.

Alcohol laws:
- You must be 21 to purchase or consume alcoholic beverages legally.
- Legally, you are presumed to be intoxicated if your blood alcohol concentration is .08%.
- Bars can serve alcohol until 2 A.M. (3 A.M. on Friday and Saturday in D.C.)

Daily newspapers: *Washington Post, Washington Times*

Sales taxes:
District of Columbia: 5.75%; hotel tax is 14.5%; food and beverage tax is 10%
Maryland: 5%; hotel tax is 5 to 8%
Virginia: 4.5%; hotel tax is 9.5 to 10%

Chamber of Commerce: D.C. Chamber of Commerce Visitor Information Center, Ronald Reagan Building and International Trade Center, 1300 Pennsylvania Avenue NW, Washington, D.C.; (866) 324–7386; www.dcchamber.org

Time: (202) 844–1212

Weather: (202) 936–1212

strong competition from big business for the Metro D.C. labor force. In reality, each was fueling the growth of the other as business realized that it would have to answer to government. At the same time government experts on industry were a labor pool in high demand by the very companies they oversaw. Many were and are wooed by the private sector, thus the infamous Washington "revolving door."

Today, about 700 foreign-owned firms or affiliates have a foothold here, and a quarter, or nearly 2,500, of the nation's trade and professional associations are headquartered in Metro D.C.

The Washington area claims more than 200 telecommunications and information giants, including America Online, Discovery Communications, and COMSAT. Journalism is big business here as newspapers, wire services, news agencies, and radio and television networks (some of the world's most prominent) call D.C. home, not to mention a complex network of bloggers. Fortune 500 companies as diverse as Exxon Mobil, Gannett, General Dynamics, Marriott, and Lockheed Martin also call the Metro area home.

But Washington's growth hasn't all been an easy, downhill coast. In the mid- to late 1980s, local business development officials used to talk of Washington's "recession-proof" economy. They touted the fact that the federal government's employment and spending base had a stabilizing effect on the economy and that the diversity of business here was too great to allow for any major slowdowns.

Well, things didn't quite turn out that way. Washington, like everywhere else, was hit hard by the recession. Commercial real estate, already dangerously overbuilt, took a beating in the early 1990s, primarily due to unleased existing space and a dramatic slowdown in new development. Defense contractors awoke to a post–Cold War New World Order and an anticipation of scarcer federal outlays. Banks failed. Engineers, architects, technicians, and journalists, among others, were handed pink slips faster than Congress writes checks. Local governments wrestled with fiscal problems. Those accustomed to the prosperity of the '80s were thinking the world was coming to an end.

But in just a few years, the Washington economy grew faster than anyone imagined.

Unemployment dropped to a record low of 2.6 percent in some suburban areas. With booming job growth, especially in the technology sector, record home construction, and a thriving, even frantic, home sales market, no one imagined Washington's economic bubble would burst.

But with job loss already on the rise since late 2000 as technology jobs disappeared, the terrorist attacks in September 2001 fueled the unemployment rate. Although the region's unemployment rate rose to 3.6 percent in the aftermath of the tech bust, the metro area now boasts one of the lowest jobless rates in the country, 3.4 percent. However, more people moved to the region than new jobs were created, thus leading to the drop in overall employment.

Over the last 20 years, the Washington area has led all metro areas in the nation in employment growth, with nearly 1.13 million jobs added between 1983 and 2003. And in the past five years, Greater Washington outperformed all other large metro regions with an increase of nearly 274,100 new jobs.

One factor keeping the unemployment rate from worsening is the enormous amount of money the government has pumped into the region to fight the war on terrorism.

Although the business development people may have blown their recession-proof theory, they were on target as far as the diversity of the economy is concerned. The region's broad mix of industry is one of the great untold economic stories of the past two decades.

Today, private-sector jobs outnumber government jobs practically four to one, with much of the job growth in high-tech and service industries. To be sure, federal employment has remained steady, but now it is only 11 percent of the total workforce compared with 21 percent in 1982. On top of that, even when you factor in the thousands of jobs supplied by local and state governments, the

i In 1800 the federal government had only 131 employees.

private sector still comes out way ahead of the game. All told, businesses employ 78 percent of Metro Washingtonians, while big government employs 21 percent.

So what does this tell us? First, we'd be kidding ourselves to dismiss the economic importance of the government's presence. Nobody spends money like federal Washington, and no one feels the effects of those shopping sprees more than our local economy. The feds spent $128.3 billion in the region in fiscal year 2004, up from $79.2 billion in 2001.

At the same time, Washington's growing stature as a high-tech and international business center has brought the benefit of a more robust and flexible economy.

A culture of entrepreneurship is growing in our region, fueled by the still-strong presence of new telecommunications and Internet-related businesses, especially in the suburbs of Northern Virginia and Maryland. Some 334,000 people work in the high-tech computer science industry, almost as many as in the federal workforce.

All this economic growth has had a revitalizing effect on the region's psyche, even as it strains our roads and school systems—especially in the outer western suburbs. The region grew by more than two million since 1990, with most of the growth happening in the western half of the region. In all, the Washington area's population was 6.02 million in 2005, up by more than 400,000 in five years.

Although the District lost 5.2 percent of its population between 1990 and 2000, outlying counties gained huge numbers of people: Loudoun County's population nearly doubled, while Prince William's grew by 30 percent. Both are projected to nearly double again by 2010.

Unfortunately, this recent growth has deepened the divisions between the "haves" and "have-nots" in the metro area. Increasingly, better-off communities lie west of Interstate 95 in the suburbs and 16th Street in the city (with some exceptions in Prince George's County). So although one half of the area enjoys robust growth, there's not enough growth in large parts of the eastern half, according to a study released by the Brookings Institution.

Racial and ethnic living patterns further divide the area. Sixty-two percent of the region's African Americans live in the District and Prince George's County, leaving the most prosperous western region largely white. A growing Hispanic community is also making its presence felt, comprising nearly 10 percent of the region's population in 2005.

Parallel with the growth in the most affluent parts of the area is the ongoing renewal of downtown D.C.—particularly in the districts bearing our leading attractions and activities.

Practically every block of the District's major historic artery, Pennsylvania Avenue, has been renovated with new plazas, office space, retail areas, theaters, restaurants, and more. The "Avenue of the Presidents," once deserted by night, has again become a thriving thoroughfare, and its renewal has sparked development throughout the rest of downtown. On Capitol Hill, Washington's historic Union Station was painstakingly restored over several years and is now the "grande dame" of all train stations. It houses Amtrak corporate headquarters and serves as their flagship station, with trains arriving and departing from beneath the magnificent, statue-lined roof.

In the District of Columbia, information and power spring not only from business and government but also from global financial institutions such as the World Bank and the International Monetary Fund. Equally vital are the city's 150-plus embassies that provide instant access to commercial and government representatives from nearly every nation.

Washington's transformation from a government- to a private-sector information-driven economy mirrors one of the most pervasive trends in our global society. The international marketplace at the turn of this century is fueled first and foremost by information. Information is power, and Washington is a wellspring of both commodities.

i If you intend to apply for a government job, request in advance the OF-612 form. You'll need to fill it out even if you've already been offered a position.

Chances are, if you're a newcomer to the Nation's Capital, you're part of this new dynamic.

The Washington Workforce

If you're looking for a job in Metro D.C., or even if you've already landed one, it's good to know a few vital statistics about the Washington workforce. Besides, a few provocative figures here and there will go a long way on the Washington cocktail party circuit.

Let's start with the big picture: Some 2.7 million people are employed in the Washington area, with roughly three-quarters working in white-collar jobs. Sounds impressive enough, but wait—it gets even more striking. The region has claimed the largest percentage of executive, administrative, managerial, professional, and technical workers among the nation's largest metropolitan areas. The proportion of scientists, technicians, and Ph.D.s working in Metro D.C. is among the highest in the nation, and nearly one in seven employees works in computer- and telecommunications-related industries. Thirteen percent of all jobs in the District are in the travel and tourism sector.

If you're a woman, you're in good company here. A full 68 percent of working-age women in greater Washington are employed, compared with 60 percent nationally. You'll find 25 of DiversityBusiness.com's Top 500 women-owned businesses in greater Washington.

With three out of five of its residents African American, the District of Columbia has long been the nation's most influential and affluent predominantly black city. Today, the entire region boasts the leading percentage of black executives, administrators, and managers. Little surprise then that the fast-growing cable network, Black Entertainment Television, is headquartered in the District. In recent years

Close-up

Brave New World

There's no question that the tragedies of September 11 had an impact on life inside the Beltway. Like the rest of the country, we struggled to understand the events that transpired and mourned for the loss of life. At the same time, we were forced to acknowledge that living in and around the Capital might make us vulnerable to future acts of terrorism. We cobbled together emergency kits and plotted evacuation strategies with our families. We stocked up on duct tape and plastic sheeting to stave off a biological attack. We learned to navigate roadblocks and street closures and came to expect long security lines at the airport.

For the most part, however, life went on as usual. We've learned to adapt to a new normal. Sure, we now have to walk through magnetometers and submit to bag checks to enter certain buildings (including the Smithsonian museums and the National Gallery of Art). We now see bomb-resistant trash cans in our Metro stations, and we've heard that some stations now have chemical sensors at work.

But most of us resisted the knee-jerk reaction to head for the hills. A survey by the Greater Washington Board of Trade found that only 15 percent of residents found themselves going downtown less often. About 8 percent said they have thought about moving out of the area because of terrorism. The strong job market and thriving cultural scene are now bringing more people to the area.

Life also changed for Washington, D.C. visitors. Ronald Reagan National Airport was shuttered in the immediate aftermath of the attacks. The popular tours of the Capitol and White House were suspended. In late 2001 and 2002, visitors came in smaller numbers. The flailing economy caused many companies to cut back on business travel, and several school districts canceled their spring break pilgrimages to the Nation's Capital due to security concerns. The visitors who did travel during this period had the city largely to themselves—and they took advantage of great hotel bargains. The average daily hotel rate in October 2001 was $149 per night, down from $167 per night in 2000.

The downturn didn't last for long. By 2003 the economy had turned the corner. Visitors were returning in droves and hotel prices were climbing again. The

Washington also has experienced a surge in entrepreneurship among its growing Asian, Hispanic, Middle Eastern, and Indian communities.

Of course, at the root of Washington's white collars is education. The metro area inarguably has the best-educated workforce in the United States. More than 17 percent of the adult population living inside the District holds graduate degrees, ranking Washington first among the states and more than double the national metro average of 8 percent.

Beyond all the grand statistics, however, are some very down-to-earth implications. More and more young people are launching their careers in Metro Washington despite the intensely competitive nature of the labor force, especially for entry-level positions.

Washington Convention Center opened its doors, allowing the city to host larger, high-yielding medical conventions. New attractions like the International Spy Museum, National World War II Memorial, and National Museum of the American Indian opened. By 2004 the average daily hotel rate reached $161 per night, up 10 percent from 2003.

For the most part, the city's tourism industry is booming. The city welcomed 15.4 million visitors in 2005, a slight increase over 2004 numbers. Hotel prices reached an all-time high in 2006, ending the year with an average daily rate of $191, up 7 percent from 2005 and up 31 percent from 2003.

What can visitors expect these days? The city is more vibrant than ever, with a revitalized downtown, a buzzing restaurant scene, and a newfound creative energy that's especially visible in homegrown art galleries, edgy theaters, and ongoing development. First-time visitors may be disappointed, however, to learn that White House tours must be arranged well in advance and that parts of the Capitol are now closed to tour groups. There's more to see than ever—new museums and attractions seem to open every year—but some of the most sought-after tours are not as easy to come by.

Visitors can also expect to pay more for their D.C. experience. As in other major cities, rising costs of gas and operations have driven up prices for hotels, restaurants, and entertainment. Fortunately there's a lot to do in Washington, D.C. that's free of charge (thanks to your tax dollars!), making the city an overall great value. You can also find good deals with a little advance planning. Hotel rates are always lower in the late summer and winter, and you can usually find bargains on the weekend, when lobbyists and conventioneers aren't in town.

It's not the same Washington, but it's still a world-class capital city and an urban center just now coming into its own. Some of us even think that our well-guarded city is one of the safest places in the world. Franklin Roosevelt once advised us that "we have nothing to fear but fear itself." If you look around at the colorful neighborhoods, ongoing development, and crowded Metro trains, you'll see that Washingtonians tend to agree.

Maybe more important, fewer are packing their bags after a couple of years. Thriving new neighborhoods inside the District lines are attracting ambitious young workers and empty-nesters alike.

Where the Jobs Will Be

Thanks to its economic diversity, experts say Metro Washington is well positioned for long, sustained economic growth over the next two decades. As the shift from federal to private-sector employment continues unabated, it's estimated there will be 1.3 million more workers out there by the year 2010, the vast majority in highly skilled occupations (including business, health care, law, and education).

Expect to see an increase in biotech jobs as well. Home to the third-largest cluster of bioscience companies in the world, the D.C.

i Politics aside, science is big business. Washington, D.C. Metro area is a booming biotechnology center, home to the third-largest cluster of bioscience companies in the world, including some of the most notable pioneers in human genome research.

Metro area is leading the way in human genome research, with new research and manufacturing facilities under development. Loudoun, Frederick, Prince William, and Stafford Counties are projected to experience the greatest job growth, with employment in the entire outer suburbs expected to expand by 138 percent in the next 20 years.

Crime in D.C.

Drug trafficking, primarily in crack cocaine, began paralyzing neighborhoods throughout the inner city in the mid '80s, and by 1988, the District of Columbia was known as the "Murder Capital of the World."

The crime rate dropped after that, and was lower in 1998 than it had been in 25 years. Unfortunately, in 2002, the city once again claimed the dubious distinction of having the most murders per capita in American cities with populations greater than 500,000. In 2006 a string of mid-summer murders prompted the District police department to declare a crime emergency. Beefed up patrols brought the situation quickly under control.

According to FBI statistics, violent crime overall in the District dropped 0.1 percent in 2005, compared with a 2.3 percent increase nationwide. The region showed a 0.2 percent decrease in serious crime, though homicides and robberies both rose.

At the same time, the Washington area's total crime, violent crime, and property crime rates are below the national average.

The best advice for visitors to Washington,

i Washingtonians opine on regional issues and other matters at www.dcist.com.

as in any big city in the world, is to use caution and common sense. Random acts of violence in usually quiet areas are of course a reality, yet by simply using everyday street smarts, locals and tourists alike should feel perfectly comfortable in Washington's tourism and business sectors.

Washington in the Twenty-first Century

In the twenty-first century, for better or for worse, Washington remains the single most important political center in the world. In Berlin and Moscow communism has been dismantled and the countries' entrepreneurs have embraced U.S.–style capitalism with gusto. In South Africa the U.S.–initiated embargo led to the abandonment of apartheid. In recent years the U.S. has taken center stage in places like the Middle East, the Balkans, and Haiti. So as Moscow fumbles over social and economic woes, and Tokyo reels from the effects of an overheated economy, Washington has its sights fixed on emerging marketplaces like China and India.

Illustrative of Washington's power is the revival of the city itself. In 2003 the behemoth new Washington Convention Center opened in the downtown Mount Vernon neighborhood. At 2.3 million square feet, the convention center is now the largest building in Washington. It covers 6 city blocks and is as long as two Washington Monuments laid end to end.

A 20,000-seat sport/entertainment complex called the Verizon Center opened in midtown in 1997, the centerpiece of an entertainment industry that generates $833 million in annual spending by visitors alone. Ronald Reagan Washington National Airport's dazzling new terminal opened in 1997 after $400 million of construction to provide new air-traffic-control facilities, a moving sidewalk system, expanded parking, shops, restaurants, and a network of convenient walkways (see the Getting Around the Metro Area chapter). If you arrive at Dulles International Airport, you'll see that an even larger expansion is ongoing there.

It's not only the residents of the area that recognize we live in a special place. An increasing number of influential publications and organizations do, as well. *Forbes* magazine thinks that moving to Washington, D.C. is good for you personally, as well as professionally; in 2006 the city topped *Forbes'* list of the best cities for finding a job and was also voted one of the ten best cities for singles. The Association of Foreign Investors in Real Estate considers D.C. the best city for investment in the United States.

NORTHERN VIRGINIA

The Monolith That Is Fairfax County

Fairfax County, which encircles the self-governed municipalities of Falls Church, Fairfax City, Vienna, and Herndon, is the dominant economic force in the metro area, housing some of the biggest employers, including Inova Health Systems, Exxon Mobil, Booz Allen Hamilton, Gannett Corporation, and Northrop Grumman IT. Each has offices with more than 2,000 employees in the county. Defense giant General Dynamics moved its national headquarters here from St. Louis. With a population of 1,006,529, it has more residents than several states and almost twice the number of the District of Columbia. Moreover, nearly one in seven Virginians lives in the county.

Since 1990 the county has added more than 10,000 new businesses and 250,000 new jobs, making it the region's largest employer. But it's more than jobs that attract people to Fairfax County. Steeped in history—this is, after all, the home of George Washington and George Mason, father of the American Bill of Rights—the county is defined by a sense of civic orderliness and a commitment to a high standard of living. When English explorer John Smith, the first European to set eyes on the area that is present-day Washington, D.C., ventured into the county in 1608, he was taken aback by the amount of wildlife and natural resources that graced the area—bounty he would later help claim for England.

i Fairfax County is more than just the largest county in Virginia. It's home to more residents than seven states: Alaska, Delaware, Montana, North Dakota, South Dakota, Vermont, and Wyoming.

If Smith were in Fairfax County today, he would also want to claim some of the finest public schools in the nation, a workforce that is among the nation's most educated and affluent, and a public safety record that is the envy of most suburban jurisdictions.

Equally alluring to newcomers—especially families—are the county's extensive parklands, myriad shopping malls—including one of the nation's largest in Tysons Corner Center—upscale neighborhoods, and abundant historical and recreational attractions.

The flip side to the county's fortunes are home costs, which are among the highest in the nation (as are housing costs in most of the metro area), with affordable housing in seriously short supply. In addition, the infrastructure lags behind the pressures of a booming population. No matter what time of day, you can find a traffic jam somewhere in Fairfax County, though matters have improved with the construction of the Fairfax County Parkway, which winds its way from the northernmost limits of the county to the southern tip.

More transportation relief is also on the way with Metrorail's new Silver Line, which will travel to Dulles Airport with stops in Tysons Corner, Reston, and Herndon.

Urban Cousins: Arlington County and the City of Alexandria

Arlington County and the city of Alexandria are the alter egos to suburban Fairfax. Much more in tune with the urban pace of Washington (they were in fact part of the District of Columbia at one time), Arlington and Alexandria command a great influence on the Nation's Capital.

i A little-known spot in Fairfax County is the historic village of Clifton at its southwestern tip. Great for a Sunday drive, the village is a patchwork of quaint houses, shops, and restaurants surrounded by winding country roads, meadows, and horses. It looks like Virginia hunt country, but it's only 35 minutes from downtown Washington, D.C.

In Arlington you can find such Washington icons as the Pentagon, Arlington National Cemetery, the Iwo Jima Memorial, and Reagan National Airport. As in Alexandria, economic activity in Arlington historically has been tied to the federal government. In addition, both jurisdictions house hundreds of national and international associations, lobbyists, and special-interest groups, as well as a fair number of federal government offices. Nevertheless, Arlington and Alexandria contain their share of private industry and government jobs. Arlington County is home to the Pentagon, the Public Broadcasting Service, and Reagan National Airport, as well as major shopping centers at Pentagon City, Clarendon, and Ballston. Next door in Alexandria—one of the nation's oldest port cities and business centers—are the headquarters for the U.S. Patent and Trademark Office and the Independent Insurance Agents of America.

Over the years, Arlington has assumed somewhat of a multiple personality. Self-contained communities such as Ballston, Crystal City, Pentagon City, and Rosslyn, each with its own central business district, bloom with shopping centers, towering offices and condos, and an inexhaustible supply of restaurants. The northern edge of the county contains upscale single-family homes, many on large lots with views of the Potomac and the District beyond, while parts of the extreme southern end border on seedy, with crime being a major concern. All told, some 195,000 people now call Arlington home. But unlike Fairfax County, which is the refuge of families with children, less than 20 percent of Arlington households have children under age 18.

Mention the word *Alexandria* and most people immediately think of Old Town, the city's charming and affluent historic district that hugs the banks of the Potomac. And for sure, history is a way of life in Old Town. Settled in 1749 by Scottish merchants, the city blossomed into one of the leading ports of Colonial America, driven in good measure by a lucrative trade in Virginia-grown tobacco. George Washington conducted a lot of business here, and Robert E. Lee grew up here, later moving to Arlington House, now part of Arlington National Cemetery. Alexandria's venerable Christ Church has been visited by almost every president. The Revolutionary and Civil Wars played out on Alexandria's streets, some of which look much the same today as they did in the early nineteenth century.

Walk around and you'll find block after block of painstakingly restored Federal-style homes interspersed between curio shops, inns, bars, restaurants, parks, churches, and museums. So picturesque is Old Town that it draws 1.5 million visitors a year. Old Town wasn't always so gentrified, though. From the 1940s through the early '70s, hard times set in and much of the area was blighted with boarded-up shops and dilapidated homes. When the revitalization bug kicked in some 20 years ago, entire blocks of houses could have been purchased for a fraction of the present-day cost of a single home here. As you can imagine, many a fortune was made in Old Town. Among the upscale renovations, there still exist some housing projects, and most of the crime in Old Town occurs here in the form of drug-related wrongdoing. Residents of nearby homes, no matter how affluent and well protected, are also subject to burglaries and muggings from time to time. For the most part, you can avoid trouble by sticking to the crowded commercial areas and steering clear of the shadowy residential streets, whose many trees and alleys provide strategic hiding places for mischief makers.

Alexandria is more than Old Town, though many visitors think the two are synonymous. Most of its 128,000 residents live in diverse outlying neighborhoods, like charming Del Rey, a trendy neighborhood adjacent to Old Town, or the West End, with its many high-rise apartments. Further confusion arises from the fact that the city of Alexandria is surrounded by Alexandria, Fairfax County. Perhaps the most famous landmark in the expanded area is the community of Mount Vernon (mailing address Alexandria), with homes ranging from modest to baronial. As the name implies, George Washington's estate—also Mount Vernon—sits smack in the middle of the area. Leading to it is a bicycle path offering Potomac River vistas, a route popular with both tourists and residents. In fact, the George Washington Memorial Parkway, and the national parkland adjoining it, make this one of the most scenic and bucolic corners of the metro area.

Prince William County

Although more than 60 percent of Prince William County residents commute at least 30 minutes to work, it's not quite the bedroom community it once was. The county has added about 18,000 jobs since 1990. At the same time, the county's population has jumped from 245,667 to 309,418, making it one of the nation's biggest gainers.

Newcomers arrive in masses here to live in nice, relatively affordable neighborhoods with improving schools and a surprisingly large number of cultural and recreational diversions. It's a good place for families just starting out, and that's reflected by the median age of residents: 32 years. The county also has the highest percentage of households with children—42.5 percent—in the region. A home that would cost $400,000 in Fairfax County might range in cost from $300,000 to $350,000 in Prince William, depending on its proximity to the county border, Interstate 66, or Interstate 95.

Prince William still contains huge tracts of undeveloped land and is home to sprawling national and state parks, including the Manas-

sas National Battlefield, one of the most important sites of the Civil War. Other attractions include the U.S. Marine Corps Museum, a minor-league baseball team, several community theater groups and museums, and the Nissan Pavilion at Stone Ridge, a state-of-the-art concert amphitheater. Here you'll also find the FBI Academy, Quantico Marine Base, and Quantico National Cemetery, which is actually larger than Arlington National Cemetery.

Prince William has been extremely proactive in efforts to lure more employers to the county. However, not every corporate entity is welcome. The Walt Disney Company was sent packing in 1994 after encountering fierce—and largely unexpected—opposition to an American history theme park it had proposed for the rolling countryside near the history-rich town of Haymarket. Easily the biggest attraction in Prince William, though, is Potomac Mills, one of the biggest outlet shopping centers in the world and—sad, but true—the single most popular tourist attraction in the entire commonwealth.

The Virginia Exurbs: Loudoun, Fauquier, and Stafford Counties

The outlying Virginia counties of Loudoun, Fauquier, and Stafford are at a crossroads as Metro Washington continues to expand in its radial fashion. Not quite totally suburban but neither completely rural anymore, the counties are what may be termed *exurban*.

In a way, we're hesitant to lump Loudoun County into this category, since it is easily the fastest-developing outer jurisdiction in either Virginia or Maryland. Between 1990 and 2000 its population nearly doubled, surging to 169,000. It's expected to grow another 94 percent by 2030. Nevertheless, with only about one-seventh the number of residents of Fairfax County, Loudoun is still mostly wide-open spaces. A vocal group of natives and newcomers would like to keep it that way. That's why you'll see the heaviest concentration of commercial and residential activity kept to the eastern stretches of the county, from Leesburg to the Fairfax County line. Here is where you'll also find Washington Dulles International Airport (although a small piece sits in Fairfax), a major catalyst behind the county's growth and a major source of employment.

Other heavy hitters headquartered in Loudoun include United Airlines, America Online, and Verizon. Government also maintains a presence here, adding thousands of homeland security and postal service jobs to Loudoun's economy.

To the south and west of Leesburg, the county seat, is a sprawling patchwork of farms, orchards, and horse pastures. It is here where Virginia's famed Hunt Country begins. South of Loudoun is Fauquier County, with its equally beautiful horse farms and country estates. New housing developments in and around Warrenton, the county's largest community, are attracting more and more Metro D.C. commuters and even a growing number of retirees. Fauquier contains some of the most scenic land in the Old Dominion, and consequently, like Loudoun, there is a considerable antigrowth sentiment here. People move out here to get away from traffic congestion, crime, and overcrowding, so they want to preserve the county's rural character. Stafford County is a bit of a different story, however. Located just south of Prince William, it is actively wooing new residents and businesses with affordable land prices, the promise of relaxed living, and easy access to I–95. Folks are responding to the offer. During the '90s, the county's population recorded one of the highest percentage gains in Virginia. Stafford enjoys a close proximity to both Washington and Richmond and is bordered immediately to the south by the city of Fredericksburg, one of the most charming and historic communities in the commonwealth. However, the access to I–95 is a mixed bless-

ing, because the road is almost always snarled with traffic. Rush hour begins at noon on Fridays, because this is also the most widely used interstate route for tractor-trailers and others traveling along the East Coast. At peak hours the drive from Stafford County to Washington, D.C. can take up to two hours, so investigate carefully before you believe claims by real estate agents of an "easy commute."

SUBURBAN MARYLAND
The "State" of Montgomery County

Although diehards on both sides of the Potomac would probably never admit it, Montgomery County is to Maryland what Fairfax County is to Virginia. In terms of population, jobs, median household income, and size, the two counties are strikingly similar. In other words, Montgomery County is an aberration of sorts. As Maryland's largest and most affluent county, one could argue—as do many lawmakers in Annapolis—that Montgomery is its own separate state. That might be overdoing it a bit, but this mega-county of about 900,700 residents is far more aligned, socially and economically, with the District and Northern Virginia than with Baltimore or any other part of the Free State.

At the same time, Montgomery in many ways is Metro D.C.'s most diverse jurisdiction. The southern half of the county is overwhelmingly white collar and decidedly urban. Here, you'll find the posh homes and estates of Potomac and Chevy Chase, the retail meccas of White Flint and Montgomery malls, and the lost-in-time Victoriana of Kensington and tiny Garrett Park (which has declared itself a nuclear-free zone). Here, you'll also find an interesting mix of both highly successful and struggling immigrants hailing from Central America, Vietnam, India, Iran, and China. Many come to work at the impressive campus of Bethesda's world-renowned National Institutes of Health or at the high-tech companies that flank I–270. Others clean the buildings, work the landscapes, and wash the dishes.

i Before you mail a letter to an address in Chevy Chase, be sure you know whether the person lives in D.C. or Maryland. The two communities border each other.

Major employers in lower Montgomery County include Marriott International; Lockheed Martin, the country's largest defense contractor; the National Naval Medical Center; and Discovery Communications, which built a new headquarters in downtown Silver Spring. In all, there were 444,500 jobs in the county in 2000.

The northern portion of Montgomery, or the "Upcounty" as locals emphatically refer to it, moves to a gentler, less urban beat. Here, it's not unusual to see large dairy farms abutting business parks, or commuters coming to a halt at cattle crossings and creeping slowly behind tractors in the spring. A few years ago, a black bear cub emerged from the woods of Seneca Creek State Park and onto a heavily trafficked road. The cub returned to the wilds unscathed, but not before setting off one of the region's more memorable traffic jams. Although the Upcounty is proud of its efforts to preserve open space—Montgomery reportedly set aside more farmland than any other suburban county in the nation—the tenor of the place is rapidly changing. Subdivisions now extend north of Gaithersburg, transforming once-sleepy areas like Germantown and Damascus into bustling bedroom communities favored by young professionals seeking affordable housing. Onetime apple orchards and wheat fields increasingly are sprouting single-family homes and shopping centers.

The Melting Pot of Prince George's County

In 1988 one of the largest commercial developers in Metro Washington broke ground on an ambitious project that came with the promise of virtually reinventing the image of Prince George's County. The huge development was to be called Port America, a stately, multipurpose business and residential community that would grace the banks of the Potomac River, within earshot of the busy Woodrow Wilson Bridge. But the national recession set in, legal hassles ensued, and Port America fell apart. Now a major develop-

i Prince George's County is full of firsts: It's where Samuel Morse sent his first telegraph message across the country's first telegraph line; it's home to the world's oldest continuously operating airport; it's the site of the first U.S. Postal Air Mail Service, the first flying school, and the first helicopter flight.

ment called National Harbor is planned for the same site and will feature hotels, entertainment, upscale shops, and a marina modeled after the Inner Harbor in Baltimore. The project is anchored by the Gaylord National Resort & Convention Center, which opens in 2008.

It's safe to say that Prince George's has still not yet totally arrived, at least not to the same degree as its more prosperous neighbors to the north and west. A chronic crime problem in the urban areas closest to Washington, coupled with some highly publicized criminal cases involving local government officials, have taken their toll on the county's image. Don't count "P.G."—as it's commonly called—and its 846,123 residents out of the picture, however.

The positives far outweigh the negatives. The county is undergoing an economic upswing, with several major federal facilities constructed here in recent years. These include the recently built 1.2 million-square-foot IRS headquarters in New Carrollton, the USDA building in College Park, and the National Archives II facility.

P.G. companies employ 350,000 workers. It is home to the University of Maryland, the state's flagship university with more than 35,000 students and a tradition-rich athletic program. Andrews Air Force Base, which is used by the president and many other government officials, the National Agricultural Research Center, NASA's Goddard Space Flight Center, and the U.S. Census Bureau also call P.G. home.

P.G., among other things, has always been the region's—if not one of the nation's—most established multiracial communities. Black, Caucasian, Hispanic, and Asian Americans live side by side and largely in harmony in Prince George's. While housing prices are still high, they're more affordable. The county's public school system has made tremendous inroads in recent years, and there's a new chief executive officer.

If you're into spectator events, chances are you'll be spending some time at Rosecroft and Laurel Park Raceways (horse racing), the new FedExField football stadium less than a mile away, and the Prince George's Equestrian Center in Upper Marlboro. These venues entertain many thousands of Washingtonians throughout the year (see the Spectator Sports chapter).

A Sense of Place in Anne Arundel County

There's a certain feeling that pervades Anne Arundel County. Maybe it's due to Annapolis, the splendid Maryland capital city, with its colonial waterfront homes, the oldest State House in continuous use in the United States (since the 1770s), and the imposing campuses of St. John's College and the United States Naval Academy. Maybe it's the quiet coves and inlets of the Magothy, Severn, and South Rivers. Or maybe it's the broad, sweeping views of the Chesapeake Bay afforded from atop hilly pastures dotted with wooden tobacco barns and thoroughbred horses. From whatever it springs, it's hard not to feel an acute sense of place in Anne Arundel, a county as beautiful as its name suggests.

Not too many decades ago, Washingtonians built summer homes here, and the county's economy was associated largely with the state government and the fishing and sailing trades of the Chesapeake Bay.

Today, Anne Arundel is grappling with a new identity. The past decade ushered in a surge in population, fueled in large part by the well-documented economic fortunes of nearby Baltimore and Washington. Many of the county's 506,620 residents now make the 25-plus-mile commute into the District and other parts of Metro Washington—a feat virtually unheard of a few decades ago. Rapid suburbanization has had its share of nasty side effects like increased crime and housing costs, but all told, Anne Arundel retains a remarkably high quality of life. Indeed, this is its main selling point. And although longtime residents vehemently resist the notion of being part of Metro D.C. or Baltimore, there is an accommodating attitude toward newcomers that are drawn to this enchanting, history-filled corner of Maryland.

Maryland's Exurbs: Frederick, Howard, and Charles Counties

As suburban Maryland continues to creep farther out into the countryside, it's markedly changing the face of at least three outlying communities: Frederick, Howard, and Charles Counties.

Bounded by Pennsylvania to the north and Montgomery County to the south, Frederick County offers the perks of a relaxed country setting—this is the land of covered bridges, inns, vineyards, and roadside produce stands—but with an undeniable air of big-city sophistication. In downtown Frederick, the county's principal city, one can munch on blue-corn tortillas and other trendy fare before taking in a gallery opening or browsing through dozens of antiques shops. From here, you're about equal distance from Gettysburg, Pennsylvania, and downtown Washington, although the commute north is much easier. In winter the ski slopes of White Tail and Liberty in Pennsylvania are only a bit more than 30 minutes away. Still, Frederick is less than an hour's drive from much of Metro D.C., and housing prices won't send your heart rate through the roof.

Howard County, lodged between Montgomery and Baltimore Counties, is easily the most established Maryland exurb. Columbia, its largest community, is a planned city developed by the same folks responsible for revitalizing the inner harbors of Baltimore and Norfolk, Virginia. In Columbia one can find the comforts of suburbia and the home investment security that goes

Convention and Tourist Bureaus/Tourist Information

Contact the following agencies to receive free, comprehensive travel and tourism information packets.

Washington, D.C.

- Visitor Information Center, 1300 Pennsylvania Avenue NW, Ronald Reagan Building, Ground Level, Washington, D.C. 20005, (202) 328–4748, www.dcvisit.com
- Washington, D.C. Convention and Tourism Corporation, 901 7th Street, NW, 4th Floor, Washington, D.C. 20001, (202) 789–7000, (800) 422–8644, www.washington.org

Northern Virginia

- Virginia Tourism Corporation, 901 East Byrd Street, Richmond, Virginia 23219, (800) 847–4882, www.virginia.org
- Alexandria Convention & Visitors Association, 421 King Street, Suite 300, Alexandria, Virginia 22314, (703) 838–4200, (800) 388–9119, www.funside.com
- Arlington Convention and Visitors Service, 1100 North Glebe Road, Suite 1500, Arlington, Virginia 22201, (703) 228–0808, www.stayarlington.com
- Fairfax County Tourism and Convention Bureau, 8300 Boone Boulevard, Suite 450, Vienna, Virginia 22182, (703) 550–2450, (800) 732–4732, www.fxva.com
- Loudoun County Convention and Visitors Association, 222 Catoctin Circle SE, Suite 100, Leesburg, Virginia 20175, (800) 752–6118, www.visitloudoun.org
- Prince William County/Manassas Convention and Visitors Bureau, 8609 Sudley Road, Suite 105, Manassas, Virginia 20110, (703) 396–7130, (800) 432–1792, www.visitpwc.com

Suburban Maryland

- Maryland Office of Tourist Development, 217 East Redwood Street, Baltimore, Maryland 21202, (866) 639–3526, www.mdisfun.org
- Annapolis and Anne Arundel County Conference and Visitors Bureau, 26 West Street, Annapolis, Maryland 21401, (410) 280–0445, (888) 302–2852, www.visit annapolis.org
- Montgomery County Conference and Visitors Bureau, 111 Rockville Pike, Suite 800, Rockville, Maryland 20850, (240) 777–2060, (877) 789–6904, www.cvbmontco.com
- Prince George's County Conference and Visitors Bureau, 9200 Basil Court, Suite 101, Largo, Maryland 20774, (301) 925–8300, (888) 925–8300, www.goprince georgescounty.com

with intense zoning regulations. Like its Northern Virginia counterpart, Reston, Columbia may be a tad sterile for some, but its numerous tree-lined parkways and quiet residential areas give the impression of country living just 25 miles from either Washington or Baltimore. Merriweather Post Pavilion, one of the nation's first outdoor concert venues, brings top-name entertainment to the county throughout the warm-weather months.

South of Prince George's County, and just 20 miles from the District line, lies Charles County, a place where not too long ago tobacco and truck farming reigned supreme. An influx of new housing developments, especially along the U.S. Highway 301 corridor between Waldorf and La Plata, and the opening of the county's first shopping mall are helping to create a bona fide suburban atmosphere. The challenge of the future for Charles County inevitably will be forging a balance between development and preservation of its long-cherished rural lifestyle.

(For information about independent cities within the above-mentioned counties, consult our Relocation chapter.)

SUGGESTED READINGS AND RESOURCES

A good number of books deal with finding a job in Metro Washington. Some of the most helpful are:

- *An Insiders' Guide to Political Jobs in Washington* by William T. Endicott, John Wiley & Sons—Former president Gerald Ford gave this rave review for this 2003 comprehensive guide: "A remarkable description of what Washington political jobs entail, how you get them, and where they lead. A public service."
- *The Book of U.S. Government Jobs: Where They Are, What's Available, and How to Get One,* by Dennis V. Damp, Brookhaven Press—Now in its ninth edition, this book on federal employment offers a practical guide for finding government work.

And of course, the Internet is an invaluable tool for Washington, D.C. job seekers. Go to www.washingtonpost.com for a comprehensive look at what's available. Federal government jobs are always posted at www.usajobs.com.

Contacts

If you'd like to receive more specific information about the Metro Washington economy, labor market, or business relocation opportu-

nities, we encourage you to contact the following agencies:

- Washington, D.C. Economic Partnership, 1495 F Street, NW, Washington, D.C. 20004, (202) 661–8670, www.wdcep.com
- The Greater Washington Board of Trade, Office of Research, Policy, and Transportation, 1725 I Street, NW, Suite 200, Washington, D.C. 20006, (202) 857–5900, www.bot.org. Or at the same address, the Greater Washington Initiative, a regional economic development marketing organization, (202) 857–5999, www.greaterwashington.org
- Maryland Department of Business and Economic Development, 217 East Redwood Street, Baltimore, Maryland 21202, (410) 767–6300, www.mdbusiness.state.md.us
- Metropolitan Washington Council of Governments, 777 North Capitol Street, NE, Suite 300, Washington, D.C. 20002-4239, (202) 962–3200, www.mwcog.org
- Virginia Economic Development Partnership, 901 East Byrd Street, Richmond, Virginia 23218, (804) 545–5600, www.yesvirginia.org

Selected Regional Economic Development Authorities

- D.C. Office of the Deputy Mayor for Planning and Economic Development, 1350 Pennsylvania Avenue, NW, Suite 317, Washington, D.C. 20004, (202) 727–6365, www.dcbiz.dc.gov
- Montgomery County Department of Economic Development, 111 Rockville Pike, Suite 100, Rockville, Maryland 20850, (240) 777–2000, www.montgomery countymd.gov/ded
- Prince George's County Economic Development Corporation, 1100 Mercantile Lane, Suite 115A, Largo, Maryland 20774, (301) 583–4650, www. pg cedc.com

- Anne Arundel County Office of Economic Development, 2660 Riva Road, Annapolis, Maryland 21401, (410) 222–7410, www.aaedc.org
- Fairfax County Economic Development Authority, 8300 Boone Boulevard, Suite 450, Vienna, Virginia 22182, (703) 790–0600, www.fairfaxcountyeda.org
- Alexandria Economic Development Partnership Inc., 1729 King Street, Suite 410, Alexandria, Virginia 22314, (703) 739–3820, www.alexecon.org
- Arlington County Economic Development, 1100 North Glebe Road, Suite 1500, Arlington, Virginia 22201, (703) 228–0808, www.smartplace.org
- Prince William County Office of Economic Development, 10530 Linden Lake Plaza, Suite 105, Manassas, Virginia 20109, (703) 792–5500, www.pwcecondev.org

HISTORY

You could read dozens of volumes about Washington, D.C., and merely scratch the surface of the rich history associated with our Nation's Capital. From high-profile local incidents to the federal government's role in national and global affairs, events emblazoned on today's front pages frequently turn up in tomorrow's historical tomes. In this chapter we won't attempt a scholarly discourse on the people and episodes that shaped our fair city. Rather, we offer a thumbnail sketch of Washington history, featuring landmark events from the District's shaky beginnings to its even shakier recent past. (For more about current conditions here, see the Metro Washington Overview chapter.)

Don't fret: You won't be quizzed! You may, however, learn a few intriguing facts about places you'll undoubtedly encounter during your forays into this unique city.

CREATING A CAPITAL

He's not only the Father of Our Country. George Washington also is the Father of Washington, the District of Columbia, in the sense that our first president chose the site for the Nation's Capital later named in his honor.

During the years immediately following the Revolutionary War, Northerners and Southerners held fierce debates over where to put the permanent capital city. Philadelphia proved a top contender, along with New York and Charlestown. The two sides finally struck a deal in 1790, an agreement forged between

> **i** The Birthnight Ball, a social celebration of George Washington's birthday, began during his lifetime and still takes place every year in Alexandria.

two of the greatest political leaders in America: Alexander Hamilton, a New York Federalist and fiscal conservative, and Thomas Jefferson, a Virginia agrarian liberal. Under the straightforward terms, Jefferson's Southerners agreed to support Hamilton's proposal that the federal government assume the war debts of the 13 original states if, and only if, Hamilton's Northerners would agree to move the capital city south, from Philadelphia to a veritable wilderness along the banks of the Potomac River.

President George Washington, a surveyor by profession, homed in on what he deemed an ideal site in 1791: a central location that proved convenient to the states and close to the Potomac River, which he considered a likely boon for commerce. Never mind that the area consisted of scattered farms and murky riverside corridors that resembled swamps to most who saw them. Washington could picture in its place a magnificent city, and he knew just the person to put his dream to paper: Pierre Charles L'Enfant, a French-born architect who had volunteered in the American Continental army. When presented with the task, L'Enfant—who had spent his childhood in the palace at Versailles, where his father served as an artist—conjured up visions of grandeur that rivaled royal European cities and raised the eyebrows of government officials. The plan he mapped out contained wide, tree-lined streets, including a mile-long avenue with a congressional building at one end and a presidential "palace" at the other. He imagined large parks adorned with statues and fountains.

L'Enfant had his own ideas of how to do things, and he increasingly ruffled feathers as he refused to follow government-ordered instructions and deadlines. Eventually, Wash-

The African American Civil War Memorial pays tribute to some of the Civil War's lesser-known heroes. COURTESY

i Washington, D.C. elected its first mayor, Walter E. Washington, in 1975. Before this election, D.C. was governed by a mayor-commissioner appointed by the president of the United States.

ington had no choice but to fire him. L'Enfant's original plan remained largely intact, however. Surveyor Andrew Ellicott and his African American assistant, Benjamin Banneker, who had mapped out the district's 10-mile-square boundaries, continued laying out the city's gridlike street designs.

THE CITY SLOWLY TAKES SHAPE

The grand city L'Enfant and Washington envisioned didn't spring up overnight. On the contrary, people were in no great rush to settle into a place characterized by damp, mosquito-infested areas, free-roaming farm animals, and more muddy roads than elegant boulevards. Even in 1800, with the Capitol's north wing completed and the government relocated from its temporary Philadelphia headquarters, one local citizen described the capital as "a town of streets without houses." George Washington also had selected the location for the White House, and although he laid the cornerstone in 1792 and lived to see the building's completion, he never occupied the presidential residence. The honor of being first to live at the historic address fell upon second president John Adams and his wife, Abigail, who found the mansion to be an inconvenient work in progress for quite some time after they arrived in 1800.

Washington, D.C. received its city charter in 1802 along with a local government that included a mayor appointed by the president and a council chosen by the residents. Although officially a city, it remained a scourge to many Congress members, who found it crowded, dirty, and unbearably hot and humid in the summer. Even Thomas Jefferson, president from 1801 to 1809, retreated to his Char-

lottesville home to escape the heat. From 1800 to 1803, the population rose from 3,000 to only 8,000 people.

A DEVASTATING FIRE

The city still possessed an ambience of incompleteness in 1814, when, two years after the start of the War of 1812, British troops invaded the city and set fire to most of the public buildings. They set the Capitol on fire, as well as the President's House (the White House's name until Theodore Roosevelt's administration). First Lady Dolley Madison, waiting for husband James to return from a trip, hesitated to leave their home even after James sent orders for her to evacuate. She refused to go before securing some of her husband's papers and Gilbert Stuart's portrait of George Washington, which has continued to hang in the White House throughout the years. Although rainy weather helped contain the fires, the Capitol and President's House received extensive damage. The Madisons finished out James's term in temporary residences, as the President's House repairs weren't complete until James Monroe took office in 1817. The Capitol took even longer to rebuild: It wasn't finished until 1830.

THE CAPITAL GROWS

As rebuilding progressed over the next few years, more and more people began to move to Washington. By 1822 the population had increased to more than 15,000 people, including many free Blacks. Over the next several years, citizens saw the beginnings of what would become some of the area's best-known attractions.

An act of Congress in 1821 created The George Washington University, which would grow into a nationally recognized school of higher education (see our Education chapter for more on the university today). The National Theatre, founded in 1835, was one of the city's first cultural attractions. It suffered through

Historical Resources

Historical societies and offices can help you dig up facts about local people and places. Following are some local resources:

- Historical Society of Washington, D.C. (801 K Street, NW, Washington, D.C., 202–383–1800, www.historydc.org)
- Montgomery County Historical Society (111 West Montgomery Avenue, Rockville, Maryland, 301–340–2825, www.montgomeryhistory.org)
- Prince George's County Historical Society (5626 Bell Station Road, Glenn Dale, Maryland, 301–464–0590, www.pghistory.org)
- Office of Historic Alexandria (220 North Washington Street, Alexandria, Virginia, 703–838–4554, oha.ci.alexandria.va.us)
- Arlington Historical Society Museum (1805 South Arlington Ridge Road, Arlington, Virginia, 703–892–4204, www.arlingtonhistoricalsociety.org)
- Fairfax County History Commission (3915 Chain Bridge Road, Fairfax, Virginia, 703–293–6383, www.co.fairfax.va.us/visitors/history/histcomm)
- Historic Prince William, Inc. (P.O. Box 1731, Prince William, Virginia 22195–1731, 703–754–8191, www.historicprincewilliam.org)

five fires and a partial collapse over the years, but still continues to entertain Washingtonians with Broadway-caliber plays and concerts (see The Arts chapter). In 1846 the government founded the Smithsonian Institution with money willed to the country by James Smithson, a British scientist who wanted the United States to build an establishment to promote knowledge. (You'll find more on Smithsonian museums and events throughout this book.)

Construction began in 1848 on the Washington Monument, deviating greatly from the proposed equestrian statue included in L'Enfant's original plan. Due to a lack of finances, the 555-foot-tall obelisk wasn't completed until 1884, and it didn't open to the public for four years after that. The city's first art gallery, the Corcoran Gallery of Art, got its start in 1859. Today, it ranks not only as the oldest, but also as one of the finest and largest. (See the Arts and Attractions chapters for more about visiting these places.)

On a sad historical note, 1841 saw the first death of a president in office. William Henry Harrison delivered his inaugural address while standing outside in cold drizzle—for about 90 minutes. One month later, he succumbed to pneumonia and Vice President John Tyler took the oath of office, during an *indoor* ceremony.

THE CIVIL WAR TAKES ITS TOLL

Washington, D.C. found itself in a precarious position as the Civil War raged from 1861 to 1865. Located 60 miles south of the Mason-Dixon Line and just 100 miles north of Richmond, the Confederate capital, the city was pulled in both directions. Washington became overcrowded with camps, temporary shelters, and hundreds of soldiers and escaped slaves who flocked to the city. Housing grew scarce and disease ran rampant. Even though the war ended in 1865, the year proved tumultuous for the city. The budding Smithsonian Institution lost its original collection of artifacts in a fire at its castle headquarters. And the country suffered a loss even more devastating: President Abraham Lincoln, attending a performance at Ford's Theatre, was fatally shot by the deranged Confederate activist John Wilkes Booth.

Civil War: Washington, D. C. at a Crossroads

For four harsh years the Washington area stood at the epicenter of the Civil War, arguably the most tragic event in our country's history. Even before the first shots were fired on Fort Sumter, South Carolina, in April 1861, the tense capital city found itself in a most precarious location—60 miles south of the Mason-Dixon line and just 100 miles north of Richmond, the Confederate capital.

Politics aside, conditions were tough in Washington. Temporary shelters, office buildings, camps, hospitals, supply depots, and hundreds of new residents suddenly appeared throughout the city, putting a strain on the housing supply and public services. Crime soared and slums grew up around the Capitol.

The war's first major battle took place about 30 miles west of Washington, near Bull Run Creek in Prince William County, Virginia, in July 1861. At the Battle of First Manassas, Union forces expected an easy victory. Instead, Union general Irvin McDowell's 35,000 soldiers were met with strong resistance from General Thomas "Stonewall" Jackson's 32,000 Confederate soldiers, whose powerful performance sent a shockwave through Washington. It was not going to be an easy fight.

The Civil War ultimately devastated neighboring Virginia. In Fredericksburg and surrounding Spotsylvania County, 50 miles south of Washington, four major battles (Fredericksburg, Chancellorsville, The Wilderness, and Spotsylvania Court House) raged between 1862 and 1864. Tens of thousands of casualties were claimed in the hundreds of battles and skirmishes, including the Battle of Second Manassas, that took place within a 60-mile radius of Washington. In fact, more Americans perished on Virginia's Civil War battlefields than in all other American wars combined.

The single most violent day of the war took place near the rural Maryland hamlet of Sharpsburg, less than 70 miles northwest of the District. Here, on September 17, 1862, at the Battle of Antietam, more than 12,000 Federal troops and 10,000 Confederates died in some of the most gruesome hand-to-hand combat ever witnessed. Never in our history have more Americans been killed in one day.

As war raged in Maryland and Virginia, the U.S. government constructed 68 forts and 98 gun batteries to protect the capital city. Civil War enthusiasts can visit Fort Dupont (Minnesota Avenue at Randle Circle, SE, 202–426–7745, www.nps.gov/nace/ftdupont.htm), which guarded the 11th Street Bridge linking the southeast neighborhood with the Federal district of Washington. The fort never saw battle but did serve as an important sanctuary for runaway slaves.

You can also roam the grounds of the strategic forts constructed in and around Rock Creek Park (202–895–6000, www.nps.gov/rocr). Fort Stevens, just east of the park at 13th and Quakenbos Streets, NW, is where General Jubal A. Early's spirited Southern forces squared off against an aggressive Union line in July

1864. Among the battle's many spectators was Abraham Lincoln, marking the first time in history that a president in office came under direct enemy fire. Battleground National Cemetery (6625 Georgia Avenue, NW) contains the graves of 41 Union soldiers who perished while defending the fort.

Fort Reno, at Belt Road and Chesapeake Street, no longer remains, but you can check out its key vantage point as the highest point in the District, more than 400 feet above sea level. Fort DeRussy, meanwhile, sits right off a bike path at Oregon Avenue and Military Road, NW, in the heart of Rock Creek Park. To the west of the park, at Western Avenue and River Road, is Fort Bayard, now a popular picnicking site. Remains of other forts still exist at Fort Slocum Park, bordered by Kansas Avenue, Blair Road, and Milmarson Place, NE; Fort Totten Park on Fort Totten Drive, south of Riggs Road; and Battery Kemble Park, bordered by Chain Bridge Road, MacArthur Boulevard, 49th Street, and Nebraska Avenue, NW. Fort Bunker Hill, no longer visible, once stood in a Northeast section now bordered by 14th, Otis, 13th, and Perry Streets.

Washington, D.C. does its part to honor the soldiers who sacrificed and the leaders who emerged during the struggle. Many of the city's squares, traffic circles, and statues are named after Union officials. Farragut Square (17th and K Streets) honors Daniel Farragut, the U.S. Navy's first admiral, who captured New Orleans from the Confederates to gain control of the lower Mississippi River. Sheridan Circle (Massachusetts Avenue and 23rd Street, NW) is named for General Phillip Sheridan, the Union commander whose ride from Winchester, Virginia, is immortalized in Thomas Buchanan Read's poem "Sheridan's Ride." There's a tribute to William Tecumseh Sherman behind the Treasury Department (15th Street and Pennsylvania Avenue, NW). McPherson Square (15th and K Streets, NW) pays tribute to Major General James B. McPherson, who served as chief engineer under General Ulysses S. Grant. McPherson commanded the army of Tennessee and was killed during a skirmish near Atlanta. Grant himself appears in a memorial just north of the Capitol Reflecting Pool. On U Street, the city's historic "Black Broadway," you'll find the African American Civil War Memorial (1200 U Street, NW, 202–667–2667, www.afroamcivilwar.org), a tribute to the more than 209,000 United States Colored Troops who fought during the great conflict. The Shaw neighborhood in which it's located is named for Robert Gould Shaw, the commander of the 54th Massachusetts Volunteer Infantry, which was immortalized in the movie Glory.

If you're a Civil War buff, you can look forward to a plethora of outings. If you're simply interested in learning a little more about the War Between the States, you'll find the Washington area an excellent instructor.

The Virginia Tourism Corporation and Maryland Office of Tourism and Economic Development publish statewide Civil War trails guides. You can get more information at www.virginia.org or www.mdwelcome.org.

i Slaves living in Washington, D.C. enjoyed their first taste of freedom on April 16, 1862, nine months before Abraham Lincoln issued the Emancipation Proclamation. "Emancipation Day" is celebrated each year in the District to mark the occasion.

CHANGES IN GOVERNMENT

Through the remainder of the 1800s, the city took shape, in terms of government and appearance, as a capital in which the nation could take pride. In 1871 Congress took control of the District, initiating plans to improve the streets and add sewers along with water and gas lines. It also annexed the neighboring tobacco port town of Georgetown, popular for its taverns and residential district. The city in 1872 began planting trees systematically, creating the beginnings of many of Washington's current vistas. The White House brightened up with electric lights in 1890, the same year that cable cars began operating. Congress changed the city's government again in 1878, creating a municipal corporation with three presidentially appointed, Senate-approved commissioners.

Washington and the nation endured yet another tragedy in 1881, when angry civil servant Charles Guiteau shot President James Garfield. Although the president hung on for two months while doctors tried to help him recover, he eventually died as a result of his two wounds, and Guiteau was executed.

On the cultural front, this period saw the 1871 founding of Howard University, now the nation's largest predominantly African American university (see the Education chapter). The Smithsonian expanded with the addition of artifacts from Philadelphia's Centennial Exposition of 1876. The National Zoological Park found a home at Rock Creek Park in 1890, and the Library of Congress opened seven years later (see Attractions). The *Washington Post*, now the city's oldest daily newspaper, first went to press in 1877 (see the Media chapter).

A NEW CENTURY

The 1900s brought still more changes to the Nation's Capital. Cars took to the now-paved roadways, and in 1908 the city opened a splendid new railroad terminal, Union Station. (Read more about this still-grand hub in the Getting Around and Shopping chapters.) The city's first park commission, created in 1901, strove to improve the city's appearance, in accordance with L'Enfant's original plan. In 1912 Washington received what would become one of its internationally known trademarks: Japanese cherry trees, a gift from the city of Tokyo. The delicate blossoms continue each spring to transform the shores of the Tidal Basin—created in 1900—into a frothy cloud of pale pink and white. By 1910 Washington's population had grown to 330,000. As the country entered World War I in 1917, new workers arrived in droves, driving the population up to more than 430,000 by 1920.

Another famous landmark made its debut in 1922: the Lincoln Memorial, with its majestic statue of the seated president, designed by American sculptor Daniel Chester French. (Seventeen years later, the memorial steps served as a concert stage for contralto Marian Anderson, who performed a free concert after the DAR refused to allow an African American woman to sing in their Constitution Hall.) The year 1922 also brought one of the city's worst tragedies: As Knickerbocker Theater patrons watched the final few minutes of a silent movie, the building's roof suddenly collapsed under the weight of piles of heavy snow. Caught off guard, the audience couldn't escape in time, and 96 people perished.

A NEW DEAL AND BEYOND

In 1932, following the Great Depression, President Franklin D. Roosevelt promised the nation a New Deal, and his Works Progress Administration program did indeed create many new jobs in the city. The '30s marked a boom in Washington construction, including many of the city's now-familiar landmarks. In 1932 the Folger Shakespeare Library opened, and the Supreme Court moved into its majestic new quarters in 1935. The National Archives Building—which houses our country's most treasured documents, the Declaration of Independence, Constitution, and Bill of Rights—also opened its doors in 1935. The government workforce grew again when we entered World War II in 1941, ushering in the city's modern era. The West Building of the National Gallery of Art, containing some of the world's greatest art treasures, welcomed its first visitors in 1941. (The East Building addition opened 30 years later, fittingly exhibiting more modern works.) In 1943 the Pentagon, one of the nation's largest office buildings, sprang up just across the river in Arlington, Virginia. In 1942 another striking monument, the Jefferson Memorial, joined the ranks of the city's best-loved landmarks. Renovations of the Capitol and White House ushered in the '50s. (Read more about all of these famous sites in the Arts and Attractions chapters.)

CIVIL RIGHTS

With the nation still divided on issues regarding race, Washington acted as a major player in the civil rights struggles of the '50s and '60s. In 1954 the U.S. Supreme Court's ruling in *Brown v. Board of Education of Topeka* led Washington to become one of the first major cities to integrate its schools. In 1963 around 200,000 civil rights supporters participated in the peaceful, historic March on Washington, which culminated at the Lincoln Memorial, as Martin Luther King Jr. delivered his stirring "I Have a Dream" speech. (The event set the stage for later, larger marches, from the 250,000-person anti–Vietnam War demonstration in 1969 to the Million Man March staged by 800,000 or more African American men and boys in 1995, and revived again in 2005. Recent marches have brought hundreds of thousands of activists to the National Mall to lobby for immigration

i The portion of Constitution Avenue that lies west of Pennsylvania Avenue was once the Washington Canal, a waterway designed to connect the U.S. Capitol with other points in the Northeast via the Potomac River.

reform, abortion rights, and an end to military involvement in Iraq.)

Later in 1963 the assassination of President John F. Kennedy in Dallas cast a pall over Washington and the entire nation. Five years later, King again offered a memorable speech in the capital city: his final sermon. Just days after addressing the congregation of Washington National Cathedral, King was assassinated in Memphis. The sad event triggered deadly, destructive riots here and in other cities, which inspired many residents to flee the city for the suburbs.

THE WATERGATE ERA

The report of a 1972 break-in by Republican campaign workers at the Democratic Party headquarters in the Watergate Hotel signaled the beginning of an embarrassing tale of corruption that would reach all the way to the White House. *Washington Post* reporters Carl Bernstein and Bob Woodward earned a Pulitzer Prize for their investigative work uncovering the country's biggest political scandal. The revelations forced President Richard M. Nixon to resign from office in August 1974.

Along with the nationally oriented changes that took place in Washington in the '60s and '70s came an evolution in the city's government. In 1961 the 23rd Amendment to the Constitution granted District residents the right to vote in national elections. Three years later, they voted in their first presidential election. A charter change in 1967 allowed the city a chief executive, assistant, and nine council members. In 1970 Washington residents elected a nonvoting representative to the U.S. House of Representatives, and 1973 brought about the Home Rule Charter, allowing the city to elect a mayor and 13-member council, but giving Congress the power to veto legislation. Under the charter, the president appoints local judges, and local criminal cases fall under the jurisdiction of the Office of the U.S. Attorney General.

The 1970s also brought positive cultural additions to Washington. The beautiful Kennedy Center for the Performing Arts opened in 1971, and the National Air and Space Museum—now one of the Smithsonian's most popular attractions—began welcoming visitors in 1976.

The nation held its collective breath in 1981, when John Hinckley Jr. shot President Ronald Reagan outside the Washington Hilton. The assassination attempt failed, and the president recovered quickly, but press secretary James Brady, shot in the head, suffered permanent brain damage. The incident served as the catalyst for the introduction of the Brady Bill, which led to a law requiring a waiting period before handgun purchases.

The following year brought the District a pair of tragedies. An Air Florida plane crashed into the Fourteenth Street Bridge shortly after takeoff, killing most of its passengers. That same day, a Metro train crashed, causing three fatalities.

WASHINGTON TODAY

Life is never dull in Washington, D.C. The Nation's Capital regularly makes headlines, not only for its role in the national and international political scenes, but also for its local events. In 1990 stunned TV audiences watched a surveillance videotape of Washing-

> **i** Edward Kennedy Ellington—better known as "Duke"—was born in Washington, D.C. in 1899. Today, a public magnet school for the arts and a bridge are named in honor of the jazz composer, musician, and bandleader, whose boyhood home still stands in northwest Washington.

ton mayor Marion Barry caught smoking crack cocaine in a Washington hotel room. Not surprisingly, Barry lost reelection, as voters chose instead Sharon Pratt Dixon, the first African American woman to become mayor of a major U.S. city. Though Barry's missteps made him the brunt of many jokes and comedy routines, he remains a popular political figure with many D.C. voters. Barry won a second term as mayor in 1994 and, after leaving the office in infamy in 1998, came back to claim a City Council seat in 2004.

Barry's successor, Anthony A. Williams, took over the city's executive office in 1999 with a mandate to improve community safety, education, housing, transportation, and employment. Williams quickly befriended Congress and the local business community and ushered in an era of prosperity and development, particularly in the city's downtown district.

Tragedy, however, was just around the corner.

No events in the city's or country's complicated history compare with the devastating happenings of September 11, 2001. When terrorists slammed jets into the World Trade Center in New York City and the Pentagon in Arlington, Virginia, everyone in Washington, D.C. braced for more turmoil. The city went into immediate high-alert mode, and many of the increased security measures continue to this day. In the aftermath of the Virginia plane crash, the region has developed a thick skin, weathering other safety and security incidents—from anthrax scares to sniper shootings to crime emergencies—with heightened awareness and extreme resiliency. (For more on the recent happenings and their effects on the city, see the Overview chapter.)

Washington remains a city of contrasts, and problems aside, the Nation's Capital also deserves to be in the spotlight for many of its innovations and contributions. The '90s witnessed the opening of the distinguished U.S. Holocaust Memorial Museum, the grand reopening of the renovated Library of Congress, dedication of the inspiring Franklin Delano Roosevelt and Women in Military Service memorials, a $400-million facelift for Ronald Reagan Washington National Airport, opening of the 20,000-seat Verizon Center sports/entertainment arena, and construction of the huge Ronald Reagan Building and International Trade Centre.

Since 2000 the city has welcomed the International Spy Museum, National World War II Memorial, National Museum of the American Indian, and the reopening of the Smithsonian American Art Museum and National Portrait Gallery, along with a breathtaking new convention center. Major League Baseball returned to the nation's capital after a 30-year absence when the Washington Nationals arrived in 2005.

Such development has not been without challenges from local taxpayers, who felt that Mayor Williams's deep involvement with business and industry had taken precedence over the city's needs to improve its schools and community services. When Williams opted not to run for reelection in 2006, Washington, D.C. voters rallied behind Adrian Fenty, a youthful, energetic City Council member who pledged to transform the public school system, create affordable housing, and improve safety and security. Mayor Fenty faces the challenge of maintaining solid relationships with local businesses and stakeholders, while addressing the needs of the community.

Whether you live here or are just passing through, now is your chance to take a closer look at Washington, D.C. and create your own personal history in this intriguing city.

THE DISTRICT'S NEIGHBORS

The areas that lie just beyond the District's borders—the city of Alexandria and counties of Arlington and Fairfax in Virginia, and the counties of Montgomery and Prince George's in Maryland—are themselves rich with history.

Alexandria was, until 1846, included in the Washington boundaries. Founded in 1749 by Scottish merchants along the banks of the

Potomac, Alexandria served as a chief port of trade during the Revolutionary years. George Washington was a prominent town figure, active in Christ Church Parish and other civic organizations.

Another resident, esteemed soldier and statesman "Light-Horse" Harry Lee, in 1799 delivered the now-famous eulogy that described Washington as "first in war, first in peace, and first in the hearts of his countrymen." Lee's son Robert Edward, commander in chief of the Confederate armies during the Civil War, spent his childhood in Alexandria. Much of colonial Alexandria still stands, and its brick side streets and quaint townhouses make Old Town Alexandria a popular tourist destination.

You'll also find remnants of Northern Virginia's past in the independent city of Falls Church. Its historic namesake, the Falls Church, dating to 1769, stands at the corner of Fairfax and Washington Streets. People still worship in the building, which also served as a colonial recruitment facility and Civil War hospital. Falls Church's surrounding counties of Arlington and Fairfax also retain vestiges of earlier times. Robert E. Lee's Arlington House, Arlington National Cemetery, and in Fairfax City and County, several houses and fort sites, still draw visitors interested in the Civil War. Glimpse the agrarian lifestyles that once flourished in these parts by watching living history programs at Fairfax County's Historic Sully, a 1794 plantation, and Claude Moore Colonial Farm at Turkey Run. (See the Attractions chapter for more information.)

Amidst the residential developments, shopping centers, and office buildings that proliferate in the modern-day counties of metro Maryland, you'll still find traces of the prehistoric wilderness once roamed by Native Americans and discovered by English settlers like Captain John Smith in the 1600s. Prince George's County, which celebrated its tricentennial in 1996, originally included land that's now part of Washington, D.C. Once a thriving tobacco society, P.G. County still boasts historic homes and plantations, like the circa-

1811 Marietta in Glenn Dale, the 1780s' Montpelier Mansion in Laurel, and, dating to 1694, Darnall's Chance in Upper Marlboro. The circa-1828 White's Ferry on the Potomac River and the C&O Canal National Historic Park transport visitors to bygone days in Montgomery County, which has evolved from an agrarian community to an industrial center nicknamed "gateway to the nation's capital."

(Read more about D.C.'s neighbors in our Metro Washington Overview chapter.)

GETTING AROUND THE METRO AREA

Natives of Los Angeles or New York may chuckle at this notion, but getting around Metro Washington can be an intimidating experience for newcomers. Even longtime residents will concede that negotiating the network of often-congested highways, byways, and bridges that serves more than 5 million people often isn't the most pleasant of tasks.

In fact, recent research studies confirm that Washington, D.C. drivers suffer from headaches with good reason. According to the Texas Transportation Institute, Washington ranks third for the amount of time—roughly 69 hours annually per person—wasted during traffic tie-ups. Traffic jams also waste fuel, at the number 4 rate of 136 gallons per commuter annually. Meanwhile, a detailed transportation study by the Greater Washington Board of Trade cites the need for new roads and Potomac bridges to keep up with the D.C. area's steady population increase.

While the region has grown dramatically over the past 30 years or so in both population and the rate of commercial and residential development, the transportation infrastructure—due to a combination of political and bureaucratic stagnation, fiscal belt-tightening, and an acute case of shortsightedness—unfortunately has not kept pace. As shopping malls, housing tracts, and office parks sprouted on the landscape, roads, mass transit, and other transportation improvements all too often became an afterthought. Subsequent changes in commuting patterns further challenged planners, as more and more suburban residents began driving to neighboring suburbs to go to work instead of into the District. Although this shift took some of the strain off downtown, it resulted in rush-hour problems never envisioned in the 1960s.

On an average day, the sheer volume of traffic can make an ordinary nonrush-hour journey aggravating. Toss in an accident (even a fender bender moved to the road shoulder), a few snowflakes, some rain, a holiday weekend, or a Friday afternoon during the summer, and you've got the makings of a potentially harrowing ordeal.

That's the bad news.

Now for the good news:

With few exceptions, Metro Washington's roads are generally clean, well maintained, and even downright scenic in places (we offer the George Washington Memorial Parkway, Dulles Greenway, and even the unusually verdant Capital Beltway in spring as prime examples). Drivers can take comfort in knowing that many of the primary roads, notably the Beltway, are patrolled by motorist-assistance units—a courtesy service provided by the Virginia State Police. The assorted trucks and vans prove a welcome sight for countless folks confronting a flat tire, spewing radiator, empty gas tank, or other vehicular challenge.

Some notable progress also has been made in improving Metro Washington's transportation network. Major stretches of roadway have been widened; once-nightmarish intersections have been transformed into the safer and far more efficient under/over configuration; and the designation of HOV (high-occupancy vehicle) lanes, requiring two or three persons to a vehicle during rush hour, has encouraged carpooling. New roads like the Dulles Greenway, Fairfax County Parkway, and Franconia-Springfield Parkway have helped ease traffic burdens in Northern Virginia.

The area's biggest road construction project, the Virginia Department of Transportation's rebuilding of the notorious Springfield

Metro trains simplify getting around Washington, D.C. and its Maryland and Virginia suburbs. COURTESY WASHINGTON, D.C. CONVENTION AND TOURISM CORPORATION

Interchange, started in 1999 and is on target for completion in late 2007. Known as the "Mixing Bowl," through which 430,000 vehicles pass daily, this area where Interstates 95, 395, and 495 converge is considered the Capital Beltway's most dangerous stretch. To keep motorists on their toes and help lower the risk of serious accidents, state and county police patrol the interchange. The department provides daily construction updates so that drivers will know when to avoid the area. Call (877) 959–5222 for the latest information or log onto www.springfieldinterchange.com.

Drivers begrudging the slow progress on the Springfield Interchange should take heart. In June 2006, the first cars crossed the Potomac on the new Woodrow Wilson Bridge, which replaced a 1961 bridge by the same name. Like its predecessor, the new Wilson Bridge is the only federally owned drawbridge in the interstate highway system. The new bridge is 20 feet higher, however, allowing for fewer traffic disruptions from bridge openings. More traffic lanes also ease the bridge's notorious bottlenecking problems. Though the new bridge is a marked improvement, the project is not yet complete; a second span will open in 2008. Obtain updated information by calling (703) 329–0300, ext. 310, in Virginia, or (301) 686–0000, ext. 203, in Maryland. Or check out the Web site at www.wilsonbridge.com.

Maryland's first major highway construction project in years is also underway. The six-lane, 18-mile Intercounty Connector (ICC) will ease congestion on the Capital Beltway by creating a toll road to directly link the I–270 and I–95 corridors in central and eastern Montgomery County and northwestern Prince George's County. Scheduled for completion in 2010, the project has raised the ire of environmentalists and homeowners impacted by the $1.8-billion construction project. Get more information about the proposed route at www.iccproject.com or call (866) 462–0020.

VDOT helps maintain smooth traffic flow through use of the high-tech Smart Traffic management system, a computerized highway monitoring and control program that oversees

For the latest news about local transportation issues—plus entertaining letters from local motorists—check out Dr. Gridlock's column, appearing in the *Washington Post* on Sundays and Thursdays.

approximately 70 miles of I–66, I–95, and I–395 and helps detect and clear accidents and disabled vehicles. Smart Traffic uses closed-circuit cameras to keep an eye on traffic conditions, traffic counters embedded in the pavement to convey important information, ramp meters to regulate the number of vehicles entering the roadway, and variable message signs that alert motorists to accidents and other traffic-related events ahead. VDOT personnel monitor the system at a control center in Arlington, where they communicate not only with the public but with service patrols, state police, and traffic reporters.

In Maryland a similar traffic-management system called CHART, short for Chesapeake Highways Advisories Routing Traffic, also uses state-of-the-art technology (message signs, cameras, and detection devices, as well as patrol vehicles) to provide quick response to accidents and other road emergencies and help reduce congestion. The statewide program covers some 400 miles of highway and another 400 miles of major arterial roadways in Maryland's eight heavily traveled traffic corridors, including such locations as I–95 and I–395 at the Woodrow Wilson Bridge, I–495 north of the American Legion Bridge, and I–95 and I–495 south of U.S. 50. From its Web site, www.chart.state.md.us, you can also view live traffic shots on some of the state's most traveled roads to help plan your daily commute and weekend beach escapes.

Future major transportation improvement proposals include adding bridges and expanding rail systems and other means of getting people out of their single-passenger vehicles. Although these plans have been hotly debated at times, they are nevertheless cause for optimism.

In the meantime, you've got to deal with the situation at hand, and that's where we hope this chapter proves helpful. There's no substitute for experience, and that's particularly true when it comes to trying to find your way around unfamiliar territory. We hope that the following information will give you a feel for the region's overall transportation system and perhaps make those initial journeys somewhat less intimidating.

First, here are a couple of suggestions. Before tackling Metro Washington from behind the wheel or from any other perspective, we suggest that you get a good map and keep it nearby. We recommend the book-style variety produced locally by Alexandria Drafting Company (ADC), "The Map People," as they proudly bill themselves. ADC's detailed and easy-to-use maps of cities, counties, and the region are invaluable resources, as well as great providers of peace of mind. Updated frequently, they're widely available at convenience stores, drugstores, supermarkets, and bookstores. For more information, contact ADC at (800) 232–6277 or visit www.adcmap.com.

You'll also be wise to keep an ear tuned to the radio for the latest traffic information, both before you leave home or office and while in the car. All it takes is one nightmarish backup and you'll soon become a devout listener. Most local stations broadcast traffic reports frequently during the morning and evening rush hours, and a few offer updates throughout the day. Some of the most comprehensive coverage is on WMAL (630 AM) and WTOP (103.5 FM, 820 AM).

ROADWAYS

The Capital Beltway and Connecting Interstates

No matter how much you may wish to avoid it, as a driver in Metro Washington you're bound to travel the Capital Beltway (I–495), that 66-mile, 55-interchange ring of asphalt so many people love to hate. Envisioned as a bypass to Metro Washington when construction began in the early 1950s, it became instead the area's Main Street—at once a transportation lifeline and the bane of our existence. We curse it for legendary traffic jams, ill-conceived interchanges and entrance/exit ramps (though many of these have been dramatically improved), and that confusing Inner and Outer Loop business (we'll clear this up shortly)—but we also can't imagine living here without the Beltway.

History and Statistics

The road opened in stages beginning in 1957, with the federal government picking up 90 percent of the $189-million construction tab; the four- and six-lane version that was completed in 1964 was subsequently widened to eight lanes. No matter the number of lanes, at times it never seems to be enough. One workday soon after opening, the Beltway carried about 48,000 automobiles; today, the average daily figure tops 200,000 and is expected to top 250,000 by 2030.

Virginia and Maryland state police have jurisdiction over the Beltway and maintain a high profile in both marked and unmarked cruisers, ready to nab drivers exceeding the 55-mph speed limit, although off-peak traffic often zooms along at 65 mph or higher speeds. Flashing lights less likely to send your blood pressure skyward are yellow and found atop specially equipped vehicles that come to the aid of stranded motorists, helping prevent ordinary breakdowns from becoming extraordinary backups.

Although tractor-trailers make up only about 6 percent of Beltway traffic, you're likely to see more trucks on the road late at night and early in the morning when traffic is lighter. Big rigs are prohibited from traveling in the far-left fast lanes of the Beltway and are also subject to spot safety inspections. Although truckers are usually considered among the best drivers on the road, accidents involving tractor-trailers do happen. The worst of these accidents can paralyze the roadways for hours on end.

Which Loop Is Which?

Sooner or later you'll hear about or see the Inner and Outer Loops, the two portions of road that comprise the Beltway. Discerning which is which is actually pretty simple. Using Washington, D.C. as a reference point (better yet, refer to your handy ADC map), with the 12 o'clock position at the top, the Inner Loop is physically closer to the city, and traffic travels in a clockwise motion. The Outer Loop, naturally, sits a bit farther out, and traffic moves counterclockwise. This is easy, right? Well, you don't have to think about it as much as you used to. To alleviate some of the confusion, the Virginia and Maryland state highway departments several years ago posted signs that tell you which loop you're traveling.

Major Roads That Intersect the Capital Beltway

You could almost say that all roads in Metro Washington lead to the Beltway. Circumnavigating Washington, D.C. like a giant lasso with numerous appendages, it slices through Fairfax County and Alexandria in Northern Virginia, and Prince George's and Montgomery Counties in Maryland. It crosses the Potomac River twice, via the American Legion (also called Cabin John) Bridge at the northern border of Fairfax County and southern border of Montgomery County, and the aforementioned Woodrow Wilson Bridge, where eastern Fairfax County and western Prince George's County meet.

The Beltway offers access to these major thoroughfares:

I-66 intersects near Tysons Corner in Fairfax County, heading east into Arlington and the District and west toward Prince William County.

I-95 overlaps the Beltway's eastern side, veering south at Springfield for drivers headed toward Richmond, and north in Prince George's County for those traveling toward Baltimore.

I-270 connects to I-495 in Montgomery

i The I-95 Corridor Coalition provides a "Northeast Travelers Alert" map with accompanying descriptions of construction projects and probable bottlenecks on the major roadways from Virginia to Maine, produced each summer and fall. Look for it at travelers information centers or visit www.i95coalition.org.

County and leads north to Frederick, where it becomes I-70.

I-295, also known as the Baltimore-Washington Parkway, heads through southern sections of the District and up through Prince George's County toward Baltimore-Washington International Airport (BWI).

I-395, also known as Henry Shirley Memorial Highway, heads north into Arlington and the District, where it becomes I-295.

The Beltway also provides access to the Dulles Toll Road and the parallel Dulles Access Road; the scenic George Washington Memorial Parkway; well-traveled U.S. 1, 29, and 50; Virginia Routes 7, 123, 236, and Maryland Route 355; and numerous secondary roads.

Bridges and Traffic

No other highway in the area carries as much clout or can get us to so many places in so short a time, barring those horrendous traffic jams. While we're mentioning traffic, we'd better point out that the two bridges across the Potomac are the sites of some of the worst Beltway backups. Maryland and Virginia finally got wise and began stationing tow trucks at either end of each span during the morning and evening rush hours to remove disabled vehicles quickly.

Keep this in mind: Coming from Virginia, you must cross a bridge to get into the District. (If you manage to accomplish this otherwise, let us know and we'll put together an

i Rock Creek Parkway earned a listing on the National Register of Historic Places in May 2005.

amazing magic act.) Your five choices, starting north and working south, are Chain Bridge, linking the McLean/Arlington areas with Canal Road and upper northwest; Key Bridge, named for "Star-Spangled Banner" author Francis Scott Key, joining Rosslyn and Georgetown; Roosevelt Bridge, in the shadows of Rosslyn, where I–66 runs into Constitution Avenue NW; stately Memorial Bridge, perhaps the most picturesque of all, stretching from Arlington National Cemetery to the Lincoln Memorial at Rock Creek Parkway; and the 14th Street Bridge, where I–395 winds past the Pentagon and crosses the Potomac near the Tidal Basin and the Jefferson Memorial.

If you drive to work, remember that the morning rush hour in Metro Washington can begin as early as 5:00 A.M. along some stretches of the Beltway and other heavily traveled routes, such as Interstates 66, 95, 270, and 395, and as early as 3:30 P.M. for the drive home. Factor in extended crunch times during inclement weather, Fridays, and holiday weekends.

Beltway Safety Tips

Now that you know a little bit about the major thoroughfares, keep in mind some pointers to lessen aggravation and enhance safety:

- Leave earlier and know where you're going.
- Gas up before you go—remember that traffic jams can eat up a lot of fuel.
- Drive courteously and be alert.
- Learn alternate routes to avoid traffic jams.
- Don't rubberneck!

One Road, Many Names

To avoid confusion on roads that intersect the Beltway, remember that the same highway can have several different names. Here are a few prime examples: Virginia Route 7 is called Leesburg Pike in the Tysons Corner area, Broad Street in the City of Falls Church, and King Street in Alexandria. Virginia Route

236 is known as Duke Street in the Alexandria area, Little River Turnpike in Annandale, and Main Street in Fairfax City. Virginia Route 123 is Ox Road in southern Fairfax County, Chain Bridge Road in the Fairfax City area and again in Tysons Corner, Maple Avenue in the Vienna town limits, and Dolly Madison Boulevard in McLean. Maryland Route 355 also is known as Wisconsin Avenue inside the Beltway, and, in Rockville and beyond, Rockville Pike and Frederick Road. Nothing like a little variety to enhance your driving pleasure, eh?

Toll Roads

Dulles Toll Road
P.O. Box 9430
McLean, VA 22102
(703) 383–2700
www.smart-tag.com/
dulles_toll_road.htm
The Dulles Toll Road (Route 267), the region's only toll road except for the connecting Dulles Greenway, exceeded popularity expectations almost immediately after opening in 1984. Despite today's heavy traffic burden, commuters in the corridor, primarily from western Loudoun County and the Fairfax County communities of Herndon, Reston, Tysons Corner, Vienna, and McLean, are much better off with the road than they were before it was built.

The 14-mile highway, with 11 exits, runs parallel to the airport-only Dulles Access Road and feeds into I–66. The toll road consists of four lanes in each direction, with the far-left lanes designated HOV-2. (Look for HOV restrictions later in this chapter.)

Attendants staff the main toll plaza, between Spring Hill Road and Route 7, 24 hours a day. Booths at other entrances and exits are attended 16 hours a day (5:30 A.M. to 9:30 P.M. daily); outside of these hours, motorists need exact change for automatic toll machines. The toll is 75 cents at the main plaza and 50 cents at all other gates.

Drivers who frequent the toll road may want to buy a high-tech Smart Tag, a tiny electronic transponder that attaches to the rearview mirror and enables cars to pass through any toll lane without stopping. An initial Smart Tag account costs $35 if paid by credit card; a check payment requires an additional $25 deposit. For information on signing up for the program, call (703) 391–7630 or (877) 762–7824, ask for an application at the tollbooth, or visit the Web site at www.smart tag.com.

Dulles Greenway
(703) 707–8870
www.dullesgreenway.com
Privately operated by Toll Road Investors Partnership II (TRIP II), this 14-mile extension of the Dulles Toll Road opened in September 1995. The four-lane highway has eight interchanges. With a 65-mph speed limit, the scenic road offers a quick route to Leesburg, and an increasing number of motorists are willing to fork over the tolls, ranging from $1.55 on weekends to $3.20 on weekdays for cars. The road is a welcome addition for folks who commute into the city from Loudoun County: You can get from Leesburg to Herndon in about half the time required for the same commute relying on Routes 7 and 28. As an added bonus, commuters can receive cashback bonuses by enrolling in the VIP Miles Frequent Rider Program. Drivers also can enroll in the Smart Tag program, described in the Dulles Toll Road listing.

Major Parkways
Fairfax County Parkway
(703) 324–1100
This 35-mile, cross-county road has opened gradually in connecting sections since September 1987. It's especially handy for folks commuting between communities in different parts of the county. The road starts in western Fairfax County and crosses over U.S. 50, I–66, and Route 123 before turning into the Franconia/Springfield Parkway (Route 7900) at Rolling Road in Springfield. Travelers can follow Route 7900 to I–95. Total estimated cost of the entire, nearly completed project, which is funded through the county and Vir-

> **i** Even a dusting of snow can send local motorists into a panic. Drive defensively and be extra careful on shady spots and bridges, which ice up fast.

ginia Department of Transportation (VDOT), is $620 million.

George Washington Memorial Parkway
(703) 289–2500
www.nps.gov/gwmp
This parkway along the Potomac is one of the prettiest routes to travel into the District, but it can also be one of the most dangerous. Watch out for aggressive drivers and treacherous curves, but don't allow our words of caution to steer you away from this road, which runs from Mount Vernon to Great Falls, Virginia. (For more about the parkway's abundant natural, recreational, and historic sites, see our Parks and Recreation and Attractions chapters.)

HOV Restrictions

If you can get people to ride with you, the HOV lanes often get you home or to work faster and reduce auto and fuel expenses, air pollution, and traffic congestion.

If you're a newcomer and wonder how you'll be able to distinguish the HOV lanes, fear not; they're well marked with signs and either physical barriers (gates, concrete dividers) or diamond-shaped lane markings. Members of the law-enforcement community will be more than happy to remind you as well. Don't take HOV restrictions lightly. Scofflaws face healthy fines plus several points on their licenses for moving violations. You'll pay $125 for a first offense, $250 for a second, $500 for a third within two years of the second, and $1,000 for a fourth violation within three years of the second! Forget about putting a mannequin or some other human substitute in your car to get around the passenger requirements. The police have seen it all and don't take kindly to motorists trying to put one over on them. Perhaps, however, you can take

ℹ️ If you're thinking of bicycling to work, call the Washington Area Bicyclist Association at (202) 628–2500 or visit www.waba.org to download maps of regional trails.

advantage of one of the rules' few exceptions. You may use HOV lanes during HOV hours if you're a motorcyclist, if you're traveling on I–66 to or from Washington Dulles International Airport for business, or if you drive a hybrid fuel vehicle bearing clean, special fuel Virginia license plates (through July 1, 2007).

Here's a summary of the regional HOV scene (restrictions apply Monday through Friday only, excluding holidays).

- I–395/I–95: HOV-3 (three or more people)

Where: A 30-mile stretch of road runs from the 14th Street Bridge in the District to Route 234 in Prince William County.

When: Two lanes, separated by barriers, operate northbound from 6:00 A.M. to 9:00 A.M., and southbound from 3:30 P.M. to 6:00 P.M.

- I–66, inside the Capital Beltway: HOV-2 (two or more people)

Where: A 10-mile length of road stretches from Theodore Roosevelt Bridge to the Capital Beltway eastbound.

When: Two eastbound lanes are designated HOV-2 from 6:30 to 9:00 A.M. Two westbound lanes are designated HOV-2 from 4:00 to 6:30 P.M.

- I–66 outside the Beltway: HOV-2

Where: An 18-mile stretch runs from the Capital Beltway to Route 234 in Manassas.

When: Outside the Beltway, the far-left lane in each direction is painted with diamonds to designate HOV travel from 5:30 to 9:30 A.M. eastbound and from 3:00 to 7:00 P.M. westbound.

- Dulles Toll Road: HOV-2

Where: The road runs from Route 28 to the main toll plaza.

When: The far-left lane is reserved for HOV-2 travel from 6:30 to 9:00 A.M. eastbound, 4:00 to 6:30 P.M. westbound.

- I–270: HOV-2 (two or more people, hybrids not exempt)

Where: In Montgomery County, Maryland, traveling south from I–370 to I–495 and north from I–495 to Clarksburg, Maryland.

When: One southbound lane is designated HOV-2 from 6:00 to 9:00 A.M. One northbound lane is designated HOV-2 from 3:30 to 6:30 P.M.

During these times, the far-right "lanes" (note the electronic green and red control signals overhead) that run for about 7 miles on I–66 are open to traffic; otherwise, these stretches of dark pavement (to distinguish them from the regular lanes) are used as shoulders only, and traffic is strictly prohibited, so please heed the signs. It can make for a dangerous situation if drivers aren't paying attention or choose to ignore the restrictions. To alleviate the nasty bottleneck conditions that have long plagued I–66, the road is being gradually widened to the west. Although the project is far from complete, newly widened lanes have opened to drivers in some of the most congested areas. Expect to see construction work and experience some related traffic tie-ups during off-peak hours along this heavily traveled corridor for quite some time.

For More Info

For answers to questions about highway travel in the region, we suggest you contact the following offices:

- Virginia Department of Transportation, 1401 East Broad Street, Richmond, Virginia, (804) 786–2801, www.virginia dot.org
- Maryland Transportation Authority, 2310 Broening Highway, Suite 150, Baltimore, Maryland, (866) 713–1596, www.mdta .state.md.us
- District of Columbia Department of Transportation, Sixth Floor, 2000 14th Street NW, Washington, D.C., (202) 673–6813, www.ddot.dc.gov

A Washington Driving Primer

Washington is indeed one of the most beautiful and well-planned cities anywhere—with its broad avenues, abundant parks, and open space—but that doesn't mean it's a pleasure to drive in, especially for newcomers.

Confusing one-way streets, traffic circles, a critical shortage of on-street parking spaces, outrageous prices for parking garages (expect to pay $15 or more a day), and other factors can frustrate the uninitiated. Finding a place to park can be both costly and aggravating, and police don't hesitate for a moment to hand out tickets. Ignore those and you may find your car towed or perhaps wearing a boot, a heavy steel clamp attached to a front wheel, preventing the car from being driven and ensuring the car owner a bit of embarrassment. All of this underscores the beauty of walking and using public transportation such as Metrorail, Metrobus, or a taxicab. Fortunately, the city's relatively small size and its grid system street layout are helpful to newcomers. With a good map, some patience, and a bit of practice, Washington is actually not a difficult place to get around.

When pondering Washington's street system, remember that the U.S. Capitol is the geographic center. The city is arranged in four sections—Northwest, Northeast, Southwest, and Southeast—with the dividing lines being North Capitol Street, South Capitol Street, East Capitol Street, and the National Mall, radiating like spokes of a wheel from the Capitol building. The Northwest, Northeast, Southwest, and Southeast used in addresses are very important. An address on M Street NW could also be found on M Street SE, so keep this in mind when mailing something, and especially when trying to get somewhere.

Streets that run north-south (14th, 15th, 18th, etc.) are numbered in sequence, while those going east-west are lettered (H, M, R, and so forth) in alphabetical order. There are no J, X, Y, or Z Streets. Streets with state names (Pennsylvania, Connecticut) are all diagonals. Circles and squares occur at the intersections of diagonal avenues and numbered and lettered streets.

THE METRO SYSTEM AND OTHER GROUND TRANSPORTATION NETWORKS

The Metro

Washington Metropolitan Area Transit Authority (Metro)
600 5th Street NW
Washington, DC
(202) 637–7000, (202) 638–3780 TTY
www.wmata.com

Metro Washington is blessed with the country's second-largest rail transit and fifth-largest bus system—Metro, short for the Washington Metropolitan Area Transit Authority (WMATA). The acclaimed Metrorail is clean, efficient, inexpensive, and, yes, even attractive. Good luck finding any graffiti, but you will see some spectacular concrete work, dramatic arched ceilings, graceful lines, and towering escalators, giving the primarily underground system a futuristic appearance.

Metro is generally safe, but deadly accidents have happened on rare occasions. Be careful not to ensnare loose clothing in the moving steps of the escalators. Keep a cautious distance from the platform edge, and make sure to enter and exit quickly. When you hear a loud electronic bell-like tone, watch for the doors to snap open or shut.

"America's Subway" first opened in 1976 and has grown to link a large portion of the National Capital Area. It's especially loved by commuters and tourists, as it offers superb access to the major business districts as well as such popular destinations as the Smithsonian,

i If you're exiting at Metro Center, Gallery Place, or L'Enfant Plaza, make note of which exit you're taking. When in doubt, ask the station manager for assistance.

i When you're riding Metro's Orange or Blue Line into Virginia, you may find your ears popping as you reach the Rosslyn station. That's when you're traveling under the Potomac River in a tunnel.

the Pentagon, the National Zoo, Ronald Reagan Washington National Airport, and Arlington National Cemetery.

Metro's general manager reports to the Metro Board, whose members include representatives from the District, Maryland, and Virginia. Area jurisdictions served by Metro pay a subsidy to the system, and residents pay a few cents extra per gallon of gasoline to help fund Metro's operation, maintenance, and expansion.

Each of Metrorail's five lines—Orange, Red, Green, Blue, and Yellow—passes through the District at some point. The recently expanded Green Line now extends from Branch Avenue in Prince George's County to Greenbelt, on the other side of P.G. County. The Orange Line stretches from Vienna, Virginia, to New Carrollton, Maryland; the Red, from Shady Grove, Maryland, to Glenmont, Maryland. The Blue Line runs from Largo, Maryland, in P.G. County to Franconia-Springfield, right off the convenient Franconia/Springfield Parkway. The Yellow Line goes from the Huntington area of Fairfax County to Mt. Vernon Square in the District. Metrorail boasts 86 stations along 106.3 miles of track. An expansion is planned to follow the Dulles Toll Road to Dulles International Airport.

The system operates from 5:30 A.M. to midnight, Monday through Thursday, 5:30 A.M. to 3:00 A.M. Fridays, 7:00 A.M. to 3:00 A.M. Saturdays, and 7:00 A.M. to midnight Sundays. The last trains leave some stations prior to midnight; refer to signs in stations for details. Trains as well as buses run on a reduced schedule on certain holidays.

i The 230-foot escalator at the Wheaton Metro Station is the largest in the Western Hemisphere.

Large brown pylons topped with Metro's distinctive "M" logo mark all station entrances. There's also good signage along roads for those stations accessible by auto.

Instead of cash or tokens, Metro operates on a farecard system. Every passenger must have a farecard to enter and exit, except children younger than age five, two of whom may travel free with a paying rider. Fares start at $1.35 and vary depending on the time of day and distance traveled. To determine your fare, look at a hard-to-miss map to determine your destination, and then check the posted fee schedule for the peak and off-peak fares to that station. Peak (rush) hours of operation are 5:30 A.M. to 9:30 A.M. and 3:00 P.M. to 7:00 P.M., Monday through Friday. Off-peak occurs all other times and on federal holidays. Although the system is far busier during the peak periods, the trains also run more often—the wait any time of day is rarely longer than 15 minutes.

Purchasing a farecard may seem confusing at first, but it's easily mastered. Farecard machines in every station accept nickels, dimes, quarters, and $1.00 and $5.00 bills; some machines also accept $10 bills, $20 bills, and credit and debit cards. Be aware, however, that change comes in coins only, and machines provide no more than $4.95 in change. Put your money in the machine or swipe your credit card and when you've pushed the "+" and "-" buttons to reach your desired fare amount, press another button to receive your card. To avoid having to run to an Addfare machine to get in or out of a station, you should consider purchasing a little more fare than you think you might need for a round-trip. Better still, just keep a farecard with $10 or $20 worth of travel stashed in your wallet or purse at all times. You never know when it might come in handy.

You also can purchase special passes, such as a $6.50 one-day pass geared toward tourists, who can ride after 9:30 A.M. on weekdays and all day on weekends and holidays, at farecard vending machines. Metro also offers various large-denomination passes that save time and expense for commuters. Purchase special passes at Metro Headquarters, 600 Fifth Street NW, Washington, D.C. It's open from 8:00 A.M. to 1:00 P.M. on weekdays and from 2:00 to 4:00 P.M. on weekends. You also can purchase special farecards at the Metro Center Sales Office, 12th and F Streets NW, Washington, D.C., open from 7:30 A.M. to 6:30 P.M. on weekdays, or at the Pentagon Sales Office at the Pentagon Concourse, open from 7:00 A.M. to 7:00 P.M. weekdays. You can purchase special passes at Giant, Safeway, or Superfresh supermarkets; by calling (202) 637–7000; and at several Commuter Stores, listed on the Web site.

Metrobus goes everywhere the rail system does, and then some, reaching far into suburban areas as well as the inner city. More than 70 percent of the buses in Metro's 1,300-plus fleet come equipped with wheelchair lifts. Bus routes and schedules are coordinated with rail routes and schedules to provide a comprehensive transportation system. Individual bus routes are detailed on brochures available at Metrorail stations and in various town, city, and county transportation offices. Metrobus fares are $1.25 for regular routes, $3.00 for express routes. Senior citizens and disabled passengers ride for 60 cents with valid IDs and transfers.

Parking is available at many Metrorail stations, but there are a few things you'll want to bear in mind before you park and ride. During the week, plan to arrive at the station early— the lots fill up quickly with commuters. Parking fees range from $2.50 to $4.00 per day, depending on the station, but it's important to know that cash and credit cards are not accepted. Instead, you'll need to purchase a SmarTrip card, a reusable, debit-style card that can also be used as a farecard. Pass the SmarTrip card across an electronic reader when you enter or exit a station and as you exit the parking lot and your fares will be deducted from the account balance. SmarTrip cards cost $5.00 and are available for purchase at vending machines at most Metro stations and at ticket sales offices. Some stations also feature

i Metro set a one-day ridership record of 850,636 on June 9, 2004, the day of Ronald Reagan's funeral.

a limited number of metered, short-term parking spaces. If you're dropping off someone, follow signs for the kiss and ride lane.

If you have questions while at a Metrorail station, don't hesitate to ask an employee in the information booth near the entrance gates. Otherwise, for general Metrorail and Metrobus details and timetables, call the ridership information line listed above or visit Metro's comprehensive Web site. Operators are on duty daily from 6:00 A.M. to 10:30 P.M. weekdays, and 8:00 A.M. to 10:30 P.M. weekends. Transit Police can be reached in emergencies at (202) 962–2121. Did you leave something behind? Call Lost and Found at (202) 962–1195.

Bus Systems
Washington, D.C.

Circulator
1250 H Street NW, 10th Floor
Washington, DC
(202) 962–1423
www.dccirculator.com
Washington, D.C.'s newest transportation option, the Circulator, was launched in 2005 to provide easy connections between downtown, Capitol Hill, Georgetown, and the National Mall on sleek, efficient buses. An east–west route runs between Georgetown and Union Station; a north–south route links the Washington Convention Center and surrounding Shaw neighborhood with the Southwest Waterfront, just south of the National Mall. A seasonal route also passes the perimeter of the National Mall. Priced at $1.00 per ride, the Circulator operates daily, every five to ten minutes, from 7:00 A.M. to 9:00 P.M. Some late-night service is also available. Cash and Metro SmarTrip cards are accepted; passes are available for purchase from ticket kiosks located at some stops.

i Parking at a Metro station? Make sure you have a SmarTrip card—you'll need it in order to exit the garage. Cards are sold in vending machines at all of the suburban stations with parking and at the sales office at Metro Center.

Visit the Web site for route information and stop locations.

Greyhound Bus Lines
1005 1st Street NE
Washington, DC
(202) 289–5154, (800) 229–9424
www.greyhound.com
Greyhound offers a less expensive, albeit more time-consuming, alternative to air and rail travel. The automated phone line lists departure times and fares for Atlanta, Boston, New York, Newark, Norfolk, Philadelphia, Pittsburgh, and Richmond. The buses also travel to and from a few suburban stations.

Northern Virginia

Alexandria Transit Company's DASH
116 South Quaker Lane
Alexandria, VA
(703) 370–3274
www.dashbus.com
DASH buses offer daily service in Alexandria and provide links to Metrobus, Metrorail, Virginia Railway Express, and the Fairfax Connector bus system. DASH takes rush-hour passengers to all Alexandria Metrorail stations, as well as the nearby Pentagon station. Base fares are $1.00, with a 25-cent supplemental charge for Pentagon service. Kids younger than age four ride for free, with up to two per paying customer. A $30 Dash Pass, available at Alexandria City Hall and other locations, is good for unlimited rides for a month. Call the city at (703) 370–3274 for information about door-to-door service for mobility-impaired passengers.

City of Fairfax CUE Bus Service
10455 Armstrong Street
Fairfax, VA
(703) 385–7859
www.fairfaxva.gov/CUEbus/CUEbus.asp
This daily service offers rides in the city of Fairfax and to the Vienna Metrorail Station and George Mason University. Regular fares are 75 cents. You can purchase convenient 10-ticket booklets through the City Treasurer's Office (703–385–7900). High school students with school IDs, elementary and intermediate students, ID-carrying seniors age 60 and older, disabled persons, and George Mason students, faculty, and staff with university IDs ride for 50 cents. Children ages three and younger ride for free when accompanied by an adult. On weekdays, passengers can ride for 50 cents from the Vienna station by presenting to the driver a Metro rail-to-bus transfer, available at the station. Disabled persons should call the service to arrange City Wheels or Metro Access transportation.

Fairfax Connector
12055 Government Center Parkway
Suite 1034
Fairfax, VA
(703) 339–7200, (703) 339–1608 TDD
www.fairfaxconnector.com
One of the largest community bus systems, with around 50 routes, the daily Fairfax Connector serves much of Fairfax County. Riders need exact cash or Metrobus passes, tokens, or commuter tickets, and rides cost $1.00 to $3.00. All buses in the Reston/Herndon area are wheelchair lift–equipped. To schedule a wheelchair-accessible ride elsewhere, call a day in advance.

OmniRide
14700 Potomac Mills Road
Woodbridge, VA
(703) 730–6664, (888) 730–6664
www.prtctransit.org
This Prince William County–based commuter bus service, managed by the Potomac and Rappahannock Transportation Commission,

provides weekday rides to Franconia-Springfield, West Falls Church, the Pentagon, Crystal City, Vienna, and the District. Fares are $5.50, free for children younger than six. A 10-ride pass costs $38. The commission also manages OmniLink, a local weekday bus service serving eastern Prince William County and Manassas, and OmniMatch, a car pool coordinating service.

Virginia Regional Transportation Association
109 North Bailey Lane
Purcellville, VA
(540) 338–1610
www.transitservices.org
This bus service offers a fixed route in Leesburg and door-to-door service throughout the county on weekdays and Saturdays. Fixed-route service includes travel from Leesburg to the county hospital east of town and from the hospital to Reston in western Fairfax County. Fares range from 50 cents to $2.00, depending on the type of trip.

Suburban Maryland

The Bus
Prince George's County Department of Public Works and Transportation
9400 Peppercorn Place, Suite 320
Landover, MD
(301) 324–2877
www.goprincegeorgescounty.com
The county's newest bus service covers routes from Upper Marlboro to the New Carrollton and Addison Road Metrorail stations. Fares are 75 cents for adults, 35 cents for senior citizens age 55 and older and disabled persons, and free for children younger than 5, one child per paying adult. Disabled residents, senior citizens, and others unable to use existing bus and rail service can contact P.G. County's Call-A-Bus service at (301) 499–8603 for transportation weekdays 8:30 A.M. to 3:30 P.M. Fares are $1.00 or 50 cents for disabled persons and seniors.

For comprehensive travel and commuting information, check out www.godcgo.com. The site features an interactive map to help you find your way to your destination, links to Metro and other regional transit system Web sites, plus helpful information about parking, bicycling trails, and a taxi fare calculator.

Ride-On
110 North Washington Street
Rockville, MD
(240) 777–7433
www.rideonbus.com
This Montgomery County bus service runs daily, supplementing Metrobus service. Fares are $1.25. Children age four and younger ride for free, up to two per fare-paying passenger. Fares for seniors and persons with disabilities are 60 cents at all times with valid IDs. You can obtain special passes, such as the Regional One Day Bus Pass for $3.00, and a 20-trip ticket for $20.00, at local Giant supermarkets, government service centers, and libraries. Riders ages 18 and younger can obtain Monthly Cruiser Passes for $10 each.

Train Service

Amtrak
Union Station, 50 Massachusetts
Avenue NE
Washington, DC
(202) 484–7540, (800) 872–RAIL,
(800) 523–6590 TDD
www.amtrak.com
The first-class Acela Express service runs at speeds up to 150 mph between Washington's grandly restored Union Station (Massachusetts Avenue and North Capitol Street NE), New York, and Boston, offering 15 daily weekday departures and few stops. Passengers also can take the 125-mph Metroliner service, with multiple departures daily. Trains travel to such cities as Baltimore, Philadelphia, Boston, Richmond, and Atlanta. An Amtrak Auto Train to Florida departs from Lorton. Call to obtain detailed schedule and fare information.

You can also pick up Amtrak trains at the following commuter stations:

- 110 Callahan Drive, Alexandria, Virginia
- Railroad Avenue, Quantico, Virginia
- 1040 Express Way, Woodbridge, Virginia
- 4300 Garden City Drive, New Carrollton, Maryland
- Hungerford Drive and Park Street, Rockville, Maryland

Maryland Commuter Rail Service (MARC)
6 Saint Paul Street
Baltimore, MD
(800) 325–RAIL
www.mtamaryland.com

Trains operate from 5:00 A.M. to midnight Monday through Friday between Washington's Union Station and Baltimore (including Oriole Park at Camden Yards and BWI Airport), serving many of the key commuter corridors of Prince George's County. Fares vary according to your destination; you can travel from Union Station to the Camden Yards station for $7.00 one way; $52.50 for a week's fares or $175 for a month's worth. MARC also links the region with Martinsburg, West Virginia and Frederick, Maryland. Two children younger than age six can travel free with a rider paying full fare.

Virginia Railway Express (VRE)
1500 King Street, Suite 202
Alexandria, VA
(703) 684–1001
www.vre.org

VRE operates two lines: the Manassas Line, between Manassas and the District, and the Fredericksburg Line, from Fredericksburg to the District.

Manassas Line stations are located in Manassas, Manassas Park, Burke Centre, Springfield, Alexandria, Arlington, and the District. Fredericksburg Line stations are in Fredericksburg, Falmouth, Stafford, Quantico, Woodbridge, Lorton, Springfield, Alexandria, Arlington, and the District. As with Metro, VRE has easy-to-spot roadside directional signs to help guide travelers to the stations, four of which are just a short walk from easy connections with Metrorail—at L'Enfant Plaza and Union Station in the District, and at Crystal City and King Street (Alexandria) in Northern Virginia. Single-ride fares range in price from $2.40 to $8.80, depending on your travel route. You can buy discounted 10-trip and monthly passes. Senior citizens, riders ages 21 and younger, and disabled people can ride for 50 percent off the regular fare.

Taxicabs

District taxi fares are based on a zone pricing system, ranging from $6.50 for a single zone to $18.90 for an eight-zone ride. You'll pay an extra $1.50 per additional person. A rush-hour surcharge of $1.00 applies from 7:00 to 9:30 A.M. and 4:00 to 6:30 P.M. on weekdays. If you're planning an interstate trip, call (202) 331–1671. Contact the D.C. Taxicab Commission, 2041 Martin Luther King Jr. Avenue SE, Washington, D.C., (202) 645–6018, dctaxi .dc.gov, with questions or complaints. A fare calculator on the Web site enables you to calculate the taxi fare between two points in the city so that you won't be "taken for a ride," so to speak.

You shouldn't have any trouble hailing a cab in the District. In the suburbs you'll most readily find them at Metro stops and the airports; otherwise, you'll need to call to arrange a pickup. Cabs in the suburban jurisdictions still use a traditional meter system.

COMMUTER AIDS

Arlington County Commuter Assistance Program
Arlington County Department of Public Works, Planning Division
2100 Clarendon Boulevard, Suite 717
Arlington, VA
(703) 228–3725
www.commuterpage.com

If your commute takes you to or through Arlington, check out CommuterPage.com for comprehensive information on transportation alternatives, traffic, weather, and fare purchasing information.

Commuter Connections
Metropolitan Washington Council of
Governments
777 North Capitol Street NE, Suite 300
Washington, DC
(800) 745–RIDE
www.commuterconnections.org

Are you interested in joining a car pool? Missed your ride home because you had to work late? Need information about local mass transit? Commuter Connections, a regional transportation information network, is ready to come to the rescue with solutions to common dilemmas. If you regularly travel to work via car alternatives, your can join the Guaranteed Ride Home program, which provides free rides home from work, up to four times annually, in cases of emergencies, illnesses, or unscheduled overtime. The network's rideshare database also helps people find car pools or van pools in their neighborhoods. Commuter Connections helps companies implement commuting and "telework" programs; provides information about Park-and-Ride lots, HOV locations, and public transit options; and publishes a quarterly newsletter.

AIRPORT OPTIONS: REAGAN, DULLES, AND BWI

Washington ranks as one of the top five domestic and international air travel markets, according to the Greater Washington Board of Trade. Naturally, air travel to and from Washington-area airports has been a shaky proposition for many passengers following September 11, 2001. Although security check-in procedures are improving, air travelers can expect long lines and more thorough inspections. In fact, most airlines strongly recommend arriving at least two hours before your scheduled departure time. (For more specifics about security measures and passenger restrictions, visit the airport's Web site.)

When traveling requires you to leave the ground, however, you'll be glad that Metro Washington is served by not one, but three

i You'll often hear Ronald Reagan Washington National Airport referred to simply as "National." It was renamed for Reagan in 1998, but the "new" name hasn't quite stuck for some of us.

major airports: Ronald Reagan Washington National; its sister facility, Washington Dulles; and Baltimore/Washington International Thurgood Marshall, commonly called BWI. This situation offers travelers some real advantages in scheduling, carrier selection, and, to a lesser degree, fares. Combined, the three airports handle about 65 million passengers annually and are served by roughly 50 scheduled airlines. The region is a major cargo hub as well, with more than a billion pounds of airfreight transported annually. Dulles, with seven air cargo buildings, gets most of the region's cargo business.

While BWI is state-owned and -operated, Reagan and Dulles are managed by the Metropolitan Washington Airports Authority (MWAA), an agency created by an act of Congress in 1987. Before the dawn of MWAA, whose board of directors features equal representation by Virginia, Maryland, and District residents, Reagan and Dulles were the only two civil airports in the nation run by the federal government. Contrary to public perception, MWAA is self-financed; no state or local tax revenues are used to fund airport activities or construction. Reagan and Dulles are very much in Northern Virginia, despite the announcement you may hear on the plane flying in, or the occasional Washington, D.C. address or phone number you may see.

For general information on Reagan and Dulles, call the Metropolitan Washington Airports Authority at (703) 417–8000 or log onto www.mwaa.com. Both Reagan and Dulles are served by the Authority's Washington Flyer Ground Transportation System (703–685–1400,

i Traffic delays are not uncommon on the routes to area airports, so leave for the airport with time to spare.

www.washfly.com), a network of buses, taxis, and limousines. Regular bus service is offered between Dulles and the West Falls Church Metrorail station. Metro also offers bus service to Dulles Airport via L'Enfant Plaza in D.C., with stops at Rosslyn, Tysons Corner, and Herndon. To get to BWI, you can take the MARC train from Union Station or a Metro express bus from the Greenbelt Metro Station. Read on for more information about each individual airport.

Baltimore/Washington International Thurgood Marshall Airport
Anne Arundel County, MD
(800) I–FLY–BWI
www.bwiairport.com

Baltimore/Washington International often seems overshadowed by Reagan and Dulles, but that's changing. In January of 2002 BWI became the first airport designated for an airline security study by the Transportation Security Administration (TSA). BWI is modern, easy to get to, easy to use, and ably serves both of its namesake markets with all major domestic carriers. More than 19 million people flew out of the airport in 2005. A 370,000-square-foot International Pier opened recently, garnering high praise from the local media. Other recent projects include parking garage expansion, motorized pedestrian walkways, and a recreational trail.

The airport boasts a handful of foreign airlines, including Air Canada, Air Jamaica, British Airways, and Icelandair. BWI has taken the lead in offering regional residents the greatest number of choices in low-cost airlines. As a result, Southwest Airlines transports nearly half (49 percent) of all passengers. Another budget carrier, AirTran, comes in second with 10 percent.

i Ronald Reagan Washington National Airport was built on land that was largely underwater and considered part of the District of Columbia. Although the airport is now geographically and legally in Virginia, it's overseen by Congress.

The fact that BWI is so user-friendly, boasts ample parking, and is served by both the Amtrak and MARC rail lines gives the airport added clout with the flying public. Garage parking is free for the first half-hour and between 10:00 P.M. and 1:00 A.M. nightly, a welcome bonus if you're just dropping off a passenger. Rates after the first 30 minutes are $2.00 per half-hour, with a maximum $20.00 for the day. The newest parking garage, at Maryland 170 and Elm Road, offers several thousand spaces at $2.00 per hour or $10.00 per day. Parking in one of Lot B's 1,400 spaces also costs $2.00 per hour, or $11.00 maximum per day. Other parking options include ESP Parking, with on-demand shuttle service at $3.00 per hour, with a $14.00 daily maximum; and Long-Term Parking, with many shuttles, at $1.00 per hour, with an $8.00 daily maximum. Eight car rental companies are on the premises, and visitors will find plenty of taxis and limousines.

While you wait, grab a bite to eat at one of the airport's fast-food restaurants or bars, or browse one of the specialty shops like the Smithsonian Museum Shop. The airport also has a game room and observation gallery to keep fidgety kids happy.

Count on driving for nearly an hour to BWI from downtown Washington or Northern Virginia—and that's without heavy traffic! The airport is in Anne Arundel County just off the Baltimore-Washington Parkway, but is also easily accessible from I–95. Ample signs posted along the Maryland portion of the Capital Beltway clearly show you which exit to take for BWI.

Ronald Reagan Washington National Airport
Arlington County, VA
(703) 417–8000
www.mwaa.com/national/index.html

The September 11 terrorist attack on the Pentagon, just a few miles away, greatly impacted Reagan National, as President George W. Bush decided to exercise extreme caution and close the bustling airport. Gradu-

GETTING AROUND THE METRO AREA

ally the airport bounced back and resumed business as usual, albeit with tighter security.

The $400-million main terminal that opened at Reagan in July 1997 is a dazzling landmark—the cornerstone of the airport authority's hefty modernization and improvement program for both Reagan and Dulles. Designed by award-winning architect Cesar Pelli, the spacious terminal, with its scalloped roof and striking control tower, proves as convenient as it is eye-catching. As passengers follow clearly marked paths to their gates, they can enjoy the skylit views in the high, vaulted ceiling; admire tiled floor medallions, colorful railing panels, murals, glass friezes, and sculptures designed by nationally known artists; browse in shops like Brooks Brothers and the National Geographic Store; and grab snacks or meals at various sit-down and take-out restaurants.

Joined to the terminal by a covered walkway, one of three parking garages offers quick access. A stone's throw from the pedestrian bridge, Metro's Blue and Yellow Lines pick up and deposit riders. Reagan, which has served the region since 1941, will only get better, not bigger, as airport officials like to say.

Reagan is the region's close-in, short-haul airport; it handles domestic traffic only, with nonstop flights limited to 1,250 miles. The number of landings and takeoffs each day is tightly controlled by federal regulations to limit noise. In Arlington County just off the George Washington Memorial Parkway and abutting the Potomac River (from which much of the airport's landmass was claimed), it could not be much closer to the heart of Washington, D.C. Under normal traffic conditions, it's about a 10-minute ride from the airport, up the parkway, over the 14th Street Bridge, and into the District. It's only about another five minutes to Capitol Hill. Reagan is unbeatable for convenience. Just ask a member of Congress or anyone who works or lives in nearby Crystal City, Rosslyn, or Alexandria. The airport is served by all the major domestic carriers and a host of commuter airlines, as well as the popular US Airways and Delta shuttles that ferry passengers hourly between Washington, New York, and Boston.

Hourly parking is $2.00 per half-hour for the first two hours, then $4.00 an hour. There's a $36.00-per-day maximum. Park in the daily garage for $5.00 per hour, with a $17.00 daily maximum. Parking at long-term lots, with free shuttles, costs $3.00 an hour, and $10.00 maximum per day.

i Superstitious? You won't find a Gate 13 at Ronald Reagan Washington National Airport!

Washington Dulles International Airport
Fairfax and Loudoun Counties, VA
(703) 417–8000
www.mwaa.com/dulles/index.html

Dulles, at the end of the airport-only access road 26 miles (about 45 minutes) from downtown Washington, is the area's full-service domestic and international hub. Dulles was the first airport built for the jet age, opening in 1962 and named after John Foster Dulles, secretary of state under President Eisenhower. Finnish-born architect Eero Saarinen sought to convey the movement of flight in his design of the stunning main terminal, which the American Institute of Architects has recognized as one of the greatest architectural achievements of the twentieth century. Beauty wasn't a harbinger of immediate success, however. Plagued by a "white elephant" label virtually from day one, Dulles languished severely until the mid-1980s, when a concerted effort was made to market and promote the airport and its rich, untapped potential.

Airlines and passengers have since been flocking to Dulles in increasing numbers as the airport further establishes itself as a major player in international aviation. Fifteen major domestic airlines (United has a substantial presence) and 19 foreign carriers serve Dulles. The roster continues to grow as the airport expands and bolsters its role as an East Coast hub for travel to Europe and the Far East. Its

11,000-acre site on the Loudoun-Fairfax border, a broad expanse of meadows and forest near established residential areas and a booming business corridor, provides room for enlargement that few airports in the world can match.

In recent years Dulles has added a new international terminal, additional parking, and a new air traffic control tower. Travelers can expect the development (and related construction) to continue as part of the Airport Authority's $3.4 billion D2 Dulles Development Program, whose projects include replacing the airport's mobile lounge system with an underground people-mover and pedestrian-walkway system and adding a new concourse to the main terminal and two new runways. Plans are also progressing to connect Dulles directly with downtown D.C. via Metro's new Silver Line, with an expected delivery date of 2015.

Meanwhile, many people still find Dulles easily accessible, thanks to the access road, which connects to I-66. Parking proves relatively hassle-free, with close-to-terminal and various reduced-price satellite options available. The terminal has a variety of eateries and shops to keep passengers occupied while waiting.

Dulles passengers can choose from numerous parking options, including a new, adjacent daily garage with 4,600 spaces. The hourly lot costs $4.00 per hour, up to $36.00 for 24 hours. Daily parking costs $5.00 per hour, with a maximum of $15.00 for 24 hours. If you'll be gone several days, opt for long-term parking, which costs $3.00 per hour, with a maximum of $9.00 for 24 hours. Your first 20 minutes are free in any of the lots. If you're running hopelessly late, you can get valet parking right in front of the main terminal. It will cost you, however: $30 for the initial 24 hours, and $17 for each day after that. At least you'll catch your flight!

Other Area Airports

Northern Virginia

Leesburg Municipal Airport
1001 Sycolin Road SE
Leesburg, VA
(703) 737-7125
www.flyvirginia.com/airport/jyo
The Leesburg Airport—also known as Godfrey Airport as a tribute to famous former resident Arthur Godfrey—boasts an FAA Automated Flight Service Station, two professional flight schools, and a variety of aircraft available for rent. A Reliever Airport, designated by the Federal Aviation Administration to relieve congestion at nearby Washington Dulles International, Leesburg has a 5,500-foot runway. The airport offers full aircraft maintenance services, an on-site conference room, and courtesy features for both passengers and flight crews.

Manassas Regional Airport
Off Route 28, 4 miles southeast of
Manassas, VA
(703) 361-1882
www.manassascity.org
One of the busiest airports in Virginia, this 830-acre airport founded in 1964 handles about 140,000 takeoffs and landings annually. It has a 5,700-foot-by-100-foot primary runway with Instrument Landing System and a terminal building that opened in September 1996. It houses the Freedom Museum (703-393-0660, 877-393-0660, www.freedommuseum.org), which opened in July of 1999. The patriotic museum honors Americans who fought and died for freedom. Hours are 10:00 A.M. to 4:00 P.M. daily. Admission is free.

The airport boasts more than 300 based aircraft, the most of any airport in the state.

The FAA Level 2 Tower is open 6:30 A.M. to 10:30 P.M., and the facility is open 24 hours a day. Fixed-base operator Dulles Aviation Inc. (703–361–2171, www.dullesaviation.com, UNICOM frequency 123.0) offers flight instruction and other services. Other flight schools on the premises include Airline Transport Professionals (703–393–6622, www.atpflightschool.com), Aviation Adventures, LLC (703–530–7737), and Manassas Aviation Center (703–361–0575, www.manassasaviation.com). Amenities include three pilot supply shops, a restaurant, two rental car companies, maintenance services, and hangar space for rent.

Suburban Maryland

College Park Airport
1909 Corporal Frank Scott Drive
College Park, MD
(301) 864–5844
**www.pgparks.com/places/historic/
hist.cpair.html**
This airport in Prince George's County boasts a museum dedicated to its storied past. College Park is the world's oldest continuously operating airport and plays nearly as important a role in aviation history as does Kitty Hawk, North Carolina. In 1909 Orville Wright came here to teach the first Army officers how to fly, and between 1909 and 1934, the airport was the site of many aviation firsts. The airport also offers instruction, sales, and a restaurant.

ACCOMMODATIONS

In this government town, the lodging industry is big business. Hotels and motels are the single largest contributor to the city's $5-billion travel and tourism sector, collecting more than $170 million in tax revenues in 2005 to fund city services.

With some 85,000 rooms spread throughout Metro Washington, hotels and motels seem to be as common as lawyers and lobbyists. There's usually room at the inn, but the lawyers, lobbyists, and other business travelers can drive rates sky-high during peak periods.

As a general rule of thumb, hotels in the suburbs, even close-in areas, are priced less than D.C. properties. That's not always the case, but it's pretty safe to say you can find a slew of real values out there as long as you don't mind being a bit off the beaten path. No matter where you stay, the area's comprehensive public transportation system (especially Metrorail and Metrobus) does an excellent job linking hotels with business and tourist areas. You'll discover that many hotels also offer their own shuttle and limousine services to destinations around the area.

While D.C. teems with tourists in the summer, business travel reaches its peak in spring and fall. Occupancy rates are at their highest during these months, and so too are room prices. Planning ahead is never a bad idea.

No matter what time of year, Metro Washington hotels do the bulk of their business Monday through Thursday hosting the area's business travelers. Most hotels cut their rates on weekends, sometimes as much as 50 to 60 percent. With that in mind, always feel free to negotiate for the best deal and always inquire about weekend, off-season, holiday, corporate, and family rates.

The best source we know to keep you informed of the latest seasonal rate discounts and other special hotel package programs is the Washington, D.C. Convention and Tourism Corporation (202–789–7000, www.washington.org). When in town, also be sure to stop by the D.C. Chamber of Commerce Visitor Information Center, located on the street level of the Ronald Reagan Building and International Trade Center at 1300 Pennsylvania Avenue NW (across from the Federal Triangle Metro Center). You can make hotel and restaurant reservations there, as well as buy tickets for local tours and even send an e-mail postcard back home. The center's number is (202) DC–VISIT. Its Web site is www.dcvisit.com.

We've divided this chapter into several categories, beginning with a section on extended-stay accommodations. For those of you who plan to house hunt in the area, who might be on a short-term work assignment, or just simply need a place to call home for a while, the extended-stay section is intended to give you an overview of some of the region's best options. Almost all the choices here include properties that have kitchenettes, many with separate living areas as well.

We follow with a section called Full-Service Hotels. This is intended for tourists, newcomers, and longtime residents alike who are looking for, or need to recommend, interesting, practical, and/or memorable places to spend a night in Metro Washington.

If you look hard enough, you'll find that the District, Northern Virginia, and Suburban Maryland all have more than their share of

---

i At 14.5 percent, D.C.'s hotel tax is one of the highest in the country. Keep this hidden cost in mind when you make your reservation.

hotel bargains—some you might even call steals. To help you along, we've listed some of our favorite values in the On a Budget section. Believe us, no one appreciates a bargain more than writers.

A short section on hostels and university inns lists some of the unsung and nontraditional accommodations found only in Washington, D.C.

Although the following lists are by no means exhaustive, we feel they represent some of the best and most viable choices available in each category.

Price Code

To give you an idea of what to expect price-wise, we've provided the following scale as a very general guide. It is based on the average cost for double occupancy, during peak season. Many offer discounts for AAA and AARP members. Prices are generally lower on weekends, in winter, and in late summer. Use these rate symbols as a guideline and bear in mind that prices fluctuate greatly. The same room may go for $300 or more per night during a peak convention period or $89 during a slower time. If your travel dates are flexible, it pays to shop around.

$ . . . . Under $125
$$ . . . . $125 to $175
$$$ . . . . $176 to $250
$$$$ . . . . More than $250

All hotels listed accept most major credit cards. Virtually every establishment listed also extends some kind of off-season rates.

EXTENDED-STAY HOTELS AND INNS

Washington, D.C.

Beacon Hotel and Corporate Quarters $$$
1615 Rhode Island Avenue NW
Washington, DC
(202) 296–2100
www.beaconhotelwdc.com

i Washington, D.C.'s hotels are busiest and rates are highest when Congress is in session and when there's a large convention in town. Hotels may also book up quickly in late March and early April when the cherry blossoms are in bloom. It's always best to plan ahead and shop around.

The product of a recent renovation, this chic and stylish property near Dupont Circle is great for weekend getaways. If you're looking for a longer stay, sign up for a 30-, 60-, or 90-day lease in one of the hotel's "corporate quarters." These rooms welcome long-term guests with perks like dishwashers, refrigerators, stovetops, and microwaves—even fireplaces. Guest rooms are quite comfortable, and it's easy to feel right at home in the neighborhood. The hotel's on-site eatery, the Beacon Bar & Grill, draws lively crowds for brunch and happy hour, while the rooftop bar serves martinis with a view.

Best Western Georgetown Hotel
and Suites $$–$$$$
1121 New Hampshire Avenue NW
Washington, DC
(202) 457–0565
www.bestwestern.com
This all-suite property offers 76 no-frills suites with kitchenettes, complimentary continental breakfasts, and valet parking. Bring along the jogging shoes and shorts, for you're only a hop and a skip from Rock Creek Park and its miles and miles of gorgeous wooded trails and running paths.

Capitol Hill Suites $$$
200 C Street SE
Washington, DC
(202) 543–6000, (800) 424–9165
www.capitolhillsuites.com
You can stay a night, a week, a month, or a year at this flexible, all-suite property just a short walk from the Capitol, the Library of Congress, the Supreme Court, Metro, and other "Hill" destinations. All 152 suites have

kitchens. It's a popular extended-stay choice among government and private sector workers with ties to Capitol Hill. To accommodate that clientele, the hotel offers complimentary continental breakfast and newspaper, valet parking, and lunch or dinner delivery from area restaurants.

Carlyle Suites Hotel $$$
1731 New Hampshire Avenue NW
Washington, DC
(202) 234–3200, (866) HOTEL–DC
www.carlylesuites.com

This art deco, all-suite hotel in the trendy Dupont Circle area offers rooms with fully equipped kitchens, a health club, a coin-operated laundry, complimentary Internet kiosks in the bar area, and free parking. From here, you're just a 3-block walk from the Dupont Circle Metro station and tons of galleries, restaurants, boutiques, and bars. Pets are accepted.

DC Digs $$
(202) 265–2415
www.dcdigs.com

If you're looking for a more personal experience during your extended stay, check out DC Digs, a hip home-away-from-home built out of a charming row house in Dupont Circle. The owners have thought of all of the extras— cozy living rooms with hardwood floors, personal fax machines, a fully stocked kitchen with pots, pans, and high-end fixtures like stainless steel sinks and granite countertops. There's a laundry facility inside and spacious walk-in closets, plus free high-speed and wireless Internet. Despite all of the luxurious personal touches, rooms are very reasonably priced and can be rented nightly, weekly, or monthly.

Embassy Suites Hotel Downtown $$$
1250 22nd Street NW
Washington, DC
(202) 857–3388
www.embassysuites.com

This West End addition to the national chain boasts two-room suites with separate living rooms (including queen-size sofa beds) and bedrooms. Standard in each suite are two color TVs, two phones with voice mail, data-port hookup, a kitchenette, iron, and hair dryer. The 318-suite property is close to everything: downtown, Dupont Circle, Foggy Bottom, and Georgetown. Guests receive complimentary cooked-to-order breakfasts, and there's room service available from the Italian restaurant on-site. Both an indoor swimming pool and health club are on the grounds. This is an especially popular place with families, which is not surprising because kids 12 and under eat for free.

Georgetown Suites $$$–$$$$
1111 30th Street NW and
1000 29th Street NW
Washington, DC
(202) 298–7800, (800) 348–7203
www.georgetownsuites.com

This is an ideal choice for extended stays that require you to be in or near Georgetown. All 214 suites, in two separate buildings, have kitchenettes with refrigerators and coffeemakers, and come equipped with irons, hair dryers, and computer outlets with free wireless Internet. The facility serves complimentary breakfast, has a coin-operated laundry, access to a nearby health club, and a multilingual staff. Georgetown Suites is frequented by corporate managers and government employees on short-term assignment. The surrounding Washington Harbour complex is a stunning waterfront development that also houses restaurants, gift shops, boutiques, and the like.

The Lansburgh $$$$
425 8th Street NW
Washington, DC
(202) 393–1800
www.thelansburgh.com

If Washington, D.C. is going to be your home for a while, live it up in one of the city's hottest neighborhoods, the Pennsylvania ("Penn") Quarter. A fixture in this neighborhood since 1860, the Lansburgh was once one of downtown's signature department stores. The building has been reconfigured to house a suite of corporate apartments. While the Lansburgh's rooms are designed with discerning business travelers in mind, leisure travelers should also consider it as an alternative to a downtown hotel. If there are vacancies, they're often willing to negotiate. You'll be rewarded with amenities like a full kitchen, washer/dryer, indoor pool and hot tub, high-speed Internet, state-of-the-art business center, and a professional concierge on hand. The Lansburgh also houses the Shakespeare Theatre Company's 449-seat stage—a bonus for theater buffs.

One Washington Circle $$$
1 Washington Circle NW
Washington, DC
(202) 872–1680, (800) 424–9671
www.onewashingtoncircle.com

All 151 units here include kitchens and some feature balconies. Just across the circle is George Washington University and Foggy Bottom Metro. Also within walking distance are the Kennedy Center, Georgetown, Dupont Circle, and parts of downtown. The on-site restaurant, Circle Bistro, draws a lively crowd of guests, neighbors, and patrons attending the nearby Kennedy Center's performances.

The Quincy $$
1823 L Street NW
Washington, DC
(202) 223–4320
www.quincysuites.com

Past visitors may remember this modest, centrally located hotel as the Lincoln Suites or the Hotel Anthony. After a top-to-bottom renovation in 2006, it reopened as the Quincy. You'll still find the amenities that made it a popular choice for business travelers, like minifridges, microwaves, and milk-and-cookie service in the evenings, not to mention its stellar location, just five blocks from the White House. Now you'll also enjoy wireless Internet and new decor.

The River Inn $$
924 25th Street NW
Washington, DC
(202) 337–7600, (800) 874–0100
www.theriverinn.com

It's not on the Potomac, but the river's not too far away. Nor is most of Georgetown and all of Foggy Bottom. All 126 units in this former apartment house are suites, each equipped with complimentary high-speed Internet and a full kitchen. Small pets are welcome. It's a nice place to unwind after an evening at the Kennedy Center, just a couple of blocks away.

Savoy Suites Georgetown $$
2505 Wisconsin Avenue NW
Washington, DC
(202) 337–9700, (800) 944–5377
www.savoysuites.com

This recently remodeled 150-suite hotel is in earshot of the inspiring Washington National Cathedral and is largely insulated from the hustle and congestion of closer-in lodgings. All suites have free Wi-Fi, and many have in-room Jacuzzis and full kitchens, and you can request fridges and microwaves. There's also a swimming pool, coin-operated laundry, Metro shuttle, and free on-site parking. Pets are welcome, too.

The State Plaza Hotel $$
2117 E Street NW
Washington, DC
(202) 861–8200, (800) 424–2859
www.stateplaza.com

Don't let the harried urban setting fool you.

ℹ️ Save yourself time and trouble by using a local reservation service to secure a hotel room during peak season, such as cherry blossom weekend. Reputable businesses such as Washington, DC Accommodations (800–554–2220, www.wdcahotels.com) will find out what you're looking for, verify availability, and book your room, often at a lower rate than you can get on your own.

Some of the places to stay in Washington, D.C., such as this room in the Hay-Adams Hotel, offer views of national landmarks. COURTESY WASHINGTON, D.C. CONVENTION AND TOURISM CORPORATION

The State Plaza Hotel, across from the State Department in Foggy Bottom, is a quiet, self-contained world unto itself. The former apartment building now houses 228 spacious suites featuring separate kitchens and dining rooms, same-day valet, shoeshine, safety deposit boxes, garage parking, complimentary breakfast, and fitness center. The hotel is often frequented by government employees, especially State Department types, on short-term assignments.

Northern Virginia

Alexandria

The Executive Club Suites $$–$$$
610 Bashford Lane
Alexandria, VA
(703) 739–2582, (877) 316–CLUB (2582)
www.dcexeclub.com
This all-suite property is at the north end of Old Town and is only a couple of minutes' drive to National Airport. Various options are available, but the best values are with extended stays. The handsome rooms feature nineteenth-century reproductions, rich jewel tones, and the kind of comfortable furniture you might find in a very nice home. What's more, you have a separate living room, kitchen, and master bedroom, just like a true apartment. Other amenities include free continental breakfast, evening reception, health club with sauna, shuttle service, and outdoor pool.

Sheraton Suites Old Town Alexandria $$$
801 North Asaph Street
Alexandria, VA
(703) 836–4700
www.sheraton.com
The Sheraton commands a superb location and has numerous amenities. Each suite has a wet bar, refrigerator, coffeemaker, iron and ironing board, two TVs with remote control, a VCR in the bedroom, and two telephones with call waiting. Guests also enjoy a pool and a health club. It's a 10-minute walk away from lower King Street, the nerve center of Old Town, and a five-minute drive from National Airport.

Arlington

The Executive Club Suites $$–$$$
108 South Courthouse Road
Arlington, VA
(703) 522–2582, (877) 316–2582
1730 Arlington Boulevard
Rosslyn, VA
(703) 525–2582
Please see the Alexandria listing.

Oakwood $$$
1550 Clarendon Boulevard
Arlington, VA
(703) 258–3000
www.oakwood.com
State department employees are frequent guests of this Arlington property, located just one Metro stop away from the department's headquarters in Foggy Bottom. It's also convenient to shopping and dining hot spots like Georgetown and Arlington's Clarendon neighborhood. One- and two-bedroom apartments come fully equipped with kitchens, washer/dryers, high-speed Internet, and weekly housekeeping services. Start your morning with complimentary breakfast and take advantage of the on-site pool and fitness center.

The Virginian Suites $$
1500 Arlington Boulevard
Arlington, VA
(703) 522–9600, (800) 606–5265
www.virginiansuites.com
Specializing in month-to-month suites, the recently renovated Virginian offers hotel convenience and basic comfort. The Rosslyn location is close to the Metro, Georgetown, and most of Arlington and Alexandria. Guests receive Metro and grocery store shuttle service, maid service, cable TV, free utilities and parking, and access to an on-site outdoor swimming pool, fitness center, and saunas.

Fairfax County

Embassy Suites/Tysons Corner $$$
8517 Leesburg Pike
Vienna, VA
(703) 883–0707
www.embassysuites.com

A Tysons Corner location—about halfway between Washington and Washington Dulles International Airport—makes this 232-suite property convenient to most points in Northern Virginia. Suites come with refrigerators and microwaves, and guests can help themselves to a free breakfast and evening happy hour reception. There's also complimentary shuttle service to the Metro and the acclaimed malls nearby, a fitness center, and indoor pool. The hotel is close to one of the world's largest office and shopping complexes, and just a few minutes' drive from Wolf Trap, the nation's only national park for the performing arts (see The Arts chapter for more information on Wolf Trap).

Marriott Residence Inn $$
Herndon/Reston
315 Elden Street
Herndon, VA
(703) 435–0044
www.residenceinn.com

Short- and long-term stays are made easy at this all-suite Marriott property about 5 miles east of Dulles Airport in the town of Herndon. One- and two-bedroom suites come with fireplaces. Pets are permitted. The Marriott has a pool and fitness area and also offers free parking, daily hot buffet breakfast, complimentary grocery shopping service, and weekday happy hours. It's near AOL and numerous other high-tech companies.

Marriott Suites/
Washington Dulles $$$
13101 Worldgate Drive
Herndon, VA
(703) 709–0400
www.marriott.com

Marriott Suites/Washington Dulles is, as the name suggests, close to the airport but also within a few minutes' drive of the surrounding technology corridor. Besides all the perks you'd expect from this national chain, the hotel is adjacent to Worldgate Athletic Club, one of the nation's largest, and close to Dulles Town Center, with numerous shopping and dining options.

Suburban Maryland

Montgomery County

Marriott Suites Bethesda $$$
6711 Democracy Boulevard
Bethesda, MD
(301) 897–5600
www.marriott.com

If you have business in Montgomery County and upper Northwest Washington, you would do well to consider Marriott Suites Bethesda as a home base. It's near the intersection of the Beltway and I–270, Marriott Corporation's world headquarters, and IBM. Guests here enjoy an indoor/outdoor swimming pool, health club, restaurant, and all the amenities you'd expect from this service-oriented national chain.

TownePlace Suites by Marriott $–$$
212 Perry Parkway
Gaithersburg, MD
(301) 590–2300, (800) 257–3000
www.towneplace.com

With spacious studio, one-bedroom, and two-bedroom suites, TownePlace provides a moderately priced home base for extended stays in Washington's northern suburbs. TownePlace has an exercise room, pool, and coin laundry. The hotel is near Montgomery County's technology corridor along I–270 and Lakeforest Mall. Pets are allowed.

Prince George's County

Comfort Inn and Suites
College Park $$
9020 Baltimore Boulevard
College Park, MD
(301) 441–8110
www.choicehotels.com

The renovated hotel offers regular rooms as

well as 33 suites. It's convenient for parents of University of Maryland students as well as travelers who prefer to stay north of the Nation's Capital. Suites offer fridges, in-room coffeemakers, and complimentary breakfast with newspaper. You'll also find a coin-operated laundry, health club, and outdoor pool.

FULL-SERVICE HOTELS
Washington, D.C.

Capital Hilton Hotel $$$$
16th and K Streets NW
Washington, DC
(202) 393–1000
www.capital.hilton.com
The 12-story, 544-room Capital Hilton is a short walk to most points downtown and just 2 blocks north of the White House. The hotel also boasts the popular Capital City Club and Spa, a notable day escape for harried locals. Not surprisingly, the hotel handles a large convention and tourist trade. Fran O'Brien's Steak House in the hotel is a hopping bar and restaurant, but more of a meet-and-greet place than a gourmet restaurant.

Channel Inn Hotel $$
650 Water Street SW
Washington, DC
(202) 554–2400, (800) 368–5668
www.channelinn.com
This basic 100-room hotel is perched right on the Southwest waterfront, with beautiful views of East Potomac Park and nearby marinas. You're also a short walk to the Metro, the venerable Arena Stage Theater, the National Mall, and the Smithsonian museums. Free parking is available, and guests can enjoy indoor as well as outdoor pools. This is also the home of the Pier 7 restaurant, which features dining and dancing.

The Churchill Hotel $$$
1914 Connecticut Avenue NW
Washington, DC
(202) 797–2000, (800) 424–2464
www.thechurchillhotel.com

This elegant, historic Dupont Circle hotel boasts a full-service business center and meeting rooms. There's a health club on the premises as well as a restaurant and piano lounge. The hotel, which was built in 1906, was renovated several years ago. Public rooms are very impressive and guest rooms are comfortable and geared to the business traveler. The Embassy Row location is equally accessible to Dupont Circle and downtown. It has 144 units, including 36 suites.

The Fairmont Washington $$$$
2401 M Street NW
Washington, DC
(202) 429–2400
www.fairmont.com
Formerly the Monarch Hotel, the grand 415-room Fairmont Washington is known for its outstanding service. The lobby is a plush, airy hall of marble, plants, and Oriental rugs, and the guest rooms mirror the decor. The hotel's Gold Level wows guests with a separate check-in and round-the-clock personal service. The real highlights here, though, are the 14,000-square-foot fitness center and the Colonnade, one of the city's most talked about destinations for Sunday brunch. You can also get your exercise with a jog through nearby Rock Creek Park. Georgetown's dining and shopping are a five-minute walk away.

Four Seasons Hotel $$$$
2800 Pennsylvania Avenue NW
Washington, DC
(202) 342–0444
www.fourseasons.com
Like so many of Washington's premium hotels, the newly renovated Four Seasons is often frequented by the rich and famous. Rock stars are a common sight here, and once upon a time Donald Trump and Marla Maples staged a much-publicized brouhaha in the lobby. Despite the occasional weirdness, the Four Seasons is all class. Guests of this Georgetown gem can expect some of the best service in Washington, an outstanding concierge, a top-rated restaurant (Seasons),

and a premier fitness center with spa services, including herbal massage and aromatherapy. The piano lounge is a hot spot for cocktails among the Washington business elite.

The Georgetown Inn $$$$
1310 Wisconsin Avenue NW
Washington, DC
(202) 333–8900, (800) 424–2979
www.georgetowncollection.com

If it's Georgetown you want, the Georgetown Inn is the place to be. The Duke and Dutchess of Windsor have even slept there. Right in the nerve center of Washington's popular nightlife district (the daylife ain't bad either), this intimate 96-unit inn offers complimentary coffee and the *Washington Post* every morning, overnight shoeshines, turndown service, and business services. Valet parking is available, an added plus in parking-scarce Georgetown.

The Grand Hyatt Washington $$$$
1000 H Street NW
Washington, DC
(202) 582–1234
www.washington.hyatt.com

The Grand Hyatt covers all the bases. It sits near the Washington Convention Center, the lively Penn Quarter restaurant and entertainment district, and is a half block from bustling Metro Center. Within a short walk are Pennsylvania Avenue and the White House, the National Theatre, the Shops at National Place (see our Shopping chapter), and the Smithsonian museums. This gigantic 888-room property is built around a 7,000-square-foot lagoon with waterfalls, with a 12-story atrium glass roof overhead. There's a swimming pool and health club, not to mention four restaurants and a martini bar. Extra perks include a kosher kitchen, marble bathrooms, and wireless Internet.

The Hay-Adams Hotel $$$$
16th and H Streets NW
Washington, DC
(202) 638–6600, (800) 853–6807
www.hayadams.com

One of our personal favorites, this ultraluxurious, ultrahistoric property overlooks Lafayette Park and the White House to the south. Diplomats, politicians, and the who's who of the Washington elite, including former presidents and presidents-elect, bunk and dine at the Hay-Adams regularly. This is the ultimate Insiders' hotel but always accommodating to all. Valet parking, a full-time concierge, nightly turndown service, and butler service are just some of the amenities. Some rooms come with kitchenettes.

The Henley Park Hotel $$$–$$$$
926 Massachusetts Avenue NW
Washington, DC
(202) 638–5200, (800) 222–8474
www.henleypark.com

The Henley Park has emerged as one of the city's leading European-style hotels. Although the guest rooms are a bit dated, this location can't be beat: less than 2 blocks from the convention center and near Union Station, Capitol Hill, and the National Mall. Guests are treated to express check-ins, minibars, overnight shoeshines, and health club privileges.

Hilton Washington Embassy Row $$$–$$$$
2015 Massachusetts Avenue NW
Washington, DC
(202) 265–1600
www.hiltonembassyrow.com

Location, location, location is the theme here. In the city's embassy district, near Dupont Circle, the Embassy Row handles a large, well-heeled international clientele, including newcomers shopping for more permanent residences. A massive renovation several years ago spruced up this already-nice hotel with 193 rooms. The rooftop bar and pool is a great warm-weather hangout and an emerging nightlife hot spot. There's also a health club on the premises.

The Hotel George features brightly colored, whimsical artwork in its guest rooms and common areas. COURTESY HOTEL GEORGE

Holiday Inn Capitol at the Smithsonian $$$
550 C Street SW
Washington, DC
(202) 479–4000
www.holidayinncapitol.com

A colleague visiting from South Dakota summed up this place best: "It's nothing super fancy, but it's a location you can't beat—right up close to the [National] Air and Space Museum." Indeed, the newly remodeled Holiday Inn Capitol knows its market. Tour groups take advantage of the take-out deli and moderate prices, considering the location. Kids pack the rooftop pool in summer, while business travelers enjoy free high-speed Internet. Nonguests can park in the hotel's garage for $22 a day, a convenience if you prefer to drive rather than take the Metro into the city for a Smithsonian visit.

Hotel George $$$$
15 E Street NW
Washington, DC
(202) 347–4200
www.hotelgeorge.com

The Hotel George made a splashy entrance on Capitol Hill as the District's first fashion-forward hotel. In 2003, the independent hotel was bought by the Kimpton Hotel Group, joining its collection of trendy boutique neighborhood properties. Built out of a vintage 1928 building, the fresh, modern Hotel George pays homage to the first president in a signature collection of brightly colored artwork. You'll find vibrant treatments of the one-dollar bill portrait hanging in the lobby and perhaps even above your bed. As luxurious Capitol Hill hotels go, the George is at the top of the list. You're likely to see a cast of Hill regulars checking in and out during the week and perhaps a celebrity or two on the weekend.

Hotel Helix $$$
1430 Rhode Island Avenue NW
Washington, DC
(202) 462–9001, (800) 508–0658
www.hotelhelix.com

It's hard to believe this fun and funky Logan Circle hotel was once a Howard Johnson. As you approach the main entrance, a curtain opens to herald your arrival—and indeed, you have arrived. This playful mod hotel is decked out with bright colors, retro prints, and lots of pop culture tributes. In the white vinyl-lined lounge, mood lighting changes from blue to yellow. Your "do not disturb" sign takes a cue from Greta Garbo, saying, "I want to be alone." Although this hotel is a popular choice for urban hipsters and gay/lesbian travelers, it's also popular with families. Rooms are spacious, equipped with plasma-screen TVs and lava lamps; some are even outfitted with bunk beds.

Hotel Lombardy $$$
2019 Pennsylvania Avenue NW
Washington, DC
(202) 828–2600, (800) 424–5486
www.hotellombardy.com

An innlike hotel for those who want to be near everything, the Hotel Lombardy has 134 rooms with kitchenettes and minibars, free newspapers, free high-speed Internet, and turndown service. Walk to the White House, West End, Foggy Bottom, downtown, and the National Mall. The Hotel Lombardy is an excellent value when you consider its location.

Hotel Monaco $$$$
700 F Street NW
Washington, DC
(202) 628–7177
www.monaco-dc.com

Even if you're not a guest at the Hotel Monaco, you ought to stop in for a peek. It's a magnificent example of how the city's earliest architecture can blend tastefully with modern design. The Hotel Monaco is housed in one of Washington, D.C.'s original buildings, the U.S. Postal Service headquarters, designed by Thomas Walter, one of the original architects for the U.S. Capitol, and Robert Mills, who designed the Patent Office Building (now home to the National Portrait Gallery and Smithsonian American Art Museum) and the Department of the Treasury. Inside the meticulously restored four-story building, you'll find original marble floors, sweeping spiral staircases, and glorious vaulted ceilings. To contrast with the classical elements, the hotel is furnished with creamy yellow and cornflower blue accents, along with unexpected splashes of red and other vivid colors. Green glass chandeliers hang in the lobby, appointed with lush purple and red sofas and chairs. Because it's part of the Kimpton Hotel Group, you'll enjoy standard features like a complimentary wine hour, free Wi-Fi, and a warm welcome for your four-legged travel companions.

Hotel Rouge $$$
1315 16th Street NW
Washington, DC
(202) 232–8000, (800) 368–5689
www.rougehotel.com

Hotel Rouge is another of the "boutique" hotels in Washington owned by the Kimpton chain, each with its own distinctive personality. The color red is red-hot at the Rouge, starting with the pop artwork and accent pillows on a white leather sofa in the lobby. Red and amber lights reflect off lime wood paneling in the elevator, and the doors open to reveal corridors lined with Chinese red silk wall coverings. Of the 137 rooms, several offer kitchenettes with stainless-steel appliances, while a few of the others are dubbed "chill rooms," each with two 27-inch flatscreen TVs, a Sony PlayStation2 that doubles as a DVD player, and access to the front-desk video game library.

Hotel Washington $$$
15th and Pennsylvania Avenue NW
Washington, DC
(202) 638–5900, (800) 424–9540
www.hotelwashington.com
One of the city's oldest hotels, the Hotel Washington sits across the street from the Treasury Department and around the corner from the White House. It is registered with the National Trust for Historic Preservation. You might find tour groups here; accordingly, ask about discounted room prices. The hotel's Roof Terrace lounge is and always has been, bar none, the best public place in the city to watch fireworks on July 4th or any of the annual parades along Pennsylvania Avenue. Bring your out-of-town guests here for an alfresco lunch with an awe-inspiring view. The 344 rooms, including 16 suites, have been renovated, and the hotel includes a fitness center with saunas.

**Hyatt Regency Washington
on Capitol Hill** $$$–$$$$
400 New Jersey Avenue NW
Washington, DC
(202) 737–1234
www.hyattregencywashington.com
The Capitol Hill edition of this international chain comes with everything you'd expect: valet parking, video checkout service, a game room and children's suite, wireless Internet, a beauty salon, swimming pool, and health club. The massive 834-room property is a block from the Capitol and 2 blocks from Union Station. The rooms are standard Hyatt but newly upgraded, which means all the business-related amenities and some extra comforts, including a dreamy bed. Thirty-two of the units are suites. As you can imagine—given its size and location—the hotel commands a huge convention and tourist business.

Jurys Normandy Inn $$
2118 Wyoming Avenue NW
Washington, DC
(202) 483–1350, (800) 424–3729
www.jurysdoyle.com
The 75-room Normandy, in upper Northwest, is lodged between Rock Creek Park and Dupont Circle. This is an intimate, European-style inn in a residential neighborhood that includes a slew of embassies. Free underground parking is available, as are on-site limousine and car rental services. Rooms come with minifridges and coffeemakers, as well as valet service and complimentary coffee, tea, and cookies every afternoon.

Jurys Washington Hotel $$$
1500 New Hampshire Avenue NW
Washington, DC
(202) 483–6000, (800) 423–6953
www.jurys.com
Owned and operated by Ireland's largest hotel group, Jurys Washington Hotel is right across the street from the Dupont Circle Metro station, close to some of the city's best art galleries, bookstores, boutiques, and restaurants. The 313 businesslike rooms come with wet bars, and there's an upscale restaurant and lively Irish pub on the premises. This hotel caters to a lot of international groups.

JW Marriott $$$$
1331 Pennsylvania Avenue NW
Washington, DC
(202) 393–2000, (800) 228–9290
www.jwmarriottdc.com
Part of downtown Washington's renaissance of the 1980s, this entry boasts 765 just refinished rooms as well as a passageway to the Shops at National Place (see our Shopping chapter). Just steps from the White House and the National Mall, the Marriott is big with conventions, tourists, and business travelers. There's a huge, marbled, multilevel lobby and lots of meeting and eating places. Not only are there a swimming pool and health club on the premises, but there are also many business amenities. Rooms are equipped with "plug and play" technology, so you can hook your laptop or entertainment equipment into a 32-inch LCD HDTV, which lets you split the screen to watch TV and work simultaneously. The hotel is directly across from the Ronald Reagan Building and International Trade Center.

L'Enfant Plaza Hotel $$$–$$$$
480 L'Enfant Plaza SW
Washington, DC
(202) 484–1000, (800) 635–5065
www.lenfantplazahotel.com

The L'Enfant Plaza Hotel is a pleasant, airy hotel near the pulse of bureaucratic Washington. Its best feature, though, is its location directly above a Metro subway station and shopping promenade. Within a short walk are the Smithsonian Castle and museum, plus the offices of NASA, the Department of Housing and Urban Development, the Transportation and Agriculture Departments, and the Federal Aviation Administration. Expect to find all the amenities for business and pleasure at this 370-room property, including a rooftop swimming pool and health club. All rooms come with minibars, stocked refrigerators, two phones, in-room safes, and a TV/radio in the bathroom. Some also have kitchens. Pets are allowed.

The Madison, A Loews Hotel $$$$
15th and M Streets NW
Washington, DC
(202) 862–1600, (800) 424–8577
www.themadisonaloewshotel.com

Elegant is the only way to describe this downtown institution featuring 353 rooms appointed with French and Asian antiques acquired by renowned collector and hotelier Marshall B. Coyne. This hotel is consistently rated in national travel magazines as a top choice of business executives. Guests should expect refrigerators and stocked bars in each room, as well as indoor valet parking and all the business amenities. What's more, it's convenient to everything in federal and corporate Washington.

Mandarin Oriental, Washington, DC $$$$
1330 Maryland Avenue SW
Washington, DC
(202) 554–8588
www.mandarinoriental.com

If you want to splurge, this is the place to do it. Opened in 2004, the Mandarin Oriental is pure luxury. Step into the light-filled, two-story lobby of this posh hotel and you'll be overwhelmed with gracious service. Guest rooms don't disappoint, either. They're outfitted with sumptuous linens and decor, including some replicas from the nearby Freer and Sackler Galleries of Art, and everything is arranged in accordance with Feng Shui principles. Although its southwest waterfront location is deemed "off the beaten path" by some, the Mandarin has proven to be popular with locals. CityZen, its acclaimed restaurant, showcases the culinary talents of Eric Ziebold, formerly of the French Laundry in Napa Valley. The Mandarin Spa is simply heavenly, offering an array of unique treatments and experiences.

Marriott Wardman Park $$$$
2660 Woodley Road NW
Washington, DC
(202) 328–2000, (800) 228–9290
www.marriott.com

At 1,350 rooms, this is Washington's largest hotel, a sprawling behemoth of brick, white columns, French doors, endless corridors, and room-size chandeliers. The setting is a grand expanse of parkland at the edge of Rock Creek. The National Zoo is 3 blocks to the north. This hotel, which offers all sorts of convention and tourist services, includes a post office, pool, health club, shoeshine stand, and hair salon. Rooms come with Starbucks coffee/tea service, voice mail, video checkout, and every other amenity imaginable for the comfort of the business traveler. Pets are allowed.

The Melrose Hotel $$$
2430 Pennsylvania Avenue NW
Washington, DC
(202) 955–6400, (800) MELROSE
www.melrosehoteldc.com

Service is key at this classic West End hotel that's just a few strides away from Georgetown. It offers valet parking, complimentary newspapers, a shoeshine service, and rooms with hair dryers and coffee machines. Classic

English and contemporary decor complement the commissioned artwork of Washington landmarks in each room.

The Morrison-Clark Inn $$–$$$$
11th Street and Massachusetts Avenue NW
Washington, DC
(202) 898–1200, (800) 222–8474
www.morrisonclark.com
This inn would be strictly a $$$$ property were it almost anywhere else in the city. However, as luxurious as it is, it is in a neighborhood undergoing gentrification, at the eastern edge of downtown near the convention center. Occupying one of the oldest buildings in Washington, the Morrison-Clark features authentic Victorian decor with all the modern amenities, including computer ports, and all the old-fashioned luxuries like complimentary newspaper and shoeshine. The restaurant here is renowned for its fine American cuisine.

Park Hyatt Washington $$$$
24th and M Streets NW
Washington, DC
(202) 789–1234, (800) 778–7477
www.hyatt.com
Another in a long list of competitive West End hotels, the Park Hyatt is one of the most elegant in the Hyatt chain. Three blocks from Georgetown, it features a wonderful restaurant and sidewalk cafe (see the Restaurants and Nightlife chapters). In the rooms you'll find the usual Hyatt amenities plus some four-star touches, including multiline phones, minibars, and complimentary fresh fruit. The hotel boasts an on-site swimming pool and a health club, as well as a beauty salon.

Phoenix Park Hotel $$$
520 North Capitol Street NW
Washington, DC
(202) 638–6900
www.phoenixparkhotel.com
For a touch of the Emerald Isle right here in Washington, check into the Phoenix Park. A recently built wing brings the total number of rooms to 150. It is 2 blocks from the Capitol and a block from Union Station and the Metro. The hotel's Dubliner Pub is widely regarded as one of the best Irish bars in Metro Washington (see the Nightlife chapter).

Renaissance Mayflower $$$$
1127 Connecticut Avenue NW
Washington, DC
(202) 347–3000, (800) 228–7697
www.renaissancehotels.com
This much-revered historic hotel is a Connecticut Avenue landmark, a place to see and be seen, and a Washington institution. The Mayflower's lobby takes up an entire block, and the property has two good restaurants and a lounge. Some of the rooms in this 657-unit hotel have kitchenettes. The White House is only 4 blocks away, and just outside the bank of brass-and-glass doors is one of Washington's nicest shopping and restaurant districts.

Renaissance Washington, D.C. Hotel $$$$
999 9th Street NW
Washington, DC
(202) 898–9000
www.renaissancehotels.com
One of the District's premiere convention and trade show sites, the Renaissance is close to the convention center, about halfway between the White House and Capitol Hill, and about 4 blocks from the Verizon Center. Twenty-five retail shops, a fitness center, food court, post office, hair salon, and indoor pool complement the 807 rooms. In each room expect all the business amenities related to computers and telephones. There's valet parking and a convenient Metro station nearby (Gallery Place). Pets are allowed.

The St. Regis Washington, D.C. $$$$
923 16th Street NW
Washington, DC
(202) 638–2626, (800) 325–3535
www.stregis.com/washington
A 178-room luxury hotel just 2 blocks from the White House, the St. Regis has set the stan-

dard for upscale lodging since it opened in 1926. In 2006 the hotel underwent a major renovation to raise the bar even higher. In addition to amenities like wireless Internet, 32-inch plasma televisions with surround-sound, DVD players, and personal fax machines, the St. Regis caters to its guests' needs with personal butler service. Guests can press the "Butler Button" on their room phones to make special requests for services like garment pressing, transportation arrangements, or coffee service with their wake-up calls.

Westin Embassy Row Washington, D.C. $$$$
2100 Massachusetts Avenue NW
Washington, DC
(202) 293–2100
www.westin.com
The name of this Embassy Row landmark has changed quite a few times. The Westin Embassy Row was previously the Westin Fairfax, before that the Ritz-Carlton, and even earlier, the Fairfax Hotel. Although some of the rooms are a bit small, the location can't be beat. And if you land an upgrade to a suite, it's blissful. Newspapers are delivered to your door, and shoeshine and limousine services are available. The hotel also boasts Westin signature amenities like the Heavenly Bed and Westin Workout powered by Reebok Gym. Some rooms come with kitchenettes.

The Willard InterContinental $$$$
1401 Pennsylvania Avenue NW
Washington, DC
(202) 628–9100, (800) 327–0200
www.washington.intercontinental.com
Along with the Hay-Adams, the Four Seasons, and a select few other properties, the Willard is among the crème de la crème of Washington hotels. Ironically, this stunning historical landmark almost fell victim to the wrecking ball before it was renovated and reopened in

> **i** The term "lobbyist" was coined in the lobby of the Willard InterContinental.

grand fashion in 1986. The 334 rooms and suites are as plush as you'd expect, with lots of mirrors, marble, and good reproduction furniture. Within a one- or two-minute walk are the White House, the Treasury Department, the National Theater, the Department of Commerce, and the National Mall. The hotel has a spa, two elegant lounges, a cafe, and a formal restaurant, the Willard Room (see Restaurants chapter).

Wyndham Washington, D.C. $$$$
1400 M Street NW
Washington, DC
(202) 429–1700, (800) 847–8232
www.wyndham.com
We tainted locals still know this best as the former Vista International Hotel, the place where former D.C. mayor Marion Barry got busted—and videotaped, no less—for using crack cocaine. That's not to knock the Wyndham, however. This is a fine, centrally located hotel that offers guests three telephones in every room and voice mail, as well as minibars, refrigerators, and all the other business amenities. It's an impressive sight, too, with its 14-story glass atrium draped in greenery. There's a fitness room with sauna, restaurant, and lounge.

Northern Virginia
Fairfax County

Hilton McLean at Tysons Corner $$$
7920 Jones Branch Drive
McLean, VA
(703) 847–5000
www.hilton.com
A Tysons Corner landmark, the 458-room McLean Hilton features a glass-domed atrium and a splashy lobby filled with marble, brass, and live plants. The rooms here are ordinary contemporary-style Hilton, but the 43 executive-level rooms offer some extras like in-room faxes and coffeemakers plus complimentary continental breakfast and evening hors d'oeuvres. There's a fully equipped health club, an indoor pool, minibars in each room, and bathroom phones as well as all the amenities business travelers expect. You'll

Linking to the Chains

Many of the hotels listed in this chapter belong to national chains. For your convenience, we've listed their toll-free telephone numbers and Web addresses below.

Best Western (800) 762–3777, www.bestwestern.com
Comfort Inn (800) 228–5150, www.choicehotels.com
Days Inn (800) 329–7466, www.daysinn.com
Econo Lodge (800) 553–2666, www.econolodge.com
Embassy Suites (800) 362–2779, www.embassysuites.com
Hilton (800) 445–8667, www.hilton.com
Holiday Inn (800) HOLIDAY, www.ichotelsgroup.com
Howard Johnson (800) 654–2000, www.hojo.com
Hyatt (800) 233–1234, www.hyatt.com
Marriott (800) 228–9290, www.marriott.com
Radisson (800) 333–3333, www.radisson.com
Ritz-Carlton (800) 241–3333, www.ritzcarlton.com
Sheraton (800) 325–3535, www.starwoodhotels.com
Travelodge (800) 578–7878, www.travelodge.com
Wyndham (800) WYNDHAM, www.wyndham.com

find a restaurant, bar, and drugstore on the premises, and you're close to shopping, movie theaters, and still more shopping at the two nearby megamalls that are the retail focal point of Tysons Corner. (See our Shopping chapter.)

Ritz-Carlton Tysons Corner　　　　$$$$
1700 Tysons Boulevard
McLean, VA
(703) 506–4300
www.ritzcarlton.com
As they are so apt to do, the folks behind the Ritz-Carlton chain like to make sure their moneyed customers have easy access to fashionable shopping areas. In this case it's the attached and oh-so-exclusive Galleria at Tysons II (Saks Fifth Avenue, Neiman-Marcus, etc.), in the heart of Fairfax County's mecca of consumerism, Tysons Corner (see our Shopping chapter). As for the hotel itself, it's typical Ritz-Carlton—fancy to the nth degree: Expect the usual grand decor, attentive serv-ice, and fine dining at Maestro, the hotel's AAA Five Diamond Award–winning restau-rant, as well as indoor pool and health club.

Its location is on one of the highest points in the area—all the better for a great view of some D.C. landmarks on a clear day, because there isn't much in the way of scenery in the immediate area, unless you count high-rise office buildings, stores, and a patchwork of busy roads. The 398 rooms feature classic English antique reproductions, marble bath-rooms, safes, minibars, and all the toiletries and business amenities. In addition, there's a business center on the premises, as well as a choice of free self-parking or valet parking. If you want to be closer to downtown D.C., check into the newly renovated Ritz-Carlton Pentagon City, attached to the Fashion Centre at Pentagon City shopping mall and offering the same amenities; 1250 South Hayes Street, Arlington (703) 415–5000.

**Sheraton Premiere at
Tysons Corner** $$–$$$
8661 Leesburg Pike
Vienna, VA
(703) 448–1234
www.starwoodhotels.com
One of Northern Virginia's most luxurious
hotels, and one of the nicest in the Sheraton
chain, the towering Sheraton Premiere
extends to guests such perks as a fitness center, indoor and outdoor pools, free parking, an
on-site rental car agency, racquetball courts,
and free transportation within a 3-mile radius.
You can't miss it—it's the glass tower at Route
7 and the toll road and one of the tallest buildings in Tysons Corner, a city in itself. It's also
close to I–66 and the Beltway. There are
restaurants and lounges on premises.

**Washington Dulles Airport
Marriott** $$$–$$$$
45020 Aviation Drive
Dulles, VA
(703) 471–9500
www.marriott.com
Talk about the Marriott advantage: This is the
only hotel on the grounds of Washington
Dulles International Airport. A large pond and
acres of wooded landscaping almost belie the
location of this 368-room hotel, though.
There's an indoor and outdoor pool, tennis
courts, fitness center, and free parking. The
terminal is a two-minute drive away, and com-
plimentary shuttle-bus service is provided.

Westfields Marriott $$$$
14750 Conference Center Drive
Chantilly, VA
(703) 818–0300
www.marriott.com
You'd never know this 335-room hotel was
part of a chain. Westfields' stately Georgian
facade and 1,100 manicured acres give the
impression of an old, established Virginia
resort. The facility, however, is the product of
the boom days of the 1980s. It exudes ele-
gance, from its state-of-the-art conference

rooms to its outstanding restaurant and
ornate guest rooms decorated in marble,
country prints, and rich carpets. Dulles Air-
port is 7 miles to the north along Route 28.
The hotel is also about equal distance from
U.S. 50 and I–66. This is an ideal venue for a
corporate retreat, large or small; a wedding
reception; or any other special occasion.
Don't miss dinner at the Palm Court (see the
Restaurants chapter). Rooms feature three
multiline phones and refrigerators. There's a
tourist desk, pro shops, a business center,
free valet parking, an indoor heated pool,
outdoor pool, spa, health club with steam
bath, tennis courts, an on-call physician, and
nearby championship golf.

Alexandria

Hilton Alexandria Old Town $$$
1767 King Street
Alexandria, VA
(703) 837–0440
www.alexandriahilton.com
If it's location you're after, the 247-room Hilton
Alexandria Old Town can't be beat. Not only
are you a short walk (or bus ride) from Old
Town's most charming shops and restaurants,
you're also directly across the street from the
King Street Metro station, giving you easy
access to Washington, D.C. and its attractions.
The guest rooms are equipped with high-speed
Internet and Wi-Fi. Guests can take advantage
of an indoor pool and fitness center.

Hotel Monaco, Alexandria $$$–$$$$
480 King Street
Alexandria, VA
(703) 549–6080
www.kimptonhotels.com
After a $22-million renovation, this former
Holiday Inn reopened as the Hotel Monaco,
Alexandria, marking the Kimpton Hotel
Group's entry into Northern Virginia. The 241-
room property blends Kimpton's signature
style with Old Town's historic charm in one of
the best locations in Alexandria. From here
you're right across the street from the town
square, the site of a colorful street market

66

held every Saturday morning, and a short walk from galleries, shops, bars, restaurants, and the Potomac waterfront.

Morrison House $$$$
116 South Alfred Street
Alexandria, VA
(703) 838–8000, (866) 834–6628
www.morrisonhouse.com

Newly acquired by the Kimpton Hotel Group, this elegant eighteenth-century-style mansion in the center of Old Town is one of the region's most-celebrated inns. Each of the 45 rooms is individually decorated with Federal-period antiques and chandeliers, and several rooms come with fireplaces and four-poster mahogany beds. The inn's cozy restaurant and lounge enhance an already intensely romantic atmosphere. Morrison House is the perfect urban getaway and the site of many honeymoons.

Arlington County

Holiday Inn National Airport $$–$$$
2650 Jefferson Davis Highway
Arlington, VA
(703) 684–7200
www.hinationalairport.com

Located in a corridor of concrete, glass, and steel, the hotel is close to Reagan National Airport, the Pentagon, Arlington National Cemetery, the Fashion Centre at Pentagon City, Crystal City Underground (shopping), and, 10 minutes to the south, Old Town Alexandria. Guests receive complimentary shuttle service to the airport and Metro, as well as laundry and valet service, voice mail, a health club, pool, and free parking. Try the '50s-style diner inside the hotel.

Hyatt Regency Crystal City $$$–$$$$
2799 Jefferson Davis Highway
Arlington, VA
(703) 418–1234
www.crystalcity.hyatt.com

Crystal City, a conglomeration of office buildings, high-rise condos, and big hotels, isn't going to win any awards for aesthetics, but it

sure is convenient. Same can be said for the Hyatt Regency here, a 685-unit hotel that offers a health club, an outdoor swimming pool, and a lounge and rooftop restaurant with a view of D.C. Guests receive complimentary shuttle service to Reagan National Airport or Metro, barely three minutes away. Crystal City is also close to the Pentagon, downtown D.C., and Old Town Alexandria.

Key Bridge Marriott $$$–$$$$
1401 Lee Highway
Arlington, VA
(703) 524–6400
www.keybridgemarriott.com

About as close to Washington as you're going to get in Virginia, the 582-room Key Bridge Marriott is a short walk (or shorter jog) across its graceful namesake span from Georgetown and just 2 blocks from the Rosslyn Metro. The hotel's riverside location affords spectacular views of the Potomac and the District beyond. There's an indoor/outdoor pool, health club, and easy access to jogging trails and bike rental facilities. Each morning, guests are treated to complimentary coffee and newspapers. Rooms have all the usual business amenities.

Ritz-Carlton, Pentagon City $$$$
1250 South Hayes Street
Arlington, VA
(703) 415–5000
www.ritzcarlton.com

See previous description under Ritz-Carlton Tysons Corner.

The Westin Arlington Gateway $$$
801 North Glebe Road
Arlington, VA
(703) 717–6204
www.westin.com/arlington

Although North Arlington's Ballston and

i The Key Bridge Marriott was the international hotel company's first property, opened in 1957 as the Twin Bridges Motor Hotel.

i Marriott, the international hotel chain, is headquartered in Bethesda, Maryland, and the Pooks Hill location nearby is one of its showcase properties.

Clarendon neighborhoods have welcomed a host of new condos, restaurants, and retail shops, the neighborhoods haven't seen much hotel development. In 2006, however, the Westin chain broke with this trend and opened the new Arlington Gateway property. The rooms are incredibly comfortable, featuring Westin's signature Heavenly Bed (and Heavenly Dog Bed) and Heavenly Bath, complete with double showerheads. It's a short walk to the Ballston Metro station and the Ballston Common Mall (see the Shopping chapter).

Loudoun County

Lansdowne Resort $$$–$$$$
44050 Woodridge Parkway
Lansdowne, VA
(703) 729–8400, (877) 509–8400
www.lansdowneresort.com
In a resortlike setting north of Dulles Airport, Lansdowne attracts a noteworthy share of meetings and conventions, especially among international firms. Luxurious rooms are complemented by an attentive staff, state-of-the-art meetings technology, two championship golf courses and a short course, indoor and outdoor pools, and a fitness center and spa. Lansdowne is part of Loudoun County's burgeoning Route 7 corridor, one of the region's fastest-growing commercial districts. You don't have to leave the premises for anything, and the fine restaurant is a special treat.

Suburban Maryland

Montgomery County

Bethesda Marriott $$$–$$$$
5151 Pooks Hill Road
Bethesda, MD
(301) 897–9400, (800) 228–9290
www.bethesdamarriott.com
This 407-room property is high atop a hill

near the Capitol Beltway, the National Institutes of Health, and White Flint shopping mall. It's a sprawling place with all manner of eateries—and we're talking exceptional cuisine—plus an indoor/outdoor pool, tennis courts, and exercise room. There's also free parking and a shuttle to the Metro.

Courtyard by Marriott
Silver Spring $$–$$$
12521 Prosperity Drive
Silver Spring, MD
(301) 680–8500
www.courtyard.com
This recently built hotel is located in a rapidly developing area of northeastern Montgomery County, closer really to College Park and the University of Maryland than downtown Silver Spring. A few of the 146 units are suites with refrigerators and microwaves. There's an indoor pool and exercise room, as well as free high-speed Internet.

Doubletree Bethesda $$$
8120 Wisconsin Avenue
Bethesda, MD
(301) 652–2000
www.doubletree.com
It's hard to get closer to the Bethesda Naval Hospital and the National Institutes of Health than this hotel, formerly the Holiday Inn Bethesda. You're also just blocks from the District line and the upscale shopping district of Chevy Chase.

Hyatt Regency Bethesda $$$$
1 Bethesda Metro Center
Bethesda, MD
(301) 657–1234
www.bethesda.hyatt.com
This bustling hotel in the heart of Bethesda's business district is atop a Metro subway station, so it couldn't be more convenient. Both Washington and the surrounding suburbs are just a few Metro stops away. Rooms come with all the business amenities now standard at most Hyatts, including video checkout, voice mail, minibars, and a striking atrium-style

lobby full of shops and services. The shopping malls at White Flint and Mazza Gallerie are only a couple of subway stops away (see our Shopping chapter), while Bethesda's cute neighborhood shops are within footsteps.

Prince George's County

Greenbelt Marriott Hotel $$$
6400 Ivy Lane
Greenbelt, MD
(301) 441–3700
www.marriott.com

This is one of the nicest full-service hotels near the University of Maryland and NASA Goddard Space Flight Center. There are 284 standard rooms in this hotel as well as concierge-level and extended-stay accommodations. You'll find a restaurant, pub, free parking, indoor and outdoor pools, a health club, tennis courts, and a business center.

ON A BUDGET

Budget properties: Sometimes you get what you pay for. Budget hotels are often no-frills ventures. Shop around for good rates on Priceline, Hotwire, or your travel Web site of choice, and you may end up with a pleasant surprise.

Washington, D.C.

Days Inn Connecticut Avenue $–$$
4400 Connecticut Avenue NW
Washington, DC
(202) 244–5600
www.daysinn.com

In the city but away from the masses, this newly remodeled 155-room edition of the national chain comes with free on-site parking, in-room safe, and voice mail. It's in upper Northwest D.C., a safe and exclusive neighborhood, and is made even more convenient by the presence of the Van Ness/UDC Metro 2 blocks away. Also close by are American University, the National Zoo, Rock Creek Park, and the restaurants and shops of Tenleytown and Cleveland Park.

Hotel Harrington $–$$
11th and E Streets NW
Washington, DC
(202) 628–8140, (800) 424–8532
www.hotel-harrington.com

The no-frills Harrington is for the budget conscious who want to be in the thick of it. It's a half-block away from Pennsylvania Avenue, about equal distance from the White House and the Capitol. There's nearby parking for $10 a day, a restaurant, bar, barber shop, and laundry room. The Harrington has always done a strong business with Europeans. More Americans should follow their lead. Families may want to try one of the 26 suites in the 260-unit hotel.

The International Guest House $
1441 Kennedy Street NW
Washington, DC
(202) 726–5808

The International Guest House is a nonprofit facility maintained by the Mennonite Church to provide clean, inexpensive lodging for international visitors in a homey atmosphere. Indeed, the large brick home with its wraparound porch is in a pleasant residential area off 16th Street NW, across the street from Rock Creek Park. Breakfast is served family style at 8:00 A.M., with guests and staff eating together. There is a large living room for lounging and reading, and a television is in the basement. Smoking and alcohol are not permitted. However, for the rock-bottom rate of $30 per person per night, you can hardly find a more reasonable bargain in a nice, safe area.

Red Roof Inn Downtown D.C. $$
500 H Street NW
Washington, DC
(202) 289–5959
www.redroof.com

Anyone who's ever stayed in a Red Roof Inn knows what to expect. Near Washington's vibrant Penn Quarter neighborhood, the hotel is less than 2 blocks from the Metro and Verizon Center, 4 blocks to the Washington

Convention Center, and 7 blocks to Capitol Hill. The inn also offers a restaurant, exercise room with sauna, and guest laundry. Small pets are allowed.

Windsor Inn $$
1842 16th Street NW
Washington, DC
(202) 667–0300, (800) 423–9111
www.windsorembassyinns.com
This is called an inn, but with 46 rooms, it's a bit large to fit into that category. The rooms are pleasant and neat, but not luxurious. The location, though a bit off the beaten path from midtown and the sights, is convenient enough to the Metro. On a nice day, you can walk the 12 blocks to the White House—a pleasant stroll past some handsome buildings. Your room comes with complimentary continental breakfast and evening sherry.

Windsor Park Hotel $$
2116 Kalorama Road NW
Washington, DC
(202) 483–7700, (800) 247–3064
windsorparkhotel.com
The Windsor Park in Washington's exclusive Kalorama neighborhood is another great European-style bargain. Close to the bustle of Adams Morgan and the shopping of Dupont Circle, the innlike setting is perfect for families with young children. All 43 simple rooms come with a small refrigerator, complimentary continental breakfast, and newspaper.

Northern Virginia

Alexandria

Hawthorn Suites Alexandria $$
420 North Van Dorn Street
Alexandria, VA
(703) 370–1000
www.hawthorn.com
If it's important to be near shopping malls and right off the interstate but not too far from D.C., then the Hawthorn should fit the bill. The 186-suite hotel in Alexandria's West End is within striking distance of I–395, one of the region's busiest arteries, and Landmark Shopping Center, one of the region's busiest malls. D.C. is just 9 miles up the road, while Old Town is but 5 miles east. The area is a fast-food mecca, but you can take solace in that all suites here come with kitchens.

Arlington

Quality Inn Iwo Jima $$
1501 Arlington Boulevard
Arlington, VA
(703) 524–5000, (800) 424–1501
www.choicehotels.com
Popular with tourists, this 141-room edition of the national chain is within an easy walk of Arlington Cemetery, the Iwo Jima Memorial, the National Mall, and even Georgetown. Rosslyn Metro is 3 blocks away. The hotel, though a bit worn, offers low prices as well as free parking, free local phone calls, in-room coffeemaker, laundry facilities, and an indoor/outdoor pool, but this is an older property and you should expect only the basics insofar as rooms are concerned—nothing fancy here.

Falls Church

Econo Lodge Metro $$–$$$
6800 Lee Highway
Falls Church, VA
(703) 538–5300, (800) 785–6343
www.econometro.com
Don't let the name rule out this property for you. This member of the popular national budget motel chain has consistently been rated as one of the best Econo Lodges in the country. Why else would inner-Beltway politicians and dignitaries and celebrities like Shirley MacLaine choose to stay here? The location couldn't be better. The 47-room lodge is at the junction of I–66 and Lee Highway, the first interchange you'll come to when entering Washington from Dulles Airport. It also puts you in proximity to the amazing French cuisine of La Cote d'Or Cafe (see Restaurants chapter) and within 2½ blocks of the East Falls Church Metro station. About half the rooms are nonsmoking, and several are wheelchair accessible.

Suburban Maryland

Bethesda

American Inn of Bethesda $–$$
8130 Wisconsin Avenue
Bethesda, MD
(301) 656–9300, (800) 323–7081
www.american-inn.com
A quick drive or ride from the District border, the American Inn is in the middle of downtown Bethesda, about a 10-minute walk from the Bethesda Metro and only a couple of minutes' drive from NIH. This is a simple property, nothing fancy, but it has a great location not far from Bethesda's famed restaurant row. Guests of the American can get microwave ovens upon request, and there's a pool for cooling off.

Gaithersburg

Motel 6 Gaithersburg $
497 Quince Orchard Road
Gaithersburg, MD
(301) 977–3311
www.motel6.com
It's nothing fancy, but even during the Cherry Blossom Festival, double rooms go for $69. Business king rooms come with an enhanced work area, data port, and speaker phone.

The National Institute of Standards and the Montgomery Fairgrounds are within walking distance. The Shady Grove Metro stop is a couple of miles away, and it's about a 40-minute ride to tourist attractions downtown. Free coffee and newspapers are available in the lobby. One small pet per room is permitted.

Silver Spring

Days Inn Silver Spring $
8040 13th Street
Silver Spring, MD
(301) 588–4400
www.daysinn.com
This Days Inn provides the basic comforts and is near much of upper Northwest D.C. and close-in areas of Montgomery County. Walter Reed Army Hospital is a mile to the south, and Takoma Park, to the immediate east, has some interesting Bohemian-tinged shops, restaurants, and nightclubs. It's also in walking distance to the National Oceanic and Atmospheric Administration.

HOSTELS/UNIVERSITY INNS

George Washington University Inn $$$
824 New Hampshire Avenue NW
Washington, DC
(202) 337–6620, (800) 426–4455
www.gwuinn.com
Formerly the Inn at Foggy Bottom, this newly renovated hotel is within walking distance from The George Washington University, Georgetown, and much of the Smithsonian. Some of the hotel's 95 rooms have kitchens, and there's also a restaurant on-site. Discounts are available to G.W. students and alumni.

Georgetown University
Conference Center $$$–$$$$
3800 Reservoir Road NW
Washington, DC
(202) 687–3200
www.conferencecenters.com/wasgu
The nation's oldest Catholic university is the obvious main attraction of this on-campus hotel run by Marriott. Mostly frequented by guests of the university and seminar participants, the conference center offers some rooms with kitchenettes plus a swimming pool and health club. All of the Georgetown neighborhood is a short walk away, and the business district of Rosslyn (Virginia) looms just across Key Bridge. Don't worry about nonstop college parties keeping you up at night; the hotel is at the far-north end of campus, in a relatively quiet residential area.

Washington International
American Youth Hostel $
1009 11th Street NW
Washington, DC
(202) 737–2333
www.hiwashingtondc.org
A clean, safe alternative for young travelers on a budget, this 270-bed dorm-style hostel is 1

block north of the Washington Convention Center and near many of the city's top restaurants. Both the rooms and huge kitchen have recently been remodeled. There's a large common area for meeting other travelers (lots of Europeans here), a 60-inch TV, and a coin-operated laundry. Free movies and tours are available and, as you can imagine, security is very tight. The price is rock bottom—$20 for members of the hostelling association and $29 for nonmembers. A free continental breakfast is served each morning.

BED AND BREAKFASTS

In a bustling place like Metro Washington, bed-and-breakfasts are a welcome escape from everyday life. Chat with the owners to learn more about neighborhood restaurants, entertainment, shopping, and the latest museum exhibits. They're pleased to share their knowledge and often will help you make arrangements. As the name implies, you can expect breakfast for two. Some also include afternoon tea or an aperitif.

Price Code

The price code is based on average room cost per night based on double occupancy.

$. . . . . Under $125
$$ . . . . $125 to $175
$$$ . . . . $176 to $250
$$$$ . . . . More than $250

Washington, D.C.

Adam's Inn $–$$
1744 Lanier Place NW
Washington, DC
(202) 745–3600, (800) 578–6807
www.adamsinn.com

i   Innkeepers are usually happy to provide a description of every room available so you can decide which atmosphere best suits you. Amenities and prices can vary widely from room to room.

Children of all ages are welcome at this comfy inn, situated in three 100-year-old buildings and completely renovated in 2002 under new owner Adam Crain. Located in a residential area of eclectic Adams Morgan, the quaint inn features 25 nonsmoking rooms, 15 of which have private baths. Amenities include an expanded continental breakfast, high-speed Internet and fax access, a sitting room with a cable TV and video player, guest kitchen and laundry privileges, and limited garage parking. Weekly rates are available.

Bed & Breakfast
Accommodations, Ltd. $–$$$$
P.O. Box 12011
Washington, DC 20005
(413) 582–9888, (877) 893–3233
www.bedandbreakfastdc.com
From budget to luxury offerings, Bed & Breakfast Accommodations, Ltd. will connect you with an array of private-home lodgings and inns. Some apartments are even available for family groups and extended-stay guests. Choices include historic properties with antiques and gardens, and some with pools. They offer more than 25 selections, such as the elegantly appointed Aaron Shipman House near Dupont Circle and the Carriage House on Capitol Hill, and convenient contemporaries like the Gallery Inn near Dupont Circle and Adams Morgan, and the Arlington Bed and Breakfast near the Ballston Metro. Various types of breakfast are included.

DC GuestHouse $$$
1337 10th Street NW
Washington, DC
(202) 332–2502, (800) 952–3060
www.dcguesthouse.com
There's a lot of character in this property, which once housed a funeral parlor in D.C.'s Shaw neighborhood. The house is tastefully decked out with treasures from the owners' art collection, with works that span the globe and include ancient relics as well as recent creations. Though the GuestHouse does make a point of honoring its guests' privacy, social

butterflies will feel right at home gathered around a cozy breakfast table or sipping wine in the living room. Six spacious rooms are tastefully decorated and outfitted with luxurious touches—even a fireplace in one room.

The Dupont at The Circle $$–$$$$
1604 19th Street NW
Washington, DC
(202) 332–5251, (888) 412–0100
www.dupontatthecircle.com
Just a block from the bustle of Dupont Circle, this upscale Victorian charmer sits on a tree-lined residential street just steps from the Dupont Metro stop. The eight luxurious guest rooms and suites are decorated with antiques; many have fireplaces and antique writing desks. Every room has a full private bath with a claw-foot or whirlpool tub and is provided with sumptuous Egyptian cotton linens. All the rooms are nonsmoking and have telephones with voice mail and data ports. Some include televisions and video players. Services include a complimentary continental breakfast, newspaper, and limited parking.

**Kalorama Guest House at
Kalorama Park** $–$$
1854 Mintwood Place NW
Washington, DC
(202) 667–6369
www.kaloramaguesthouse.com
In the lively Adams Morgan neighborhood, just a block from the restaurant district, this elegant, nonsmoking 30-room inn is furnished in Victorian antiques. Once inside, expect peace and quiet. Fifteen rooms, including the five suites, have private baths. The suites contain TVs and phones. Complimentary continental breakfast, cookies and lemonade, and evening sherry are served in the parlor and garden. The Kalorama Park's sister property at Woodley Park is located just a few blocks away, offering an additional 18 rooms cut from a similar mold.

i If you drive to D.C., be sure to ask about parking at in-town bed-and-breakfasts. Many are in residential areas with limited parking.

**Swann House Historic Dupont
Circle Inn** $$$
1808 New Hampshire Avenue NW
Washington, DC
(202) 265–4414
www.swannhouse.com
Housed in an 1883 Dupont Circle mansion, the Swann House is nothing if not romantic—an ideal destination for an urban honeymoon, an anniversary celebration, or even an engagement. The inn's nine rooms are equipped with carved fireplaces, whirlpool baths, and sumptuous feather beds. Each room sports its own thematic decor. Breakfast is bountiful, and guests can also nibble on refreshments and sip cocktails in the evening. Summer visitors can even take advantage of an outdoor swimming pool.

Northern Virginia

Bed & Breakfast Association of Virginia
P.O. Box 1077
Stanardsville, VA 22973
(888) 660–BBAV
www.bbonline.com/va/bbav
Contact this association for a free directory of more than 200 member inns throughout the state, including several in the Northern Virginia area.

Fairfax County

Bailiwick Inn $$$–$$$$
4023 Chain Bridge Road
Fairfax, VA
(703) 691–2266
www.bailiwickinn.com
This early-nineteenth-century brick house is wedged in the center of Fairfax City's charming but often overlooked historic district, just across Route 123 from the old courthouse. Geared toward romantic getaways, the Bailiwick has 14 guest rooms, each named for a

local historical figure, all with feather beds and some with Jacuzzis and fireplaces. George Mason University and its beautiful Center for the Arts are right up the road, and the Vienna Metro station is less than 10 minutes away. The rate includes a filling gourmet breakfast. Children are not permitted, and smoking is allowed only on the garden terrace.

Loudoun County

The Norris House Inn $$–$$$
108 Loudoun Street SW
Leesburg, VA
(703) 777–1806, (800) 644–1806
www.norrishouse.com
Right in the middle of Leesburg's historic district, the Norris House Inn (built in 1760) has guest rooms with elegant beds, antiques galore, and fireplaces. It's a nice spot for a romantic night away but also conducive to small meetings and family celebrations. Guests have full access to the distinguished dining room, parlor, library, sunroom, and an expansive veranda overlooking beautiful gardens. Its Stone House Tea Room, next door, is open by reservation and on special weekends each month. Washington is about an hour away.

Surburban Maryland

Longwood Manor
Bed and Breakfast $–$$$
2900 DuBarry Lane
Brookeville, MD
(301) 774–1002, (866) 774–1002
www.bbonline.com/md/longwood
Only 16 miles from Washington, D.C., Longwood Manor features three guest rooms, all with private baths, cable TV, and individual air-conditioning. Built in 1817, the large, formal residence, complete with a white-

columned facade, originally served as the home of Thomas Moore, who invented the first refrigerator. Special features include a spacious outdoor swimming pool, a large meeting room, and event catering. Guests receive an expanded continental breakfast.

Pleasant Springs Farm $$$
16112 Barnesville Road
Boyds, MD
(301) 972–3452
www.PleasantSpringsFarm.com
Surrounded by 30 acres of gardens, meadows, nature trails, and streams, this restored log cottage can accommodate a couple or a family with well-behaved children. Dating to 1768 and featured on HGTV in 2002, the cabin includes two log sitting rooms, one of which boasts a fireplace. One bedroom has a queen-size bed and full bath, while a second offers a full bed and half-bath. The building has window air-conditioning. Full homemade breakfasts, delivered by the innkeepers, include such dishes as eggs Benedict, scalloped potatoes, and quiche seasoned with herbs grown on-site. Guests can purchase farm products such as hand-spun and -dyed wool yarn, and cheese and soap made from goat milk. The inn closes January through March.

The Reynolds of Derwood
Bed and Breakfast $
16620 Bethayres Road
Derwood, MD
(301) 963–2216
www.reynolds-bed-breakfast.com
Conveniently located in a quiet suburban neighborhood just minutes from the Shady Grove Metro station, this three-room, family-oriented inn without age restrictions features several amenities for active guests. Highlights include a putting green, driving range, exer-

cise room, sauna, and two outdoor hot tubs; a park is right across the street. The President's Room showcases authentic memorabilia from the many years when innkeeper Joan Reynolds's parents worked for the White House. The window offers a view of the 25-foot, illuminated waterfall outside. An adjoining Quilt Room, stocked with toys, can be added for guests with children. The downstairs Williamsburg Room is wheelchair accessible. Both rooms include TVs with VCRs, and guests have access to a collection of 450 videos. Continental breakfasts—custom ordered on the inn's Web site—can be eaten in the sunroom or outdoors at tables near the waterfall. Reynolds, whose art studio is on-site, sells her paintings, drawings, and notecards of local historic places.

RESTAURANTS

From Chinatown to Adams Morgan, Capitol Hill to Georgetown, Rockville to Old Town Alexandria, and Tysons Corner to Bethesda, a veritable dining world in miniature awaits you. Whatever cuisine you crave, you're likely to find it in Metro Washington, mainly because so many residents are originally from elsewhere. Despite this, it took until the mid-1990s for Washington to be recognized as a city for fine dining. In recent years, however, the city has truly arrived.

Magazines like *Gourmet, Bon Appétit*—and their readers—have begun to sit up and take notice, and several Washington chefs have won international reputations. It had to happen sooner or later, given the area's demographics. Metro Washington offers a customer base that is diverse, well traveled, and affluent. Suffice it to say there are plenty of folks here who appreciate good food and who can afford to dine out regularly. Not to say that you can't dine reasonably. There are some bargains, especially among Washington's ethnic eateries. You'll also find the national chains, from the economical Chili's to the deluxe steak houses like the Palm, Morton's, and Ruth's Chris Steak House. But if you're from anywhere except New York, Tokyo, or London, get ready for sticker shock. Even the folksiest eateries are likely to be pricier than you'll find back home.

Before we get into the meat of this chapter, though, a few words about the ingredients.

Please keep in mind: This is in no way an exhaustive listing. We'd probably still be writing if that was the objective! Instead, we've dished up an eclectic buffet, if you will—a little of this and a little of that—to give you a taste for what's available. Still, we've barely scratched the proverbial surface—or rather,

removed that first delicious layer—of what Metro Washington has to offer in the way of calories, carbohydrates, and cholesterol.

The restaurants that made the cut are a mix of recognized local favorites (in some cases, institutions), very personal choices, and a smattering of others in the District, Suburban Maryland, and Northern Virginia. With a few exceptions, none of the major national chain establishments (including fast-food outlets, sandwich/pizza joints, and full-service family restaurants such as Ruby Tuesday, Outback Steakhouse, etc.) are represented. We want to introduce you to places you're unlikely to find anywhere else.

(Be sure to check out our Close-up on kids' dining in the Kidstuff chapter also.)

All establishments listed accept most major credit cards unless otherwise noted.

Restaurants are divided first by geographic areas: Washington, Northern Virginia, and Maryland. Within each area we've broken down the list by ethnic cuisine, and restaurants under each ethnic heading are in alphabetical order. One final note—seafood restaurants used to be a separate category, but fish is now so prevalent on most menus that we've simply grouped these restaurants according to the type of ethnic cuisine they specialize in.

Bon appétit!

Price Code

To give you an idea of what to expect price-wise, we've provided the following scale as a very general guide. Prices shown are for a complete dinner for two, including appetizers, wine, beer or spirits, and dessert, but excluding tax and tip. All, of course, are subject to change.

$. . . . . $50 or less
$$ . . . . $51–$75

$$$ . . . . $76–$125
$$$$ . . . . More than $126

WASHINGTON, D.C.
American/Continental

Acadiana $$$
901 New York Avenue NW
Washington, DC
(202) 408–8848
www.acadianarestaurant.com
This downtown newcomer captures the flavors of Louisiana in classic dishes like shrimp and grits, fried green tomatoes and jambalaya, and serves them in a dining room that's reminiscent of a classy home on the Bayou—albeit one that's been built out of a slick new office building. The flavors you'll find here are authentic, but they're done up with the grace and style you'd expect in one of the city's finest restaurants. Fresh biscuits are brought out to greet each diner, and they're heavenly when slathered with red pepper and cream cheese spread. Desserts are authentic as well, from tasty crème brulée and lemon doberge cake to classic beignets. Lunch is served Monday through Friday and dinner is served Monday through Saturday; brunch is served Sunday.

Ben's Chili Bowl $
1213 U Street NW
Washington, DC
(202) 667–0909
www.benschilibowl.com
Ben's is a Washington, D.C. institution—a gathering place for neighborhood workers, politicians, celebrities, and students. Opened in 1958, it weathered the riots that afflicted the U Street neighborhood in the late 1960s. Now it attracts a diverse clientele, particularly late at night, when young adults stop here for a late bite after a night on the town. The signature dish here is the chili half-smoke (half hot dog, half sausage, served on a bun and smothered with chili, onions, and mustard). Also try the chili cheese fries and the handmade milkshakes for a decadent treat.

i Celebrated tour guide Tony Pitch leads culinary walking tours through Adams Morgan several times each year, revealing the history of the neighborhood with stops at some of the more interesting eateries. Visit www .residentassociates.com to see when the next tour is coming.

Blue Duck Tavern $$$
Park Hyatt Washington
1201 24th Street NW
Washington, DC
(202) 419–6755
When the Park Hyatt Washington closed for renovation, Chef Brian McBride of the hotel's Melrose Restaurant left to perfect his technique. The hotel reopened with a new destination restaurant, Blue Duck Tavern, designed by Tony Chi and again featuring McBride at the helm. On the menu, you'll find tasty creations like pork loin with bourbon-soaked peaches. Dessert is also a treat; a warm chocolate cake comes with a splash of bourbon flamed tableside. Ice cream is hand-cranked and delivered to the table in a glass bowl for sharing. The restaurant is open daily for breakfast, lunch, and dinner.

Café Saint-Ex $$
1847 14th Street NW
Washington, DC
(202) 265–7839
www.saint-ex.com
This comfortable Logan Circle gathering place takes its name from author/pilot Antoine de Saint-Exupéry, and you'll notice an aviation theme in its decor. The restaurant itself is cozy and unpretentious—a good place to meet a friend for brunch or to listen and groove as DJs take over the downstairs lounge space, Gate 54. When the weather is pleasant, you can sit outside and people-watch. The restaurant is open for lunch Tuesday through Sunday and for dinner nightly.

A U Street legend, Ben's Chili Bowl has served up half-smokes and milkshakes since 1958. COURTESY WASHINGTON, D.C. CONVENTION AND TOURISM CORPORATION

Capital Grille $$$$
601 Pennsylvania Avenue NW
Washington, DC
(202) 737–6200
www.thecapitalgrille.com

Yes, Capital Grille is part of a chain, but we've decided to include it. Why? In a very short time it has become one of the trendiest places around Capitol Hill, the kind of establishment where you're likely to run into the town's top lobbyists, along with the legislators they're trying to influence. Nowadays some of Washington's most important powerbrokers are women, and you'll find them here, too, but this place has the atmosphere of a men's club—dark wood, dark green, and, yes, even hunting trophies. From the street you're greeted with a view of the meat-aging room, complete with moldy rinds that will be expertly cut away to provide you with flavorful—and humongous—cuts of beef. Even vegetarians will find something to like here if they are able to overlook the carnivorous atmosphere. The baked potatoes weigh a pound, and salads are a meal in themselves. Similar fare is served at the Tysons Corner location, 1861 International Drive, McLean, Virginia (703) 448–3900. Capital Grille is open for lunch weekdays and dinner nightly.

Cashion's Eat Place $$$
1819 Columbia Road NW
Washington, DC
(202) 797–1819
www.cashionseatplace.com

Ann Cashion is one of the town's most innovative chefs, and she has won many honors to prove it, both locally and nationally. Her namesake restaurant serves dinner nightly and Sunday brunch but is closed Monday.

The dining room is curved and spills into the street on warm summer evenings, thanks to a front wall of sliding glass doors that open onto the patio. The crowd is as eclectic as the Adams Morgan neighborhood that is home to the restaurant. There are sleek women in black dresses, along with young execs in khakis and the occasional business-suited lawyers. The real attraction, however, is the food. It has a down-home, Southern touch, but there's always an interesting fillip, often in the chef's choice of vegetable accompaniments.

The handwritten menu changes regularly; recently, the halibut fillet was pan-roasted with wild mushrooms in a vin blanc sauce and served with sautéed spinach, and the rack of pork was marinated with orange, thyme, and garlic and served with glazed fennel and a black olive, ouzo, and orange sauce. There are all kinds of exotic meats, like buffalo, sweetbreads, and guinea hen. What really makes dining here memorable, though, is Cashion's flair for seasoning. She manages to make her dishes distinctive, but she's so skilled at combining flavors that you're not quite sure what the ingredients are.

Chadwicks $$
3205 K Street NW
Washington, DC
(202) 333–2565
www.chadwicksrestaurants.com

It's tough to avoid comparisons with the local Clyde's chain (see below), but Chadwicks should view it as a compliment. It's easy to find something to like in this warm, inviting Georgetown saloon/restaurant, be it the woodsy atmosphere, the selection from the bar, or the hamburgers. Indeed, this may be one of the best burgers in town, thick and charbroiled to your taste. The rest of the menu is the usual saloon fare, served in generous portions: seafood, soups, salads, pasta, and the like. Chadwicks serves lunch and dinner daily, and Sunday brunch. The only hard part for the uninitiated may be find-

ℹ Want to find out what Washingtonians think about their dining establishments, or have a question about a local restaurant? Log onto www.chowhound.com/midatlantic/boards/dc/dc.html. *Washington Post* restaurant critic Tom Sietsma also takes readers' questions in his online chat, hosted each Wednesday at 11:00 A.M. at www.washingtonpost.com.

Even spies get hungry. The infamous Aldrich Ames met his KGB handlers at Chadwicks in Georgetown and betrayed ten of his American colleagues over lunch.

ing this place, which sits literally beneath the Whitehurst Freeway near the foot of Wisconsin Avenue.

CityZen $$$$
1330 Maryland Avenue SW
Washington, DC
(202) 787–6868

When CityZen opened in the Mandarin Oriental Washington D.C., it made critics concede that the Nation's Capital had truly arrived as a restaurant town. After all, the city managed to attract the culinary talents of Eric Ziebold, who earned acclaim under legendary chef Thomas Keller at the French Laundry in Napa. Both CityZen and Ziebold have amassed an impressive list of awards and achievements from top culinary magazines. Expect an ever-changing, multi-course dining experience that's nothing short of elegant, prepared with ingredients that are fresh and often unusual. The dining room is open Tuesday through Saturday for dinner; it is closed Sunday and Monday.

Clyde's of Georgetown $$
3236 M Street NW
Washington, DC
(202) 333–9180
www.clydes.com

Here's a D.C. institution that was smart enough to bring its success to the suburbs. Although all of the locations inside and outside the Beltway have proven to be a hit, none have quite the charm of this street-front saloon in the very crux of trendy Georgetown. Serving lunch and dinner daily, and Sunday brunch, it's a raucous, lively place—a little bit meat market, a little bit family fun center—all housed in nooks and alcoves that feature touches of stained glass, extravagant art, and, often, wall-to-wall people. Beyond the irresistible bar area, Clyde's beckons with its own brand of award-winning chili, steaks, burgers,

salads, sandwiches, and homemade desserts. Clyde's makes a special effort to buy its produce from local farmers, so the veggie dishes can be among the freshest in town. The food's not always perfect—and almost never exceptional—but the place is a blast, and its appeal is broad. Patrons include college students, families, and business types.

Dean & DeLuca Cafe $
3276 M Street NW
Washington, DC
(202) 342–2500
www.deandeluca.com

Shopping in Georgetown and want to grab a quick bite? Do you need some takeout to stock your hotel room? This self-service counter, serving lunch and dinner daily in one of D.C.'s premier gourmet markets, will fit the bill with passable-to-yummy soups, sandwiches, salads, and fresh baked goods. The Cafe also provides classy catering for cocktail parties and wedding receptions. For those who need an extra shot of energy, there's also an espresso bar.

Georgia Brown's $$$
950 15th Street NW
Washington, DC
(202) 393–4499
www.gbrowns.com

If upscale soul food's your bag, this is the place, but if you prefer traditional preparations, you may be startled by some of the innovations at Georgia Brown's. You'll find black-eyed peas, grits, and collards—and one of the city's most decadent Sunday brunches. Give the brown-sugar-grilled pork chops and hearty Carolina gumbo a try, if you make it through the spread of brunch classics like eggs and crunchy French toast. Georgia Brown's also serves lunch weekdays and dinner nightly.

Kinkead's $$$
2000 Pennsylvania Avenue NW
Washington, DC
(202) 296–7700
www.kinkead.com

Seafood is the specialty of imaginative Robert Kinkead, one of Washington's premier chefs, and a Boston transplant. His casual restaurant serves lunch Monday through Saturday, Sunday brunch, and dinner nightly. Just 4 blocks from the White House, Kinkead's is always packed, and the wooden booths and floors make for some noisy rooms. The atmosphere, however, is beside the point in a place that transforms seafood into such a melting, rich, heavenly experience. Kinkead runs this restaurant with military precision, as you can see through the open kitchen. The kitchen staff wear headphones to communicate above the clatter, turning out seafood timed to perfection. Try the skate wing if they have it or, in season, the soft-shell crab. The seasonings are bold and exotic, and the appetizers are almost too pretty to eat.

Komi $$$$
1509 17th Street NW
Washington, DC
(202) 332–9200
www.komirestaurant.com

Chef Johnny Monis is part of a class of talented young chefs in Washington, D.C. who operate their own restaurants. After your dining experience at Komi, you'll find it hard to believe that Monis hasn't yet reached his 30th birthday. Among the other restaurants on 17th Street, Komi stands out as a star. The dining room itself is intimate and sparsely decorated, letting the cuisine take center stage. Monis's Greek roots shine through with hints of the Mediterranean in his creations and in the largely Greek wine list. You can order a la carte or indulge in a five-course tasting menu; on Fridays and Saturdays, only the tasting menu is served.

Matchbox $$
713 H Street NW
Washington, DC
(202) 289–4441
www.matchboxdc.com

Matchbox is suitably named—a narrow, three-story restaurant on the edge of Chinatown.

While pizza is the main course here, the prime attractions are the mini-hamburgers, available in orders of three, six, and nine and served on toasted brioche, piled high with parmesan cheese–coated fried onions. If you opt for pizza, you'll find a fine selection of meat, cheese, and vegetarian toppings, and the crust is thin and crisp. Matchbox is open for lunch and dinner Monday through Saturday.

Mr. Smith's of Georgetown $$
3104 M Street NW
Washington, DC
(202) 333–3104
www.mrsmiths.com

You won't be able to see the lovely patio garden from the street, yet it's the main draw at this saloon/eatery in Georgetown. You'll find standard pub fare here at reasonable prices and, at night, a piano bar. In fact, Maryland-raised Tori Amos sang here as a teenager. If you like fancy cocktails, this place features daiquiris and other frozen drinks in a dozen varieties. Mr. Smith's serves lunch and dinner daily and Sunday brunch.

Old Ebbitt Grill $$
675 15th Street NW
Washington, DC
(202) 347–4800
www.ebbitt.com

When they say old, they mean it—since 1856. Old Ebbitt Grill bills itself as "Washington's oldest saloon," and although that may be subject to argument, especially since its renovation (handsome forest green upholstery, mahogany booths, and Victorian lamps), its stellar reputation and prime location are not. Just 2 blocks from the White House, this casually elegant establishment long ago made a name for itself with roasts, steaks, fresh seafood, homemade pastas, soups, burgers, deli-style sandwiches, and homemade desserts. Check out the famed Oyster Bar—even if you don't a have a taste for this particular Chesapeake Bay delicacy.

Old Ebbitt Grill is open for breakfast Monday through Friday, lunch Monday through

Saturday, dinner nightly, and Saturday and Sunday brunch. With a 3:00 A.M. closing time on Friday and Saturday, it's understandably popular with the hungry after-theater crowds. In the Grill's atrium you'll find Ebbitt Express, serving freshly prepared, wholesome take-out food for breakfast, lunch, and dinner.

Old Glory $$

3139 M Street NW
Washington, DC
(202) 337–3406
www.oldglorybbq.com

Great barbecue, sandwiches, and burgers; a lively, casual atmosphere; and fascinating history-rich decor combine to make George-town's Old Glory something to shoot fire-works about. If you take your barbecue seriously, you'll want to sample all six of the sauces here: Each follows the recipe of a dif-ferent barbecue region, like Memphis and Texas. Corn muffins, biscuits, and hush pup-pies are the real thing, but save room for the mouthwatering desserts. This is a noisy, fun spot, so be sure to add it to the list of places to consider for birthday celebrations or other get-togethers. Old Glory is open for lunch Monday through Saturday, dinner nightly, and Sunday brunch.

Polly's Café $

1342 U Street NW
Washington, DC
(202) 265–8385
pollyscafe.com

Polly's Café typifies the ethnically diverse, rapidly gentrifying Shaw/Cardozo neighbor-hood along U Street. It's a restaurant and bar where bikers and brokers seem to feel equally at home. There's the usual range of burgers, chicken, and seafood, with a revolv-ing selection of specials, such as chicken stuffed with spinach. Open for dinner daily and for brunch on Saturday and Sunday. For night owls and folks who've just been to the nearby Lincoln Theater, Polly's Café stays open until 3:00 A.M. on Friday and Saturday nights.

Prime Rib $$$$

2020 K Street NW
Washington, DC
(202) 466–8811
www.theprimerib.com

This is a place for high rollers, and you'll sense it as soon as you see the flashy blondes at the lively bar and lots of fit, fiftyish men . . . with lots of money. People dress up for dinner here: dark suits, slinky black dresses, and even a bit of glitter. The dining room has the feel of an old-time lovers' ren-dezvous, with its draperies and martinis and baby-grand piano—but it's too crowded for an effective hideaway. The food here is as much an attraction as the ambience. You won't find better prime aged beef, and there's live Maine lobster and fresh Florida seafood flown in daily. Don't forget the tradi-tional accompaniments either: mouthwater-ing mashed potatoes and creamed spinach. Prime Rib is open for lunch weekdays and dinner Monday through Saturday.

Restaurant Nora $$$$

2132 Florida Avenue NW
Washington, DC
(202) 462–5143
www.noras.com

Nora Pouillon, the chef and founder of Restaurant Nora, was one of the first in the city to insist on organic ingredients. From free-range poultry to farm-fresh chèvre, Nora has always produced the best and most healthful food. Her cozy restaurant has the same honest, farmhouse feeling, with its dec-orative handicrafts, dark wood floors, and Windsor chairs. As is often the case with sim-ple beauty, this eatery attracts the rich and famous, from former president Clinton to media mogul Barry Diller. Dishes are sophisti-cated without necessarily being too calorie laden, with influences from India, France, and, of course, the United States. In general the cuisine will suit those who prefer their foods less seasoned. Those who savor strong flavors may even find some dishes a bit bland. If you go, be sure to save room for one of the special fresh-fruit desserts. Restaurant Nora is open for dinner Monday through Saturday, and closed on Sunday. (See our Close-up on Nora in this chapter.)

1789 Restaurant $$$$
1226 36th Street NW
Washington, DC
(202) 965–1789
www.1789restaurant.com

Perhaps it's the location, a two-story Federal town house in a quiet residential area of upper northwest in the shadows of Georgetown University. Then, once you treat your palate to the food, that immediately carries equal weight. Whatever the reason, 1789 captivates with its country-inn charm and elegance and the efficient, first-class service. Although named for the year the university was founded, 1789 offers a truly modern American menu, serving dinner nightly, with such classic treats as pheasant, venison, fish, veal, soft-shell crabs, lobster, and homemade soups. Be sure to leave room for the breads and desserts, all whipped up on the premises. 1789 is open for dinner nightly.

Starland Cafe $
5125 MacArthur Boulevard NW
Washington, DC
(202) 244–9396
www.starlandcafe.com

Remember the hit song "Afternoon Delight" by the Starland Vocal Band in the 1970s? The Starland Cafe is co-owned by Washingtonian Bill Danoff, who was in the group and also penned other songs, such as "Take Me Home, Country Roads." The cafe is located in a comfortable residential neighborhood near the Potomac, northwest of Georgetown. Brunch on Saturday or Sunday offers Belgian waffles, smoked salmon, and eggs Benedict. Or go for the live acoustic jazz and blues on Friday nights. You may just get a table next to Danoff himself.

Vidalia $$$
1990 M Street NW
Washington, DC
(202) 659–1990

You'd never guess there was a bright dining room in the basement of this midtown office building, but that's just the impression you'll get when you walk through the door of Vidalia. Although a recent million-dollar makeover has done away with the restaurant's farmhouse decor, you'll still find the same heavenly aromas wafting from the kitchen. The restaurant's elegant cream, gold, and blue pallet complements Vidalia's haute Southern cuisine. Unlike much Southern cooking, which relies on frying and slow simmering, Vidalia serves dishes with real finesse and its own creative touches. You'll be off to a good start with a basket of cornbread and buttermilk biscuits so sinful you may be tempted to make a meal of them. For a main course you'll find all sorts of great, rich Southern-influenced dishes. The seafood is juicy and prepared just right, and these may be the best sweetbreads in town. Vegetable accompaniments are always unusual, but rarely low-cal, so don't look for salvation here. It may be wise to wear something loose; you may feel a size larger at meal's end. Vidalia is open for lunch weekdays, dinner nightly.

Willard Room $$$$
InterContinental Hotel
1401 Pennsylvania Avenue NW
Washington, DC
(202) 637–7440
www.washington.interconti.com/dining

The Willard Room is almost daunting in its grandeur: soaring ceilings decorated with medallions and carved moldings, elaborate chandeliers, silken draperies, and table settings fit for royalty. The cooking is also rich and elaborate—a cuisine that hearkens back to the turn of the century when course after lavish course was served. You'll find all the

Close-up

Nora Pouillon: A Pioneer in Healthy Cooking

Nora Pouillon is a pioneer. Twenty-eight years ago, she opened her Restaurant Nora in a Washington, D.C. town house, insisting on organic products free from hormones and antibiotics. It was quickly crowded for lunch and for dinner. In 1995 Pouillon opened Asia Nora, and in 1999 Restaurant Nora became the first certified organic restaurant in the nation, with at least 95 percent of all its products certified organic.

Nora Pouillon strives to get the message out on organic foods. COURTESY RESTAURANT NORA

Restaurant Nora offers elegant dining in a twentieth-century carriage house in the Dupont Circle area. It is decorated with museum-quality Amish and Mennonite quilts, while Asia Nora has an exotic and romantic atmosphere with Asian art objects displayed around the restaurant. The service in both restaurants is knowledgeable, friendly, and professional. The wine list focuses on "boutique" wineries that grow their grapes organically. Most of the produce comes from local, organic farmers. The chicken, duck, veal, pork, and beef are raised by Amish farmers in Pennsylvania and Virginia, using organic feed and no antibiotics, growth-promoting hormones, or GMOs (genetically modified organisms). Pouillon has pioneered the link between farmers and restaurants and

rare epicurean treats here—game, truffles, and vegetables in fancy shapes and combinations. Eye-popping desserts are wheeled to your table on a dessert cart that looks like it came straight from Paris, both in its construction and its contents. It's all lovely, and yet no one dish is a standout. If you're out to

If you have Kennedy Center tickets for a Sunday matinee, try brunch right there at the Roof Terrace Restaurant. It's a lavish affair that includes a tour of the kitchen.

impress a client or a date, you couldn't choose better surroundings, but if it's a truly memorable meal you're after, there may be better choices for the money. The Willard Room is open for breakfast and lunch weekdays, and dinner Monday through Saturday.

Zola $$$
800 F Street NW
Washington, DC
(202) 654–0999
Zola abuts the International Spy Museum and pays tribute to the world of espionage itself.

has introduced her customers and other chefs to local, seasonal, organic foods.

The Viennese-born chef is always on a mission, always striving to share the message about organic foods, sustainable living, and a holistic approach toward life. Typical of Pouillon is her role as a founding member of Chefs Collaborative, an organization of chefs that promotes organic agriculture. Even the water used in her restaurants comes from an Aquapure system especially designed for her. "It is essential that our water is pure, free of chlorine, bacteria, and all heavy metals. We feel that our water is better than any bottled brand! Just try it!" says Pouillon.

Pouillon is quick to stress that she practices what she preaches, even in her private life. Chefs are notorious for their late hours and indulgent diets, but Pouillon, a mother of four, says she has always been conscious of a healthy lifestyle for the sake of her family. Her daily ritual begins with yoga or synergy dance, and she is a big believer in outdoor exercise and activities.

Fitness magazine pronounced Pouillon one of America's healthiest chefs, and her unique organic lifestyle has been the topic of featured articles in *Natural Health*, *Yoga Magazine*, *Organic Style*, and *Sinra* (Japan's top food and living magazine). Such accolades are nothing new to Pouillon, who has been praised in publications as diverse as *Gourmet*, *USA Today*, *Travel & Leisure*, the *Washington Post*, the *Wall Street Journal*, *Food & Wine*, the *San Francisco Examiner*, and *W Magazine*. In 2003 she was honored by the Campaign for Better Health as the first recipient of the Nora Pouillon Award for Sustainable Living. The Organic Trade Association honored her with a leadership award in 2004.

Pouillon demonstrates in her book *Cooking with Nora* how easy it is to cook meals that are both organic and low in fat. "I hate hidden calories in restaurants and try not to do the same to my customers," she told *Washington Woman* magazine. "Being a woman I think makes me more sensitive to the 'fat' subject." And that is a philosophy we can all appreciate.

Named for the French author Émile Zola, who championed the cause of a falsely accused spy, the restaurant also includes art works made of shredded CIA documents. Food is strictly cutting-edge American, from lobster macaroni and cheese to crispy veal meatloaf sliders served with Maytag blue cheese potato salad. Even if you're not visiting the Spy Museum, the restaurant is convenient to other attractions within a couple of blocks, such as the Verizon Center and Smithsonian American Art Museum. Open weekdays for lunch and daily for dinner.

African

Dukem Ethiopian Market $$
1114–1118 U Street NW
Washington, DC
(202) 667–8735
www.dukemrestaurant.com

Washington, D.C. boasts the largest concentration of Ethiopian restaurants in the world—outside of Ethiopia. Many of them are clustered on U Street. Dishes are eaten by tearing off a piece of *injera*, a spongy bread that tastes a bit like a sour crepe, and dipping it into communal servings of meat dishes like

Zola is one of the many restaurants that have helped Metro Washington become known for its fine dining opportunities. COURTESY WASHINGTON, D.C. CONVENTION AND TOURISM CORPORATION

kitfo (made with ground beef and cottage cheese) and vegetable dishes like seasoned greens and lentils. The dishes themselves are also served on a piece of *injera* that acts as a plate. Many of Dukem's customers are Ethiopian—and that's always a good sign.

Etete $$
1942 9th Street NW
Washington, DC
(202) 232–7600

Etete may not be what you'd expect from an Ethiopian eatery. It looks more like a stylish downtown restaurant than an authentic ethnic neighborhood outpost. It's worth a visit, though, particularly if you're new to Ethiopian cuisine. The friendly wait staff will talk you through the menu and will alter the spice level to the uninitiated palate. The *injera* is tasty, but not as sour and dense as some you'll encounter. Try the lamb dishes, seasoned with hints of jalapeño and *berbere* spices. Vegetarians will have ample choices, but we'd recommend the *azifa*, a lentil dish flavored with onions, jalapeños, bell peppers, lemon juice, and spicy mustard, which you won't see on the menu at every Ethiopian restaurant in town. Etete is open daily for lunch and dinner.

Meskerem $$
2434 18th Street NW
Washington, DC
(202) 462–4100
www.meskeremonline.com

National recognition and awards galore have done a lot to enhance the reputation of this Ethiopian restaurant, which some critics rank as the nation's finest. If you enjoy such dining adventures, one visit will have you singing its praises too. Enjoy the big, floppy crepelike bread for scooping up the various hot and mild meat dishes (including beef, lamb, and chicken), the lentils and green vegetables, and all that glorious sauce. You can't beat the prices. Lunch and dinner are served daily.

Zed's Ethiopian Cuisine $$
1201 28th Street NW
Washington, DC
(202) 333–4710
www.zeds.net

Only alphabetical order put Zed's at the end of the list for recommended Ethiopian dining. Although it offers less ambience than some of its competitors, it always scores high where it matters the most for a restaurant: food. In particular, the rich sauces, beef dishes, and a unique offering of broiled short ribs help place Zed's ahead of many of its contemporaries. Zed's serves lunch and dinner daily.

Asian (includes Chinese, Japanese, Vietnamese, and Thai)

Asia Nora $$$$
2213 M Street NW
Washington, DC
(202) 797–4860
www.noras.com

Before the sushi craze, Americans equated Asian restaurants with budget fare, and most do still prove relatively economical. This is not so at Asia Nora. The setting is a breathtaking cocoon of rosy wood, gold pillars, intimate lighting, and eye-catching art—and the food lives up to the surroundings. You'll find precious Japanese-style plates decorated with art of the edible kind.

Since the owner is the same Nora (see the Close-up in this chapter) who began the organic food craze in Washington two decades ago, you can be sure of fresh fish and vegetables. You'll find dishes that tend more toward Japanese or Thai, like the ginger-flamed filet mignon and shichimi onions, as well as those with a more Indian influence, like the curry

i Feast on ethnic cuisine in Metro Washington and you'll find your dinner check to be quite reasonable. In general the best values can be found at Indian, Thai, Chinese, Vietnamese, and other Asian restaurants.

served with traditional accompaniments like chutney and basmati rice. Asia Nora is open for dinner Monday through Saturday but closed on Sundays.

Ching Ching Cha $
1063 Wisconsin Avenue NW
Washington, DC
(202) 333–8288

This serene little tearoom is a welcome respite from the crowded hustle of Georgetown. Guests partake of the classic Chinese tea ritual here, choosing from 33 teas from China and Taiwan. There's a raised platform with two low tables and lots of pillows for sitting and laid-back sipping. Sweets and snacks are available, as well as light "Tea Meals" that include a choice of three vegetables and one of the three feature dishes, with jasmine rice and a bowl of soup.

Full Kee $
509 H Street NW
Washington, DC
(202) 371–2233
www.fullkeedc.com

Ask anyone in the know where to find the best soups and dumplings in Chinatown and they'll point you in the direction of Full Kee. Customers line up outside this simple, cash-only restaurant for wonton or hot and sour soup. You'll also find the dishes you'd expect at any Chinese eatery here, including some of the best lunch bargains in the city.

Haad Thai $$
1100 New York Avenue NW
Washington, DC
(202) 682–1111

Not only is this one of the most popular Thai restaurants in downtown Washington, it's also one of the most vibrantly decorated. Big windows, room-size murals, and artistic fixtures

i **George W. Bush hasn't been spotted much out on the town, but he and Laura have been known to show up at Peking Gourmet Inn in Virginia.**

make for a lively, trendy atmosphere. The food is just as vibrant as the space. Flavors explode in your mouth, not just with hot chilis, but also with lemongrass and all those other wonderful Thai spices. Like most Asian restaurants, Haad Thai offers a menu with a mind-boggling array of selections, but any of the curries and coconut-based dishes will please lovers of Thai cuisine. Haad Thai is open for lunch Monday through Saturday, and dinner nightly.

Kaz Sushi Bistro $$
1915 I Street NW
Washington, DC
(202) 530–5500
Kazsushibistro.com

There are a few great places for sushi in this city, and Kaz is at the top of the list. The decor is deceptively plain, but Chef Kaz Okochi's creations are downright artistic, crafted from the freshest fish and the finest rice. Kaz's signature dishes include tuna sushi with kalamata olives and even foie gras. Vegetarians will find about a dozen sushi options, made with mushrooms, eggplant, and tofu. For a true culinary adventure, sign up for an eight-course tasting menu.

Makato $$$
4822 MacArthur Boulevard NW
Washington, DC
(202) 298–6866

It's likely no one will recommend this tiny Japanese gem, but that's because few people know of it. It's hard to find, even when you do know where to look, but it's worth the trouble. The door is your first hint that this is the real thing. It's made of pale wood and rice paper and is unmistakably Japanese. Inside, you must remove your shoes before you enter the minuscule dining area. The seats are padded stools unless you sit at the sushi bar. Here your best bet is to go for the tasting menu, a 10-course meal of specialties that you may never see outside Japan. You'll get a chance to sample everything from soup to a delicate, perfect serving of exotic fruit or homemade fruit ice at meal's end. Lunch is served Tuesday through Saturday, dinner is served Tuesday through Sunday, and it is closed on Monday.

Perry's $$$
1811 Columbia Road NW
Washington, DC
(202) 234–6218
www.perrysadamsmorgan.com

An Asian restaurant named Perry's? Well, yes, in a way. Perry's, at the throbbing heart of Adams Morgan, offers pretty darned good sushi and other Asian dishes, along with international standards like pasta. Some dishes are a wonderful fusion of East and West. Perry's is for those who like to party hearty and, in summer, there's no better place than the rooftop garden sparkling with fairy lights. For a touch of decadence, there's a drag show at Sunday brunch. It's open for dinner and the Sunday brunch.

Spices Asian Restaurant & Sushi Bar $$
3333-A Connecticut Avenue NW
Washington, DC
(202) 686–3833

Spices is a real crowd pleaser—especially if your crowd is looking for quality sushi, tasty pad thai, and classic Chinese selections in the same place. Although the chic restaurant looks like it would come with a pricey menu, you'll be pleasantly surprised. Make this your stop if you're catching a movie at the Uptown Theatre or if you're looking for a place to recharge after a visit to the National Zoo. The restaurant is open for lunch and dinner daily.

Sushi-Ko $$$
2309 Wisconsin Avenue NW
Washington, DC
(202) 333–4187

As the name implies, sushi is the word at Sushi-Ko, and few in town do it better: eel, toro, sea urchin, shrimp, salmon, quail eggs, flying-fish roe, and even monkfish liver. In fact, when Japanese dignitaries come to Washington for official visits, Sushi-Ko does the catering. Although many people have been converted by the "Try it, you'll like it"

urging of their fellow diners, not everyone has embraced the sushi phenomenon. Not to worry—Sushi-Ko also offers decidedly tasty non-sushi creations, many of which are the chefs' own fusions of Japanese and American cooking styles and ingredients. This is a cramped, no-frills place, but it's always packed with people who know Japanese cuisine. Sushi-Ko is open for lunch Tuesday through Friday and dinner nightly.

Tony Cheng's Mongolian Barbecue $
619 H Street NW
Washington, DC
(202) 842–8669

To be certain, there's no shortage of barbecue joints in Metro Washington, but you'll be hard pressed to find the Mongolian style (yes, Mongolian) offered anywhere but Tony Cheng's. Here's how it works: You fill your plate with the raw ingredients of your choice from a buffet, then you take it to the chef who grills it. It's as good as it is different, but don't just take our word as gospel. Tasting is believing. Expect generous offerings of meat, vegetables, and tangy sauces, and if you have trouble deciding, opt for the all-you-can-eat deal. Tony Cheng's is open for lunch Monday through Saturday, dinner nightly, and Sunday dim sum (Chinese dumplings filled with a variety of delectable meats and vegetables), served from 11:00 A.M. to 3:00 P.M.

Vietnam-Georgetown $$
2934 M Street NW
Washington, DC
(202) 337–4536

This was one of the first Vietnamese restaurants in Washington, and it remains popular, perhaps in part because of the appealing garden in back that, on summer evenings, is strung with fairy lights. The food is quite tasty—the usual Vietnamese restaurant fare of spring rolls and sweet and sour dishes and fresh grilled seafood. If you enjoy Southeast Asian food and the bustle of downtown Washington, then you won't be disappointed. It is open daily for lunch and dinner.

French

Bistrot du Coin $$
1738 Connecticut Avenue NW
Washington, DC
(202) 234-6969
www.bistrotducoin.com

This lively Dupont Circle bistro is a neighborhood fixture. It's open every day, teeming with colorful customers and a flamboyant staff. Customers represent a cross-section of the neighborhood, gay and straight, old and young, feasting on steamed mussels, hangar steak, decadent tartines, and pâté creations. It's quintessentially European, with large glass windows opening onto the street and water bowls and leash hooks outside for four-legged guests.

La Chaumiére $$$
2813 M Street NW
Washington, DC
(202) 338-1784

This country inn/bistro in the heart of Georgetown is a perennial favorite in the competitive, come-and-go world of French restaurants. With its midroom fireplace and its walls decorated with antique farm tools and copper molds, this is the perfect spot to come in out of the cold. Expect attentive and warm service, and hearty and reliable French peasant fare like cassoulet and couscous, tripe, quenelles of pike, and choucroute garnie. If these earthy offerings don't tempt, there is more conventional fare, often rich with garlic, butter, and other delicious staples of French country cooking. Lunch is served weekdays, dinner is served Monday through Saturday. La Chaumiére is closed on Sunday.

La Fourchette $$
2429 18th Street NW
Washington, DC
(202) 332-3077

You'll think you're in Montmartre at this quaint little spot in Adams Morgan. Walk past the entrance and the garlic wafts out, inviting you in. As befits a French restaurant, there are tables outside where you can watch the wide cross-section of humanity on busy 18th Street. Inside, murals of cafe scenes dominate the walls. The tables are tiny and the chairs are the kind you'd find in a Paris bistro. The menu, too, looks like it came straight from Paris: cheese-filled onion soup, crepes, bouillabaisse, escargots, and pâtés. You can't go wrong. La Fourchette is open for lunch weekdays and dinner nightly.

Lavandou $$
3321 Connecticut Avenue NW
Washington, DC
(202) 966-3002
lavandourestaurant.com

This adorable neighborhood restaurant, serving lunch weekdays and dinner nightly, is tucked away in a strip of old shops north of the National Zoo, but don't let the facade fool you. Inside, you'll find hearty provençale bistro cooking in a dollhouse setting that may be a little too close for those seeking complete privacy, but just right for those who want the full flavor of casual French dining. This is the kind of homey cooking that carries the punch of garlic and balsamic vinaigrette, cured meats, white beans, and wine. The sautéed veal sweetbreads are served with polenta and shitake mushroom terrine and tomato coulis. With the seared sea scallops, you'll find braised leeks and a zesty lemon parsley sauce. Open Monday through Friday for lunch and dinner.

Le Paradou $$$$
678 Indiana Avenue NW
Washington, DC
(202) 347-6780
www.leparadou.net

Executive Chef Yannick Cam is credited with bringing fine French cuisine to Washington. He left the D.C. restaurant scene in the 1990s, then roared back in 2005 with the opening of Le Paradou. It's easily the finest French restaurant in downtown, and arguably the best in the city. Start with luscious creations like perfectly fashioned crab raviolis, accented with lobster claws drizzled with basil-scented butter and ripe tomatoes. A fillet of sole is served alongside scallops and squids stuffed with pine nuts and lavender flower lobster saffron sauce. If you're coming for a special occasion or looking for a little indulgence, try the chef's six- or nine-course tasting menu. The main dining room is meant for romance, complete with star-like lights shining overhead.

Marcel's $$$$
2401 Pennsylvania Avenue NW
Washington, DC
(202) 296–1166
www.marcelsdc.com
Marcel's promises "French cuisine with a Flemish flair," and chef/owner Robert Wiedmaier certainly delivers. Start your meal with boudin blanc, a classic Flemish sausage dish served here with celery root puree, truffle, and red wine essence. For the main course, try the veal osso bucco, accompanied by wild forest mushrooms and Yukon Gold potatoes, or opt for the rack of lamb, paired with lamb sausage and chive potato puree. The Foggy Bottom location makes this a good choice for dinner if you're off to the Kennedy Center, and there's an excellent three-course menu developed for the purpose. Priced at $48 per person, the menu also includes sedan service to the Kennedy Center.

Montmartre $$$
2002 P Street NW
Washington, DC
(202) 544–1244
Capitol Hill residents were saddened when Montmartre left its location near Eastern Market for its new home in Dupont Circle. After all, it was the most sought-after Saturday night reservation in the neighborhood. Dupont Circle residents are now discovering Montmartre's French bistro classics like duck confit with white beans, hangar steak, and pommes frites cooked to a perfect crisp.

German

Cafe Berlin $$$
322 Massachusetts Avenue NE
Washington, DC
(202) 543–7656
www.cafeberlindc.com
No, you haven't been transported from Capitol Hill to Germany; it just feels that way when you step into Cafe Berlin. Like most restaurants located in town houses, this one has that cozy, warm feeling that immediately charms. The hearty fare—good and reasonably priced—and, of course, the beer selection make this eatery worth a try for those who enjoy German food, both new and traditional, in an Old World setting. Lunch is served Monday through Saturday, and dinner is served daily.

Old Europe $$$
2434 Wisconsin Avenue NW
Washington, DC
(202) 333–7600
www.old-europe.com
Praise and popularity are old hat for Old Europe, unwavering in its appeal, at the same spot for more than half a century in upper Georgetown. This place, some will contend, embodies all that an Old World German restaurant should be, except maybe for the American locale. Just use your imagination, though, and enjoy various wursts, schnitzel, dumplings, pork, and other filling creations, not to mention the homemade pastries and an extensive wine and beer list. And we can't forget the lively, infectious music. Lunch and dinner are served nightly at Old Europe.

Hispanic/Caribbean/ Tex-Mex

Cactus Cantina $$
3300 Wisconsin Avenue NW
Washington, DC
(202) 686–7222
www.cactuscantina.com
Lively crowds flock to this funky Cleveland Park retreat with their sights set on Tex-Mex delights, and Cactus Cantina doesn't disap-

point. Standard fare includes generous portions of enchiladas, tacos, ribs, and fajitas. There's also a mesquite grill that turns out tasty salmon, shrimp, ribs, and quail. It's open daily for lunch and dinner.

Cafe Atlantico $$$
405 8th Street NW
Washington, DC
(202) 393–0812
www.cafeatlantico.com

If you're looking for creative Central and South American cuisine, look no further. You can tell that Chef Katsuya Fukushima has a sense of adventure. Bite into the Dominican conch fritters and let the warm, liquid center explode in your mouth. The classic Brazilian dish *feijao* is on the menu as well, but it's broken down into its basic components: black beans and pork, white rice, oranges, and sautéed collard greens, served with chicken or pork belly. The cocktail menu also meanders off the beaten path, tossing crushed pineapple into its *caipirinhas* and topping its margaritas with a salty emulsion.

California Tortilla $
728 7th Street NW
Washington, DC
(202) 638–2233

3501 Connecticut Avenue NW
Washington, DC
(202) 244–2447
www.californiatortilla.com

There's a lot of personality at this local chain, known for its generously stuffed burrito, tacos, and fresh salads. The self-proclaimed "spunky" owners are known to woo customers with gimmicks like free frozen treats

i Try a new restaurant during Washington, D.C. Restaurant Week, when nearly 200 of the region's top eateries offer fixed-price lunches for about $20 and dinners for about $30. Restaurant Week takes place twice a year, in January and August.

during the summer and free chips and salsa if you make an animal sound or deliver a secret password at the cash register. Favorites here include the grilled chicken Caesar burrito and the southwestern chicken salad.

Ceiba $$$
701 14th Street NW
Washington, DC
(202) 393–3983
www.ceibarestaurant.com

Ceiba takes its name from a tree native to South America, purported to have magical powers. True to its name, many of the dishes seem purely magical. The *queso fundido* arrives at the table in a sizzling skillet with the zesty aroma of poblano peppers. Empanadas are perfectly crispy, stuffed with succulent beef, and the sampler of ceviches is light and refreshing. Grilled shrimp is brought to the table on sugarcane skewers. Fish lovers will delight in the whole red snapper, served with tomatoes, olives, peppers, and pickled jalapeño. Save room for sunny desserts like key lime tart and guava cheesecake.

Rosa Mexicano $$$
575 7th Street NW
Washington, DC
(202) 783–5522
www.rosamexicano.com

A transplant from New York, Rosa Mexicano has built a large fan base in D.C., thanks to its savory upscale Mexican cuisine, fresh guacamole prepared tableside, and pomegranate margaritas. Basic dishes like chicken and steak tacos come served in a skillet with bubbling hot cheese, served with a stack of tortillas. Tortilla soup is thick and pleasing. A grilled fillet is doused in heavenly mushroom tequila cream sauce. The restaurant itself is a sight to behold, decked out in vibrant shades of blue, red, orange, and yellow with elements of running water. It's located across the street from the Verizon Center, and the joint's bound to be jumping if there's a game or concert.

Taqueriz Distrito Federal $
3463 14th Street NW
Washington, DC
(202) 276–7331
Columbia Heights is the historic center for the Latino community in Washington, D.C. Though the neighborhood's face has changed, you can still taste its heritage in some of the neighborhood eateries. Come here for a tasty taco, burrito, or tostada, served with beef, pork, and spicy chorizo and all of the fixings and chased with a tasty *horchata*, a cold cinnamon rice milk drink.

Indian

Bombay Club $$$
815 Connecticut Avenue NW
Washington, DC
(202) 659–3727
www.bombayclubdc.com
Located mere footsteps from the White House, the Bombay Club sets the standard for elegant Indian dining in the nation's capital at remarkably affordable prices. Tandoori dishes are delectable, particularly the tempting fish preparations. You can't go wrong with the classics here, either, like the assortment of curries, chicken tikka masala, and lamb vindaloo. Or try something more exotic, like mustard shrimp bathed in coconut milk, seasoned with ginger, garlic, mustard seed, and curry leaves.

IndeBleu $$$
707 G Street NW
Washington, DC
(202) 333–2538
www.bleu.com/indebleu
Downtown hot spot IndeBleu is sleek and stylish, with a pulsing downstairs lounge scene and an elegant upstairs dining room. Chef Vikram Garg serves elegant, contemporary Indian fare with French accents. Whether it's French, Indian, or a combination you're craving, the menu can take you in many directions. Appetizers include a lobster and shrimp tower dressed with mango or a wild

mushroom *dosa*. Follow it up with braised veal shanks with kumquat chutney and garlic mashed potatoes or seared striped bass with cornbread and a mussel bouillabaisse. Stick around after dinner to be a part of the lounge scene. Cocktails are pricey, but deliciously creative. We recommend the blackberry *mojitos*.

Rasika $$$
633 D Street NW
Washington, DC
(202) 637–1222
www.rasikarestaurant.com
Rasika is the latest venture for restaurateur Ashok Bajaj, who earned a place in the hearts and stomachs of D.C. diners with restaurants like the Bombay Club and the Oval Room. Taking its name from the Sanskrit word for spices, Rasika follows in the same tradition. In fact, it was named the city's top new restaurant in 2006 by Zagat. On the menu you'll find delightful fare like a salad crafted with warm bananas and avocados; fried baby spinach with yogurt and chutney; mango shrimp with fruit, garlic and coriander accents; and, in an unusual twist, duck served with a cashew and saffron sauce.

The White Tiger $$
301 Massachusetts Avenue NE
Washington, DC
(202) 546–5900
The White Tiger is affordable and charming, tucked into a row of Capitol Hill shops and eateries. You'll find a lot of northern Indian fare on the menu. They offer the usual spread of biryanis and tandoori dishes and an ample spread of vegetarian selections, but each dish is presented with its own unique blend of delicate seasonings. The cozy restaurant aims for an aura of elegance, presenting its entrees on regal gold platters and serving water in goblets. It's particularly pleasing in summer, when the outdoor patio beckons diners with gentle white lights and terrific people-watching opportunities.

Italian

Al Tiramisu $$$
2014 P Street NW
Washington, DC
(202) 467–4466
www.altiramisu.com

You'll feel like you're in one of those white-washed underground wine cellars that they so cleverly convert into restaurants in Europe. The effect is romantic and oh-so-intimate. This Dupont Circle restaurant is the brainchild of Chef Luigi Diotaiuti, Italian born, and trained in some of the best restaurants in the world, not to mention the Ritz Escoffier Ecole de Gastronomie Française in Paris. Your first course should be pasta—it's like silk here, both in terms of the subtle melding of flavors and the just-right texture. Next should be a dish of fish, the restaurant's specialty. Try the linguine with baby clams. The desserts are all delicious, and this small, friendly place is eager to please. They serve lunch on the weekdays and dinner nightly.

Galileo $$$$
1110 21st Street NW
Washington, DC
(202) 293–7191
www.robertodonna.com

Galileo's Roberto Donna is one of Washington's stars. He is in demand all over the world as a guest instructor, speaker, and—of course—chef. Aside from Galileo, he owns a slew of other restaurants in town, many less expensive. Galileo is his flagship, however, and it continues to be one of the city's premier Italian restaurants. You cannot be certain that every detail of every meal will be flawless, but when this restaurant is on point, it's stellar. What's more, Donna is a trendsetter, a visionary, and that makes his restaurant worth a

i | Dining havens such as Arlington, Bethesda, Adams Morgan, and Georgetown have scores of restaurants representing every nationality in short distance of one another.

splurge. If you're a fan of risotto, you won't find any better version outside of Italy. Galileo is open for lunch weekdays and dinner nightly.

i Ricchi $$$$
1220 19th Street NW
Washington, DC
(202) 835–0459
www.iricchi.net

Why go to Florence when you can taste the fortunes of her cuisine right here in the District? This bright, airy restaurant takes pride in serving an authentic taste of Tuscany. The setting is inviting country-casual with some luxurious touches: pink tablecloths, flowers, wooden chairs with rush seats, and lots of copper and plants. As for food, it's tough to go wrong here, especially if you try the cheeses, the pasta, the olive oil, the quail, veal, rabbit, and the pork. Especially popular, though, is the fish cooked on a wood-burning grill. i Ricchi has taken Tuscan cuisine in a classy setting to new heights. i Ricchi is open for lunch weekdays, dinner Monday through Saturday, and closed Sunday.

Obelisk $$$$
2029 P Street NW
Washington, DC
(202) 872–1180

Now for something completely different. You won't find a wide range of choices here; in fact, this restaurant offers a fixed price menu from which you choose one of three items for each course. How can they get away with such restraint? This tiny town house dining room is always full, so it must be the cooking. You sense that the people who put this together take artistic pride in their creation, and so they should, from the decor of elegant rusticity to the food. Let's start with the bread: It's crusty and aromatic, accompanied by top-shelf olive oil. It's also, of course, made in-house. It's hard to recommend any one dish because the menu changes all the time, and if you're looking for flashy, extravagant cooking, you won't find it here. For subtle, genuine quality, Obelisk is a sure bet. The restaurant serves dinner Tuesday through Saturday and is closed on Sunday and Monday.

Middle Eastern/Mediterranean

Lebanese Taverna Restaurant $$
2641 Connecticut Avenue NW
Washington, DC
(202) 265–8681
www.lebanesetaverna.com

This lively, attractive establishment has served notice as a serious contender in the Middle Eastern market, a category that seems either to enchant diners or completely turn them away. For the faithful, Lebanese Taverna will surely please with its own brand of moussaka (a Greek staple)—sans the usual ground beef—and other delicious eggplant dishes, spicy sausages, a variety of vegetable kebabs, and, of course, a wood-fired oven that brings out all the right aromas. Also, be sure to sample the wonderful Lebanese breads. It's hard to complain, given the reasonable prices, good cooking, and the cordial and efficient service. There are also locations in Virginia at 5900 Washington Boulevard (703–276–8681) and 1101 South Joyce Street (703–415–8681) in Arlington, at Tysons Galleria in Tysons Corner (703–847–5244), and in Rockville, Maryland, at 1605 Rockville Pike (301–468–9086). Lunch is served Monday through Saturday and dinner nightly.

Mama Ayesha's $$
1967 Calvert Street NW
Washington, DC
(202) 232–5431
www.mamaayeshas.com

There's nothing fancy or formal about this folksy Middle Eastern restaurant perched on the edge of the Adams Morgan neighborhood. In fact, it's easy to feel right at home. If you find the menu overwhelming, settle on the combination platter (shish kebab, couscous, stuffed grape leaves, and the house specialty, the kifta kebab) or the mixed grill (shish kebab, kifta kebab, and shish taouk,

served with grilled vegetables and rice). If the food doesn't win you over, we bet you'll fall for the spacious outdoor patio.

Marrakesh $$$
617 New York Avenue NW
Washington, DC
(202) 393–9393
www.marrakeshwashington.com

Dinner at Marrakesh is an event and a festival of new sensations. First, there are the low, cushy sofas and the equally low tables; then, there's the bit about eating with your hands. At the beginning of the meal, the waiter brings water and towels to accommodate the custom. Finally, there's the teasing belly dancer who, of course, selects several men from the audience as stage props to the hilarity of everyone else. The food? Oh, yes, it's good, too. The roasted chicken in preserved lemons and olives, the lamb bursting with spices, the flaky bastilla (a savory-sweet concoction of phyllo pastry and meat dusted with sugar) all serve to make the seven-course meal an exotic foray. Marrakesh is open for dinner daily and will open at lunch for parties of 10 or more. This restaurant does not accept credit cards.

Zaytinya $$$
701 9th Street NW
Washington, DC
(202) 638–0800
www.zaytinya.com

This eye-catching restaurant, named for a Turkish word for olive oil, is perched on a busy downtown corner. Stop by during the day for a light lunch, or check out its pulsing bar scene after hours. On the menu you'll find an overwhelming spread of Greek, Turkish, and Lebanese *mezze*, or small portions begging to be shared among friends. You'll find a lot of things to come back for. Baskets of steaming bread arrive at the table; the olive oil brought out for dipping is splashed with pomegranate puree. We recommend that you don't stop there, however, but order the hummus or roasted red peppers with feta cheese for dipping as well. We're also partial to the *manti*, tiny puffs of beef pasta bathed in a yogurt and garlic sauce, and the shrimp, prepared with a hint of dill.

Spanish

Jaleo $$$
480 7th Street NW
Washington, DC
(202) 628–7949
www.jaleo.com

Jaleo introduced tapas to the D.C. mainstream when it opened its doors in 1993. Since then it's added locations in Arlington and Bethesda. The menu features more than 70 little bites designed to be savored and shared. Cold tapas like beet salad dressed with Cabrales cheese, oranges, walnuts, and sherry vinaigrette join the expected classics, like bread with tomato and Iberian ham and Spanish tortilla. Warmer cravings will be satisfied by chorizo served with mashed potatoes, croquettes of ham and chicken, and garlic shrimp. Order a pitcher of sangria to share.

Taberna del Alabardero $$$
1776 I Street NW
Washington, DC
(202) 429–2200
www.alabardero.com

Taberna del Alabardero, in the minds of many critics and everyday patrons alike, is considered a serious candidate for the title of nation's finest Spanish restaurant. Although traditional cuisine from Spain may be a new dining experience for some, the growing popularity of tapas bars is making Spanish fare more commonplace. Recipes are from the Iberian peninsula, which means fresh sardines, roasted duck, whole suckling pig, rabbit, and several kinds of paella. The setting is as upscale as any French restaurant, and the service is top drawer. Lunch is served weekdays, dinner is served Monday through Saturday, and it's closed Sunday.

NORTHERN VIRGINIA
American/Continental

Amphora Restaurant $$$
377 Maple Avenue West
Vienna, VA
(703) 938–7877

Amphora's Diner Deluxe $–$$
1151 Elden Street
Herndon, VA
(703) 925–0900
www.amphorabakery.com

If you've got a late-night craving, you'll probably find just the right dish at one of these popular diners, open 24 hours and usually bustling no matter what time of day. The menus feature a huge selection of treats, from a la carte and breakfast items to filling Greek specialties. We love the mouthwatering moussaka, but if we're in need of comfort food, we can't resist the open-faced roast beef or turkey sandwiches, served with mashed potatoes and gravy. Many folks visit for the desserts alone, particularly the decadent layer cakes, pies, and pastries, baked at the neighboring Amphora Bakery at 403 Maple Avenue West, Vienna, (703) 281–5631, or in the Herndon restaurant.

The Herndon location boasts an added bonus: It looks like an eatery right out of a movie. It's probably the most gorgeous diner you'll ever see. Sleek neon lights accent the facade, while inside, smooth, dark wood gives the place a surprising air of elegance.

The Amphora chain also includes several fast-food Knossos and Village Chicken restaurants, specializing in great-tasting, budget-priced Greek food and rotisserie chicken dinners. Locations are sprinkled throughout Northern Virginia.

Artie's $$
3260 Old Lee Highway
Fairfax, VA
(703) 273–7600
www.greatamericanrestaurants.com/artiesmain/arties-main.htm

Artie's serves up classic American fare, including one of the finest brunches in the D.C. Metro area. On the menu, you'll find classics like crab cakes, blackened prime rib, barbecue ribs, and roasted pork, along with homemade soups and salads. The dessert course brings tasty creations like deep-dish apple pecan pie and a flourless chocolate waffle. The atmosphere is friendly and inviting, perfect for large parties or families dining with children.

Carlyle Grand Cafe $$
4000 28th Street
Arlington, VA
(703) 931–0777
www.greatamericanrestaurants.com/
carlyle/cm.htm
One of the cornerstone establishments in the ever-changing urban village of Arlington, Carlyle Grand Cafe is convenient city dining without parking headaches (ample, free, and convenient spaces nearby). Just a stone's throw from I–395, the restaurant features fresh, modern, and simple decor and quality food (meats, seafood, pasta, sandwiches, etc.). The hot beignets served in lieu of bread for Sunday brunch are impossible to resist. As for the menu, it offers a wide variety of New American cuisine, from Thai-flavored dinner salads to savory pastas. Choose to dine downstairs, where the popular bar limits the seating and makes for a livelier time, or upstairs where it's decidedly quieter but equally enjoyable. Carlyle Grand Cafe is open for lunch Monday through Saturday, dinner nightly, and Sunday brunch.

Chutzpah Deli $
12214 Fairfax Town Center
Fairfax, VA
(703) 385–8883

8100 Boone Boulevard
Tysons Corner, VA
(703) 556–3354
www.chutzpahdeli.com
The Chutzpah Deli brings a little slice of New York to the Virginia suburbs. Owners brag

that the bagels are imported from New York, and Chutzpah's menu brims with what the deli calls "Jewish soul food." Regulars rave about the chicken soup (better than Mom's?), tasty corned beef sandwiches, and lox, eggs, and onions. Enjoy complimentary bowls of pickles and coleslaw on your table while you wait for your order. Hours vary by location.

Clyde's $$
1700 North Beauregard Street
Alexandria, VA
(703) 820–8300

11905 Market Street
Reston, VA
(703) 787–6601

8332 Leesburg Pike
Vienna, VA (Tysons Corner)
(703) 734–1900
www.clydes.com
These suburban versions of the original District Clyde's have done well, to say the least. The older Tysons location and the newer one in Reston—a cornerstone establishment in the Town Center—have faithful patrons and are wildly popular happy-hour, late-night, and brunch destinations. (See the Washington listing for details.) Like the downtown and Chevy Chase, Maryland branches, these two, especially Tysons, are decorated with lavish amounts of glossy wood and glass. The menus are pretty much alike at all branches. Clyde's is open for lunch and dinner nightly and Sunday brunch.

Evening Star Café $$$
2000 Mount Vernon Avenue
Alexandria, VA
(703) 549–5051
www.eveningstarcafe.net
Evening Star Café is a cheery, inviting eatery in Alexandria's artsy Del Ray neighborhood. The cuisine is classic American fare, with tasty, satisfying dishes with interesting contemporary twists. Hearty short ribs come paired with butternut squash and scallion risotto, while the roast duck breast is served

with sour cherry bread pudding. On a breezy summer evening, the restaurant's outdoor patio is particularly inviting. Stop by the adjoining wine shop, Planet Wine, for a souvenir to take home.

Fish Market $$
105 King Street
Alexandria, VA
(703) 836–5676
www.fishmarketoldtown.com

Like hundreds of other Old Town buildings, the one that houses the ever-popular Fish Market has a storied past. It was at one time a focal point of the colonial-era seafaring trade, when Alexandria was a port city and market of widespread importance. The city still buzzes here in the lower King Street area, but these days the activity is centered around the flourishing restaurant and small retail business. Fish Market consists of several rooms, including a packed raw bar and a balcony overlooking the heavy pedestrian traffic on King Street. Waiting in line here is not at all uncommon, especially on weekends, so plan accordingly. The raw bar is stocked with spicy shrimp, oysters on the half shell, and all manner of fresh seafood. The restaurant proper offers lots of fried specialties, often accompanied by that Southern favorite, hush puppies. Chowders, too, are thick and hearty here. You can get more low-calorie fare, but it somehow doesn't seem to match the raucous, checkered tablecloth ambience. It's open for lunch and dinner daily.

Hard Times Cafe $
3028 Wilson Boulevard
Arlington, VA
(703) 528–2233

1404 King Street
Alexandria, VA
(703) 837–0050

428 Elden Street
Herndon, VA
(703) 318–8941

6362 Springfield Plaza
Springfield, VA
(703) 913–5600

14389 Potomac Festival Plaza
Woodbridge, VA
(703) 492–2950
www.hardtimes.com

Chili in one of a dozen incarnations is the best reason to go to Hard Times Café. But there's nothing wrong with that reason, is there? Visit one of these down-home joints, which are dark and loud and lots of fun, for a casual—very casual—evening or a quick bite accompanied by Hank Williams tunes on the jukebox. No one will frown if you wipe your bowl clean with a chunk of yummy cornbread. We're partial to the Cincinnati-style chili, served with shredded cheese and onions atop a dish of spaghetti. They are open for lunch and dinner daily. See the Suburban Maryland section for Maryland locations.

Heart in Hand $$$
7145 Main Street
Clifton, VA
(703) 830–4111
www.heartinhandrestaurant.com

A favorite of former First Lady Nancy Reagan, romantic Heart in Hand specializes in American cuisine with a Southern touch. The bread basket at the beginning of the meal may be the highlight, but soups are hearty and good, and the restaurant features great homemade desserts. You can't help but get sentimental and warm all over as you're served in this historic farmhouse in the quaint community of Clifton, the heart of Fairfax County's affluent horse country. Heart in Hand is open for lunch and dinner Tuesday through Saturday and Sunday brunch. It's closed Monday.

J. R.'s Stockyards Inn $
8130 Watson Street
McLean, VA (Tysons Corner)
(703) 893–3390
www.jrsbeef.com

There's Morton's of Chicago across the street

and then there's J. R.'s, the budget alternative. At this casual, kid-friendly restaurant, the beef is fresh from the family-owned packing plant, and it's aged and cut in-house. Try their fresh seafood, chicken, lamb chops, barbecue, or gourmet salads. Nothing fancy here, just good food and lots of it. It's open for lunch weekdays and dinner nightly.

Kilroy's $
5250-A Port Royal Road
Springfield, VA
(703) 321–7733
www.kilroys.com
Whether you come with your kids for the Sunday brunch buffet, to watch Monday Night Football, or to dance to live bands playing '80s and '90s tunes, Kilroy's has it all. There are a total of 36 TVs in its lounge and dining room, and you can reserve one to watch your favorite team. Kilroy's is open for lunch and dinner daily and may be most popular for its moderately priced brunch, which includes omelettes to order, Belgian waffles, eggs Benedict, and nearly a dozen other items.

Morton's of Chicago $$$$
8075 Leesburg Pike
Vienna, VA (Tysons Corner)
(703) 883–0800

11956 Market Street
Reston, VA
(703) 796–0128

1631 Crystal Square Arcade
Arlington, VA
(703) 418–1444
www.mortons.com
Here's one of the exceptions to our no-national-chains pledge made at the beginning of this chapter. We didn't list Morton's location in D.C. because there are so many superb steak houses in the District, but if you want this kind of quality in Northern Virginia, there's only Morton's. It's a big-night-on-the-town kind of place without the commute and parking hassles. If this legendary steak house can't satisfy that hankering for prime dry-aged beef,

you might as well buy some cattle and a do-it-yourself guidebook. The waiter who brings the cuts of meat to your table on a trolley presents the menu with drama. Along for the ride is a live lobster just waiting for someone to soak it in butter. As with other Washington-area steak houses, the vegetable accompaniments and salads (all a la carte) are served in portions generous enough to satisfy a sumo wrestler. Our favorite here is the Delmonico or, for bigger appetites, the porterhouse. But other meats and seafood are also top drawer. For dessert Morton's soufflés are always popular, but must be ordered with the meal, and by the time you've made your way through the entree, you may regret the extra course. If you want to try the D.C. locations, one is in Georgetown at 3251 Prospect Street NW (202–342–6258), and the other at 1050 Connecticut Avenue (202–955–5997). The Virginia locations are open for lunch weekdays and dinner nightly.

Ray's the Steaks $$$
1725 Wilson Boulevard
Arlington, VA
(703) 841–7297
Ray's is considered the best steak house in the region by some of its most discerning diners. Unlike downtown's power-dining emporia, dimly lit and decked out with sumptuous furnishings, Ray's focuses on the meat, which owner Michael Landrum purchases, butchers, and ages himself. You'll see the biggest difference between Ray's and its downtown counterparts when the bill arrives; prices are considerably lower here. The entrees are served with shareable sides of creamed spinach and mashed potatoes.

Red, Hot & Blue $$
1600 Wilson Boulevard
Arlington, VA
(703) 276–7427

169 Hillwood Avenue
Falls Church, VA
(703) 538–6466

4150 Chain Bridge Road
Fairfax, VA
(703) 218–6989

6482 Lansdowne Centre
Alexandria, VA
(703) 550–6465
www.redhotandblue.com
Barbecue fan? You won't find better than
Red, Hot & Blue. By now a Washington institution, this crowded joint in Arlington serves
succulent ribs, pulled pork and chicken, and
brisket. The ribs are served wet (with sauce)
or dry (rubbed with spices, no sauce). Sauces
and seasonings are perched on each table so
you can customize your order. There are
other locations in the Metro area (see Suburban Maryland listings), but we think the original one on Wilson Boulevard in Arlington is
best. Open for lunch and dinner daily.

Restaurant Eve $$$$
110 South Pitt Street
Alexandria, VA
(703) 706–0450
www.restauranteve.com
Restaurant Eve is one of the reasons why Old
Town Alexandria merits a special trip for culinary tourists. Chef Cathal Armstrong was
named one of *Food & Wine* magazine's best
new chefs in 2006, and you'll quickly understand why. The menu is anything but ordinary, a mix of unusual dishes like veal
sweetbreads with fried oysters and sinfully
rich pork belly. While there's a lot to tempt
you on the dessert menu, the most popular
choice is the Birthday Cake, a three-layer creation just for one, topped with bright pink
buttercream icing and colorful sprinkles. Diners can indulge in a five- or nine-course set
menu in the chef's tasting room or piece
together their own decadent menu in the
casual, comfortable bistro.

Silver Diner $
3200 Wilson Boulevard
Arlington, VA
(703) 812–8600

14375 Smoketown Road
Dale City, VA
(703) 491–7376

12251 Fair Lakes Parkway
Fairfax, VA
(703) 359–5999

8101 Fletcher Avenue
McLean, VA
(703) 821–5666

8150 Porter Road
Merrifield, VA
(703) 204–0812

11951 Killingsworth Avenue
Reston, VA
(703) 742–0805

6592 Springfield Mall
Springfield, VA
(703) 924–1701
www.silverdiner.com
Like the Maryland locations (see our entry
under Suburban Maryland), these restaurants
have the feel of an old-time diner. We especially like the Silver Diner for breakfasts and
desserts. Waffles and French toast are great
here. If you're visiting later in the day, try
their meatloaf and mashed potatoes, burgers
and shakes, or humongous sandwiches. The
3:00 A.M. closing time on weekends makes
Silver Diner a favorite stop for night owls. Silver Diner is open for breakfast, lunch, and
dinner daily.

Southside 815 $$
815 South Washington Street
Alexandria, VA
(703) 836–6222
www.southside815.com
Southside isn't the place to go if you're
watching your waistline. If you're a trans-
planted southerner with a craving for
chicken-fried steak, succotash stew, and
sweet potato biscuits, however, you've found
your place. You'll find a slate of fare ranging
from barbecue ribs and pot roast to jamba-
laya and seared tuna. Be sure to order a bas-

ket of bread with your meal; biscuits and cornbread come served piping hot with apple butter and peach pepper jelly. It's hard to save room for dessert, but the peach pound cake with caramel sauce and ice cream is worth a trip back.

Tuscarora Mill $$
203 Harrison Street
Leesburg, VA
(703) 771–9300
www.tuskies.com
Tuscarora Mill is one of Leesburg's best-loved dining spots. Soaring beamed ceilings, dark wood, and old farm tools let you know you're in horse country. This casual spot is great for thick sandwiches, burgers, fries, and other well-executed American dishes. The desserts of the mile-high, fudgy ilk are the highlight. You wouldn't make a special trip to Leesburg to eat here, but the town is crammed full of history, boutiques, and antiques shops, so go exploring before or after your meal. Tuscarora Mill is open for lunch and dinner nightly.

2941 Restaurant $$$
2941 Fairview Park Drive
Falls Church, VA
(703) 270–1500
www.2941restaurant.com
This excellent, modern American and French restaurant is located in the basement of a Virginia office building. But don't let its address scare you off. Built on a hillside, glass walls on three sides overlook a lovely lake and waterfall. It's pricey for the suburbs, but the fresh, intriguingly combined ingredients may be worth it for a special dinner or business lunch. Open weekdays for lunch and nightly for dinner.

Union Street Public House $$
121 South Union Street
Alexandria, VA
(703) 548–1785
www.usphalexandria.com
Union Street is one of the area's most popular neighborhood saloons and restaurants.

Choose a lively and often-crowded bar scene downstairs, quieter dining in the raw bar and grill room upstairs, or something in between in the sometimes overlooked backroom oyster bar. An array of huge dinner salads and sandwiches graces the menu, along with the usual saloon fare like buffalo wings, fritters, pastas, burgers, and some grilled meats. Highlighted here are a dozen or so draft beers, including the house exclusive—the rich and delicious Virginia Native. It is open for lunch and dinner daily and Sunday brunch.

Warehouse Bar and Grill $$
214 King Street
Alexandria, VA
(703) 683–6868
www.warehousebarandgrill.com
This pleasant restaurant bills itself as New Orleans–style and offers Louisiana specialties, but the decor is casual, understated classic American, with the exception of the nice gallery on the second floor overlooking the space below. The place has a fun atmosphere, a hopping bar scene, and is a great place to drop in if you're in the neighborhood. Snag a window table to take in the interesting sights along King Street. Open for lunch Monday through Saturday, dinner nightly, and Sunday brunch.

Asian

Bangkok 54 $
2919 Columbia Pike
Arlington, VA
(703) 521–4070
www.bangkok54restaurant.com
When you walk into Bangkok 54, you'll be impressed with how attractive it is, adorned with silver Buddha figurines and delicate orchids. You'll also be relieved to learn that the food is an appealing departure from traditional Thai fare. Try the Pad Cha, a mix of pan-seared scallops, mussels, shrimp, and calamari, topped with a red chili sauce, or the soft-shell crabs, deep fried and drizzled with garlic chili sauce.

Bee-won Secret Garden $
6678 Arlington Boulevard
Falls Church, VA
(703) 533–1004

We dare you to try to find this restaurant in any other guide, because it is truly a secret in this area. Tucked into a strip mall, this is not a place you'd wander into by accident. Once inside, the decor is pleasant but simple, with a sushi bar, a scattering of booths, a long table in the center, and smaller tables against the wall—all in light wood. The reason to come here is the sparkling fresh sushi as well as Korean and Japanese cooked dishes, all at rock-bottom prices.

The fresh fish tank at the entrance is not just for show. There is an Asian custom that many Westerners find abhorrent—that of serving whole fish that are still alive. Vital organs are separated from the meat but left intact enough so the fish lives as it is eaten, assuring the ultimate in freshness. This is definitely not for everyone, but some Asians consider it a delicacy, and at Secret Garden you can have it. As you might imagine, this is a restaurant that caters to a great many Asians, so if it's authenticity you want, this is the place. Bee-won is open for lunch and dinner daily.

Busara $$
8142 Watson Street
McLean, VA
(703) 356–2288

11964 Market Street
Reston, VA
(703) 435–4188
www.busara.com

Fans of the Washington Busara (2340 Wisconsin Avenue, 202–337–2340), with its wild murals and ultramodern seating, have quickly made hits of the Virginia branches of this innovative Thai restaurant. On the menu are all the traditional Thai favorites like curries, pad Thai, or larb gai, but there are also some imaginative fusion dishes. For lunch or dinner try one of the meal-size salads or make a meal of the dough-wrapped appetizers that range from shrimp to chicken to veggies. If you order curry or one of the other sauced dishes, specify how hot you want it to be or use the chili-pepper scale on the menu as a guide. Busara serves lunch and dinner daily.

Duangrat's $$
5878 Leesburg Pike
Falls Church, VA
(703) 820–5775
www.duangrats.com

New Thai restaurants spring up all the time in Metro Washington, but Duangrat's continues to shine. Maybe it's the gracious, almost formal decor, with its rosy tablecloths, flowers, and generously upholstered chairs; then again, it's probably the food as much as anything. There are always interesting daily specials—try the spicy soft-shell crab if it's available—and the menu is as long and varied as in any Thai restaurant, with a few extra soups and stews thrown in. Compare the standard Thai dishes here with those in other restaurants, and you'll see why Duangrat's is so popular. Batters are always light and fresh, peanut sauce is never cloying, and the crab-stuffed chicken wings are head and shoulders above anyone's in town. Duangrat's serves lunch and dinner daily.

Hee Been $$
6231 Little River Turnpike
Alexandria, VA
(703) 941–3737

This is where Northern Virginia's large Korean community comes to celebrate special occasions, and you'll understand why once you've experienced Hee Been. Korean barbecues are always fun, grilled at the table and accompanied by a dozen condiments. The difference at Hee Been is that nothing is done by rote, and no one is rushed. Let the waiter be your guide as to what's good. You're sure to have an adventure. If language is a barrier and you want to venture beyond barbecues, try the soups—some as thick as stews, others brothlike and delicate. Whatever you choose, don't miss the short ribs, which are a star here. Hee Been is open for lunch and dinner daily.

Matuba $
2915 Columbia Pike
Arlington, VA
(703) 521–2811
Matuba is open for lunch weekdays and dinner nightly. Please see the Suburban Maryland listing.

Nam Viet $
1127 North Hudson Street
Arlington, VA
(703) 522–7110
www.namviet1.com
The name may be turned around, but we've figured it's for a reason: That's exactly what you'll be inclined to do after your first dining experience at Nam Viet. Go back again. And soon. The food is as consistently good as the atmosphere is relaxing and unpretentious, and the prices reasonable. Don't miss the bon dun, the great selection of soups, or the skewered meats grilled with fragrant herbs. You can enjoy your meal outside in warm weather, but the indoor dining room is several steps above the utilitarian atmosphere found in some of the other low-cost neighborhood restaurants. Nam Viet is open for lunch and dinner daily.

Peking Gourmet Inn $$
6029-6033 Leesburg Pike
Falls Church, VA
(703) 671–8088
www.pekinggourmet.com
The Peking duck here remains the standard against which to measure all others—crispy on the outside, lean on the inside, and carved at tableside. The appetizers are very good, too, especially the dumplings, the sesame shrimp toast, and the hot and sweet cabbage. Peking Gourmet Inn takes pride in growing its own leeks and garlic sprouts, and they are featured in several main courses, but the meats can sometimes be flabby—it's often hit or miss here. Still, the place has kept its prices low enough so that mistakes won't spoil your evening, and if you choose right, you'll love your meal. Be sure to make reservations for dinner. Despite the endless array of dining rooms, it's always crowded and there's always a line. That should tell you something right there. Lunch and dinner are served daily.

Pho 75 $
1711 Wilson Boulevard
Arlington, VA
(703) 525–7355

382 Elden Street
Herndon, VA
(703) 471–4145
You don't choose this Vietnamese restaurant for the atmosphere. It's basic, very basic. And you don't go for variety. The only thing you can order, appropriately enough, is pho. But you can bet the pho's darned good here. In case you haven't tried it, pho is a soup based on beef broth and studded with wonderfully aromatic Asian spices like lemongrass, coriander, and anise. But lest you think you'll leave hungry, imagine a soup so thick with noodles, meat, and veggies that it easily makes a meal. If you want to spice it up even more, there's a variety of condiments that comes with each order, as well as bottles of sauce on the tables. Price-wise, the whole thing just barely breaks into the double digits, so it's an unbeatable bargain. (See the Suburban Maryland section for locations in Hyattsville and Rockville.) Pho 75 is open for breakfast, lunch, and dinner nightly until 8:00 P.M.

Sunflower Vegetarian Restaurant $
2531 Chain Bridge Road
Vienna, VA
(703) 319–3888
www.crystalsunflower.com
Vegetarians from throughout Metro Washington have heard about the Sunflower, and many of them make the trip to Vienna to dine here. Sunflowers decorate the dining room in various shapes and sizes, from the cheery

vases at the tables to the art on the walls. Sauces and seasonings are superbly created for entrees like the Songbird, a mix of wheat gluten and soy protein sautéed with peanuts and watercress in a kung pao–flavored sauce, and the wheat gluten sautéed with black bean sauce. Meat-eaters will find a lot to like about this place, too. General Tso's Surprise and Sweet and Sour Sensation taste much like their similarly named non-vegetarian counterparts when made with Sunflower's white mushroom and soy protein nuggets. If the healthy ingredient names don't look familiar, not to worry—there's a glossary at the back of the menu.

Tachibana $$$
6755 Lowell Avenue
McLean, VA
(703) 847–1771
Tachibana, in upscale McLean, is a low-key, western-style dining room curved around a sushi bar. Although there are many Japanese specialties, the point is the sushi, which is well executed, fresh, and often displays a variety not found elsewhere in the suburbs. Try any of the sushi chef's specials and you won't be disappointed. Unlike many Asian restaurants, the service is unhurried, and the plush carpeting and upholstered chairs lend themselves to long, quiet conversations. You can also sit at the surprisingly roomy sushi bar and watch the master at work. Tachibana is open for lunch and dinner daily.

Tara Thai $$$
226 Maple Avenue
Vienna, VA
(703) 255–2467

7501-E Leesburg Pike
Falls Church, VA
(703) 506–9788

4001 North Fairfax Drive
Arlington, VA
(703) 908–4999
The decor here makes a statement. It looks

like an aquarium: deep blues and greens, very moody, very pretty. There's also a touch of Africa in the zebra-striped banquettes. It's all very young, fun, and vibrant. The food is vibrant, too, bursting with chilis, lemongrass, lime, and cilantro. A standout is the shrimp— big, juicy, and cooked just right. If you like whole fish, this is the place to have it. It is smothered in all those tongue-teasing spices, and even after you're full, you can't stop picking at it, the flavor's so memorable. All the seafood is good here, befitting the aquarium theme. After dinner, Tara Thai pays tribute to America's endless sweet tooth by offering a variety of unusual desserts. Most feature tropical fruits and flavorings, and all are delectable, though some may not suit western palates. Owner Nick Srisawat has also expanded his concept into suburban Maryland: One is at 9811 Washington Boulevard in Gaithersburg (301–947–8330), and another is in downtown Bethesda at 4828 Bethesda Avenue (301–657–0488). Tara Thai is open for lunch and dinner every day.

Woo Lae Oak $$
1500 South Joyce Street
Arlington, VA
(703) 521–3706

8240 Leesburg Pike
Vienna, VA
(703) 827–7300
This is a great stop if you happen to be shopping at Pentagon City or Tysons Corner, but both locations of Woo Lae Oak alone are also worth a trip. Step inside and you'll know from the fragrant smoke that there's a whole lot of grilling going on. Korean-style barbecue is a favorite here, and the sushi is a good way to start the meal. It's served on ice, and portions are generous. This eatery has a long menu featuring many noodle dishes and soups, so ask your waitress for recommendations or watch what the Koreans around you are ordering. It serves lunch and dinner daily.

French

Hermitage Inn   **$$$$**
7134 Main Street
Clifton, VA
(703) 266–1623
www.hermitageinnrestaurant.com
Just across the street from the village of
Clifton's other top restaurant, Heart in Hand,
Hermitage Inn offers romance that's more
Continental than country. Housed in a white,
two-story former hotel once visited by Presidents Grant and Hayes, Hermitage Inn features a wide veranda and second-story
balcony, along with a beautifully landscaped
patio garden just right for warm summer
evenings. Inside, you'll find a plantation-style
dining room cooled by softly whirring ceiling
fans and French doors, and warmed by flat-
tering pastel decor and fireplaces. In winter
you may prefer to dine instead in the publike
wine bar/restaurant on the first floor, complete with its own wood-burning fireplace.

The food here is a mixture of French and
Mediterranean cuisine, with a number of daily
specials. Salads, even the most basic, are creative and tasty. There are interesting game
specials from time to time that are worth a try,
but the real treat here is the wine list, which
offers nearly 20 different selections by the
glass as well as some unusual bottles. Enjoy
soaking in the atmosphere and leave renewed
by the peaceful, romantic setting. It's open for
dinner Wednesday through Sunday, Sunday
brunch, and is closed Monday and Tuesday.

La Bergerie   **$$$**
218 North Lee Street
Alexandria, VA
(703) 683–1007
www.labergerie.com
La Bergerie is an old classic that always
pleases. After more than two decades, you
might expect it to fade or get sloppy, but the
food here is always a delicious surprise. The
origins are Basque, that region between Spain
and France that produces food rich with gar-
lic, tomatoes, bell peppers, and seafood.
There are also the elegant French standards

like sole in creamy sauce or coq au vin. All this
is served in a setting that is cozy and formal.
The walls are brick, lending warmth. As in the
best restaurants, the tables are generous and
well spaced, and there are leather banquettes
scattered about the dining room. Service is
very proper and traditional, and some of the
waiters are of the European breed that makes
a lifelong career in elite restaurants, taking
great pride in their professions, as they
should. End your meal with one of La Ber-
gerie's desserts—many of which are made
in-house. The tarts are particularly good. They
serve lunch and dinner Monday through Sat-
urday and dinner Sunday.

La Cote d'Or Cafe   **$$$**
2201 West Moreland Street
Arlington, VA
(703) 538–3033
www.lacotedorcafe.com
Striking arrangements of roses, pretty table
settings, and intimate lighting all add up to a
downtown atmosphere—at downtown
prices—right in the Virginia suburbs. The
food lives up to the surroundings, as befits
highly esteemed Washington chef, Raymond
Campet, who decided to set up shop in
Virginia.

There are all sorts of elegant classics featuring game, duck, and high-quality beef. The
daily specials are particularly good but often
pricier than the regular menu. The dishes are
expertly sauced, such as the game meats with
savory berry glazes or the seafood with but-
tery garlic accents. Desserts, even the simple
berries in sabayon sauce, can be a real treat.
Several critics consistently rate this restaurant
among the best in Washington. It serves lunch
and dinner daily.

L'Auberge Chez François   **$$$**
332 Springvale Road
Great Falls, VA
(703) 759–3800
www.laubergechezfrancois.com
Accessible only by a twisting two-lane road—
one of many in woodsy, fashionable and oh-so-

affluent Great Falls—L'Auberge Chez François continues to reap awards and praise as the years go by, and it never seems to falter in its appeal. There's an unmistakable country inn warmth and romance that permeates the soul. The French cuisine hails from Alsace, that province along the German border that specializes in game and richly sauced vegetables. The waitstaff is dressed in keeping with the theme: dirndl skirts, colorful vests, and the whole bit. Menu selections are endless, all accompanied by garlic bread, salad, after-dinner sweets, and a slew of side dishes. Stick with traditional Alsatian fare—duck, pork, or anything in puff pastry—and you can't go wrong. Desserts are equally representative of the region, with lots of fruit tarts and soufflés that are definitely worth a try. Reservations for weekends should be made a month in advance (unless you want to wait till the last minute and hope for a cancellation), but it's worth the wait. L'Auberge Chez François is the kind of place you anticipate with a smile. It's open for dinner Tuesday through Sunday and is closed Monday.

Le Gaulois $$
1106 King Street
Alexandria, VA
(703) 739–9494

The minute you walk through the door and onto the hardwood floors at Le Gaulois, you feel as though you've found refuge from the city bustle in a country French auberge—no easy feat for a street-side restaurant. Friendly, quiet, and accommodating to a new degree, Le Gaulois serves creative and very reliable French-influenced cuisine at reasonable prices. The menu changes here with the seasons, and as you'd expect, winter entrees are hearty offerings in warm sauces infused with wine and garlic. Summer is the time to try seafood poached or grilled, then spiked with zesty herbs. If you're seeking authentic French peasant fare, try the organ meats. Not many places offer such a wide selection. Accompaniments can range from crisp, buttery veggies to those homey parsleyed pota-

toes. This is country French cooking at its best, with prices that don't break the bank. Le Gaulois is open daily for lunch and dinner.

Le Refuge $$
127 North Washington Street
Alexandria, VA
(703) 548–4661
www.lerefugealexandria.com

If Le Gaulois is peaceful, then Le Refuge is the exact opposite. It's a wild place where you may feel as though you're dining in your neighbor's lap. It makes for lots of conversations and laughter between tables, though, and you'll have a good time. The food here is typical brasserie fare, with good, solid cooking that is quick and inexpensive. Veggie accompaniments are French classics like calorie-laden Lyonnaise potatoes (deliciously sinful!) or green beans swimming in butter. You really can't go wrong here when the bill is so very reasonable. Le Refuge is open for lunch and dinner Monday through Saturday and is closed on Sunday.

Hispanic/Caribbean/Tex-Mex

Anita's $
9278 Old Keene Mill Road
Burke, VA
(703) 455–3466

13921 Lee Jackson Highway
Chantilly, VA
(703) 378–1717

701 Elden Street
Herndon, VA
(703) 481–1441

10880 Lee Highway
Fairfax, VA
(703) 385–2965

5 Fort Evans Road NE
Leesburg, VA
(571) 209–5092

521 Maple Avenue East
Vienna, VA
(703) 255–1001
www.anitasrestaurants.com

Vienna was the original home of this popular local chain of "New Mexico"–style Mexican food outlets, but the town couldn't keep Anita's to itself for long. Soon, other suburban communities began to experience what they were missing. Although the fare may not satisfy Tex-Mex aficionados used to the zestier, eye-watering concoctions, it is nevertheless consistently good and inexpensive, the service is efficient, and the setting is relaxed and inviting. You can't help but overdo it on the homemade chips and salsa before the entrees arrive, but be sure to leave room for the sweet, puffy sopaipillas that beg to be topped with honey. Anita's serves lunch and dinner nightly.

El Guajillo $$
1727 Wilson Boulevard
Arlington, VA
(703) 807–0840
www.waheeyo.com

El Guajillo takes its name from a spicy chili pepper and delivers an equally spicy Mexican experience. In addition to the expected lineup of enchiladas and tamales, check out the shrimp and goat cheese enchiladas and New York strip steak with mushroom chipotle sauce. Your chips and salsa are served with a side of habañero sauce so that you can spice it up to suit your tastes. The chefs also give you ample opportunities to experiment with mole, the classic chocolate and nut sauce. Here it's made in two other varieties, one seasoned with tomatillo and pumpkin seeds and another crafted with three different chilies.

El Pollo Rico $
932 North Kenmore Street
Arlington, VA
(703) 522–3220

This modest, Peruvian-owned cafe is among the best of the area's bargain rotisserie-chicken restaurants. El Pollo Rico ("Delicious Chicken") does a brisk carryout business, but you can also sit at one of the handful of small tables scattered around the simple room. The menu is limited, and the only real reason to

come is the house specialty: marinated, charcoal-fired rotisserie chicken that's perfectly flavored and practically melts in your mouth. With it, you can have fries, empanadas, or tamales. If you're in Maryland, try the Wheaton location at 2541 Ennalls Avenue (301–942–4419). El Pollo Rico serves lunch and dinner nightly. It does not accept credit cards.

Rio Grande Cafe $$
4301 North Fairfax Drive
Arlington, VA
(703) 528–3131

1827 Library Street
Reston, VA
(703) 904–0703
Please see Suburban Maryland listing.

South Austin Grill $$
801 King Street
Alexandria, VA
(703) 684–8969

Austin Grill Springfield
8430 Old Keene Mill Road
Springfield, VA
(703) 644–3111
www.austingrill.com

These Tex-Mex spots are always jumping, and there's a reason why. At the South Austin Grill, the bar downstairs is crammed with attractive 20- and 30-somethings, and the margaritas are good and plenty. Upstairs, there's almost always a wait for a table. Those in the know appreciate the authenticity of Austin Grill. To be won over requires a mere sample of any of the expertly prepared and presented enchiladas, fajitas, burritos, chili, and even the zesty appetizers. It's also one of the greenest restaurants around. In 2003 the six restaurants in the chain became some of the first in the nation to be powered exclusively by wind energy. The chain also donates some proceeds to the Chesapeake Bay Foundation. The Austin Grill can also be found in D.C. in Glover Park at 2404 Wisconsin Avenue (202–337–8080) and 750 E Street

NW (202–393–3776), in the heart of Bethesda at 7278 Woodmont Avenue (301–656–1366), and in Silver Spring at 919 Ellswoth Drive (240–247–8969). Open for lunch and dinner daily.

Sweetwater Tavern $$
14250 Sweetwater Lane
Centreville, VA
(703) 449–1100

3066 Gatehouse Plaza
Falls Church, VA
(703) 645–8100

45980 Waterview Plaza
Sterling, VA
(571) 434–6500
www.greatamericanrestaurants.com
The same team who dreamed up such popular eateries as the Carlyle Grand Cafe and Best Buns Bread Company has ventured into Southwestern cuisine with Sweetwater Tavern. As usual, these owners know how to do it right, with high-quality, imaginative variations on the old standards. The decor glows with rich wood and leather, amber lighting, and Indian rugs. Wrought-iron chandeliers feature Western scenes, as do the etched glass dividers on the booths. There's a highly rated microbrewery on premises, not to mention the spicy, smoky dishes such as ribs, quesadillas with poblanos, Tex-Mex egg rolls, and smoked salmon. Desserts are big and mouthwatering. Don't even try to resist the chocolate waffle filled with the richest of chocolate ganache—that's pure chocolate, butter, and cream to you and me. Sweetwater Tavern is open for lunch and dinner nightly and Sunday brunch.

Tortilla Factory $
648 Elden Street
Herndon, VA
(703) 471–1156
www.thetortillafactory.com
Other parts of the region will hopefully have a Tortilla Factory to call their own some day, but until then, it's worth a trip to this town

near Dulles Airport. Tacos, fajitas, enchiladas, burritos, nachos, salsa—the Tortilla Factory prepares them all in the zesty Sonoran tradition—and the results are memorable. Plus, you get a ton for the money in this casual, friendly setting. The restaurant serves lunch and dinner daily and also hosts live folk music—sometimes by renowned acts—on Tuesdays.

Italian

**Generous George's Positive Pizza
and Pasta** $
3006 Duke Street
Alexandria, VA
(703) 370–4303
www.generousgeorges.com
It's an odd name indeed, but the gigantic portions of superb pizza and pretty good pasta—served atop a pizza crust—are nothing to laugh at. You'll be too busy chewing, swallowing, and smiling in between. The pizza's the whole point of coming here, and at least one member of your party should order it. The toppings are all fresh and high quality. If you pass on the pizza, try the chicken Florentine. The quirky, eclectic decor—a true mishmash of the odd, the colorful, and the bizarre—and a fun family atmosphere, for kids in particular, make Generous George's a hit every time. One visit and you'll understand why people gladly sweat the lines on weekends. It is open for lunch and dinner daily. (See our Kidstuff chapter for more on family dining here.)

Il Radicchio $
1801 Clarendon Boulevard
Arlington, VA
(703) 276–2627
www.robertodonna.com
Il Radicchio is a bargain-priced eatery that still manages to seem trendy. The concept here is simple: Order an all-you-can-eat bowl of spaghetti and pair it with one of a dozen or so sauces offered. There's variety enough to satisfy anyone, from those who prefer simple pesto to those who think spaghetti ain't

spaghetti unless it has tomato sauce. Il Radicchio caters to families, busy bees in need of a quick meal, and young up-and-comers who want lots to eat and don't want to pay a lot. The pizzas are good, too. Lunch is served Monday through Saturday and dinner nightly.

Italian Store $

3123 Lee Highway
Arlington, VA
(703) 528–6266
www.italianstore.com

You'll be glad you discovered this little Italian restaurant and shop, nestled in an Arlington shopping center. Locals flock here for pizza by the slice or for delicious pies to take home, and the kitchen manages to strike a balance between tomato and cheese on its perfectly kneaded crust. Sandwiches are also delicious, lightly seasoned with oil and oregano on Italian hard rolls. Stop by on your way to a dinner party for a bottle of wine or a couple of cannolis.

Maestro $$$$

1700 Tysons Boulevard
McLean, VA
(703) 917–5498
www.ritzcarlton.com/hotels/tysons_corner

Chef Fabio Trabocchi couldn't have chosen a better name for his restaurant than AAA Five Diamond Award–winning Maestro. There's nothing short of masterful on the menu here, borrowed from Italian traditions and accented with each season's freshest bounty. Expect a few surprises on the prix fixe, multi-course menu, presented under headings that describe Trabocchi's inspirations: creation, tradition, evolution, and harvest. We've been served a crawfish salad with a vial of green tomato soup as a chaser. A fitting match to the menu, Maestro's wine cellar boasts more than 800 wines from Italy, France, and the United States.

Paolo's Ristorante $$

1898 Market Street
Reston, VA
(703) 318–8920
www.paolosristorante.com

Paolo's Reston branch is inviting, with its outdoor tables in the town square, its cafe-style seating just outside the front doors, and the curved, sunny room within. There's also a bar that hops on weekends, complete with loud music and attractive guys and gals out on the town.

As soon as you're seated, you'll be served Paolo's signature breadsticks, soft and warm, along with a zesty green-olive tapenade. The main courses feature lots of pastas, some quite imaginative, along with meat that's mostly grilled and infused with light sauces. Balsamic vinaigrette plays a big role in the cooking here, and that's just great as far as we're concerned. Pizzas cooked in wood-burning ovens are a house specialty, and the crusts are smoky, thin, and delicious, just as you'd expect. You can make a meal of Paolo's salads—which range from steak over greens to grilled chicken with Greek-style accompaniments—and you'll always be offered fresh grated Parmesan as a garnish. Also try the Georgetown location, at 1303 Wisconsin Avenue (202–333–7353). Paolo's serves lunch and dinner daily and Sunday brunch.

Tivoli Restaurant $$$

1700 North Moore Street
Rosslyn, VA
(703) 524–8900
www.tivolirestaurant.net

It's a tribute to Tivoli's quality that it has managed to endure for more than two decades hidden away in this Rosslyn high-rise. Perhaps it helps to have a bakery and carryout service of the same name on the ground floor—advertisement for the good things to come upstairs. This handsome dining room, rendered even more inviting by the wrap-around windows and the strategically placed mirrors, is a good place to take clients or a first date. Tivoli bills itself as a northern Italian restaurant, and you'll find many dishes napped in the rich sauces of that region. There are risottos and stuffed pastas, as well as old standards of the fettucine Alfredo ilk. You'll also find some continental classics that you don't often see anymore, like veal Oscar. This is a place to linger and enjoy your meal, an elegant, leisurely experience at prices that are surprisingly reasonable. They serve lunch weekdays and dinner Monday through Saturday. Tivoli is closed Sunday.

Middle Eastern/Indian/Afghan

Bombay Bistro $$
3570 Chain Bridge Road
Fairfax, VA
(703) 359–5810
www.bombaybistro.com
You could come to Bombay Bistro every day for a month and never exhaust the menu possibilities. This is superb and very serious Indian cuisine, with some prepared in a tandoori oven, some curried, and some grilled over charcoal. The main courses are so filling that there is always some left over. The solution? Bring a large group, split the main courses, and sample the appetizers and those wonderful, smoky Indian breads (which you do have to order—they aren't free). The standouts among the main courses are the lamb dishes. Lamb nilgiri khorma is an irresistible type of curry served with green masala alive with fresh coriander. Whole fish is enhanced by a marinade that features ginger, garlic, and yogurt. Tandoori specialties can sometimes be a bit dry, but they're so tasty that you can almost overlook the flaw. This is a casual, fairly nondescript place, but there are some low tables in a back nook that are very romantic, and the food makes every meal seem special. This location is less crowded than the Bombay Bistro in Rockville, Maryland, at 98 West Montgomery Avenue (301–762–8798). Lunch and dinner are served daily.

Layalina $$
5216 Wilson Boulevard
Arlington, VA
(703) 525–1170
www.layalinarestaurant.com
Arlington residents in search of delicious Middle Eastern food will sooner or later find their way to Layalina. Chef and owner Rima Kodsi serves up recipes of her own creation that reflect the most popular tastes of the Middle East, such as hummus accented with pomegranate juice, baba ghanouj, and *kafta bil jawz*, a blend of beef, walnuts, pepper, and mint. Side dishes and accents like yogurt are made in-house, and the lamb dishes are particularly tasty.

Nizam's $$
523 Maple Avenue West
Vienna, VA
(703) 938–8948
You'll find plenty of people who will argue that Nizam's is the region's best Turkish restaurant. Small and attractive as a jewel box, Nizam's is famous for its house special, doner kebab. Slices of lamb are marinated in yogurt and Turkish spices, then stacked on a vertical rotisserie spit and slow-roasted. The result is fragrant, crusty, juicy slices of meat served with pita bread and yogurt seasoned in the Middle Eastern style. Although doner kebab is such a major project, Nizam's prepares it every evening. You'll also do fine with such delicacies as marinated lamb in a variety of styles, beef tenderloin, stuffed grape leaves, and assorted eggplant preparations. Nizam's is open for lunch Tuesday through Friday, dinner Tuesday through Sunday; it is closed Monday.

Pasha Cafe $$
3911 North Lee Highway
Arlington, VA
(703) 528–1111
The cuisine here harks from Egypt and is very similar to other Middle Eastern cuisine, so expect the usual array of delicious appetizers like hummus, tabbouleh, and baba ghanouj.

The fun is in mixing and matching dishes. The menu suggests various combinations that provide a taste of just about everything. Meals are filling and delicious, though somewhat oversalted. Try the kofte, kebabs, or on the lighter side, lemony chicken. The waiters, many of whom are Egyptian, are warm, hospitable, and happy to guide you. One problem: Waits for a table can be long, and the line crowds into the front end of the one-room dining area. Ask for a table away from the door and arrive early or late to avoid a long spell of standing. Pasha Cafe serves lunch Monday through Saturday and dinner nightly.

SUBURBAN MARYLAND
American/Continental

Bethesda Crab House $$
4958 Bethesda Avenue
Bethesda, MD
(301) 652–3382

It offers famed Chesapeake Bay crabs, yes, but Bethesda Crab House is also a popular late-night dining option; it is open till 11:00 P.M. seven days a week. If you order the crabs, you'll be given a tableful along with the implements to crack 'em open, so wear washable duds. Be aware that dwindling crab catches are forcing prices higher quickly, although the restaurant does offer $20 "all-you-can-eat" specials.

Black's Bar & Kitchen $$
7750 Woodmont Avenue
Bethesda, MD
(301) 652–5525
www.blacksbarandkitchen.com

Oysters encrusted in cornmeal. Plump shrimp rolled in plantain chips. Angus beef tenderloin glazed with Cabernet and blue cheese. These diverse flavors all encompass owner Jeff Black's native Gulf Coast Texas, and he has imported them to Bethesda. With its tastefully framed fishing photos from the early twentieth century, antique metal table

fans, and an expansive Victorian sofa that looks like it might have come straight from a New Orleans brothel, the restaurant exudes an air of the bygone South. Old jazz favorites from Billie Holiday and Duke Ellington play softly on the sound system. But the food is pure twenty-first century, fusing an amalgam of tastes. For example, there's the shrimp taco salad, petite taco shells filled with grilled gulf shrimp, poblano chilies, sweet corn, and avocado in a cilantro-lime vinaigrette over mixed baby greens. There's also a tortilla-crusted mahi mahi filet on a bed of Texmati rice, wilted spinach, and black beans, drizzled with mango and ginger broth. Black and his wife, Barbara, also own another standout restaurant, Addie's, in a converted bungalow in Rockville (11120 Rockville Pike, 301–881–0081). This comfortable restaurant focuses more on creative American cooking of all stripes. Both restaurants are open for lunch weekdays and dinner nightly.

Clyde's of Chevy Chase $$
5441 Wisconsin Avenue
Chevy Chase, MD
(301) 951–9600
www.clydes.com

This is as much an elegant entertainment center as a restaurant. There's a model train that circles overhead, and the theme is carried through in the booths, which are replicas of Orient Express parlor cars. Gleaming model airplanes hang from the ceiling, and stunning posters, prints, and hand-painted murals adorn the walls. The newly relocated Chevy Chase location is a hit, as are the other branches. The food here is good and varied, but a special treat is the vegetarian platter, offering all sorts of gems at a very reasonable price; otherwise, as at the other Clyde's locations, you do best when you stick to pub fare—steak, salads, and sinful desserts—all particularly festive in a setting like this. Clyde's serves lunch Monday through Saturday, dinner nightly, and Sunday brunch.

Crisfield Seafood Restaurant $$
8012 Georgia Avenue
Silver Spring, MD
(301) 589–1306
www.crisfieldseafoodrestaurant.com

Crisfield used to be one of those seafood places so basic and utilitarian in decor that you knew the food had to shine—especially at these downtown prices. Well, it's lost some of its luster, but if your namesake is the tiny Maryland community that claims to be the crab capital of the solar system, you'd better serve some world-class crabs. And Crisfield still does. Maybe that's why it's still going strong after more than 60 years in business. If you're in the neighborhood, there's no better place for crab and crab dishes, but it's not worth a trip. Crisfield serves lunch weekdays and dinner Tuesday through Sunday.

David Craig $$$
4924 St. Elmo Avenue
Bethesda, MD
(301) 657–2484
www.dcbethesda.com

A longtime figure in the D.C. restaurant scene, David Craig built a following during his stints at Pesce, Tabard Inn, and Black's Bar and Kitchen. On the menu in his namesake restaurant, you'll find an array of interesting seasonal recipes, like a risotto with lobster, prosciutto, artichokes, and fava beans; or braised veal cheeks with semolina gnocchi and swiss chard in the winter and a salad of arugula, summer squash, tomatoes, peaches, and bacon in summer. Desserts are simple and pleasing creations like rich chocolate bread pudding mellowed by vanilla ice cream and drizzled with caramel sauce.

Hard Times Cafe $
4920 Del Ray Avenue
Bethesda, MD
(301) 951–3300

4738 Cherry Hill Road
College Park, MD
(301) 474–8860

1117 Nelson Street
Rockville, MD
(301) 294–9720
www.hardtimes.com

See the Suburban Virginia section for information about this local chain of chili restaurants.

Louisiana Express Company $
4921 Bethesda Avenue
Bethesda, MD
(301) 652–6945
www.louisianaexpresscompany.com

No, you haven't been transported back to "Lew-zee-ann-uh." It just seems that way at Louisiana Express Company, where authentic Cajun treats—crawfish, po' boys, jambalaya, soft-shell crab sandwiches, the works—are served up in a down-home atmosphere. Stop by early for a full breakfast or on Sunday for a knockout brunch. It serves breakfast and lunch Monday through Friday, dinner nightly, and brunch on Saturday and Sunday.

O'Brien's Pit Barbecue $
387 East Gude Drive
Rockville, MD
(301) 340–8596
www.obrienspitbarbecue.com

Casual and inexpensive, O'Brien's has endured for years as a popular stop for some of the tastiest Texas-style barbecue around. There is other, newer competition, but O'Brien's holds its own with favorites like chili dogs, pork spareribs, and beef brisket. Side orders like beans and rice and spicy onion rings have plenty of pizzazz, too. O'Brien's is open for lunch and dinner nightly.

Old Angler's Inn $$$$
10801 MacArthur Boulevard
Potomac, MD
(301) 299–9097 or 365–2425
www.oldanglersinn.com

Old Angler's Inn sits snugly in the woods across the lane from the C&O Canal towpath. It looks like an enchanted cottage from a fairy tale, with its half-timbered accents and stone walk. You can cozy up next to the roaring fire-place in fall and winter or enjoy patio dining by a fountain in spring and summer. Back inside, the spiral staircase leads from a sitting area featuring big, soft couches, to an intimate, albeit bustling, dining room where the mood continues to captivate. The prices at Old Angler's Inn may give you a little predinner heartburn—this is a "jackets required" kind of place—but then again, when you consider the setting, service, and wonderful menu selections such as rack of lamb, venison, quail, and rabbit, the financial bite seems somehow less painful. Seafood is treated with respect, carefully herbed and never overcooked. Seared tuna and several other dishes feature Asian spices that show the chef's range of skill with any number of cooking styles. If you just can't decide what looks best, let the chef choose for you with his nightly tasting menu. Sated, you can relax into one of those down-filled couches and enjoy an after-dinner digestif. It serves lunch and dinner Tuesday through Saturday, Sunday brunch, and is closed Monday.

Olney Ale House $
2000 Olney-Sandy Spring Road
Olney, MD
(301) 774–6708

Susan Sarandon ate here. So did eccentric British actress Tallulah Bankhead after starring in a play at the Olney Theatre across the street. And Presidents Hoover, Truman, and Eisenhower are also said to have dined in one of the incarnations of the Olney Ale House. A homey, cozy restaurant with a stone fireplace, the Olney Ale House also lures less luminary diners, and the crowd in the waiting area often overflows outside past the restaurant's beer garden. The Olney Ale House's trademark—besides its bevy of beers—is its bread: hot, crusty, home-baked loaves for $3.00 (small) and $5.00 (large) that are available both in the restaurant and to take out. They range from the delectably sweet and airy oatmeal molasses, available all the time, to daily specials such as wheat bread stud-

ded with plump raisins and bits of carrot. The menu offers an array of vegetarian dishes, including a not-too-fiery chili and a portobello mushroom sandwich. There's also fried chicken, crab cakes, and beef stew. Open Tuesday through Sunday for lunch and dinner. Closed Mondays.

Persimmon $$
7003 Wisconsin Avenue
Bethesda, MD
(301) 654–9860
www.persimmonrestaurant.com

Opened in 1998, Persimmon is one of the longest-standing members of the Bethesda restaurant row. Nearly a decade later, it's still one of the most popular places in the neighborhood. Hints of Asia appear in the dishes, like the salmon that's crusted with shitake mushrooms and hoisin, bathed in a scallion miso broth with shrimp dumplings. As diners await their selections, they're served crusty white bread and chicken pâté—an interesting twist on the classic bread and butter combo. If you've got a sweet tooth, save room for the homemade ice cream and sorbet.

Red, Hot & Blue $$
16809 Crabbs Branch Way
Gaithersburg, MD
(301) 948–7333

677 Main Street
Laurel, MD
(301) 953–1943

If you like barbecue, this is the place to come for lunch or dinner. Please see the Virginia listing.

Silver Diner $
11806 Rockville Pike
Rockville, MD
(301) 770–2828

14550 Baltimore Avenue
Laurel, MD
(301) 604–6995
www.silverdiner.com

This is a recent Washington-based chain that

looks like an old-time diner. The Rockville Silver Diner sits at the edge of a busy shopping center and is almost always crowded. Breakfasts and desserts are tops here, with the rest being pretty standard stuff. In keeping with the diner theme, there's meatloaf and mashed potatoes, burgers and shakes, and humongous sandwiches. Waffles and French toast are great here and can be had at any time of the day. The 3:00 A.M. closing time on weekends makes Silver Diner a favorite stop for night owls. There are also seven Silver Diners in Virginia. Silver Diner is open for breakfast, lunch, and dinner daily.

Thyme Square Cafe $$
4735 Bethesda Avenue
Bethesda, MD
(301) 657–9077
www.thymesquarecafe.com
Whimsical painted pea pods curve around the windows, and giant pears and peppers flank the door. Inside, more larger-than-life veggies form a mural, giant paper peppers are suspended from the ceiling, and the booths are upholstered in a cherry and pear print. For those striving for five fruits and vegetables a day, this is a good place to meet that nutritional quota. The restaurant is largely vegetarian, with a smattering of fish and chicken entrees. But there's no granola or tempeh in sight. Instead, the cafe offers a global cuisine—from China to Cuba—that's low on fat and high on flavor. There's crisp artichoke polenta with spinach, Moroccan tagine, spicy pad Thai noodles, and wood-oven-roasted chicken pizza with sun-dried tomatoes and shaved artichokes. It's open Monday through Saturday for lunch Sunday for brunch, and nightly for dinner.

Tower Oaks Lodge $$
2 Preserve Parkway
Rockville, MD
(301) 294–0200
www.clydes.com
With its cedar beams, enormous stone fireplaces, antique wooden boats suspended

from the ceiling, and wraparound windows facing a nature preserve, there's little about the Tower Oaks Lodge that reminds diners they're in the heart of Rockville. And that's just the intention of this new member of the Clyde's group of restaurants around the Washington area. It's built to resemble the lodges in the Adirondacks from the turn of the twentieth century. Entrees range from the usual burgers to the more adventurous pork loin chop served with ham-and-cheese bread pudding and sautéed spinach. There's also a delicious Atlantic salmon with ratatouille and tomato couscous with arugula pesto. Tower Oaks Lodge is open for lunch and dinner daily.

Ray's the Classics $$$
8606 Colesville Road
Silver Spring, MD
(301) 588–7297
Ray's the Classics opened as a Maryland complement to Arlington's wildly popular Ray's the Steaks (see the description under Northern Virginia). The Maryland outpost promises the same commitment to quality techniques and ingredients, but the menu steps beyond steak to look at other classic dishes. The atmosphere is also a bit grander—you're likely to see a few more jackets and ties at this location. You won't go wrong here with fried chicken, crab cakes, and, of course, the steaks—and the reasonable prices—are sublime.

Asian

Benjarong $
885 Rockville Pike
Rockville, MD
(301) 424–5533
www.benjarongthairestaurant.com
This Thai restaurant in a Rockville shopping center is unexpectedly elegant. The decor is pastel and cheery with linen-covered tables set comfortably apart to allow for private conversation. Spices here are combined masterfully, and you really can't go wrong no matter what you order. Shrimp is presented in almost a dozen ways, as are whole fish, squid, and soft-shell crab. Pork and beef play

a lesser role, but there are several interesting duck dishes, including a shredded duck appetizer with carrots, spring onions, chili paste, and lime juice. If you want incendiary spicing you'll have to ask, because dishes have been toned down a bit for Western palates. Benjarong serves lunch Monday through Saturday and dinner nightly.

China Bistro/Mama's Dumplings $
755 Hungerford Drive
Rockville, MD
(301) 294–0808

The Chinese dishes at this Rockville restaurant are satisfying enough, but if you're like most customers, you're really coming here for the handmade dumplings. You're in good company; just take a look around at the Chinese customers who flock here for a taste of Mama's eight varieties. The most popular choice, Mama's Special Dumplings, come stuffed with pork, shrimp, cabbage, and chives. Other varieties include beef and celery, pork and dill, and a vegetarian special loaded with mushrooms and bean curd. You can also purchase uncooked dumplings to prepare at home.

Green Papaya $$
4922 Elm Street
Bethesda, MD
(301) 654–8986

A restaurant with a name like Green Papaya ought to bring a smile to your face. Reasonably priced and tastefully decorated, it's a pleasant spot that works well for a casual date, a business meeting, or even a family outing. On the menu, you'll find an appealing mix of sweet and spicy dishes. Duck is prepared with a hint of lemongrass, while garden rolls are accompanied by a delectable peanut sauce. Come early; this popular eatery usually attracts a crowd.

Mama Wok and Teriyaki $
595 Hungerford Drive
Rockville, MD
(301) 309–6642

If nothing else, you gotta love the name. This restaurant—which features Chinese and Japanese cuisine—has more to offer than that, however. If you're not squeamish, there's live seafood prepared to your liking, and the selection's not limited to fish, as in many other restaurants. According to the season, you're likely to find oyster, clams, crab, or shrimp. Even if you don't want to meet your meal before you eat it, the other seafood items are sparkling fresh, and simple preparations show them to good advantage. The decor here is as plain as could be, but when there's such fresh seafood to be had at rock-bottom prices, who cares about atmosphere? It's open for lunch and dinner daily.

Matuba $
4918 Cordell Avenue
Bethesda, MD
(301) 652–7449
www.matuba-sushi.com

For top-notch Japanese cuisine at bargain prices, Matuba can certainly dish it out. Budget sushi is almost an oxymoron, but not at Matuba, which offers sushi and sashimi in a large variety of combinations. Sushi rolls are a special treat, executed with flair. At Matuba, you can afford sushi as a first course and go on to sample tempting cooked seafood as a second course—the soft-shell crab, for example. There's another Matuba in Arlington (see our listing under Northern Virginia). Matuba is open for lunch and dinner Monday through Saturday.

Pho 75 $
1510 University Boulevard
Hyattsville, MD
(301) 434–7844

771 Hungerford Drive
Rockville, MD
(301) 309–8873

See the Virginia listing for information on this no-frills local chain that serves hearty, aromatic bowls of this Vietnamese soup.

i If you've had it with trying to park your own car in Bethesda's popular restaurant district, spend an extra $5.00 or $6.00 on valet parking and save yourself a headache. Public and private lots fill up fast and are so crowded they are difficult to navigate.

Sabang $
2504 Ennalls Avenue
Wheaton, MD
(301) 942–7859
www.sabangrestaurant.com
If you enjoy Thai, Vietnamese, or virtually any other Asian cuisine, you'll like Indonesian. The trouble is in finding a restaurant that serves it. You needn't look any farther than Wheaton's Sabang for inexpensive, interesting creations in this unique gastronomic genre. Sabang is an exceptionally pretty and festive space—maybe it's the Indonesian aesthetic of jewel-like colors, handmade textiles, and intricately carved furniture. As for the cooking, Indonesian is so unfamiliar to most Westerners that it's not a bad idea to order the rijstaffel, an amalgam of dishes that allows you to sample a broad range. If that doesn't appeal, try the satays, skewered meats with dipping sauce of peanuts and chilis. If you're still confused, ask your server; the staff here is warm, helpful, and eager to share this cuisine with you. Sabang serves lunch and dinner daily.

Sam Woo $$
1054 Rockville Pike
Rockville, MD
(301) 424–0495
Sam Woo's selections are among the area's best in Korean cuisine (grilled at your table if you'd like), and you'll know it at once when you walk in and see all the Korean diners there. There's a broad selection of main course soups and casseroles, many that are sure to please seafood lovers. Or choose from an extensive selection of Japanese entrees, including chicken teriyaki, sushi, and tempura. Try the weekday buffet for a truly

different kind of lunch break. Sam Woo is open for lunch and dinner daily.

Seven Seas Chinese Restaurant $$
1776 East Jefferson Street
Rockville, MD
(301) 770–5020
www.sevenseasrestaurant.com
This restaurant is well known in the Washington area for its seafood, and you know it's fresh from the minute you walk in and spot the large fish tank full of ocean delicacies. Seven Seas serves both traditional Chinese and Japanese fare, including dim sum and sushi. This small storefront restaurant has also branched out even more into calorie-conscious offerings, both vegetarian and with meat. Seven Seas is open for lunch and dinner daily.

Suporn's $
2302 Price Avenue
Wheaton, MD
(301) 946–7613
You've probably gathered by now that Wheaton and Rockville are meccas for Asian restaurants, and there are many Thai offerings among them. Suporn's is a bargain-priced eatery that offers some interesting dishes and a great deal of range. Start with one of Suporn's many salads, some flavored with lime, cilantro, anise, chilis, peanuts, or in most cases, a combination of several harmonious seasonings. Go on to hot, spicy soup or skip to a main course that features noodles, curries, or stir-fry. The prices here are so low, you can try it all. Suporn is open for lunch Tuesday through Saturday, dinner Tuesday through Sunday, and it's closed Monday.

Tako Grill $$
7756 Wisconsin Avenue
Bethesda, MD
(301) 652–7030
www.takogrill.com
As the name implies, Tako Grill ventures beyond its considerable sushi menu to feature an equally wide array of grilled foods.

There are grilled meats, seafood, and a surprising variety of vegetables, many so exotic that they're not found elsewhere in Washington—certainly not grilled. At one time fans would stand in line to eat here because the restaurant accepts no reservations, but it was recently expanded, so the wait shouldn't be as long. Try going on a weeknight just to be sure. Open for lunch Monday through Friday and dinner daily.

Tara Thai $$
4828 Bethesda Avenue
Bethesda, MD
(301) 657–0488

9811 Washingtonian Boulevard
Gaithersburg, MD
(301) 947–8330
The Maryland suburbs around Washington have lots of good, basic Asian restaurants, but here's one with glamor. For more on Tara Thai, please see its Virginia listing. It serves lunch Monday through Saturday and dinner nightly.

Taste of Saigon $$
410 Hungerford Drive
Rockville, MD
(301) 424–7222
tasteofsaigon.com
This light, pretty Vietnamese restaurant is always crowded despite its hard-to-find location in the middle of a Rockville parking lot. The prices are good—which accounts for some of its popularity—but with so many reasonably priced Asian restaurants in Rockville, that's not all there is to it.

There's the fashionable contemporary dining room with plenty of light and cheery linens on the tables, the outdoor patio with stylish umbrellas, and there's the food. Try the whole fish bathed in spices and scallions, intriguing soups crammed with noodles and meat, and stir-fries bursting with fresh veggies. There's also a location at 8201 Greensboro Drive in McLean, Virginia. Both serve lunch and dinner daily.

Vegetable Garden $
11618 Rockville Pike
Rockville, MD
(301) 468–9301
www.thevegetablegarden.com
At the Vegetable Garden, plants rule. The menu, devoid of all meat, dairy, MSG, and refined sugar, is instead stuffed full of organic bell peppers, portobello mushrooms, tofu, and brown rice. The restaurant is one of the only ones in the Washington area to serve not just vegan cuisine, but primarily organic produce. It even offers several macrobiotic dishes.

Expect mainly Chinese fare on the 80-item menu, starting with vegetarian wonton soup with potatoes, black mushrooms, carrot, celery, tofu, and a touch of cilantro for flavor rather than the traditional pork. Kung Pao Tofu ditches the meat but leaves all the fire behind, with cayenne peppers, a colorful assortment of green, red, and yellow bell peppers, and plenty of peanuts. The Vegetable Garden's menu also includes a smattering of non-Asian dishes, such as a veggie-gyro sandwich and portobello mushroom burger. The Vegetable Garden is open for lunch and dinner daily.

French

Jean-Michel $$$
10223 Old Georgetown Road
Bethesda, MD
(301) 564–4910
This restaurant may be located in a shopping center, but it's a very classy one and this is a classy restaurant. Step through the door and you'll think you're in one of those chic Paris eateries that tourists never find. The crowd is well heeled, the room is alive with conversation, and the lighting is flattering and rosy. Owner Jean-Michel Farret has been a presence in Washington for decades, and he once reigned supreme in one of those downtown French restaurants that bit the dust with the three-martini lunch. He now offers cuisine on a slightly more modest scale, but you won't feel shortchanged. Try any of the beef or seafood dishes here—they're especially good. It serves lunch weekdays and dinner nightly.

La Ferme $$$
7101 Brookville Road
Chevy Chase, MD
(301) 986–5255
www.lafermerestaurant.com

La Ferme is nestled into a wealthy residential section of Montgomery County, one of the few commercial enterprises in the neighborhood, but it's hardly a drop-in kind of place. There's something both fresh and luxurious about the country French decor—you couldn't ask for a more inviting setting. As befits a restaurant in this cosmopolitan and very upscale area, the food is excellent. Cuts of meat are well trimmed for the utmost in tenderness and taste. Veal is often pallid elsewhere, but at La Ferme it shines. Seafood classics like Dover sole are done right here, but you can also find more modern, simply grilled fish. Restaurants that serve chateaubriand aren't exactly rare in the Washington area, but they aren't common either. La Ferme does it and does it well. This is the kind of spot that's lovely for a special occasion or for an escapist lunch on a lazy summer day. Lunch is served Monday through Friday and dinner Monday through Sunday.

La Miche $$$
7905 Norfolk Avenue
Bethesda, MD
(301) 986–0707
www.lamiche.com

Think of dried flowers, lively prints, and baskets, and you've pictured La Miche. This French charmer, near the National Institutes of Health, has stayed ahead of the competition for nearly three decades by sticking to the basics of French cooking, like lobster bisque, cream sauces, puff pastries, and meats redolent of garlic. You probably won't find anything unfamiliar on this menu—just calories-be-damned French cooking that takes you back to the old days. La Miche is open for lunch Tuesday through Friday and dinner nightly except for Sunday.

Le Vieux Logis $$$
7925 Old Georgetown Road
Bethesda, MD
(301) 652–6816

Even in restaurant-packed Bethesda, Le Vieux Logis makes you do a double take. That's because it looks like a slice of Alsace with its half-timbered facade and flower-filled window boxes. Flowers are everywhere, and what a nice greeting! Inside, there are other reminders of Alsace in the cooking, which has a somewhat German accent; for example, many of the meat dishes are paired with sauces that contain fruit or mustard. Mushrooms are used liberally in both appetizers and main courses. Try the mushroom soup, a creamy concoction with a haunting flavor. If seafood's your fancy, you'll find several dishes infused with citrus. They are lighter than the meat dishes and also very good. This is interesting, unusual French cuisine, and you won't find a more pleasant setting. They serve dinner nightly except for Sunday.

Italian

Cesco $$
4871 Cordell Avenue
Bethesda, MD
(301) 654–8333

There's no more agreeable patio on Bethesda's restaurant row than that at Cesco, and the interior decor is just as inviting, with wonderful arches and plenty of windows. The menu here departs a bit from the Italian standards—there are some interesting ingredients and presentations. For example, one of the appetizers is a delectable work of art: a cylinder of baked Parmesan cheese filled with endive and other greens. The bruschetta brings to mind the Italian flag: red, white, and green. One piece has a fresh tomato topping, another is punctuated with broccoli rabe, and another with cannellini beans. If it's meat you're craving, try the sinful filet of beef layered with eggplant and tomato in a Gorgonzola cheese sauce. Cesco is open for lunch Tuesday through Friday and dinner nightly.

C. J. Ferrari's $
143111 Baltimore Avenue
Laurel, MD
(301) 725–1771
www.cjferraris.com

There's nothing fancy about this bargain-priced eatery in Prince George's County, but surprising care is taken with several dishes. Anything tomato-based is a good bet here—the sauce is springy and flavorful. Try one of the seafood dishes, like scallops in a delicious wine sauce, zinged with a bit of mustard. You'll want to sop up that extra sauce with a slice of the restaurant's crusty bread. What put Ferrari's on the map, though, is the white pizza, a garlicky, cheesy version that puts others to shame. For dessert, try the home-made ice cream. Ferarri's is open for lunch Tuesday through Friday, dinner Tuesday through Sunday. It is closed Monday.

Geppetto's $
10257 Old Georgetown Road
Bethesda, MD
(301) 493–9230

Imagine pepperoni piled so high it's hard to see the pizza itself. Although such generosity seems terribly wasteful except for perhaps eaters of above-average girth, it's tough for lovers of deep-dish pizza and pasta not to adore Geppetto's. The pleasure begins from the moment you step inside this casual cafe at the upscale Wildwood Shopping Center and take in the delightful aroma. This is not a place for those seeking delicate refinements in Italian cooking. It's Italian-American abbondanza at its best. Make sure you see the exhibit of puppets in the back dining room, including, of course, Pinocchio. Lunch and dinner are served daily.

Il Pizzico $$
15209 Frederick Road (also known as Rockville Pike)
Rockville, MD
(301) 309–0610
www.ilpizzico.com

Outside Il Pizzico's windows, traffic on Route 355 in northern Rockville careens past strip malls and car dealerships. Inside the restaurant, though, faux windows set in the walls offer painted views of sunlit terraced Italian hillsides. And the small storefront with a generic sign outside belies the white linen tablecloths and white-coated waiters within. Although the menu is not expansive, you can hardly go wrong, especially with the veal, fish, and pasta that is made on-site. The wild mushroom–stuffed ravioli with pistachio cream sauce is rich and satisfying—coupled with an icy glass of Pinot Grigio, it's pure heaven. Ask about the daily specials, the wine list, and, lest we forget, the desserts. Il Pizzico is open for lunch Monday through Friday; dinner Monday through Saturday. Closed Sunday.

Pines of Rome $
4709 Hampton Lane
Bethesda, MD
(301) 657–8775

Pines of Rome has stuck to its guns through cooking fads from nouvelle to northern Italian to fusion. Never has it deviated from the old Italian-American standard: pasta with heavy red sauce served on checkered tablecloths. Sure, there's a white pizza that's pretty good and a robust spaghetti carbonara, but that's about as adventurous as you want to get here. This is a place to bring kids when you want to eat cheaply, quickly, and plentifully. It's open for lunch and dinner nightly.

Sergio's Ristorante Italiano $$$
8727 Colesville Road
Silver Spring, MD
(301) 585–1040

If you're going to a movie at the AFI Silver Theatre in Silver Spring, think about stopping here for a bite before the show. It's the sort of place you might overlook, housed in the unassuming Hilton Silver Spring. If you walk on by, however, you'd miss out on some of the region's finest Italian fare. Owner Sergio Toni serves a loyal neighborhood clientele fresh pasta dishes doused in delightful sauces brimming with fresh ingredients, including real butter and cream. Ravioli are delightfully plump, stuffed with ground veal and pork, perfectly seasoned—and the pasta is made fresh daily by the owner himself. Veal dishes are sublime.

That's Amore $$
15201 Shady Grove Road
Rockville, MD
(240) 268–0682

10400 Little Patuxent Parkway
Columbia, MD
(410) 772–5900
www.thatsamore.com

You'd better pack an appetite when you go to That's Amore. Even then, one dish may be enough to serve your entire party. For cheap eats, the food here is very good, and the atmosphere is raucous and friendly, with lots of families. The cooking is heavy on the garlic, tomato sauce, and cheese—nothing subtle about this place. The menu contains all the Italian standards like eggplant and veal parmigiana, but the underlying ingredients hardly matter when the toppings are so robust. Try anything that features lemon-butter sauce and you'll probably be happy. The meal-size salads are stocked with lots of goodies like olives, onions, and tomatoes. If you want to sample everything from soup to nuts, bring your extended family and share, or you'll never get through it. There are also Virginia locations at 150 Branch Road SE in Vienna (703–281–7777) and 46300 Potomac Run Plaza in Sterling (703–406–4900). Open for lunch and dinner daily.

Tragara $$$$
4935 Cordell Avenue
Bethesda, MD
(301) 951–4935
www.tragara.com

This may be the most extravagant—and the most formal—Italian restaurant in the Maryland suburbs, and it's one of the prettiest, with two levels, generous floral arrangements, and light, bright decor. The food is mostly northern Italian, which means rich white sauces, grilled meats, and a delicate

hand with seasoning. You may end up spending more here than you think you should, but if you're looking for a special occasion Italian restaurant in Maryland, nothing comes close in terms of overall atmosphere and cuisine. Tragara is open for lunch weekdays and dinner nightly.

Middle Eastern/Indian

Aangan Indian Restaurant $
4920 Saint Elmo Avenue
Bethesda, MD
(301) 657–1262

In Hindi, the word "aangan" means courtyard, and with its potted palms, climbing vines, and flickering lanterns, Aangan Indian Restaurant re-creates a lush patio. The enveloping rattan chairs, stone archways set into the stucco walls, and wicker blinds enhance the tropical feel and impart a welcome, warm atmosphere in the dead of winter. The food also plays its part in heating the place up. Aangan concentrates on the cuisine of northern India, its spice palette filled with ginger, garlic, cumin, and curry. Many of the dishes focus on lamb or chicken, often cubed and served as kabobs. Open daily for lunch and dinner. The weekday lunch buffet is a particular bargain.

Bacchus $$
7945 Norfolk Avenue
Bethesda, MD
(301) 657–1722

In the minds of many Washingtonians, the art of Middle Eastern cooking—in this case, Lebanese—begins and ends at Bacchus. Count on quality and satisfaction in whatever menu selection catches your eye at this bustling restaurant. Bacchus specialties include the creative kebabs of beef, chicken, and lamb; savory sausages; stuffed cabbage; and baby eggplant. Bacchus knows how to mix spices and textures for a knockout effect. The absolute must here is the assortment of *mezze*, appetizers like fragrant hummus with ground beef and toasted almonds on top, baba ghanouj, or hot, flaky phyllo stuffed with cheese. You can make a complete dinner of appetizers and not feel deprived. Bacchus is open for lunch weekdays and dinner nightly.

Bombay Bistro $$
98 West Montgomery Avenue
Rockville, MD
(301) 762–8798
www.bombaybistro.com
Bombay Bistro is open for lunch and dinner nightly. Please see the listing in the Virginia section.

Spanish

Andalucia $$$
12300 Wilkins Avenue
Rockville, MD
(301) 770–1880
Rockville has a Spanish star in Andalucia, which serves consistently good food (emphasizing the gastronomic delights of southern Spain) with the grace and flair of a matador. This place, with its wonderful guitar music in the evenings, isn't nearly as informal as the other restaurants in the Hispanic category. Don't overindulge in the good and garlicky appetizers—you have to save room for such specialties as paella and zarzuela. Don't overdo it on those tasty entrees, either; the desserts—especially the cakes—are a delightful way to top it all off. It is open for lunch and dinner every day except Monday.

Tex-Mex/Hispanic

Acajutla Mexican Restaurant $
18554 Woodfield Road
Gaithersburg, MD
(301) 670–1674
As we've noted, the D.C. Metro area is home to a large South and Central American com-munity—and some charming neighborhood restaurants that serve authentic fare. Although much of the menu here is Mexican, you'll find a handful of enticing Salvadoran dishes like deep-fried yucca served with chicken and rel-ished cabbage. You can't go wrong with Mexi-can classics like sizzling fajitas, either.

Mi Rancho $$
8701 Ramsey Avenue
Silver Spring, MD
(301) 588–4744
For no-frills standards, Mi Rancho is a good bet. The menu reads like a "greatest hits" list of Tex-Mex favorites: beef nachos, pork tamales, steak fajitas, and an endless supply of chips and salsa. If you're avoiding red meat, the kitchen does a good turn with fish dishes like whole snapper and shrimp soup. Wood paneling and exposed beams give it a rustic feel, and the outdoor patio is especially inviting in warm weather.

Rio Grande Cafe $$
4870 Bethesda Avenue
Bethesda, MD
(301) 656–2981
It used to be that an hour-long wait was stan-dard for a table at Rio Grande Cafe. Some of the furor has died down, but this casual eatery remains popular. One of the highlights here is the tortilla machine, which produces warm, fresh . . . you guessed it . . . tortillas to accompany the fajitas and other Tex-Mex fare. You'll find the usual tacos, enchiladas, burritos, plus a few unexpected items like frog legs and quail. This place is loud, busy, and frenetic, so it might not be the place for an intimate evening. It is open for lunch Mon-day through Saturday, dinner nightly, and Sunday brunch.

NIGHTLIFE

In a place where shuffling papers and climbing corporate ladders are forms of recreation, nightlife may not seem like a top priority for many people. Believe it or not, even stressed-out, career-minded Washingtonians know how to have a good time away from the office, embracing the work hard/play hard philosophy with ample gusto.

Although the nightlife here is plentiful and diverse, don't expect a heavy dose of Los Angeles–style glitz or New York–style up-'til-dawn decadence. Instead, like the dining scene, after-hours diversions in Metro Washington include a little bit of everything, from cutting-edge music halls and stand-up comedy venues, to funky watering holes, sports saloons, yuppified fern bars, and high-energy dance clubs.

First, here are a few things to keep in mind before venturing out for an evening on the town. As a general rule, the District offers the widest variety of nightlife, but you can almost always expect to pay a bit more for such things as drinks, cover charges, and live entertainment. Case in point: Single beers exceeding the $5.00 mark are common, especially at some of the city's tonier clubs—and if they don't get you at the bar, there's a good chance you paid for it at the door.

Suburban establishments are generally a

i Can't decide where to go? Try the Boomerang Party Bus, a party-on-wheels that takes you to four or five different bars between 8:00 P.M. and 1:15 A.M. Boomerang provides your transportation and introduces you to a new group of friends, plus you'll beat the lines and cover charges and even get discounted drinks at some of the city's hottest spots, all for $25 (www.ridetheboomerang.com).

bit less expensive. Whether you live in the Virginia exurbs or far-flung Maryland counties, chances are your nightlife will occur in one of three places: Montgomery County, Maryland; Washington, D.C.; or the Northern Virginia suburbs immediately surrounding Washington—that is, Arlington or Fairfax Counties and Old Town Alexandria. Accordingly, we've used only three geographical divisions in the listings that follow: Washington, D.C., Northern Virginia, and Suburban Maryland.

"Last call for alcohol," as the saying goes, is typically around 2:00 A.M. in the city, and 1:00 to 1:30 A.M. in the 'burbs. Some of the downtown haunts may not finish shooing people out the door until 3:00 or 4:00 A.M., but alcohol cannot be legally served after 3:00 A.M. in the District.

Incredibly, soft drinks aren't always that much cheaper than booze at many bars and clubs in Metro Washington, although they certainly should be in this age of heightened awareness about the lunacy of drinking and driving. Some places do, however, occasionally offer free, unlimited nonalcoholic beverages to the designated driver in a group, so it pays (in more ways than one) to inquire.

The scourge of underage drinking and the increasingly tough penalties levied against those who serve minors have convinced many business owners—grocery, convenience, and liquor store operators included—to be extra cautious about who's buying. So take the request to see your driver's license as a compliment, not an insult. On your drive home don't be surprised if you encounter roadblocks where police check for drunk drivers—it's a common practice on weekends in the Metro Washington area.

In 2007 Washington, D.C. joined the list of major U.S. cities that have banned smoking in public places—including bars and restaurants. Nonsmokers are delighting in the clean air, while smokers have resigned themselves to stepping outside. (In this chapter you'll find a few listings for hookah bars and cigar clubs—which, as of press time, were exempt from the new regulations. We encourage you to double-check before you head out.) Bars and restaurants in Montgomery County, Maryland, are also smoke-free.

For updates on what's happening in the local nightlife scene and advice from local experts, we encourage you to check in with washingtonpost.com's "Going Out Gurus." Nightlife reporters offer advice for weekend plans during a live chat every Thursday at 1:00 P.M. If you miss the chat, check the Web site for a transcript. You can also check the "Weekend" and "Washington Weekend" sections of the *Washington Post* and *Washington Times*, respectively, or pick up a copy of the *Washington City Paper*.

As with the Restaurants chapter, this is far from an exhaustive roundup of Metro Washington nightspots, and again we've tried to emphasize the local places. Entries bearing an asterisk (*) beside their name are also covered in the Restaurants chapter, so please refer to that section for more details.

WASHINGTON, D.C.
Live Music and Dancing

Apex
1415 22nd Street NW
Washington, DC
(202) 296–0505
www.apex-dc.com
Although it changed its name from Badlands to Apex and expanded the dance floor, this is still one of the gay dance clubs that newcomers to Washington will hear of first. That's because it's always crowded and always rocking. There's a little something for everyone, from a music video room to pool tables. The crowd is fairly young, in shape, and attractive. There are often theme nights ranging from

country and western to karaoke. The club is open Thursday through Sunday nights, with a weekend cover charge of up to $10.

Black Cat
1811 14th Street NW
Washington, DC
(202) 667–7960
www.blackcatdc.com
This eclectic nightclub ranges from swing music to alternative rock, depending on which night you go. On swing music nights you'll find people sipping champagne and smoking cigars. On rock nights it's a whole different crowd—a very young one, with lots of black jeans in evidence. To keep up with what's going on here, you'll need to call for the weekly schedule. It is open nightly, and tickets are $5.00 to $15.00.

Blues Alley
1073 Wisconsin Avenue NW
Washington, DC
(202) 337–4141
www.bluesalley.com
You could easily miss the aptly named Blues Alley, as it's hidden in a Georgetown alley, halfway between K and M Streets off Wisconsin Avenue. For decades this intimate supper club has been the city's top spot for the best in local and national jazz and blues acts, including the likes of Tony Bennett, Wynton Marsalis, and Charlie Byrd. Reservations are a must, especially on weekends and when top talent is on the bill. Blues Alley is open nightly, and tickets are $20 to $30.

Bukom Cafe
2442 18th Street NW
Washington, DC
(202) 265–4600
www.bukom.com/bukom
Washington has a large community that hails from Africa, and many of its members can be found at this hot spot in Adams Morgan when the place rocks with live reggae music from Wednesday to Saturday. The atmosphere

starts out relaxed, but it picks up as the band plays on and the night progresses. Dress is casual as could be. There is no cover charge.

Chief Ike's Mambo Room
1725 Columbia Road NW
Washington, DC
(202) 332–2211
www.chiefikes.com

This funky Adams Morgan nightclub draws a casual crowd ranging in age from 20-something to around 40. On weekends there's some very hip live music. Bands vary from reggae to rock. If you don't like the music here, you can wander down the street to any number of other locales for live tunes. It is open nightly, with a weekend cover charge of $3.00 to $5.00.

Chloe Restaurant Lounge
2473 18th Street NW
Washington, DC
(202) 265–6592

There's a good chance you'll encounter a line at this spacious Adams Morgan club, which boasts one of the best floor plans in the neighborhood—pieced together from three separate row houses, with all of the activity centered on a two-story dancing and dining space accented by lights that change color. If you prefer a bird's-eye view of what's going on in the club, take the stairs to a mezzanine level. Or, better yet, snag a space on the back patio.

Dubliner Pub
520 North Capitol Street NW
Washington, DC
(202) 737–3773
dublinerdc.com

For a taste of the Emerald Isle without stepping on a plane, head for this popular pub.

i Although last call in Washington dance clubs is usually 2:30 A.M. on weekends, most places don't pick up speed until at least 11:00 P.M.

The Dubliner is in the Phoenix Park Hotel and is considered by many to be the region's most authentic Irish pub and dining experience. Although Irish cuisine may be beside the point, Irish folk music appeals to many and is featured here nightly. It is open nightly, with no cover charge.

The Fireplace
2161 P Street NW
Washington, DC
(202) 293–1293

The Fireplace has been around for decades, first as a bar and lounge for all sorts, now as a bar and lounge for a mostly gay crowd. The salient feature of this place is, in fact, the fireplace visible at the corner of the building (it looks like an outdoor fireplace at first) on P and 22nd streets. Inside, you'll find a very dark series of rooms and a couple of bars on two stories. The clientele here is definitely on the prowl, so if you're looking for a place to meet new people, this may be it. You'll find a mix of neighborhood locals and tourists from nearby hotels, along with a somewhat raffish element. The Fireplace is open nightly, with no cover charge.

Irish Times
14 F Street NW
Washington, DC
(202) 543–5433

This low-key pub features live Irish music Thursday through Saturday. Entertainment is mostly of the acoustic guitar variety, and the crowd is an easy mix of downtown suits, chinos, and bluejeans. Irish Times is open nightly, with no cover charge.

Kramerbooks & afterwords Cafe & Grill
1517 Connecticut Avenue NW
Washington, DC
(202) 387–1400
www.kramers.com

Here's a fun twist: a bookstore with live music from Wednesday to Saturday. Long before Borders and the other big chains came along and tried it, this Dupont Circle

If you're looking for diverse nightlife, spend a night out in the Adams Morgan neighborhood. COURTESY
WASHINGTON, D.C. CONVENTION AND TOURISM CORPORATION

mainstay dreamed up the idea of teaming these two great forms of entertainment. Expect a laid-back approach with lots of acoustic guitar and folk music—nothing too intrusive. The cafe serves three meals a day and has great coffee and desserts. It is open nightly (24 hours on Fridays and Saturdays), with no cover charge.

Madam's Organ
2461 18th Street NW
Washington, DC
(202) 667–5370
www.madamsorgan.com
SORRY, WE'RE OPEN, reads a sign on the door at this Adams Morgan mainstay, named one of the best bars in the country by *Playboy* magazine. The bar is decked out with taxidermy creations, comical signs, and a hodgepodge of items you'd expect to find in your eccentric aunt's attic. Many patrons come here for the live music, served up nightly, in varieties that range from bluegrass to acoustic blues to Latin jazz.

9:30 Club
815 V Street NW
Washington, DC
(202) 393–0930
www.930.com
If alternative rock is your thing, you won't want to miss the 9:30 Club. The crowd here varies by show, but the atmosphere is always intense. Playing in this redesigned space are cutting-edge bands. It is open nightly, and ticket prices usually range from $12 to $40, depending on the show.

Twins Jazz
1344 U Street NW
Washington, DC
(202) 234–0072
www.twinsjazz.com
While other D.C. jazz clubs may have greater notoriety, music fans in the know are partial to U Street's Twins Jazz. Owned by twin sisters from Ethiopia, Twins serves up a delicious selection of Ethiopian food to complement the mellow jazz tunes. Walls are decorated with works by local artists and photos of jazz legends. Sunday afternoons attract talented amateurs for jam sessions that truly showcase the local jazz flavor.

Nightclubs

Birreria Paradiso
3282 M Street NW
(202) 337–1245
www.eatyourpizza.com
Beer lovers usually make a pilgrimage to the Brickskeller (see next listing), but this newcomer is also worth a trip. Housed in the lower level of the Georgetown location of the ever-popular Pizzeria Paradiso, the Birreria serves 16 varieties of beer on draft (with a menu that changes regularly) and stocks about 80 bottles, each well suited to match the delicious brick-oven pizzas.

The Brickskeller
1523 22nd Street NW
Washington, DC
(202) 293–1885
www.thebrickskeller.com
The Brickskeller remains the city's consummate beer-lover's nirvana, offering more than 700 brands from around the world. It's handy for washing down fare like pizza, sandwiches, and buffalo burgers. Be sure to check out the unbelievable beer can collection lining the walls. The Brickskeller is open nightly, with no cover charge.

Cafe Saint-Ex
1847 14th Street NW
Washington, DC
(202) 265–7839
www.saint-ex.com
An aviation theme takes over at this Logan Circle restaurant and bar, named for French author/pilot Antoine de Saint-Exupéry. Upstairs you'll find a well-stocked bar and a friendly, unassuming, and affordable menu. After dinner, head downstairs to Gate 54, an intimate lounge space serviced by talented DJs.

Eighteenth Street Lounge
1212 18th Street NW
Washington, DC
(202) 466–3922
www.eslmusic.com

A chapter on D.C. nightlife wouldn't be complete without a mention of Eighteenth Street Lounge, or "ESL." While clubs come and go, ESL has earned a permanent place among the city's best and most exclusive clubs, partly due to its connections with its former owners, electronica/house duo Thievery Corporation. And because they'd like to keep it that way, the club keeps an aura of exclusivity. There's no sign on the door outside, and if you do find it, you can expect to be heavily scrutinized by the doorman.

Felix and the Spy Lounge
2406 18th Street NW
Washington, DC
(202) 483–3549
www.thefelix.com

Felix has developed into an Adams Morgan mainstay, with a cool lounge vibe and a fashionable cocktail menu. Many of the specialty drinks pay homage to James Bond and his various enemies—what you'd expect, more or less, in a place that bills itself as a "spy lounge." This is a good bet for dancing, whether you're looking for hip-hop, reggae, soul, or live music from Latin jazz or alternative bands.

Five
1214B 18th Street NW
Washington, DC
(202) 331–9882
www.fivedc.com

This Dupont Circle club is a good choice if you're more concerned with having a good time than with dressing to impress. Dancers pack three levels, with an island-themed dance party on the rooftop, which is heated on cooler nights. Another thing that sets Five apart: It stays open until 5:00 A.M., when most other D.C. clubs have locked up their doors for the night. Expect to pay a cover

---

> **i** The Brickskeller claims to hold the world's record for the largest beer menu, with more than 700 varieties from around the globe in stock.

charge of about $10, or check local newspapers for free or discounted entry passes.

Fly Lounge
1802 Jefferson Place NW
Washington, DC
(202) 828–4433
flyloungedc.com

At press time, this was the hottest ticket in town. Located in Dupont Circle, the airplane-themed lounge has earned praise in hip-hop magazine *Vibe* and was even written up in the *New York Times*. Step inside and you'll feel as if you've climbed aboard a 747, complete with servers in stewardess-inspired uniforms and free bags of mixed nuts, delivered in an ultra-chic, ultra-cool atmosphere with some of the hottest DJs in town.

H Street Martini Lounge
1236 H Street NE
Washington, DC
(202) 397–3333
www.hstreetlounge.com

H Street is one of D.C.'s most talked-about emerging nightlife destinations, and the H Street Martini Lounge is one of the places you can credit. Boasting a menu of more than 54 martinis, the lounge is classy and upscale, yet manages to gel with the quirky neighborhood vibe. On Wednesday nights you can take free hand-dancing lessons, or catch live jazz and blues music on Thursday and Friday nights.

Helix Lounge
1430 Rhode Island Avenue NW
Washington, DC
(202) 462–9001
www.loungedc.com

Another addition to the D.C. nightlife scene brought to you by the Kimpton Hotel Group,

ℹ️ The newest hot strip for nightclubs is 12th Street NE. You'll also find a lot of new clubs opening on U Street NW.

Helix Lounge takes its design and mood cues from the funky, fabulous, pop art–inspired Hotel Helix, where it serves as the in-house restaurant. During the summer, neighborhood residents and guests sip, munch, and mingle with their four-legged companions on the Helix's dog-friendly patio. The lounge's walls and seating areas are lined with white vinyl, which changes color, thanks to some neat lighting effects. On the cocktail menu you'll find fruity, creative concoctions that change with the season.

LOVE
1350 Okie Street NE
Washington, DC
(202) 636–9030
www.lovetheclub.com
LOVE took over the glorious warehouse-turned-club space once known as Dream, which was known to attract celebrities and musical tourists from across the country. Fortunately for nightlife lovers, Love picks up where Dream left off. It's beautifully appointed with rich wood accents and lush colors, spreading across four floors, each with its own personality. Guests are smartly dressed and often arrive in stylish luxury cars, but club-goers should be careful around here. The neighborhood hasn't yet risen to match the standards you'll find inside. Cover charges are $10 to $20, but you can usually find tickets good for free admission on the club's Web site.

Modern
3287 M Street NW
Washington, DC
(202) 338–7027
This addition to Georgetown's club scene may be modern, but it's not postmodern. No techno DJs or light show wizardry here. There are, however, some funky touches, with a

bubble chair suspended in air in the corner and retro mod plastic couches scattered around. The DJs spin a familiar range of funk, soul, disco, and pop, and Georgetown University students and 20-something professionals crowd the small dance floor. Open nightly, with some events free and others with a $5.00 to $10.00 cover charge.

Science Club
1136 19th Street NW
Washington, DC
(202) 775–0747
www.scienceclubdc.com
Leave it to cerebral Washington to give a hip new nightspot a name like this. The owner chose the name in tribute to its Victorian setting, reminiscent of an exclusive members-only club. While the name manages to attract a few curious science-types, the broader client base is what you'd expect in any stylish Dupont Circle gathering place. At the bar you'll sit on metal stools acquired from a high school chemistry lab, and there's a chalkboard available for your equation-solving or doodling pleasure. There's no cover charge, though drinks can be a bit pricey.

Showbar Presents the Palace of Wonders
1210 H Street NE
Washington, DC
(202) 398–7469
There's no place in Washington quite like Showbar. At times it's more like a carnival or sideshow than a bar. There are women's arm wrestling contests on Tuesday evenings and quiz nights on Wednesdays. Decor isn't what you've come to expect in a bar. Here you'll find shrunken heads, Peruvian mummies, and a taxidermy unicorn. To entertain guests on weekends, Showbar will trot out performers like sword swallowers and drag queens.

The Reef
2446 18th Street NW
Washington, DC
(202) 518–3800
thereefdc.com
The Reef is one of Adams Morgan's largest

bars and its most eco-friendly destination, espousing an all-organic, all-natural philosophy for its menu and its upkeep. You won't find any beers in bottles here (but 16 varieties on draft), and napkins are made with recycled paper. Each of the Reef's three floors takes on the personality of a different climate zone—a jungle-like lower level, an aquatic-themed main bar, and a desert-themed rooftop deck.

Third Edition
1218 Wisconsin Avenue NW
Washington, DC
(202) 333–3700
www.thethirdedition.com
Nightclubs come and go in Washington, but the Third Edition in Georgetown has managed to pack 'em in for more than three decades. Maybe it's the Wisconsin Avenue location right near the busy M Street intersection, or maybe it's the glass doors, thrown open to let the music out and the crowd in. Whatever the reason, Third Edition draws a fairly well-groomed crowd of mostly 20- and 30-somethings, including lots of students from nearby Georgetown University. It is open nightly, with a cover charge of $5.00 on Friday and Saturday.

Sports Bars

Buffalo Billiards
1330 19th Street NW
Washington, DC
(202) 331–7665
www.buffalobillards.com/dc
Cowboys would feel right at home here with the pinto-printed upholstery, peeled log chairs, and, of course, a Southwestern menu of bar munchies and a few more substantial dishes. As the name implies, this is primarily a pool hall. There are the requisite music and TVs, of course, and a singles bar atmosphere. It is open nightly, with no cover charge.

Fanatics
1520 K Street NW
Washington, DC
(202) 638–6800

This sports bar advertises itself as having plenty of babes, beers, and billiards. All three are probably true, because it is connected to Archibald's—a strip joint that's been around since 1969. For those whose idea of entertainment involves spectator sports of a different kind, however, there are 30 TVs, seven satellites, five pool tables, and darts. It is open nightly, with no cover charge.

Piano Music and Mellow Lounges

Aroma
3417 Connecticut Avenue NW
Washington, DC
(202) 244–7995
Aroma is a grown-up place for a grown-up crowd—you don't have to worry about your feet sticking to a beer-soaked floor here. It's billed as a comfortable neighborhood gathering place—albeit one that woos its patrons with trendy martinis, soft lighting, and soothing piano music during the week and dance tunes spun by a DJ on Fridays and Saturdays. If the bar gets too crowded, head to the back of the lounge, where you'll find a cozy spread of 1960s-inspired furnishings perfect for conversation.

Bourbon
2348 Wisconsin Avenue NW
Washington, DC
(202) 625–7770
www.bourbondc.com
If you're a fan of Kentucky's finest liquor, you owe it to yourself to check out this Glover Park bar. Stop in to try about 50 varieties of bourbon and a handful of Tennessee whiskeys—including some highly rare (and pricey!) labels. You'll also find a dozen wines by the glass (served on draft) and a nice selection of beers. Bourbon opened a second location in Adams Morgan (2321 18th Street NW, 202–332–0800)—a mellow addition to

i In the 1980s the "Brat Pack" gathered at Third Edition to film St. Elmo's Fire.

the neighborhood's lively—occasionally raucous—nightlife district.

Busboys and Poets
2021 14th Street NW
Washington, DC
(202) 387–7638
www.busboysandpoets.com

We're not sure how to classify this place. It's part bookstore, part bar, part cafe, and part performance space, often used as a gathering space for community activists. A new addition to 14th Street, Busboys and Poets takes its name from poet Langston Hughes, who once lived in the neighborhood. Adjacent to the main dining room, there's a room outfitted with a stage and sound system for open-mike nights—and as one of few establishments in the country to have a resident poet on staff, the quality of what you're served up is quite good.

Degrees
Ritz-Carlton, Georgetown
3100 South Street NW
Washington, DC
(202) 912–4100

You'd expect the Ritz-Carlton, Georgetown, to be a classy place to get a drink—and you'd be absolutely right. The bar takes its name from the "fire" theme that's carried out throughout the hotel, which was built out of the former site of the Georgetown incinerator. There's something decidedly elegant about this place—you'll see it in the creative cocktails, the well-dressed clientele, the swanky red leather barstools and furnishings. It's a great place to unwind after a dinner in Georgetown or to meet a friend or client you're looking to impress.

Kinkead's*
2000 Pennsylvania Avenue NW
Washington, DC
(202) 296–7700
www.kinkead.com

Upstairs is one of Washington's best restaurants; downstairs is a spacious, woodsy bar with a jazz combo Tuesday through Saturday. Despite the proximity to George Washington University, this is a crowd of adult professionals. Yet it's a casual scene, rarely jam-packed, and quiet enough for conversation. Drop in after dinner in the restaurant or when you're in the neighborhood. There is no cover charge.

Mr. Smith's of Georgetown*
3104 M Street NW
Washington, DC
(202) 333–3104
www.mrsmiths.com

This may be Washington's most popular piano bar—it's certainly the oldest. It's also a piano bar in the traditional sense, with everyone gathering 'round the player and chiming in. The lights are low, the drinks include every fancy concoction imaginable (and some that aren't), and the crowd is convivial. You'll fit right in, no matter where you come from or what you're wearing. It is open nightly, with no cover charge.

Cigar Bars

Chi-Cha Lounge
1624 U Street NW
Washington, DC
(202) 234–8400

This ever-so-hip place is in D.C.'s hottest club district. The crowd is mostly young and Euro—and just about everyone is smoking something, whether it be cigarettes, cigars, or even, on certain nights, a hookah filled with Arabic tobacco. On Tuesdays live jazz adds to the cool (attitude, not temperature), dark atmosphere. It is open nightly, with no cover charge.

Off the Record
16th and H Streets NW
Washington, DC
(202) 942–7599
www.hayadams.com

The Hay-Adams is one of Washington's most historic and luxurious hotels—they know how to do things right here. Off the Record, with its low-lit, men's club atmosphere, offers not only cigars, but a generous selection of single-malt scotch, champagnes, and wines by the glass. Many are hard-to-find labels and can cost more than $20. Martinis alone are $10. The Hay-Adams is right across Lafayette Square from the White House, and the patrons here look like the kind of successful folk who may have come from an appointment at 1600 Pennsylvania Avenue. It is open Monday through Saturday, with no cover charge.

Ozio Restaurant & Lounge
1835 K Street NW
Washington, DC
(202) 822–6000
Inside Ozio you'll find a very dark lounge with booths and tables placed around a small dance floor. The place starts to rock after midnight, when a mix of Euro types and K Street expense account executives crowd the dance floor. There's a wide selection of gin and vodka martinis, including a couple of original Ozio recipes. It is open Monday through Saturday.

Comedy Clubs

The Improv
1140 Connecticut Avenue NW
Washington, DC
(202) 296–7008
www.dcimprov.com
This club—yes, we admit, it's part of a national chain—brings top acts to Washington in a convenient midtown location. You can have dinner if you attend the early shows or wait for the 10:30 performance on weekends and dine at one of the great restaurants nearby. Acts here are often comedians you've seen on TV, and you'll recognize most of the names. And if you have aspirations to be a stand-up comic yourself, you can try one of the new classes offered at the Improv. It is open Tuesday through Saturday, and tickets are $15 to $25.

> ℹ️ On weekends driving your car can be a bad decision in such traffic-choked hubs as Georgetown, Adams Morgan, and Old Town Alexandria, so carpooling and park-and-walk strategies are best.

NORTHERN VIRGINIA

Alexandria's Old Town area is Northern Virginia's answer to Georgetown. That ought to give you an idea of the richness of the nightlife in this charming and beautiful area. As with Georgetown, a sidewalk stroll along the narrow, sometimes cobblestone streets will reveal a world unto itself. The hub of Old Town's nocturnal activity is located on the river side (east) of Washington Street, also known as the George Washington Memorial Parkway, especially lower King Street and the surrounding few blocks.

Not all of Virginia's nightlife is in Old Town, though. There are also pockets of activity in Rosslyn and just 10 minutes farther west in Clarendon. People who are serious about nightlife still head into D.C., but the suburbs have enough to keep you occupied for at least a few evenings on the town. Because of the more limited offerings, we haven't created as many categories as for downtown Washington, D.C. For example, piano lounges are not a category, but are rather listed under live music. One category you will find here that's missing from D.C. is dinner theaters—we haven't found any in Washington D.C., whereas Northern Virginia has a couple. As we mentioned in the introduction, we have not broken down Northern Virginia by county for two reasons: The first is that distances are insignificant for the most part, and the second is that nightlife is limited enough that any further breakdown would result in some categories having only one listing—or perhaps none. That isn't to say that fun can't be found in the 'burbs, though. Just read on if you want proof.

Live Music and Dancing

Basin St. Lounge
219 King Street
Alexandria, VA
(703) 549–1141

For a more formal setting than some of those listed previously, Basin St. Lounge in Old Town offers live jazz and Louisiana cuisine one floor below the 219 Restaurant. The decor here is particularly inviting, featuring a brick courtyard and wall accents; a dark, sophisticated lounge; and a restaurant upstairs furnished in New Orleans–style French reproductions. It is open in the evenings Tuesday through Saturday. The cover charge is $7.00 on Friday and Saturday.

The Birchmere
3701 Mount Vernon Avenue
Alexandria, VA
(703) 549–7500
www.birchmere.com

In an area known as Arlandria (Arlington/Alexandria border), this has become one of the top national venues for bluegrass, zydeco, country, folk, pop, and blues performers, all in a down-to-earth, casual setting. The once crowded space has undergone a major expansion and renovation. Now you'll find a pool hall, German beer garden, and plenty of room for the crowds that gather here for top-of-the-line performers such as David Crosby, Doc Watson, and the Nighthawks. The schedule is determined by show times, and tickets are $20 to $45.

Clarendon Ballroom
3185 Wilson Boulevard
Arlington, VA
(703) 469–2244
www.clarendonballroom.com

It's art deco and it's huge. There's a lot going for the Clarendon Ballroom. The 20,000-square-foot former carpet outlet hosts swing dances twice a week and has live rock and DJs on the weekends. The building retains its original 1930s pressed-tin ceiling in gold leaf, and the 1,000-person-capacity ballroom is decked out in art deco touches. It also rents out to private parties, complete with catering. Cover is $5.00. Closed Monday.

Fat Tuesday's
10673 Braddock Road
Fairfax, VA
(703) 385–8660
www.fatsfairfax.com

Near George Mason University, Fat Tuesday's is another major force in live rock and R&B music on Wednesday to Sunday nights. This is a much smaller setting than some of the concert halls listed in this category, and it couldn't be more casual. The crowd is a mix of blue-collar workers and students. Take pitchers of beer; hot music; a dark, noisy bar; and a location at University Mall and you get the idea of what kind of atmosphere to expect at Fat Tuesday's any day of the week. It is open nightly, with a cover charge of $3.00 to $5.00 Wednesday through Sunday.

Fish Market*
105 King Street
Alexandria, VA
(703) 836–5676
www.fishmarketoldtown.com

This Old Town spot always seems to be full of jolly people ready to party, and the ragtime piano player adds to the mood on Wednesdays through Saturdays. You can dine on seafood while you enjoy the old-time saloon atmosphere, the humor, and the cheerful music. It is open nightly, with no cover charge.

Galaxy Hut
2711 Wilson Boulevard
Arlington, VA
(703) 525–8646
www.galaxyhut.com

Galaxy Hut has built a solid reputation among fans of indie rock—and among young professionals seeking solitude from spiffy new restaurants and national chains. The place isn't much to look at, but it's one of the region's best places to catch a live music show (presented Saturday through Monday nights). When live acts aren't performing, Galaxy Hut still offers good reasons to visit—karaoke, and on Tuesdays you can bring your own iPod and take a turn as DJ.

IOTA
2832 Wilson Boulevard
Arlington, VA
(703) 522–8340
www.iotaclubandcafe.com
For live alternative country and rock music, make your way across the Potomac to IOTA, one of the region's most celebrated live music venues. Local and national acts love playing this intimate venue; it's where Washington, D.C. first grooved to the sounds of John Mayer, Jason Mraz, and Norah Jones. IOTA boasts one of the broadest demographics of any D.C.–area club—thanks in part to the "all ages" shows it hosts on weekend afternoons, catering to families with children.

Ireland's Own
132 North Royal Street
Alexandria, VA
(703) 549–4535
www.pattroysirishpub.com
Fans of live Irish-themed acoustic music, Irish food, and Irish drink can get their fill at Ireland's Own in Old Town Alexandria. St. Patrick's Day, in particular, is an occasion at this bar. This is a casual neighborhood place, comfortable for people of any age. It is open nightly, with a $5.00 cover charge on weekends.

Jaxx
6355 Rolling Road
Springfield, VA
(703) 569–5940
www.jaxxroxx.com
You wouldn't expect to find a progressive rock concert hall in suburban Virginia, especially conservative Springfield, but Jaxx is just such a place. Patrons are young college students, grunge wannabes, and others in that general age group. On occasion former big

names like Johnny Winter and Eddie Money appear. Show times determine openings, with cover charges from $10 to $20.

Lobby Lounge
1700 Tysons Boulevard
McLean, VA
(703) 506–4300
www.ritzcarlton.com
The Ritz-Carlton at Tysons Corner is a showplace of antiques, art, and Oriental rugs, and the Lobby Lounge is as lovely a refuge as the rest of the hotel. Tables are spaced for intimacy and the piano music is low key but high quality. The pianist here has a range from gospel to classic, but the playing is never intrusive. It is open nightly, with no cover charge.

Murphy's of Alexandria
713 King Street
Alexandria, VA
(703) 548–1717
www.murphyspub.com
As if it weren't cozy enough to have an intimate sweaters-and-jeans-type place along the cobbled walks of Old Town, this place also features a wood-burning fireplace and Irish music nightly. Like Ireland's Own, listed earlier, this is a hot spot on St. Patrick's Day after the parade. It is open nightly, with no cover charge.

The Shark Club
14114 Lee Highway
Centreville, VA
(703) 266–1888

8111 Lee Highway
Falls Church, VA
(703) 641–8888

8794 Sacramento Drive
Alexandria, VA
(703) 360–8283

1440 Central Park Boulevard
Fredericksburg, VA
(540) 548–2228
With four D.C.-area locations, the Shark Club

offers casual dining and billiards all under the watchful eyes of Jaws-like creatures painted on the walls. DJs spin dance music on the weekends. There are live bands and full-service restaurants at some locations. Try the salsa dance lessons on Thursdays at the Falls Church location.

Tiffany Tavern
1116 King Street
Alexandria, VA
(703) 836–8844
www.tiffanytavern.com
This cozy spot at the west end of Old Town isn't very well known outside the neighbor-hood, but it's usually crowded, thanks to the intimate space. It's the only bar in the Wash-ington area that hosts bluegrass bands every weekend. Dress down or dress up as you please. There is no cover charge.

Meet and Greet
You won't find live music at these places except on special occasions. However, you may find dancing, and, if so, we've indicated it; otherwise, the point is to check out the crowd, have a few drinks, and maybe even strike up a conversation with a stranger.

Chadwicks
203 South Strand Street
Alexandria, VA
(703) 836–4442
www.chadwicksrestaurants.com
Chadwicks is as inviting as the Georgetown original, with bars upstairs and down. On weekends, 20- and 30-somethings pack the place. Beer is the drink of choice and the dress is khakis to business suits. It is open nightly, with no cover charge.

Clyde's*
8332 Leesburg Pike
Vienna, VA (Tysons Corner)
(703) 734–1901

11905 Market Street
Reston, VA
(703) 787–6601

1700 North Beauregard Street
Alexandria, VA
(703) 820–8300
www.clydes.com
Whether you choose the location, in Alexan-dria, in Reston Town Center, or in Tysons Corner, Clyde's is a hopping place for the check-'em-out crowd. Tysons is more upscale, with the peak action on weeknights for after-business, 30-plus patrons. The decor is extravagant art nouveau, and business suits are the norm—it's a prosperous-looking bunch here. Reston and Alexandria, which are more family-oriented eateries, also have handsome, lively bars, but expect chinos rather than custom-made suits, and leggings rather than dresses. Clyde's is open nightly, with no cover charge.

Continental
1911 North Fort Myer Drive
Arlington, VA
(703) 465–7675
www.modernpoollounge.com
Welcome to one of the most unusual lounges in the area, with purple felt billiards tables, surfboard-shaped tables, columns painted like palm trees, and two silver bars sparkling with a confetti of silver glitter. Patrons may not be surprised to learn that the establish-ment was inspired by Disneyland's Tomorrow-land and Fantasyland. Depending on who's feeding it quarters, the jukebox pumps out lounge music or alternative rock. Open nightly.

Dr. Dremo's Taphouse
2001 Clarendon Boulevard
Arlington, VA
(703) 528–4660
www.drdremo.com
The eclectic, offbeat bars Bardo Rodeo and Ningaloo occupied this space before it was transformed into Dr. Dremo's Taphouse. The

new management jettisoned the small art gallery and sushi and added more pool tables.

Fast Eddie's Billiards Cafe
9687 Lee Highway
Fairfax, VA
(703) 385–7529

7255 Commerce Street
Springfield, VA
(703) 912–7529

14114 Lee Highway
Centreville, VA
(703) 266–1888
www.fasteddies.com

This is a fun hybrid of pool hall, bar, and restaurant. It's hard not to have a good time here, even if shooting pool isn't your thing. If it is, there are plenty of tables, but you can almost always count on a wait during prime time on Friday and Saturday nights. Also expect efficient, cheerful service; tasty chow; and a better singles atmosphere than one might expect. It's best to go in a small group to make it easier to meet the attractive group shooting a round at the next table. Also visit the Fast Eddie's in Washington, D.C. at 1520 K Street NW, (202) 638–6800. Fast Eddie's is open nightly, with no cover charge.

Gua-Rapo
2039 Wilson Boulevard
Arlington, VA
(703) 528–6500
latinconcepts.com/guarapo

Gua-Rapo is a recent addition to the Arlington nightlife scene, but its quick rise to success hasn't been much of a surprise. Developed by the owners of D.C. hot spots Chi-Cha Lounge and Gazuza, Gua-Rapo brings a hip Latin vibe to the Court House neighborhood of Arlington. If you arrive hungry, you'll be relieved to find an agreeable assortment of Latin-inspired tapas on the menu.

Joe Theismann's
1800 Diagonal Road
Alexandria, VA
(703) 739–0777
www.joetheismanns.com

This restaurant and bar, named after the former Redskins quarterback and current football announcer, offers great sports viewing and karaoke. On Friday nights expect a dark, clubby scene for the over-30 set. Dress ranges from casual to business suits. The Old Town location attracts a clientele that's a bit more affluent than that of the original restaurant in Baileys Crossroads, which was sold to another company. It is open nightly, with no cover charge.

P. J. Skidoos
9908 Lee Highway
Fairfax City, VA
(703) 591–4516
www.pjskidoos.com

This restaurant and bar has become something of a contemporary disco when it comes to music and the dance atmosphere. It boasts a busy club scene and rates as a prime spot for singles—professionals and students—in their 20s and 30s, not to mention anyone with a hankering for hearty munchies. There's sometimes a decent live rock band on Saturday nights. It is open nightly, with no cover charge.

Summers Grill and Sports Pub
1520 North Courthouse Road
Arlington, VA
(703) 528–8278
www.summers-restaurant.com

Summers has built a reputation in its twenty-plus-year history as the place to go to watch sports—particularly sports with strong international followings like soccer and Formula One racing. Inside you'll find a gallery of flat-screen TVs, along with an appealing selection of draft beers and classic bar fare. Don't be surprised to find the bar open on Saturday and Sunday mornings, when European fans come in droves to watch their favorite teams face off.

Sweetwater Tavern*
14250 Sweetwater Lane
Centreville, VA
(703) 449–1100

3066 Gatehouse Plaza
Falls Church, VA
(703) 645–8100

45980 Waterview Plaza
Sterling, VA
(571) 434–6500

Neither Centreville nor Falls Church are hot spots for nightlife, so Sweetwater Tavern—a restaurant and brewpub—is a welcome addition in both locations. The restaurant features very good Southwestern cuisine and sinful desserts, while the bar attracts singles and couples alike, not to mention folks who want to watch sports in a convivial atmosphere. You'll find a handsome, Wyoming-style ambience with big wrought-iron chandeliers, vaulted ceilings, and all manner of Wild West art. These are casual, suburban places, so dress down. It is open nightly, with no cover charge.

Union Street Public House*
121 South Union Street
Alexandria, VA
(703) 548–1785
www.usphalexandria.com

This has long been one of Old Town's most popular singles spots, and there seems to be no end in sight for the accolades. Crowded? Yes. But the wait that's not unusual during prime time is worth it, if only for the spirited bar ambience, the extensive and offbeat beer selections, and the friendly help. If the front bar is too much, try the often-overlooked oyster bar in back. It's smaller and less lively, but the beer is just as good and it's easier to find a seat or a quiet corner. It is open nightly, with no cover charge.

Whitlow's on Wilson
2854 Wilson Boulevard
Arlington, VA
(703) 276–9693
www.whitlows.com

If it's a young, lively neighborhood bar scene you're looking for, you'll find a lot to like in Whitlow's. It's one of the Clarendon neighborhood's most popular watering holes—a place where you can consistently find reasonably priced food and drinks, good music, and a friendly game of pool or Foosball to join.

Dinner Theater/Comedy Clubs

The Comedy Spot
4238 Wilson Boulevard
Arlington, VA
(703) 294–5233
comedyindc.com

Take a break from the bar scene and go for a good laugh instead. Located inside the Ballston Common Mall, the Comedy Spot hosts comedy acts Thursday through Monday nights, including ComedySportz, which delivers jokes and gags appropriate for audiences of all ages. In addition to the family-friendly humor, you can also find comedy hypnosis and adults-only acts.

Lazy Susan Dinner Theater
U.S. 1 at Furnace Road
Woodbridge, VA
(703) 550–7384
www.lazysusan.com

Lazy Susan has been around forever, and it remains a popular destination for residents of Northern Virginia who enjoy musicals. Dinner and the show together make for a nice evening. They are open nightly, except on Monday. Tickets are $36.95, except on Saturdays, when they cost $39.95.

SUBURBAN MARYLAND

The Maryland suburbs don't possess quaint pedestrian areas like Georgetown in Washington, D.C. or Old Town Alexandria in Virginia; as a result, there are few clubs. But that doesn't mean you can't find nightlife. There are essentially two hubs of nighttime activity in the Maryland suburbs, each radically different from the other. For affluent Montgomery County, Bethesda and Rockville have grown into a sprawling "downtown" of sorts, so it's not surprising that this urban-style suburban core offers its share of nighttime diversions. A little farther from Washington is College Park, the home of the 35,000-student University of Maryland. Here, too, the nightlife rocks, with partying students filling the bars along U.S. 1, also known as Baltimore Avenue. We've also mentioned some notable places outside both hubs.

Live Music and Dancing

Allie's Bethesda Marriott
5151 Pooks Hill Road
Bethesda, MD
(301) 897–9400
www.marriott.com

This is a sprawling hotel that draws lots of conventioneers. It's also one of the few in the Maryland suburbs to consistently offer live piano music. The crowd here is mature, and the dress is casual to business suits. This isn't a raucous piano bar, but rather a spot for conversation and easygoing entertainment. There's also a dance spot in the hotel, which can be lively when the hotel is full. It is open nightly. There is no cover charge.

Chick Hall's Surf Club
4711 Kenilworth Avenue
Bladensburg, MD
(301) 927–6310
www.chickhallssurfclub.com

You won't find many places in the D.C. Metro area that can classify themselves as "honky-tonks" in good faith. Chick's is a notable exception. Rock, country, and R&B acts take the stage here—and on weekends, you'll hear the talented Chick Hall himself playing guitar in the house band. The dance floor rocks with patrons of all ages—many of whom are regulars here.

Flanagan's Harp & Fiddle
4844 Cordell Avenue
Bethesda, MD
(301) 951–0115
www.flanagansharpandfiddle.com

Harp & Fiddle picks up where Flanagan's, a longtime Bethesda favorite, left off. Neighborhood redevelopment forced Flanagan's to close its doors, but the owners have managed to recapture much of its appeal in their latest venture, Harp & Fiddle. Like its predecessor, Harp & Fiddle features acoustic and folk music in a comfy pub setting. Food isn't bad here either, and the dress is casual, so it's a great stop for a lazy weekend evening or a bite after work. It is open nightly, with no cover charge.

The Royal Mile Pub
2407 Price Avenue
Wheaton, MD
(301) 946–4511
www.royalmilepub.com

This attractive and comfortable oasis in downtown Wheaton features live Celtic music and jazz four to five times a month. Every third Sunday, a traditional Irish session is led by well-known local musician Dennis Botzer. Most Saturdays also feature traditional Irish or Scottish music. Rarely is there a cover charge. The pub is open seven nights a week and has a surprisingly interesting menu. Berry salad on wild greens with goat's cheese isn't your usual pub fare. The owner's son is a culinary school graduate and has helped shape the menu.

Meet and Greet

Dave & Buster's
White Flint Shopping Center
11301 Rockville Pike
Rockville, MD
(301) 230–5151
www.daveandbusters.com

Dave & Buster's is a multimedia, multisensation event. It's almost too much to absorb in one visit. An 11-screen video wall in the Players Bar, a mystery theater with audience participation on weekends, virtual reality, billiards, and all manner of games attract families, singles, and date-night couples. Dave & Buster's serves weekday lunches until 5:00

P.M., dinners until late into the night, giant servings, giant drinks . . . and the list goes on. Dress is casual, though the neighborhood is one of the most upscale in the country, so you don't have to worry about being over-dressed if you've just come from work. It is open nightly, with no cover charge except on Friday and Saturday after 10:00 P.M., when the cover is $5.00.

Europa Lounge
7820 Norfolk Avenue
Bethesda, MD
(301) 657-1607
www.cafeeuropabethesda.com
Bethesda's burgeoning restaurant scene has given rise to a handful of clubs that are per-fect after-dinner gathering places. Europa fits right into the mix—an upscale lounge that's perfect for sipping a martini or glass of wine when it's just too early to call it a night. You'll also find a soothing soundtrack of jazz music, and weekends frequently bring live perform-ances by top local talent.

Glen Echo Spanish Ballroom
7300 MacArthur Boulevard
Glen Echo, MD
(301) 492-6229
www.glenechopark.org
Opened in 1933, Glen Echo Park's gloriously restored Spanish Ballroom is unlike any other nightlife venue you'll find in Metro D.C. It's a throwback to an earlier era, a gathering place for seasoned ballroom, swing, and folk dancers of all ages, as well as those who are interested in learning a few steps. The music is always performed live—sometimes by large orchestras and other times by small combos.

The Hangar Club
6410 Old Branch Avenue
Camp Springs, MD
(301) 449-6970
www.hangarclub.com

How do you categorize a place like this? We haven't included strip joints for male clients, so why the Hangar Club, which features male strippers on Thursday to Saturday nights? Well, it's the only club we know in the area that caters almost exclusively to straight women, so it's unique. Its decency level, as some might put it, is a notch above many of the clubs for men featuring female dancers—here they don't take quite everything off, but it's indeed enough to send the female patrons into a tizzy. Dancing and gawking—and plenty of high-pitched screaming—are the norm here.

This cavernous establishment hosts hun-dreds of bachelorette parties and girls-night-out get-togethers each year. More than 30 brands of beer help keep the whistles wet. It is open Friday and Saturday, with an admission charge of $16 in advance, $18 at the door, and $25 for premium seating.

Hollywood Contemporary Ballroom
2126 Industrial Parkway
Silver Spring, MD
(301) 622-5494
www.hollywoodballroom.com
Dancing is the point here. It's a 7,200-square-foot, floating maple dance floor, where ball-room lessons (rumba, swing, tango, fox trot) are offered each night for an hour until the dancing-in-earnest takes over. The group is old, young, and everything in between—peo-ple who love to dance and those who want to learn. There are also special nights just for singles. Dress is mostly casual, but don't be surprised if a couple in formal wear float by. It is open Wednesday and Friday through Sun-day. Cover charges vary.

Jokes On Us Comedy Club
312 Main Street
Laurel, MD
(240) 568-5081
www.jokesonuscomedyclub.com

In stuffy, button-down Washington, things can seem a bit humorless at times. There are few comedy clubs here, but that doesn't mean people don't like to laugh. Featuring local comedians to nationally known acts, Jokes On Us is a recent addition to the Washington area's paltry assortment of comedy offerings. It has two comedy shows nightly Friday through Sunday, with ticket prices ranging from $10 to $30.

94th Aero Squadron
5240 Paint Branch Parkway
College Park, MD
(301) 699–9400

This dance club's intriguing aviation/military theme—a nod to the nearby College Park Airport, which is the nation's oldest in continuous operation—includes a prop plane outside and a World War I ambulance inside. A mix of white-collar patrons and, of course, plenty of students from the nearby University of Maryland helps keep the place hopping. There is no cover charge, and it is open seven nights a week.

Dinner Theaters

Blair Mansion Restaurant
7711 Eastern Avenue
Silver Spring, MD
(301) 588–6646
www.mansionmysteries.com

This restaurant, which for years was a special occasion family place, fell out of style a few years back, but it caught a second wind when the management dreamed up the Blair Mansion Mysteries. These shows will never see Broadway, but they should appeal to the whole family with lots of laughs and audience fun. Ticket prices include full dinner, tip, tax, and even hors d'oeuvres. Performances are held every Friday and Saturday and occasionally on Thursday and Sunday. Tickets are $54.95, including tax and gratuity. (See the Kidstuff chapter for information about Now This! Kids! performances here.)

SHOPPING

If you're a shopaholic looking to kick your habit, forget about coming to the Nation's Capital! Whatever the object of your desire, you're certain to find it here. Metro Washington's thousands of retail establishments include everything from megamalls, factory outlets, and neighborhood shopping centers to department stores, tony designer boutiques, discount retailers, bulk-buy membership warehouses, and antiques havens.

In this chapter we offer a shopping tour of Metro Washington, spotlighting major malls and popular retail districts as well as some of the D.C. area's most interesting specialty stores, with categories listed alphabetically.

MALLS AND PRIME SHOPPING DISTRICTS

Metro Washington

Washington, D.C. boasts shopping options in almost every corner of town, from Chevy Chase to Northeast. They're thriving places, attracting both tourists and city residents.

For example, Connecticut Avenue from Dupont Circle south to Pennsylvania Avenue NW and the blocks surrounding it offer a delightful mix of boutiques, salons, bookstores, and very pricey designer shops, such as Burberry. Farther east, Macy's takes up a city block at 12th and G Streets NW. The area also includes plenty of smaller stores and restaurants, including H&M and West Elm, as well as the convenient Metro Center Metrorail station.

Georgetown's Wisconsin Avenue and M Street NW serve as the hub for dozens of boutiques, antiques shops, bookstores, art galleries, restaurants, and jewelry stores stretching north to New Mexico Avenue, south to K Street, east to 28th Street, and west to 34th Street. Don't miss an excursion here, if only to people-watch and window shop. Unique local retail concepts are common to the city's emerging neighborhoods, where low rent and a strong sense of community have kept major chains away. You'll find funky home furnishings and used-clothing stores in the trendy Logan Circle neighborhood, particularly along 14th and U Streets. New boutiques have taken root near Eastern Market on Capitol, a terrific shopping destination in its own right.

Besides the great districts we've described, Washington's malls are destinations in and of themselves. Here are some of the biggest and best.

Mazza Gallerie
5300 Wisconsin Avenue NW
Washington, DC
(202) 966–6114
www.mazzagallerie.com
This glass-fronted structure is home to upscale retailer Neiman Marcus. You'll find more than 20 other posh stores and boutiques here—including Pampillonia Jewelers, Williams-Sonoma Grande Cuisine, the Saks Fifth Avenue Men's Store, Krön Chocolatiers, and AMC's 11-screen luxury theater features leather seating and cafe meals. Friendship Heights is the closest Metro station.

The Old Post Office Pavilion
1100 Pennsylvania Avenue NW
Washington, DC
(202) 289–4224
www.oldpostofficedc.com
Rescued from demolition in the 1960s, this historic destination offers the city's second-highest vantage point. Take the glass elevator up to the 315-foot clock/bell tower and enjoy the view! The pavilion, near the Federal

Triangle Metro stop, also features more than a dozen souvenir shops, services, and a large food court.

The Shops at Chevy Chase Pavilion
5335 Wisconsin Avenue NW
Washington, DC
(202) 686–5335
www.ccpavilion.com

A lot of people think this mall, and its neighbor across the street—Mazza Gallerie—are in Maryland, but they're right over the line. And they're top of the line, too. The Pavilion houses fashion bargain-hunter haunt Steinmart, as well as a number of artsy boutiques for women's clothing, housewares, gourmet foods, and shoes. Anchored by the popular Pottery Barn, the mall features more than 45 businesses, including Embassy Suites, J. Crew, Talbots, the Cheesecake Factory, Starbucks, and a food court. Take Metro to the Friendship Heights station.

The Shops at Georgetown Park
3222 M Street NW
Washington, DC
(202) 298–5577
www.shopsatgeorgetownpark.com

There is no question that this is downtown's (as opposed to Chevy Chase, D.C.'s) most posh and complete mall. It's right in the heart of Georgetown and features four floors decorated in lavish Victorian style. Standard mall stores here include the likes of the upscale Ann Taylor, Anthropologie, and J. Crew. The mall also houses businesses like New York–based Intermix and Fornash designs, featuring bags and gifts by a D.C. designer. If you get hungry, stop at one of eight eateries discreetly tucked away on the bottom floor, or grab a quick bite at gourmet grocery, cafe, and carryout Dean & DeLuca. The mall's multilevel underground garage offers discounted parking: $1.00 an hour during the first two hours, with a $10 purchase.

i A new Web site, e-newsletter, www.discount.com, is the ultimate resource for serious shoppers in the region, packed with information on sample sales, trunk shows, and new store openings.

The Shops at National Place
1331 Pennsylvania Avenue NW
Washington, DC
(202) 662–1250

This mall adjacent to the massive J. W. Marriott Hotel and the National Press Building bustles with 60 shops, including Filene's Basement and fascinating independent boutiques, mostly featuring women's clothing and jewelry. Office workers crowd the big food court during the noon hour. The National Press Club is adjacent to this facility, adding more shops to the mix.

Union Station
Massachusetts Avenue and First Street NE
Washington, DC
(202) 289–1908
www.unionstationdc.com

Housed in the glorious 1908 beaux arts train station, the mall here features national chain clothing boutiques, a bookstore, a music store, a nine-screen cinema, restaurants, and a food court—more than 100 shops in all. A separate section, the East Hall, offers a variety of jewelry and craft stalls, many selling unique ethnic merchandise. You'll find souvenirs and memorabilia at the U.S. Mint shop (specializing in unique coin-themed items), and Made in America (brass and pewter Washington-themed desk accessories, patriotic gifts, jewelry, and apparel).

Despite its additional role as a shopping hub, Union Station chugs on as a working railroad station too, accommodating not only Metrorail but several commuter lines and Amtrak (see the Getting Around the Metro Area chapter). Although the station operates around the clock and the restaurants and theaters stay open fairly late, the stores operate

Dating to 1873, Eastern Market at 7th and C Streets SE, in Washington D.C., is the city's only remaining original public market. COURTESY WASHINGTON, D.C. CONVENTION AND TOURISM CORPORATION

during regular mall retail hours. (So much for that 3:00 A.M. credit card fix.) Visit during December, when Union Station holds its annual Christmas in Norway celebration and colossal model trains exhibit. (Our Kidstuff chapter's dining guide describes the mall's family-oriented restaurants and food court.)

Northern Virginia

The most varied and interesting shopping district in Northern Virginia isn't even a mall—it's Old Town Alexandria. Begin at the easternmost end of King Street and work your way up. Most intersecting streets, including major thoroughfare Washington Street, also contain a seemingly endless array of stores. You'll find antiques shops, clothing boutiques for kids and adults, bookstores, art galleries, craft shops, gourmet food emporiums, and, when you get hungry, all manner of restaurants (see the Restaurants chapter).

The flagship of the area is the waterfront Torpedo Factory Art Center and the adjacent minimall, at the intersection of Union and King. (See our Arts chapter for more information.) Local artists feature their work in side-by-side galleries, all housed under one roof. Painters, sculptors, photographers, potters, and jewelers all showcase their talents here. On weekends look for street performers who enjoy entertaining the passersby.

Some of Old Town's most popular and charming shops include Fetch Dog & Cat Bakery-Boutique, 101A South St. Asaph Street, (703) 518–5188, specializing in all-natural, organic pet treats and upscale accessories; Kingsbury Chocolates, 1017 King Street, (703) 548–2800, a purveyor of fine homemade chocolates and confections; and Why Not?, 200 King Street, (703) 548–4420, an enchanting children's shop packed with fine clothing, toys, books, and one-of-a-kind gifts. The Winterthur Museum Store, 207 King Street, (703) 684–6092, an offshoot of the store at the Winterthur Museum in Delaware, stocks elegant American decorative-art house-

ware reproductions from 1640 to 1860. (See our Kidstuff chapter for information about children's specialty stores in Old Town.) Arlington's Clarendon is a popular destination for city dwellers who hop on the Metro's Orange Line for easy access to Crate and Barrel, the Apple Store, and the Container Store, along with dozens of specialty shops.

In the northwestern part of the county, Reston Town Center (off Reston Parkway between the Dulles Toll Road and Baron Cameron Avenue; www.restontowncenter .com) resembles a fresh downtown business district, with its pedestrian-friendly layout, striking architecture, and numerous public gathering spots, including a large fountain. Nearly 60 shops and restaurants—mostly specialty retailers such as the Gap, Banana Republic, Victoria's Secret, and craft boutiques—line the broad avenues. The food scene includes outdoor cafes like Clyde's and Paolo's Ristorante (see Restaurants). The Equity Office Garage features 550 free parking spaces as well as retail stores and restaurants.

Still growing, Town Center also contains office space, residential areas (condo mania), a 13-screen cinema, and the posh Hyatt Regency Reston Town Center. The open-air Equity Office Pavilion houses free concerts during the summer and an outdoor skating rink during the winter (see the Parks and Recreation chapter).

Not far from Reston, rapidly growing Loudoun County boasts one of the area's newest regional malls, a large outlet center, and lots of big shopping plazas, especially in the Highway 7 corridor that includes the communities of Ashburn, Sterling, and Sterling Park.

You'll also still find small towns and villages alive with their own brand of retail activity. Historic downtown Leesburg (intersection of Highways 7 and 15) offers more than 100 merchants, primarily specialty retailers stretching along Market and King Streets. (See the Antiques section in this chapter.)

Virginia's Prince William County offers two fun and funky shopping districts. Old Town

Manassas (Highway 29, 7.5 miles off I–66 in the city's downtown area), features nearly two dozen merchants, mostly of the crafts and antiques variety. Also in Prince William County, the historic riverfront community of Occoquan (just off I–95, about 10 miles south of the Capital Beltway, but also accessible from the extreme southern end of Highway 123) boasts more than 100 merchants in a charming Victorian setting.

Northern Virginians do most of their shopping at malls, however, and they have several from which to choose.

Ballston Common Mall
4238 Wilson Boulevard, at
North Glebe Road
Arlington, VA
(703) 243–8808
www.ballston-common.com

Just a 1-block walk from the Ballston Metro station (Orange Line) at Fairfax Drive and North Stuart Street, the mall features 136 stores, including anchor Macy's. The ground level of the four-story mall boasts a food court. There's also the Regal Cinemas Ballston Common 12, a posh movie theater featuring stadium seating and state-of-the-art sound.

Shops include fashion and accessory stores like Claire's and Rainbow, and specialty shops such as the Official Washington Redskins Store and Agape Bears. Among the many restaurants, you'll find Texas Bar-B-Q Company and trendy Rock Bottom Restaurant & Brewery.

The Crystal City Shops
U.S. 1, between 15th and 23rd Streets
Arlington, VA
(703) 922–4636
www.thecrystalcityshops.com

In the concrete and steel maze known as Crystal City, just off Jefferson Davis Highway (Route 1), are Crystal City Shops North (on Crystal Drive, between 15th and 18th Streets) and Crystal City Plaza Shops (corner of Crystal Drive and 23rd Street), two subterranean shopping experiences linked by a climate-controlled walkway. A new outdoor "Main Street" retail area is in the same vicinity. Visit more than 130 stores, cafes, and restaurants. Specialty stores include Puppet Heaven and Khoury Brothers Fine Jewelers, as well as Ship's Hatch, carrying hard-to-find nautical items. Because these stores are covered by high-rise apartment and office buildings, they're hard to find, so it's good they're connected to Metrorail's Crystal City station (Blue and Yellow Lines) at 18th Street and Jefferson Davis Highway. Parking in two underground garages is free on weekends and after 4:30 P.M. weekdays.

Dulles Town Center
21100 Dulles Town Circle
Dulles, VA
(703) 404–7120
www.shopdullestowncenter.com

Just up the road from Washington Dulles International Airport is a huge, two-story shopping complex. Anchored by Macy's, Lord & Taylor, JCPenney, Sears, and Nordstrom, the mall also houses H&M and around 185 specialty shops, restaurants, and entertainment.

Fair Oaks Mall
Intersection of U.S. 50 and I–66
Fairfax, VA
(703) 359–8300
www.shopfairoaksmall.com

Macy's, Lord & Taylor, Sears, and JCPenney anchor this megamall of more than 150 stores and services, including an office for laser eye surgery. Specialty retailers include the likes of Papyrus (gifts and stationery), Sephora (cosmetics), People's Pottery, and standard mall favorites like the Gap, Talbots, Godiva, Jos. A. Bank, and Bath & Body Works. The mall features several dining options but no food court. Visit during the holiday season for the annual display of lifelike stuffed animals, adored by kids.

If you can't find what you're looking for at Fair Oaks, supplement your shopping spree at several shopping centers within a couple of miles. The neighboring Fair Lakes area includes a two-story Kohl's department store, featuring clothing and housewares, at 12551 Fairlakes Circle, Fairfax. Right next door to Kohl's, Galyan's offers just about anything you'd ever want in the way of sporting or outdoor goods. Down the street, you'll find Fairlakes Shopping Center, with a Toys "R" Us Kids World superstore, Target, Wal-Mart, World Market, and Designer Shoe Warehouse.

Fashion Centre at Pentagon City
1100 South Hayes Street
Arlington, VA
(703) 415–2400
www.fashioncentrepentagon.com
Arlington County's premier retail showcase, Pentagon City, as it's customarily called, is one of the area's most exciting and dynamic shopping showplaces, a visual wonderland complete with towering skylights, palm trees, a sunlit food court, six-screen cinema, and 170 stores spread over four levels. Anchor tenants are Macy's and Nordstrom; specialty shops include the likes of Coach, bebe, Victoria's Secret, Bath & Body Works, and MAC Cosmetics. If all that walking and buying has left you too exhausted to drive home, the snazzy Ritz-Carlton Hotel is right next door. You'll find dozens more shops at the adjacent Pentagon Centre, such as Hudson Trail Outfitters, World Market, and Designer Shoe Warehouse, plus an ice-skating rink. You can take the Metro right to the mall, making it a popular shopping destination for commuters.

Landmark Mall
5801 Duke Street at I–395
Alexandria, VA
(703) 354–8405
www.landmarkmall.com
Alexandria's only enclosed shopping mall is Landmark Mall, which some residents of neighboring Fairfax County happily call their own as well. The three-level mall offers a wealth of (free) covered and surface parking and some 120 stores and restaurants (but no movie theaters), including anchor tenants Macy's, Lord & Taylor, and Sears. You'll find

Some local shopping malls offer valet parking, a feature you may find handy during the busy holiday season.

specialty stores like As Seen on TV and mall favorites like the Gap and Old Navy. Special programs include a summer farmers' market and mall concerts. The mall is conveniently located right off I–395.

Springfield Mall Regional Shopping Center
Intersection of Franconia and Loisdale Roads
Springfield, VA
(703) 971–3000
www.springfieldmall.com
This mall houses more than 230 stores, including three anchors, Macy's, JCPenney, and Target. Largely geared toward families, it features game arcades, a play tower, and a beautiful carousel. It also sponsors more than 20 family-oriented events annually, including a monthly kids' club and, during the holiday season, a store just for children. The mall offers two food courts, a multiscreen movie theater, and specialty stores like the Gap, Aeropostale men's and women's clothing, and the Virginia Department of Transportation Informational Store. (See the Getting Around chapter.)

Conveniently, just across Frontier Drive (by Macy's) from the mall is a mini shopping center. It's anchored by Best Buy, one of the growing number of retailers offering rock-bottom prices on major appliances and consumer electronics. You'll also find Kohl's just minutes away.

Tysons Corner Center
Intersection of Highways 123 and 7
Vienna, VA
(703) 893–9400, (888) 2TYSONS
www.shoptysons.com
Tysons Corner is one of the shining jewels in Fairfax County's economic crown. Shoppers from throughout the region flock to Tysons Corner Center and its more than 290 stores, including Nordstrom, Bloomingdale's, Lord &

Taylor, and L.L. Bean, the Maine-based catalog company.

Recent additions include Mexx, West Elm, Barnes & Noble, Esprit, and Urban Outfitters. The mall's restaurants include the megapopular Rainforest Cafe, described in our Kidstuff chapter.

Tysons is one of the area's oldest shopping malls (dating to 1968), but you wouldn't know it. Like so many of its peers, Tysons experienced a rebirth during the mid-1980s and a subsequent major addition in 2005. Among the most welcome changes were the addition of parking decks and the conversion of underground truck tunnels into rows of specialty shops.

Tysons Galleria
2001 International Drive
McLean, VA
(703) 827–7700
www.tysonsgalleria.com
Just across Chain Bridge Road (Route 123) from Tysons Corner Center and adjacent to the Ritz-Carlton Hotel, this 100-store showplace is upscale to the nth degree. Its anchors include Macy's, Saks Fifth Avenue, and Neiman Marcus. Other retailers include Betsey Johnson, Burberry, Lacoste, Hugo Boss, Elan salon and day spa, and the only Vidal Sassoon salon in the D.C. market. The restaurants here are first-rate, including the likes of Maggiano's Little Italy, Legal Sea Foods, and P.F. Chang's China Bistro.

If the two Tysons malls don't hold your interest, cross Highway 7 and you'll discover a series of strip malls housing car dealers, restaurants, hotels, specialty stores, and large chain outlets such as Borders Books & Music and Marshall's.

Suburban Maryland

Maryland's got malls all right, but it also has some of the priciest shopping streets around.

D.C.'s answer to Michigan Avenue, the Chevy Chase Shopping District features more than 200 stores and restaurants along Wisconsin Avenue, where Chevy Chase, Maryland, and the Chevy Chase district of D.C. meet. At 5555 Wisconsin Avenue, Saks Fifth Avenue has anchored the upscale area for more than three decades. This huge, stately store possesses almost all the cachet of the original on New York's Fifth Avenue, and its very presence has served as a catalyst for dozens of other exclusive shops to locate nearby. The new Collection at Chevy Chase brought many of the top names in luxury shopping together in one place (see this chapter's listing). Across Wisconsin Avenue you'll find women's shops where clerks bring dresses out from the back for you to try on, and service is always the utmost in personal courtesy. Saks-Jandel, 5510 Wisconsin Avenue, is a Washington retailer known worldwide as a premier furrier and designer boutique. Wander south from there, or cross the street, and you'll be immersed in yet more glamor, culminating in D.C.'s Mazza Gallerie and the Shops at Chevy Chase Pavilion (see this chapter's listings), just across the state line and only 2 blocks away. The Friendship Heights Metro station is right next door.

Drive north from Chevy Chase on Wisconsin Avenue and you'll hit Bethesda. No matter which way you look, you'll see blocks and blocks of stores selling furniture, Oriental rugs, furs, art, clothing, shoes, toys, books, and anything else you can dream up. This shopper's paradise goes on for approximately 2 square miles, culminating at Wilson Boulevard to the west and Cordell Avenue to the north.

No matter how great a shopping district, on a blowy winter day or a sticky summer afternoon, a mall can be a refuge. Here are some of the biggest and best in metro Maryland.

Beltway Plaza Mall
6100 Greenbelt Road
Greenbelt, MD
(301) 345–1500
www.beltwayplazamall.com
Serving nearby University of Maryland and Prince George's County, this bargain-conscious mall features stores like Target,

Marshalls, Burlington Coat Factory, and Value City. Children can play games and ride rides at Jeepers! indoor amusement park, and adults can work out at a Gold's Gym with a glass-enclosed basketball court. As an added convenience, the mall boasts the area's largest Giant Food grocery. In all, the mall houses more than 100 fashion and specialty stores as well as 14 movie theaters.

The Collection at Chevy Chase
5471-5481 Wisconsin Avenue
(301) 215–4122
www.thecollectionatchevychase.com
The Collection opened its doors in 2005 in the hopes that the region's fashion-hungry population would need no longer travel to New York for haute couture. Boasting tenants like Barneys Co-Op, MaxMara, Jimmy Choo, Cartier, and Bulgari, the shopping development has dubbed itself the "Rodeo Drive of the East Coast." Even if the price tags are beyond your budget, it's worth a trip to see the spectacular fashions, the beautiful people, and the stores' remarkable designs.

Lakeforest
701 Russell Avenue
Gaithersburg, MD
(301) 840–5840
www.shoplakeforest.com
In northern Montgomery County, two-story Lakeforest Mall offers anchor stores Lord & Taylor, Macy's, Sears, and JCPenney, plus a whopping 160 other stores, five theaters, and more than a dozen restaurants. Specialty stores are along the lines of Ann Taylor, Talbots, and Brookstone. The mall is sister to Fair Oaks Mall in Fairfax, Virginia (see earlier listing).

Westfield Shoppingtown Montgomery Mall
7101 Democracy Boulevard
Bethesda, MD
(301) 469–6025
www.westfield.com/montgomery
With 183 specialty stores, Montgomery Mall may require a full day to explore. Check out

i Many area department stores offer discounted shopping days for senior citizens. Some malls also feature monthly senior events, such as free movies or health programs.

anchors Nordstrom, Sears, and Macy's, along with specialty stores like Crate and Barrel, J. Crew, Guess?, Ann Taylor, and the Limited. The mall also houses a movie theater and restaurants like California Pizza Kitchen and Legal Sea Foods. Youngsters love cruising the mall in complimentary strollers resembling red sports cars.

Westfield Shoppingtown Wheaton Plaza Shopping Center
11160 Viers Mill Road
Wheaton, MD
(301) 946–3200
www.westfield.com/wheaton
This mall houses more than 120 stores, including anchors Macy's, JCPenney, and Target. It features the usual mall specialty stores, as well as cinemas and several restaurants. Wheaton Plaza underwent remodeling in 2000.

White Flint
11301 Rockville Pike
North Bethesda, MD
(301) 468–5777
www.shopwhiteflint.com
Anchored by Bloomingdale's, Lord & Taylor, and a giant Borders Books & Music and Cafe, the three-level upscale mall houses 100 stores and restaurants. In addition to mainstream stores like the Gap and Banana Republic, White Flint also features the trendy adult amusement center/restaurant Dave & Buster's (see the Nightlife chapter), a five-theater Loews Cineplex, and the Roxsan Day Spa. The mall holds annual programs such as camp, college, and bridal expos, and offers a VIP frequent shoppers program.

OUTLET MALLS

They literally bring 'em in by the busloads at outlet malls, particularly huge Potomac Mills near Woodbridge, Virginia, and its sibling, Arundel Mills in nearby Arundel County, Maryland. Because people are willing to drive long distances to visit these places, and because there aren't too many of them in Metro Washington, we haven't broken them down by geographic region, but we've listed them alphabetically. All of the following destinations are within an hour of the Washington area.

Arundel Mills
7000 Arundel Mills Circle
Hanover, MD
(410) 540–5110
www.arundelmills.com
Although slightly smaller than its Virginia counterpart, Arundel Mills also specializes in name-brand outlet stores, including some places you won't find anywhere else in the region. This lively, colorful mall features fun offerings like Medieval Times Dinner & Tournament and Dave & Buster's Grand Sports Cafe. Anchors include the 130,000-square-foot Bass Pro Shops Outdoor World, featuring everything for fishing and hunting enthusiasts; Off 5th–Saks 5th Avenue Outlet; Books-A-Million; Old Navy; and Muvico Egyptian 24 Theaters, the area's largest movie theater, which even features a children's playroom. Among clothing and specialty stores you'll find H&M, a Banana Republic Factory Store, Ann Taylor Loft, Jones New York Country, Skechers USA, and Kirkland's Outlet. Grab a bite to eat at the large food court.

Leesburg Corner Premium Outlets
241 Fort Evans Road NE, at Highway 7 and U.S. 15
Leesburg, VA
(703) 737–3071
www.premiumoutlets.com
This outdoor outlet center features 110 stores, including designer clothing names like Barneys New York Outlet, Off 5th–Saks Fifth Avenue, Kenneth Cole, Tommy Hilfiger, Polo Ralph Lauren, Liz Claiborne, and Burberry. Other specialty stores feature housewares, country decorating accessories, party goods, jewelry and hair accessories, and gourmet food items. Eat at the mall's five-eatery food court, or at one of many restaurants nearby.

Potomac Mills
2700 Potomac Mills Circle
near Woodbridge, VA
(703) 496–9301
www.potomacmills.com
It says something about the power of shopping when one of the most popular tourist destinations in history- and scenery-rich Virginia is an outlet mall, namely Potomac Mills. Several million people shop here annually.

Just 12 miles south of Washington off I-95 (you can't miss the signs), Potomac Mills more than lives up to its billing as a paradise for shoppers, especially those with a penchant for savings. More than 200 off-price and outlet stores include the likes of L.L. Bean, Off 5th–Saks Fifth Avenue Outlet, Polo Ralph Lauren, Tommy Hilfiger, Nautica, and Nordstrom Rack. You'll also find Old Navy, T. J. Maxx, Marshalls, and the Sports Authority. A 15-screen theater provides entertainment. Potomac Mills also offers more than 20 restaurants and food-court eateries and full concierge service, including foreign currency exchange.

Swedish furniture retailer IKEA, previously one of Potomac Mills's biggest anchor stores, now occupies a building just a few feet outside the mall. With 300,000 square feet of retail space, double the size of the old location, IKEA features more than 10,000 furnishings, housewares, toys, accessories, and gourmet food items. The store even showcases its products in model homelike settings. The restaurant serves delicious Swedish meatballs and other specialties as well as children's meals. While parents shop, kids can hang out in a large play area with a Swedish farmhouse theme.

Prime Outlets Hagerstown
495 Prime Outlets Boulevard
Hagerstown, MD
(888) 883–6288
www.primeoutlets.com

Conveniently located just off I–70 West, this collection of more than 100 outlet stores features such names as Gap, Bass, Black and Decker, Jones New York, Brooks Brothers, Polo Ralph Lauren, and Dexter. Folks in the far reaches of Montgomery County may find this place more convenient than the Virginia centers.

ANTIQUES DISTRICTS

Washingtonians have an insatiable appetite for antique paintings, furniture, and bric-a-brac, as demonstrated by the numerous districts and shops specializing in such merchandise. Maybe folks are inspired by the many historic buildings and neighborhoods in the region, or maybe they've just got to have accessories to accent the conservative colonial architecture prominent in even the newest homes. The region offers antiques emporiums for the most serious of collectors as well as those who just like to dabble.

Antiques shops often buy at public auctions, then mark up the items as much as 100 percent, a necessity when you consider that they must pay rent, salaries, insurance, and all the other incidentals associated with owning a business. Still, antiques shops are a good place to get an education on quality and construction. Many are sleepy little stores where the proprietors are happy to share their knowledge. Owners realize that a browser today may be a paying customer tomorrow, so don't be shy about asking questions.

If variety is what you're after, you'll want to stroll through one of Washington's several antiques districts. One of the foremost is Georgetown in Washington, D.C., which has stores on every block offering serious furniture and accessories like grandfather clocks, nineteenth-century paintings, and sterling. These are the shops that furnish those man-

i Turn a day trip into a weekend getaway when visiting some of the popular outlet malls in Pennsylvania and West Virginia—maybe you can even fit in some skiing.

sions hidden along the side streets, so expect to fork over major bucks.

If your budget is more restrained, you might venture to Howard Avenue in Kensington, Maryland. This is one of the foremost antiques districts in the mid-Atlantic, with store after store featuring genuine antiques, reproductions, lighting, and other accessories. It's serious, but not as rarefied as Georgetown. Head to the lower, warehouse end of Howard Avenue for serious antiques shopping, especially if you are looking for big pieces and a wider selection. The downtown Antique Row, by contrast, has lots of cute, smaller shops full of collectibles. On the streets branching out from Howard, you'll discover furniture makers and restoration experts who provide value for the money. Nothing here is cheap, but the quality is good and the service excellent.

In Virginia, Loudoun County is making an effort to become the antiques capital of the Old Dominion. You'll find well-stocked shops throughout historic downtown Leesburg. Along the western stretches of U.S. 50 in Loudoun, hunt-country delights are the name of the game in the Middleburg Historic Shopping District. The tiny burg offers a fair number of stores for its size, many along Washington and Madison Streets. Middleburg's antiques specialties run the gamut from hunt prints and accessories to period furniture and jewelry.

The cobbled streets of Old Town Alexandria in Virginia will lead you to dozens of antiques shops. King Street from the west end of town to the river offers stores that stock everything from genuine Persian rugs (pre-embargo antiques) to French, English, and American period furniture. The streets intersecting King (Washington, Asaph, Royal), as well as those parallel to it (Cameron, Prince), likewise have many specialty antiques stores with merchandise such as chandeliers, mirrors, tableware, and art. Quality varies from store to store, and the search here could easily occupy several days, depending on how long you linger at each shop.

For a real antiquing adventure, try your hand at an auction. One of the most popular auction houses is downtown Washington, D.C.'s Adam A. Weschler & Son, Inc. (909 E Street NW, 202–628–1281, www.weschlers .com). Since 1890, Weschler's has been a premier spot for those interested in fine antique furniture, jewelry, paintings, and decorative items. Auctions take place every Tuesday, and the business also holds special catalogue events. This highly reputable house offers some very nice pieces, but the people who shop here—including dealers—usually know what they're doing, so bargains may be snapped up from under your nose if you're an amateur.

You can also sift through someone else's treasures at some of the region's outdoor markets. Join the local antiquing crowd each Sunday at the Georgetown Flea Market (www .georgetownfleamarket.com, 202–775–FLEA), a longtime Georgetown fixture that has relocated to Arlington, Virginia. Antiques dealers fill the parking lot opposite the Court House Metro station with jewelry, furniture, and other treasures. The market is open year-round from 8:00 A.M. to 4:00 P.M. Antiques are also part of the appeal at Capitol Hill's Eastern Market, which plays host to vendors and treasure-hunters on weekends.

BOOKSTORES AND NEWSSTANDS

We thought it appropriate to offer a handy guide to some of the area's best bookstores and newsstands—those places with such a wealth of resources (including maps, out-of-town newspapers, and local see-and-do/history guides) that they're invaluable to newcomers. Visit them often enough and you'll make friends with some of the most helpful and knowledgeable people around.

Remember, too, that Washington's many museums and universities feature gift shops and bookshops worth exploring. We've listed a couple of noteworthy ones in this category as well as in the section on museum shops.

Of course, you've heard of the large chains—and they're wonderful in terms of size and variety of stock. In Washington, Maryland, and Virginia, you'll find numerous branches, mostly in malls, of superstores like B. Dalton Bookseller, Barnes & Noble, Borders Books & Music, and Tower Records and Books. Most of these places have cushy reading chairs, coffee shops, and plenty of special events—they're great places to while away a lazy afternoon. You'll find one nearby whether you're in Washington, Maryland, or Virginia, so consult the phone directory.

Aside from these chains, Washington is also blessed with a wealth of fine independent bookstores, many of which offer similarly inviting atmospheres. The following are among those we especially enjoy.

Washington, D.C.

ADC Map & Travel Center
1636 I Street NW
Washington, DC
(202) 628–2608, (800) 544–2659
www.adcmap.com
This little shop has been around for about forty years and continues to be a popular browsing spot for those who love to travel. Not only does the store carry every kind of map imaginable, it also features a nice selection of travel books, including narratives and guides. The store is closed on Sundays. Located on Farragut Square, the store is right next door to the Farragut West Metro station.

Bridge Street Books
2814 Pennsylvania Avenue NW
Washington, DC
(202) 965–5200
www.bridgestreetbooks.com
This intimate bookstore at the edge of Georgetown specializes in humanities and social science topics such as politics, cultural

theory, literature, philosophy, poetry, and history. It's open daily.

Chapters: A Literary Bookstore
445 11th Street NW
Washington, DC
(202) 737–5553
www.chaptersliterary.com
Chapters specializes in poetry, literary fiction, and foreign language books. Recently moved from its former K Street location, Chapters also has a small gift section, as well as books on tape. It's open daily. Metro Center is the closest Metro stop.

Franz Bader Bookstore
1911 I Street NW
Washington, DC
(202) 337–5440
If it's a gorgeous picture book you're after, this is the place. Franz Bader specializes in books on the visual arts—design, graphics, photography, and architecture—and most of their selections are breathtaking. Even if you don't buy, this place is worth a look for the sheer beauty of the photographs you'll see. It's closed on Sundays. Farragut West is the closest Metro station.

Glover Books & Music
2319 Wisconsin Avenue NW
Washington, DC
(202) 338–8100
Not only does this store have a wide selection of popular books for adults and children, it also features sheet music, videos, computer software, and tickets for shows and sports events. Conveniently located in the cozy Glover Park neighborhood of upper Georgetown, Glover's is open daily.

International Language Centre
1753 Connecticut Avenue NW
Washington, DC
(202) 332–2894
www.newsinform.com
If you're a foreign tourist in Washington, you may want to stop in here for books, maga-

Scoop up bargains at local estate and yard sales held on Saturday mornings throughout the metro area.

zines, videos, and newspapers in more than 200 languages. If you're an American going abroad, drop by to get a feel for the culture you'll be visiting. Open daily, it's just 2 blocks from the Dupont Circle Metro stop.

Kramerbooks & afterwords Cafe & Grill
1517 Connecticut Avenue NW
Washington, DC
(202) 387–1400
www.kramers.com
This Washington mainstay is crowded day and night, thanks to its great full-service restaurant and outdoor cafe and its central location at the hub of Dupont Circle activity. Political books and big bios are always featured in the window, as are tomes on economics, philosophy, religion, and gay/lesbian studies. The selection here is large enough to include plenty of beach reading and guides to everything under the sun. It's open daily. Take the Metro to the Dupont Circle station.

The Newsroom
1753 Connecticut Avenue NW
Washington, DC
(202) 332–1489
One of the city's foremost newsstands, this spot features newspapers from most major U.S. cities, as well as a huge variety of periodicals, including publications written in foreign languages. It also specializes in maps of major cities. Its Dupont Circle location draws a colorful mix of browsers, and the management tolerates lengthy browsing.

News World
1001 Connecticut Avenue NW
Washington, DC
(202) 872–0190
Like the Newsroom, this store features thousands of titles—magazines and newspapers—from around the world.

Olsson's Books & Records

1307 19th Street NW
Washington, DC
(202) 785–1133 (books),
(202) 785–2662 (music)

418 7th Street NW
Washington, DC
(202) 638–7610
www.olssons.com

This popular shop is the oldest and one of the largest independents in the Washington Metro area, with more than 100,000 titles in stock. You're bound to find what you're looking for in both the music and book departments at Olsson's. Check out the large cookbook section, as well as plenty of selections on subjects ranging from the military to psychology and self-help. Both locations are close to parking or Metro stations.

Politics & Prose Bookstore & Coffeehouse

5015 Connecticut Avenue NW
Washington, DC
(202) 364–1919, (800) 722–0790
www.politics-prose.com

This bookstore is highly thought of by Washington's intelligentsia, thanks to the personal touch of the owners and their savvy blend of the latest and most popular books, as well as the obscure. Washington authors always get the spotlight here, and the store holds frequent readings, coffees, and signings by local and national celebrities. The store, open daily, takes pride in being the city's largest independent bookseller. As an added bonus, it's got free parking in back.

Reiter's

1990 K Street NW
Washington, DC
(202) 223–3327
www.reiters.com

Reiter's claims to have more than 60,000 scientific and technical books, including tomes on computers, math, physics, engineering, medicine, nursing, business, and psychology. They'll also make a special effort to hunt down anything not in stock. It's open daily,

and close to both the Farragut North and Farragut West Metro stops.

Reprint Bookshop

455 L'Enfant Plaza SW
Washington, DC
(202) 554–5070

Ignore the name, which originates from the fact that the shop only sold paperbacks when it opened nearly 50 years ago (and paperbacks are, of course, reprints of hardcover books). Now, the store sells all kinds of popular fiction, nonfiction, literature, and, naturally, paperbacks. Specialties include African American literature as well as computer guides. Convenient to the L'Enfant Plaza Metro station, the store is closed on Saturdays and Sundays.

Second Story Books Inc.

2000 P Street NW
Washington, DC
(202) 659–8884
www.secondstorybooks.com

Another Dupont Circle institution—the store's been here for about 30 years—Second Story features old and rare books, first editions, fine bound volumes, or those that are just plain used. The three-store chain's president, Allan Stypeck, is one of the Book Guys heard on National Public Radio. If you're looking for something unique or just hard to find, try this shop. If a branch in Maryland is more convenient, drop in at 12160 Parklawn Drive, Rockville (301–770–0477), or 4914 Fairmont Avenue, Bethesda (301–656–0170).

Trover Shop

221 Pennsylvania Avenue SE
Washington, DC
(202) 547–BOOK
www.trover.com

This family-owned and -operated shop has been around for nearly 50 years. It continues to be popular with busy Capitol Hill office workers as well as lobbyists, lawyers, and White House types. Right near the Library of Congress, this Pennsylvania Avenue shop specializes in political science, though you also can find plenty of lunch-hour escape reading.

Northern Virginia

George Mason University Bookstore
Johnson Center
4400 University Drive
Fairfax, VA
(703) 993–2666
www.gmu.bkstore.com
Beyond a couple of large chain stores, there aren't many bookstores in this section of Fairfax, so the university bookstore is quite a blessing—a well-stocked emporium that also carries accessories and stationery. Not only will you find textbooks, but also popular and classic fiction as well as nonfiction. It's closed on Sundays.

Old Town News
721 King Street
Alexandria, VA
This newsstand, conveniently located among the boutiques and restaurants of Old Town Alexandria, carries a wide variety of international newspapers and magazines, as well as a large stock of those published in the United States.

Olsson's Books & Records
106 South Union Street
Alexandria, VA
(703) 684–0077 (books)
(703) 684–0030 (music)

2111 Wilson Boulevard
Arlington, VA
(703) 525–4227 (books)
(703) 525–3507 (music)

Ronald Reagan Washington National Airport
(703) 417–1087
To learn more about the Virginia locations of this local favorite, please see the Washington, D.C. listing.

Suburban Maryland

Book Nook
9933 Rhode Island Avenue
College Park, MD
(301) 474–4060
If you're stocking up on books for a week at the beach, the Book Nook is a good stop. You won't find rare folios here, but you will find an impressive selection of paperbacks for adults and children—and an especially large selection of romance novels. The staff is knowledgeable and friendly, and the prices can't be beat.

Maryland Book Exchange
4500 College Avenue
College Park, MD
(301) 927–2510
www.marylandbook.com
The University of Maryland is one of the largest in the nation, with some 40,000 students, so it makes sense that this bookstore would be equally comprehensive. You'll find more than 125,000 titles here—that's right, we haven't mistakenly added any zeroes. The store stocks plenty of text and reference books, fiction and nonfiction best-sellers, used books, and school supplies.

Second Story Books
12160 Parklawn Drive
Rockville, MD
(301) 770–0477

4914 Fairmont Avenue
Bethesda, MD
(301) 656–0170
Please see the Washington, D.C. listing.

FURNITURE AND HOME DECORATING

With so many people moving in and out of the D.C. area all the time, it's no wonder that furniture stores here thrive. You'll find stores to fit every budget—sprawling furniture warehouses to high-style designer shops.

Of course, nearly every mall has a Pottery Barn or Crate and Barrel, both great stores for picking up smart home accents at reasonable prices. Instead of describing these well-known retailers, we'll try to give you an overview of stores particular to the region, hit the high-lights, and get you started. By no means is this a comprehensive list, and for more ideas, consult your telephone directory, the home section in Thursday's *Washington Post*, the ads in *Washingtonian* magazine, and the regional advertising pages in *Architectural Digest*. Note that our list is alphabetical rather than geographical. If you're like us, borders don't matter in your quest for just the right piece!

Apartment Zero
406 7th Street NW
Washington, DC
(202) 628–4067
www.apartmentzero.com

Finding quality contemporary furniture at reasonable prices can be a daunting task. Luckily, there's Apartment Zero, a downtown home furnishings emporium catering to the young, hip, condo-owning crowd. While some of the stylish furnishings do come with high price tags, you'll find some well-priced, functional pieces that will make your home decidedly chic.

Country Curtains Retail Shop
Arlington Forest Center
Arlington Boulevard (U.S. 50)
at Park Drive
Arlington, VA
(703) 522–7111
www.countrycurtains.com

Fans of the Stockbridge, Massachusetts–based curtain company's cheerful catalogues should visit the D.C. area's only immediate Country Curtains shop. You'll view lots and

lots of inspiring window displays as well as coordinating furnishings and accessories.

Danker Furniture
1211 South Fern Street
Arlington, VA
(703) 416–0200

21080 Dulles Town Center Mall
Dulles, VA
(571) 323–6000

1500 Ritchie Highway
Annapolis, MD
(410) 757–1674

1582 Rockville Pike
Rockville, MD
(301) 881–6010
www.danker-furniture.com

This place is as swank as a large furniture store gets. It specializes in high-style and high-quality pieces, ranging from Chippendale to ultracontemporary. The showroom is beautifully decorated—inspiring, in fact, and designers on the premises can help you envision what the pieces will look like in your own home.

Go Mama Go!
1809 14th Street NW
Washington, DC
(202) 299–0850
www.gomamago.com

Go Mama Go! doesn't fit the mold of a traditional furniture and home furnishings store. Step inside and you'll feel like you're inside an international marketplace. Bright, colorful home furnishings and housewares are crafted from recycled glass and natural products like cork and bamboo. Nifty handbags, funky jewelry, lightly scented candles, and beautiful tea sets are arrayed atop functional tables and shelves—many of which are also for sale.

The Hardwood Artisans
3622 King Street
Alexandria, VA
(703) 379–7299

i Eastern Market, at 7th and C Streets SE in Washington, D.C., is open daily except Mondays, for seasonal produce, flea market items, and much more.

14080-E Sullyfield Circle
Chantilly, VA
(703) 803–7785

15005 Farm Creek Drive
Woodbridge, VA
(703) 643–1044

12266K Rockville Pike
Rockville, MD
(301) 770–0337
www.hardwoodartisans.com

Are you short on space? Consider drop-down, foldout furniture. The store specializes in cabinets primarily and can construct a multipurpose piece to fit the tiniest studio apartment. Merchandise includes entertainment units, dressers, bookcases, and Murphy, trundle, and platform beds—or you can have it all combined in one wall system. The solid hardwood pieces don't come cheap, but they're built to last. The Woodbridge store is closed on Sundays.

Home Rule
1807 14th Street NW
Washington, DC
(202) 797–5544
www.homerule.com

One of the first businesses to open up in the now-thriving 14th and U Street corridor, Home Rule takes its name from D.C.'s long battle for self-government. The shop stocks a delightful selection of kitschy home products, from chopstick sets for kids and mesh trash cans to organization tools, organic soaps, and cleaning products.

Marlo Furniture Warehouse & Showroom
5650 General Washington Drive
Alexandria, VA
(703) 941–0800

3300 Marlo Lane
Forestville, MD
(301) 735–2000

13450 Baltimore Avenue
Laurel, MD
(301) 419–3400

725 Rockville Pike
Rockville, MD
(301) 738–9000
www.marlofurniture.com

You won't be in Washington a day before you see or hear ads for Marlo. This store seems to be open around the clock, seven days a week, and is always pushing a special sale. It's no wonder—there's room after room of merchandise here, and it's gotta be moved! You really will find some good bargains, in styles ranging from colonial to the latest trends.

Muleh
1831 14th Street NW
Washington, DC
(202) 667–3440
www.muleh.com

Asian-inspired furnishings are in focus at this trendy furniture store. Owner Christopher Reiter built a loyal following with his first shop, located in Bethesda, then followed the real estate boom into the Logan Circle neighborhood for his second venture. Many of the featured pieces are designed by Filipino Kenneth Cobonpue, while others come from leading designers in Bali. Since the store's opening, Reiter has also added a line of clothing and accessories.

Reincarnations
1401 14th Street NW
Washington, DC
(202) 319–1606
www.reincarnationsfurnishings.com

What began as a yard sale and a simple furniture refinishing business has become a must-visit for furniture shoppers in the region. While owner Christopher Torres no longer refinishes pieces, his store carries an eclectic mix of new and restored pieces and unusual home furnishings. While the overall effect is very high end, the prices are affordable. Stop by during the holiday season to see some of the city's most original decorations.

For unique clothing and funky home furnishings, check out the independent boutiques on U Street. COURTESY
WASHINGTON, D.C. CONVENTION AND TOURISM CORPORATION

Saah Unfinished Furniture
2330 Columbia Pike
Arlington, VA
(703) 920–1500

5641-F General Washington Drive
Alexandria, VA
(703) 256–4315
www.saahfurniture.com
If you're a do-it-yourselfer, then Saah may
have just what you want. This family-owned
business carries unfinished armoires,
hutches, shelves, entertainment centers,
tables, and chairs in pine, oak, aspen, and
birch. Prices are reasonable, value is good,
and you'll have the satisfaction of seeing your

handiwork every day. The Arlington store is
closed Sundays.

Theodore's
2233 Wisconsin Avenue NW
Washington, DC
(202) 333–2300
www.theodores.com
Theodore's has been at the vanguard of
Washington's contemporary furniture scene
for 38 years. No fake colonial stuff here—just
sleek, eclectic, innovative pieces that you
won't find just anywhere. Its location in
upper Georgetown makes it a popular spot
for trendies in the surrounding neighbor-

hood, but people are also willing to travel to this one-of-a-kind shop.

Urban Country Designs Ltd.
7801 Woodmont Avenue
Bethesda, MD
(301) 654–0500
www.urbancountrydesigns.com
This eclectic design studio features top-quality furniture that's a blend of antique, ethnic, and a touch of contemporary. Here they strive for an entire design concept rather than simply a sofa or a dining room table, so you'll find wall, window, and floor treatments, as well as decorators to help you pull it all together.

MUSEUM SHOPS

Any overview of shopping in our Nation's Capital has to include a mention of the city's great museum and gallery shops, particularly those at any of the Smithsonian's vast collection of properties. These places aren't just for tourists. Locals love them as well, especially for gifts that are hard to find anywhere else, including books, jewelry, china, framing-quality posters and prints, and assorted novelties. (See our Arts and Attractions chapters for more on the museums that house these shops.)

Bureau of Engraving and Printing
14th Street and Independence
Avenue SW
Washington, DC
(202) 874–3019
www.bep.treas.gov
Buy sheets of uncut $1.00 and $2.00 bills, always fun for the kids to see.

Donald W. Reynolds Center (Smithsonian American Art Museum and National Portrait Gallery)
8th and F Streets NW
Washington, DC
(202) 633–1000
www.reynoldscenter.org
Downtown's newest museum collection is home to an impressive new shop. Browse

through tomes on American art and photography or pick up art-inspired jewelry, handbags, and stationery. Because the museums and shops stay open until 7:00 P.M., it's also a great choice for last-minute souvenirs.

Hillwood Museum and Gardens
4155 Linnean Avenue NW
Washington, DC
(202) 686–8500
www.hillwoodmuseum.org
This former residence of Marjorie Merriweather Post (the cereal heiress) features a large collection of French and Russian decorative arts, and reproductions are on sale in the gift shop. You'll remember your visit with the Fabergé-style egg pendants and other items relating to the permanent collection.

Hirshhorn Museum
950 Independence Avenue NW
Washington, DC
(202) 633–1000
hirshhorn.si.edu
The Hirshhorn Museum features modern art, and the jewelry in the gift shop reflects it. It's quirky and interesting, especially the earrings, which are not the kind of merchandise you'll find in a shopping mall.

John F. Kennedy Center for the Performing Arts
Rock Creek Parkway and New Hampshire
Avenue NW
Washington, DC
(202) 467–4600
www.kennedy-center.org
Visit the Kennedy Center for a good selection of gifts with music, dance, theater, and opera themes.

Mount Vernon Inn Gift Shop
George Washington Memorial Parkway
Alexandria, VA
(703) 780–0011
www.mountvernon.org
The gift shop at George Washington's estate has reproductions of his key to the Bastille,

Martha Washington's cookbook, china and silver, and toys and souvenirs. The Christmas ornaments make nice mementos.

National Air and Space Museum
6th Street and Independence Avenue SW
Washington, DC
(202) 633–1000
www.nasm.si.edu
Kids love the stuff here, from the freeze-dried ice cream like the astronauts eat to the kites and other flight-related objects. Books and videos also will appeal to the aspiring pilots and astronauts on your gift list.

National Archives Museum Store
7th Street and Constitution Avenue NW
Washington, DC
(202) 357–5271
www.nara.gov
Here you'll find great replicas of the Declaration of Independence, the U.S. Constitution, and the Bill of Rights, along with posters, postcards, handmade jewelry, and pottery. The shop also stocks a variety of games, gifts, greeting cards, books, clothing, and crafts.

National Building Museum
401 F Street NW
Washington, DC
(202) 272–2448
www.nbm.org
Some folks visit this museum especially to browse the Museum Shop, which is widely known for its wonderful selection of unusual building toys and other architecture-oriented gifts.

National Gallery of Art
600 Constitution Avenue NW
Washington, DC
(202) 737–4215
www.nga.gov
The basement shops of the National Gallery carry a vast collection of inexpensive prints and postcards of masterpieces that are suitable for framing. You'll also find stationery, jewelry, scarves, and glorious picture books.

National Geographic Society
17th and M Streets NW
Washington, DC
(202) 857–7588
www.nationalgeographic.com
For superb wall maps, globes, books, and educational children's toys, the National Geographic Society can't be beat.

National Museum of the American Indian
4th Street and Independence Avenue SW
Washington, DC
(202) 633–1000
www.nmai.si.edu
Shop for Native American creations and objects of interest at the newest museum on the National Mall. This fantastic museum caters to deep-pocketed, serious collectors with its Chesapeake Museum Store, where some of the featured jewelry, textiles, pottery, sculptures, and other handcrafted works of art cost hundreds—if not thousands—of dollars. For lower-priced books and gifts, try the Roanoke Museum Store on the museum's second level.

National Museum of African Art
950 Independence Avenue SW
Washington, DC
(202) 633–1000
www.nmafa.si.edu
Every home could benefit from a few eclectic accents, and you'll find just the right touch of ethnic artistry here. Look for textiles, dolls, crafts, and jewelry from Africa. You're sure to get compliments on these exotic items.

National Museum of Women in the Arts
1250 New York Avenue NW
Washington, DC
(202) 783–5000
www.nmwa.org
The shop just inside the museum's front doors features several cases of unique jewelry designed by artists. Decorative objects, books, stationery, clothing, and other gifts also cram the shelves in this tiny but well-stocked store.

The Stephen Decatur House Museum
748 Jackson Place NW
Washington, DC
(202) 842–0920
www.decaturhouse.org
This museum store on Lafayette Square, across from the White House, sells reproduction home accessories of the eighteenth and nineteenth centuries.

Washington National Cathedral
Wisconsin and Massachusetts
Avenues NW
Washington, DC
(202) 537–6267
www.cathedral.org/cathedral
The shop here stocks unusual Gothic and Medieval products such as stuffed gargoyles, colorful window decorations, and stained-glass-patterned scarves. If you're home decorating, pick up one of the dramatic tapestries or Gothic stone garden accessories.

SECONDHAND STORES

Outlet malls may offer bargains, but if you want something more offbeat, you may want to check out the area's numerous second-hand shops.

Clothing

Many shops in the area offer great bargains in designer clothing. Expect to pay about one-third of what you'd shell out for a comparable new item. Some of the more upscale include the following:

Encore Resale Dress Shop
3715 Macomb Street NW
Washington, DC
(202) 966–8122
This 40-year-old store on a genteel Cleveland Park side street features great bargains on designer clothes, furs, and accessories. You'll find names like Chanel, Escada, and Ungaro, and glamorous accessories like scarves, handbags, leather goods, and unworn shoes. Don't expect "vintage" here: Nothing is older

than two years. Open Monday through Saturday; the store accepts clothing by appointment.

Inga's Once Is Not Enough
4830 MacArthur Boulevard NW,
2nd Floor
Washington, DC
(202) 337–3072
www.ingafashiontherapist.com
Socialites from ritzy Foxhall bring their once-used gowns and designer suits here for resale. Owner Inga Guen refers to her ultra-upscale shop, featured in such publications as *Harper's Bazaar* and *Financial Times of London,* as "a touch of luxury at a budget price." Savvy shoppers travel from New York City, England, and Paris in search of stunning, one-of-a-kind fashion finds. Expect some real bargains, including barely worn Chanel, Christian Lacroix, Armani, Bill Blass, Ungaro, and more. Accessories include handbags by the likes of Gucci and Prada. The store is closed on Sundays.

Meeps & Aunt Neensie's Fashionette
2104 18th Street NW
Washington, DC
(202) 265–6546
www.meepsonu.com
Vintage clothing lovers will fall for Meeps, one of the most popular shops of its kind in Washington, D.C. Meeps built a loyal following among neighborhood residents when it opened on U Street in 1992 and has since expanded to a larger clientele and a bigger home a few blocks away. Fashions here are truly vintage—think flirty 1950s dresses and 1970s jeans, plus retro sunglasses, hats, wigs, and even bridal gowns. The shop also stocks some items by local designers that blend well with the vintage looks.

Polly Sue's Vintage Shop
6915 Laurel Avenue
Takoma Park, MD
(301) 270–5511
Funky Takoma Park, Maryland, is home to

many eclectic used-clothing stores, but Polly Sue's is one of the best. Beyond classic pieces from the 1960s and '70s, you'll also find a handful of Victorian dresses from the 1850s and other unusual items. Polly Sue's selects its merchandise with men in mind, too, boasting one of the most extensive collections of vintage menswear in the region, including hats and accessories.

Secondi
1702 Connecticut Avenue NW
Washington, DC
(202) 667–1122
www.secondi.com

You'll find high-style consignment clothing for women at this small boutique, tucked away 2 blocks north of Dupont Circle. Look for designers like Donna Karan, Coach, Banana Republic, Ann Taylor, Country Road, Kate Spade, and Prada. The store is open daily.

Furniture

Consignment Galleries
3226 Wisconsin Avenue NW
Washington, DC
(202) 364–8995

This shop displays quality furniture and accessories in a charming showroom that gives you a good idea of how the other half lives. The nice thing is that you can have a piece of the good life for less-than-new prices. Even if you're only looking for something small, this place is worth a stop. You'll find French and Italian accessories, oil paintings, many styles of lamps, Oriental screens, sterling, crystal—just about any style and period you can imagine. Consignment Galleries also stocks a variety of traditional-style furniture pieces. The store is closed on Sundays.

The Cordell Collection
4911 Cordell Avenue
Bethesda, MD
(301) 907–3324

In the heart of Bethesda you'd expect to find the best in used furniture, and this shop

delivers. Artfully blended antiques, reproductions, and collectibles inspire the imagination. Prices are not cheap, but some of the pieces are in the category of "they just don't make 'em like that anymore." The store is closed on Sundays.

Upscale Resale
8100 Lee Highway
Falls Church, VA
(703) 698–8100
www.upscale-resale.com

Maybe it's the catchy name, but this has become one of the premier shops in Metro Washington for high-quality secondhand furniture. This store is picky about what it carries, and its showroom is attractive and classy. A lot of wealthy people live in Washington, and some of them appear to have left their discards here on consignment—maybe the remainder have picked up a few pieces here?

SPAS AND SALONS

Beauty products are easy to find—any department store or salon has them. If you're like most people, you stick to certain brands and you know where to find them. What about beauty services? If you're looking for sessions that can last anywhere from an hour to a day, and that may include manicures, waxing, facials, and massage, you'll need a day spa—a wonderful place to unwind from Washington's frenetic pace. Here are some of the top names in the Washington area. Several of the city's top hotels, such as the Mandarin Oriental, Four Seasons, St. Regis, Ritz-Carlton, and Willard InterContinental also operate exceptional destination spas. Most serve both men and women and offer gift certificates to give as special presents. Expect to pay anywhere from $70 to more than $100 for a facial, $80 to $100 for an hour-long massage, and $280 to upwards of $400 for a whole day of pampering.

Beauty Spas

Andre Chreky
1604 K Street NW
Washington, DC
(202) 293–9393
www.andrechreky.com

Andre Chreky opened this cozy oasis just a couple of blocks from the White House, in the thick of the K Street lobbying district. Although it's one of the city's busiest and most popular hair salons, it manages to deliver a truly relaxing experience. Soft piano music plays as a romantic fireplace beckons. Sip cappuccino or espresso while you wait for a soothing massage, invigorating facial, or pedicure. With its prime location and late—even Sunday—hours, you're likely to see politicians and media personalities milling around the place as well.

Celadon Spa
1180 F Street NW
Washington, DC
(202) 347–3333
www.celadonspa.com

Celadon does a remarkable job of calming the hustle and bustle of downtown Washington, D.C. While it's a good choice for a quick haircut or lunchtime manicure, Celadon is best known for its facials and skin and body treatments. Hot stone massages, microdermabrasion, body masques, and skin regimens from the top European lines set this sleek, stylish salon apart.

Elizabeth Arden Red Door Salon & Spa
5225 Wisconsin Avenue NW
Washington, DC
(202) 362–9890

Fairfax Square, 8075 Leesburg Pike
Vienna, VA
(703) 448–8388

Spectrum Center
Reston, VA
(703) 467–8488

Wildwood Shopping Center
10213 Old Georgetown Road
Bethesda, MD
(240) 644–1319

Pentagon Row
1101 South Joyce Street, Suite B-36
Arlington, VA
(703) 373–5888

Fairfax Corner
Fairfax, VA
(703) 968–2922
www.reddoorsalons.com

Remember those 1940s movies where women would sit in a steam box with their cold cream–slathered faces poking out? Chances are, they were in Elizabeth Arden, who started the whole day spa concept decades ago. Well, the Washington salon is still going strong, though a lot of competition has come along in the interim. Maybe it's because of that same competition that this salon, once so pricey, is now relatively reasonable.

Georgette Klinger
Advanced Aesthetics
The Collection, Level Two
5481 Wisconsin Avenue
Chevy Chase, MD
(240) 482–8450
www.georgetteklinger.com

The Hungarian-born Klinger founded her first salon in New York and was an immediate hit with all manner of celebrities. She has since brought her skincare methods and products to Washington, where the salon is equally successful. Whatever beauty treatment you can imagine, you can find at Klinger. On your first visit you'll be asked to fill out a skincare questionnaire, much as you would in a dermatologist's office. The questionnaire becomes part of your "chart," which is kept on file for future reference.

The atmosphere at Klinger is soothing, feminine (though there are male clients, too), and ultraclean. The specialty here is facials, some of which last more than an hour and involve the use of aromatic herbs or fruit acids. There are also manicures, pedicures, and haircuts and cosmetic makeovers available. Ask about packages, and you'll save some money.

Lillian Laurence Ltd.
2000 M Street NW
Washington, DC
(202) 872–0606
www.lillianlaurence.com
Lillian Laurence was a day spa before the term was invented. It's always been on the cutting edge of beauty treatment and continues to be so, offering facials, massage, body wraps, mud packs, body polishing, waxing, and nonsurgical face-lifts. It's a pleasant refuge, conveniently located in the lower level of a midtown office building.

Patricia's Skin Care Center
1620 Wisconsin Avenue NW
Washington, DC
(202) 298–6773
You're not likely to find a more personal approach to skin care than that of Patricia Alvarez, owner of Patricia's Skin Care in Georgetown. Appointments for her signature hour-and-a-half facial are highly sought after, but worth the effort. More of a doctor than an esthetician, Alvarez views the skin as the outer manifestation of each client's habits and lifestyle. You won't find a hard sell for a specific product line or a standardized approach; it's all about personal attention here.

Sugar House Day Spa & Salon
111 North Alfred Street
Alexandria, VA
(703) 549–9940
www.sugarhousedayspa.com
Housed in an Old Town row house, this full-service day spa and salon is cozy and inviting. Sugar House's signature service is the Sugar House Scrub, an intense, invigorating exfoliation with a mixture of sugar crystals and oils designed to leave you feeling smooth and smelling slightly sweet. You'll also find a full menu of facials for mature skin as well as

teenage skin, and a tempting array of massages, plus hair and nail services.

Hair Salons

Following is a list of Washington salons most often mentioned in national beauty magazines. They serve both men and women. The aforementioned spas are also good places for hair pampering.

Bang Salon and Spa
1612 U Street NW
Washington, DC
(202) 299–0925

601 F Street NW
Washington, DC
(202) 737–2264
www.bangsalonspa.com
Bang has earned acclaim from the budget-conscious, fashion-forward, and beauty media alike for filling a unique void. In a town where $80 haircuts aren't unusual, Bang charges just $25 for men's cuts and $35 for women's—and it does so in a stylish, trendy setting. The original location on U Street was joined by a second outpost in downtown's new Gallery Place development.

Daniel's Salon
1831 M Street NW
Washington, DC
(202) 296–4856
In a handsome town house, Daniel's is three stories packed with beauty services. It's always bustling with patrons of both sexes, generally up-and-coming executives from the surrounding office district.

Okyo Beauty Salon
2903 M Street NW
Washington, DC
(202) 342–2675
www.okyosalon.com
This bright, spare-looking loft attracts all sorts of Washington celebs. It's acclaimed for fine cuts and coloring, as well as long waits for appointments. Call well in advance.

Roche Salon
3050 K Street NW, Washington Harbour Plaza
Washington, DC
(202) 775–0775
www.rochesalon.com
This salon is a fantasyland, complete with paintwork to simulate blue skies and brightly colored cabanas (changing rooms) that make you think of a day at the beach. Don't let the whimsy fool you, though: Cuts and color are taken seriously here, and the salon is regularly named in national magazines as one of Washington's best. What's more, they won't try to chop off your long hair or give you an unsuitable, hard-to-manage style. *InSalon* magazine named Roche Salon's informative Web site the best in the beauty industry. It even offers cyberspace makeovers!

Salon Jean Paul
4820 Yuma Street
Washington, DC
(202) 966–4600
This has been a favorite of the Washington establishment for many years. In upper northwest D.C., Salon Jean Paul attracts a number of patrons from the affluent residential area surrounding it.

UNIQUE STORES

Some stores just don't fit into any category, or if they do, they're the only ones in it. The stores listed below either offer more of their specialty than anyone in Metro Washington, or they offer unusual or unique merchandise.

Artcraft Collection
132 King Street
Alexandria, VA
(703) 299–6616

11960 Market Street
Reston, VA
(703) 964–0145

Historic Savage Mill
8600 Foundry Street
Savage, MD
(410) 880–4863
www.artcraftcollection.com
A whimsical array of furnishings (including unique, handmade designs by Texan David Marsh), home furnishings, jewelry, glassware, and more greets visitors to these colorful shops. Each store is packed to the gills with eye-catching stuff created by more than 400 contemporary artisans. If you're looking for unique gifts, you'll find items ranging in price from around $16 to hundreds of dollars. You can even register your preferences at the company's Web site.

The Artisans
Langley Shopping Center
1368 Chain Bridge Road
McLean, VA
(703) 506–0158
www.artisansofmclean.com
The artistry of American craftspeople highlights this shop in McLean. You'll find wearable art, gifts, housewares, and jewelry—all of it unique. Candlesticks are sculptures containing glass and semiprecious stones, and brooches are striking enough to make a memorable outfit of any little black dress. Not everything here is costly, however. Polymer clay jewelry starts at $15, and you'll also find a nice selection of hair accessories and journals.

Backstage Inc.: The Performing Arts Store
545 8th Street SE
Washington, DC
(202) 544–5744
www.backstagebooks.com
This costume store, located 2 blocks from the Eastern Market Metro station, will actually make your costume to order, if you wish. Or you can choose from the large selection of ready-made disguises and all kinds of accessories, including wigs, masks, makeup, and dancewear. The shop is closed on Sundays.

The Brass Knob
2311 18th Street NW
Washington, DC
(202) 332–3370
www.thebrassknob.com
You've selected the perfect furniture, wall coverings, and draperies for your new house, but how do you pull it all together? It's the details that count, and the Brass Knob can provide them. The store carries a wide variety of antique lighting fixtures, stained and beveled glass, doorknobs, and hardware. You'll also love the architectural accents here, such as fireplace mantles, porcelain sinks, tiles, ornamental ironwork, and carved stone. Visit the sister store, the Back Doors Warehouse, 57 N Street NW, Washington, D.C. (202–265–0587), for larger items such as claw-foot bathtubs and fences.

Chocolate Moose
1743 L Street NW
Washington, DC
(202) 463–0992
www.chocolatemoosedc.com
You'll find a wonderful selection of gifts—yes, some of them made out of chocolate!—at this downtown emporium. Shop for funky alarm clocks and glassware, baby gifts, Magic 8 Balls, and tasty chocolate treats, plus a laugh-out-loud selection of greeting cards.

The Christmas Attic
125 South Union Street
Alexandria, VA
(703) 548–2829

House in the Country
107 North Fairfax Street
Alexandria, VA
(703) 548–4267
www.christmasattic.com
Christmas lasts year-round in these two magical Old Town shops. The Christmas Attic features hundreds of gorgeous ornaments and decorated trees with themes ranging from Victorian lace to gold-and-glass, musical instruments, and toys. Its sister store, House in the Country, carries country-style gifts, collectibles, and decor items as well as Christmas merchandise. Both stores even smell like Christmas, thanks to strategically placed potpourri and, during the fall, bushels of apples at the doors.

Distinctive Bookbinding
1755 S Street NW
Washington, DC
(202) 466–4866
www.distinctivebookbinding.com
This shop will take you back to an era when people prided themselves on the quality of their stationery and penmanship and on the leather-bound volumes in their libraries. You'll find exotic Florentine writing paper of the highest quality here, as well as all sorts of writing accessories, including scented ink. If you already own some worn first editions, this is the place to have them rebound and restored. The store is closed on Saturdays and Sundays.

Fahrney's Pens Inc.
1317 F Street NW
Washington, DC
(202) 628–9525, (800) 624–PENS
www.fahrneyspens.com
Other stores in Washington sell fine pens and pencils, but Fahrney's is an institution. Appropriately located near the National Press Building, this shop has been around since 1929, and the service is just as personal today as it was then. It specializes in writing instruments from Montblanc, Parker, Cross, Sheaffer, Waterman, and Pelikan. The store is closed on Sundays.

Fleet Feet
1841 Columbia Road NW
Washington, DC
(202) 387–3888
www.fleetfeet.com
If you're looking for the perfect pair of running or walking shoes, or a little friendly advice for getting into shape or training for a marathon, jog over to Fleet Feet in Adams Morgan. Staffed by runners and athletes

who'll let you take the shoes out for a test run before you commit, Fleet Feet will also invite you back on Sunday mornings for a 5-mile group run. Opened in 1984, it's owned and operated by Phil and Jan Fenty—the proud parents of D.C. mayor Adrian Fenty.

Mark Keshishian & Sons Inc.
Oriental Rugs
4507 Stanford Street
Chevy Chase, MD
(301) 654–4044, (301) 951–8880
www.orientalcarpets.net

Sometimes it seems as though there's an Oriental rug dealer on every corner in Washington and the surrounding 'burbs. Many of them are excellent, but Keshishian is widely considered the cream of the crop when it comes to appraising, variety of merchandise, and restoration. The store carries antiques of the first quality as well as more contemporary pieces. The staff is friendly, knowledgeable, and what is most important, willing to share information.

Music Box Center
1920 I Street NW
Washington, DC
(202) 783–9399

Choose from more than 1,500 music boxes, both antique and modern, and then personalize your choice with one of more than 500 melodies. Browse through the selection and you'll be surprised at the variety of shapes and sizes of these pretty boxes. The shop is closed on Sundays.

Park Place
5100 Wisconsin Avenue NW
Washington, DC
(202) 342–6294

You won't believe the selection of garden furniture, fixtures, and accessories here. Browse among classic styles in teak, wicker, and metal, and decorative pieces like lampposts, massive flower pots, and stained-glass panels. The shop also carries Tiffany-style interior lamps. Whether you have an estate or a tiny kitchen garden, you're sure to find the whimsical or dramatic touch you need here.

Pulp
1805½ 14th Street NW
Washington, DC
(202) 462–7857
303 Pennsylvania Avenue SE
(202) 543–1924
www.pulpdc.com

Pulp brings a fun, playful selection of cards, paper products and gifts to shoppers on 14th Street. Nothing is sacred here; you'll find products that poke fun at politicians, bosses, and religious and military figures alike. You'll also find a selection of art by local talent and interesting music in the air (and for sale).

The Surrey
10107 River Road
Potomac, MD
(301) 299–8225
www.onlinethesurrey.com

Potomac is traditional horse country, and this high-toned shop caters to those wealthy enough to belong to that set. You'll find all manner of riding clothes and equipment, including leather jackets and pants, boots, riding crops, and cold weather gear.

Teaism Tea Shop
400 8th Street NW
(202) 638–7700
www.teaism.com

Find the perfect gift for tea lovers at this purveyor of fine loose teas and related accessories. Teapots and boxes imported from China and Japan are also available for sale,

i If you live in Virginia but think you might save a few bucks by stocking up on distilled spirits at independently operated liquor stores in the District or Maryland, be aware that there are limits on the amount of alcohol that can be purchased for transport across state lines. It's a good idea to first check with local authorities to see what the law allows.

along with candles and home accessories that strive for the perfect zen effect. The shop is attached to the Penn Quarter outpost of the restaurant and tearoom of the same name.

Tennis Factory
2500 Wilson Boulevard, Suite 100
Arlington, VA
(703) 522–2700
www.tennisfactory.com
Tennis players will be agog at the selection of women's, men's, and children's clothing, shoes, and rackets here. Trained staff help shoppers choose from every brand imaginable. Still not sure? Rent a demo racquet. Get your own racquet restrung overnight.

Tiny Jewel Box
1147 Connecticut Avenue NW
Washington, DC
(202) 393–2747
www.tinyjewelbox.com
Yes, there are dozens of jewelry stores in Metro Washington, and every mall seems to have at least three, but the Tiny Jewel Box is special. It carries modern designer jewelry, of course, but the real attraction here is the area's largest collection of antique and estate jewelry. The business has bought and appraised such items since 1930. You can find art nouveau brooches, rings, and earrings for as little as $200, but you also can spend tens of thousands of dollars for some of the shop's diamond and platinum pieces.

Yes Organic Market
3425 Connecticut Avenue NW
Washington, DC
(202) 363–1559

1825 Columbia Road NW
Washington, DC
(202) 462–5150

648 Pennsylvania Avenue SE
Washington, DC
(202) 546–9850
A lot of mainstream grocery chains have jumped on the organic food/herb/vitamin bandwagon, and they do a wonderful job. A look at the telephone directory will reveal dozens of listings for health food stores, but we have to take our hats off to one of the most long-lived and consistent shops in the Washington area, Yes Organic Market. Its three locations prove its success—many health food boutiques fade away after a couple of years. Yes sells organic produce and groceries, diet products, bulk food, and herbs, vitamins, and bodycare items. Refuel at the deli and juice bar.

ZYZYX Inc.
Wildwood Shopping Center, 10301A Old Georgetown Road
Bethesda, MD
(301) 493–0297
It may be the very last entry in a Maryland suburban phone book, but ZYZYX is tops with shoppers seeking unique gifts and home accents. The colorful store carries unique pottery, jewelry, and other artistic, fun stuff.

ANNUAL EVENTS

How many times have you seen photos of the president emerging from the massive portals of the Washington National Cathedral, surrounded by Secret Service and cabinet officials? Imagine attending Christmas Eve services in that same house of worship, surrounded by the very newsmakers you've glimpsed on CNN. If that doesn't sound like your cup of tea, rest assured that in Washington, D.C., you'll have plenty to do and see. Year-round you'll find parades, festivals, and ceremonies, many of which you may have seen on television—like the annual lighting of the national Christmas tree.

Many who come to Washington plan their trips around special celebrations and exhibitions. From the exuberance of the Chinese New Year to the ceremonial splendor of the Marine Color Guard on parade, Washington visitors and residents can choose from an endless variety of fascinating, amusing distractions. The beauty of touring the area is that some of the most exciting and well-known events are free and open to the public.

Here you'll find a month-by-month calendar of events in the Washington Metro area. In the monthly categories you'll find geographic subdivisions: Washington, D.C., Northern Virginia, and Suburban Maryland. Most events are free, but 2006 adult admission fees are shown for those that aren't. Please note that for the most part we have not included dates and times because they so often change from year to year. Instead, you'll find contact numbers for people and organizations who can provide a wealth of information.

JANUARY
Washington, D.C.

Chinese New Year Parade
H Street NW, between 5th and 8th Streets
Washington, DC
(703) 851–8777
The Lunar New Year is a time to close accounts, pay debts, clean house, honor ancestors, prepare exotic foods, and thank the gods for a prosperous year. The residents of Washington's Chinatown do it all in style, with traditional firecrackers, drums, and colorful dragon dancers that make their way through the streets flanked typically by more than 10,000 onlookers. The date of the event varies according to the new moon and sometimes happens in February.

Martin Luther King Jr.'s Birthday Observance
Department of Interior Auditorium
18th and C Streets NW
Washington, DC
(202) 619–7222
www.nps.gov/ncro
Local choirs, guest speakers, and a military color guard salute the memory of the influential civil rights leader. Student programs are held at the Lincoln Memorial throughout the month.

Washington, DC Restaurant Week
Various locations
Washington, DC
(202) 789–7000
www.restaurantweekdc.org
Break your New Year's resolution with this dining extravaganza, held each January and

The National Cherry Blossom Festival celebrates the blossoming of more than 3,000 Japanese cherry trees in downtown D.C. COURTESY WASHINGTON, D.C. CONVENTION AND TOURISM CORPORATION

August when Congress is out of session (and thus, expense account lunches with lobbyists die down). More than 100 of the top restaurants in the metro area offer special three-course lunch and dinner menus priced to correspond with the year. For example, in 2007 you'll find lunches priced at $20.07 and dinners for $30.07.

Suburban Maryland

Historic Annapolis Antiques Show
Medford National Guard Armory
Hudson Street
Annapolis, MD
(410) 435–2292
This giant of an antiques show—7,700 square feet of exhibit space—is set most appropriately in a city that's one of the nation's premier antiques meccas. You'll find dealers from all over the United States showing wares as varied as nineteenth-century French furniture to Shaker, Chinese export, and American country styles. You'll also find, appropriately enough (Annapolis is a yachting capital), marine artifacts and maps and a myriad of other decorative items, such as porcelains, Oriental rugs, and paintings. The show runs for three days and opens with a preview party for serious private collectors, charging a $65 admission fee that allows you into the following day's shows. The show benefits the Historic Annapolis Foundation, which advocates public education about Annapolis history. Admission to the show is $8.00.

FEBRUARY

Washington, D.C.

Abraham Lincoln's Birthday
Lincoln Memorial
23rd Street and Independence
Avenue NW
Washington, DC
(202) 619–7222
www.nps.gov/ncro
A wreath-laying ceremony and reading of the Gettysburg Address are highlights of the 16th

i Many of the Metro Washington area's gourmet supermarkets offer unusual, creative picnic meals packed for outdoor events. Whole Foods Market, Balducci's, Dean & DeLuca, and Giant's Someplace Special are some of the most well known for prepared foods.

president's birthday celebration on February 12, at his namesake memorial. The site is inspiring with its view of the Reflecting Pool, the Washington Monument, and the U.S. Capitol. Inside, the 19-foot marble statue is set against inscriptions of Lincoln's second inaugural address and the Gettysburg Address.

Washington Boat Show
Washington Convention Center
801 Mount Vernon Place NW
Washington, DC
(703) 823–7960
www.washingtonboatshow.com
Surrounded by rivers, and with the Chesapeake Bay just a short drive away, Metro Washington is boat-crazed. This five-day event has become a tremendous draw in a town where people have the money to spend on grown-up toys. It showcases next year's models of hundreds of boats, from dinghies to motor yachts. If you're a serious buyer, you can often snag great buys at the show. Flash your wallet and representatives from the big boat makers will be ready to negotiate. If you're not in that league, you can still purchase nautical accessories and pick up brochures from yacht charter companies. Admission is $10.

Northern Virginia

George Washington's Birthday Parade
Wilkes and St. Asaph Streets
Old Town Alexandria, VA
(703) 991–4474
www.washingtonbirthday.net
Old Town plays host to the nation's largest birthday parade, honoring a native son and

America's first president. The cobblestoned streets of Old Town, flanked by eighteenth- and nineteenth-century historical buildings, including private residences, make a perfect backdrop for the celebration. The route begins in a beautiful residential section of town and ends at Gadsby's Tavern, a nationally designated historical building dating from the eighteenth century. It is now a restaurant with costumed servers and eighteenth-century-style minstrels. Make sure to bundle up because it can be cold and windy in February.

GMC Capital Home & Garden Show
Dulles Expo Center
4320 Chantilly Place Center
Chantilly, VA
(800) 274–6948
www.capitalhomeshow.com
The Capital Home Show is a good place to see what's new in remodeling and decorating products and services. The show offers more than 300 exhibitors for homeowners to speak with to receive free expert advice, helpful hints, and tips for projects for inside and out. The show is also held in September. Admission to the three-day event is $10 for adults.

Mount Vernon Open House
Mount Vernon Estate
George Washington Memorial Parkway
Alexandria, VA
(703) 780–2000
www.mountvernon.org
After the parade in Old Town on George Washington's Birthday, head south to George Washington's lovely estate on the Potomac for an afternoon of period costumes, music, and food. Admission is free of charge on this special day, which usually includes a performance on the bowling green by the U.S. Army Old Guard Fife and Drum Corps and the Commander-in-Chief's Guard. A tour of the house is worth the wait, and "George Washington" will be on the grounds all day to receive your birthday wishes.

MARCH
Washington, D.C.
D.C. Spring Antiques Fair
The D.C. Armory
2001 East Capitol Street SE
Washington, DC
(301) 933–9433
The area's most popular antiques show, this three-day display features almost 200 dealers from the United States, England, France, and Canada. You'll find an eye-popping array of collectibles from delicate sterling, porcelains, and Oriental rugs to fine furniture. Browsers are welcome, but it's also a good place to connect with dealers in far-flung areas who will be more than happy to ship you their wares as well as notifications of their latest finds. Admission is $6.00. The event also takes place in October and December.

National Cherry Blossom Festival
Various parks and downtown locations
Washington, DC
(202) 547–1500
www.nationalcherryblossomfestival.org
Perhaps Washington's most visible fete, the National Cherry Blossom Festival honors the extraordinary blooming of the city's 3,000 Japanese cherry trees—surely one of the most beautiful sights in America. The capstone event is the Cherry Blossom Festival Parade (usually the first Saturday in April), but scores of related parties and ceremonies begin the last week of March. The trees bloom anywhere from late March to early April, depending on Mother Nature. A word to the wise: If at all possible, take Metrorail into Washington and walk to the Tidal Basin. It's a short jaunt from most stops downtown, and you'll save yourself the agony of trying to find a parking space.

St. Patrick's Day Parade
7th to 17th Streets and Constitution Avenue NW
Washington, DC
www.dcstpatsparade.com

Salute the Irish and sport the green in style during this always-festive downtown parade that features traditional dancers, bagpipers, and floats galore. The parade, which lasts about three hours, has been a major Washington event for more than 30 years. Afterwards participants and spectators alike spill into the bars and eateries that flank the parade route. High school bands from around the country join in, as well as bands from Ireland. It's not nearly as big as the one in New York, but it manages to clog traffic for most of the day, so take the Metro.

Smithsonian Kite Festival
Between 4th and 7th Streets NW on the National Mall
Washington, DC
(202) 661–7585
www.kitefestival.org
Now part of the National Cherry Blossom Festival, the Kite Festival is another much-heralded signal of spring, as colorful kites dip and soar next to the Washington Monument. Kite makers and flyers of all ages compete for prizes and trophies.

Washington Home & Garden Show
Washington Convention Center
801 Mount Vernon Place NW
Washington, DC
(703) 823–7960
www.washingtonhomeandgardenshow.com
This extravaganza of color and scent features gardening experts, landscape designers, and, of course, masses of flowers and plants. This four-day show features almost 600 exhibitors in a space larger than two acres. Over half of that space is filled with gardens that have been forced into bloom—breathtaking gardens that can include waterfalls and bridges, magnificent statuary, and dramatic trees. The home show component includes decorating and remodeling exhibits and information. Cost is $10.

ℹ️ Want to see cherry blossoms but don't want to see crowds? There are also clusters of cherry trees in other parts of the metro region, like the National Arboretum and Brookside Gardens.

Northern Virginia

St. Patrick's Day Parade
King and West Streets
Old Town Alexandria, VA
(703) 237–2199
www.ballyshaners.org
Usually held a day or two before the D.C. parade, Old Town's festivities extend beyond the parade route and into the city's extremely popular Irish pubs, such as Murphy's and Ireland's Own.

Woodlawn Plantation Annual Needlework Exhibition
George Washington Memorial Parkway and U.S. 1
Alexandria, VA
(703) 780–4000
www.woodlawn1805.org
Needlework crafts from the eighteenth century to the present day are on display at this lovely plantation, about 3 miles east of the Mount Vernon estate. The exhibition includes works by amateur and professional stitchers, as well as celebrities like Maureen Reagan, the former president's daughter. Admission is $7.50 and $3.00 for students through grade 12.

Suburban Maryland

Annual Quilt Show
C. Elizabeth Reig Special Center
2614 Kenhill Drive
Bowie, MD
(301) 262–4194
www.southerncomforters.org
Heirloom and contemporary quilts are showcased in this popular Prince George's County show. Admission is $5.00.

APRIL

Washington, D.C.

Shakespeare's Birthday Celebration
Folger Shakespeare Library
201 East Capitol Street SE
Washington, DC
(202) 544–4600
www.folger.edu
The Capitol Hill building is an attraction in itself, with its replica of Shakespeare's Globe Theatre, but during the birthday celebration, the library also offers music, theater, children's events, food, and special exhibits. Admission is free.

Smithsonian Craft Show
National Building Museum
401 F Street NW
Washington, DC
(888) 832–9554
www.smithsoniancraftshow.org
Some 100 juried exhibitors show their crafts at this prestigious juried event, which features fiber, ceramics, glass, jewelry, leather, metal, paper, textiles, and wood. Admission is $15.

Walkingtown, DC
Cultural Tourism DC
Various locations
(202) 661–7581
www.walkingtowndc.org
Each April and September or October, Washington, D.C.'s tour guides create a free day of walking tours in neighborhoods throughout the city, led by tour guides and knowledgeable local experts.

Washington International Film Festival
(Filmfest D.C.)
Theaters and reception halls
Washington, DC
(202) 628–FILM
www.filmfestdc.org
Washington is the focus of the cinematic world during this two-week festival of international and American film. Washington is one of the top U.S. movie markets and one of the most filmed cities in the world. Films are shown at venues throughout the city.

White House Easter Egg Roll
The White House (Southeast Gate)
East Executive Avenue NW
Washington, DC
(202) 456–7041
www.whitehouse.gov/history/tours/special-events.html
Children ages three through six, accompanied by adults, gather on the White House South Lawn for the annual Easter Egg Roll. This is easily the best opportunity in town for youngsters—and, for that matter, parents—to play at the president's house. Each child receives free souvenirs. The event also includes concerts by nationally known family entertainers like Tom Chapin, storytelling by celebrities like Jamie Lee Curtis, strolling costumed characters, and educational exhibits. Arrive as early as you can. It's not uncommon for the line to start the night before. Free tickets usually run out well before 9:00 A.M.

White House Spring Garden and House Tours
The White House
1600 Pennsylvania Avenue
Washington, DC
(202) 456–7041
www.whitehouse.gov
The spectacular gardens of the presidential home are open to the public during these annual tours (usually for two days during the second week of the month). Highlights include the Jacqueline Kennedy Rose Gardens and the spectacular West Lawn Gardens.

Northern Virginia

Easter Sunrise Service
Arlington National Cemetery
Memorial Drive
Arlington, VA
(703) 607–8000
www.arlingtoncemetery.org
The cemetery's Memorial Amphitheatre, an

inspiring setting, awaits early-morning worshipers. The service is conducted by a changing roster of prominent Washington ministers
and includes a moving, dignified tribute by
the Army's Old Guard.

Historic Garden Week in Virginia
Statewide
(804) 644–7776
www.vagardenweek.org
The finest in Virginia homes and gardens are
spotlighted during this week-long festival.
Our favorites include the gardens at such
area plantations as Mount Vernon, Gunston
Hall, and Oatlands. Call to find out more
about tours in Northern Virginia. Admission is
$10 to $30 depending on the tour chosen.

MAY
Washington, D.C.
"The Commandant's Own"
U.S. Marine Corps Barracks
8th and I Streets SE
Washington, DC
(202) 433–6060
www.mbw.usmc.mil/parades
Reservations are recommended, but admission is free to these extraordinary Friday
night parades, beginning in May and running
through August. Here is your chance to see
the elite of the United States military in a 75-
minute performance of music and precision
marching. The evening parade begins with a
concert by "The President's Own" United
States Marine Band. After the concert, "The
Commandant's Own" United States Drum and
Bugle Corps and the Marine Corps Silent Drill
Platoon perform.

Reservations must be made in writing or
online and requested at least three weeks in
advance. Address requests to Protocol Office,
Marine Barracks, 8th and I Streets SE, Washington, D.C. 20390–5000 or fax to (202)
433–4076. The request should include the
name of the party (either group or individual),
the number of guests, a complete return

address, and a point of contact with a telephone number.

Georgetown Garden Day
Various locations
Washington, DC
(202) 965–1950
www.georgetowngardentour.com
The private gardens of this famous neighborhood are on display in this inspiring tour.
You'll be surprised by the extensive landscapes hidden behind Georgetown's walled
courtyards and gardens. Some go an impos-
sibly long way—you'd never guess it from the
outside. Guided and self-guided tours are
available. Admission is $30.

Memorial Day Ceremonies
Vietnam Veterans Memorial
Constitution Avenue and Henry Bacon Drive
NW
Washington, DC
(202) 619–7222
www.nps.gov/ncro
Speeches, military bands, and a keynote
address are the centerpieces of this solemn
event. Directories help you find names on the
walls, and you can request a name rubbing.

Memorial Day Weekend Concert
West Lawn of the Capitol, Capitol Hill
Washington, DC
(202) 619–7222
www.nps.gov/ncro
As a kickoff to the summer tourist season,
this popular concert features the globally
acclaimed National Symphony Orchestra in
an unforgettable setting under the stars.

If you're moving to the area or planning to make many trips here, sign
up for Cultural Tourism D.C.'s weekly
events e-mail update at www.cultural
tourismdc.org to learn about museum
happenings, concerts, lectures, performances, tours, and more.

> **i** While attending summer outdoor concerts, consider applying bug spray to keep the gnats and mosquitoes away. They can be fierce!

Washington National Cathedral Flower Mart
Massachusetts and Wisconsin
Avenues NW
Washington, DC
(202) 537–6200
www.cathedral.org
Each year, the mart's theme is a salute to a different country, featuring flower booths, entertainment, and decorating demonstrations.

Northern Virginia

"The Commandant's Own"
Iwo Jima Memorial
U.S. 50 at Arlington National Cemetery
Arlington, VA
(202) 433–4075
www.mbw.usmc.mil
Beneath the shadows of the dramatic Marine Corps War Memorial, commonly known as the Iwo Jima Memorial, you'll be awed by the precision and discipline of the Marine Corps Silent Drill Platoon, stirred by the patriotic music of the Drum and Bugle Corps. These concerts will rivet you, and your children will remain fascinated for the entire hour. The site itself offers an inspiring view of the Nation's Capital and the Potomac River in the setting sun. Bring a picnic dinner and blanket—there's plenty of space on the lawn. See this event weekly, May through August.

Memorial Day Ceremonies
Arlington National Cemetery
Memorial Drive
Arlington, VA
(703) 607–8000
www.arlingtoncemetery.org
Wreath layings at the John F. Kennedy grave site and the Tomb of the Unknowns are part of the ceremonies that wind down with a service at the Memorial Amphitheatre. The

president usually delivers the keynote address.

The Virginia Gold Cup
90 Main Street
Warrenton, VA
(800) 69–RACES
www.vagoldcup.com
Usually held the same day as the Kentucky Derby, this premier steeplechase of Virginia and the international community has blossomed into one of the largest sporting and social events in Metro Washington. Held at Great Meadow, riders compete for a $50,000 purse, which, if they win the Gold Cup's counterpart in England, nets them another £30,000. Great Meadow is in the heart of the state's gorgeous hunt country, about an hour west of Washington in Fauquier County. Admission is $65 per car in advance. The International Gold Cup takes place at Great Meadow on the third Saturday in October.

Suburban Maryland

Andrews Air Force Base Open House
Andrews Air Force Base
Camp Springs, MD
(301) 981–4511
www.andrews.af.mil
This air show is an impressive display of American military and technological might. You'll see all those bombers and fighter planes you read about in the news, as well as precision formation flying by the crack Air Force Thunderbirds. As is often the case with sites and events in Metro Washington, you need to be early to avoid traffic.

JUNE
Washington, D.C.

DC Caribbean Carnival
Emery Park, Georgia and Missouri Avenues NW
Washington, DC
(202) 726–2204
www.dccaribbeancarnival.com
Washington's large Caribbean population

turns out in full force for this annual carnival that is reminiscent of Caribbean and Brazilian celebrations, though on a smaller scale. Participants wear elaborate costumes with sequins and peacocklike feather headpieces.

Dupont-Kalorama Museum Walk Day
Various locations on Dupont Circle
Washington, DC
(202) 667–0441
www.dkmuseums.com
D.C.'s most historic arts district extends a gracious welcome through house tours, craft demonstrations, and concerts on the first weekend in June. A shuttle service is provided.

Military Band Concerts
Locations vary
Washington, DC
(202) 619–7222
www.usafband.com
www.usarmyband.com
www.marineband.usmc.mil
www.navyband.navy.mil
Summer brings a daily dose of free concerts to Washington. On any night of the week, you can catch a patriotic performance by the U.S. Army Band, U.S. Air Force Band, U.S. Marine Corps Band, or U.S. Navy Band. The concerts are set against patriotic backdrops like the Washington Monument Sylvan Theatre, the U.S. Capitol, and the National World War II Memorial. Call the National Park Service or visit the bands' Web sites for an up-to-date schedule.

The Shakespeare Theatre Company
Free-for-All
Carter Barron Amphitheatre
16th Street and Colorado Avenue NW
Washington, DC
(202) 547–1122
www.shakespearedc.org
Carter Barron and D.C.'s Shakespeare Theatre Company collaborate to stage free, professional performances of Shakespearean masterpieces for two weeks every June. These open-air productions draw huge

crowds, in spite of the fact that you have to drive into D.C. to pick up those free tickets the same day as the performance.

Smithsonian Folklife Festival
National Mall
Between Independence and Constitution
Avenues
Washington, DC
(202) 275–1150
www.folklife.si.edu
The rich cultural and folklife heritage of the Americas is played out on the National Mall in the form of lectures, concerts, working villages, and hands-on exhibits. You'll see performances and exhibits from obscure societies you may not have known existed, as well as the more familiar ones, like Cajun or Navajo Nation. The festival runs through the 4th of July and attracts upward of 1 million people.

Northern Virginia

Antique Car Show
Sully Plantation
Route 28 (Sully Road)
Chantilly, VA
(703) 437–1794
A car-lover's fantasyland unfolds at this historic plantation in western Fairfax County, in the shadows of Washington Dulles International Airport. You'll find about 450 cars, ranging from the era of the Model-T to 1954. Admission is $8.00.

Celebrate Fairfax! Festival
Fairfax County Government Center Grounds
Government Center Parkway
Fairfax, VA
(703) 324–3247
www.celebratefairfax.org
This is not exactly a country fair, but then again, Fairfax County hasn't been rural for quite some time. Instead of livestock and produce, you'll get your fill of high-tech laser shows, fireworks, arts and crafts, business, government service, and community informa-

Close-up

Drama on Parade: Silent Drill at Sunset

These U.S. Marines move in such crisp and perfect unison that they almost look like robots. The hush of the audience is absolute. Faces are rapt, awestricken at the finesse of the Silent Drill Platoon. In the setting sun the bayonets fixed atop the M-1 rifles gleam like mirrors. The platoon stands erect and still—not a muscle seems to twitch.

Despite the heat of the summer evening, they are in full dress: white gloves, white caps and slacks, and the famous navy jackets. Above the scene towers the U.S. Marine Corps War Memorial, the famous bronze sculpture that captures the moment in World War II when U.S. Marines raised the flag on the Japanese island of Iwo Jima. It's a perfect backdrop for the dramatic demonstration that takes place at sunset on the green lawn below. The marines hold the sunset parades here, each Tuesday evening in summer, in tribute to the men who fought at Iwo Jima, as homage to those whose "uncommon valor was a common virtue." (The base of the sculpture bears the quotation in gold lettering.)

The parade begins with the platoon marching onto the green from an area behind the memorial. First come the Battle Colors, the Official Colors of the Corps. The streamers and silver bands that grace the Colors represent every battle, campaign, and expedition the corps has participated in since its founding more than two centuries ago. The Color Sergeant has the responsibility of carrying the National Colors, and by virtue of that billet is considered the senior sergeant in the Marine Corps. Then, clad in red jackets and white slacks, the U.S. Marines Drum and Bugle Corps, known as "The Commandant's Own," parade to a series of toe-tapping marches and popular tunes. Their choreography is intricate, and the marching patterns are fascinating to watch.

The climax of the evening is unquestionably the Silent Drill Platoon, a corps of elite military performers. They stand on the field alone, their bearing ramrod straight, their positioning accurate to a hair's breadth. Their silent exercise begins, a breathtaking drill punctuated only by the sound of the rifles thumping into their owners' gloved hands. The Rifle Inspector, who stands facing his 24-person team, issues no verbal commands. The rifles twirl, change hands, and

tion booths. There's also plenty of music, games, and rides along the midway for the kids and the young at heart.

Civil War Camp Day
Fort Ward Museum and Park
4301 West Braddock Road
Alexandria, VA
(703) 838–4848

Fort Ward was one of several Union fortifications that encircled Washington during the Civil War. This living history reenacts Union and Confederate camp life, complete with artillery drills. Suggested donation is $2.00

come to rest in a ruler-straight row pointing at the evening sky. Onlookers gasp with each twirl of the bayonets—risky maneuvers that miss the marines by only centimeters.

Each member of the platoon has spent six weeks training for 12 to 14 grueling hours a day. Training doesn't end there. New members must practice for six months before they are permitted to perform before the public. The goal is to spin the rifle and march without looking at the weapon. The group makes it look effortless, but around 50 percent of the marines recruited for the Silent Drill Team fail to graduate to the ranks. Mistakes during the parades are seldom seen, although if one does occur, it is then up to the marine to save face with another dazzling maneuver.

The highlight of the 11-minute drill is the moment when the Rifle Inspector comes to a stop before a single member of the team. The marine throws his rifle, spinning it into the air. The Rifle Inspector catches it with one hand, and there is the sharp report of metal as it hits. It's a strong, authoritative sound. Not a breath is heard from the audience as the two marines exchange the rifle, tossing it, spinning it, twisting it in different patterns and directions. When it is over, the audience exhales in relief that there were no mishaps, and then erupts in giddy applause.

The Tuesday evening Sunset Parades have been a summer tradition in Washington since 1957. They are free and no reservations are required, because there is only lawn seating. Those who plan ahead, however, can make reservations to attend the somewhat more elaborate Friday Evening Parades, held at the Marine Barracks in Washington, D.C. The Friday Evening Parades are 15 minutes longer than the Sunset Parades, and searchlights add to the drama. More marines also participate, including Private First Class Chesty XII, a brindle-and-white pedigreed English bulldog who serves as the official mascot of the Marine Barracks of Washington, D.C.

During the closing ceremony the marines march away and the searchlights are extinguished as a lone bugler comes out and plays "Taps."

For information on parking, reservations, and transportation, contact the Marine Barracks at (202) 433–6060.

Red Cross Waterfront Festival
Oronoco Bay Park
Base of Oronoco Street at the waterfront
Old Town Alexandria, VA
(703) 549–8300
www.waterfrontfestival.org
One of Alexandria's top summer events, the Red Cross Waterfront Festival brings in a weekend full of music (including some top-name rock, country, folk, and reggae acts), ethnic foods, canoe rides, juried arts and crafts, fireworks, tall ships, and even a 10K run to work off all the calories. Admission is $10.00 for adults and $5.00 for children.

JULY

Washington, D.C.

Annual Soap Box Derby
Begins at Constitution Avenue NW
Between New Jersey and Louisiana Avenues
Washington, DC
www.dcsoapboxderby.org
It takes an act of Congress each year to close the easternmost section of Constitution Avenue for this race, and each year Congress passes a joint resolution enabling the event—which proves that politicians aren't all sourpusses. Approximately 50 children from ages 9 to 16 participate in the "Gravity Grand Prix," as it's sometimes called, racing a course from Constitution and New Jersey Avenues NW to Louisiana Avenue NW. The route runs between the Russell Senate Office Building and the U.S. Capitol, and the event lasts all day. The kids build their own cars, some from kits and some not, and many have even recruited local businesses as sponsors. Participants take this 60-year-plus tradition seriously and put a lot of effort into their entries, but the event couldn't be more fun.

Brassene Les Halles Bastille Day
12th Street and Pennsylvania Avenue NW
Washington, DC
(202) 347–6848
www.leshalles.net
Washington has a large French-speaking community, plus many French restaurant fans, so this Gallic Independence Day celebration on July 14 draws plenty of participants. Enjoy live entertainment and watch waiters bearing trays race and tackle an obstacle course on Pennsylvania Avenue.

i Don't wait till the last weekend of the Smithsonian Folklife Festival to come down to the National Mall for arts, crafts, foods, and entertainment from around the world. That would be the hot and jam-packed July 4th weekend. Come a week earlier and enjoy it at an easier pace.

National Independence Day Celebration
The National Mall
Between Independence and Constitution Avenues NW
Washington, DC
(800) 215–6405
www.july4thparade.com
Washington fittingly plays host to the nation's largest 4th of July party, with a parade down Constitution Avenue, colonial military maneuvers, concerts at the Sylvan Theatre next to the Washington Monument, and an evening performance by the National Symphony Orchestra on the west steps of the Capitol. The day ends with a spectacular 45-minute fireworks exhibit that has been known to draw more than a million onlookers—on both sides of the river.

Waterlily Festival
Kenilworth Park and Aquatic Gardens
1900 Anacostia Drive SE
(202) 426–6905
www.nps.gov/kepa
A true off-the-beaten-path experience, Kenilworth Aquatic Gardens is a fascinating blooming ground for aquatic plants—the only National Park site of its kind, nestled against the Anacostia River. Each July the Waterlily Festival draws crowds to see the splendid flowers in peak bloom.

Northern Virginia

Vienna's Fourth of July Celebration
Waters Field
Cherry and Center Streets
Vienna, VA
(703) 255–6300
www.viennava.gov
One of suburban Washington's oldest July 4th celebrations, Vienna presents a viable small-town alternative to the pressing crowds and traffic associated with the downtown D.C. festivities. There's music and also some surprisingly good fireworks.

Suburban Maryland

Frederick's 4th—An Independence Day
Celebration!
Baker Park
121 North Bentz Street
Frederick, Maryland
(301) 694–2489
www.celebratefrederick.com
If you want a somewhat lower-key version of
the downtown July 4th festivities, try this
suburban version, with activities for children,
capped by a decent fireworks display that
draws thousands each year.

AUGUST
Northern Virginia

Arlington County Fair
Thomas Jefferson Center
3501 South 2nd Street
Arlington, VA
www.arlingtoncountyfair.org
Arlington's urban multicultural heritage is the
reason for this four-day fair typically held the
third week of the month. Craftspeople and
exhibits are indoors, while food vendors are
outside.

Suburban Maryland

Maryland Renaissance Festival
Crownsville Road, off Maryland Highway
450 East
Crownsville, MD
(410) 266–7304, (800) 296–7304
www.rennfest.com
The Free State slips into a medieval state of
mind during this well-attended festival usually held the last weekend of August and
extending into October. Jousting events, jug-
glers, and medieval foods and crafts are just
some of the many delights awaiting visitors
at this 20-acre "village" located in the heart

i A great way to view Independence
Day fireworks is from a boat on the
Potomac River, but whether you intend to
make a group tour or hire your own, try
to make reservations months in advance.

of suburban Crownsville. Admission is $17.00
for adults, $8.00 for children ages 7 to 15,
and free for kids 6 and under.

Montgomery County Agricultural Fair
Montgomery County Fairgrounds
Exit 10-11 off I–270
Gaithersburg, MD
(301) 926–3100
www.mcagfair.com
There's still plenty of rural character in this
highly urbanized county, as evidenced by the
size and popularity of this old-fashioned
country fair. You'll find livestock judging,
pony rides, a petting zoo, gardening displays,
old-time handcraft and baking exhibits,
amusement park rides, games of chance,
concerts, and plenty of food concessions.
Admission is $7.00 for adults and children 8
and up and $3.00 for children ages 2 to 7.
Parking costs $5.00.

Rotary Crab Feast
U.S. Navy-Marine Corps Stadium
Farragut Road
Annapolis, MD
(410) 841–2841
www.annapolisrotary.com
Lovers of Maryland's prized crustacean
should bring a hefty appetite to the world's
largest crab feast, held for over 50 years.
More than 185,000 gallons of crab soup and
325 bushels of Maryland blue crabs are con-
sumed at this spicy event, which benefits the
Annapolis Rotary Club.

SEPTEMBER
Washington, D.C.

Adams Morgan Day
On 18th Street NW between Columbia Road
and Florida Avenue NW
Washington, DC
(202) 232–1960
www.adamsmorgandayfestival.com
This giant ethnic festival, a salute to Adams
Morgan's multicultural character, is a hot
ticket with the city's young and hip crowd.
Expect to hear great music—reggae, jazz,
R&B, and salsa—and be tempted by some of
the city's best international cuisine.

Black Family Reunion
Washington Monument grounds
15th Street and Constitution Avenue NW
Washington, DC
(202) 737–0120
www.ncnw.org/events/reunion.htm
Since 1986 African American families have
gathered at the Washington Monument for
this annual event, organized by the National
Council of Negro Women. Themed pavilions
tackle issues like health, education, and economic empowerment, while music, activities,
and family entertainment make it a fun event
for all ages.

Kalorama House and Embassy Tour
Kalorama Neighborhood, Woodrow Wilson
House
2340 S Street NW
Washington, DC
(202) 387–4062
www.woodrowwilsonhouse.org
Historic Kalorama is still one of D.C.'s most
exclusive and interesting neighborhoods.
Homes and gardens in this area are lavish
and beautifully maintained. You begin at the
Woodrow Wilson House, a museum property
of the National Trust for Historic Preservation. Admission is $22 in advance and $25 on
the day of the tour.

Kennedy Center Open House
John F. Kennedy Center for the Performing
Arts
2700 F Street NW
Washington, DC
(202) 467–4600
www.kennedy-center.org
Stroll the towering red-carpeted halls of
Washington's premier performing arts center,
and then enjoy the free concerts and performances at this annual open house.

Labor Day Weekend Concert
West Lawn of the Capitol
Capitol Hill
Washington, DC
(202) 619–7222
The National Symphony Orchestra officially
closes Washington's summer tourist season
with a rousing selection of classical and patriotic arrangements. This event is packed, so
plan to come early, maybe with a blanket and
a picnic, and take public transportation or
you'll be caught in the mother of all traffic
jams.

Rock Creek Park Day
Nature Center, Rock Creek Park
5200 Glover Road NW
Washington, DC
(202) 426–6829
www.nps.gov/rocr
The nature center is headquarters for a slate
of environmental, recreational, and historical
programs during this daylong tribute to one
of the world's largest and most beautiful
urban parks. Each year Rock Creek Park Day
commemorates the founding of the park in
1890.

Northern Virginia

Fall for the Book
George Mason University
4400 University Drive
Fairfax, VA
(703) 993–3986
www.fallforthebook.org

This annual festival celebrating literacy, reading, and writing features free events for all ages. The wide range of programs includes author readings, signings, book appraisals, poetry slams, roving storytellers, workshops, and puppet shows.

International Children's Festival
Wolf Trap Farm Park for the Performing Arts
1624 Trap Road
Vienna, VA
(703) 642–0862
www.artsfairfax.org
At America's only national park for the performing arts, kids take center stage for a three-day outdoor festival celebrating the global arts. Sponsored by the Arts Council of Fairfax County, the popular event features a variety of performances and educational workshops presented by groups from the local area, throughout the U.S., and around the world. Most of the performance groups are largely made up of children. Admission is $12 for adults and $10 for children age three and older.

Occoquan Fall Craft Show
Mill, Union, Washington, and
Commerce Streets
Old Town Occoquan, VA
(703) 491–2168
www.occoquan.com
More than 350 juried artisans, representing 30 states, exhibit their wares in front of some 100,000 shoppers in this tidy and historic waterfront community. This weekend fair just might be the largest craft show on the East Coast. Admission is free.

Oktoberfest
Reston Town Center
Market Street
Reston, VA
(703) 787–6601
www.clydes.com
More than 20,000 people usually attend this four-day beer, polka, and sauerbraten festival in lively Reston Town Center. This is a big,

open area where you can let the kids run, and there's plenty to amuse them, from balloons to dancers and musicians. Admission is free.

Vienna Fall Carnival
Nottoway Park
9601 Courthouse Road
Vienna, VA
(703) 281–1333
www.viennava.gov
Carnival rides, popcorn, funnel cakes, and hot dogs are what this four-day event is all about. You can enjoy all the rides you want for $20 the first night of the event, which fell on September 7 in 2006. Admission is free the remaining three days, but you have to pay for all the rides.

Virginia Scottish Games
Fort Ward
4301 West Braddock Road
Alexandria, VA
(703) 912–1943
www.vascottishgames.org
The Virginia Scottish Games used to be held annually in July, but organizers moved it to September in 2006 in hopes of milder weather. No matter the month, it's still a treat to watch Northern Virginia embrace its Scottish heritage at this weekend fete. Entertainment highlights include Highland dancing, bagpiping, fiddling, and athletic events. Scottish foods, crafts, and genealogy exhibits are also part of the popular festival. Admission is $5.00 to $15.00.

Suburban Maryland
Kensington Labor Day Parade
On Plyers Mill Road and
Connecticut Avenue
Kensington, MD
(301) 949–2424
www.tok.org/Labor_day_parade/index.php
Each Labor Day for some 40 years, this old-fashioned, small-town parade has wound through the suburb of Kensington. With fire engines, antique cars, unicycles, marching bands, and dozens of other participants, the

parade especially appeals to kids, who scramble after candy and trinkets thrown by the marchers. Beware that because the parade falls just a couple months before elections, politicians are usually out in full force this day, taking the opportunity to stump for your vote.

Kunta Kinte Heritage Commemoration and Festival
Anne Arundel County Fairgrounds
Route 178
Crownsville, MD
(410) 349–0338
Made into a household name with the airing of TV's 1977 landmark ministries *Roots*, Kunta Kinte was brought into the harsh New World at the Port of Annapolis. Formerly held in August, the festival now takes place in September to honor Kunta Kinte's actual arrival date, September 29. In honor of Kunta Kinte and generations of succeeding African Americans, you'll find educational programs, crafts exhibits, and demonstrations, along with entertainment ranging from gospel singers to calypso. Admission is $7.00 for adults and $3.00 for seniors and children.

Maryland Seafood Festival
Sandy Point State Park
U.S. 50 at the Chesapeake Bay Bridge
Annapolis, MD
(410) 266–3113
www.mdseafoodfestival.com
The bounty of the Chesapeake Bay is baked, steamed, grilled, broiled, sautéed, and fried at this waterside park, next to the western end of the towering Bay Bridge. Admission is $10.00 for adults and $4.00 for children under seven.

Prince George's Community College Blue Bird Blues Festival
Prince George's Community College
301 Largo Road
Largo, MD
(301) 322–0856
www.pgcc.edu

It's a blues festival, but there are also children's activities, food, and crafts. The one-day event features a half-dozen or so local bands. Admission is free.

Prince George's County Fair
Prince George's Equestrian Center
U.S. Route 4
Upper Marlboro, MD
(301) 952–7900
www.countyfair.org
Like neighboring Montgomery County, urbanized Prince George's still holds on to its rural origins. Begun in 1842, this county fair is the oldest in the state of Maryland, and you'll find many old-time traditions like livestock contests, 4-H shows, and horticultural displays. (The county was once a major producer of tobacco, and vestiges of that tradition can still be seen in areas far beyond the Beltway.) Admission is $5.00.

Senior Beacon InfoExpo
White Flint Mall
North Bethesda, MD
(301) 949–9766
www.seniorbeacon.com
This annual expo hosted by the *Senior Beacon* newspaper draws thousands of senior citizens for free health screenings, seminars on everything from retirement finances to controlling clutter, and dozens of exhibitors. The expo is also held in the same week at Springfield Mall in Virginia.

OCTOBER
Washington, D.C.
Annual Lombardi Gala
Various locations throughout Washington, DC
(202) 687–1067
lombardi.georgetown.edu
All proceeds from this benefit go to the Lombardi Cancer Center at Georgetown University Medical Center. The Lombardi Center is one of only 40 centers in the nation designated as a comprehensive cancer center by

the U.S. National Cancer Institute, a part of the National Institutes of Health. The gala features a dinner and a silent auction of many high-ticket items. Admission is $400.

Duke Ellington Jazz Festival
Various locations
Washington, DC
(202) 232–3611
www.dejazzfest.org

Washington, D.C. native Duke Ellington serves as inspiration for this annual jazz festival, which draws some of the genre's biggest names. Performances take place in popular venues like the Kennedy Center and Lincoln Theatre, as well as outdoor venues like the Sylvan Theatre on the grounds of the Washington Monument.

Library of Congress National Book Festival
National Mall between 7th and 14th Streets NW
Washington, DC
(888) 714–4696
www.loc.gov/bookfest

The world's largest library spills out onto the National Mall each year in late September or early October with a special daylong celebration of the written word. Noted authors are on hand to read from their collections, and budding authors are encouraged to share their stories as well. First Lady Laura Bush serves as honorary chair of this event.

Washington International Horse Show
Verizon Center
Washington, DC
(301) 987–9400
www.wihs.org

Equestrian teams from the United States and Europe compete in a week of events, with plenty of sideline shows for laypeople and kids. There are competitions in dressage and jumping and exhibition events. Admission ranges from $15 to $60, depending on dates and seat locations.

i Some of the best local blues can be heard for free at Carter Barron's outdoor theater in the summer.

Northern Virginia

Marine Corps Marathon
Iwo Jima Memorial
U.S. 50 at Arlington National Cemetery
Arlington, VA
(800) RUN–USMC
www.marinemarathon.com

Thousands of world-class runners snake through the downtown streets and parks in what has become one of the nation's most prestigious marathons. Although most of the action takes place in Washington, the race begins and ends at the Iwo Jima Memorial in Arlington. Registration is $75 for runners.

Theodore Roosevelt's Birthday Celebration
Theodore Roosevelt Island
George Washington Memorial Parkway
Arlington, VA
(703) 289–2550
www.nps.gov/this

The scenic urban wilderness sanctuary of Roosevelt Island plays host to this birthday party honoring the nation's first environmental president. Hike along trails in this 88-acre preserve, view the 17-foot bronze statue of Roosevelt, then stop and chat with the Roosevelt look-alike who plays the former president for the day. There's even birthday cake!

Vienna Halloween Parade
Branch and Maple Avenues
Vienna, VA
(703) 255–6300
www.viennava.gov

Vienna claims the region's oldest (since the 1940s) and largest (several thousand strong) Halloween Parade, which wends its way along a stretch of the town's main thoroughfare.

Waterford Homes Tour and Crafts Exhibit
Route 662 to High Street
Waterford, VA
(540) 882–3018
www.waterfordva.org
More than 50 years ago a group of Waterford residents had the foresight to set up a preservation foundation in Loudoun County to save this picturesque National Historic Landmark village from suburbia. The annual event, which features more than 100 juried artisans, benefits ongoing restoration and preservation efforts. Admission is $13 in advance and $15 on the day of the tour and show. Children 12 and under are admitted free.

Suburban Maryland

Taste of Bethesda
Fairmont, Norfolk, and St. Elmo Streets
Bethesda, MD
(301) 215–6660
www.bethesda.org
Tens of thousands of food experts flock to this food and music festival showcasing more than 50 prime restaurants in Bethesda. Admission is free, and food tickets are sold in bundles of four for $5.00.

U.S. Sailboat Show/U.S. Power
Boat Show
Annapolis City Dock, Dock Street
Annapolis, MD
(410) 268–8828
www.usboat.com
Held on consecutive weekends, with the sailors going first, these are the largest in-water boat shows in the nation. With boats and nautical products from the world's leading manufacturers, Annapolis turns into a festival for the water-loving set. General admission is $16 for adults and $8.00 for children 12 and under.

NOVEMBER

Northern Virginia

Alexandria Antiques Show
Holiday Inn Hotel and Suites
625 First Street
Old Town Alexandria, VA
(703) 549–5811
www.historicalalexandriafoundation.org
You guessed it—more antiques and crafts from the heirloom gold mine of the mid-Atlantic. The furniture here is often quite formal, in keeping with the Old Town setting, with lots of oil paintings and European pieces. Admission is $12.

Veterans Day Ceremonies
Vietnam Veterans Memorial
Constitution Avenue and Henry Bacon Drive NW
Washington, DC

Arlington National Cemetery
Memorial Drive
Arlington, VA
(202) 619–7222
www.nps.gov/ncro
Both solemn and celebratory, the ceremonies attract thousands of veterans, military VIPs, general spectators, and, often, the commander-in-chief of the armed forces (a.k.a. the president).

Suburban Maryland

Sugarloaf's Autumn Crafts Festival
Montgomery County Fairgrounds
Exit 10 or 11 off I–270
Gaithersburg, MD
(301) 990–1400
www.sugarloafcrafts.com
This is it—the granddaddy of all Metro D.C. craft shows, featuring 500 juried artisans. It'll take you two hours just to walk the grounds, let alone browse and shop. Admission is $7.00. Other, smaller shows are offered throughout the year.

Even serious and patriotic places get in the holiday spirit in Washington, D.C. COURTESY WASHINGTON, D.C. CONVENTION AND TOURISM CORPORATION

DECEMBER

Washington, D.C.

National Christmas Tree Lighting/Pageant of Peace
The Ellipse, behind the White House
Between 15th and 17th Streets NW
Washington, DC
(202) 619–7222
www.nps.gov/whho/pageant
The president lights the giant National Christmas Tree and officially kicks off the Christmas season. From early December to New Year's Day, the Ellipse is the site of nightly choral concerts, a nativity scene, live reindeer, a burning yule log, and lighted Christmas trees from each of the nation's states and territories.

Washington Auto Show
Washington Convention Center
801 Mount Vernon Place NW
Washington, DC
(202) 237–7200
www.washingtonautoshow.com
Each year, this massive exhibition introduces car buffs to next year's models, as well as wildly imaginative concept cars that may one day come to market in modified form. There are often autograph signings by Washington celebrities, live radio broadcasts, and, of course, those glamorous human models in their glittering outfits. Admission is $10.

Washington National Cathedral Christmas Celebration and Services
Washington National Cathedral
Massachusetts and Wisconsin
Avenues NW
Washington, DC
(202) 537–6200
www.cathedral.org
The Christmas Eve service here, at Washington's answer to the great cathedrals of Europe, is simply breathtaking; however, passes are required to attend, and you should write for them in November if you expect to snag one of the 3,400 seats available for either the 6:00 P.M. or 10:00 P.M. service on Christmas Eve. At the earlier service the cathedral's 24-member girls' choir performs; the later service features 40 singers of the men's and boys' choir.

Up to six tickets per person may be requested by sending a self-addressed, stamped envelope to Christmas (the year), Washington National Cathedral, Massachusetts and Wisconsin Avenues NW, Washington, D.C. 20016. Be sure to include your own name, address, and a daytime phone number with your request. Requests are not accepted via fax or e-mail. Also specify which service you would like to attend. On Christmas Day, there are services at 9:00 A.M., noon, and 4:00 P.M., and none require passes. The 9:00 A.M. is televised and features a choir, while the two later services have only organ music and hymns.

Northern Virginia

Alexandria Scottish Christmas Walk
Campagna Center
418 South Washington Street
Alexandria, VA
(703) 549–0111
www.scottishwalk.org
A gathering of the clans—bagpipes and all—takes over the streets and alleys of Old Town for one of the holiday season's most festive events. Adjunct activities include a designer tour of homes and a Christmas marketplace of decorations and ornaments at the Campagna Center (no admission fee). The Historic Alexandria Candlelight Tours continue the magic the very next week. Check www.funside.com for more Alexandria holiday events.

Northern Virginia Christmas Craft Market
Expo Center
Willard Road and Route 28
Chantilly, VA
(757) 417–7771
www.emgshows.com
More than 250 fine artists and craftspeople display their work, including Christmas collectibles and a seemingly infinite number of home decorating ideas for the holidays. Spe-

cialty food vendors also offer gift food packages and stocking stuffers. Admission to the three-day show is $7.00.

Suburban Maryland

Christmas Lights Parade
Annapolis City Dock
Dock Street
Annapolis, MD
(410) 280–0445
www.visit-annapolis.org
Annapolitans decorate their yachts with Christmas lights for this highly visual, and often chilly, evening on the Chesapeake Bay.

Festival of Lights
Washington Mormon Temple Visitors' Center
9900 Stoneybrook Drive
Kensington, MD
(301) 587–0144
www.washingtonlds.org
Tens of thousands of lights adorn the grounds of this Oz-like temple looming above the Capital Beltway. Inside the visitor center are Christmas trees bearing decorations from around the world. The temple itself is open only to those of the Mormon faith. (See the Worship chapter for more information.)

The Castle serves as an information center for visitors to the Smithsonian museums on the National Mall.

ATTRACTIONS

You'll never lack for something to do in Metro Washington. Just when you think you've seen it all, a new monument opens or the Smithsonian Institution hosts a special exhibition. In this chapter we fill you in on some of the region's most popular attractions, from monuments and museums to famous historic sites. At the end we've included information on some of the leading commercial tour operators. See the Metro Washington Overview chapter for information about the numerous convention and visitors bureaus and tourism offices that serve the Washington area.

You'll also find some important attractions featured prominently in other chapters. Washington's major art museums, such as the National Gallery, are described in our Arts chapter. Our Kidstuff chapter details the family-oriented exhibits and programs at many museums listed here. We cross-reference such entries where applicable.

Price Code

Because admission prices change so frequently, we offer the following price code to give you a general idea of what you can expect to pay at area attractions. You may be surprised, however, at how many are free!

$. . . . . Under $5.00
$$ . . . . $5.00 to $7.99
$$$ . . . . $8.00 to $12.00
$$$$ . . . . $12.00 and higher

WASHINGTON, D.C.

Monuments

Franklin Delano Roosevelt
Memorial   Free
West Potomac Park,
along the Tidal Basin
1850 West Basin Drive SW
Washington, DC
(202) 426–6841
www.nps.gov/fdrm/home.htm

Dedicated in May 1997, this tribute to FDR's presidency is notable for being the city's first completely wheelchair-accessible monument. When the memorial opened, however, the president's disability was conspicuously absent. Four years later, a life-size statue of the president in his wheelchair was added to appease critics. As you walk through the impressive memorial, you'll also be greeted by the likeness of Fala the terrier. Eleanor Roosevelt is also honored—the first time a presidential memorial included the First Lady.

On seven and a half acres near the Jefferson Memorial, the monument features four outdoor "galleries" representing each term of FDR's presidency. Gardens, pools, and fountains accent the pathway that connects the different sections; in fact, early visitors found the water so inviting on hot summer days that park police issued an order banning people from splashing in the fountains! Photo opportunities abound here: Tourists especially enjoy posing with the life-size figures in the breadline sculpted by George Segal. You'll find the memorial right off the path that circles the Tidal Basin, which is a must-see during cherry blossom season in April. Rangers staff the site from 8:00 A.M. to midnight daily, except on

> ℹ️ There are 19 statues at the Korean War Veterans Memorial, but the reflective black granite wall makes it look like there are 38 figures—representing the 38th parallel, the pre-war border between North and South Korea.

December 25. The site has special parking for disabled visitors, but regular spaces in the vicinity fill up quickly. If you don't mind walking, take the Metro to the Smithsonian station.

Korean War Veterans Memorial   Free
French Drive SW
Washington, DC
(202) 426–6841
www.nps.gov/kwvm/home.htm
Dedicated in 1995, this startling tribute to the 1.5 million U.S. men and women who served during the Korean War features a stainless-steel patrol of 19 lifelike statues, designed by World War II veteran Frank Gaylord. Depicting members of the four branches of the armed forces, the scattered sculptures face a black granite wall that's etched with photographic images of actual American servicemen and -women. The site, featuring a circular Pool of Remembrance and grove of trees, is near the Lincoln Memorial Reflecting Pool. Staffed hours are 8:00 A.M. to midnight daily, except December 25. Foggy Bottom is the closest Metro stop.

Lincoln Memorial   Free
On 23rd Street and Independence Avenue NW
Washington, DC
(202) 426–6841
www.nps.gov/linc/home.htm
The somber, seated Civil War president looks past the stairs that have served as a site for many public demonstrations and across the vast Reflecting Pool. An equally captivating vista is the one in the opposite direction, straight across Memorial Bridge and up to Arlington House on the hill overlooking Arlington National Cemetery.

Completed in 1922 and modeled after the Parthenon in Athens, the memorial, designed by architect Henry Bacon, includes walls that are inscribed with the Gettysburg Address and Lincoln's Second Inaugural Address. Daniel Chester French's 19-by-19-foot marble statue has eyes that really do seem to follow you as you walk past, gazing up at the serious face. Staffed by National Park Service rangers from 8:00 A.M. to midnight daily except December 25, the memorial includes a bookstore on the lower level along with restrooms, concessions, and additional exhibits. To avoid parking hassles, take the Metro to the Foggy Bottom stop.

The National Law Enforcement Officers Memorial   Free
E Street between Fourth and Fifth Streets NW
Washington, DC
(202) 737–3400
www.nleomf.com/
The National Law Enforcement Officers Memorial, dedicated in 1991, features a tree-lined pathway leading past a granite wall displaying the names of fallen officers. Tragically, the list is expansive, with more than 17,000 names, including the first police officer ever killed in the line of duty, back in 1794. The memorial, open 24 hours daily, is at Judiciary Square, between E and F Streets and 4th and 5th Streets NW, right next to a Metro station. A visitor center features exhibits relating to many of the slain officers. It also houses a gift shop. Hours are 9:00 A.M. to 5:00 P.M. Monday through Friday, 10:00 A.M. to 5:00 P.M. Saturdays, and noon to 5:00 P.M. Sundays and holidays, except New Year's Day, Thanksgiving, and Christmas.

National World War II Memorial   Free
17th Street and Independence Avenue NW
Washington, DC
(202) 426–6281
www.nps.gov/nwwm
Dedicated on Memorial Day weekend 2004, the newest memorial on the National Mall honors the 16 million who served in uniform,

D.C.'s newest national monument, the National World War II Memorial, pays tribute to the men and women who served and sacrificed overseas and on the home front. COURTESY WASHINGTON, D.C. CONVENTION AND TOURISM CORPORATION

the 400,000 killed in action, and supporters who sacrificed on the home front. Two 43-foot pavilions mark the entrances to the memorial, representing the Atlantic and Pacific theaters of action. Surrounding the memorial plaza, you'll find 56 granite pillars representing the states and territories. The memorial's centerpiece is the Freedom Wall, a field of 4,000 stars, each one representing 100 lives lost in action.

Thomas Jefferson Memorial   **Free**
Southern end of 15th Street SW
Washington, DC
(202) 426–6821
www.nps.gov/thje/home.htm
Breathtaking any time, but especially at

night, the Jefferson Memorial has an undeniable aura, sensed by locals and tourists alike. Inspired during our first visit to the city, we huddled with our touring high school youth group on the memorial's moonlit front steps and harmonized on "Let There Be Peace on Earth."

The architectural firm that blueprinted the National Gallery of Art also designed this memorial, built in the style of Jefferson's Rotunda at the University of Virginia and dedicated in 1943 on Jefferson's 200th birthday.

> **i** Climb the 87—or "four score and seven"—steps at the Lincoln Memorial.

Marble walls inscribed with Thomas Jefferson's writings surround the 19-foot bronze likeness of our third president. Created by Rudolph Evans, the statue crowns a 6-foot pedestal. Looking from the memorial across the Tidal Basin affords an unforgettable illuminated view of downtown Washington. Add blossoming cherry trees and a warm, sunny spring day and you're talking tingles up and down the spine.

The memorial is open 24 hours a day, staffed from 8:00 A.M. to midnight daily, except on December 25. You can purchase Jefferson-related books and other items in the bookstore on the lower level and in the gift shop upstairs near the rotunda. The site also has exhibits, restrooms, and concessions. Parking, as usual, is scarce, so think about taking the Metro to the Smithsonian station.

U.S. Navy Memorial and
Naval Heritage Center   Free
701 Pennsylvania Avenue NW, Suite 123
Washington, DC
(202) 737–2300
www.lonesailor.org

This interesting memorial at Market Square, open 24 hours, features the largest map of the world, inlaid in granite on the plaza. The Lone Sailor, a beautiful Stanley Bleifeld sculpture, keeps sentry. Nearby, two walls hold 22 bronze-sculpture panels, a representation of American naval history, and a salute to those who have served or will serve in the navy. Fountains and pools further accent the plaza. Inside the adjacent Naval Heritage Center, guests can view free movies daily at noon. The center, which also features interactive videos, a log room, and a gift shop, is open 9:30 A.M. to 5:00 P.M. Monday through Saturday, March through October, 9:30 A.M. to 5:00 P.M. Tuesday through Saturday, November through February. The closest Metro station is Archives/Navy Memorial.

Vietnam Veterans Memorial   Free
Bacon Drive and Constitution
Avenue NW
Washington, DC
(202) 426–6841
www.nps.gov/vive/home.htm

Just a short walk from the Reflecting Pool and the Lincoln Memorial, the Vietnam Veterans Memorial, or simply "The Wall," has become one of the most visited monuments in the city since its controversial opening in 1982, attracting more than 1.7 million people annually. Built with private funds, the structure—designed by a young architecture student named Maya Ying Lin—is composed of simple black granite panels embedded in the earth and etched (in chronological order) with the names of the more than 58,000 Americans who perished in the war. A few steps away, a pair of amazingly lifelike bronze sculptures depict servicemen and -women in wartime action scenes. The Wall is often the site of some of the most moving personal tributes ever witnessed at a very public place. A new memorial center designed to enhance the visitor's experience is currently under development. Construction is expected to begin in 2008. The memorial is staffed from 8:00 A.M. to midnight daily, except on Christmas. Nearby you'll find concessions, restrooms, and a bookstore. The closest Metro station is Foggy Bottom.

Washington Monument   Free
15th Street NW
Washington, DC
(202) 426–6841
www.nps.gov/wamo/home.htm

Even newcomers can't miss this 555-foot signature landmark.

Certainly one of the most photographed icons anywhere, the marble tower—the tallest freestanding masonry structure in the world—contains nearly 200 memorial stones from many states as well as numerous countries and organizations. An elevator ride to the 500-foot level rewards visitors with an unsurpassed view of Washington and environs.

You need a ticket to go inside the monument. Pick up as many as six from the kiosk on 15th Street, normally open 8:00 A.M. to 4:30 P.M. Or, make reservations in advance by calling the National Park Reservation service at (800) 967–2283 or visit reservations.nps.gov. A reserved ticket will cost a few dollars. The monument's regular hours are 9:00 A.M. to 4:45 P.M. September through March and 8:00 A.M. to midnight April through August. A bookstore, exhibits, concessions, and restrooms are nearby. The site is closed December 25. The Smithsonian Metro is the closest station.

Federal Sites

Bureau of Engraving and Printing   Free
14th and C Streets SW
Washington, DC
(202) 874–2330, (866) 874–2330
www.moneyfactory.com
Few people ever get closer to so much money than they do at the Department of the Treasury's Bureau of Engraving and Printing, which boasts a recently renovated gallery from which to watch currency being printed. A 35-minute guided tour, one of the most popular in Washington, offers visitors a look at the fascinating process involved in the production of U.S. currency as well as stamps. Hours vary seasonally, but tours generally start every 20 minutes from 9:00 A.M. to 2:00 P.M. Monday through Friday, except federal holidays. They also take place from 5:00 to 6:45 P.M. from May through August.

Tickets, required March through August, are free but available only on a first-come, first-served basis. The ticket booth on Raoul Wallenberg Place (formerly 15th Street) is open from 8:00 A.M. until all tickets are distributed, Monday through Friday. Tours end in the visitor center, open from 8:30 A.M. to 8:00 P.M. during peak season and 8:30 A.M. to 3:00 P.M. during nonpeak months, where you can purchase fun souvenirs like pens filled with shredded currency. Smithsonian is the nearest Metro station.

i Contact your congressional representative's office to request congressional passes and tickets for special tours of the White House and U.S. Capitol. They're in limited supply, and you must ask for them at least three months in advance.

Congressional Cemetery   Free
1801 E Street SE
Washington, DC
(202) 543–0539
www.congressionalcemetery.org
This cemetery on the Anacostia River in Southeast D.C. is a final resting place for more than 60,000 Americans, including more than 60 senators and representatives.

Scores of interesting American personalities found here include such notables as John Philip Sousa, J. Edgar Hoover, Mathew Brady, and several Native American chiefs. At Congressional Cemetary you also can view the grave of Vice President Elbridge Gerry of Massachusetts, the man who gave us the term *gerrymander,* a reference to voting-district alterations that give one political party an unfair advantage and often result in oddly shaped jurisdictions. The cemetery is open from dawn to dusk. The office and library are open from 10:00 A.M. to 2:00 P.M. Monday, Wednesday, and Friday, and 9:00 A.M. to 1:00 P.M. on Saturday.

Department of State   Free
22nd and C Streets NW
Washington, DC
(202) 647–3241
www.state.gov/www/about_state/diprooms/tour.html
This massive agency, responsible for creating and carrying out U.S. foreign policy, is partly accessible to the general public. A must-see for eighteenth-century furniture aficionados, free 45-minute tours of the elegant eighth-floor diplomatic reception areas begin at 9:30 and 10:30 A.M. and 2:45 P.M. Monday through Friday, except federal holidays. The tour is

not recommended for children unless they're older than 12, and strollers are not permitted. Call to make required reservations at least four weeks in advance, if possible. Written materials about the many interesting aspects of the department are available by calling the Public Information Division at (202) 647–6575.

Federal Bureau of Investigation   Free
J. Edgar Hoover FBI Building
935 Pennsylvania Avenue NW
Washington, DC
(202) 324–3447, (202) 324–1016 TDY
www.fbi.gov/aboutus/tour/tour.htm
The J. Edgar Hoover Building is as intriguing as the man himself. It's undergoing major renovations, however, and is temporarily closed for tours. Call for updated information on the reopening. When it's available, the free, one-hour excursion through America's top law-enforcement agency offers an inside look at crime-fighting techniques and crime laboratories, a peek at photos of the FBI's Ten Most Wanted Fugitives, and a thrilling live firearms demonstration, viewed safely from behind glass. After the tour, visit the gift shop for FBI souvenirs. Like so many of the city's other popular tours, this one requires early arrival to ensure ticket admission. Walk here from Metro Center, Federal Triangle, Gallery Place, or the Archives/Navy Memorial Metro stations.

The Interior Museum   Free
1849 C Street NW
Washington, DC
(202) 208–4743
www.doi.gov/interiormuseum
Housed in the Department of Interior's main building, constructed during the FDR administration, this unique museum features exhibits of surveying equipment, maps, historical documents, natural history, and American Indian cultures. Visitors can view many of the original 1930s features, such as art deco–style metal silhouettes and intricately detailed dioramas that depict Interior bureaus.

The museum is open from 8:30 A.M. to 4:30 P.M. Monday through Friday and 1:00 to 4:00 P.M., with family activities, the third Saturday of each month. It's closed on federal holidays. Adults must show photo IDs to enter. Call two weeks in advance to arrange guided tours or to see the New Deal murals. Farragut West is the nearest Metro stop.

Library of Congress   Free
Independence Avenue at 1st Street SE
Washington, DC
(202) 707–8000
www.loc.gov/loc/visit
Another one of Thomas Jefferson's legacies to Washington, his personal collection of books grew into the world's largest library, totaling some 120 million items in 460 languages. One million people annually visit the library's three buildings, all of which house topical reading rooms open to adults older than high-school age. The Thomas Jefferson Building houses a visitor center and 90-seat theater where you can watch a film about the library. Don't miss the marble-floored Great Hall, where you can view such treasures as the Gutenberg Bible and the room's magnificent stained-glass ceiling. Other highlights include the main reading room, a large gift shop, a performing arts gallery, and special rooms that display some of the library's important collections. Take a free guided tour at 10:30 and 11:30 A.M. and 1:30, 2:30, and 3:30 P.M. Monday through Friday; and at 10:30 and 11:30 A.M. and 1:30 and 2:30 P.M. on Saturdays. Call TTY (202) 707–6362 in advance to arrange for sign-language interpretation, available at 2:30 P.M. Monday and 11:30 A.M. Friday. Borrow a free audio wand to listen to famous speeches and music displayed in American Treasures. The building is open from 10:00 A.M. to 5:00 P.M. Monday through Saturday, and closed on Sundays and federal holidays. Visitors should enter the Carriage entrance at 1st Street and go to the information desk, where tours start.

The library's Madison and John Adams Buildings offer reading rooms, and the Madison also contains exhibitions and a cafeteria. Call (202) 707–6400 for reading room hours and instructions on how to obtain a required

Reader Identification card if you plan to do research or read at the library.

Located on Capitol Hill near the U.S. Capitol, the library is close to the Capitol South Metro stop.

The National Aquarium $
Department of Commerce Building
14th Street between Constitution and Pennsylvania Avenues NW
Washington, DC
(202) 482–2825
www.nationalaquarium.com
Now affiliated with the centerpiece of Baltimore's Inner Harbor that shares the same name, this is the nation's oldest aquarium, established in 1873. It's one of the city's lesser-known attractions, due in part, perhaps, to its basement location. Some 70 tanks house more than 270 species of aquatic creatures, including alligators, sea turtles, and denizens of the Touch Tank, a children's favorite that offers a thrilling hands-on experience with underwater life. Be sure to check on times for the popular shark feedings. (See our Kidstuff chapter for a complete description.)

National Archives Building Free
700 Pennsylvania Avenue, with entrance on Constitution Avenue, between 7th and 9th Streets NW
Washington, DC
(202) 357–5000, (866) 325–7208
www.archives.gov
The three most important documents in America—the Declaration of Independence, the Constitution, and the Bill of Rights—now reside in helium-filled, sealed glass encasements in the beautiful Rotunda of this well-guarded building. To keep the precious parchments out of harm's way, the Charters of Freedom are lowered 20 feet each evening into a special bombproof, fireproof vault. After a major renovation, visitors can view all four pages of the Constitution in new, state-of-the-art encasements. To show that it's more than just the Charters of Freedom, the Archives also opened a new exhibition, the

Public Vaults, which displays more than 1,000 records, photographs, and recordings from its permanent collection. A new movie theater hosts Oscar-nominated documentary screenings and historic film showcases.

The Rotunda also houses the 1297 Magna Carta and the *American Originals* exhibit of other important historical documents. For a totally different experience, trace your family history in the cavernous Research Room, or simply take advantage of one of the free lectures, films, or other exhibits.

For a schedule of public events, visit www.archives.gov/calendar. The Rotunda is open 10:00 A.M. to 7:00 P.M. in spring and summer; it closes at 5:30 P.M. from Labor Day through March 14. Researchers can access the collections Monday through Friday from 9:00 A.M. to 5:00 P.M. It's closed on Sundays and federal holidays. The nearest Metro stop is Archives/Navy Memorial.

The Old Post Office Pavilion Free
1100 Pennsylvania Avenue NW
Washington, DC
(202) 289–4224
oldpostofficedc.com
This 12-story landmark soaring above America's Main Street was built in 1899 as the nation's postal headquarters. Since concerned citizens stepped in to save the building from demolition in 1934, it has been masterfully renovated to feature shopping, dining, and entertainment attractions. Ride the glass elevator up to the tower's 12th-floor observation deck for a dramatic view. The Pavilion is open from 10:00 A.M. to 8:00 P.M. Monday through Saturday, noon to 7:00 P.M. Sunday March through August; it closes an hour earlier in fall and winter. Federal Triangle is the nearest Metro station.

Organization of American States Free
Art Museum of the Americas
17th Street and Constitution Avenue NW
Washington, DC
(202) 458–3000
www.museum.oas.org
The incredible art and culture of the Ameri-

ℹ️ You'll find Washington, D.C.'s central point clearly marked on the basement floor of the United States Capitol.

cas—Canada, the Caribbean, Latin America, and the United States—unfolds at this impressive compound across from the Ellipse. The main building boasts a monumental entrance hall and huge Palladian windows and features changing exhibitions. Be sure to visit the Art Museum of the Americas, housed in a separate building at 201 18th Street NW. Hours are 10:00 A.M. to 5:00 P.M. Tuesday through Sunday. The museum is closed Mondays, federal holidays, and Good Friday. To arrange a guided tour, call (202) 458–6016. Farragut West is the nearest Metro stop.

While in the vicinity, walk across Virginia Avenue and take a look at the striking statue of Simon Bolívar, the liberator of much of South America.

Supreme Court of the United States   Free
1st Street and Maryland Avenue NE
Washington, DC
(202) 479–3211
www.supremecourtus.gov/visiting/visiting.html

The weightiest legal decisions in the land are handed down behind the imposing columned facade of this renowned building. Although their work is of paramount importance, the nine justices don't deliberate for a full calendar year, but go into session only between October and June. They typically hand down orders and opinions on Mondays, an exciting time to visit. When the nation's highest court is not in session, free lectures are given on weekdays every hour on the half-hour from 9:30 A.M. to 3:30 P.M. When court is in session, line up early on the Front Plaza for limited seating. You can choose to hear a full argument, or just watch for a few minutes. The building, open from 9:00 A.M. to 4:30 P.M. weekdays except holidays, also has exhibits, a film, a gift shop, and food. Union Station and Capitol South are the nearest Metro stations.

The United States Botanic Garden Conservatory   Free
Maryland Avenue and First Street SW
Washington, DC
(202) 225–8333
www.usbg.gov

This showcase for living plants sits on the grounds of the U.S. Capitol. Highlights include almost 4,000 plants housed in a climate-controlled environment, a new three-acre National Garden showcasing unusual and ornamental plants, a gift shop, themed gardens, and features designed for safety and accessibility. The conservatory holds numerous workshops, tours, lectures, and family activities. Hours are 10:00 A.M. to 5:00 P.M. daily. The nearest Metro stations are Federal Center Southwest and Capitol South.

United States Capitol   Free
East End of the Mall on Capitol Hill
Washington, DC
(202) 225–6827
www.aoc.gov/cc/visit/index.cfm

Perhaps the strongest competitor to the Washington Monument in terms of world-wide recognition, the Capitol looms majestically over the city as its tallest building, something that will never change, thanks to the farsighted vision of early planners of the federal district. Tours of the great halls and the magnificent renovated Central Rotunda of this regal edifice take place from 9:00 A.M. to 4:30 P.M. Monday through Saturday. All visitors must join a ticketed, guided tour to see its interior. Wait in line at the Capitol Guide Service kiosk, which opens at 9:00 A.M., near the intersection of First Street SW and Independence Avenue. Following your tour, you can visit the House and Senate chambers. A massive, underground Capitol Visitor Center is in the works, with completion expected in September 2007. Expect the tour ticket distribution system to change—for the better—if you visit when the center is open. Tours will be available to larger groups, and you'll have a climate-controlled, interactive center to ease your wait.

In addition to the Rotunda, your guide will point out the colorfully detailed Brumidi Corridors, featuring painted walls designed in the 1850s by Italian artist Constantino Brumidi. Many of the works have been restored to their original appearance. You'll also see such highlights as the dimly lit Old Supreme Court Chamber, restored to look just as it did in the mid-nineteenth century; the National Statuary Hall, featuring sculpted tributes to notable Americans; and the President's Room, an ornate chamber that many presidents used for late-night bill signing.

For a peek at Congress in action, obtain a pass through the office of your representative or senator. You don't need a pass to visit the House and Senate galleries when Congress isn't in session. Capitol South and Union Station are the closest Metro stations.

U.S. Department of Agriculture   Free
12th Street and Jefferson Drive SW
Washington, DC
(202) 720–4197
www.usda.gov/oo/visitorcenter/
Trace America's agrarian roots at the Department of Agriculture's Visitor Information Center, located in the Administration Building. Exhibits and displays change regularly. This monolithic agency is housed in one of the largest structures in Washington, just a short walk from the National Mall. Hours are 9:00 A.M. to 3:00 P.M. Monday through Friday.

U.S. Information Agency   Free
330 Independence Avenue SW
Washington, DC
(202) 203–4959
www.voanews.com
The American propaganda machine comes alive on the Voice of America tour at the U.S.I.A., which now boasts the Multimedia Broadcast Center and Visitor Center. The 45-minute tour tells the story of how the VOA's shortwave radio systems and television programs, magazines, and books are used to gain support abroad for American policies. Take a tour at noon or 3:00 P.M. Monday

through Friday except holidays; call (202) 203–4990 to make required reservations or visit www.voanews.com to reserve online.

The White House   Free
1600 Pennsylvania Avenue NW
Washington, DC
(202) 456–7041, (202) 456–2121 TDD
www.whitehouse.gov
Known as the President's Palace in its early days, this masterpiece of federal architecture each year hosts scores of dignitaries, entertainers, and other luminaries. Burned by the British during the War of 1812, the White House has been home to every president and his family except George Washington.

The White House now offers tours for parties of 10 or more, which must be requested through your Congress member up to six months in advance. Visit the Web site for a virtual look at the seven rooms normally included.

If possible, take a virtual tour or actual tour during December to see the halls decked in holiday splendor.

The visitor center, open from 7:30 A.M. to 4:00 P.M. daily, features a video presentation and exhibits about the White House, as well as a gift shop. (See our Annual Events chapter for details about the Easter Egg Roll and garden tours.)

Directly south of the White House grounds is an expanse of parkland known as the Ellipse, the site of the annual Pageant of Peace holiday celebration (see our Annual Events chapter). One of the Ellipse's little-known features is the Settlers' Memorial, a granite marker located near 15th Street. Here you will find inscribed the names of the 18 landowners whose corn and tobacco farms ultimately became the land that is today's Washington, D.C.

Federal Triangle is the closest Metro stop.

i The White House was originally called the President's Palace. President Theodore Roosevelt dubbed it the White House in 1901.

Museums and Galleries

The Smithsonian Institution—on the National Mall

Arts and Industries Building   Free
900 Jefferson Drive SW
Washington, DC
(202) 633–1100, (202) 633–5285 TTY
www.si.edu/ai
You'll feel as though you've stepped back in time when you enter this Victorian-style building, next to the Castle (see following entry). Although it still shows traces of its previous incarnation as a re-creation of the 1876 Philadelphia Centennial Exposition, the museum now houses various temporary exhibitions.

The Arts and Industries building is currently closed for renovation, but programming continues in the museum's Discovery Theater.

The Castle   Free
1000 Jefferson Drive SW
Washington, DC
(202) 633–1000, (202) 633–5285 TTY
www.si.edu/visit/infocenter/sicastle.htm
Take one look at its imposing reddish-brown, Norman Gothic exterior and you'll know how this building got its name. The Castle has been a fixture on the Mall since 1855 and now almost seems out of place in the company of some of the more modern architecture. But what a story it has to tell. This is the original building of the Smithsonian Institution, which now encompasses 16 museums and the National Zoo in Washington, D.C. and the capital region, making it the largest museum complex in the world and an unparalleled national treasure. An ideal place for newcom-

> **i** Become a Smithsonian Resident Associate to enjoy benefits like a subscription to *Smithsonian* magazine, discounts on museum shop purchases, and free events just for members. Annual membership is $51 for individuals. Call (202) 357–3030 or visit www.resident associates.org.

ers to begin exploring the Smithsonian collection, the Castle houses a high-tech visitor information center, as well as the crypt of James Smithson, the Englishman whose donations led to the birth of the institution that bears his name. It's open daily except Christmas, from 10:00 A.M. to 5:30 P.M.

**Freer Gallery of Art and
Arthur M. Sackler Gallery**   Free
Jefferson Drive at 12th Street SW
Washington, DC
(202) 633–1000
www.asia.si.edu
These two museums share a focus on Asian and Near Eastern art, also displaying works by nineteenth- and twentieth-century American artists. (See the Arts chapter for a complete description. The Kidstuff chapter describes family programs.)

**Hirshhorn Museum and
Sculpture Garden**   Free
Independence Avenue SW
Washington, DC
(202) 633–1000, (202) 633–5285 TTY
www.hirshhorn.si.edu
Visit this gallery to view works by many of the great nineteenth- and twentieth-century artists. (See our Arts chapter for a complete description, and Kidstuff for details about family programs.)

National Air and Space Museum   Free
6th Street and Jefferson Drive SW
Washington, DC
(202) 633–1000, (202) 633–5285 TTY
www.nasm.si.edu
Humankind's insatiable fascination with flight has made the National Air and Space Museum one of the most visited museums in the world. Its more than two dozen galleries—including the magnificent glass-walled lobby where dozens of aircraft hang in suspended animation—showcase the evolution of aviation and space technology.

The collection features the history-making plane flown by Charles Lindbergh, the *Apollo*

11 command module, a space station, and the wiry "flying fuel tank" that was flown on a record-breaking nonstop flight around the world. New exhibits include the *Wright Brothers and the Invention of the Aerial Age,* which features interactive experiments. Free highlights tours take place daily, starting at the tour desk in the South lobby. Special tours can be arranged by calling the Tours and Reservations office at (202) 633–2563. Check the museum's daily events schedule for times of the exciting Samuel P. Langley IMAX Theater and Albert Einstein Planetarium shows, which require tickets that cost up to $9.00. The museum is open from 10:00 A.M. to 5:30 P.M. daily, except on December 25. The closest Metro stop is L'Enfant Plaza.

Because the museum no longer has room to accept large items for display, it built an annex on the grounds of Washington Dulles International Airport. The $312-million Steven F. Udvar-Hazy Center opened in December of 2003, showcasing such initial exhibits as the Space Shuttle Enterprise.

National Museum of African Art — Free
950 Independence Avenue SW
Washington, DC
(202) 633–1000, (202) 633–5285 TTY
www.nmafa.si.edu
This unique museum dedicated to African culture and art features permanent exhibits and rotating shows. (See our Arts and Kidstuff chapters for more information.)

National Museum of American History — Free
14th Street and Constitution Avenue NW
Washington, DC
(202) 633–1000, (202) 633–5285 TTY
www.americanhistory.si.edu
Visitors of all ages love the exhibits of American culture, politics, and technology brought to life at the ever-popular National Museum of American History. From White House dishes to an original Model T, from Archie Bunker's armchair to Mr. Rogers' sweater, the exhibits are as varied and interesting as history itself. The museum closed for renovations in September 2006 and is scheduled to reopen in 2008. If you're visiting during its closure, head across the Mall to the Air and Space Museum, where several of the most popular artifacts are installed in a temporary exhibition, *Treasures of American History.*

National Museum of the American Indian
4th Street at Independence Avenue SW
Washington, DC
(202) 633–1000, (202) 357–1729 TTY
www.nmai.si.edu
In 2004 the National Mall welcomed its newest museum, the breathtaking National Museum of the American Indian. More than a museum, it's a rich cultural center that explores the traditions and contemporary issues of indigenous groups across the Americas, from the Arctic to South America. When you step inside, you'll find yourself bathed in natural light in the Potomac Rotunda, where Native artisans and performers share their talents with demonstrations and performances every day. The museum itself is divided into thematic sections. *Our Universes* looks at philosophy and spirituality. In *Our Peoples,* Native peoples relate the last 500 years of their history. *Our Lives* explores twenty-first-century life for eight Native communities. Be sure to check out Mitisam, the museum's cafe, which boasts one of the best spreads and varieties of all eating options on the National Mall. It's open daily from 10:00 A.M. to 5:30 P.M., except for December 25.

National Museum of Natural History — Free
10th Street and Constitution Avenue NW
Washington, DC
(202) 633–1000, (202) 633–5285 TTY
www.mnh.si.edu
You'll know you've arrived at the National Museum of Natural History when you look up and see the colossal stuffed elephant in the rotunda—and it only gets more intriguing from there. This treasure house contains more than 81 million items documenting

 Close-up

The Janet Annenberg Hooker Hall of Geology, Gems, and Minerals

Dazzling: That's the word that immediately comes to mind when you visit the Janet Annenberg Hooker Hall of Geology, Gems, and Minerals at the Smithsonian Institution's National Museum of Natural History. After a two-year, $13-million renovation, the 20,000-square-foot hall opened in September 1997 with new, well-lit displays of old favorites like the Hope Diamond and recent acquisitions. It continues to draw crowds.

Hooker, for whom the hall is named, died in 1997, just a few weeks after the new exhibit opened. She contributed $5 million to the privately funded project and also donated Cartier-designed yellow starburst diamonds and, several years ago, the Hooker Emerald, a jaw-dropping 75.47-carat stone surrounded by 20 baguette diamonds in a platinum setting.

The exhibit begins in the Harry Winston Gallery, named for the jeweler who in 1958 donated what would become one of the Smithsonian Institution's most popular attractions: the Hope Diamond. The flawless blue gem takes center-stage here, rotating inside a circular display vault, while surrounding onlookers marvel at the illuminated 45.52-carat stone's clarity. Written displays tell all about the Hope Diamond's intriguing history. Also in this room you'll find such large natural treasures as a 1,300-pound slab of quartz, a sheet of nearly pure copper, and a natural sandstone formation resembling abstract art.

If you enjoy window shopping at elegant jewelry shops, you'll love the National Gem Collection. An amazing array of treasures glistens from inside illuminated display cases. The one-of-a-kind, art deco–style Clagett Bracelet features an exotic hunt scene, painstakingly created of 626 diamonds, 73 emeralds, 48 sapphires, and 20 rubies. Nearby, flashes of light emanating from the 22,892.5-carat American Golden Topaz may temporarily blind you. Among the collection's royal jewels, Marie Antoinette's pear-shaped diamond earrings create tiny rainbow-

humankind and the natural environment.

The Discovery Center houses the Samuel C. Johnson IMAX theater. Watch 2-D and 3-D and interactive films on a six-story screen! Daytime tickets are available up to two weeks in advance and cost up to $9.00. Other highlights of the center include a cafe in a six-story, glass-domed atrium and huge gift shops. Friday nights feature live jazz performances.

Prepare to be dazzled as you enter the Janet Annenberg Hooker Hall of Geology, Gems, and Minerals. It's filled with some of the

most impressive jewelry most people will ever lay eyes on, as well as an enormous collection of natural gems and minerals (see the Close-up in this chapter).

The museum's other highlights include dinosaur skeletons (an even bigger hit with youngsters thanks to Barney-mania and the gargantuan success of Steven Spielberg's dino flicks), displays of early man, a live coral reef, and a newly refurbished Hall of Mammals.

The museum's immensely popular insect zoo underwent a dramatic metamorphosis

hued points of light throughout the case. Empress Marie-Louise's crown, a wedding gift from husband Napoleon I, contains—count 'em—more than 1,000 diamonds. An empress can never have too many diamonds, though: Celebrating the birth of the couple's first son, Napoleon presented his wife with a necklace bearing 172 of the glittering stones, weighing more than 263 carats!

The gem collection—which also includes numerous rubies, sapphires, emeralds, and aquamarines in various sizes and cuts—by itself would impress most visitors. The equally awesome Minerals and Gems Gallery follows it. Here you'll see cases filled with more colors, shapes, and sizes of natural formations than you'd dream possible. (It's a great place to take kids for a visual scavenger hunt!) The Mineral Rainbow display showcases such samples as fluorescent blue azurite, purple quartz, avocado pyromophite, coral crocoite, lemon yellow sulphur, and red rhodochrosite.

Elsewhere in the room look for wulfenite that resembles a pile of peanut brittle, and precariously piled iron pyrite cubes that look like a carefully cut and stacked sculpture.

After mingling with the minerals, check out the mine gallery, where you can walk through a simulated mine and see what stones look like underground. The new hall also includes a gallery devoted to plate tectonics, the scientific concept that explains such phenomena as earthquakes and volcanos. Here you can create your own earthquakes and touch a 3.96-billion-year-old rock, the world's oldest. You'll end your tour in the Moon, Meteorites, and Solar System Gallery, where you can look at moon rocks and stardust.

The hall also includes computer programs, films, and interactive exhibits. A Rocks Gallery contains hands-on displays.

that culminated in a grand reopening in late 1994 as the O. Orkin Insect Zoo. It's named after—that's right—the founder of Orkin Pest Control (Otto Orkin, to be precise), perhaps the most familiar of all monikers in the bug-bagging business. The zoo includes a 14-foot model of an African termite mound that children can crawl through, a live beehive (behind glass, thankfully), a Southwest desert diorama, and a rain forest exhibit complete with live giant cockroaches and leaf-cutter ants. (See our Kidstuff chapter for more on this and other kid-pleasing attractions.)

Guided highlights tours usually take place at 10:30 A.M. and 1:30 P.M. Tuesday through Friday. Meet in the Rotunda. The museum is open from 10:00 A.M. to 5:30 P.M. daily, except December 25. Federal Triangle is the nearest Metro stop.

The museum's Naturalist Center, a hands-on study facility, is at 741 Miller Drive, Leesburg, Virginia (800–729–7725). It's open at no charge from 10:30 A.M. to 4:00 P.M. Tuesday through Saturday, closed Sundays and federal holidays.

S. Dillon Ripley Center
(The Smithsonian
International Gallery)   Free
1100 Jefferson Drive SW
Washington, DC
(202) 633–1000, (202) 633–5285 TTY
www.si.edu/ripley/start.htm
You'll find the International Gallery as well as
the Smithsonian Associates membership and
education branch at this underground site,
between the Castle and Freer Gallery of Art.
The gallery hosts a variety of traveling exhibitions. Entered through a copper-topped kiosk,
it's open from 10:00 A.M. to 5:30 P.M. daily. The
center also houses the Smithsonian Institution
Traveling Exhibition Service (SITES), International Center, and conference rooms.

The Smithsonian Institution—off the National Mall

Anacostia Community Museum   Free
1901 Fort Place SE
Washington, DC
(202) 633–4820, (202) 357–1729 TDD
www.si.edu/anacostia
At the small Anacostia Community Museum,
you'll find intriguing changing cultural and
historical exhibitions focusing on regional
and national topics related to African American culture. It is open from 10:00 A.M. to 5:00
P.M. daily, except December 25.

Donald W. Reynolds Center for American
Art and Portraiture   Free
8th and F Streets NW
Washington, DC
(202) 633–1000, (202) 663–5285 TTY
www.reynoldscenter.org
The National Portrait Gallery and Smithsonian
American Art Museums reopened in July
2006 following a six-year renovation as the
Donald W. Reynolds Center for American Art
and Portraiture. The name is a mouthful, but
the museums are amazing. The National Portrait Gallery houses the only complete collection of presidential portraits outside of the
White House. In the Smithsonian American
Art Museum you'll find a breathtaking array
of American art, from pre-colonial portraits
to modern-day multimedia presentations.
The museum is open daily from 11:30 A.M. to
7:00 P.M., except for December 25. (See our
Arts chapter for a complete description.)

National Postal Museum   Free
2 Massachusetts Avenue NW
Washington, DC
(202) 633–1000
www.si.edu/postal
The National Postal Museum opened in July
1993 with great fanfare. Philatelists queued
up for several hours to get special first-day-
of-issue commemorative stamps. The
museum documents the founding and development of the modern postal system and
features interactive displays and the largest
stamp collection in the world, including all
U.S.–issue stamps since 1847. It's open from
10:00 A.M. to 5:30 P.M. daily, except December 25. (See Kidstuff for more on the
museum's many child-friendly exhibits.)

National Zoological Park   Free
3000 block of Connecticut Avenue NW
Washington, DC
(202) 633–1000
www.nationalzoo.si.edu
Although the National Zoo suffered a spate of
bad press, new leadership and ongoing
development have helped appease critics
while giving visitors new reasons to visit.
More than 2,400 animals of 400 species call
the National Zoo home, including notable
recent additions like Asian elephant calf Kan-
dula, Sumatran tiger cub Berani, and giant
pandas Mei Xiang, Tian Tian, and their cub
Tai Shan, who was born at the zoo in 2005.
The pandas have a starring role in the zoo's
new six-acre Asia Trail, where visitors can get
a close-up look at endangered species like
clouded leopards, red pandas, Asian small-
clawed otters, and sloth bears. Bison, prairie
dogs, and grasses highlight the *American
Prairie* exhibition. Another addition, Think
Tank, features interactive and observation
exhibits related to how animals think.

Other especially popular exhibits include the Reptile Discovery Center, Pollinarium, ape house, and the big cats. Be sure to leave time for a stroll through a re-created rain forest in the Amazonia exhibit.

The wild animals on display aren't the only endangered species around here; ditto for parking spaces. Do yourself a huge favor and take Metro to the Cleveland Park station, a less-taxing walk than the uphill schlep from the Woodley Park/Zoo station (on the Red Line). From there it's a pleasant 10-minute walk down the street. Visit early in the morning to avoid crowds and to see the animals at their liveliest: The grounds are open from 6:00 A.M. to 6:00 P.M. daily mid-September through April, and 6:00 A.M. to 8:00 P.M. the rest of the year. Most animal buildings are open from 10:00 A.M. to 4:30 P.M. mid-September through April, 10:00 A.M. to 6:00 P.M. the rest of the year. Friends of the National Zoo (FONZ) offers numerous special programs in the visitor center, during and after zoo hours; call (202) 633–3034 for information about membership, which includes parking privileges. Visit the gift shop for a variety of animal-related souvenirs. (See Kidstuff for additional information.)

Renwick Gallery   Free
Pennsylvania Avenue and 17th Street NW
Washington, DC
(202) 633–1000
www.americanart.si.edu/collections/renwick
This off-the-Mall gallery showcases American design, crafts, and contemporary arts. (See our Arts chapter for a complete description.)

Other Museums, Galleries, and Attractions

B'nai B'rith Klutznick National
Jewish Museum   Free
1640 Rhode Island Avenue NW
Washington, DC
(202) 857–6572, (866) 533–6249
www.bnaibrith.org/museum/index.cfm
The permanent collection of this museum features items spanning some 4,000 years of Jewish culture and history. The museum is

currently under construction and closed to visitors, but it is open to researchers by appointment.

DAR Museum   Free
1776 D Street NW
Washington, DC
(202) 879–3241
www.dar.org/museum
This museum of the Daughters of the American Revolution features state-named period rooms decorated with lovely furnishings, china settings, and other accent pieces. Tell your docent if there's a certain room you wish to visit during your tour. The museum is open from 9:30 A.M. to 4:00 P.M. Monday through Friday and 9:00 A.M. to 5:00 P.M. Saturdays, with guided tours of the period rooms given from 10:00 A.M. to 2:30 P.M. weekdays and 9:00 A.M. to 4:30 P.M. Sundays. The building closes on federal holiday weekends. (See our Kidstuff chapter for details about children's programs here.)

Decatur House Museum   Donation
1610 H Street NW
Washington, DC
(202) 842–0920
www.decaturhouse.org
Located on Lafayette Square near the White House, the Decatur House is one of only three residences in the United States designed by Benjamin Henry Latrobe, dubbed the "father of American architecture." The original owner, naval hero Stephen F. Decatur, was killed in a duel in 1820. The museum is open Tuesday through Saturday from 10:00 A.M. to 5:00 P.M. and Sunday from noon to 4:00 P.M.

Dumbarton Oaks
$$ (Free November through March 14)
1703 32nd Street NW
Washington, DC
(202) 339–6401
www.doaks.org
Dumbarton Oaks' resplendent gardens are famous among garden lovers throughout the

world. It's easy to lose yourself on the intoxicating grounds of this nineteenth-century Georgetown mansion (which is also a renowned research center for Byzantine and pre-Columbian art and history). There's an orangerie, a rose garden, groves of cherry trees, and fragrant magnolias scattered throughout. The gardens are open from 2:00 P.M. to 6:00 P.M. March 15 through October 31, and 2:00 P.M. to 5:00 P.M. November 1 through March 14. At press time the mansion was closed for renovations but was expected to reopen in 2007.

Hillwood Museum and Gardens   **$$$$**
4155 Linnean Avenue NW
Washington, DC
(202) 686–5807
www.hillwoodmuseum.org
You'd never expect to find a place like this in the middle of a major city. Cereal heiress Marjorie Merriweather Post's former Washington, D.C. residence houses a jaw-dropping collection of Russian imperial art and eighteenth-century French decorative arts, including fine china, religious relics, and jewel-encrusted Fabergé eggs. After you tour the house, take time to unwind in the lush gardens of the 25-acre estate.

International Spy Museum   **$$$$**
800 F Street NW
Washington, DC
(202) 393–7798, (866) SPYMUSEUM
www.spymuseum.org
If you thrill to tales of international espionage or fantasize about becoming the next James Bond or Mata Hari, don't miss this intriguing museum, one of the city's newest and quite popular attractions. You'll see lots of real-life gadgets, including a KGB buttonhole camera, a ring gun, and cipher machines. There's even a shoe transmitter, reminiscent of Maxwell Smart's disguised phone. Exhibits in the eye-catching museum, which has won several design and public relations awards, take visitors through the history of espionage and include hands-on activities for kids and adults.

Special programs (free–$$$$), held frequently, include book signings and lectures on such topics as John F. Kennedy's assassination and Israeli intelligence. Don't miss the museum store, which features all kinds of cool gadgets. A cafe and popular full-service restaurant, Zola, also are on-site. The museum's hours vary by season, opening as early as 9:00 A.M. and closing as late as 8:00 P.M. The hours may also fluctuate to accommodate private events. Check the Web site (where you can also beat the lines by pre-purchasing your tickets!) before you visit.

National Building Museum   **Free**
401 F Street NW
Washington, DC
(202) 272–2448
www.nbm.org
Created by an act of Congress in 1980, this is the only national museum of its kind, offering a variety of exhibits and programs about building aspects from architecture to urban planning. Housed in the beautiful 1887 structure originally occupied by the Pension Bureau, the museum is known for its spectacular 316-by-116-foot Great Hall, a frequent site of presidential inaugural balls. Its 75-foot-high Corinthian columns are among the world's tallest indoor pillars. The museum's permanent exhibitions include *Washington: Symbol and City,* a must-see for anyone interested in the stories behind the capital's monuments and famous buildings. Changing exhibitions focus on such topics as engineering and home improvement.

The museum boasts an interesting gift shop and a cafe featuring light meals and snacks. Guided tours, which start next to the fountain in the Great Hall, take place at 12:30 P.M. Monday through Wednesday; at 11:30 A.M., 12:30 P.M., and 1:30 P.M. Thursday through Sunday. Other free programs include films, concerts, lectures, and family activities (see our Kidstuff chapter). Hours are 10:00 A.M. to 5:00 P.M. Monday through Saturday, and 11:00 A.M. to 5:00 P.M. Sunday. The museum is closed on Thanksgiving, December 25, and

Downtown's International Spy Museum is one of the city's most popular attractions. COURTESY WASHINGTON, D.C. CONVENTION AND TOURISM CORPORATION

January 1. Taking the Metro couldn't be more convenient: Walk out of the Judiciary Square station and you're right there!

National Children's Museum $$–$$$
L'Enfant Plaza
Washington, DC
(202) 675–4120
www.ncm.museum
This attraction, created with D.C.'s youngest visitors in mind, has left its former location near Union Station for a striking new location across the street from the National Mall. Look for the new facility to open in 2009.

National Gallery of Art Free
4th Street and Constitution Avenue NW
Washington, DC
(202) 737–4215
www.nga.gov
Housing one of the world's greatest art collections, the National Gallery is another of Washington's amazing free attractions. (For a complete description, see our Arts and Kidstuff chapters.)

National Geographic Society   Free
17th and M Streets NW
Washington, DC
(202) 857-7588
www.nationalgeographic.com/explorer
At the headquarters of this venerable institution, you'll find Explorers Hall, a geography and map lover's paradise. Exhibits, ranging from earth science and cultural geography to environmental and social issues, change regularly and never fail to fascinate. Like so many wonderful attractions in Washington, it boasts free admission. It's open from 9:00 A.M. to 5:00 P.M. Monday through Saturday and holidays, except Christmas, 10:00 A.M. to 5:00 P.M. Sunday. (See the Kidstuff chapter for more information.)

National Museum of
Women in the Arts $-$$
1250 New York Avenue NW
Washington, DC
(202) 783-5000
www.nmwa.org
This is the world's first museum devoted entirely to works by women artists. (You'll find a thorough description in our Arts chapter.)

The Navy Museum   Free
Building 76, Washington Navy Yard
805 Kidder Breese SE
Washington, DC
(202) 433-4882
www.history.navy.mil/branches/
nhcorg8.htm
Housed in the former Naval Gun Factory, this museum offers a fascinating look at United States naval history from the American Revolution to the present day. More than 5,000 artifacts on display include gun mounts, full-size equipment models, decorations and awards, uniforms, and artwork. Tour exhibits include such topics as polar exploration (including Admiral Richard E. Byrd's Antarctic hut), World War II, space travel, and undersea study.

A favorite rainy-day destination for families, the museum features hands-on activities, plenty of space for active kids, and a gift shop with fun souvenirs (see our Kidstuff and Shopping chapters). Don't miss the Washington Navy Yard's neighboring attractions, including the decommissioned destroyer Barry (DD-933), the first marine railway, and a gate designed by Benjamin Latrobe. Museum hours are subject to change. Call in advance to arrange for an escort, a new security precaution. Parking is free and generally plentiful. Eastern Market is the closest Metro station.

Newseum $$$$
6th Street and Pennsylvania Avenue NW
Washington, DC
(888) NEWSEUM
www.newseum.org
This blockbuster attraction opens in its new home in downtown Washington, D.C. in September 2007. The seven-level museum, located on Pennsylvania Avenue between the White House and the U.S. Capitol, goes behind the scenes to show how news is made and disseminated, underscoring the importance of the First Amendment. Its largest gallery traces more than 500 years of news history through more than 40,000 historic newspapers. There's an entire gallery dedicated to Pulitzer Prize–winning photojournalism and other displays that look at the growth of TV, radio, and Internet news. Budding journalists can practice broadcasting or seeking out award-winning photos in an extensive hands-on gallery.

The Octagon $-$$
1799 New York Avenue NW
Washington, DC
(202) 638-3221
www.archfoundation.org/octagon
History and architecture buffs alike will find plenty of interesting features at this National Historic Landmark, the country's oldest architecture museum. Designed by William Thornton, first architect of the U.S. Capitol, the building served as James and Dolley Madison's temporary home after the British burned the President's House during the War of 1812. In fact, Madison signed the war-ending Treaty of

Ghent at the Octagon. A five-year, $5-million restoration, which ended in 1996, included repainting rooms in true period hues.

The adjacent icehouse holds a gift shop, and the site's enclosed garden features a vending cart and seating for outdoor dining. Visitors can view furnished period rooms, as well as architecture- and design-related exhibitions that rotate twice a year. The American Architectural Foundation operates the museum, which is open from 10:00 A.M. to 4:00 P.M. Tuesday through Sunday. Tours begin on the hour and half-hour. Please note that the building isn't elevator-equipped, and therefore is not completely wheelchair accessible. You should be able to find metered on-street parking. Taking the Metro to Farragut North or Farragut West will require you to walk a few blocks.

The Phillips Collection $$$–$$$$
1600 21st Street NW
Washington, DC
(202) 387–2151
www.phillipscollection.org
Renoir's beloved *Luncheon of the Boating Party* highlights the permanent collection at this intimate art museum. (Read more about it in our Arts chapter.)

Sewall-Belmont House $
144 Constitution Avenue NE
Washington, DC
(202) 546–1210
www.nps.gov/sebe/
Almost lost amid the grandeur of Capitol Hill, this eighteenth-century building now houses the headquarters of the National Woman's Party and contains mementos of the equality movement, including writings and heirlooms belonging to Susan B. Anthony and Alice Paul, the woman who penned the Equal Rights Amendment. The mansion was once the abode of Albert Gallatin, the treasury secretary who masterminded the finances of the $15-million Louisiana Purchase in 1803.

The building also houses the country's first feminist library. The museum is open to guided tours only, which run hourly at 11:00 A.M.,

i The Octagon is reputedly one of the most haunted places in Washington. Original owner John Tayloe's daughter jumped (or fell) to her death from atop the grand staircase after her father voiced his disapproval of her suitor.

noon, and 1:00 and 2:00 P.M. Tuesday through Friday, and at noon, 1:00, 2:00, and 3:00 P.M. Saturday. The tours last approximately an hour and are recommended for ages eight and older. Visit the gift shop for history books, women's crafts, and unique souvenirs like replica jail door pins. The nearest Metro stops are Union Station and Capitol South. Wheelchair access is limited.

The Textile Museum $$
2320 S Street NW
Washington, DC
(202) 667–0441
www.textilemuseum.org
You'll be amazed by the intricate handwork exhibited in this museum's collection of Oriental carpets and other important textiles. (See our Arts chapter for a description.)

**United States Holocaust
Memorial Museum**   Free
100 Raoul Wallenberg Place SW
Washington, DC
(202) 488–0400
www.ushmm.org
As compelling as it is disturbing, the U.S. Holocaust Memorial Museum documents the horrors of the Holocaust through photographs, film, interactive exhibits, and incredible artifacts. Built with private funds and opened in the spring of 1993, the museum occupies a two-acre parcel right next to the Bureau of Engraving and Printing, just off the National Mall. The five-story building, between 14th and 15th Streets, is itself a fascinating architectural statement and tribute to the victims. Due to the graphic nature of some displays, the tour is not recommended for children younger than 11. An interactive exhibit, *Remember the Children: Daniel's*

Story, is designed for ages 8 and older. The museum also houses resource and research facilities and a theater and auditorium for special programs. Grab a light meal in the dairy cafe, open from 8:30 A.M. to 4:30 P.M. The museum shop features books and other Holocaust-related items.

Visitors must obtain tickets to tour the museum's permanent exhibition; they're free, albeit not always easy to come by. Pick them up at the 14th Street entrance beginning at 10:00 A.M. on the day of your visit, or obtain them in advance through Tickets.com (800–400–9373). The museum is open from 10:00 A.M. to 5:30 P.M. daily. The museum is closed on Yom Kippur and Christmas. Parking is scarce, so take the Metro to the Smithsonian station, 1 block away.

**The United States
National Arboretum   Free**
3501 New York Avenue NE
Washington, DC
(202) 245–2726
www.usna.usda.gov
The arboretum, a national site operated by the United States Department of Agriculture, showcases a lush variety of plants, flowers, and trees. Another of the city's amazing free attractions, the 446-acre living museum bursts into an incredible blaze of color during the spring azalea and summer rhododendron seasons, prime times to plan a visit. Look for one of the site's most unusual displays: 22 freestanding Corinthian columns, originally part of the United States Capitol. The arboretum's renowned annual plant sale, held during the spring, features bargains galore and many unusual species of trees, shrubs, and perennials—some cultivated on-site. For just $4.00, you can learn more about the arboretum and see many of its highlights aboard a tram. During the 35-minute narrated tour, you'll learn about the arboretum's history, mission, and research, and the display gardens and collections. You can go back and visit your favorite parts when the ride is over.

The park's grounds are open from 8:00 A.M. to 5:00 P.M., except on Christmas. The National Bonsai and Penjing Museum is open from 10:00 A.M. to 3:30 P.M. daily. The arboretum also boasts a gift shop, open 10:00 A.M. to 3:30 P.M. on weekdays and until 5:00 P.M. on weekends. The administrative building is open 8:00 A.M. to 4:30 P.M. Monday through Friday and on weekends spring through fall. Free tours and classes take place on weekends.

Neighborhoods

Embassy Row   Free
Along Massachusetts Avenue NW
Washington, D.C.
Nearly 50 of the city's approximately 150 embassies are clustered along this 2-mile stretch of prime real estate, hence the designation Embassy Row. From the grand and ornate to the simple but elegant, the homes make for a wonderful walking tour, especially in the spring and fall. Look (very closely in some cases) for the flag and coat of arms that designate each diplomatic mission. From an architectural perspective, some of the more noteworthy embassies include those of Brazil, Japan, Britain, Austria, Pakistan, and Turkey. (See our International Washington chapter for more information.)

Georgetown   Free
M Street and Wisconsin Avenue NW
Washington, DC
(202) 298–9222
www.georgetowndc.com
A thriving tobacco port and completely independent Maryland community when Washington was established as the Nation's Capital in the late 1700s, Georgetown is the city's oldest and best-known neighborhood and one that's synonymous with wealth, power, and prestige. Locals and out-of-towners alike come here to stroll the narrow, cobblestone streets; view the elegant homes; and sample the incredible array of nightclubs, bars, art galleries, restaurants, funky shops, and elegant boutiques. Keep an eye out for that precipitous set of steps made famous in a memorable but gruesome scene from *The Exorcist,*

the classic devil flick starring Linda Blair.

The nerve center of Georgetown is at M Street and Wisconsin Avenue NW, through the years the spillover site of some spirited post–Super Bowl, New Year's Eve, and Halloween celebrations. Besides those steps we mentioned, prime attractions in this part of town include venerable and beautiful Georgetown University (whose graduates include former president Clinton), described in our Education chapter, and C&O Canal National Historic Park, described in our Parks and Recreation chapter.

Amid the noisy drama of M Street lies the Old Stone House, 3051 M Street NW (202–426–6851), built in 1766 and believed to be the oldest building in the District. Step into the backyard and you'll enter another world. A quiet garden, maintained by the National Park Service, overflows with seasonal plants, exotic butterflies, and birds. It's a great place for a brown-bag lunch. When you're finished, take a tour of the historic house that many parapsychologists claim is one of the most haunted buildings in Washington. It's open 9:30 A.M. to 5:00 P.M. daily, except January 1 and December 25. Admission is free.

You'll also find Dumbarton Oaks, at 1703 32nd Street NW (202–339–6401, www.doaks .org), the aristocratic former home of Mr. and Mrs. Robert Woods Bliss. Now owned by Harvard University, the 16-acre property features a museum with pre-Columbian and Byzantine collections, open 2:00 to 5:00 P.M. Tuesday through Sunday, with free admission. It also features beautifully landscaped gardens, accessible from an R Street entrance, open 2:00 to 6:00 P.M. mid-March through October and 2:00 to 5:00 P.M. November through early March. Admission is $7.00 for adults, and $5.00 for children and seniors. Call the docents' office at (202) 339–6409 for information about tours.

Religious Sites

See our Worship chapter for more information about these and other historic places of worship.

 Georgetown is the oldest neighborhood in the city, founded in 1751.

The Basilica of the National Shrine of the Immaculate Conception   **Free**
4th Street and Michigan Avenue NE
Washington, DC
(202) 526–8300
www.nationalshrine.com
With a lofty bell tower, ornately carved entryway, and vibrantly decorated dome, the country's largest Roman Catholic church takes your breath away even before you go inside. Enter you must, however, to see the many treasures of this Byzantine-Romanesque house of worship. Guided tours take visitors throughout the building to see stained-glass art, mosaics, and sculptures, most of which honor Mary, the Mother of Jesus. Highlights include more than 50 chapels, each designed to express a unique vision of Mary; the world's largest mosaic portrait of Jesus, the Byzantine *Christ in Majesty;* and pillars of different types of marble, symbolizing the universality of the church.

The building is open from 7:00 A.M. to 6:00 P.M. daily November through March, and from 7:00 A.M. to 7:00 P.M. daily April through October. Free guided tours, which last 30 minutes to an hour, take place from 9:00 to 11:00 A.M. and from 1:00 to 3:00 P.M. Monday through Saturday, and 1:30 to 4:00 P.M. Sunday. Call in advance to arrange group tours. You also can pick up a brochure for a self-guided tour. Carillon concerts are held on Sunday afternoons.

Visit the gift shop for a variety of Catholic-oriented merchandise. A cafeteria offers breakfast and lunch. Free, on-site parking is available. The nearest Metro stop is Brookland-CUA.

Franciscan Monastery   **$**
14th and Quincy Streets NE
Washington, DC
(202) 526–6800
www.myfranciscan.org
Guided tours, lasting about 45 minutes, include a look at full-scale replicas of Holy

Land shrines such as the Roman Catacombs. This is a beautiful, peaceful enclave that many Washingtonians know nothing about. Tours take place on the hour except at noon from 10:00 A.M. to 3:00 P.M. Monday through Saturday, and from 1:00 to 3:00 P.M. Sundays. Admission is free, with a suggested donation. Brookland is the nearest Metro station.

Washington National Cathedral $
Massachusetts and Wisconsin
Avenues NW
Washington, DC
(202) 537–6200
www.cathedral.org/cathedral
This magnificent Gothic stone church took 83 years to build, and it's filled with unique and stunning art. The cathedral offers a wide assortment of tours on a regular basis. Your best bet is to take a general highlights tour to receive a 30- to 45-minute overview of the building's features, like its more than 200 stained-glass windows, including a Space Window, an abstract tribute to the *Apollo 11* mission that contains a moon rock.

The cathedral is open from 10:00 A.M. to 5:30 P.M. Monday through Friday, 10:00 A.M. to 4:30 P.M. Saturday, and 8:00 A.M. to 6:30 P.M. Sunday. Regular tours, beginning at the west entrance doors, take place from 10:00 to 11:30 A.M. and 12:45 to 3:30 P.M. Monday through Saturday, and from 12:45 to 2:30 P.M. on Sundays. No tours are given on Palm Sunday, Good Friday afternoon, Easter, Thanksgiving, or Christmas. The suggested donation for most tours is $3.00 for adults and $1.00 for children. The cathedral offers specialized tours and programs like Tour and Tea. Call for times and costs. (See our Kidstuff and Annual Events chapters for more information about cathedral programs and special events.)

i Take the kids on a gargoyle tour of the National Cathedral. There's even one that looks like Darth Vader.

Civil War Sites

Abraham Lincoln *Emancipation Group*
Statue
Lincoln Park, East Capitol Street between
11th and 13th Streets NE
Washington, DC
Emancipated citizens paid for this $18,000 statue, the first D.C. tribute to America's 16th president, dedicated in 1876. Created by prominent sculptor Thomas Ball, the bronze work depicts the president holding the Emancipation Proclamation as a freed slave kneels at his feet.

African American Civil War Memorial
U Street and Vermont Avenue NW
Washington, DC
(202) 667–2667
Unveiled with great fanfare in 1998, this memorial honors the more than 200,000 African American soldiers who fought as Union troops during the Civil War. It's set in the city's historic Shaw neighborhood, named for Robert Gould Shaw, the white colonel who led his 54th Massachusetts Volunteer Infantry in the ill-fated attack on a Confederate fortification depicted in the acclaimed film *Glory*. The site features the *Spirit of Freedom* sculpture by Kentucky artist Ed Hamilton, as well as two curved granite walls bearing the names of the men who fought in the United States Colored Troops.

The accompanying African American Civil War Memorial Freedom Foundation Museum and Visitors Center, 1200 U Street NW, displays artifacts and photos and offers screenings of Civil War videos. Hours for the free museum are 10:00 A.M. to 5:00 P.M. weekdays and 10:00 A.M. to 2:00 P.M. on Saturday.

Ford's Theatre
511 10th Street NW
Washington, DC
(202) 426–6924, (202) 347–4833 (box office)
www.fordstheatre.org
Forever memorialized as the place where President Lincoln was shot by John Wilkes Booth, Ford's is a must-see for any Civil War

history buffs. On April 14, 1865, Abraham and Mary Todd Lincoln and their guests, Major Henry Reed Rathbone and Clara Harris, arrived at Ford's Theatre to see a performance of the critically acclaimed comedy *Our American Cousin*. Less than two hours later, Lincoln was shot and Rathbone was stabbed. Lincoln was carried across the street to the Petersen House, where he was pronounced dead the next day.

Today Ford's Theatre, a National Historic Site, is largely restored to the way it looked during the night of the assassination. It is still a performing theater, with plays scheduled throughout the year. (See the Arts chapter.) The recently renovated lower-level museum displays some 3,000 Lincoln-related items, such as the .44-caliber Derringer Booth used to shoot the president. At the Petersen House (516 10th Street NW) you can view the room where the president died. The free sites generally are open daily from 9:00 A.M. to 5:00 P.M., but they're closed on Christmas. Call ahead, though, because the theater also closes during matinees, rehearsals, and special occasions.

Frederick Douglass National Historic Site
1411 W Street SE
Washington, DC
(202) 426–5961
www.nps.gov/frdo

Former slave Frederick Douglass became a famed abolitionist, editor, orator, and advisor to Abraham Lincoln. Douglass's 21-room home, Cedar Hill, reopened in February 2007 after a major renovation. Visitors discover a vast collection of personal items and artifacts from this turbulent period in American history. Watch an introductory film at the visitor center, where you'll also find a statue of Douglass, exhibits of memorabilia, and a gift shop filled with books about Douglass and his cause. U.S. National Park Service rangers lead engaging 30-minute tours of the white brick house. Cedar Hill, a National Historic Site in the southeast neighborhood of Anacostia, affords a stunning view of downtown to the north. The site is open

daily mid-April through mid-October from 9:00 A.M. to 5:00 P.M.; mid-October through mid-April from 9:00 A.M. to 4:00 P.M.; and closed New Year's Day, Thanksgiving, and Christmas. Admission is $2.00.

NORTHERN VIRGINIA
Museums and Other Attractions

Alexandria Black History Museum   Free
902 Wythe Street
Alexandria, VA
(703) 838–4356
oha.alexandriava.gov/bhrc

For an introduction to the city's rich African American heritage, stop by this center, where exhibits help convey the significance of historical figures and events, while a library next door offers a wealth of information. It's open from 9:00 A.M. to 5:00 P.M. Tuesday through Saturday. Braddock Road is the closest Metro stop.

Arlington National Cemetery
Free, $–$$ parking and tours
Memorial Drive
Arlington, VA
(703) 607–8000
www.arlingtoncemetery.org

With its sea of white headstones spread across 612 wooded, hilly acres overlooking the capital city, Arlington National Cemetery is perhaps the most famous burial site in the world, and one of Washington's most popular tourist attractions. This is the final resting place for more than 260,000 American military personnel who served in conflicts from the Revolutionary War to the present. Among the many famous graves are those of President John F. Kennedy and his brother Robert; President William Howard Taft; 16 astronauts, including Mercury's Virgil "Gus" Grissom and those aboard the space shuttle *Challenger*; and prize-fighter Joe Louis.

It's also the site of the Women in Military Service Memorial, the country's first national memorial honoring all women who have served their country in the armed services. Dedicated in October 1997, the memorial at the cemetery's main gateway includes a hall of honor, a 196-seat theater, exhibit space, and details and photos about registered servicewomen.

Also on the cemetery grounds is the Tomb of the Unknowns, where crowds gather to view the somber Changing of the Guard every hour on the hour from October 1 through March 31 and every half-hour during the day and hourly at night from April 1 through September 30. (The tomb made headlines in 1998 with the discovery that the "unknown" bones of a Vietnam soldier buried there actually belong to Air Force First Lieutenant Michael J. Blassie, whose plane was shot down in 1972.)

Majestic Arlington House, Robert E. Lee's former home, sits high on a hill facing the Lincoln Memorial. When Lee left to command the Confederate forces, the neoclassical mansion and its several thousand acres of surrounding property were seized by Federal troops and became the headquarters for the Army of the Potomac. Three Union forts were built on the land, and casualties (both Northern and Southern) from local battles were buried here beginning in June 1864. Arlington House is also where Pierre Charles L'Enfant, the French architect who drafted the original plans for Washington, is buried.

Continuous 30-minute Tourmobile tours run daily (except on Christmas) from 8:30 A.M. to 6:30 P.M. April through September and from 8:30 A.M. to 4:30 P.M. October through March. Tours depart from the Arlington Cemetery visitor center, where you'll also find exhibits and a gift shop. Admission to the cemetery is free, but there's a fee for parking and tours. The cemetery is open from 8:00 A.M. to 5:00 P.M. October through March and 8:00 A.M. to 7:00 P.M. April through September. It has its own Metro stop.

Carlyle House $–$$
121 North Fairfax Street
Alexandria, VA
(703) 549–2997
www.nvrpa.org/museum.html
One of the first houses built in Alexandria, this replica of a Scottish manor home, dating

from 1753, was the residence of John Carlyle and his wife Sara Fairfax. Among its other uses, the house served in 1755 as the headquarters of General Braddock, leader of the British forces during the French and Indian War. We recommend you take a guided tour of the home and its terraced garden. Hours are from 10:00 A.M. to 4:30 P.M. Tuesday through Saturday and noon to 4:30 P.M. on Sunday. Tours begin every half-hour.

Christ Church Free
118 North Washington Street
Alexandria, VA
(703) 549–1450
www.historicchristchurch.org
George Washington and Robert E. Lee both attended this church, which dates to the mid-1700s. It's open from 9:00 A.M. to 5:00 P.M. Monday through Saturday, and 9:00 A.M. to 4:00 P.M. Sunday. Admission is free, but the church welcomes contributions. (See our Worship chapter for additional information.)

Colvin Run Mill Historic Site $–$$
10017 Colvin Run Road
Great Falls, VA
(703) 759–2771
www.co.fairfax.va.us/parks/history.htm
Visit this working, water-powered nineteenth-century gristmill on the weekend, and you'll often find special events like Civil War encampments, ice-cream making, wood-carving lessons, and outdoor concerts. Stop by the general store for old-fashioned candy, handmade crafts, and fun gift items, as well as a display of old tins, bottles, and utensils. The site is open daily from 11:00 A.M. to 5:00 P.M. (4:00 P.M. in January and February), except Tuesdays. Mill tours are offered on the hour from 11:00 A.M. to 4:00 P.M. (See our Kidstuff chapter for information about programs for youngsters.)

Fort Ward Museum and Historic Site Free
4301 West Braddock Road
Alexandria, VA
(703) 838–4848
oha.alexandriava.gov/fortward

Named after the first Union officer killed in the Civil War, Fort Ward was one of dozens of Union fortifications that suddenly popped up following the North's embarrassing defeat at the Battle of First Manassas, just 30 miles to the west. Armed with 36 guns, it was the fifth-largest fort surrounding the Nation's Capital.

Today visitors can see much of the same structure as it appeared more than 100 years ago. A self-guided walking tour takes about 45 minutes. The Fort Ward Museum contains an impressive collection of Civil War artifacts and photographs. The grounds of the 45-acre park are open 9:00 A.M. to sunset daily, and the museum is open 9:00 A.M. to 4:00 P.M. Tuesday through Saturday, noon to 5:00 P.M. Sunday. It's closed Thanksgiving, Christmas, and New Year's Day. Admission is free. Guided tours can be arranged, at least a month in advance, for groups of ten or more.

Gadsby's Tavern Museum $–$$
134 North Royal Street
Alexandria, VA
(703) 838–4242
www.gadsbystavern.org

The social nerve center of colonial Alexandria, Gadsby's is noted as "the finest tavern built in the colonies." Gadsby's was the site of numerous balls, meetings, and political functions. Among the luminaries who unwound here were the Marquis de Lafayette, John Paul Jones, Aaron Burr, George Mason, Francis Scott Key, Henry Clay, and, of course, George Washington. The tavern—now functioning as a museum—has been restored to its colonial condition and is open for tours. The 200-year-old George Washington Birthnight Banquet and Ball is still held here every year and is one of the most prestigious social events in Virginia.

Other special events include dance classes, costumed reenactments, teas for girls and their dolls, and summer camps with colonial themes. The museum is open from 11:00 A.M. to 4:00 P.M. Tuesday through Saturday and from 1:00 to 4:00 P.M. Sunday November through March; from 10:00 A.M. to 5:00 P.M.

Tuesday through Saturday and 1:00 to 5:00 P.M. Sunday April through October. It's closed on Mondays and major holidays, and occasionally during private rentals.

Stop by the adjacent Gadsby's Tavern Restaurant, 138 North Royal Street (703–548–1288), for a colonial bite to eat, served by costumed waiters.

George Washington Masonic National Memorial   Free
101 Callahan Drive
Alexandria, VA
(703) 683–2007
www.gwmemorial.org

Beltway travelers passing Alexandria can't miss this tall granite tower, standing majestically atop a hill just outside of Old Town. Modeled after the ancient lighthouse in Alexandria, Egypt, the familiar landmark was erected by Freemasons throughout the nation to honor their fraternal brother, who served as Worshipful Master of the Alexandria-Washington Lodge No. 22 in 1788 and 1789. (Ironically, the very hill upon which the monument sits could have held the U.S. Capitol, but Washington vetoed the site!)

Visitors see several of Washington's personal and family possessions, portraits, and Masonic relics. Among the artifacts displayed in the Replica Lodge Room are the clock that Washington's doctor stopped the moment Washington died and the little silver trowel that Washington used to lay the cornerstone of the U.S. Capitol. A Mason-led tower tour is the only way for visitors to view the nine-story memorial's upper levels, which house more Washington-related displays, Masonic organizations' exhibits, a Masonic library, and a top-floor observation deck. Children especially enjoy the detailed mechanical model of an Imperial Shrine Parade, complete with tinier renditions of those unique tiny Shriners' cars.

The memorial is open from 10:00 A.M. to 4:00 P.M. daily except New Year's Day, Thanksgiving, and Christmas. Visitors can take guided 45-minute tours of the tower and observation deck at 10:00 A.M., 11:30 A.M.,

1:30 P.M., and 3:00 P.M. Note that the building is only partially wheelchair accessible, and eating, drinking, and smoking are prohibited inside. Parking is free and plentiful, and the King Street Metro station is a short walk. Admission is free, but you're welcome to make a donation.

Gunston Hall Plantation $$–$$$
10709 Gunston Road
Lorton, VA
(703) 550–9220
www.gunstonhall.org
George Mason, a framer of the Constitution and the father of the Bill of Rights whose namesake university is also in Fairfax, built this southeastern Fairfax County landmark in 1755. With its period furnishings, formal gardens, and exhibits, Gunston Hall serves as a landmark connection with the region's colonial past. The home is more than just a museum or monument, though. It's also a favorite spot for small meetings, parties, and receptions. Request a schedule of annual events, featuring such seasonal favorites as a kite celebration in March and Christmas programs in December. The plantation is open 9:30 A.M. to 5:00 P.M. daily, except New Year's Day, Thanksgiving, and Christmas. Home tours begin every half-hour.

Lee-Fendall House Museum and Garden $
614 Oronoco Street
Alexandria, VA
(703) 548–1789
www.leefendallhouse.org
Built in 1785 by Philip Richard Fendall, cousin of "Light Horse Harry" Lee, this historic home served as a residence to Lee family members until 1903, with one Civil War–related exception: In 1863 the Union Army took over the property and turned it into a hospital. Today visitors view the restored home in its 1850–1870 residential appearance.

A popular site for weddings and private parties, the house and gardens also host special holiday events and educational programs. Hours are 10:00 A.M. to 4:00 P.M. Tuesday through Saturday and 1:00 P.M. to 4:00 P.M. Sunday. Call ahead on weekends, as the museum often closes on Saturday and Sunday for special events. Admission for guided tours is $4.00 for adults, $2.00 for ages 11 to 17, and free for children younger than 11.

The Lyceum Free
201 South Washington Street
Alexandria, VA
(703) 838–4994
oha.alexandriava.gov/lyceum
Alexandria's history museum showcases a permanent collection of city-related artifacts, including locally produced furniture and housewares. The building itself served as a hospital for Union soldiers during the Civil War. Changing exhibits focus on various cultural and historical topics. The museum also hosts special events in its lecture hall. Visit the gift shop for local souvenirs. The Lyceum is open from 10:00 A.M. to 5:00 P.M. Monday through Saturday and from 1:00 to 5:00 P.M. Sunday. It's closed on Thanksgiving, December 24 and 25, and January 1.

Mount Vernon $$–$$$$
Southern end of the George Washington Memorial Parkway
Alexandria, VA
(703) 780–2000
www.mountvernon.org
One look at the view from the green expanse of lawn and you'll see why George Washington chose this site for his gracious riverside plantation, which has become America's most-visited historic house. Washington's final resting place, Mount Vernon offers a wealth of information about the life of the man as well as the turbulent colonial period. Present-day archaeological digs on the site continue to tell us more. A new, high-tech interpretive center, opened in 2006, also goes beyond the image of the president as a senior statesman to portray him as a youthful, vigorous young soldier and surveyor.

After touring the mansion, sit a spell on the long, white-columned porch, where you can take in the most glorious view of the Potomac. Garden enthusiasts will enjoy walking through the estate's many authentic gardens and looking at original trees from Washington's day. The wonderful *George Washington: Pioneer Farmer* exhibit features a round, 16-sided barn, farm animals, and fields of crops, between the mansion and the Potomac Wharf. Open year-round, the site offers hands-on activities March through November. Mount Vernon features special events throughout the year, including a wreath-laying ceremony for Washington's birthday and candlelight tours during December.

Mount Vernon is open from 8:00 A.M. to 5:00 P.M. April through August; 9:00 A.M. to 5:00 P.M. during March, September, and October; and 9:00 A.M. to 4:00 P.M. November through February. Annual passes and group discounts are available. Visit Mount Vernon's gift shop for colonial-themed merchandise. Visitors can dine at the colonial Mount Vernon Inn or a snack bar at the visitor center.

Oatlands Plantation $–$$$
On Route 15 near Leesburg, VA
(703) 777–3174
www.oatlands.org
About 6 miles south of Leesburg, in Loudoun County, this classic revival home built in 1803 is one of the state's foremost historic plantations. Four acres of formal terraced English gardens accent the grounds and architecture. Oatlands is the site of various events and gatherings throughout the year, including annual plays and a needlework exhibition. It's open from late March through December from 10:00 A.M. to 5:00 P.M. Monday through Saturday, and from 1:00 to 5:00 P.M. Sundays.

The Pentagon Free
Arlington, VA
(703) 695–1776
www.defenselink.mil/pubs/pentagon/index.html
With 17½ miles of corridors housing more than 23,000 Defense Department employees, the Pentagon remains the largest single-structure office building in the world. Sadly, public tours here are suspended indefinitely following the terrorists' attack of September 11, 2001. School, church, and veterans groups may take tours by reservation only.

Ramsay House Visitors Center Free
221 King Street
Alexandria, VA
(703) 838–4200
www.funside.com
Visit this historic house to peek into the life of William Ramsay, the town overseer, census-taker, postmaster, and member of the committee of safety. Ramsay was a close friend of George Washington and hosted the president-elect in his home the last night before the inauguration. You'll also find numerous free pamphlets about local tourist sites, restaurants, and lodgings. Open daily except Thanksgiving, Christmas, and New Year's Day from 9:00 A.M. to 5:00 P.M.

Stabler-Leadbeater Apothecary Shop $
105 South Fairfax Street
Alexandria, VA
(703) 836–3713
www.apothecarymuseum.org
From 1792 to 1933 this early pharmacy dispensed medicine to Alexandrians, including loyal customers James Monroe, Robert E. Lee, and George Washington's family. When it closed, it was the second-oldest apothecary shop in the United States and the oldest in Virginia. Today the shop is a museum exhibiting an array of colonial medical implements and patent medicines. It also contains the most comprehensive collection of apothecary jars in the nation.

It's open from 10:00 A.M. to 5:00 P.M. Tuesday through Saturday and 1:00 to 5:00 P.M. Sunday and Monday. November through March, the museum is closed on Monday and Tuesday.

Theodore Roosevelt Memorial   Free
Theodore Roosevelt Island in the Potomac
River
Arlington, VA
(703) 289–2500
www.nps.gov/gwmp/tri.htm
This obscure, enchanting monument to America's environmental president is set amid a densely wooded island in the middle of the Potomac River between the Roosevelt and Key Bridges. Besides a giant statue of the gregarious 25th president, the island is laced with 2½ miles of trails—perfect for jogging or a leisurely walk. Its marshy shoreline offers excellent views of the Washington and Northern Virginia skylines. Open from sunrise until dark, Roosevelt Island is accessible only from the Virginia side via a footbridge. A bicycle/pedestrian bridge spanning the G.W. Parkway near the north end of the parking lot offers an easy connection to Rosslyn, Key Bridge, and Georgetown, just beyond.

U.S. Marine Corps Memorial
Iwo Jima Statue   Free
U.S. 50 at Arlington National Cemetery
Arlington, VA
(703) 289–2500
www.nps.gov/archive/gwmp/usmc.htm
Officially known as the U.S. Marine Corps War Memorial, this is the largest bronze statue in the world and depicts the raising of the American flag on Mount Suribachi during World War II. Presented to the nation by members and friends of the Marine Corps, the statue was created by Felix de Weldon, based on the famous photograph by Joe Rosenthal. Nearby, the Netherlands Carillon was a thank-you gift from the Dutch people for America's aid during World War II. In season, a gorgeous field of tulips lies at the base of the bell tower. At night the illuminated statue proves a striking sight for passersby.

Woodlawn Plantation and Frank Lloyd
Wright's Pope-Leighey House $–$$$$
9000 Richmond Highway
Alexandria, VA
(703) 780–4000
www.woodlawn1805.org
www.popeleighey1940.org
Another of southern Fairfax County's architectural icons, Woodlawn Plantation was the Georgian estate home of Nellie Custis Lewis, granddaughter of George and Martha Washington. William Thornton, architect of the U.S. Capitol, designed the richly appointed mansion, a virtual neighbor of Mount Vernon. Our favorite time to visit is during March, when hundreds of hand-stitched entries in the annual needlework exhibition decorate the rooms. Browse in the gift shop downstairs, and, only during March from 11:30 A.M. to 2:00 P.M., enjoy lunch in the final room on the tour.

The spacious grounds also feature the Pope-Leighey House, designed by Frank Lloyd Wright in 1939. Hours are 10:00 A.M. to 5:00 P.M. daily March through December; both houses are closed in January and February.

SUBURBAN MARYLAND
Museums and Other Attractions

Beall-Dawson House and
the Stonestreet Museum of
19th-Century Medicine $
103 West Montgomery Avenue
Rockville, MD
(301) 762–1492
www.montgomeryhistory.org
This authentically restored brick house, dating to 1815 and furnished in the Federal style, is the headquarters of the Montgomery County Historical Society. The adjacent museum offers fascinating insight into early surgical practices and medical treatments. The site also has a gift shop. Hours are from noon to 4:00 P.M. Tuesday through Sunday. Admission is free for Montgomery County Historical Society members.

Chesapeake Bay Bridge-Tunnel $
Maryland Route 50
Anne Arundel/Queen Anne's
Counties, MD
(757) 331–2960
www.cbbt.com
Officially, the William Preston Lane Jr. Memorial Bridge, the Bay Bridge, as it's affectionately known, connects Metro Washington with the rural charms of Maryland's Eastern Shore and the Atlantic Coast resorts of the Delmarva Peninsula. The approximately 4.3-mile twin spans offer a spectacular view of the world's largest estuary. The bridge is in the midst of a $45-million rehabilitation project. Motorists pay a toll before heading eastbound.

College Park Aviation Museum $
1985 Corporal Frank Scott Drive
College Park, MD
(301) 864–6029
www.collegeparkaviationmuseum.com
If you like aviation history but dread the crowds at the National Air and Space Museum, consider this little museum near the College Park Metro station as an alternative. It's adjacent to the College Park Airport, the nation's oldest continually operating airfield, which opened in 1909. It's here that the first mile-high flight took place and where the Wright Brothers perfected the art of flying after their experiments in Kitty Hawk. Kids will love its hands-on approach; they can activate talking likenesses of Wilbur Wright at the touch of a button and try on flight helmets and goggles. The museum is open daily except major holidays from 10:00 A.M. to 5:00 P.M.

Goddard Space Flight Center
NASA Visitors Center   Free
Soil Conservation Road
Greenbelt, MD
(301) 286–9041
www.nasa.gov/centers/goddard/visitor/home/index.html
Visitors to this museum learn about the history of American rocketry, from its humble beginnings on Robert Goddard's Massachusetts farm in 1926 to current research involving the Hubble Space Telescope. Visit the gift shop for space-related souvenirs. The center is open 10:00 A.M. to 3:00 P.M. Tuesday through Friday and 12:00 P.M. to 4:00 P.M. Saturday and Sunday from September 1 through June 30. From July 1 through August 31, it's open 10:00 A.M. to 5:00 P.M. Tuesday through Saturday and is closed on Sunday and Monday. The visitor center is also closed on all Federal holidays. Call for information. (See our Kidstuff chapter for information about hands-on activities and model rocketry programs.)

Maryland State House   Free
State Circle
Annapolis, MD
(410) 974–3400
www.mdarchives.state.md.us/msa/homepage/html/statehse.html
The beautiful Maryland State House is yet another reason to visit the historic sailing mecca of Annapolis. The focal point of Maryland's government, this is the nation's oldest state house in continuous legislative use. It even served as capitol of the United States for several months in 1783–84 and is the place where George Washington resigned his commission as commander of the Continental Army and where the Treaty of Paris was ratified, ending the Revolutionary War. Be sure not to miss the great exhibits depicting Annapolis during colonial times. The visitor center is open from 9:00 A.M. to 5:00 P.M. Monday through Friday and from 10:00 A.M. to 4:00 P.M. on Saturday and Sunday. Free 25-minute tours take place at 11:00 A.M. and 3:00 P.M. daily. Each adult must show a picture ID.

National Institutes of Health   Free
Natcher Conference Center (Building 45)
45 Center Drive, off Rockville Pike
Bethesda, MD
(301) 496–1776
www.nih.gov

NIH is where doctors, scientists, and technicians wage war against some of society's most devastating illnesses and disorders, including cancer, AIDS, heart disease, diabetes, arthritis, and Alzheimer's disease. This sprawling federal research complex—a branch of the U.S. Department of Health and Human Services—is perhaps the nation's preeminent medical resource.

NIH's National Library of Medicine (8600 Rockville Pike, Bethesda, 888–346–3656), is the largest medical library in the world and features a reading room and a department specializing in historic and rare books. The NIH's visitor information center offers a slide show, films, and a "working" lab. Free overviews are available for walk-in visitors at 9:30 A.M. on Tuesday and Thursday. An overview and tour of the clinical research center is offered on Monday, Wednesday, and Friday at 11:00 A.M.; special-interest tours also can be arranged. The Visitor Information Center is open from 8:30 A.M. to 4:00 P.M.

National Wildlife Visitor Center   **Free**
Patuxent Research Refuge
Route 197
Laurel, MD
(301) 497–5772
patuxent.fws.gov
There's a wildlife research facility amid the din of Metro Washington? Indeed. This agency of the U.S. Department of the Interior conducts vital investigations involving a variety of endangered species. It's open from 10:00 A.M. to 4:30 P.M. daily, November through mid-March, and until 5:30 P.M. mid-March through October. It is closed December 25. Admission is free, but there's an overall charge for guided tram tours through the woods. (See Kidstuff for more information.)

U.S. Naval Academy   **Free**
Bordered by King George Street
and the Severn River
Annapolis, MD
(410) 263–6933
www.usna.edu

It's hard not to feel exceedingly patriotic when you set foot on the gorgeous grounds of this National Historic Site where naval officers have been trained since 1845. The academy chapel dominates the scene; below the building lies the crypt of John Paul Jones. Other campus highlights include a museum featuring models, swords, and paintings; Bancroft Hall, where the Brigade Noon Formation takes place; numerous monuments dedicated to naval heroes and battles; and Navy-Marine Corps Memorial Stadium. The Armel-Leftwich Visitor Center, 52 King George Street (Gate l), houses a theater, gift shop, and exhibits. The visitor center is open daily from 9:00 A.M. to 5:00 P.M. In January and February it closes at 4:00 P.M. Guided tours, with times varying seasonally, are available daily except Thanksgiving, December 25, and January 1. Be prepared to show a photo ID.

TOUR OPERATORS

It takes a while to find your way around any new place, so until you get your bearings straight, what better way to get an overview of all the top attractions than to take a professionally guided tour?

The following companies provide regular, scheduled sightseeing excursions for the general public:

Alexandria Colonial Tours   **$$**
201 King Street, 3rd Floor
Alexandria, VA
(703) 519–1749
www.alexcolonialtours.com
Guides attired in colonial costumes lead candlelit Ghosts and Graveyard walking tours, recommended for ages seven and older and offered on Friday, Saturday, and Sunday nights April through mid-November. The tours chronicle documented eerie happenings in Old Town Alexandria and end in a graveyard! Group tours are available by appointment. Tours last approximately one hour.

Anecdotal History Tours $$–$$$$
9009 Paddock Lane
Potomac, MD
(301) 294–9514
www.dcsightseeing.com
Local historian Anthony Pitch leads two-hour walking tours of the Adams Morgan district and Georgetown on Sundays from mid-March through mid-December and by appointment. The guide specializes in "anecdotal history," focusing on homes of famous Washingtonians past and present.

Bike the Sites Inc. $$$$
Old Post Office Pavilion
1100 Pennsylvania Avenue NW
Washington, DC
(202) 842–BIKE
www.bikethesites.com
For a more leisurely way to see Washington, you might consider a bicycle tour of the monuments, memorials, and museums. Or, rent a cycle for your own self-guided tour. Tours are recommended for ages nine and older, and adults must accompany children.

Capitol River Cruises $$–$$$$
Washington Harbour
3050 K Street NW at 31st Street
Washington, DC
(301) 460–7447, (800) 405–5511
www.capitolrivercruises.com
The 91-person *Nightingale II*, a riverboat originally built for sightseeing excursions to Mackinac Island, takes passengers on 45-minute, narrated cruises along the Potomac River from Georgetown to Ronald Reagan Washington National Airport and back.

D.C. Ducks $$$$
2640 Reed Street NE
Washington, DC
(202) 832–9800
www.historictours.com/washington/
dcducks.htm
Ride in the area's only amphibious touring vehicles—part bus, part boat, they must be

i The DUK-W vehicles used for the D.C. Ducks tour were originally built for use in World War II.

seen to be believed. Tours depart from Union Station April through October.

Gray Line Worldwide $$$$
Gray Line Terminal
Union Station, 50 Massachusetts
Avenue NE
Washington, DC
(301) 386–8300, (800) 862–1400
www.graylinedc.com
This internationally known sightseeing tour company offers a variety of D.C. tours and packages, including double-decker bus tours and Washington After Dark coach tours.

Odyssey Cruises $$$$
Gangplank Marina
600 Water Street SW
Washington, DC
(888) 741–0281
www.odysseycruises.com
This long, sleek ship is low enough to pass under the 14th Street Bridge, so you get to travel the Potomac River from Georgetown to Old Town Alexandria. Savor an elegant meal and dance to live music as you view the passing sights from the glass atrium dining rooms, or enjoy the fresh air as you take a walk around the quarter-mile deck.

**Old Town Trolley Tours
of Washington** $$$$
2640 Reed Street NE
Washington, DC
(202) 832–9800
www.historictours.com/
A lively, old-fashioned trolley with gold lettering will be a big hit with the kids. The hop-on, hop-off format makes it easy to canvas the city's most famous sites, on and off the National Mall.

Potomac Party Cruises, Inc. $$$$
Zero Prince Street
Alexandria, VA
(703) 683–6076
www.dandydinnerboat.com
The *Dandy* offers popular lunch, brunch, and dinner and dancing cruises along the Potomac, from Old Town Alexandria to Georgetown and back. The riverboat is climate-controlled for year-round tours.

Potomac Riverboat Company $–$$$$
Alexandria City Marina
King and Union Streets
Old Town Alexandria, VA
(703) 684–0580
www.potomacriverboatco.com
The *Matthew Hayes* riverboat offers 90-minute narrated excursions on the Potomac between Alexandria and Georgetown. A 50-minute cruise takes passengers to Mount Vernon, where they can explore George Washington's home before reboarding for the return trip. To learn more about historic Alexandria, take the 40-minute narrated *Admiral Tilp* cruise along the waterfront area. Tours run April through October.

Scandal Tours of Washington $$$$
1602 South Springwood Drive
Silver Spring, MD
(202) 783–7212
www.gnpcomedy.com/scandaltours.html
Take a humorous look at landmarks involved in Washington scandals, such as Monica Lewinsky–related sites, Gary Hart's town house, and the Watergate. The tours run spring through fall.

Spirit Cruises $$$$
Pier 4, 6th and Water Streets SW
Washington, DC
(866) 211–3811
www.spiritofwashington.com
This ship seats 600 people and travels to Alexandria as guests enjoy a lavish dinner buffet and live entertainment.

Tourmobile Sightseeing $$–$$$$
1000 Ohio Drive SW
Washington, DC
(202) 554–5100, (888) 868–7707
www.tourmobile.com
Free all-day reboarding is offered by this service, which is the only one authorized by the U.S. National Park Service to board and discharge people on the National Mall and in Arlington National Cemetery.

Washington Photo Safari $$$$
4545 Connecticut Avenue NW #620
Washington, DC
(202) 537–0937, (877) 512–5969
www.WashingtonPhotoSafari.com
Learn how to take postcard-quality photos using your own camera, while touring the city with a professional photographer. Tours focus on various topics, such as Monuments and Memorials and Churches of the Nation's Capital.

Washington Walks $$–$$$$
(202) 484–1565
www.washingtonwalks.com
Experienced guides lead daily scheduled walks with such titles as the White House Un-Tour, A Moveable Feast, and the Most Haunted Houses.

THE ARTS

A rich and diverse arts scene is flourishing in Metro Washington, from repertory theaters and burgeoning artists' colonies to the esteemed National Symphony Orchestra and National Gallery of Art, not to mention such renowned venues as the John F. Kennedy Center for the Performing Arts and Wolf Trap National Park, the nation's only national park for the performing arts.

Washington, D.C. offers more museums and public galleries than any other North American city. Visitors come from all over the globe to view the National Gallery's many treasures and once-in-a-lifetime retrospectives. Although the National Gallery alone would be enough to secure our city's reputation as a visual arts center, Washington is also home to such esteemed galleries as the Smithsonian Institution's art museums, the Corcoran, the Phillips Collection, and the National Museum of Women in the Arts. Up-and-coming visual artists can be found at galleries in such areas as Dupont Circle and Georgetown in D.C., and Old Town Alexandria in Virginia.

Our city has produced more than its fair share of past and present cultural luminaries, especially in the areas of stage, screen, and studio. Among those with ties to the area, whether by birth or stints working or attending school here, are actors Warren Beatty and big sister Shirley MacLaine, Goldie Hawn, Robert Prosky, Sandra Bullock, and Helen Hayes, for whom Washington's equivalent of the Tony Award is named; singers Pearl Bailey, Toni Braxton, Mary Chapin Carpenter, Eva Cassidy, and Roberta Flack; opera stars Placido Domingo and Beverly Sills; jazz legends Duke Ellington and Ella Fitzgerald; guitar virtuoso Danny Gatton; and folk singer Tom Paxton.

Anchored by the aforementioned Kennedy Center and Wolf Trap, Metro Washington knows no music unfamiliar to its discerning ears. Each week you can uncover at least one major concert that fits your taste or mood, whether it be rock, country, opera, classical, bluegrass, R&B, rap, world beat, or folk.

If all the world's a stage, and if Washington is indeed the nerve center of the globe, then it stands to reason that the Nation's Capital should have a relatively unparalleled theater scene. While we don't have the equivalent of the Great White Way, you'll find the D.C. theater experience to be rewarding in a different way. Our theater companies often tackle evocative subjects and difficult themes. They also host their share of world and U.S. premieres from playwrights who aren't afraid to be irreverent or controversial. Because D.C. theater companies are not-for-profit, you usually won't see the same fanfare you'll find in a Broadway show, with the exception of national touring productions.

Metro Washington enjoys increasingly close ties to Hollywood. It only seems logical that film stars including John Lithgow, Susan Sarandon, and Jon Voight cut their theatrical teeth at Washington's own Catholic University, whose drama department is among the finest in the nation.

Hollywood has taken a liking to Metro Washington, which has become one of the largest film markets in the nation, rivaling Los Angeles, New York, and Chicago.

This city of monuments and magnificent vistas is also one of the most filmed locations in the world. Chances are you won't live here

i Love the arts? Sign up for Gold Star Events (www.goldstarevents.com), a weekly e-mail service offering discounts on select performances at many area theaters and performing arts venues.

long before you spot a movie crew in Georgetown, Capitol Hill, Old Town Alexandria, Annapolis, or along the National Mall. Recent films, such as *Thank You for Smoking, Wedding Crashers,* and *National Treasure* feature Metro Washington as a backdrop.

In this chapter you'll find an overview of Metro Washington's performing arts, galleries, and movie houses. You'll also want to check out our Nightlife chapter for the lowdown on Washington's club scene, where you'll find a wide range of entertainment. Check out our Attractions chapter for profiles of museums and other cultural institutions.

PERFORMING ARTS VENUES

Washington, D.C.

DAR Constitution Hall
18th and D Streets NW
Washington, DC
(202) 628–4780
www.dar.org

Near the White House and next to the DAR National Headquarters and Museum, this renovated concert hall—the city's largest—hosts a wide variety of musical performances, from classical to pop. Aerosmith, Whitney Houston, Jerry Garcia, the Lincoln Center Jazz Orchestra with Wynton Marsalis, Rick James, Elvis Costello and Burt Bacharach, and the United States Air Force, Army, and Navy bands all have presented shows here. It's been said that Vladimir Horowitz, the legendary pianist, preferred to perform in this classy and surprisingly intimate atmosphere. Avoid parking hassles by taking the Metro to Farragut West. (See our Attractions and Kidstuff chapters for information about the neighboring DAR Museum.)

Ford's Theatre
511 10th Street NW
Washington, DC
(202) 347–4833 (box office)
(202) 638–2941 (Ford's Theatre Society)
www.fordstheatre.org

Walk into this theater where John Wilkes Booth assassinated President Abraham Lincoln on April 14, 1865, and you'll view a room appearing eerily the same as it did on that ill-fated night. The painstaking restoration includes the Presidential Box, adorned with patriotic bunting, gold drapes, and a portrait of George Washington. Nobody's allowed to sit in Lincoln's seat, although many visitors wish they could.

Today Ford's remains an active and immensely popular theater, a tribute to Lincoln's love for the performing arts. The 699-seat theater each year stages four or five musical revues and plays that Lincoln most likely would have enjoyed. Recent examples include a revival of the historical musical *Shenandoah* and an ambitious production of *The Grapes of Wrath,* staged as a tribute to the theater's restorer, Frankie Hewitt, who died in 2003. Annual events include a presidential gala and a megapopular holiday staging of Dickens's *A Christmas Carol.* Satirist Mark Russell usually performs during inaugural week.

Ticket prices range from $25 to $52, depending upon the production, seating area, and performance time. Shows start at 7:30 P.M. Tuesday through Saturday, 2:30 P.M. Saturdays and Sundays, and noon on weekdays. For tickets visit www.ticketmaster.com or call (202) 347–4833. Ford's does not offer parking, but you'll find two public lots within a block. The nearest Metrorail stops are Metro Center and Archives-Navy Memorial. For information on touring the theater and its museum, call the National Park Service (202–426–6924).

George Washington University's Lisner Auditorium
21st and H Streets NW
Washington, DC
(202) 994–6800
www.lisner.org

Students aren't the only listeners who flock to Lisner's eclectic lineup, from university concerts, plays, and ballets to international acts like Ondekoza: Demon Drummers of Japan and popular performers like Rickie Lee

Jones and the Pat Metheny Group. The concert hall boasts 1,490 seats, which offer good views but not a lot of legroom. Look for the whimsical hippopotamus statue out front. If you're driving, you may be lucky enough to find on-street parking. Otherwise, opt for the University Garage on I Street between 22nd and 23rd Streets, or take Metrorail's Orange or Blue Line to Foggy Bottom-GWU, just 3 blocks away. Ticket prices vary, but GW students can receive discounts by presenting their student IDs at the box office.

The John F. Kennedy Center for the Performing Arts
New Hampshire Avenue at Rock Creek Parkway
Washington, DC
(202) 467-4600
www.kennedy-center.org

Sitting majestically along the Potomac just south of Georgetown, this "living memorial" to the nation's 34th president proves just as impressive inside. Even if you don't attend a performance, you'll enjoy strolling through the Grand Foyer and flag-laden Hall of States and Hall of Nations. This unique arts center offers much more than beautiful hallways, however.

Topping the list is the center's 2,500-seat Concert Hall, which has earned rave reviews onstage boxes and lower-priced chorister seats onstage behind the musicians. An adjustable, multipaneled stage canopy enhances sound. Seats feature swing-away arms, and specially designed ramps permit easy wheelchair access. Visit the elegantly decorated Israeli Room on the Box Tier and Chinese Lounge on the Second Tier.

The world-renowned National Symphony Orchestra (202-416-8100), performs in the Concert Hall from September through May. The 18-concert season typically features such guests as pianist Emanuel Ax, violinist Joshua Bell, and the Guarneri String Quartet, and such works as Mozart's Piano Concerto No. 20 in D minor, K. 466; Beethoven's Eroica symphony, and world premieres like Danielpour's *Voices*

Look for free concerts every week, in a variety of musical genres, presented throughout the Washington area by first-rate bands and ensembles of the U.S. Army, Air Force, Navy, and Marines.

of Remembrance. Tickets range in price from $20 to $80. Consider a subscription if you plan to attend concerts frequently and want to be assured of the best seats. During the summer the symphony performs the annual Capitol Fourth concert on the U.S. Capitol's West Lawn and appears at Wolf Trap Farm Park for several outdoor shows. Marvin Hamlisch conducts the NSO Pops.

The Kennedy Center's 2,318-seat Opera House—how about that 1,735-bulb chandelier?—primarily hosts Broadway productions such as *Annie Get Your Gun* and *Titanic*, as well as several national and international dance troupes. Shows often appear here before their Broadway premieres.

The Opera House also is home to the Washington National Opera (202-416-7800), with popular tenor Placido Domingo as its artistic director. A typical season includes seven operas, such as *Rigoletto, Le Cid,* and *Otello*. Tickets for most operas sell out, so if you plan to attend several performances, purchase a subscription package. Call (202) 295-2400 or (800) 876-7372. Individual tickets, if you're lucky enough to get them, cost anywhere from $45 to $300, with the less-expensive seats often filled by subscribers.

The Eisenhower Theater also showcases a variety of productions, including crowd-pleasers like the *Sing-Along Wizard of Oz,* at which boisterous, costumed fans belted out the tunes while watching the classic move on a big screen. The Terrace Theater and Theater Lab accommodate smaller shows, like the long-running *Shear Madness*, a comic whodunit set in a beauty salon.

The center also hosts numerous events sponsored by the Washington Performing Arts Society (202-833-9800, www.wpas.org), which brings a diverse array of international

Musicals, Plays, and Lincoln History at Ford's Theatre

"God bless us, every one!" shouts an exuberant Tiny Tim, ushering in the holiday season for delighted theatergoers who look forward to an annual tradition at one of Washington, D.C.'s most historic theaters.

The staging of Charles Dickens's beloved *A Christmas Carol*, one of the most popular events at Ford's Theatre, is one of many reasons to visit the historic site. Every year the cozy, elegant theater in the city's bustling Penn Quarter hosts a variety of musicals and dramas, many of which showcase American icons or cultures. A must-see destination for both history buffs and theater lovers, the building draws 1,160,000 visitors every year, making it the city's most visited theater/museum/tour off the National Mall, according to the Downtown DC Business Improvement District.

Best known as the site of President Abraham Lincoln's assassination on April 14, 1865, the original theater closed and the building for many years housed government offices. Restored and reconstructed with more than $2 million authorized by a 1964 act of Congress, the historic theater reopened in 1968. Frankie Hewitt, who died in 2003, founded the Ford's Theatre Society, the not-for-profit corporation that produces Ford's live entertainment under a public/private partnership with the owner/operator, the Department of the Interior, National Park Service. In 2002 and 2003 Ford's underwent extensive renovations, including such features as new theatrical lighting and sound systems, seating and restrooms for disabled patrons, new heating and cooling systems, and a refurbished Lincoln museum.

Recent changes at the theater extend to its shows. Ford's recently staged a new production of the holiday classic *A Christmas Carol: A Ghost Story of Christmas*. Dickens himself makes an appearance in this adaptation by Michael Wilson, which also keeps the author's full name for the production in its title. History buffs will appreciate the effort; Dickens actually did travel to Washington for a public reading when the novel was first published.

The production features a lovely Victorian set and beautifully detailed period costumes that add to the authentic flavor of this faithful retelling. The men's costumes include perfectly tailored waistcoats with brass buttons, topped by dramatic, capelike overcoats. The women's full-skirted outfits feature sumptuous fabrics in rich hues and patterns like gold and lively plaids. Musical interludes showcase English carols nicely harmonized by cast members and accompanied by pit musicians.

Ford's Theatre pays tribute to its most famous patron's love of the performing arts by producing shows Lincoln himself would have enjoyed attending. Lincoln might even have seen *A Christmas Carol*, as Dickens was his contemporary. Most of Ford's productions, however, are contemporary plays and musicals written by Americans and/or focusing on American events and personalities, both famous and little known. *George Gershwin Alone*, Hershey Felder's fascinating one-man show about the life and music of the great American composer, proved so popular

The renovated Ford's Theatre, the site of Abraham Lincoln's assassination in 1865, stages American plays and musicals. COURTESY WASHINGTON, D.C. CONVENTION AND TOURISM CORPORATION

in its 2003 debut that the theater brought it back for an encore engagement in 2004. Another recent one-man show, *Trying*, starred 85-year-old Academy Award nominee James Whitmore as elder statesman Francis Biddle.

Although the majority of the theater's shows are dramas, it also produces standout musicals, including 23 world premieres and some—*Joseph and the Amazing Technicolor Dreamcoat* and *The American Dance Machine*—that jumped to Broadway. The theater recently staged a revival of *1776*, the rousing musical about how our country's forefathers created the Declaration of Independence. A spring 2007 offering, *Jitney*, is co-presented with D.C.'s African Continuum Theatre Company in tribute to the late American playwright August Wilson.

Since 2004, Ford's has operated under the artistic direction of Paul Tetreault, who was former managing director of the Alley Theatre in Houston. He has planned an emphasis on the theater's American identity.

Ford's is worth a visit even when the stage is dark, as the lower level features a newly renovated exhibition on Lincoln's assassination. Display cases hold numerous writings and artifacts related to the incident. Visitors also can view a tribute to Hewitt and look at posters from past productions. Free self-guided tours of the museum and theater take place daily, from 9:00 A.M. until 5:00 P.M., except during performances. Call the National Park Service on-site, (202) 426–6924, to confirm availability. The theater is at 511 10th Street NW, Washington, D.C.

acts to performance sites throughout Metro Washington. The Washington Ballet (202–362–3606, www.washingtonballet.org) presents shows here in the fall, winter, and spring, including such titles as *Carmen, Leaves Are Falling,* and *The Young Lions Roar.* The company, led by Artistic Director Septime Webre, also performs *The Nutcracker* annually at the Warner Theatre. Individual ticket prices generally range from $29 to $75, depending on the show and its location.

The Kennedy Center's "Performing Arts for Everyone" initiative is highlighted by daily free concerts at 6:00 P.M. on the Millennium Stage. You don't even need a ticket!

To get a close-up look at the center's many outstanding features, take a free, guided, hourlong tour, offered by the Friends of the Kennedy Center from 10:00 A.M. to 1:00 P.M. Saturdays and Sundays, 10:00 A.M. to 5:00 P.M. weekdays. You don't need reservations, but you can call (202) 416–8340 or TTY (202) 416–8524 for more details. The center boasts two restaurants: the Roof Terrace for elegant dinners, and KC Cafe for casual dining. Visit the two gift shops, open from 10:00 A.M. to 9:00 P.M., for a variety of performing arts–related merchandise.

The center offers three levels of underground parking, priced at $15, but it tends to fill up quickly. Your best bet is to park at the nearby Columbia Plaza Garage, 2400 Virginia Avenue NW. You also can take the Metro to the Foggy Bottom–George Washington University station and catch the Kennedy Center Show Shuttle, which operates from 9:45 A.M. to midnight Monday through Friday, from 10:00 A.M. to midnight Saturday, from noon to midnight on Sunday, and from 4:00 P.M. to midnight on holidays.

Don't miss visiting the center during December, when it's all decked out for the holiday season. You'll also find some of the Kennedy Center's most popular programs, like the annual free Messiah Sing-Along (tickets are distributed early in the month—and they go fast!), the Paul Hill Chorale's Christmas Candlelight Concerts, and the Oratorio Society of Washington's Music for Christmas. December also marks the annual gala for recipients of the Kennedy Center Honors, awarded in 2006 to Zubin Mehta, Dolly Parton, Andrew Lloyd Webber, Steven Spielberg, and William "Smokey" Robinson. (See our Kidstuff chapter for information about children's shows at the Kennedy Center.)

The National Theatre
1321 Pennsylvania Avenue NW
Washington, DC
(202) 628–6161
(800) 447–7400 (for ticket charges)
www.nationaltheatre.org
The National, the city's oldest theater, has been bringing stage entertainment to Washingtonians since 1835; in fact, every president since then, with the exception of Dwight Eisenhower (and we're not sure why), has attended a show here at "The Theatre of Presidents." The National gives the impression of a Broadway theater. Whether you're sitting in the orchestra, mezzanine, or balcony of the 1,676-seat theater, you'll enjoy first-rate acoustics and elegant details like crystal chandeliers.

The National's forte is booking big musicals such as *Les Miserables; Bring in 'Da Noise, Bring in 'Da Funk; Rent; Chicago; Ragtime;* and perennial favorite *Cats.* The theater has played host to several world premieres, including *Showboat* in the 1920s, and, more recently, *Crazy for You* and *Whistle Down the Wind.*

The National also hosts three entertainment series in its second-floor Helen Hayes Gallery. Admission is free, on a first-come, first-served basis. Check the Web site for the schedule. Saturday Morning at the National features family shows at 9:30 and 11:00 A.M., generally during the fall and mid-January through mid-April. Monday Night at the National showcases various performers at 6:00 and 7:30 P.M. Weekly film screenings highlight the Summer Cinema series.

Arrange a tour, given for groups of 10 or more, by calling (202) 783–6854. You'll view a slide show about the National's history (the theater was rebuilt five times after devastating fires in the 1800s), get a behind-the-scenes look at the theater, and even learn about friendly resident, opening-night ghost John McCullough, an actor reportedly murdered by a fellow performer in the basement.

If you're driving to the theater, you'll find convenient parking right across the street at the Ronald Reagan Building and International Trade Center. (It's a federal building, so don't be alarmed if security guards give your car a once-over.) Several nearby garages, including one right behind the theater, also offer parking, or take the Metro to the Metro Center station.

Verizon Center
601 F Street NW
Washington, DC
(202) 397–SEAT
www.verizoncenter.com

One of the city's most heralded additions, the spacious athletic arena also hosts concerts by the likes of Simon and Garfunkel, the Dixie Chicks, Paul McCartney, Cher, and Shania Twain. Tickets for such headliners don't come cheap: Expect to pay $80 to $200 apiece for the best seats. (See our Spectator Sports chapter for complete information on the center and the teams that play here.)

Warner Theatre
13th and E Streets NW
Washington, DC
(202) 783–4000
www.warnertheatre.com

A former vaudeville and movie palace just around the corner from the National, the beautifully restored, gilt- and chandelier-accented Warner now specializes in concerts by the likes of Boz Scaggs and Tom Jones, and Broadway productions such as *Cabaret*. The theater seats 1,850 people. Ticket prices vary according to the event. Parking and Metro opportunities are the same as those for the National.

Northern Virginia

George Mason University's Center for the Arts
Route 123 and Braddock Road
Fairfax, VA
(703) 993–8888
www.gmu.edu/cfa/

Touted as the "Kennedy Center of Northern Virginia," this showcase for local as well as nationally known acts offers a pleasant alternative for folks who'd rather avoid D.C.'s traffic and parking hassles—though you should be forewarned that rush hour shows create traffic problems of their own! We've found this to be one of the area's most comfortable theaters, with roomy seating affording excellent views and acoustics from both the balcony and orchestra levels. The center continues to attract prominent artists such as Moscow State Radio Symphony and Choruses, Vienna Radio Symphony Orchestra, Canadian Brass, Mark Morris Dance Group, Carnegie Hall Jazz Band, and Irish band Altan. Tickets, generally ranging in cost from $20 to $90, are available by subscription or individually, with prices varying according to the performance.

The 50-year-old Fairfax Symphony (703–827–0600), Virginia's answer to the National Symphony, performs here with up-and-coming as well as renowned guest artists. The university's resident theatrical company, Theater of the First Amendment, performs critically acclaimed contemporary works, including world premieres like Anna Theresa Cascio's *Crystal* and original musicals for families, in a building just behind the center. Inexpensive parking is available at an adjacent parking deck, which connects to the center via a pedestrian bridge.

Patriot Center at George Mason University
4400 University Drive
Fairfax, VA
(703) 993–3000
www.patriotcenter.com

This 10,000-seat arena hosts a variety of events in addition to the men's and women's

Many area community centers boast resident theater companies whose performances prove highly entertaining, yet easy on the budget.

Patriots' home basketball games. The center's annual event slate features 25 shows, mostly by nationally known popular performers the likes of David Bowie and Avril Lavigne. Family programs like *Walt Disney's World on Ice* and *Sesame Street Live* take place several times a year. (See our Spectator Sports chapter for more on the center's sporting events.)

Suburban Maryland

The Prince George's Publick Playhouse for the Performing Arts
5445 Landover Road
Cheverly, MD
(301) 277–1710
www.pgparks.com/places/artsfac/publick.html
Better known as Publick Playhouse, this Maryland-National Capital Park and Planning Commission–sponsored, 462-seat entertainment showcase specializes in family concerts and plays by visiting performers and drama troupes, including local community theater. Tickets vary in price according to the event, and discount subscriptions are available.

Strathmore Hall Arts Center
10701 Rockville Pike
North Bethesda, MD
(301) 530–0540
www.strathmore.org
This beautiful, circa-1902 mansion is home to a superb new 1,976-seat music center, as well as more intimate venues for musical performances. At the Music Center you can catch performances by major national artists or listen to the Baltimore Symphony Orchestra in its Metro Washington residence. Other resident companies offering regular performances include the National Philharmonic, Washington Performing Arts Society, Levine School of Music, CityDance Ensemble, Mary-

land Classic Youth Orchestras, and interPLAY, an ensemble of 50 adults with cognitive disabilities. The Gudelsky Concert Pavilion hosts outdoor concerts and movie screenings during the summer.

Changing exhibits of visual arts can be seen in the second-floor Gudelsky Gallery Suite, first-floor Invitational Gallery, and along hallways and stairways. Among the center's other programs are Afternoon Tea at 1:00 P.M. Tuesdays and Wednesdays, with instrumental performances in the Dorothy M. and Maurice C. Shapiro Music Room, at $18 per person; and Art After Hours, featuring performances in the cafe beginning at 7:30 P.M. Wednesdays ($10). The galleries and gift shop are open from 10:00 A.M. to 4:00 P.M. Mondays, Tuesdays, Thursdays, and Fridays; from 10:00 A.M. to 9:00 P.M. on Wednesdays; and from 10:00 A.M. to 3:00 P.M. on Saturdays.

OUTDOOR STAGES
Washington, D.C.

Carter Barron Amphitheatre in Rock Creek Park
4850 Colorado Avenue NW
Washington, DC
(202) 426–0486
www.nps.gov/rocr/cbarron.htm
In beautiful Rock Creek Park, this popular outdoor stage sponsors an annual summer musical festival, including many top names in jazz, soul, and R&B, Saturday and Sunday nights. The theater seats 3,700. Annual free events include performances of a Shakespearean work by the Shakespeare Theatre Company, the D.C. Blues Festival, and National Symphony Orchestra concerts. Note that tickets for paid concerts are nonrefundable, rain or shine. Plenty of free parking is available.

RFK Stadium
2400 East Capitol Street SE
Washington, DC
(202) 547–9077
www.washington.nationals.mlb.com
Due east of the Capitol, this 56,000-seat for-

mer home of the Washington Redskins and current home to the Washington Nationals baseball team and DC United Soccer team also is used occasionally for huge rock concerts and musical events. Bruce Springsteen played here during his 2003 tour. In October 2001 RFK hosted an all-day benefit for victims of the September 11 attacks. Michael Jackson headlined the all-star event, which also featured such performers as 'N Sync, Bette Midler, Aerosmith, and Destiny's Child. Acoustically, well, RFK is a football stadium, but as a venue for megaconcerts, it plays its role rather well.

Sylvan Theatre
The National Mall
Washington, DC
(202) 426–6839
With the Washington Monument looming in the background, this outdoor theater stages a number of military, Big Band, and pop concerts during warm-weather months.

Northern Virginia
Nissan Pavilion at Stone Ridge
7800 Cellar Door Drive
Bristow, VA
(703) 754–1288
www.nissanpavilion.com
The 25,000-seat amphitheater made its debut in June 1995, presenting Metro Washington music fans with yet another attractive warm-weather venue for rock, pop, and country music concerts. It's three times the size of the more prominent Wolf Trap National Park for the Performing Arts (see the following listing) and features two 30-by-40-foot video screens. It also offers a separate sound system just for the lawn. Concerts feature such performers as Shania Twain, Cher, Lauryn Hill, Bob Dylan, Paul Simon, Jimmy Buffett, and James Taylor.

Ticket prices range from free (for radio-sponsored festivals and occasional National Symphony shows) to $50 and up. Children 12 and younger are admitted free to some shows, like those given by James Taylor and Aretha Franklin. Give yourself plenty of time to travel, as traffic on I–66 frequently backs up for miles, causing many a frustrated concert-goer to miss out on part of the show. Your best bet is to call the pavilion for alternate directions or arrive early for "tailgating." As an added convenience, some events offer valet parking.

Wolf Trap National Park for the
Performing Arts
1551 Trap Road
Vienna, VA
(703) 255–1868
www.wolf-trap.org
This beautiful National Park Service facility, with its open-air Filene Center wooden pavilion and lawn seating, brings to the Virginia suburbs some of the world's leading musical entertainers during the spring and summer. The park's annual summer concert series officially kicks off with a formal gala, followed with a concert by a big-name act, such as the O'Jays in 2006. This series is virtually free of musical boundaries. Mary Chapin Carpenter may perform on a Friday night, followed by a Saturday night journey through Lake Wobegon with Garrison Keillor, a Sunday afternoon blues concert, and a Monday evening with Peter, Paul, and Mary. Concerts by the National Symphony Orchestra sometimes accompany films, such as classic Looney Tunes cartoons or NASA space footage, shown on a big screen.

Concertgoers often tote elegant picnics, turning the lawn into a patchwork quilt of blankets and baskets. An on-site restaurant catered by Ovations features a first-rate dinner buffet. Ticket prices vary, starting at about $15 for some lawn seats. Note that everyone, regardless of age, must have a ticket to enter. Also, be forewarned that rarely does rain drown out a concert: If you have lawn seats during a downpour, prepare to get soaked or pay extra to upgrade your tickets to pavilion seats—if they're still available.

A smaller indoor concert hall just down the road, the intimate Barns of Wolf Trap

(703–938–2404), serves primarily as a fall-and-winter showplace for folk and acoustic musicians such as Tom Chapin and Richie Havens. (See our Kidstuff chapter for information about children's programs at Wolf Trap.)

Suburban Maryland

Merriweather Post Pavilion
10475 Little Patuxent Parkway
Columbia, MD
(410) 715–5550
www.merriweathermusic.com
In the Howard County planned community of Columbia, a short drive from Montgomery County, Merriweather is Maryland's answer to Wolf Trap. One of the country's pioneer outdoor music halls, Merriweather is one of six locations to receive a 2005 nomination for "Best Large Outdoor Concert Venue" from the concert industry trade magazine *Pollstar*. Its summer rock and pop concert series (harder-edged than Wolf Trap's) attracts enormous crowds from the Washington-Baltimore corridor. The lineup features from 20 to 65 shows, including hot acts like the Black-Eyed Peas, Kenny Chesney, Mariah Carey, Phish, and Kanye West. Boomers also can count on a few old favorites, however, like Rod Stewart, the Allman Brothers Band, and the ever-popular Jimmy Buffett. Admission prices range from about $20 for lawn seats to $40 or more for pavilion tickets.

THEATER

Washington, D.C.

Arena Stage
1101 6th Street SW
Washington, DC
(202) 488–3300
www.arenastage.com
Across the street from the Southwest waterfront, the nationally recognized and critically acclaimed Arena Stage presents a mix of

classical and contemporary shows, including the provocative works of David Mamet and August Wilson and classic musicals like *South Pacific* and *Camelot*. The three-theater complex has proven to be a hotbed for emerging talent and previously untried productions and boasts more than 50 Helen Hayes Awards for its efforts. It's also the first theater outside of New York City to receive a Tony Award for Theatrical Excellence, awarded in 1976. Molly D. Smith has been the artistic director since 1998.

Recent productions include August Wilson's *Gem of the Ocean* and a daring new staging of *Cabaret*. Tickets, available by subscription, average around $40 to $50 if purchased singly. Arrive ticketless 90 to 30 minutes before a show, and you might get lucky: During this time period most Fichandler and Kreeger performances offer a limited number of half-price tickets. Arena's "fivetwentyfive" program features $10 tickets for patrons between the ages of 5 and 25 with valid IDs. They go fast, but if you call or drop by before 5:25 P.M. the day of the show (or the day before a weekend matinee), you may be able to get your hands on a couple. Call (202) 488–3300 for further details. The theater seats 800 in its Fichlandler theater in the round, and 500 in the Kreeger. A third stage, the Old Vat, features works by visiting troupes. Free on-street parking usually is easy to find in the neighborhood. Disabled patrons can park in the theater's lot. Waterfront is the closest Metro station.

The Folger Shakespeare Library
201 East Capitol Street NW
Washington, DC
(202) 544–4600
www.folger.edu
If you're a fan of the master British playwright, get thee to the Folger Theatre, where you can watch innovative productions of the Bard's plays and other works presented by visiting troupes. The intimate wooden theater on Capitol Hill, modeled after a true Shakespearean stage, seats 250 people. Expect

shows like *King Lear,* featuring the Classic Theater of Harlem, or classic stagings of *A Midsummer Night's Dream* and *The Tempest.* Tickets start at $32.

Theater is just the tip of the arts iceberg here, however. The library itself, open only by appointment to scholars, features the largest collections of early editions of Shakespeare. The public can visit the reading rooms annually during Shakespeare's Birthday Open House in April (see Annual Events chapter). The Folger holds rotating exhibits on period topics such as old-fashioned remedies, cooking, and music. The PEN/Faulkner Novel Reading Series features nominees for the nation's largest juried fiction award, and a poetry series includes poets of national fame. The library also sponsors family programs on such topics as "Exploring Shakespeare's Plays." The Folger Consort Group, meanwhile, presents a slate of concerts of medieval, Renaissance, and baroque music.

Admission is free. Public tours take place at 11:00 A.M. Monday through Friday and 11:00 A.M. and 1:00 P.M. Saturdays, and tours of the Elizabethan Herbal Knot Garden take place at 10:00 and 11:00 A.M. every third Saturday from April through October. Shakespeare etc., the library's gift shop, sells Folger editions of Shakespeare's plays and other merchandise related to the Bard. The building is open from 10:00 A.M. to 4:00 P.M. Monday through Saturday and is closed on federal holidays. On-street parking is available, and the nearest Metro stations are Capitol South and Union Station.

GALA Hispanic Theatre
3333 14th Street NW
Washington, DC
(202) 234-7174
www.galatheatre.org
The city's only Spanish-language theater offers both classic and contemporary plays by Spanish and Latin American playwrights, including some premieres. Hugo Medrano is the artistic director.

¿No habla español? Not to worry: English

i More than 20 area theaters participate in Stages for All Ages, a program sponsored by the *Washington Post* and the League of Washington Theaters to introduce young people ages 17 and under to live, professional theater throughout the metropolitan area. From January through May the theaters offer a free ticket to a young person with each adult ticket purchased for select performances. For information on upcoming events or to request a brochure, call the Stages for All Ages Hotline at (202) 334-5885 or visit www.lowt.org.

translations appear as supertitles above the stage. Tickets start at $20, with discounts available for seniors, children, and groups of 10 or more. The theater also sometimes features community nights, with greatly reduced ticket prices.

The Shakespeare Theatre
450 7th Street NW
Washington, DC
(202) 547-1122
shakespearedc.org
Buy your tickets early for productions of this critically acclaimed theater company, which specializes in Shakespearean and other classic drama by the likes of Ibsen and Williams. The company, which has won 51 Helen Hayes Awards in 19 years, performs five main-stage plays annually, under the artistic direction of Michael Kahn. Recent productions have featured such plays as Ibsen's *An Enemy of the People* and Shakespeare's *Titus Andronicus.*

Shows such as *Othello* sell out quickly, with just $10 standing-room-only seats available at the last minute. (SRO tickets are available one hour before sold-out shows for cash only, with a limit of two per person.) Regular tickets, if you're lucky enough to get them, range in price from $30 to $70.

In a revitalized section of downtown near the National Gallery of Art, the 449-seat theater is home to Washington's resident Shakespeare company. It's housed at the Lansburgh,

The Shakespeare Theatre is one of Washington D.C.'s most popular sites for live performances of classic drama. COURTESY WASHINGTON, D.C. CONVENTION AND TOURISM CORPORATION

a former department store building that is a longtime Washington icon. In October 2007 the Shakespeare Theatre Company will open a new facility across the street. The new Harman Center for the Arts will encompass the existing Lansburgh stage and a new 776-seat theater, the Sidney Harman Hall. With the larger stage, the company will be able to accommodate growing audiences and visiting companies with other technical needs. The construction will also give rise to several new spaces for educational programs, seminars, and other events.

Parking is available on-site in a garage accessible from 8th Street. The nearest Metro stations are Gallery Place-Chinatown and Archives-Navy Memorial. The theater also presents two weeks of free performances of a Shakespearean play each June at Carter Barron Amphitheatre in Rock Creek Park.

The Studio Theatre
1333 P Street NW
Washington, DC
(202) 332–3300
www.studiotheatre.org

This 29-year-old regional theater strives to combine quality and affordability in its broad range of productions. With two 200-seat theater spaces, it offers an intimate setting for plays like Athol Fugard's *Master Harold and the Boys* and Harold Pinter's *Betrayal*. Joy Zinoman is founder and artistic director of the theater, which produces five to six plays annually on its main stage. The Studio Theatre Acting Conservatory offers professional instruction, and Secondstage features works by emerging playwrights. Ticket prices range from $34 to $65. Limited free parking is available at a store lot at 15th and P Streets. The nearest Metrorail station is Dupont Circle.

Woolly Mammoth Theatre Company
641 D Street NW
Washington, DC
(202) 289–2443
www.woollymammoth.net

This cutting-edge theater, now in its new

i Cutting-edge and alternative performance arts are in the spotlight each July when Washington, D.C. hosts the Capital Fringe Festival, a ten-day series of offbeat productions from local, regional, and international artists. Tickets to most performances are $15 or less.

home in downtown's Penn Quarter, specializes in world and national premieres, including offerings such as Regina Porter's *Man, Woman, Dinosaur* and *Dead Funny* by Terry Johnson. Howard Shalwitz is artistic director. Productions take place on various stages. Tickets generally cost from $32 to $52, but each show also features two "pay what you can" previews. Patrons under 25 can also secure seats for $10 for select performances. Side balcony "stampede seats" are available an hour before each show to patrons of any age for $10. The theater also offers a variety of acting classes at $269 for eight weeks.

Northern Virginia

Signature Theatre
2800 South Stafford Street
Arlington, VA
(703) 820–9771,
(703) 218–6500 (box office)
www.sig-online.org

This highly acclaimed 17-year-old company has racked up more than 50 Helen Hayes Awards in its relatively short lifespan, including eight awards in 2006 alone for its production of *Urinetown*. In 2007 it moved into a new complex in Arlington's Shirlington neighborhood, featuring two black-box theaters, expanded facilities for artists, production, and education, and a rare treat for theatergoers: ample parking. Signature, under the artistic direction of Eric D. Schaeffer, is well regarded for its productions of Sondheim shows and other musical theater revivals, as well as new plays. The company performs three musicals and two plays annually, including such productions as *Into the Woods* and the little-known Rodgers and Hammerstein

ℹ️ Washington's suburbs are rich with community orchestras and bands, most of which perform concert series in auditoriums at community centers and high schools.

musical *Allegro*. Single-show tickets are $27 to $65, but nonsubscribers often find that performances sell out early.

The company also holds *STAGES,* a series of free public readings of new plays at 7:30 P.M. on most Mondays. Signature also offers a drama education program for high school students.

Suburban Maryland

Olney Theatre Center for the Arts
2001 Olney-Sandy Spring Road
Olney, MD
(301) 924–3400
www.olneytheatre.org
Suburban Maryland's best-known playhouse, this nonprofit, professional theater in the Montgomery County countryside is a staple for quality theater. Expect solid productions of favorites the likes of *Death of a Salesman* and *Peter Pan*. Ticket prices range from $34 to $44 for adults, with discounts for students and seniors. Shows take place Tuesday through Sunday and include matinee performances on Thursdays and weekends.

The center also houses the country's oldest theatrical touring company, the 55-year-old National Players; the Potomac Theatre Project, which specializes in experimental works; school performances; acting workshops; and a free Summer Shakespeare production.

The suburban location offers a welcome bonus: lots of free on-site parking!

Round House Theatre
4545 East–West Highway
Bethesda, MD
(240) 644–1100
www.roundhousetheatre.org
This Montgomery County repertory company has entertained audiences for more than 30 years, claiming 23 Helen Hayes Awards. It specializes in contemporary works and new

translations of classics such as *The Cherry Orchard* and *Our Town*. The theater, under the artistic direction of Blake Robison, presents six to eight shows annually. Performances take place in two locations: a 400-seat theater for Subscription Series productions at the corner of East–West Highway and Waverly Street in downtown Bethesda and a 100- to 150-seat flexible space for Cabaret Series shows at 8641 Colesville Road, Silver Spring, next door to the new AFI Silver Theatre and Cultural Center. Paid parking for both locations is available at nearby lots and garages. Ticket prices range from $15 to $50, with discounts for those under 25 and seniors.

The theater also conducts classes for adults and children and participates in a school outreach program.

MAJOR GALLERIES AND MUSEUMS

Washington, D.C.

Arthur M. Sackler Gallery
1050 Independence Avenue SW
Washington, DC
(202) 633–1000
www.si.edu/asia
Distinctively international, the Sackler Gallery features a permanent collection of masterpieces of Asian and Near Eastern art that spans from the beginning of civilization to the present. Works include jades, bronzes, lacquerware, sculpture, paintings, and furniture. Many of the exhibits are on loan from various sources, while nearly 1,000 are gifts from museum namesake Dr. Arthur M. Sackler. This Smithsonian museum, which opened in 1987, connects underground with the neighboring Freer. The museum also houses a comprehensive research library and hosts numerous public programs. Admission is free, and it's open from 10:00 A.M. to 5:30 P.M. daily, except December 25. The museum is close to the L'Enfant Plaza and Smithsonian Metro stations. (See the Kidstuff chapter for details on family programs.)

Corcoran Gallery of Art
500 17th Street NW
Washington, DC
(202) 639–1700
www.corcoran.org/museum

Of all the fine arts showcases that the Nation's Capital has to offer, the Corcoran ranks as the largest and oldest private gallery. It boasts an amazing selection of American paintings and sculpture and a smaller assortment of European pieces. It also hosts numerous special solo and group exhibitions, featuring a wide array of works by local, national, and international artists. Some shows feature students of the Corcoran School of Art, the city's sole professional school of art and design.

Recent exhibitions included, among others, the enormously popular *Modernism* and jovial sculptor J. Seward Johnson Jr.'s *Beyond the Frame: Impressionism Revisited,* featuring three-dimensional tableaus based on famous paintings.

The gallery also hosts frequent concerts, lectures, and family programs (see the Kidstuff chapter). Visit the gift shop and cafe, which features a popular brunch on Sundays. The Corcoran is open from 10:00 A.M. to 5:00 P.M. Wednesday through Sunday, and 10:00 A.M. to 9:00 P.M. on Thursday. It is closed Monday, Tuesday, Thanksgiving, December 25, and January 1. Admission is $8.00 for adults, $6.00 for seniors, and $4.00 for students ages 13 to 18. The nearest Metro stations are Farragut West (17th Street exit) and Farragut North (K Street exit).

Freer Gallery of Art
Jefferson Drive at 12th Street SW
Washington, DC
(202) 633–1000, (202) 357–1729 TDD
www.si.edu/asia

The Freer Gallery of Art showcases a world-renowned collection of Asian works such as Chinese paintings, Japanese screens and Egyptian glass, and nineteenth- and early-twentieth-century American art by painters such as John Singer Sargent and James McNeill Whistler. The granite-and-marble

i For a unique interactive experience, check out *Dance of the Labyrinth,* a computerized walking labyrinth in artist Sandra Wasko-Flood's studio at 57 N Fine Art, 57 N Street NW, near the Union Station Metro. Call (703) 217–6706 or e-mail info@labyrinthsforpeace.org to make an appointment. Admission is free, but a donation is requested. The studio also features labyrinth art for sale and Wasko-Flood's collection of labyrinth books and journals for browsing. You can see pictures of the artwork at www.waskoart.com.

building, one of the Smithsonian Institution's museums on the National Mall, opened in 1923. The undisputed highlight is Whistler's gorgeous Peacock Room, a lavish dining room designed by the artist for Frederick R. Leyland during the nineteenth century.

The museum regularly hosts special events like concerts and films; pick up a schedule or look online for information about upcoming programs here and at other Smithsonian museums. Highlights tours begin at 12:15 P.M. daily except Wednesdays, July 4, Thanksgiving, New Year's Day, and other federal holidays. Museum hours are 10:00 A.M. to 5:30 P.M. daily except December 25. Admission is free. Your best bet is to take the Metro to the Smithsonian station, practically right outside the museum's door. (See the Kidstuff chapter for information about family programs.)

Hirshhorn Museum and Sculpture Garden
7th Street and Independence Avenue SW
Washington, DC
(202) 357–2700
hirshhorn.si.edu

This striking doughnut-shaped building is yet another hard-to-miss Smithsonian landmark along the National Mall. The Hirshhorn, established in 1974, specializes in modern art, including nineteenth- and twentieth-century paintings and sculpture by such greats as de Kooning, Pollock, and Rothko.

Adjoining the building and just to the north, the idyllic Sunken Sculpture Garden features works by the likes of Matisse, Moore, and Rodin. Like all Smithsonian museums, the Hirshhorn offers special programs such as film screenings and lectures. Take a free walk-in tour, offered weekdays at 10:30 A.M. and noon, and Saturdays and Sundays noon and 2:00 P.M. Tours operate less regularly in the winter; garden tours are available in spring and fall. Hours are 10:00 A.M. to 5:30 P.M. daily except December 25. The museum is a short walk from the L'Enfant Plaza or Smithsonian Metro stops. (Our Kidstuff chapter describes family activities here.)

The Kreeger Museum
2401 Foxhall Road NW
(202) 337–3050, (800) 337–3050
www.kreegermuseum.org

This 12-year-old museum, housed in a distinctive white, post-modern building on gorgeous Foxhall Road, displays the extensive modern art collection of David and Carmen Kreeger. Highlights include paintings by such artists as Monet, Renoir, Kandinsky, and Miró; sculptures by the likes of Calder and Rodin; and African artworks. The Kreeger also hosts special shows, such as *Gene Davis: Interval* in 2007.

The museum holds Open Hours on Saturdays from 10:00 A.M. to 4:00 P.M. You can visit at other times by calling (202) 338–3552 and making a reservation for a docent-guided tour, offered Tuesday through Friday at 10:30 A.M. and 1:30 P.M., and Saturdays at 10:30 A.M. Suggested admission for the 90-minute tour is $8.00 per person, $5.00 for seniors and students. You don't need a reservation to take a tour on Saturdays when optional tours—with the same suggested admission—take place throughout the day. All ages are welcome during Open Hours and special events for families, but only children 12 and older are welcome during tours. The museum has free parking but does not house a gift shop. While the main floor is wheelchair accessible, visitors can reach the lower level only by staircase.

National Gallery of Art
4th Street and Constitution Avenue NW
Washington, DC
(202) 737–4215
www.nga.gov

In 2003 the National Gallery completed a four-year renovation of the sculpture galleries on the ground floor of the West Building. Utilizing natural light and open space, the 24,000 square feet of exhibits showcase more than 900 works, including many new acquisitions. The galleries feature 10 sections: Late 19th Century and Lost Wax, Auguste Rodin, Degas and Contemporary Painter-Sculptors, Early Modern Figures, 18th and 19th Century, 18th-Century Furniture and Sculpture, Chinese Porcelains, Late Renaissance and Baroque, Renaissance, and Medieval and Renaissance.

In 1999 the 6.1-acre Sculpture Garden was opened at 7th Street and Constitution Avenue NW, next to the West Building. Beautifully landscaped with 35 native species of trees, shrubs, and other plants, the garden features 17 modern sculptures and a central fountain/ice rink. A pavilion includes restrooms and a cafe.

Visitors enjoy strolling curving pathways to view such works as Barry Flanagan's *Thinker on a Rock,* a pensive hare who serves as a whimsical homage to Rodin's familiar sculpture. Roy Lichtenstein's *House I* looks like a cartoon abode come to life. *Typewriter Eraser, Scale X* by Claes Oldenburg and Coosje van Bruggen resembles a giant-sized rolling eraser, complete with curved bristles. The garden, a gift of the Morris and Gwendolyn Cafritz Foundation, also contains sculptures by such artists as Alexander Calder, Louise Bourgeois, Joan Miró, and David Smith.

Actually two buildings, the National Gallery of Art is one of the world's preeminent cultural attractions, housing a collection vast

i Volunteers—like you, perhaps?—
lead tours at the National Gallery of Art. Call (202) 842–6247 or visit www.nga.gov/education/docent.shtm.

The National Gallery of Art houses one of the world's largest and most revered collections of art. COURTESY WASHINGTON, D.C. CONVENTION AND TOURISM CORPORATION

and rich enough to command repeated visits. Created in 1937 by a joint resolution of Congress, the gallery grew from the bequest of prominent financier Andrew Mellon (Paul Mellon's father) and opened in 1941. You'll not find a better cultural bargain anywhere: Admission is always free.

The gallery's magnitude and diversity of exhibitions can make a visit daunting, especially for the first-time tourist. We recommend starting at the Micro Gallery, conveniently located off the West Building's main entrance off the National Mall. Here you can preview more than 1,700 works on an interactive computer screen and design a personalized tour, complete with a map, of art you'd especially like to see. Search for works categorized

according to artists, subjects, or time periods, and learn more about the artists' backgrounds.

The original West Building features some of the best in American and European painting, sculpture, and graphic arts from the thirteenth through nineteenth centuries, including works by Botticelli, Raphael, and Rembrandt, and the only da Vinci painting on exhibit outside Europe. The popular impressionism collection includes famous works by Renoir, Monet, Manet, Cassatt, Pissaro, and others. You'll also see well-known American works like Gilbert Stuart's presidential portraits. The East Building, designed by I. M. Pei and completed in 1978, showcases modern art, including a giant Calder mobile. This building also hosts many of the museum's major exhibitions, such as recent shows featuring retrospectives of works by Rousseau, Toulouse-Lautrec, and Roy Lichtenstein.

A dramatic fountain- and skylight-enhanced underground automated walkway connects the two buildings. Here you'll also find informal dining and a great gift shop featuring beautiful books and postcards and reasonably priced, framing-quality prints. Another gift shop, featuring an even more extensive selection of prints and postcards, is on the West Building's ground floor. Other dining options include the Garden Cafe in the West Building and a coffee bar in the East Building. Call (202) 216–5966 for restaurant information and (202) 842–6002 for gift shop details.

The museum holds numerous special programs, most of which are free of charge. Obtain information by calling (202) 737–4215, or you can request a free monthly calendar of events by calling (202) 842–6662, or just look online. A Sunday evening concert series (202–842–6941) features free performances by the National Gallery Orchestra at 7:00 P.M. on most Sundays, October through June. Arrive at the West Garden Court as early as 6:00 P.M.; admission is first-come, first-served. The East Building Auditorium offers free screenings of art films on weekends and some weekdays. Admission is also on a first-come, first-served basis. Call (202) 842–6799 for a schedule. (See our Kidstuff chapter for a description of family-oriented features.)

Enhance your visit with a free guided tour of the West or East Buildings, or the Italian Renaissance, Nineteenth-Century French, and American collections. Dates and times are subject to change, so visit an information desk to find out about the current schedule.

i You'll find some of Washington's most intriguing artwork in the city's historic houses of worship. See our Attractions and Worship chapters for more about the stained-glass windows at Washington National Cathedral and mosaics at the Basilica of the National Shrine of the Immaculate Conception.

You can rent audiotours in the Rotunda, at $5.00 or $3.00 for a family tour.

The National Gallery of Art and Sculpture Garden hours are 10:00 A.M. to 5:00 P.M. Monday through Saturday, and 11:00 A.M. to 6:00 P.M. Sundays. Take the Metro to the Judiciary Square, Archives, or Smithsonian stations.

National Museum of African Art
950 Independence Avenue SW
Washington, DC
(202) 633–1000
www.nmafa.si.edu

This is a fascinating highlight on any Smithsonian tour if only for one reason: It's the one national museum dedicated solely to the collection, study, and exhibition of the art and culture of Africa. The gallery's permanent exhibitions include *Images of Power and Identity,* featuring visual arts from south of the Sahara; aesthetic, everyday African objects such as chairs, snuff containers, and drinking horns; and treasures from the ancient city of Benin. Visit the museum's gift shop for hard-to-find art objects and books. The museum is open from 10:00 A.M. to 5:30 P.M. daily, except on December 25. It's close to the Smithsonian Metro station. (See Kidstuff for information on family activities.)

National Museum of Women in the Arts
1250 New York Avenue NW
Washington, DC
(202) 783–5000
www.nmwa.org

Four centuries of works by women artists, including O'Keeffe, Cassatt, and Le Brun, highlight this exquisite museum, the first of its kind. Recent special exhibitions have featured paintings by Frida Kahlo, Berthe Morissot, and Italian women artists from the Renaissance to the baroque; sculptures by Nancy du Pont Reynolds; sixteenth-century paintings by Lavinia Fontana and other women artists of Bologna; and photographs by Sarah Charlesworth. The museum marked its 20th anniversary in 2007. In what could be the answer to a trivia question, the collection is housed, ironically enough, in a former Masonic temple. Highlights include frequent education programs, a library and research center (by appointment only), a quarterly magazine called *Women in the Arts,* a cafe, and a gift shop that specializes in unique jewelry. Metro Center is the closest Metro stop.

Hours are from 10:00 A.M. to 5:00 P.M. Monday through Saturday and noon to 5:00 P.M. Sundays. It's closed January 1, Thanksgiving, and December 25. Admission is $8.00 for adults and $6.00 for seniors and students; children ages 18 and younger get in free. (You'll find additional information in the Kidstuff chapter.)

The Phillips Collection
1600 21st Street NW
Washington, DC
(202) 387–2151
www.phillipscollection.org
In the shadows of Embassy Row, the former home of Duncan Phillips features a diverse collection of masterpieces of French impressionism, postimpressionism, and modern art. In April 2006 the Phillips welcomed back Renoir's *Luncheon of the Boating Party,* the best-known work from its permanent collection, along with about 50 other key works when it unveiled its new addition.

Be sure to inquire about the museum's wonderful free Sunday concerts, gallery talks, and tours. The museum has a small eatery and a gift shop. Admission to the special exhibitions is $12 for the general public, $10 for seniors and students, free for ages younger than 18, and is voluntary on weekdays. The museum is open 10:00 A.M. to 5:00 P.M. Tuesday, Wednesday, Friday, and Saturday; 10:00 A.M. to 8:30 P.M. Thursday; and noon to 7:00 P.M. Sunday. It's closed on most holidays. The Dupont Circle Metro stop is just a block away.

Renwick Gallery
Pennsylvania Avenue and 17th Street NW
Washington, DC
(202) 633–1000
americanart.si.edu

i Opened in 1874, the Renwick Gallery of Art originally housed the private art collection of William Wilson Corcoran, an early collector of American art. The collection moved to the present-day Corcoran Gallery of Art at 17th Street and New York Avenue in 1890.

Leave the present and step into the late nineteenth century. The Renwick Gallery, a Smithsonian museum established in 1972, is a showcase of American design, crafts, and contemporary arts. The Grand Salon and the Octagon Room boast period furnishings and decorations from the 1860s and 1870s. The building itself dates to 1859 and is the original site of the Corcoran Gallery. The museum, which has a gift shop, is open from 10:00 A.M. to 5:30 P.M. daily, except on December 25. It's near the Farragut West Metro station.

Smithsonian American Art Museum and National Portrait Gallery
8th and G Streets NW
Washington, DC
(202) 633–1000
americanart.si.edu and
www.npg.si.edu/
These two museums reopened in July 2006 as the Donald W. Reynolds Center for American Art and Portraiture. Housed in the painstakingly restored Patent Office Building, you'll be as wowed by the works as their surroundings. The National Portrait Gallery houses the only complete collection of presidential portraits outside of the White House, but it also takes a turn with contemporary portraiture, highlighting the field's top names and showcasing images of Tom Wolfe, Snoop Dogg, and other household names. In the magnificent third floor's Great Hall, you'll find portraits of leading twentieth-century figures in science, politics, entertainment, and sports.

The Smithsonian American Art Museum houses an intriguing collection. The oldest works are simple wood paintings from seventeenth-century Puerto Rico. Colonial

Smithsonian American Art Museum/ National Portrait Gallery

American art fans had reason to rejoice in July 2006, when the Smithsonian Institution lifted the veil off of two magnificent jewels. The Smithsonian American Art Museum and National Portrait Gallery, the museum system's two repositories of American art treasures, had been closed to the public since 2001. Nearly six years later, they made a smashing return. The museums reopened collectively as the Donald W. Reynolds Center for American Art and Portraiture.

Although the art is impressive, the building itself is worth a trip for a lesson in American history, ingenuity, and perseverance. Originally constructed as the U.S. Patent Office in 1836, it quickly became a major attraction where inventors showcased their creations, drawing more than 100,000 visitors a year and hosting major gatherings like Abraham Lincoln's 1865 inaugural ball. Restored to its former glory, the glorious Greek Revival building retains the spirit of the past but fits easily into what is now the heart of Washington, D.C.'s Penn Quarter—the city's hottest spot for entertainment, dining, theater, and performance and visual art.

To keep pace with the Penn Quarter's bustling nightlife, the Reynolds Center museums keep later hours than the other museums in the Smithsonian system, staying open until 7:00 P.M. each night. And tipping a hat to the district's lively restaurant scene, the museum is home to the Portico, a seasonal outdoor cafe and lively neighborhood gathering place. It boasts a 22-foot bar, a schedule of evening jazz concerts, and chairs designed by Harry Bertoia, an artist whose work is on display in the American Art Museum's Lincoln Gallery.

Beyond their remarkable history and neighborhood appeal, the museums are a must-see for any American art lover. The National Portrait Gallery is home to portraits of notable Americans past and present—including Shaquille O'Neal and Marilyn Monroe—and the nation's only complete collection of presidential portraits outside of the White House, including the famous "Lansdowne" portrait of George Washington. Other permanent and temporary exhibitions showcase notable figures in sports, entertainment, the civil rights movement, and other thematic fields.

works include Gilbert Stuart portraits and Thomas Cole landscapes. Following a theme of western expansion, the museum houses 400 Indian paintings from George Catlin's collection, plus spirited frontier landscapes by Albert Bierstadt and Frederic Remington. Pivotal Gilded Age and impressionist works by Childe Hassam, Winslow Homer, John Singer Sargent, and Mary Cassatt show the country's march toward industrialism and prosperity.

New Deal masterpieces by Thomas Hart Benton, Jacob Lawrence, and Edward Hopper depict life in rural outposts and urban centers alike. Twentieth-century artists like Marsden Hartley, Georgia O'Keeffe, and Wayne Thiebaud and contemporary artists like David Hockney and Nam June Paik also play an important role in this collection, as do masters of folk art. James Hampton's spiritual sculpture, *The Throne of the Third Heaven,* a collec-

The Gallery also balances historical portraiture with modern trends in the field. The permanent collection includes *American Origins, 1600–1900*, a virtual journey through America's history that spans 17 galleries. But to keep portraiture fresh and contemporary for its patrons, there's also a chance for patrons to see works by contemporary portrait artists.

The Smithsonian American Art Museum boasts the largest American art collection in the world. But it's more than a museum—it celebrates the talent and artistic accomplishments of beloved American artists like Edward Hopper, Georgia O'Keeffe, and George Catlin, known for his works of Native Americans.

Another thing that sets these museums apart: They're as much about preservation as exhibition. You'll get a rare behind-the-scenes look at how the art you enjoy in the galleries is preserved and protected. The on-site Lunder Conservation Center does just that, featuring state-of-the-art laboratories and studios viewable through full-length glass walls. And even those doing the hard work will look their finest—renowned designer Isaac Mizrahi was commissioned to craft custom aprons to be worn by conservators.

Also part of the complex, the Luce Foundation Center for American Art lets you experience works of art not usually displayed. The center's namesake, Hank Luce, was an ardent advocate of bringing stored art into public view—and that's exactly what you'll see. If paintings are your passion, the Luce Foundation Center's screens are densely covered. Fond of sculpture or folk art? The center's shelves are never in short supply. Portrait miniatures, bronze medals, and jewelry are arranged in drawers that slide open at the touch of a button.

Those who attended Abraham Lincoln's second inaugural ball on the center's third floor in 1865 were unaware that they were setting a standard that was to be met nearly 150 years later. It's a standard of excitement, ingenuity, and a dynamic, bustling spirit of revelry. The Reynolds Center's dramatic return indicates that the standard continues to be raised.

tion highlight, is a life-size throne crafted from recycled materials and aluminum foil.

The museum's Luce Foundation Center for American Art is a visible art storage space that features some 3,300 artworks: paintings densely hung on screens; sculptures, contemporary crafts, and art objects arranged on shelves; and portrait miniatures, bronze medals, and contemporary jewelry in drawers that slide open with the touch of a button. The Lunder Conservation Center is a working art restoration center where visitors can watch restoration experts at work. To complement their lively downtown neighborhood, the museums keep later hours, open daily from 11:30 A.M. to 7:00 P.M.

ℹ The National Portrait Gallery is the only place outside of the White House where you'll find a portrait of every president.

The Textile Museum
2320 S Street NW
Washington, DC
(202) 667–0441
www.textilemuseum.org
This small, elegant museum houses renowned collections of textile art, including rare Oriental carpets. Visitors can explore hands-on activities in an interactive gallery. The museum also offers frequent lectures and monthly family programs. Suggested admission is $5.00 per person. Hours are from 10:00 A.M. to 5:00 P.M. Monday through Saturday, and from 1:00 to 5:00 P.M. Sundays.

THE GALLERY SCENE

Metro D.C.'s flourishing arts community and gallery scene sometimes get overlooked due to some of the region's more internationally visible art treasures. Here we list galleries from the area's most prominent art districts.

Washington, D.C.

DC Arts Center
2438 18th Street NW
Washington, DC
(202) 462–7833
www.dcartscenter.org
This nonprofit center cultivates the local artistic community by providing a professional venue for artists and performers, giving budding artists necessary support to hone their craft and learn useful business skills. Residents and visitors can take advantage of the center's offerings: a 750-square-foot visual arts gallery, a 50-seat black-box theater, and a host of special public events. The gallery is open Wednesday through Sunday from 2:00 P.M. to 7:00 P.M., with later hours when performances are on.

Flashpoint
916 G Street NW
Washington, DC
(202) 315–1310
www.flashpointdc.com
This downtown arts space showcases works by local artists while also providing training and strategy development for cultural organizations and working artists. Step inside the gallery to see the works of local artists or catch an experimental theater performance in the theater lab space. Flashpoint also offers classes in yoga, belly dancing, and other creative disciplines. You'll notice residents coming and going from the Mather Building, which was constructed with 12 artist residences as the city's Cultural Development Corporation's first live/work housing project for artists. The facility is open from noon to 6:00 P.M. Tuesday through Sunday, with later hours for classes and performances.

Foundry Gallery
1314 18th Street NW
Washington, DC
(202) 463–0203
www.foundry-gallery.org
One of the Dupont Circle galleries, this 36-year-old artists' cooperative features abstract and experimental art, as well as representational contemporary art. It's open from 12:00 P.M. to 6:00 P.M. Wednesday through Sunday.

Hemphill Fine Arts
1515 14th Street NW
Washington, DC
(202) 234–5601
www.hemphillfinearts.com
Hemphill opened in 1993 as a showplace for emerging, mid-career, and established artists. One of Hemphill's goals was to mount socially relevant exhibitions. It's now part of 14th Street's emerging gallery scene, sharing a building with Adamson Gallery (202–842–9220, www.adamsoneditions.com), G Fine Art (202–462–1601, www.gfine

artdc.com), and micro-gallery Curator's Office (202–387–1008, www.curatorsoffice.com).

Touchstone Gallery
406 7th Street NW, 2nd floor
Washington, DC
(202) 347–2787
www.touchstonegallery.com
This multiartist cooperative gallery each month features two single-artist shows of contemporary, modern work. The 31-year-old gallery also occasionally hosts invitational shows featuring international artists. Its hours are 11:00 A.M. to 5:00 P.M. Wednesday through Friday, and from noon to 5:00 P.M. Saturdays and Sundays. The gallery is part of the Pennsylvania Quarter District, between the White House and Capitol Hill. It's one of several galleries participating in a gallery walk from 6:00 to 8:00 P.M. every third Thursday.

Northern Virginia

Arlington Arts Center
3550 Wilson Boulevard
Arlington, VA
(703) 248–6800
www.arlingtonartscenter.org
This gallery, in a renovated schoolhouse, showcases ambitious works of regional artists. The building also contains studio space for up to 14 artists. Hours are from 11:00 A.M. to 5:00 P.M. Tuesday through Saturday.

First Friday Gallery
Walk Downtown
Downtown Leesburg, VA
(703) 777–7838
www.leesburgfirstfriday.com
The Loudoun Arts Council sponsors this ongoing event, held from 6:00 to 9:00 P.M. the first Friday of each month except January. Visit nine galleries and specialty shops in historic downtown Leesburg for show openings, wine, and hors d'oeuvres and book signings. Pick up a map at any participating merchant.

The Greater Reston Arts Center (GRACE)
Market and St. Francis Streets
Reston, VA
(703) 471–9242
www.restonarts.org
In Reston Town Center, the lively downtown hub of one of the nation's first planned communities, this gallery features changing exhibitions of contemporary works. In December of 2003 the nonprofit center moved into a brand-new, larger building. GRACE sponsors an annual spring arts festival and sells unique artistic holiday gifts each December. Hours are from 11:00 A.M. to 5:00 P.M. Tuesday through Saturday.

McLean Project for the Arts
McLean Community Center
1234 Ingleside Avenue
McLean, VA
(703) 790–1953
www.mcleanart.org
MPA presents themed exhibitions of works by regional and international artists in its Emerson Gallery. The nonprofit organization also sponsors community classes for adults and children, and special events such as lectures and tours. The gallery is open from 10:00 A.M. to 4:00 P.M. Tuesday through Friday and 1:00 P.M. to 5:00 P.M. Saturdays.

Medlin Art Ltd.
2 Loudoun Street SE
Leesburg, VA
(703) 771–8696
www.loudouncounty.com/art/medlin.htm
This 23-year-old gallery, which recently relocated, specializes in limited edition prints by such artists as P. Buckley Moss and Paul Landry. Hours are 10:00 A.M. to 6:00 P.M. Tuesday through Saturday. The gallery closes on Sundays and Mondays.

i Prints and paintings of Washington-area attractions make ideal souvenirs. Check out gallery spaces at local community and recreation centers for affordable works by local artists.

ℹ️ You'll find intriguing street performers—including a glass harp player—during weekends along the waterfront behind the Torpedo Factory Art Center in Old Town Alexandria.

The Potomac Gallery
26 South King Street
Leesburg, VA
(703) 771–8085
www.thepotomacgallery.com
This 17-year-old gallery in the heart of historic downtown Leesburg carries originals and limited editions, specializing in local art and Civil War–themed works. The store also offers custom framing. It's open 10:00 A.M. to 6:00 P.M. Monday through Saturday, noon to 5:00 P.M. Sundays.

Torpedo Factory Art Center
105 North Union Street
Alexandria, VA
(703) 838–4565
www.torpedofactory.org
If you enjoy watching artists at work, you'll love visiting this nationally known attraction in historic Old Town Alexandria. Once a waterfront munitions factory, the massive building now houses studio and gallery spaces for more than 160 professional artists, including painters, sculptors, glass makers, jewelry makers, and potters. The view of the Potomac and bustling harbor provides an added bonus as you observe and chat with artists. Most work is for sale, including bargains like pottery seconds.

The Art League (703–683–2323, www.theartleague.org), a local arts organization headquartered here, offers classes for children and adults. The Art League gallery holds juried exhibitions and sells a wide variety of affordable original works by regional artists. The building also houses Alexandria Archaeology, Room 327 (703–838–4399, www.alexandriaarchaeology.org), where visitors can look at museum exhibits on the city's history and watch archaeologists at work in the laboratory. The organization also offers hands-on courses. The museum is open to the public from 10:00 A.M. to 3:00 P.M. Tuesday through Thursday, from 10:00 A.M. to 5:00 P.M. Friday and Saturday, and from 1:00 to 5:00 P.M. on Sunday.

Admission to the Torpedo Factory is free. The building is open from 10:00 A.M. to 3:00 P.M. Tuesday through Friday, 10:00 A.M. to 5:00 P.M. Saturday, and 1:00 P.M. to 5:00 P.M. Sunday, although individual studio hours vary. The building is closed on New Year's Day, Easter, July Fourth, Thanksgiving, and Christmas.

Suburban Maryland

Creative Partners Gallery
4600 East–West Highway
Bethesda, MD
(301) 951–9441
www.creativepartnersart.com
This lively Bethesda-based gallery is designed to bring emerging artists together with emerging collectors. Would-be patrons will enjoy a pleasing array of ceramics, furniture, photography, sculpture, and painting by juried artists, who also mount exhibitions each month. Creative Partners also supports the artistic community with workshops, artist talks, and other useful programs and services. The gallery is open Tuesday through Saturday from noon to 6:00 P.M.

The Glass Gallery
5335 Wisconsin Avenue NW
Washington, DC
(202) 237–1119
www.artline.com/galleries/glass/glass.html
As its name implies, the gallery focuses on glass in its many forms: blown, cast, fused, etc. It features about nine openings annually and carries works by artists from throughout the United States and five or six other countries. It's open from 10:00 A.M. to 8:00 P.M. Monday through Friday, 10:00 A.M. to 6:00 P.M. Saturday.

Glen Echo Park
7300 MacArthur Boulevard
Glen Echo, MD
(301) 634–2222
www.glenechopark.org

"Unique" describes in a nutshell this National Park Service arts site, which began as a National Chautauqua Assembly in 1891, evolved into an amusement park, and now promotes visual and performing arts. You can watch artists work in their studios inside yurts, funky little huts topped with rounded, grass-covered roofs. Other studios fill space in buildings that once served as game arcades, rides, and concessions. You'll also find resident artists' and instructors' works exhibited in the Gallery and Bookshop in the Stone Tower, one of the site's original buildings. It's open from noon to 5:00 P.M.

The annual Labor Day Art Show fills the park's former bumper car pavilion with a variety of works by local artists. Pick up a free quarterly catalog for information about special events and scheduled art, music, and dance workshops, and classes for adults and children, or look online to see what's going on. To learn more about the park's history, watch the 60-minute *Glen Echo on the Potomac* at 4:00 P.M. on Saturday and Sunday, or take a ranger-conducted tour at 2:00 P.M. on Saturday and Sunday. Plenty of free parking is available. (See our Kidstuff chapter for information about the park's antique carousel and children's theaters, then check out Parks and Recreation for details on dances held in the restored ballroom.)

AT THE CINEMA

If you're a film buff, you'll want to check out the following events and theaters. Also, contact the city's major art museums, described earlier in this chapter, for information about their film series.

Washington, D.C.

AMC Loews Uptown Theatre
3426 Connecticut Avenue NW
Washington, DC
(202) 966–5400

Don't let the boxlike, drab facade fool you. Inside, this theater offers what you'd expect from the heyday of Hollywood: velvet-backed seats, an ornate and towering proscenium, a plush reception area, and a huge screen. It's easily the area's best film-watching venue. The theater is a quick walk from the Cleveland Park Metro station.

Avalon Theatre
5612 Connecticut Avenue NW
Washington, DC
(202) 966–6000
www.theavalon.org

The Avalon has a unique comeback story. Opened in 1933, the historic theater was closed down by the Loews company in 2001. Patrons rallied to save this neighborhood fixture with the help of local developer Douglas Jemal. The theater was renovated and reopened in 2003, giving rise to a new luxury movie experience, complete with freshly gilded furnishings, plus seats that bear the names of the patrons who contributed to the theater's return. The main theater is likely to show edgier recent releases, while you're more likely to find art films and independent productions in the smaller second-story theater.

Landmark E Street Cinema
555 11th Street NW
Washington, DC
(202) 452–7672
www.landmarktheatres.com

This new theater lures a steady crowd for independent, foreign, and documentary films, quickly earning a role in downtown's thriving entertainment district. The deceptively large facility is hidden behind a downtown storefront; eight auditoriums (ranging in size from 96 to 260 seats) are located underground. Hit the concession stands for

ℹ️ Free outdoor concerts take place every summer weekend at such locations as Reston Town Center's Equity Office pavilion, the courthouse lawn in downtown Leesburg, and the Alexandria waterfront. Check the *Washington Post's* weekend section on Fridays for a schedule.

healthy treats like veggie dogs or grab a bite before or after the show at a nearby eatery.

Washington International Film Festival (Filmfest D.C.)
P.O. Box 21396
Washington, DC 20009
(202) 628–FILM
www.filmfestdc.org
This two-week celebration of American and international film, from the alternative to the mainstream, takes place in late April to early May. The city becomes the focus of the movie world, with scores of screenings, seminars, and receptions held throughout town. Screenings take place at theaters, museums, and auditoriums throughout town, and most cost $9.00.

Northern Virginia

AMC Loews Shirlington 7
2772 South Randolph Street
Shirlington, VA
(703) 671–0978
Here's another hot spot for new independent and foreign films, notable for its location in the village of Shirlington. Before or after the show, grab a bite at one of the trendy sidewalk cafes featuring anything from sushi to tapas.

Arlington Cinema 'n' Drafthouse
2903 Columbia Pike
Arlington, VA
(703) 486–2345
www.arlingtondrafthouse.com
At this popular moviehouse/restaurant, you

can sit at a table munching nachos, pizza, and buffalo wings; throwing back a beer or two; even smoking, while watching second-run films on a big screen. Special features include midnight flicks and big-screen Redskins games.

Cinema Arts Theatre
Fair City Mall
Route 236 (Main Street) and
Pickett Road
Fairfax, VA
(703) 978–6991
www.cinemaartstheatre.com
We head to this friendly neighborhood theater, owned by local film buffs, when we want to catch the latest art release or first-rate mainstream flick. The remodeled theaters feature amenities like loveseat-style chairs, seats with attached trays, and an eclectic menu offering sushi, cracker and cheese plates, gourmet desserts, and fancy coffees. The cinema hosts a popular Sunday morning film club, which screens upcoming indie and foreign films.

Suburban Maryland

American Film Institute Silver Theatre and Cultural Center
8633 Colesville Road
Silver Spring, MD
(301) 495–6720
www.afi.com/silver
A crowning jewel in Silver Spring's recent renaissance, the AFI Silver Theatre is a must-see for any serious movie enthusiast. The original Silver Theatre first opened its doors in 1938, and classics shown here couldn't look better on another screen. You'll also find an ongoing assortment of Hollywood hits, foreign films, and documentaries, along with special events like the SilverDocs film festival and special tributes to notable performers and directors. Inside the building you'll find three theaters, the largest seating 400 and boasting a giant, 41-foot-wide screen. The smaller

theaters, seating 200 and 75, are outfitted with stadium seating.

Muvico Egyptian 24 Theatres
Arundel Mills
7000 Arundel Mills Circle
Hanover, MD
(443) 755–8992
www.muvico.com
Although located in Anne Arundel County just outside Metro D.C., this posh, enormous complex is worth the drive. With 24 screens, it's easily the largest theater in the area, and it boasts amenities galore. Check out the Egyptian-themed decor, stadium seating, and supervised children's playroom, where kids get to hang out while their parents enjoy a movie. While you're there, visit the mall's designer outlet stores.

LITERARY ARTS
Suburban Maryland
The Writer's Center
4508 Walsh Street
Bethesda, MD
(301) 654–8664
www.writer.org
This 31-year-old nonprofit organization for people in the literary and graphic arts fields sponsors poetry, fiction, and play readings by local and nationally known writers. The center also hosts workshops and events like the annual Mid-Atlantic Small Press Conference and Book Fair, offers a book gallery of literary magazines and works by local authors, gives technical assistance, and publishes a newsletter for members. Most events are open to the public; members receive admission discounts. Membership is $40 annually for individuals, $25 for students, and $50 for families.

A WORD ABOUT TICKETS
The most convenient way to get tickets to Washington area shows is over the phone via TicketMaster at (202) 397–7328, or on the Web, www.ticketmaster.com; or (800) 955–5566, www.tickets.com. Unfortunately, with any of these services, expect to fork over a surcharge of a few dollars. You can always buy at the box office, but sometimes finding same-day tickets, especially during the tourist season and for big shows, can be tricky. Your best bet is to reserve seats as far in advance as possible.

If you're like us, though, and place a premium on discount tickets, then head over to TICKETplace (202–842–5387, www.cultural alliance.org/tickets), at the corner of 7th and D Streets NW, near the Archives-Navy Memorial and Gallery Place Metro stations. (Take the Metro if you want to avoid parking hassles!) Here you can find reduced-rate tickets for day-of-performance shows only; the cost is typically half the regular price plus a service charge of 10 percent of the full ticket price. You can't make advance purchases, with the exception of a few Sunday and Monday performance tickets available on Saturday, and you must conduct all transactions by cash, traveler's checks, or debit cards. The outlet is open from 11:00 A.M. to 6:00 P.M. Tuesday through Friday, 10:00 A.M. to 5:00 P.M. Saturday, and it's closed Sunday and Monday, Thanksgiving, Christmas, and New Year's Day. You never know exactly what you'll find available, but sometimes that's part of the fun! If you're a student, senior, or enlisted military employee, you may not have to venture to TICKETplace for half-price tickets. Inquire at the box office or ticket charge service about availability. Some theaters also offer last-minute "student rush" and "standing-room-only" tickets.

Washington, D.C.'s free, patriotic, and educational attractions make the city a great value for traveling families. COURTESY WASHINGTON, D.C. CONVENTION AND TOURISM CORPORATION

KIDSTUFF

Washington may be filled with politicians, lawyers, and lobbyists, but any parent knows that the capital's real movers and shakers aren't even old enough to vote. Endlessly energetic and inquisitive, kids are always ready to leap into action, while moms and dads scramble to arrange safe, educational, and—most of all—fun outings. In this chapter you'll find dozens of destinations listed under a variety of categories. Whether you're passing through or planning to stay awhile, you're sure to find adventures just right for your family.

MARVELOUS MUSEUMS

Your kids just want to have fun; you want them to learn too. They can do both at these great museums, where hands-on activities and special family programs make visits entertaining and enlightening. And here's a bonus: Many feature free admission, so you needn't feel obligated to stay for hours if the little ones get fidgety. (Be sure to check our Attractions and Arts chapters for complete information on many of these and additional museums and galleries you may find intriguing.)

Washington, D.C.

The Smithsonian Institution

The Smithsonian museums feature numerous interactive exhibits and special activities with kid appeal. Start at the Castle to collect information and devise a sightseeing plan. Or do your research at home at www.si.edu, which features a kids' page as well. Above all, don't expect to see it all in one outing. Your best bet is to limit a visit to two or three hours, avoiding crowds by arriving first thing in the morning or late in the afternoon.

Most Smithsonian museums are open from 10:00 A.M. to 5:30 P.M. daily, except Christmas. Admission is free. The Smithsonian Metro stop is a quick walk from most Smithsonian museums. (See our Attractions, Arts, and Annual Events chapters for additional information.)

**The Smithsonian Information Center
1000 Jefferson Drive SW
Washington, DC
(202) 633–1000
www.si.edu/visit/infocenter/sicastle.htm**
Before your museum visit, call or stop by the Smithsonian Information Center (a.k.a. the Castle) at the listed address (or look online for kid's programs). You'll find an 18-minute orientation video, electronic maps, helpful touch-screen computers, and a variety of brochures. Hours are 8:30 A.M. to 5:30 P.M. Outside, stroll through the beautiful Enid A. Haupt Garden or go for a whirl on the circa-1940s Allan Herschell carousel in front of the neighboring Arts and Industries Building. The ride operates daily, year-round, weather permitting. A ticket costs $2.00.

**Freer Gallery of Art and Arthur M. Sackler Gallery
Jefferson Drive and 12th Street SW
1050 Independence Avenue SW
Washington, DC
(202) 633–1000
www.asia.si.edu**
Visit the information desks at these two connected museums of Asian art to obtain a variety of free children's activity sheets on such subjects as Japanese screens, scrolls, Hindu gods, and gallery terminology. The museum gift shops carry *The Princess and the Peacocks,* a children's book about the Freer's

ornate Peacock Room, designed by James McNeill Whistler. The popular ImaginAsia program, for youngsters ages 6 through 14 and their parents, features a different themed tour and related craft each month. Drop-in sessions generally take place Saturday and Sunday afternoons, with additional days available during summer.

Hirshhorn Museum and Sculpture Garden
7th Street and Independence Avenue SW
Washington, DC
(202) 633–1000
www.hirshhorn.si.edu

You may need to caution your kids not to touch the assorted pieces in the outdoor Sculpture Garden, which looks a lot like a funky playground. Children can do lots of looking, however, and they'll see and learn plenty of interesting things about modern art by using the museum's wonderful *Family Guide,* available free of charge at the information desk. The eye-catching folder contains a dozen or more colorful "artcards," each of which features a picture of an art work, information about the artist, observations about the piece, and at least one activity.

Look for kid-pleasers like Alexander Calder's fish mobile, Andy Warhol's *Marilyn Monroe's Lips,* and Joan Miró's sculpture, *Lunar Bird.* The museum hosts free, monthly "Young at Art" family programs on Saturdays, featuring hands-on activities for children ages six to nine accompanied by adults. Call (202) 633–1000 for reservations, which are required. Free drop-in activities for families take place regularly in the museum's Improv Art Room.

National Air and Space Museum
7th Street and Independence Avenue SW
Washington, DC
(202) 633–1000
www.nasm.si.edu

This most popular Smithsonian museum awes kids as soon as they walk in and spy all the hanging aircraft. They can experience firsthand the principles of flight by visiting the interactive How Things Fly gallery, where they can work the controls on a real Cessna and perform numerous experiments, like sending Gumby aloft in a miniature hot-air balloon. Related activity sheets describe additional fun to try at home.

Elsewhere in the museum, kids enjoy walking through a space lab and touching a moon rock. The museum offers free highlights tours, which can be tailored toward children, daily at 10:15 A.M. and 1:00 P.M. Check the daily schedule for IMAX theater and planetarium shows, which require tickets.

National Museum of African Art
950 Independence Avenue SW
Washington, DC
(202) 633–1000
www.nmafa.si.edu

Kids like looking at kinetic sculptures, colorful masks, and patterned clothing. The museum regularly offers drop-in, family-oriented events, such as storytelling and the Let's Read About Africa reading program. Kids' activity sheets related to special exhibits sometimes are available at the information desk.

National Museum of American History
14th Street and Constitution Avenue NW
Washington, DC
(202) 633–1000
americanhistory.si.edu

Known as "America's Attic," this museum is a perennial family favorite, packed with hands-on activities, pop culture symbols, and patriotic treasures that kids love. If you're visiting before summer 2008, however, this museum will be closed for renovation. Check the Web site for construction updates and stay tuned for a new-and-improved museum that promises even more family-friendly activities. In the meantime, you can also visit the National Air and Space Museum to see a special exhibition of 150 artifacts from the National Museum of American History, including kid-pleasers like Dorothy's Ruby Red Slippers, Kermit the Frog, and the Droids from *Star Wars.*

National Museum of the American Indian
4th Street and Independence Avenue SW
Washington, DC
(202) 633–1000
www.nmai.si.edu

The newest Smithsonian Museum on the National Mall celebrates Native cultures, including traditions like dance, music, and storytelling that prove delightful diversions for young visitors. The circular Lelawi Theater re-creates a Native campfire experience with a 12-minute multimedia presentation. In the sunlit Potomac Rotunda, you'll often catch theater, dance, and other cultural demonstrations. Stop for a bite to eat in the museum's Mitisam Cafe, whose menu features kid favorites like chicken fingers and french fries, along with grown-up dishes like buffalo chili and grilled salmon.

National Museum of Natural History
10th Street and Constitution Avenue NW
Washington, DC
(202) 633–1000
www.mnh.si.edu/

Kids love this museum from the moment they walk in and spot the rotunda's giant elephant. From there, head for the popular dinosaur hall, where you'll find a diplodocus, an allosaurus, and other prehistoric skeletons. The first floor also houses the museum's newly renovated mammal displays, featuring taxidermied animals. Upstairs, the Number 1 kid-pleasing attraction is the O. Orkin Insect Zoo, filled with live creepy crawlies. Look for bugs and their relatives, such as hissing cockroaches and centipedes, and don't miss the tarantula feedings, weekdays (except Mondays and Thanksgiving) at 10:30 and 11:30 A.M. and 1:30 P.M., and weekends at 11:30 A.M. and 12:30 and 1:30 P.M. Many youngsters also enjoy discovering the many shapes, colors, and textures of gems and minerals in an exhibit featuring a few interactive components. The museum also boasts a six-story Discovery Center, which houses an IMAX theater, an interactive Immersion Cinema, a cafe in a glass-domed atrium,

and a huge gift shop with lots of cool stuff for kids. Stay tuned for a new Ocean Hall in 2008.

National Postal Museum
2 Massachusetts Avenue NE
Washington, DC
(202) 633–1000
www.postalmuseum.si.edu

Right across the street from Union Station (see this chapter's dining guide), this entertaining museum usually proves much less crowded than Smithsonian museums on the Mall. Visit the information desk for a brochure highlighting exhibition elements children appreciate. Older kids can search for answers to true-or-false questions in the *Check It Out!* pamphlet. The museum's many kid-pleasing exhibits include a "wooded" trail that simulates a colonial mail route, a stagecoach that's a great prop for photos, interactive computer games, a puzzlelike stamp collection, and a railway mail car to explore. Children also like to look at Owney, a taxidermy postal dog who collected more than 1,000 "dog" tags during his travels aboard mail trains. Computer kiosks in the lobby create postcards that can be mailed from the museum.

The museum usually holds at least one family activity each month.

Other Kid-Friendly Museums in Washington

National Children's Museum
L'Enfant Plaza
Washington, DC
(202) 675–4120
www.ncm.museum

This kid-friendly favorite left its longtime home near Union Station to construct a dazzling new facility, currently slated to open in 2009. Its new location—directly across Independence Avenue from the National Mall—will be a welcome treat for families who prefer to explore the city on foot. Check the museum's Web site for construction updates and to learn more about the new facility.

i If you're going to be in D.C. for an extended stay in the summer, take advantage of the incredible assortment of day camp options. The Shakespeare Theatre Company, International Spy Museum, and Washington National Opera are just a few of the organizations that offer amazing educational opportunities for school-age children.

Corcoran Gallery of Art
17th Street and New York Avenue NW
Washington, DC
(202) 639–1700
www.corcoran.org

The city's oldest private art gallery is small enough not to overwhelm youngsters, who enjoy its large landscape paintings and works featuring children and animals. Visit the information desk to inquire about family-oriented brochures, sometimes available for special exhibitions.

The museum's free, ongoing Sunday Traditions program, held at 2:30 on some Sunday afternoons, features performances, workshops, and storytelling designed for families with children age four and older. Call (202) 639–1727 for a schedule of upcoming events or to make required reservations. Occasional daylong, drop-in Family Day celebrations include workshops, storytelling, and other activities built around a theme such as "Artists of Our Town."

DAR Museum
1776 D Street NW
Washington, DC
(202) 628–1776
www.dar.org/museum/

Docents lead guided tours of the museum's period rooms, which are tailored to visitors' ages and interests. Children especially enjoy the Touch of Independence area, where they can play with a genuine nineteenth-century, hand-painted Noah's Ark; roll a hoop with a stick; and enjoy a tea party with dolls, using a miniature Blue Willow china set. Nearby, the New Hampshire Toy Attic displays numerous

antique toys, dolls, and games. Other period rooms feature musical instruments, tea party settings, and children's furniture that appeals to kids. Tours are held on weekdays from 10:00 A.M. to 2:30 P.M. and Saturdays from 9:00 A.M. to 4:30 P.M.

Call the museum for information about children's programs, such as the popular Colonial Adventure for ages 5 to 7 (held the first and third Saturdays of each month), Junior Girl Scout programs, and summer quilt camp for kids ages 10 to 15.

International Spy Museum
800 F Street NW
Washington, DC
(202) 393–7798, (866) SPYMUSEUM
www.spymuseum.org

"Spy Kid" wannabes will get a thrill checking out the amazing espionage gadgets displayed at one of the city's newest museums. The "School for Spies" collection of more than 200 artifacts includes such intriguing items as a wristwatch camera, lipstick pistol, and CIA disguise kit. Visitors can pretend they're spies by trying activities such as code breaking and spy hunting. Children and parents will recognize some of the toys and games promoting films and TV shows like Mission: Impossible. The museum frequently holds special programs, including KidSpy School workshops featuring such topics as disguises and science used in spying. Don't miss the museum store, which features a wide array of kid-pleasing spy stuff. The museum is recommended for ages 12 and older.

National Aquarium
Department of Commerce Building,
Room B-077
14th Street between Constitution and Pennsylvania Avenues NW
Washington, DC
(202) 482–2825
www.nationalaquarium.com

Children have an easy time seeing exhibits at the nation's first public aquarium, which recently formed an alliance with the better-known and much larger National Aquarium in Baltimore. Kids can observe more than 270 species of fish, invertebrates, amphibians, and reptiles. A Touch Tank features horseshoe and hermit crabs, starfish, and pencil urchins, all of which may be handled by little hands. Look for the electric eel, which emits an audible charge, and the popular alligator exhibit. Kids also enjoy watching shark feedings Saturdays, Mondays, and Wednesdays at 2:00 P.M. The annual summer Shark Day includes hands-on activities and costumed characters.

The aquarium is open 9:00 A.M. to 5:00 P.M. daily, except Christmas and Thanksgiving. Admission is $5.00 for adults, $2.00 for children ages 2 to 10, and free for ages younger than 2. Visit the gift shop for fun and fishy souvenirs. The aquarium is adjacent to the Ronald Reagan International Trade Center, which houses a popular food court, and is close to the Federal Triangle Metro stop.

National Building Museum
401 F Street NW
Washington, DC
(202) 272–2448
www.nbm.org

Kids love to roam the open space in the museum's great hall and touch tactile models of Washington monuments in the Washington: Symbol and City exhibit.

Free children's activity booklets, available at the front desk, feature such topics as patterns, building history, architectural terms, and museum treasure hunts. Call for a schedule, costs, and registration information regarding the museum's monthly family programs, which include haunted house–building workshops, gingerbread house construction, and other fun activities. The gift shop is well known for its vast selection of intriguing building toys, among other unusual items.

National Gallery of Art
4th Street and Constitution Avenue NW
Washington, DC
(202) 737–4215
www.nga.gov/kids/kids.htm

Kids will be less intimidated by this awe-inspiring, free museum's large scale if you start your family outing in the Micro Gallery in the West Building Art Information Room. Here, visitors can have fun using the touch-screen computer monitors to view art works featuring their favorite animals or other subjects and learn more about the artists. Design a personalized tour featuring a printed map showing the locations of works your children want to see.

Stop by an art information desk, on the main level of the West Building or on the East Building's ground level, to pick up a copy of "Inside Scoop," a children's guide to key exhibitions. Among children's favorite works in the West Building are Sir Peter Paul Rubens's *Daniel in the Lions' Den,* John Singleton Copley's *Watson and the Shark,* and Gilbert Stuart's presidential portraits. In the East Building youngsters like the untitled red Alexander Calder mobile and Jackson Pollock's splattered *Lavender Mist.* Call (202) 789–3030 for a schedule of family programs held in conjunction with special exhibits. The museum also hosts a monthly Saturday children's film series and other special family activities.

The gallery offers special audio tours for kids and families, available at the Acoustiguide desk in the West Building ($3.00 per tour, $2.00 for additional headphone set). The museum shops also carry art history and activity books for young art lovers.

Bringing a baby or toddler? Free strollers for museum use are available at every entrance in both buildings. Hungry kids enjoy visiting the Cascade Cafe/Espresso Bar to eat a snack or meal while they watch a mesmerizing waterfall outside a large window. (See the din-

i Washington Walks offers walking tours for children ages 4 to 9, including "The White House Un-Tour," a look at the interesting people and animals that have occupied the executive mansion, and "In Fala's Footsteps," a tour of the FDR Memorial through the eyes of the famous first pooch.

ing guide in this chapter.) Outside, visit the sculpture garden, which includes a kid-pleasing giant spider.

National Geographic Society's Explorers Hall
17th and M Streets NW
Washington, DC
(202) 857–7588
www.nationalgeographic.com/explorer
Geographica: The World at Your Fingertips features numerous kid-pleasing hands-on exhibits, including video touch screens exploring assorted topics, a simulated tornado, and a black-box aquarium containing lifelike images of different fish for children to "catch." An interactive amphitheater, Earth Station One, boasts an impressive 11-foot globe and simulated space flight. The free museum also offers changing exhibits. Hours are 9:00 A.M. to 5:00 P.M. Monday through Saturday and holidays, 10:00 A.M. to 5:00 P.M. Sundays, closed Christmas. The closest Metro stop is Farragut North.

National Museum of Women in the Arts
1250 New York Avenue
Washington, DC
(202) 783–5000
www.nmwa.org
Visit the information desk for a free *Exploring Art* booklet that includes activities related to kid-pleasing works such as Lilly Martin Spencer's realistic painting *The Artist and Her Family at a Fourth of July Picnic,* Frida Baranek's untitled abstract wire sculpture, and Gabriele Munter's landscape *Staffelsee in Autumn.* Call (202) 783–7370 for recorded information about upcoming events, including family programs held monthly on Sundays.

i Looking for a unique photo opportunity? Kids love to climb into the lap of the 12-foot bronze Albert Einstein Memorial at the National Academy of Sciences at 2100 C Street NW in Washington, D.C.

The Navy Museum
Building 76, Washington Navy Yard
805 Kidder Breese SE
Washington, DC
(202) 433–4882
www.history.navy.mil/branches/nhcorg8/htm
Ships ahoy! Kids may not care much about the U.S. naval history presented at this recently renovated museum, but they love to climb aboard the hulking antiaircraft guns. Young visitors enjoy other hands-on activities, such as the popular submarine room, where children can pretend to steer a sub and operate assorted buttons and toggle switches on genuine instrument panels. Two periscopes offer a revolving view of the Navy Yard outside. Kids also like to drive their parents crazy by repeatedly sounding the Klaxon, a diving alarm that blares an ear-piercing "WhaOOOOOOga!" throughout the museum.

Visitors can take self-guided scavenger hunts using brochures obtained at the information desk.

Important: Unless you have a military or Department of Defense ID, you must call to make a reservation, a recently added security precaution.

Northern Virginia

Steven F. Udvar-Hazy Center
14390 Air and Space Museum Parkway
Chantilly, VA
(202) 633–1000
www.nasm.si.edu/udvarhazy
If you've got an aspiring pilot or astronaut on your hands, it's worth the trip to see this amazing annex of the Smithsonian's National Air and Space Museum near Dulles Airport. Opened in 2003 as a repository for the articles that couldn't fit in the facility in the National Mall, you'll find such aircraft as the Enola Gay, an SR-71 Blackbird, an Air France Concorde, and the Space Shuttle *Enterprise.* Kids can watch planes take off and land from Dulles in an observation tower or catch an IMAX film.

Suburban Maryland

Discovery Creek Children's Museum of Washington
The Stable at Glen Echo
7300 MacArthur Boulevard,
Glen Echo Park
Glen Echo, MD
(202) 364–3111
www.discoverycreek.org

Set in one of the area's most intriguing parks (see related entries later in this chapter), this unique, program-based museum serves as a hands-on science, natural-history, and art-learning lab for families and school groups. Visitors participate in workshops related to elaborate exhibits replicating actual environments. In addition to the eco-inspired exhibitions, kids can tackle hiking trails and explore a special Children's Garden equipped with an underground tunnel, aquatic habitats, a giant sandpit, and a tree house.

Live animals further enhance the programs. Hours are 10:00 A.M. to 3:00 P.M. Saturdays and Sundays. The museum reserves other times for school programs and popular birthday parties. Most activities are geared toward children ages 3 to 11 and cost $3.00 per child for museum members, $5.00 for non-members. Adults get in free of charge. A one-year family membership is $75 and includes members-only programs, a subscription to the programming newsletter, and discounts.

NASA Goddard Space Flight Center Visitor Center
8800 Greenbelt Road
Greenbelt, MD
(301) 286–9041
www.nasa.gov/centers/goddard/home/index.html

Kids interested in space and rocketry will enjoy the museum's interactive exhibits pertaining to Goddard's involvement in the space program. Visitors can build and launch a space satellite via a computer game and sit in a *Gemini* space capsule that includes an audio recording simulating liftoff in a *Titan* rocket. Model rocket enthusiasts hold launches the first Sunday of each month at 1:00 P.M. The museum also arranges educational birthday parties.

National Wildlife Visitor Center
10901 Scarlet Tanager Loop
Laurel, MD
(301) 497–5760
patuxent.fws.gov

Budding naturalists will have fun pushing buttons and playing with interactive videos in exhibits that focus on global environmental problems, habitats, endangered species, and life cycles. A guided electric tram tour travels through the woods and around the lake of the surrounding Patuxent Research Refuge (described further in our Attractions chapter), operated by the U.S. Fish and Wildlife Service. Tram tickets are $3.00 for teens and adults, $2.00 for seniors 55 and older, and $1.00 for children 12 and younger.

Play Wise Kids
6570 Dobbin Road
Columbia, MD
(410) 772–1540
www.playwisekids.com

This hands-on museum/indoor play center in Howard County, in the Maryland suburbs, features lots of themed play stations for young children. With 24,000 square feet of space in which to roam, it labels itself "Maryland's largest activity center of its kind." It's open from 9:30 A.M. to 5:00 P.M. Monday through Friday, 9:30 A.M. to 7:00 P.M. Saturdays, and 11:30 A.M. to 6:00 P.M. Sundays. Admission is $3.00 for adults, $8.95 for children ages two and older, $5.95 for children age one, and free for babies younger than 12 months. A popular party site, it features rooms with themes like the Polar Icecaps and Ocean Treasures.

FABULOUS FARMS

Leave the bustling city and suburbs behind and head for a close-at-hand yet more pastoral experience at one of the following historic sites or working, pick-your-own-produce farms.

Farm Museums and Plantations

Northern Virginia

The Claude Moore Colonial Farm at Turkey Run
6310 Georgetown Pike
McLean, VA
(703) 442–7557
www.1771.org
Your kids will think they've stepped back in time as they watch a poor farm family of 1771 work their land, tend to their livestock, and perform their chores at this living-history site. The authentic-looking reenactors, often including children, are happy to answer the questions of curious, modern-day visitors. Youngsters enjoy looking at the farm animals and participating in special events like harvest time and periodic eighteenth-century market fairs. Be prepared for a lot of walking on gravel paths that wind around the six-acre farming area. (Take a tip from the staff and don't even bother trying to push an umbrella stroller along the frequently muddy paths.)

Hours are 10:00 A.M. to 4:30 P.M. Wednesday through Sunday, early April through mid-December. The farm is closed during bad weather and on Thanksgiving. Admission is $3.00 for adults and teens, $2.00 for seniors and children ages 3 to 12; tots 2 and younger get in free. Admission for special programs usually is $5.00 for adults, $2.50 for seniors and children.

Kidwell Farm at Frying Pan Park
2709 West Ox Road
Herndon, VA
(703) 437–9101
www.co.fairfax.va.us/parks/
fryingpanpark.htm
Children love visiting this small, working model of a 1930s family farm, which features a barnyard full of pigs, goats, dairy cows, sheep, draft horses, chickens, and peacocks, and many baby animals in the spring. It's also home to the official Presidential Turkey, which arrives after its traditional Thanksgiving pardon. Special programs include hayrides, blacksmithing demonstrations, and occasional "Putting the Animals to Bed" story times for children. Events are free or require a nominal charge. Call for a schedule. Daily farm hours are 10:00 A.M. to 6:00 P.M. Admission is free.

Mount Vernon
Southern end of the George Washington Memorial Parkway
Mt. Vernon, VA
(703) 780–2000
www.mountvernon.org
George Washington's historic estate and gardens have become increasingly kid-friendly, with year-round interactive programs. Throughout the summer children can visit the Hands-On History Tent to harness a fiberglass mule, play colonial games, try on period clothing, and make wooden buckets, among other activities. They also can measure themselves next to a life-size likeness of the first president. Year-round, kids can visit the George Washington: Pioneer Farmer exhibit, which features, March through November, hands-on activities such as fence building, corn cracking, and fish-net making. Youngsters especially like looking at the farm animals, including such rare breeds as Ossabaw hogs and Hogg Island sheep. Even a visit to the mansion and outbuildings becomes fun for kids when they follow the Treasure Map of Mount Vernon, a souvenir brochure available free of charge at the main gate. Mount Vernon's new Donald W. Reynolds Museum and Education Center, opened in 2006, includes 23 new galleries (many of them interactive) that illustrate Washington's career as a soldier and a statesman. Admission is $13.00 for folks 12 and older, $12.00 for seniors 62 and older, and $6.00 for children ages 6 through 11.

Sully Historic Site
3601 Sully Road, Route 28, across from Washington Dulles
International Airport
Chantilly, VA
(703) 437–1794
www.co.fairfax.va.us/parks/sully
Young visitors to this restored 1794 plantation home of Northern Virginia's first congressman enjoy year-round family-oriented weekend programs on such topics as Toys and Games of Yesteryear, Quill Pen Writing, and Ice-Cream Making. During the summer, Sully offers a variety of hands-on educational activities for children ages 8 to 12. See the summer issue of *Parktakes*, a guide to Fairfax County parks, for details. To obtain a copy, call (703) 222–4664. Admission to the site is $5.00 for adults, $4.00 for students 16 and older, and $3.00 for children and seniors. Hours are 11:00 A.M. to 4:00 P.M. daily, except Tuesdays and some holidays.

Suburban Maryland

National Colonial Farm of the Accokeek Foundation
3400 Bryan Point Road
Accokeek, MD
(301) 283–2113
www.accokeek.org
Mount Vernon's neighbor directly across the Potomac River, this colonial tobacco farm, part of the National Park Service, features many barnyard animals such as cows, sheep, geese, chickens, roosters, and lovely EllieMae, the Ossabaw hog. Look for baby critters in the spring. Weekend tours feature rotating demonstrations about such topics as herbs, colonial lighting, and textiles. Call for information about upcoming special programs such as Children's Day and seasonal celebrations. Admission is $2.00 for adults and 50 cents for children younger than 12. Hours, subject to seasonal changes, generally are 10:00 A.M. to 4:00 P.M. Saturdays and Sundays spring through fall. Staff members who serve as docents are available only during weekends. Visitors can take a ferry across

the river to Mount Vernon during the summer; call for times.

Oxon Hill Farm
Oxon Cove Park and 6411 Oxon Hill Road
Oxon Hill, MD
(301) 839–1176
www.nps.gov/oxhi/
This turn-of-the-twentieth-century working farm, owned by the National Park Service, offers daily hands-on events for children, who enjoy seeing the many barnyard animals. Kids can help milk a cow, feed chickens, and gather eggs. Call for more information about these and special weekend events. Admission is free. The farm is generally open daily, 8:00 A.M. to 4:30 pm., closed New Year's Day, Thanksgiving, and Christmas.

Farm-Fresh Fun

Visit these farms in October for special children's activities, usually requiring a weekend admission fee of $6.00 to $8.50 per person. They also feature fresh or pick-your-own crops in the spring and summer.

Northern Virginia

Cox Farms
15621 Braddock Road
Centreville, VA
(703) 830–4121
www.coxfarms.com
The annual fall festival, throughout October,

> **i** Enjoy Loudoun County's beautiful rural scenery during the annual Spring Farm Tour and fall Farm Color Tour of the Loudoun Valleys. Kid-pleasing highlights include hayrides, berry and pumpkin picking, straw mazes, pony rides, face painting, and lots of live animals, such as llamas, peacocks, burros, and all the standard barnyard favorites. For free brochures, including directions to and descriptions of each location, call the Loudoun Tourism Council at (800) 752–6118.

The D.C. Miniguide to Kids' Dining

"I'm tired! I'm thirsty! I'm hungry!"

What parent doesn't dread these words, especially when they're pronounced by a whining child in the middle of a sightseeing expedition? Here's your challenge: Find a restaurant—now!—with kid- and adult-pleasing food, fast and friendly service, reasonable prices, and diversions to keep your youngster entertained until the meal arrives.

Such a task can prove difficult even when you're close to home, let alone touring a new city. Fortunately, Washington and its surrounding suburbs offer countless options for family dining, from neighborhood eateries to familiar chains. Follow our tips and recommendations and you'll find that eating out with kids can be fun—really!

• Build mealtimes into your itinerary, and try to find out in advance if kids' meals or favorite a la carte items are available at whatever attraction you're visiting. With planning, you won't be caught off guard by a hungry child in the middle of touring a museum that doesn't have a restaurant.

• Eat at "off" times to avoid unsettling crowds. You'll find restaurants in popular tourist areas packed to the gills during the noon hour and between 6:30 and 8:30 P.M. Eat a late lunch or early dinner and you'll have a much shorter wait for your food.

• Find out if a restaurant features free or discounted children's meals during certain times. Many chains in the Washington area offer great specials during the week to entice families to dine on otherwise slow nights.

• To reduce the waiting time, especially when a restaurant is crowded, order the kids' meals or an appetizer such as soup as soon as you're seated. A cup of ice and a spoon also help stave off boredom for a while.

• Traveling with an infant or toddler? Avoid restaurants with few or no high chairs and booster seats, as such establishments generally aren't used to accommodating young children. Find out if the women's and men's rooms have changing tables, and ask whether the dining area or restroom offers a discreet place to nurse a baby. Many restaurants with salad bars allow toddlers to eat for free, a welcome option for parents whose children like to nosh on cheese, crackers, and fresh fruit or sliced vegetables.

• Carry a small backpack with a few emergency snack items like crackers, cereal bars, and packets of juice-fortified gummy treats. Also include some small games or toys and a pad of paper and pen or pencil for each child. Elementary-age youngsters can hone their reading and writing skills by copying everyone's orders from the menu. Or, have your youngster draw or write about someplace you've just visited. You can also use your waiting time to write postcards to mail to friends or to your child as a unique way of recording the trip.

• As soon as you enter an eatery, locate the restrooms. Some kids enjoy visiting restaurant bathrooms just to check them out.

- Have realistic expectations. Don't count on a child to tolerate sitting for more than 45 minutes.
- Ask for a souvenir menu or place mat, inexpensive collectibles that prove easy to display or store. You might wish to circle and label each family member's meal.
- Kids love the decor, fish tanks, and fortune cookies at Chinese restaurants. Order steamed chicken and vegetables, sauce on the side, and let the youngsters poke around with chopsticks. (You'll be surprised at how much they eat!)
- The following restaurants are favorites of Metro Washington families, who appreciate their dependable service and kid-pleasing food. Note that, contrary to our usual policy, we do include some chains here because of their special features for kids. In general expect to pay from $2.50 to $6.00 for a child's meal featuring a burger or chicken fingers, fries, and drink.

WASHINGTON, D.C.

Hard Rock Cafe
999 E Street NW, Washington, DC
(202) 737–7625
www.hardrock.com
Where else can children order guitar-shaped chicken tenders? They're among several choices offered on the back of the coloring book/menu. Big kids have a blast exploring the restaurant's rock 'n' roll memorabilia, heavy on Jimi Hendrix, Elvis, and the Beatles. Many youngsters collect Hard Rock pins, available in the gift shop. Watch for Breakfast with Santa in December.

National Gallery of Art
4th Street and Constitution Avenue NW, Washington, DC
(202) 737–4215
www.nga.gov
If you're visiting museums on the National Mall, the Cascade Café/Espresso Bar in the gallery's Concourse is a good bet for a quick bite. We've watched one of the world's pickiest little eaters polish off a meal of favorite a la carte items like fresh fruits and french fries. Lines at the various self-service stations—salads, sandwiches, hot meals, desserts, etc.—usually move quickly once diners figure out what they're doing. Look for a seat near the huge window with a view of a mesmerizing waterfall outside.

Union Station
50 Massachusetts Avenue NE ,Washington, DC
(202) 371–9441
www.unionstationdc.com
This bustling train and Metro station also holds a shopping mall and numerous restaurants, including a huge food court with a wide selection of kid favorites.

(Cont'd)

(Pick up a bag of freshly baked cookies at Vaccaro's Italian Pastry Shop.) If you pre-fer a full-service restaurant, visit America (202–682–9555), which offers great views of the U.S. Capitol upstairs. Downstairs, children can color on white butcher paper table coverings. The menu of more than 200 a la carte items, about $4.00 and up, features state specialties such as Maryland crab cakes and Virginia chicken pot pie. Kids can get a half-size portion of any pasta dish, including plain spaghetti. Young diners also like peanut butter and jelly, hot dogs, grilled cheese, macaroni and cheese, and miniature hamburgers. The National Postal Museum, with many hands-on exhibits, is right across the street. (See listing in this chapter.)

NORTHERN VIRGINIA
IKEA Washington
Potomac Mills
2901 Potomac Mills Circle
Woodbridge, VA
(703) 494–4532
www.ikea-usa.com
The restaurant in this huge, popular Swedish furniture and housewares store fea-tures a brightly decorated dining area with kid-size chairs and children's meals of Swedish meatballs. The store also offers a free supervised ballroom and play area, where youngsters can romp while parents shop.

Paradiso Ristorante
6124 Franconia Road, Alexandria, VA
(703) 922–6222
www.paradisoristorante.com
Can't get a babysitter? This restaurant just down the street from Springfield Mall is your dream come true: Kids ages 3 to 10 eat at plastic picnic tables, color, and watch the latest videos in a children's dining area while their parents enjoy a quiet meal in an adjacent room. A waitress/babysitter supervises the youngsters, and parents keep an eye on things from a picture window that's a mirror on the kids' side. Children's meals, which include ice cream, are $7.00. We recommend you call ahead for reservations and availability.

Rainforest Cafe
Tysons Corner Center
1961 Chain Bridge Road, McLean, VA
(703) 821–0247
www.rainforestcafe.com
This so-called Wild Place to Shop and Eat captivates kids from the moment they catch the lifelike crocodile in front. Don't expect things to quiet down once you're inside: The dining areas feature animatronic gorillas who periodically holler and beat their chests, elephants who screech and raise their trunks, and flashes of

realistic lightning, among other special effects and sounds that create a tropical atmosphere. A favorite destination for birthday celebrations, the restaurant offers a kids' menu with such fun selections as dinosaur-shaped chicken nuggets and Chocolate Banshee Screamer Sundaes. Don't miss the talking tree, real aquarium, and assorted surprises in the fun gift shop.

SUBURBAN MARYLAND

B. J. Pumpernickel's New York Style Deli & Diner
18169 Town Center Drive, Olney, MD
(301) 924–1400

Kids eat free at dinner, Monday through Wednesday, at this deli-diner. While the youngsters pick a meal, including a drink and cookie, from the Kids' Korner selections, you'll have to make up your mind about which of more than 300 items to choose from the regular menu.

Franklins
5123 Baltimore Avenue, Route 1, Hyattsville, MD
(301) 927–2740
www.franklinsbrewery.com

Kids love eating at this unique restaurant, with its eclectic menu, including inexpensive children's meals. Set in a building that used to house Hyattsville Hardware, the restaurant accompanies a brewery and recently expanded general store. The hardware store's original fixtures, including nail bins and wooden boxes, now hold such items as candy, toys, and cooking gadgets.

Stained Glass Pub Too
3333 Olney Sandy Springs Road
Olney, MD
(301) 774–3778

This friendly neighborhood eatery features a clown performance from 6:00 to 8:00 P.M. Fridays. Kids often get balloon animals and can order from a children's menu.

MUTIPLE LOCATIONS

We also recommend the following chains, with multiple locations throughout the metro area. Check the phone book for the nearest spot.

Bertucci's Brick Oven Pizzeria
www.bertuccis.com

Here's a novel way to stave off boredom: Children can fiddle with a ball of dough while waiting for their entrees. The finished creations can be cooked in the oven and taken home as keepsakes.

(Cont'd)

(Cont'd)

Clyde's
www.clydes.com
This popular local chain specializes in fresh, seasonal dishes. Kids enjoy looking at the decorations, such as model airplanes, and coloring on placemats.

Fuddruckers
www.fuddruckers.com
Families flock to these burger restaurants where youngsters enjoy free cookies, balloons, game rooms, funky decors, and on some nights, clowns.

Romano's Macaroni Grill
www.macaronigrill.com
The servers write their names upside down on the white paper tablecloths, upon which kids enjoy doodling as they await their meals. Don't be surprised if your waiter or waitress bursts into song or tap dances. Children get a kick out of the restrooms, where they listen to an audio Italian lesson. Visit early, especially on weekends, when the wait for tables often runs 40 minutes or more.

Shoney's
www.shoneysrestaurants.com
These family restaurants often offer Kids' Night promotions, including free or discounted meals, balloons, lollipops, and visits from a costumed Shoney Bear.

Silver Diner
www.silverdiner.com
Resembling old-fashioned diners, complete with at-the-table jukeboxes, these friendly eateries feature kids' meals served with cardboard cars and coloring place mats. Each location also features a weekly kids' night with special activities.

features numerous slides, climbable hay bales, hay swings, animals, face painting, and live entertainment on weekends, along with cider, apples, and pumpkins for visitors. A tractor-drawn hayride drives through a pond and includes an encounter with a spaceship, complete with "aliens" who chase after gleefully screaming kids aboard the hay wagon. Plan to spend several hours!

Suburban Maryland

Butlers Orchard
22200 Davis Mill Road
Germantown, MD
(301) 972–3299
www.butlersorchard.com
Butlers holds one of the area's most popular pumpkin festivals on weekends during October. Kids love to go for rides in a hay wagon and Cinderella's fiberglass mouse-pulled

pumpkin coach, feed billy goats and other farm animals, jump in a hayloft, navigate a tunnel and straw maze, and look at the many characters who populate Pumpkin Land.

RAINY-DAY RAVES

Actually, you needn't wait for a rainy day to visit these children's stores and craft places, big and small, all of which offer indoor fun through story times, creative activities, and other special events.

Books and Toys

Barnes & Noble Booksellers
3040 M Street NW
Washington, DC
(202) 965–9880

555 12th Street NW
Washington, DC
(202) 347–0176

5345 Wisconsin Avenue NW
Washington, DC
(202) 686–6542

3651 Jefferson Davis Highway
Alexandria, VA
(703) 299–9124

12193 Fair Lakes Promenade Drive
Fairfax, VA
(703) 278–0300

6260 Arlington Boulevard
Falls Church, VA
(703) 536–0774

1851 Fountain Drive
Reston, VA
(703) 437–9490

6646 Loisdale Road
Springfield, VA
(703) 971–5383

4801 Bethesda Avenue
Bethesda, MD
(301) 986–1761

21 Grand Corner Avenue
Gaithersburg, MD
(301) 721–0860

12089 Rockville Pike
Rockville, MD
(301) 881–0237
www.bn.com
Free story hours, young adult book clubs, interactive music and movement classes, and craft sessions take place regularly in the children's departments of most stores in this large chain. Costumed characters and well-known authors also make occasional appearances. Visit to obtain a monthly events calendar.

Borders Books & Music
600 14th Street NW
Washington, DC
(202) 737–1385

18th and L Streets NW
Washington, DC
(202) 466–4999

5333 Wisconsin Avenue NW
Washington, DC
(202) 686–8270

1201 South Hayes Street
Arlington, VA
(703) 418–0166

5871 Crossroads Center Way
Baileys Crossroads, VA
(703) 998–0404

11054 Lee Highway
Fairfax, VA
(703) 359–8420

6701 Frontier Drive
Springfield, VA
(703) 924–4894

8311 Leesburg Pike
Vienna, VA
(703) 556–7766

4420 Mitchellville Road
Bowie, MD
(301) 352–5560

534 North Frederick Avenue
Gaithersburg, MD
(301) 921–0990

11301 Rockville Pike
Kensington, MD
(301) 816–1067

20926 Frederick Road
Germantown, MD
(301) 528–0862
www.borders.com

These nationally known bookstores carry a large selection of children's volumes, and each features at least one weekly free story time for preschoolers. On Saturdays many of the stores hold free special events such as craft workshops, book signings by children's authors, puppet shows, storytelling, and visits from costumed characters like Curious George and the Cat in the Hat. Times vary at individual stores; stop by for a schedule.

Northern Virginia

Aladdin's Lamp Children's Books & Other Treasures
2499 Harrison Street
Arlington, VA
(703) 241–8281

Run by a children's librarian, Aladdin's Lamp is one of the area's few remaining independent, family-owned children's bookstores. The shop carries more than 20,000 titles and hosts frequent special programs, most of which are free. Reservations are recommended for story hours, usually held Wednesdays and Saturdays at 11:00 A.M. for ages two and a half to six. Workshops for older children often feature authors or community volunteers who share special talents and feature such topics as origami, sports, and American Girls.

The store also carries puppets, stickers, bookmarks, and a large selection of unusual Baltic amber jewelry made by the owner's family. Hours are Monday, Wednesday, Friday, and Saturday, 10:00 A.M. to 6:00 P.M.; Tuesday and Thursday, 10:00 A.M. to 8:00 P.M.; and Sun-

day 11:00 A.M. to 4:00 P.M. Ask for a newsletter describing special events.

Imagination Station
4524 Lee Highway
Arlington, VA
(703) 522–2047
www.kinderhaus.com

This neighborhood children's bookstore holds book signings and parties with costumed characters. The shop carries a large selection of foreign-language books. Hours are Monday through Friday, 10:00 A.M. to 7:00 P.M., Saturdays 10:00 A.M. to 6:00 P.M., and Sundays 11:00 A.M. to 4:00 P.M. Call for a quarterly newsletter. Visit the neighboring, affiliated Kinder Haus Toys, with two floors of playthings and children's clothing at 1220 North Fillmore Street in Clarendon (703–527–5929), which is open 10:00 A.M. to 7:00 P.M. Monday through Friday, 10:00 A.M. to 6:00 P.M. Saturdays, and 10:00 A.M. to 4:00 P.M. Sundays.

A Likely Story
1555 King Street
Alexandria, VA
(703) 836–2498
www.alikelystorybooks.com

This independent children's bookstore in Old Town features seasonal activities, monthly costumed-character appearances, and 8 to 10 author visits annually. The shop, which has been in business for more than 20 years, holds story times twice a week. A drop-in program Tuesdays and Wednesdays at 11:00 A.M. offers songs and finger plays for infants to age three. Reservations are requested for programs held Saturday at 11:00 A.M., usually with themed crafts for ages three to six. The store also holds events for parents and teachers. While grown-ups browse, kids can visit the store's hermit crabs or hang out in a play space stocked with toys. The store also carries an expanded game section, featuring Alexandria-designed Binary Arts games. Hours are 10:00 A.M. to 6:00 P.M. Monday through Saturday and 1:00 to 5:00 P.M. Sundays. Call for a newsletter, published five times a year.

Once Upon a Time
120 Church Street NE
Vienna, VA
(703) 255–3285
www.once.uponatime.com
A realistic tree and beautiful displays of collectible dolls, miniatures, and stuffed animals charm visitors who enter this compact but well-stocked 25-year-old toy store. Each month, Once Upon a Time hosts at least one creative special event. Children attending Madeline Day in the spring meet the popular book character and sample French pastries. Breyer horse collectors celebrate their shared interest with a party featuring carrots, apples, and sugar cubes. The store is open Monday through Saturday from 10:00 A.M. to 5:00 P.M. (10:00 A.M. to 7:00 P.M. Thursdays), and Sundays from noon to 5:00 P.M., except during August. Stop by after taking in a children's concert at Wolf Trap National Park for the Performing Arts (see the subsequent Sensational Shows section as well as the Arts chapter).

Why Not?
200 King Street
Alexandria, VA
(703) 548–4420
Kids "ooh" and "aah" over the whimsically detailed plush animal scenes in the window of this charming 45-year-old corner store, right in the heart of historic Old Town Alexandria. Inside, you'll find two floors of specialty clothing, books, and toys, including many display models that have been placed throughout the store for children to try; toddlers get to test some, too, in an enclosed "playpen" area while their parents shop. The store boasts a fun selection of hip retro toys, like Curious George items. Hours vary seasonally, but usually are from 10:00 A.M. to 5:30 P.M. Mondays, 10:00 A.M. to 9:00 P.M. Tuesday through Saturday, and noon to 5:00 P.M. Sundays.

Suburban Maryland
Whirligigs & Whimsies
Wildwood Shopping Center
10213 Old Georgetown Road
Bethesda, MD
(301) 897–4940
American Girl Days, costumed-character appearances, and book signings by well-known children's authors are among the free special events that take place at least once a month at this specialty toy store. Although the shop doesn't publish a newsletter, its mailing list customers receive advance notification of activities. A pleasant stop after a visit to nearby Cabin John Regional Park (see the listing later in this chapter), the store is open Monday through Wednesday, Friday, and Saturday from 10:00 A.M. to 6:00 P.M. and Thursday from 10:00 A.M. to 7:00 P.M.

ARTFUL ADVENTURES
Pottery Painting
Creativity is the name of the game at the following studios, offering ideal outings for kids who like to say, "I made it myself." Choose a white-clay figurine or serving piece, pick your colors, and start painting; the studio staff does the cleanup, glazing, and firing. Studio fees include unlimited paint, use of supplies, and glazing and kiln firing. The bisque item(s) you pick to paint cost extra—usually anywhere from $3.00 to $45.00. All supplies are nontoxic, and most clear glazes are lead-free. Birthday party packages are available at all locations. Note that you may have to wait a few days to pick up your completed masterpiece.

All Fired Up
3413 Connecticut Avenue NW
Washington, DC
(202) 363–9590

4923 Elm Street
Bethesda, MD
(301) 654–3206
www.allfiredupdc.com

Hours vary by location and season. A flat fee, ranging from $6.00 to $60.00, covers the cost of your item, supplies, and studio time.

Northern Virginia

Clay Cafe Studios
13894 Metrotech Drive (in the Sully Place Shopping Center)
Chantilly, VA
(703) 817–1051

101 North Maple Avenue
Falls Church, VA
(703) 534–7600
www.claywire.com

In addition to pottery painting, these studios also offer mosaic projects, which kids can complete during classes or drop-in visits. The studio fee is $6.00 per hour. Hours are Monday through Thursday, 11:00 A.M. to 7:00 P.M.; Fridays and Saturdays, 11:00 A.M. to 9:00 P.M.; and Sundays, noon to 5:00 P.M.

Paint Your Own Pottery
10417 Main Street
Fairfax, VA
(703) 218–2881
www.ciao-susanna.com

Hours are Mondays 10:30 A.M. to 5:00 P.M.; Tuesday through Friday, 10:30 A.M. to 6:00 P.M.; Saturdays, 10:00 A.M. to 6:00 P.M.; and Sundays, noon to 6:00 P.M. The studio fee is $7.00 for the first hour, $1.00 for each additional 10 minutes. Ask about specials, such as half-price kids' days, or visit the Web site for discount coupons.

Other Crafts

Cathedral Medieval Workshop
Washington National Cathedral
Massachusetts and Wisconsin
Avenues NW
Washington, DC
(202) 537–2934
www.cathedral.org/cathedral

The Cathedral Medieval Workshop's seven hands-on stations give families a close-up look at the creative process behind the mag-nificent gothic building's art and architecture. Designed for children five and older accompanied by adults, the activity center lets visitors create gargoyles from self-drying clay, carve limestone with a mallet and chisel, design a gothic bookmark, hammer copper on an anvil, make a crayon rubbing of a brass engraving, construct arches with blocks and a wooden frame, and piece together stained glass.

As you leave the workshop, pick up pamphlets featuring cathedral-related family activities, from puzzles to scavenger hunts. Kids who enjoy Disney's The Hunchback of Notre Dame especially like Eight Great Gargoyles—A Self-Guided Tour for the Young at Heart, featuring some of the most popular of the 107 gargoyles and countless grotesques that adorn the building's exterior.

The drop-in workshop, in the northwest crypt, is open to the public year-round on Saturdays from 10:00 A.M. to 2:00 P.M. The admission fee of $5.00 per person includes a ball of clay and paper for the bookmark and brass rubbing. The cathedral also holds a monthly Family Saturday, featuring stories, a tour, and an art project built around a theme such as Groovy Gargoyles or Beauty and the Bestiary. Geared toward ages four through eight, the $6.00 sessions take place from 10:00 to 11:30 A.M. and from noon to 1:30 P.M. Call (202) 537–2934 to make a reservation. (See the Attractions, Annual Events, and Worship chapters for other activities.)

Reston Storefront Museum & Shop
Lake Anne Village Center
1639 Washington Plaza
Reston, VA
(703) 709–7700
www.RestonMuseum.org

Visit this community museum between 10:00 A.M. and noon on Saturdays for free drop-in children's art workshops. Local artist Pat Macintyre provides materials and encouragement as youngsters create a different project each week. Activities often relate to local historical topics or seasonal themes. Browse the free museum to learn about the unique planned community of Reston. Other family-oriented Lake Anne activities on Saturdays from spring through early fall include a farmers' market from 8:00 A.M. to noon, handcrafters, and pedal-boat rentals. The Lakeside Pharmacy next door to the museum features inexpensive meals and snacks at a soda fountain and outdoor cafe.

AWESOME AMUSEMENTS

When the kids need to let off some steam, visit one of these amusement places for nothing but fun and games. Unless otherwise noted, prices vary widely according to the type of activity, age of participant, and time of day. Hours also vary seasonally. Your best bet is to call ahead with specifics on your visit. (See our Parks and Recreation chapter for more ideas.)

Sportrock Climbing Centers
5308 Eisenhower Avenue
Alexandria, VA

45935 Maries Road
Sterling, VA
(703) 212–7625
www.sportrock.com
Kids—and grown-ups too—literally climb the walls at these indoor recreation centers, where the walls resemble rocky surfaces just waiting to be scaled. Check out Kids' Nite on Fridays from 6:30 to 8:30 P.M., when children ages 6 to 14 get vertical with help from experienced instructors. The cost is $20.00 per child. Call for information about summer camps and classes. Hours are noon to 11:00 P.M. Monday through Friday, noon to 8:00 P.M. Saturdays and Sundays. Admission is $16.00 to $18.00 for ages 13 and older, $7.00 for ages 12 and younger. Parents must sign a waiver whenever kids participate.

Northern Virginia

Centreville Mini Golf & Games
6206 Multiplex Drive
Centreville, VA
(703) 502–7888
If you're not already on vacation, you may feel like you are when you play the 18-hole, resort-style miniature golf course, landscaped to resemble a lush, natural setting complete with waterfalls. Ready for something completely different? Head inside for a game of Laser Storm, a futuristic tag game using laser beams and accented by special lighting effects. Active kids 10 and younger can climb all over a three-story indoor playground, while less adventurous family members try their skills at arcade games that offer redemption tickets.

Suburban Maryland

Jeepers
6000 Greenbelt Road
Greenbelt, MD
(301) 982–2444

700 Hungerford Drive
Rockville, MD
(301) 309–2525
www.jeepers.com
What's faster than a rolling grape? How about a flying banana? Banana Squadron is one ride you'll find at these indoor amusement parks, which also feature kid-size roller coasters, bumper cars, and a few other jungle-themed moving attractions. Rambunctious youngsters enjoy climbing about the mazelike playground's many tunnels and chutes and playing arcade games for coupons to redeem for prizes.

Six Flags America
13710 Central Avenue
Largo, MD
(301) 249–1500
www.sixflags.com/america
Kids needn't fret over being too little for this theme/water park's thrill rides: Looney Tunes Movie Town features rides and a live show

Kids enjoy the Northern Virginia Regional Park Authority's Downpour water park at Algonkian Regional Park in Sterling, Virginia. COURTESY NORTHERN VIRGINIA REGIONAL PARK AUTHORITY

especially for children. Crocodile Cal's Out-back Beach House, a five-story interactive play area, offers more than 100 water-powered attractions, including a barrel that dumps 1,000 gallons of water on unsuspecting passersby every few minutes. Still not wet enough? Play on the slides and submarine in the 10,000-square-foot Kids' Cove pool. You'd be wise to avoid Six Flags on summer weekends, when lines frequently require waits of 45 minutes or longer. Park personnel tend to get cranky in the heat, too. (See our Parks and Recreation chapter for more about this park, formerly known as Adventure World.)

SENSATIONAL SHOWS

Watching plays, puppet shows, and other live performances stimulates children's powers of imagination and promotes a love of the arts. We've selected a few of our favorite places to see entertaining, high-quality productions for families. (Check out the Arts chapter for additional ideas.)

Washington, D.C.

Discovery Theater
Smithsonian Institution's Arts and Industries Building
900 Jefferson Drive SW
Washington, DC
(202) 357–1500
discoverytheater.si.edu

Now in its 25th year, this theater puts on 30 shows annually, including five or six original works written or directed by local actors. Popular field trips for local schoolchildren, the performances include puppet shows, dance, plays, and storytelling by various artists, many of whom are nationally known. Shows take place weekdays at 10:00 and 11:30 A.M. and some Saturdays at 11:30 A.M. and 1:00 P.M. during the school year and in June and July. Admission is $6.00 for adults and $4.00 for children, and reservations are recommended. Call the number listed for information about upcoming programs. The closest Metro stop is Smithsonian.

John F. Kennedy Center for the Performing Arts
2700 F Street NW
Washington, DC
(202) 467–4600
www.kennedy-center.org

Think you can't afford to take the whole family to a show at this internationally renowned showcase for the performing arts? Check out the free programs offered on the Millennium Stage. The series features something different every night, including children's performers. The center also features plays and concerts for kids throughout the year in its newly opened family theater. Recent Kennedy Center Youth and Family Programs have included such popular tales as *Alexander Who's Not Not Not Not Not Not Going to Move* and *The Giving Tree*. The Washington Chamber Symphony holds an annual series of educational Concerts for Young People, featuring such themes as the Mighty Strings and Beethoven's Symphony No. 5. The symphony's Family Series includes a traditional Holiday Sing-a-Long so popular it sells out four months in advance. The center also holds Broadway-caliber musicals such as *The King and I* and Disney's *Aida;* tickets are pricey, but worth considering for a special occasion. (See our Arts chapter for more about the Kennedy Center's programs.)

Northern Virginia

Classika Theatre
4041 28th Street South
Arlington, VA
(703) 824–6200
www.classika.org

Founded by Russian-born actress Inna U. Shapiro, this critically acclaimed theater specializes in adaptations of beloved fairy tales like *Little Red Riding Hood* and *The Snow Queen,* as well as original works. The theater presents both live-action and puppet shows, as well as thought-provoking plays for adults. It also holds a variety of drama classes and a summer camp. Tickets for children's productions range from $10 to $15, and performances take place on Fridays, Saturdays, and Sundays. You'll find the theater in the Village at Shirlington, a retail district filled with interesting restaurants and shops.

ComedySportz
Ballston Common Mall, 4238 Wilson Boulevard
Arlington, VA
(703) 486–4242
www.cszdc.com

You never know just what to expect at this wacky, family-friendly improv club set in the "Old Vic," a former Victoria's Secret store now decorated in a sports theme. Teams of talented comic players compete against each other in a series of refereed, improvised games using suggestions from the audience. The shows play like G-rated versions of the Drew Carey–hosted TV show *Whose Line Is It Anyway?* In fact, anyone who "says or does something lewd, crude, or of a downright 'naughty' nature out of the context of the scene" has to wear a brown paper bag labeled "Potty Mouth." Performances take place Thursdays at 8:00 P.M., Fridays at 9:00 P.M., and Saturdays at 7:30 and 10:00 P.M. Admission is $8.00 on Thursdays, $12.00 on Fridays and Saturdays. Take the Metro to the Ballston stop, or park in the garage for $1.00.

Wolf Trap National Park for the Performing Arts
1551 Trap Road
Vienna, VA
(703) 255–1868
www.wolftrap.org

The National Park Service's venue for the performing arts features many kids' shows, including those of the 32-year-old Children's Theatre-in-the-Woods outdoor summer show and workshop series. Call (703) 255–1827 in late May for a schedule of puppet shows, plays, songs, stories, dancing, and clowning. Admission is $5.00. Reservations for the series fill up quickly. The park's primary summer concert series in the open-air Filene Center sometimes includes children's performers. Kids' shows also take place during the

fall and winter in the Barns of Wolf Trap just down the road. The park's International Children's Festival, held annually during a September weekend (see our Annual Events chapter), features an eclectic array of young performers from around the world. Kids can also create a variety of beautiful craft projects in a hands-on tent staffed by adult volunteers. Admission is charged. (See the Arts chapter for additional information about Wolf Trap.)

Suburban Maryland

Adventure Theatre
Glen Echo Park
7300 MacArthur Boulevard
Glen Echo, MD
(301) 320–5331
www.adventuretheatre.org

Headquartered in a former amusement park penny arcade, 55-year-old Adventure Theatre is the oldest continuous children's theater in the Washington area. Semiprofessional actors annually perform eight shows, many of which are based on classic stories for young people and recommended for ages 4 to 12. Recent and upcoming offerings dramatize such tales as *The Lion, the Witch and the Wardrobe; The Adventures of Beatrix Potter and Her Friends; Anne of Green Gables; Jack and the Beanstalk;* and *The Wizard of Oz.* The audience sits on carpeted steps to watch the performances, which take place Saturdays and Sundays at 1:30 and 3:30 P.M. Tickets are $8.00 a person regardless of age. After the show, kids enjoy meeting the performers, who are more than happy to sign autographs. (See the subsequent Puppet Co. Playhouse and Glen Echo Park entries for related information.)

BAPA's Imagination Stage
4908 Auburn Avenue
Bethesda, MD
(301) 280–1660
www.ImaginationStage.org

Watch a world-premiere musical at BAPA's Imagination Stage sponsored by the children's theater of the Bethesda Academy of

Performing Arts (BAPA). The children's theater formerly occupied a small performing space at White Flint shopping mall but recently opened a large complex in nearby Bethesda. In addition to housing two theaters, the new building also features performing arts classrooms, a gift shop, and a cafe. Imagination Stage presents six productions per season, ranging from adaptations of contemporary children's stories such as *Junie B. Jones & A Little Monkey Business* to multicultural folktales like *Mufaro's Beautiful Daughters*. The 27-year-old organization also offers drama classes and camp as well as a performing company of hearing-impaired teens. Performance times are 10:30 A.M. Tuesdays through Fridays, 3:30 P.M. Saturdays, and 12:30 and 3:30 P.M. Sundays. Tickets are $10 to $20. The adjacent public parking lot is free on weekends.

Now This! Kids!
Blair Mansion Inn
7711 Eastern Avenue
Silver Spring, MD
(202) 364–8292
www.nowthisimprov.com

If you missed the debut performances of *The Ugly Princess and the Mean Carrot* and *The Duck Who Burped,* you won't get another chance to see the shows. They're among the one-time-only titles presented by Now This! Kids!, the area's only totally improvised musical theater company for kids. Using suggestions from children in the audience, the wacky adult troupe creates on-the-spot songs, comic sketches, and fairy tales. The company received the International Special Events Society's award for best entertainment and WRC-TV Channel 4's nod for Best Bet for Children's Entertainment.

The troupe works its magic on young audiences ages 5 to 12 each Saturday during a luncheon theater that attracts a lot of birthday parties. (Performers make up an original song about each birthday child.) Ticket prices range from $11 to $18, and reservations are requested. They also perform once a month at Arlington Cinema & Drafthouse, with tickets priced from $6.00 to $14.00.

The Puppet Co. Playhouse
Glen Echo Park
7300 MacArthur Boulevard
Glen Echo, MD
(301) 320–6668
www.thepuppetco.org

A hop, skip, and a jump from the neighboring Adventure Theatre, the Puppet Co.'s claim to fame is its status as the only East Coast theater between Atlanta and New York that performs only puppet shows. The Puppet Co. recently moved into a brand-new, spacious theater. The three-person company creates unique marionettes and puppets for year-round shows, featuring both original stories and new takes on classic fairy tales like *Jack and the Beanstalk* and *Little Red Riding Hood*. The company's popular annual production of *The Nutcracker* includes stunning special effects.

Children sit on the carpeted floor, and adults squeeze in behind the kids and on the sides, where they won't block the little ones' view. Warning: Some toddlers and preschoolers may become frightened by the realistic witch and giant puppets used in many shows. Afterward, kids can meet the puppeteers and say hello to a marionette or two.

Shows are performed Wednesday through Friday at 10:00 and 11:30 A.M., and Saturday and Sunday at 11:30 A.M. and 1:00 P.M. Reservations are recommended. Admission is $8.00.

PERFECT PARKS

When the weather's great and your children get tired of their own backyard or hotel room, head for a park. We've selected a sampling of family favorites, filled with such dependable kid-pleasers as playgrounds, pools, merry-go-rounds, and nature centers. (Be sure to check the Parks and Recreation chapter for more information on these and other parks.)

Washington, D.C.

National Zoological Park
3001 Connecticut Avenue NW
Washington, DC
(202) 633–1000
natzoo.si.edu

With its 5 miles of winding, sloping pathways, the zoo proves a great destination for burning off energy. Time your visit to see a kid-pleasing animal demonstration, such as the Asia Trail interpreters' talks on giant pandas, sloths, and other creatures, and cheetah feedings. School-age youngsters in particular enjoy hands-on attractions in the popular Amazonia, the Reptile Discovery Center, the Invertebrate Exhibit, and the Kids' Farm.

The Friends of the National Zoo membership program ($40 annually) holds numerous children's programs, including camps and family overnights and camp-outs. (See the Attractions chapter for more details about zoo hours and features.)

Rock Creek Park
3545 Williamsburg Lane NW
Washington, DC
(202) 895–6070
www.nps.gov/rocr

This huge, popular urban park holds a gallery, historic mill, horse riding facility, and planetarium and nature center, all of which feature programs for children. The Rock Creek Gallery holds a children's art festival in June and a summer art camp. The Rock Creek Nature Center, open 9:00 A.M. to 5:00 P.M. Wednesday through Sunday, features hands-on activities and special events for kids. Call (202) 895–6070 for information about programs there and at the Planetarium. (See the

i Many area parks house nature centers with hands-on exhibits and children's programs that describe local natural history, plants, and wildlife. Call the nearest parks and recreation department for a nearby location. (See the Parks and Recreation chapter for phone numbers.)

Parks and Recreation chapter for more about this park, which closes on New Year's Day, July 4th, Thanksgiving, and Christmas.)

Northern Virginia

Burke Lake Park
7315 Ox Road
Fairfax Station, VA
(703) 323–6600
www.co.fairfax.va.us/parks/burkelake

A favorite with Fairfax County families, this park features numerous kid-pleasing attractions, including a carousel, a *C.P. Huntington* train ride that goes through a tunnel and woods, and an ice-cream parlor for snacks or birthday parties. Youngsters also love to ride the pontoon tour boat on the lake and feed bread to the many ducks and Canada geese that flock around the marina. The park hosts a children's festival in the spring, nature camps and Saturday morning kids' concerts during the summer, and a Ghost Train Ride near Halloween. The park is open 7:00 A.M. to dark daily. Call for times and prices of the rides, which operate throughout the summer and during some weekends in the spring and fall. Non-county residents pay an $8.00 per car admission fee. (See the Parks and Recreation chapter for more information.)

Colvin Run Mill Historic Site
10017 Colvin Run Road
Great Falls, VA
(703) 759–2771
www.co.fairfax.va.us/parks/crm

Grab some homemade ice cream at Thelma's country store just down the road, then stroll the grounds around this working, water-powered gristmill. Children enjoy feeding crushed grain to the resident millpond ducks. On many Sundays throughout the summer, the Northern Virginia Woodcarvers offer free carving lessons to kids and adults. The site frequently holds special events on weekends, including child-only holiday shopping in the old-fashioned General Store that sells candies, toys, and fun gifts. The site is open daily, 11:00 A.M. to 5:00 P.M., except Tuesdays. The park closes at 4:00 P.M. in winter. Mill tours, offered on the hour from 11:00 A.M. to 4:00 P.M., cost $5.00 for adults, $4.00 for any students 16 and older, and $3.00 for children and seniors.

Lake Accotink Park
7500 Accotink Park Road
Springfield, VA
(703) 569–0285
www.co.fairfax.va.us/parks/accotink
The Lucky Duck Mini Golf Course highlights this kid-pleasing park, which also offers a carousel, tour boat, snack bar, and playgrounds. The park hosts a summer concert series that's popular with families. (See our Parks and Recreation chapter for additional information.)

Lake Fairfax Park
1400 Lake Fairfax Drive
Reston, VA
(703) 471–5415
www.co.fairfax.va.us/parks/lakefront.htm
The park's Western-themed Water Mine Family Swimmin' Hole features several slides, bubblers, water cannons, and shallow play areas geared toward children ages 10 and younger. The park itself is an all-round kid-pleaser, offering rides on a miniature train, carousel, and sightseeing pontoon boat for nominal fees, plus a new marina with canoe-launch facilities. Call for hours, which vary throughout the summer months. Admission to the pool is $13.00 for adults, $11.00 for visitors shorter than 48 inches in height, and free for children younger than age two. Admission is $8.00 after 5:00 P.M. Admission includes unlimited rides on the park's tour boat, train, and carousel. (See the Parks and Recreation chapter for more information.)

Meadowlark Gardens Regional Park
9750 Meadowlark Gardens Court
Vienna, VA
(703) 255–3631
www.nvrpa.org/meadowlark.html
Here's a favorite spot for stroller-pushing parents, who get their day's exercise navigating more than 2 miles of winding walkways around landscaped gardens and three small lakes that attract ducks and geese. Kids have fun getting sprayed by a fountain, crossing stepping stones over shallow water, and watching the waterfowl and fish from a wooden gazebo overlooking Lake Caroline. Although you can't carry food into the park, you can munch in the air-conditioned visitor center snack room. Youngsters also like browsing the toys and nature-related items in the gift shop. Call for hours, which vary seasonally. Admission, charged from April through October, costs $5.00 for visitors ages 18 to 59, and $2.50 for those ages 7 to 17 and 55 and older. (See the Parks and Recreation chapter for more information.)

River Farm
7931 East Boulevard Drive
Alexandria, VA
(703) 768–5700
www.ahs.org/river_farm/index.htm
Kids love visiting the children's gardens on the grounds of the American Horticultural Society's headquarters, just down the road from George Washington's home, Mount Vernon (see the listing under Farm Museums and Plantations, in this chapter). Among the interactive, themed plots are the crawl-through Bat Cave; a sea-themed garden in a boat; a fairy tale garden; an Alphabet Garden featuring plants starting with each letter; and Beau Beau's Garden, accented by a yellow-brick road leading to a fortlike bridge that crosses a dry riverbed containing fun discoveries. Bring a picnic to enjoy as you gaze out at the Potomac River. The gardens are open only from 9:00 A.M. to 5:00 P.M. and, during summer, Saturdays from 9:00 A.M. to 1:00 P.M. Kids' educational programs are $5.00.

SplashDown Waterpark
7500 Ben Lomond Drive
Manassas, VA
(703) 361–4451
www.splashdownwaterpark.com

At this 13-acre park, a popular family destination, a popular family destination on sticky summer days, visitors can cool off in the 770-foot Lazy River and slip and slide through two 70-foot-tall water slides. A kids' area features four water slides. Children also enjoy getting splashed by "raindrops" and "bubblers." Umbrellas and pavilions offer much-needed shade. The park is open Memorial Day weekend through Labor Day. Hours vary while school is still in session, but during the summer the park is open 11:00 A.M. to 7:00 P.M. Sunday through Thursday, and 11:00 A.M. to 8:00 P.M. Fridays and Saturdays. Admission is $13.50 for people taller than 48 inches, $10.50 for visitors shorter than 48 inches, $7.00 after 3:00 P.M., and free for children 2 years old and younger.

Suburban Maryland

Cabin John Regional Park
7400 Tuckerman Lane
Rockville, MD
(301) 299–0024
www.mc-mncppc.org
An old-fashioned miniature train takes visitors on a 2-mile ride through a forest and past the large, inviting playground. Play equipment includes a complex Action Playground for school-age children, plus slides, swings, and storybook-themed climbing equipment for preschoolers. Children enjoy looking for scampering chipmunks, which are in plentiful supply throughout the park. Cabin John Station, where the train boards, doubles as a garage, and kids like to watch the big metal doors roll shut after the day's last ride. The station also houses a snack bar. A nearby waste container features a talking pig that "eats" litter. (See the Parks and Recreation chapter for more information.)

Glen Echo Park
MacArthur Boulevard at
Goldsboro Road
Glen Echo, MD
(301) 492–6282
www.nps.gov/glec/
The sound of the antique Dentzel carousel's Wurlitzer band organ beckons visitors before they even catch sight of the prancing ponies, ostriches, and rabbits. This enchanting park, a former trolley-line amusement park now operated by the National Park Service, is full of quirky fun, from the resident artists' studios in grass-covered yurts to the restored Spanish Ballroom that hosts big band and folk dancing every week. It's a nice spot for birthday parties after a show at the Puppet Co. or Adventure Theatre or a visit to Discovery Creek Children's Museum of Washington (see the previous Marvelous Museums and Sensational Shows sections). Just watch out for the yellow jackets! The magnificent, completely restored carousel operates Wednesday and Thursday from 10:00 A.M. to 2:00 P.M. and Saturday and Sunday from noon to 6:00 P.M. May and June. It also operates on Fridays from 10:00 A.M. to 2:00 P.M. in July and August. In September it runs Saturday and Sunday from noon to 6:00 P.M. Other attractions are open all year. (See the Arts chapter for more information.)

Robert M. Watkins Regional Park
301 Watkins Park Drive
Upper Marlboro, MD
(301) 218–6702 (Nature Center)
www.pgparks.com/places/parks/
watkins.html
Eenie, meenie, minie, moe: With so many choices, kids may have a hard time deciding what to do first. Stop at the Lottsford-Largo Train Station for tickets to take a ride on the *C. P. Huntington,* a miniature version of the classic locomotive. Grab a treat at the snack bar, then go for a spin on the antique carousel. Visit Old Maryland Farm to look at live barnyard animals, play miniature golf, or stop by the nature center. (This park also is listed in the Parks and Recreation chapter.)

Water Park at Bohrer Park at
Summit Hall Farm
502 South Frederick Avenue
Gaithersburg, MD
(301) 258–6445
www.ci.gaithersburg.md.us

Gaithersburg residents flock to this pool and its special features, like two twisting 250-foot water slides, a frog slide, water fountains, and a seal that spouts water. The surrounding grounds offer a playground with a ball pit and climbing equipment, concession stand, miniature golf course, and five-hole "kiddie" course. Costs and hours vary, so please call ahead.

Wheaton Regional Park
2000 Shorefield Road
Wheaton, MD
(301) 680–3803
www.mc-mncppc.org/parks/facilities/
regional_parks/wheaton
Line up at the beautiful train depot for a ride on the miniature locomotive. It's just one of many kid-friendly attractions at this popular Montgomery County park. You'll also find a snack bar and carousel (open, along with the train, throughout the summer), a huge playground, and an ice-skating rink (open October through March). Walk or drive to the adjacent nature center and Brookside Gardens, both of which offer bountiful children's programs, including a delightful butterfly garden. Wherever you go in the park, expect crowds on weekends. (Look for more on this park in the Parks and Recreation chapter.)

SPECTATOR SPORTS

Just because government and politics tend to dominate the character of Metro Washington and outsiders' perceptions of it, don't underestimate the importance of leisure activities—spectator sports especially—to residents. You'll find every level of competition here, from outstanding high school and college action to professional teams representing a variety of sports.

In 2005 the Nation's Capital welcomed the Washington Nationals, Major League Baseball's newest team. Washington has experienced several diverse sports milestones in recent years. In keeping with its international presence and status as the Nation's Capital, the city recently hosted worldwide and national sporting events, including the NBA All-Star Game and the ACC men's basketball conference tournament, along with the Presidents Cup PGA tournament.

Washingtonians, by and large, hold a special place in their collective heart for one sport and one team in particular. For at least six months a year, the sports scene focuses intensely on our beloved Washington Redskins, proud member of the NFL's finest division, the NFC East. In a bittersweet turn of events in 1997, the team's new Jack Kent Cooke Stadium (later renamed Redskins Stadium and later renamed FedExField) opened—just 160 days after its 84-year-old namesake died of a heart attack. The Redskins won the stadium opener, beating the Cardinals 19–13 in overtime.

Despite its inconsistent performance and a well-publicized series of coaching changes, the team enjoys an almost divine status among its faithful fans. After all, the Redskins have been in Washington for more than 60 years and boast a solid winning tradition fueled by three Super Bowl victories (all under the reign of inimitable coach Joe Gibbs, who returned to lead the team in 2004) in five appearances.

Nonfans, don't despair. You'll soon discover that an ideal time to go grocery shopping or roam the malls is during a Redskins game, when a large part of the local population is at home glued to the TV.

Before becoming further immersed in Redskins mania, we should also mention Metro Washington's representatives in the National Basketball Association and Women's National Basketball Association, the Washington Wizards and the Washington Mystics. Hockey fans can root for the previously mentioned Capitals, the National Hockey League's local team. Conveniently, they all have the same home, the Verizon Center. Here you also can watch the popular Georgetown University Hoyas basketball team.

Baseball fans were eager to welcome the Washington Nationals, marking the end of professional baseball's 30-year absence from the Nation's Capital. The team's new home on the Anacostia waterfront is scheduled to open in 2008, but local crowds have embraced the team in its retro-fitted home at RFK Stadium. Of course, the D.C. area is home to plenty of Baltimore Orioles fans, who frequently travel north to Camden Yards to catch a game. Also at RFK, soccer fans also get their kicks watching Major League Soccer team D.C. United.

Devotees of the diamond will also be happy to know that Minor League Baseball has a strong presence in Metro Washington, with the Potomac Nationals, Bowie Baysox, Frederick Keys, and Hagerstown Suns all within a short drive. Intercollegiate athletics are a big part of the sports scene as well, and the region's many colleges and universities afford plenty of opportunities for the spectator.

Schools with the most prominent athletic programs include the University of Maryland, Georgetown University, George Washington University, Howard University, and George Mason University. Meanwhile, Johns Hopkins University, just up the road in Baltimore, is a perennial lacrosse powerhouse; and to the south in Charlottesville, the University of Virginia wields a big stick in lacrosse, as well as soccer, basketball, and football.

You also can live out your sports fantasies with a variety of other events, including horse and auto racing, golf, and tennis, to name a few. So, having discarded the stodgy, white-collar, work-reigns-supreme label that seems permanently affixed to Washingtonians, let's take a closer look at an abundant sporting roster. The following provides an overview of spectator sports in Metro Washington (see our Parks and Recreation chapter for general recreational pursuits).

BASEBALL

Major League

Washington Nationals
RFK Stadium
2400 East Capitol Street SE
Washington, DC
(202) 675-5100
www.nationals.com

Baseball fans in Metro Washington rejoiced when Major League Baseball announced plans to relocate the Montreal Expos to Washington, D.C. in 2005. The new team, the Washington Nationals, will move into a sleek new home on the Anacostia waterfront in time for the 2008 season. In the meantime they've settled into RFK Stadium, where their predecessors, the Washington Senators, once played. While the stadium is short on amenities, it's easy to get there on the Metro. Take the Orange or Blue Line to the Stadium-Armory stop. While the Nats' first two seasons didn't bring much glory, they did bring the promise of future success. Third baseman Ryan Zimmerman was a finalist for 2006 National League Rookie of the Year, and new

i Each summer the political newspaper *Roll Call* puts on the Annual Congressional Baseball Game, a spirited, bi-partisan battle that raises money for charity. The game was first played in 1962.

manager Manny Acta comes from several successful seasons with the Mets. Single game tickets start at just $5.00 and go up to $55, with more than 13,000 seats priced at $10.00 or less.

Baltimore Orioles
Oriole Park at Camden Yards
333 West Camden Street
Baltimore, MD
(202) 397-7328 or (703) 573-7328 (tickets), (410) 685-9800 (information)
www.theorioles.com

Unable to root, root, root for a home team until recently, many Washingtonians support the Baltimore Orioles. Although the Nationals' arrival and the lackluster performance by the Orioles have caused attendance to slide, a trip to Camden Yards is a treat for any baseball fan.

Going to see an O's game is much easier and more enjoyable than it used to be for Metro Washingtonians. Oriole Park at Camden Yards is a good half-hour closer than Memorial Stadium, the team's home for 38 years, and it sits in a wonderful attraction-filled area easily accessed by rail, bus, and automobile.

From Northern Virginia, Suburban Maryland, and the District, just take the Baltimore/Washington Parkway north into Baltimore and the stadium is right there looming in front of you as you near the downtown area. It's a straight shot and the route is well marked. You also can take I-95 into Baltimore, but this route is a bit longer and subject to more traffic hassles. Want to ride the train? Just take Metrorail to Union Station, where you pick up a MARC (Maryland's passenger railroad system) train to the Baltimore station literally right next to the stadium; the trip takes about 45 minutes.

The Washington Nationals are Major League Baseball's newest team. COURTESY WASHINGTON, D.C. CONVENTION AND TOURISM CORPORATION

Camden Yards seats about 48,000 people, a perfect size for baseball, and offers a great view from virtually every seat. Modern yet old-fashioned in an architectural sense, it's truly a ballpark designed for the way baseball was meant to be played, on real grass, with the city skyline as a backdrop. (The seating areas are smoke-free, by the way; smoking is permitted only on the concourse.) Even the stadium's location is interesting. Camden Yards sits in a historic area of downtown Baltimore and masterfully incorporates the nearly 100-year-old B&O Warehouse, which looms just beyond the right-field wall. Refurbished during construction of the stadium, the warehouse now houses office space for the team, along with a cafeteria, lounge, and the exclusive, members-only Camden Club. During the early 1900s, a piece of land that's now part of the outfield was the site of a watering hole called Ruth's Cafe, operated by the father of baseball's immortal George Herman "Babe" Ruth, a Baltimore native.

Tickets, which generally go on sale during the winter for the following season, range in price from $9.00 to $45.00 for single games. Periodic bargain nights feature left-field upper reserved and bleacher seats for a reduced price. Kids ages 12 and younger can join the O's Dugout Club. The $17.00 membership fee includes a membership card, hat, ball, and a general admission ticket to ten pre-selected games. Call the information number above, or get more information online.

Minor Leagues

Northern Virginia

Potomac Nationals
G. Richard Pfitzner Stadium
7 County Complex Court
Woodbridge, VA
(703) 590–2311
www.potomacnationals.com

Think there's no such thing as an old-fashioned, up-close baseball game? Head to Pfitzner Stadium to watch the Cannons, the Class A affiliate of the Washington Nationals. These Minor League games provide inexpensive family entertainment and a chance to watch future big-leaguers in action: Past Cannons players include Bernie Williams, Barry Bonds, and Bobby Bonilla.

The Cannons play 70 games each season—mid-April to early September—at the 6,000-seat stadium off Davis Ford Road in Woodbridge. Carolina League opponents include the Durham Bulls, made famous by the hit movie *Bull Durham* that starred Kevin Costner.

Never mind that the team finished its 2006 season with a 64–76 record, hasn't reached a playoff since 1995, and hasn't won a championship since 1989. The Cannons still draw sellout crowds, especially on Saturday nights, which feature such promotions as minibat and baseball cap giveaways. Fans enjoy the goofy between-innings contests, like mock sumo wrestling and dizzy-bat races. Ticket prices range from $7.00 ($6.00 for kids ages 6 to 14 and seniors ages 55 and older) to $11.00, with supermarket-sponsored discounts available on some weeknights. Children ages 5 and younger get in free.

The team caters to kids, with a special alcohol-free family seating area, a no-smoking policy, a kids' club, and frequent promotions. Youngsters who wait near the locker room after the game often meet players, who, unlike most Major League superstars, usually prove more than happy to sign autographs. They've even been known to supply the baseballs!

i Although fans clamored for Washington's new baseball team to be called the Senators, they had to settle for the Nationals. The name "Senators," along with the team franchise, was sold to today's Texas Rangers.

Suburban Maryland

Bowie Baysox
Prince George's Stadium
4101 Northeast Crain Highway
Bowie, MD
(301) 805–6000
www.baysox.com

The Baysox, a Class AA affiliate of the Baltimore Orioles, play in the Eastern League. Like the Cannons, the Baysox offer fun family entertainment and average right around .500 or lower. The team finished its 2006 season with a 67–74 record. Harold Baines, Armando Benitez, and Mike Mussina all wore the Baysox uniform early in their careers. Tickets range in price from $6.00 to $15.00 for general admission, with discounts available some weeknights. Children ages 12 and younger who wear their baseball or softball team jerseys get free general admission to the 10,000-plus-seat stadium Monday through Thursday, as do any kids ages 5 and younger at all games. Just for kids, the stadium includes an amusement area with a carousel, jungle gym, games, face painting, and concession stand. There's also a fan club for kids 12 and under.

Frederick Keys
Harry Grove Stadium
21 Stadium Drive
Frederick, MD
(301) 662–0013, (877) 8GOKEYS
www.frederickkeys.com

The Orioles' Class A affiliate, the Keys compete in the Carolina League, which includes the rival Cannons. Fans have watched the likes of Brady Anderson, Armando Benitez, and David Segui before they were stars. Ticket prices range from $9.00 ($5.00 general admission for children ages 6 to 12, military, and seniors older than 60) to $11. Children ages 5 and younger get in free, and so do kids ages 12 and younger who wear their Little League shirts and caps. Popular promotions, such as fireworks nights, sell out in advance. The Junior Keys Club, $12.00 for kids ages 12 and younger, includes a T-shirt and free admission to Sunday games.

The Hagerstown Suns
Municipal Stadium
274 East Memorial Boulevard
Hagerstown, MD
(301) 791–6266, (800) 538–9967
www.hagerstownsuns.com

Visit the Suns' 77-year-old Municipal Stadium to see a piece of baseball history: This is where Willie Mays played his first professional game. A Class A affiliate of the New York Mets, the Suns play in the South Atlantic League. They've boasted such future stars as Curt Schilling, Mike Mussina, Arthur Rhodes, Billy Ripken and Cal Ripken Jr., José Mesa, and Bob Milacki. Ticket prices range from $5.00 to $7.00 for general admission seating, to $9.00 for reserved seats. The Hagerstown Suns Kids Club, $10 annually, features a T-shirt, certificate, and card entitling the bearer to $1.00 admission to games. The team is gaining a reputation for its wacky fan promotions, such as beer and wing-tasting events.

BASKETBALL
Professional

Washington Mystics
Verizon Center, 601 F Street NW
Washington, DC
(202) 266–2200
www.wnba.com/mystics

One of the WNBA's first teams, the Washington Mystics have managed a couple of runs at the playoffs in 2000 and 2002, led by University of Tennessee all-star Chamique Holdsclaw, and again in 2004 and 2006, led by Duke University standout Alana Beard. They've also turned in some dismal performances, finishing dead last in 1998 and 2003. No matter the team's record, and although Holdsclaw has since left the team, the Mystics manage to draw some of the largest crowds in the league. Individual game tickets range in price from $10 to $110. The season runs from June through August.

The Washington Wizards
Verizon Center, 601 F Street NW
Washington, DC
(202) 397–SEAT, (703) 573–SEAT
www.nba.com/wizards

The Washington Wizards, whose only recent glory had been Michael Jordan's two-year stint as a player and team president, are enjoying new success under another Jordan—coach Eddie Jordan, a native Washingtonian who guided the team to its back-to-back playoff appearances in the 2004–05 and 2005–06 seasons. The team is led by all-star guard Gilbert Arenas and forwards Antawn Jamison and Caron Butler, who combine to score more than 64 points a game on average.

The franchise has won only one championship, way back in 1978 when the team was known as the Bullets. That doesn't stop fans from flocking to the Verizon Center to cheer on the team. Available tickets for home games range from $10 seats in the upper levels to $850 court-side seats. And one thing's for certain about the Wizards: They play hard and they're fun to watch, winning or not.

Collegiate

American University
Bender Arena, 4400 Massachusetts Avenue NW
Washington, DC
(202) 885–TIXX (tickets)
(202) 885–DUNK (sports updates)
www.aueagles.com

The men's basketball team finished its 2005–06 season with a 12–17 record.

Led by coach Melissa McFerrin, the women's basketball team finished their 2005–06 season with a 12–16 record.

Tickets for individual men's and women's basketball games cost $9.00 to $12.00 for reserved seats. Games take place in the newly refurbished Bender Arena.

In 2006 American University captured the Patriot League title in men's cross-country, placing 26th in the NCAA finals. They've also enjoyed recent success in women's lacrosse and soccer and men's tennis and volleyball.

Georgetown University
Verizon Center, 601 F Street NW
Washington, DC
(202) 397–SEAT, (703) 573–SEAT
www.guhoyas.com

The Verizon Center's other roundball tenant, Georgetown University, has earned a reputation as one of the nation's strongest programs and one that demands that athletes work as hard in the classroom as they do on the court—a rarity in major college athletics today. John Thompson, who was the physically imposing and highly regarded coach of the Hoyas for 27 years, deserves much of the credit. Under Thompson's direction, Georgetown won a national championship, became a regular in post-season play, and remained a force in the formidable Big East Conference. Thompson's son, John Thompson III, carries on his father's legacy as head coach.

Georgetown alumni appear on team rosters throughout the NBA—Allen Iverson, Alonso Mourning, Dikembe Mutombo, and the legendary Patrick Ewing, to name a few.

Under Thompson III, the Hoyas have rediscovered their winning ways, advancing to the Sweet 16 in the 2006 NCAA tournament and earning a top-ten ranking to start the 2006–07 season. The women's team is coached by Terri Williams-Flourney, who compiled a 22–33 record in her first two seasons.

Tickets to Hoyas home games cost $5.00 for students to $100. Tickets to women's games played on-campus at the McDonough Center cost $2.00 to $5.00 for students.

Other sports in which the Hoyas excel include men's and women's lacrosse and women's volleyball.

i Legendary Georgetown coach John Thompson's son—also named John—now calls the shots for the Hoyas.

George Mason University
Patriot Center
4400 University Drive
Fairfax, VA
(703) 993–3000
www.gomason.cstv.com

Patriot mania gripped George Mason University, spreading through Fairfax County and much of the nation in 2006 when the men's basketball team earned an unexpected entry into the Final Four. Coach Jim Larranaga joined the program in 1997 and led the team to its first Colonial Athletic Association conference title and NCAA tournament appearance in 1999. The team earned return trips to the NCAA tournament in 2001 and 2006, when it became the first CAA team and only the second 11th-seeded team to reach the Final Four, toppling powerhouses Michigan State, North Carolina, and Connecticut on the way.

Under Coach Debbie Taneyhill, a former Patriot point guard, the women's team finished the 2005–06 season at 12–17, but they returned four starters in 2006–07.

Lucky for spectators trying to keep up with the action, George Mason's home arena in Fairfax is the comfy 10,000-seat Patriot Center, the only sports/entertainment facility of its kind in Northern Virginia. The men's team plays about 15 home games, with tickets selling for $11.00 each, $6.00 for seniors and youths 18 and younger. The women's team plays about 12 home games, with tickets priced at $5.00, $2.00 for youths 18 and younger. The arena hosts special sporting events such as the Harlem Globetrotters, tennis, and beach volleyball tournaments and gymnastics programs.

George Washington University
Smith Center
Washington, DC
(202) 994–6050
www.gwsports.com

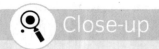

Inside Washington's Verizon Center

The $200-million, 1-million-square-foot, 20,000-seat Verizon Center debuted December 2, 1997, to kudos all around from the fans who watched the Washington Wizards handily defeat the Seattle SuperSonics. The massive, brightly lit sports and entertainment center signaled the start of a downtown revitalization. The arena's location—at 7th and F Streets NW, just a hop, skip, and jump from the Gallery Place–Chinatown Metro station—proves quite convenient, particularly for those who work in the city. Most suburbanites need drive only as far as their closest Metro station.

Here are more reasons to check it out:

• Sports—The NBA Washington Wizards, WNBA Washington Mystics, NHL Capitals, and Georgetown Hoyas all play here. If you miss any action on the floor, you can look up at one of the four 12-by-16-foot screens on the 15-ton video scoreboard cube that hangs from the center of the ceiling. It's the biggest of its kind!

The basketball playing surface dismantles to reveal a permanent ice hockey rink underneath, used by the Capitals.

• Concerts—The arena hosts some of the region's hottest concerts, including The Who, Rod Stewart, Bob Seger, and Justin Timberlake in 2007. Barry Manilow presented the venue's inaugural musical event, followed a month later by country singer Alan Jackson. Billy Joel also has appeared a few times.

• Special events—The arena hosts skating championships, professional wrestling, Disney on Ice, and the Ringling Brothers and Barnum & Bailey Circus.

• Miscellaneous features—The center—built in compliance with the Americans with Disabilities Act—features 175 to 204 wheelchair-accessible seats for disabled patrons and their companions. Call (202) 661–5065 or TTY (202) 661–5066. Other services for the disabled include Braille signs and menus, TTY phones, 12 elevators, assisted-listening devices, and lowered counters.

The building boasts 24 restrooms, with extra toilets in the women's rooms. Three restrooms are designed for family use.

Your best bet, as we mentioned earlier, is to take the Metro to the center. The adjacent stop, Gallery Place–Chinatown, is on the Red, Yellow, and Green Lines. If taking the Metro from the suburbs, give yourself at least an hour: Crowds can be heavy, and trains slower, before big events. If you choose to drive, you'll find more than 7,000 parking spaces in lots and garages within a 10-minute walk. The center's own 500 spaces, accessible on 6th Street between F and G Streets, are open to the public only during the day and nonevent weekend hours. Taxi stands for center visitors are at the corner of 5th and F Streets and 8th and F Streets. Concerned about safety? The center is equipped with a police command post, complete with two holding cells!

Contact the Verizon Center information line at (202) 628–3200 or visit www.verizoncenter.com.

Not to be excluded from Metro Washington's major college basketball lineup, George Washington University is an emerging program in its own right.

Under charismatic coach Karl Hobb, the Colonials delivered one of the region's strongest performances in 2006, ending the season ranked 19th nationwide with a 26–2 record. The team fell to Duke in the second round of the 2006 NCAA tournament, but captured back-to-back Atlantic 10 tournament crowns.

Led by 18-year coach Joe McKeown, the women's team finished the 2005–06 season at 23–9, falling in the second round of the NCAA tournament to Tennessee. The Lady Colonials earned a top 25 ranking early in the 2006–07 season.

Catch the Colonials in action at the cozy Smith Center, located in the heart of the Northwest Washington campus. Tickets for men's games are $18 and $12. Admission to women's games is $9 for adults, $6 for youths.

Howard University
Burr Gymnasium
6th and Girard Streets NW
Washington, DC
(202) 806–7140
www.bisonmania.com
These small but powerful Mid-Eastern Athletic Conference Bison teams have played inconsistently in recent years. Coached by Gil Jackson, the men were 7–22 in 2005–06, Jackson's first season. The Lady Bison fared better. They finished their 2005–06 season at 14–15. Tickets for both men's and women's Bison games are $8.00 general admission and $12.00 reserved.

University of Maryland
Comcast Center
College Park, MD
(301) 314–7070, (800) 462–TERP (tickets),
(800) 314–TERP (updates)
www.umterps.com
Another of the region's prominent basketball programs is the University of Maryland,

which holds court at the 17,100-seat Comcast Center.

Under the leadership of Coach Gary Williams, a former Terp himself, Maryland has become one of the premier teams in the Atlantic Coast Conference. The Terps earned berths in the NCAA tournament for 11 consecutive seasons, 1993 through 2004, including seven trips to the regional semifinals, two trips to the Final Four, and an NCAA title in 2002.

On the heels of the men's 2002 championship, the Lady Terps earned some successes of their own. Under Coach Brenda Frese, the team has appeared in four consecutive NCAA tournaments, clinching the national title in 2006. With many of their starters returning, the team began the 2006–07 season ranked number one in the country.

Tickets to the men's games are $26 to $33, if they're available! Tickets to the women's games are $8.00 for adults and $4.00 for ages 17 and younger and senior citizens.

While basketball usually gets top billing, the Terps' football program also merits some attention. The team earned bowl appearances in 2002, 2003, and 2004 and finished the 2006 season ranked 21st in the country. The men's soccer team has made it to the Final Four four times since 1998, winning the title in 2005. The field hockey team has appeared in 11 Final Fours, claiming back-to-back championships in 2005 and 2006, while the women's lacrosse team clinched seven straight national titles from 1995 through 2001.

FOOTBALL

Washington Redskins
FedExField
Arena Drive
Landover, MD
(301) 276–6050
www.redskins.com
Hail to the Redskins! In 1999 the team sold for a record $800 million to a partnership led by 34-year-old communications mogul Daniel M. Snyder of Bethesda. The young owner began stirring things up as soon as he took over the

ℹ️ If you plan on driving to FedExField for a Redskins game, get there about two hours before kickoff so you can beat most of the traffic and have plenty of time to take part in the traditional tailgating festivities.

franchise, which had been in the Jack Kent Cooke family for almost 30 years. Snyder changed the arena's name from Jack Kent Cooke Stadium to Redskins Stadium, then again to FedExField. He also made major staff overhauls, intent on turning the organization around after its disappointing 1998 season, when the Redskins opened with seven straight losses and finished with a 6–10 record.

New management lit a fire under the players, and the '99 Skins made the playoffs for the first time in six seasons but lost their second game to Tampa Bay. In 2000, the team finished 8–8, and Head Coach Norv Turner lost his job after the thirteenth game. Turner's departure set the stage for Snyder's infamous "revolving door" at the helm. Succeeding Turner was Kansas City Chiefs veteran Marty Schottenheimer, who was excused after one season. Former University of Miami coach Steve Spurrier was up next, turning in disappointing results in 2002 and 2003. Joe Gibbs, the Redskins' legendary coach, agreed to step out of retirement and take over the team in 2004. Gibbs brought the Redskins back to the playoffs in 2006, though the following season was a letdown.

Win or lose, the Skins boast a loyal, enthusiastic following. Trying to be one of the 80,000 fans who jam the stadium for every home game, however, is tough to do, since few if any tickets are available to the general public. A limited number go on sale each sum-

ℹ️ If you happen to score tickets to a Redskins game, keep an eye out for the Hogettes. This group of rabid 'Skins fans wear muumuus, wigs, pig noses, and other garish attire and make their spirit known throughout the stadium.

mer for the one or two home preseason games in August, but they usually sell out too. So you've got to act fast. Lucky season ticket holders pay upwards of $40 per ticket (executive suites cost from $59,950 to $159,950), but don't count on season tickets' availability. You're more likely to find yourself on a waiting list. You can buy tickets through brokers, but they'll cost you a pretty penny. The good news about consistent sellouts is you never have to be concerned about home games being blacked out on local TV—an unfortunate reality in some NFL markets. Perhaps most compelling is that in a region where political party, race, gender, or socioeconomic status too often divide people, the Redskins have remained a unifying force that transcends these and other barriers.

The eye-catching, contemporary new stadium, built in just 17 months, took years of planning and false starts, but overall, fans seem pleased with the results. On the plus side, the stadium offers roomier seats, highly visible scoreboards in each end zone, 38 concession stands with food ranging from traditional stadium fare to crab cakes and Mexican food, larger restrooms, and for those with the big bucks, two tiers of luxury seats. On the down side there's traffic, traffic, traffic! With no nearby Metrorail access, the stadium offers limited transportation options. Your best bet is to arrive early to beat the congestion and find parking.

HORSING AROUND

Horse-racing enthusiasts are in luck. Maryland is home to several equine venues. (Virginia has approved horse betting as the latest form of gambling, but the first local tracks have yet to open; the sport is illegal in the District.)

Steeplechase events, usually held in the spring and fall in the hunt country of Metro Washington, are as much social gatherings as they are sporting spectacles. Kentucky we're not, yet the influence of the equine industry is astounding in Virginia and Maryland. Entire towns such as Middleburg, Warrenton, and Keswick in Virginia, and Upper Marlboro and Potomac in Maryland, are dedicated to the care, training, and competition of the sport horse. Both states are home to a large number of equine-related organizations and happenings, far too many to list. Check local newspapers, especially the weekend/calendar sections, for steeplechase dates and locations.

Here are some of the region's most popular arenas and events.

Northern Virginia

Contact the Loudoun Tourism Council, (800) 752–6118, for a free "Welcome to Virginia Horse Country" brochure, or find horse attractions featured on its Web site, www.visit loudoun.org. Here are a few Loudoun County highlights:

The Fairfax Hunt
Morven Park International Equestrian Center
41793 Tutt Lane
Leesburg, VA
(703) 787–6673
www.fairfaxhuntraces.org
This annual event, usually held the third Saturday of April, features racing over hurdles and timber. Post time is 2:00 P.M. Admission is $10 in advance and $15 at the gate.

Morven Park International Equestrian Center
41793 Tutt Lane
Leesburg, VA
(703) 777–2414
www.morvenpark.org
Spectators enjoy tailgating parties before the annual steeplechase race, held the second Saturday of October. The 1,200-acre estate, especially lovely in the spring and fall, also boasts an elegant, historic governor's mansion, the Museum of Hounds and Hunting (currently under renovation), and the Winmill Carriage Collection, featuring well-preserved antique vehicles. Tours take place on the hour, noon to 4:00 P.M., Friday through Monday from early April through early December.

Holiday tours are featured later in December. Tours cost $5.00 for adults and $1.00 for children ages 6 to 12.

The Virginia Gold Cup Races and The International Gold Cup Races
The Virginia Gold Cup Association
90 Main Street
Warrenton, VA 20188
(540) 347–1215
www.vagoldcup.com
Virginia's premier steeplechase events take place at Great Meadow Event Center in the Plains, 40 miles west of Washington, D.C. Hobnob with the area's rich and famous at the Virginia Gold Cup Races, held the first Saturday in May, and at the International Gold Cup Races, held the third Saturday in October. Races run from 1:00 to 5:00 P.M., preceded by special events such as Jack Russell Terrier Races. Tickets run from $65 for a general car pass that admits up to six passengers, to thousands of dollars for corporate tents.

Suburban Maryland

Laurel Park
Route 198 and Laurel Racetrack Road
Laurel, MD
(301) 725–0400
www.laurelpark.com
Live thoroughbred racing takes place Wednesdays through Sundays January through March, late June through late August, and October through December. Admission is $3.00 for grandstand and clubhouse seats. You may wish to reserve a table at one of the on-site bars or restaurants (fees apply). The 9-furlong track is open all year, with simulcast racing when live races aren't held. Minimum betting usually is $2.00. A free Pony Pals kids' club features a monthly Sunday morning stable tour, craft activity,

i When the Washington International Horse Show comes to town, the streets surrounding the Verizon Center take on a different appearance (and smell) as horse trailers move in.

and live entertainment for children ages 2 to 12, accompanied by an adult. Preferred parking is $2.00.

Pimlico Race Course
Hayward and Winner Avenues
Baltimore, MD
(410) 542–9400
www.pimlico.com
The showcase event at this historic course (dating to 1743) is, of course, the Preakness, the second jewel in thoroughbred racing's Triple Crown, held the third Saturday in May. Tickets are hard to come by for this prestigious event, but you can watch other thoroughbred racing during April, May, and most of June. Simulcast races are televised the rest of the year. Admission is $3.00 for grandstand and clubhouse seats. Reservations are recommended for the enclosed dining room, which charges a seating fee. See the Laurel Park entry for information about kids' club activities, which also take place at this course. Preferred parking is $2.00.

Rosecroft Raceway
6336 Rosecroft Drive
Fort Washington, MD
(301) 567–4000
www.rosecroft.com
Just a few minutes from the Wilson Bridge, off Capital Beltway exit 4A, this 55-year-old raceway features live harness racing starting at 5:20 P.M. Monday and Tuesday and 7:20 P.M. Saturday, most of the year. Patrons also can watch simulcast thoroughbred races. Admission is $3.00, and minimum bets are $1.00. You also can watch the races from an enclosed dining room, which offers televisions at each table; reservations are recommended. Call (301) 567–4045. Seats are $2.00. General parking is free.

The Show Place Arena
14900 Pennsylvania Avenue
Upper Marlboro, MD
(301) 952–7900
www.showplacearena.com

This 5,800-seat, multipurpose arena often plays host to horse-riding competitions. Call for a rundown of upcoming events.

The Washington International
Horse Show
Verizon Center
601 F Street NW
Washington, DC
(301) 987–9400, (202) 397–SEAT
www.wihs.org
This annual event, held for more than a week each fall, features some of the world's top show jumpers, hunters, and dressage riders, not to mention those entertaining canine show-stealers, the racing Jack Russell terriers. This is a fun event that the whole family can enjoy. Tickets for the evening shows usually run $20 and up. Daytime event admission is $15. Tickets go on sale in mid-August, but also are available at the door.

ICE HOCKEY

Capitals
Verizon Center
601 F Street NW
Washington, DC
(202) 397–SEAT, (703) 573–SEAT
www.washingtoncaps.com
Like the Redskins, the Capitals also came under new ownership during the summer of 1999. Longtime majority owner Abe Pollin sold the franchise to America Online executive Ted Leonsis, local businessman Jon Ledecky, and Capitals president Dick Patrick.

The Caps proudly signed star players Jaromir Jagr and Peter Bondra, who helped stage a playoff run in 2002–03, but the success was not sustained. Both players were traded in 2004, along with league-leading scorer Robert Lang. After weathering the NHL labor dispute in 2004–05, the Caps have seen some promise in rising Russian stars Alexander Ovechkin, who finished third in the NHL in scoring during his rookie season, and Alexander Semin. Nevertheless, the team finished the 2005–06 season in last place in its division, despite losing some close contests.

As a thanks to their devoted fans, some prices still remain affordable. Single-game tickets range from $10 for "eagle's nest" seats to $90. The team also offers Family Night deals.

RUNNING

Marine Corps Marathon
Downtown Washington, DC
next to the National Mall
(800) RUN–USMC
www.marinemarathon.com
This fall classic, sometimes referred to as the "People's Marathon," remains accessible to everyday runners as well as serious contenders. Registration begins in February and fills up quickly. Those who would rather watch than actually attempt to run 26 miles and 385 yards, will find abundant prime vantage points along the course, which begins and ends in Arlington but canvases a large section of the National Mall area downtown.

SOCCER

D.C. United
RFK Stadium
2400 East Capitol Street
(202) 587–5000
www.dcunited.com
Washington is well on its way to becoming a soccer town, thanks to D.C. United, its four-time Major League Soccer champion team. The 1994 World Cup games played in Washington and other U.S. cities were a huge success by any measure—a surprise, perhaps, to some people except die-hard fans, including those among the region's diverse and substantial immigrant population. Now soccer ("football" to the rest of the world) is beginning to catch on with the American public, in part because of the infant Major League Soccer league.

Washington's MLS team couldn't have gotten off to a much better start: It won three MLS Cups in four years, then triumphed again in 2004. In 2006 it fell to Kansas City in the playoffs.

The team plays April through early fall at RFK Stadium, former home of the Washington Redskins. Tickets range in price from $13 to $40.

STOCK CAR RACING

Hagerstown Speedway
15112 National Pike
west of Hagerstown, MD
(301) 582–0640
www.hagerstownspeedway.com
Stock cars roar into action on Sunday afternoons during spring and fall, and Saturday nights late February through September at this track about an hour's drive from Washington. General admission for regular events is $9.00, with children younger than 12 admitted free. Special events like TNT Monster Trucks and World of Outlaw Sprints take place every other weekend. The track is a half-mile clay oval, semibanked.

Old Dominion Speedway and Dragstrip
10611 Dumfries Road,
Route 234
Manassas, VA
(703) 361–7753
www.olddominionspeedway.com
Stock car and drag racing take place Fridays, Saturdays, and some Sundays, March through September.

TENNIS

Legg Mason Tennis Classic
William H.G. FitzGerald Tennis Center
16th and Kennedy Streets NW
Washington, DC
(202) 721–9500
www.leggmasontennisclassic.com
Tennis anyone? If the answer is yes, then the showcase event to see is the Washington Tennis Classic, held each July or August at this 7,500-seat facility, on the fringes of beautiful Rock Creek Park. The lineup usually features several stars of the tennis world,

including the likes of Andre Agassi and Andy Roddick in addition to lower-ranked players and some solid local talent. Tickets run from $9.00 to $45.00 per session.

WATERSPORTS

It's free, it's exciting, and it's a lot closer than you think. Here are some good bets.

Washington, D.C.

Jack's Boathouse
3500 K Street NW
Washington, DC
(202) 337–9642
www.jacksboathouse.com

If you're looking to create your own aquatic adventure, rent a canoe or kayak at one of the boathouses that are perched along the Potomac River. Our favorite is Jack's, a quirky, friendly, family-owned Washington, D.C. institution that opened its doors in 1945. Public figures—from media personalities to politicians—count themselves among Jack's customers. You'll find Jack's beneath the Key Bridge, which links Georgetown with Arlington, Virginia. Boat rentals are $15 for the first hour, $10 for the second hour, or $35 all day.

Washington Boat Show
Washington Convention Center
Washington, DC
(703) 823–7960
www.washingtonboatshow.com

If you enjoy browsing larger and more expensive pleasure craft, keep an eye out for this annual trade show, held each February. It includes entertainment, too, such as Twiggy, the waterskiing squirrel.

Northern Virginia

Great Falls Park
Old Dominion Drive and
Georgetown Pike
Great Falls, VA
(703) 285–2965
www.nps.gov/gwmp/grfa

For a different kind of thrill, head over to this national park in the well-heeled Fairfax County community of Great Falls and watch gutsy kayakers and occasional canoeists attempt to negotiate the wicked Great Falls of the Potomac River, just north of Washington. Definitely not for the faint of heart.

Even if you show up and don't spot any boaters, you won't have wasted a trip. The water and surrounding countryside are spectacular in themselves and worth a look any time of year. (See our Parks and Recreation chapter for more on this park.)

Suburban Maryland

United States Powerboat Show
City Dock
Annapolis, MD
(410) 268–8828
www.usboat.com/shows/pbhomes.htm

The boating mecca of Annapolis lays claim to hosting the world's largest in-the-water exhibition, held in October at the City Dock. Admission is $16.00 for adults, $8.00 for children.

United States Sailboat Show
City Dock
Annapolis, MD
(410) 268–8828
usboat.com/shows/sbhomes.htm

Boating purists get their due in October with this show, also held at the City Dock. Admission is the same as that for the powerboat show.

PARKS AND RECREATION

From small, leafy plots of land in the inner city to the giant state and regional parks found in the suburbs, our fair capital area features an abundance of lush, green spaces, beckoning both nature lovers and outdoor-sports enthusiasts. With almost 90,000 protected acres, Washington, D.C. rates as one of the country's greenest metropolitan areas, according to the Greater Washington Board of Trade. No other American urban area can claim as many National Park Service properties as can Metro Washington. It's one of the many perks of being in or near the Nation's Capital, where nearly 30 percent of all land is controlled by the National Park Service.

Metro Washington also boasts scores of recreation centers offering gymnasiums, swimming pools, fitness rooms, sports leagues, classes, and summer camps.

This chapter presents a brief survey of prominent national, state, regional, and local parks in the National Capital area and follows with information about recreation centers and other resources for leisurely pursuits. Note that when we don't list park hours, you'll find the park open from dawn until dark.

PARKS

Washington, D.C.

Chesapeake & Ohio Canal National Historical Park
Georgetown Visitor Center
1057 Thomas Jefferson Street NW
Washington, DC
(202) 653–5190
www.nps.gov/choh
In the 1800s construction of the Chesapeake & Ohio Canal linked Washington with the western reaches of the Potomac River. The canal stretches 184 miles from Georgetown to Cumberland, Maryland, passing through 74 lift locks. In 1971 the entire length became a national park, and today the C&O Canal and Towpath are among Washington's and Suburban Maryland's most coveted recreational retreats. The gravel path is an inviting destination for hikers and joggers. The canal itself, meanwhile, makes for gentle canoeing and kayaking.

In April 1999 the park officially became a "trash-free" site with no waste receptacles: All visitors must take their garbage with them when they leave. If you forget your own bag, pick one up at designated stations in the park.

Go back in time with an hourlong guided ride aboard the Georgetown, an authentic replica of a mule-pulled, 80-person canal boat operated by costumed interpreters. The schedule varies seasonally, but the boat generally runs from early May through mid-November. Admission is $8.00 for adults, $6.00 for seniors, and $5.00 for children ages 4 to 14. The park also hosts frequent special events such as Civil War walks, lockhouse tours, and fishing contests. The park is closed on New Year's Day and Christmas.

Visit Thompson Boat Center, Virginia Avenue and Rock Creek Parkway (202–333–9543, www.thompsonboatcenter.com), to rent boats or bicycles. All-terrain bikes, which you can rent for $8.00 per hour or $25.00 per day, and cruisers, which you can rent for $4.00 per hour or $15.00 per day, are available March through November. Rent canoes, kayaks, and rowing shells for between $8.00 and $26.00 an hour, spring through mid-October.

The C&O Canal's towpath in Georgetown proves popular for warm-weather strolls. COURTESY WASHINGTON, D.C.
CONVENTION AND TOURISM CORPORATION

Kenilworth Park and Aquatic Gardens
Intersection of Douglas Street and Anacostia Avenue NE
Washington, DC
(202) 426–6905
www.nps.gov/kepa/

Metro Washington sits amid a region of beautiful and fragile wetlands. At this lovely site in Northeast D.C., naturalists can spend hours traversing nearly 12 acres of aquatic gardens featuring dozens of species of pond and marginal plants, such as tropical and hardy water lilies and hyacinths. The park's ancient lotuses regularly draw visitors from Asia. Kenilworth is the only national park devoted to cultivating and propagating aquatic plants.

Arrive first thing in the morning in the summer to get a good look at both night- and day-blooming water lilies. More than 40 natural ponds attract water birds, frogs, turtles, and curious kids. Take a guided tour at 9:00 and 11:00 A.M. and 1:00 P.M. on weekends and holidays, Memorial Day to Labor Day. Call ahead to arrange tours at other times, depending on staff availability. The park is open daily from 7:00 A.M. to 4:00 P.M. The visitor center, featuring an exhibit area and bookstore, is open from 8:00 A.M. to 4:00 P.M. The park is closed on New Year's Day, Thanksgiving, and Christmas.

Surrounded by approximately 77 acres of marshland, Kenilworth is part of Anacostia Park, 1900 Anacostia Drive SE, Washington, D.C., (202) 426–9365, www.nps.gov/anac. Covering approximately 1,200 acres along the Anacostia River, the park features the 18-hole Langston Golf Course, exotic waterfowl, a boat ramp, picnic areas, playgrounds, an outdoor pool, playing fields and courts, and an outdoor pavilion used for roller skating and special events.

The National Mall and Memorial Parks
900 Ohio Drive SW
Washington, DC
(202) 426–6841
www.nps.gov/nama

The National Park Service's D.C.-area domain begins with the National Mall, that vast esplanade as envisioned by the capital city's French designer, Pierre Charles L'Enfant. The 3-mile, 146-acre expanse of green extends westward from the foot of Capitol Hill to the Lincoln Memorial and Potomac River. It contains the highest density of museums and monuments in the world. (See our Annual Events, Arts, Attractions, and Kidstuff chapters for more on those.)

The Mall, as you'll probably discover, is every bit as humble as it is inspiring. Designed to be used by the people, it draws pet walkers, joggers, Frisbee tossers, and kite fliers. Informal games of soccer, volleyball, softball, and touch football are almost as common a sight here as the museums and monuments. From spring through fall, Capitol Hill staffers, among others, use the Mall for their various athletic leagues. Less active folks can park themselves on benches and watch the ever-changing flurry of passing activity.

The Mall is also the site of some of the nation's most important public gatherings. In 1963 Dr. Martin Luther King Jr. led one of the largest public demonstrations in U.S. history on these hallowed grounds (see our History chapter). Every four years, the East Mall, at the base of the Capitol Building, is the site of presidential inaugural swearing-in ceremonies. Whatever your political affiliation, the ceremony and the setting make for an unforgettable Washington experience. In 2006 the National Park Service launched a campaign to create a 50-year, forward-looking vision of the National Mall, soliciting opinions from experts—and the tax-paying public—about what they'd like to see on this hallowed ground. While the results will no doubt unravel at "government" pace, we're excited to track the plan's progress.

Between the Washington Monument, National World War II Memorial, and Lincoln

i Kenilworth Aquatic Gardens' Water Lily Festival, held each July, attracts water plant lovers from throughout the United States.

ℹ️ Look for gorgeous plantings of seasonal flowers at National Park Service–maintained sites throughout Washington. In the spring, more than a million daffodils adorn the Potomac's west bank.

Memorial, you'll find the beautifully land-scaped, 50-acre Constitution Gardens, just north of the long Reflecting Pool and near the Vietnam Veterans Memorial. Look for ducks, geese, and other water birds swimming in the gardens' six-and-a-half-acre lake, which also holds an island adorned with a memorial to the 56 signers of the Declaration of Independence. Waterfowl also frequent the Reflecting Pool and the nearby Tidal Basin, around which thousands of delicate Japanese cherry trees burst into bloom each spring (see our Annual Events chapter for details about the National Cherry Blossom Festival). Look for the Tulip Library, which boasts more colors and varieties of the flower than you'd dream possible. If you'd like to take in the sights from the water, rent a pedal boat at the Tidal Basin Boat House, 1501 Maine Avenue, (202) 479–2426. They're generally available from 10:00 A.M. to 6:00 P.M. during good weather, April through October. Hourly rates are $8.00 for a two-seater and $16.00 for a four-seater.

On the fringes of the river end of the National Mall, West Potomac Park contains the beautifully designed Franklin Delano Roosevelt Memorial, described in our Attractions chapter. Opposite the FDR Memorial, the new Washington, D.C. Martin Luther King Jr. National Memorial will soon take shape. East Potomac Park, south of the Tidal Basin, features picnic areas, a playground, an outdoor pool and tennis courts, a pathway for biking and exercising, and a unique, kid-pleasing statue, *The Awakening*, which resembles a giant about to get up from his underground resting place. (See this chapter's Golfing section for information about the East Potomac Park Golf Course.)

Rock Creek Park
3545 Williamsburg Lane NW
Washington, DC
(202) 895–6239
www.nps.gov/rocr
The city's second most visible green space, Rock Creek Park, covers more than 2,000 acres of rolling hills, woods, meadows, and the namesake boulder-strewn creek in the center of Northwest. President Benjamin Harrison signed the legislation creating Rock Creek Park in 1890, making it one of the nation's oldest city parks. It's also one of the world's largest urban parks, boasting plentiful amenities like its popular trails, frequented by hikers, bikers, and horseback riders. Its bike trail is also part of a larger trail network, connecting the District with both Maryland and Virginia. The park also holds picnic and play areas, an equestrian center (202–362–0118, www.rockcreekhorsecenter.com), a golf course (see this chapter's listing under Golfing), and tennis courts.

Historic Peirce Mill (202–895–6000) was closed for renovations at press time. Call ahead for hours and activities; the buildings are open periodically during the restoration. Visit the Rock Creek Nature Center, 5200 Glover Road, (202) 895–6070, to explore the Discovery Room and take part in daily programs such as guided nature walks. It's open from 9:00 A.M. to 5:00 P.M. Wednesday through Sunday except New Year's Day, July 4th, Thanksgiving, and Christmas. The adjacent planetarium specializes in free educational shows for ages four and older at 1:00 P.M. on Saturdays and Sundays, and for ages seven and older at 4:00 P.M. on Saturdays, Sundays, and Wednesdays. The planetarium also holds monthly stargazing sessions. The Carter Barron Amphitheater, 4850 Colorado Avenue NW, (202) 426–0486, hosts concerts throughout the summer, as well as several performances of a free Shakespearean play each June.

(See our Attractions, Kidstuff, and Spectator Sports chapters for more information on attractions within this urban forest.)

Rock Creek Park is packed with miles of inviting hiking and biking trails. COURTESY WASHINGTON, D.C. CONVENTION AND TOURISM CORPORATION

Northern Virginia

Algonkian Regional Park
47001 Fairway Drive
Sterling, VA
(703) 450–4655, (703) 430–7683 (pool)
www.nvrpa.org/algonkian.html
Set along the Potomac in eastern Loudoun County, this Northern Virginia Regional Park Authority (NVRPA) park features an outdoor pool, miniature golf, picnic tables and shelters, a 2-mile nature trail, boat ramp, and boat and RV storage. The 500-acre park's riverfront cabins, available for rent year-round, offer a pleasant family camping experience. Call at 3:00 P.M. seven days in advance to arrange a tee time for the 18-hole, par 72 golf course, or book online at the park's Web site.

Bull Run Regional Park
7700 Bull Run Drive
Centreville, VA
(703) 631–0550, (703) 631–0552 (pool)
www.nvrpa.org/bullrunpark.html
Not far from Manassas National Battlefield Park, NVRPA's Bull Run features scenic hiking trails and several acres of springtime wildflowers. A large outdoor pool includes a tropical island–themed water slide. Visitors also enjoy trying their skills at miniature and disc golf and skeet- and trap-shooting at the Bull Run Shooting Center (703–830–2344), open 3:00 P.M. to 8:00 P.M. Tuesday, Wednesday, and Thursday; 2:00 P.M. to 8:00 P.M. Friday; and 9:00 A.M. to 5:00 P.M. Saturday and Sun-

i Covering 1,754 acres, Rock Creek Park is even larger than New York's Central Park.

day. The park also offers group and family camping. Call (703) 631–0550 for group reservation information. The main park is open mid-March through November. Nonarea residents must pay an entrance fee of $7.00 daily, $14.00 weekly.

Burke Lake Park
7315 Ox Road
Fairfax Station, VA
(703) 323–6600
www.co.fairfax.va.us/parks/burkelake

A favorite with local fishing and boating enthusiasts, this 888-acre Fairfax County Park Authority (FCPA) park features a 218-acre lake. Rent rowboats or take a guided pontoon-boat tour of the lake, which includes an island sanctuary for waterfowl. (Ask your tour guide to tell you about the interesting objects at the bottom of the manmade body of water.) The park also offers a campground, picnicking, play areas, and more than 4 miles of hiking trails. (See our Kidstuff chapter for more on the park's kid-pleasing attractions. See our golf listings in this chapter for information about the park's course.) Non–Fairfax County residents pay $8.00 per vehicle on weekends and holidays.

Cameron Run Regional Park
4001 Eisenhower Avenue
Alexandria, VA
(703) 960–0767
www.nvrpa.org/cameron.html

A favorite spot for cooling off on steamy summer days, Cameron Run attracts hundreds of families to its Great Waves water park, which features a wave pool, four-story water slide, and liquid playground for youngsters. It's open 11:00 A.M. to 7:00 P.M. daily through most of the summer; admission is $12.75 for visitors taller than 4 feet, $10.25 for those shorter than 4 feet, and free for children younger than two. Batting cages and a beautifully landscaped miniature golf course are open 10:00 A.M. to 11:00 P.M. daily during the summer, and for more limited hours during the spring and fall. Golf games are $5.50 for

patrons age 16 and older, $4.50 for ages younger than 16. Batting-cage tokens cost $1.00 apiece for 16 balls. You'll find the park just off I–495, minutes from family-geared motels and the Eisenhower Avenue and Van Dorn Street Metrorail stations.

George Washington Memorial Parkway
Turkey Run Park
McLean, VA
(703) 289–2500
www.nps.gov/gwmp

In Northern Virginia, the George Washington Memorial Parkway and its adjacent Mount Vernon Trail provide spectacular riverside hiking and biking trails extending from the riverbanks opposite Theodore Roosevelt Island southward 18.5 miles to Mount Vernon. You'll also find boating opportunities and nature preserves like Dyke Marsh on the river's west bank, where you may spot resident waterfowl and other critters. The 7,200-acre national park area also features such historic sites as Robert E. Lee's home, Arlington House, and Claude Moore Colonial Farm (see the Kidstuff chapter).

George Washington's Grist Mill
5514 Mount Vernon Memorial Highway
3 miles west of Mount Vernon, VA
(703) 780–3383
www.dcr.state.va.us/parks/georgewa.htm

This interpretive historical site at Mount Vernon offers tours of a reconstructed mill once used by the first president, who resided just down the road at his Mount Vernon estate. Near the gristmill, archaeologists have also uncovered the foundation of Washington's whiskey distillery and have begun the process of restoring it to learn more about this component of plantation life. Tickets to see the gristmill are $4.00 for adults and $2.00 for children ages 6 to 11. If you're purchasing a ticket to tour Mount Vernon, you can also visit the gristmill for $2.00 extra for adults and $1.50 extra for children.

Great Falls Park
Old Dominion Drive and
Georgetown Pike
Great Falls, VA
(703) 285–2966
www.nps.gov/grfa

We love to surprise our out-of-town company with a visit to one of the most impressive natural sights in Metro Washington: the cascading Great Falls of the Potomac, plunging (in some places more than 35 feet) through a series of jagged rocks and gigantic boulders that make up Mather Gorge. It's not Niagara, but it'll do! You also can view the falls from the Maryland side of the river at the C&O National Historical Park; visit both, and decide which vista you prefer. The park is a favorite with outdoor sports enthusiasts, from kayakers to rock climbers. Just pay careful attention to the posted warning signs: The water can be as dangerous, even deadly, as it is beautiful.

Stop by the park's visitor center, open from 10:00 A.M. to 4:00 P.M., with longer hours during the warmer months, to see a 10-minute slide show, a children's area, and exhibits relating to the park's natural resources and to the Patowmack Canal, a project over which George Washington presided. The park boasts an interesting history, including a stint as an amusement park. Rangers lead daily talks as well as special programs on weekends and holidays all year. The park intermittently charges admission of $5.00 per car or $3.00 per pedestrian, jogger, or bicyclist, valid for three consecutive days and also good for entrance to the C&O Canal National Historic Park on the other side of the falls. You can obtain an annual park pass, good for Great Falls and the C&O Canal, for $20. The park is open daily from 7:00 A.M. to dusk, except on Christmas. The gates are locked at dark.

Green Spring Gardens Park
4603 Green Spring Road
Alexandria, VA
(703) 642–5173
www.greenspring.org

This 27-acre garden-filled Fairfax County park proves a beautiful and popular spot for strolls and outdoor weddings. Demonstration gardens offer inspiration to both budding gardeners and those with green thumbs. The historic Manor House, open select days and hours, features a gift shop, art exhibits, and special programs such as Full English teas. Visit the Horticulture Center from 9:00 A.M. to 4:30 P.M. Monday through Saturday, noon to 4:30 P.M. Sunday.

Huntley Meadows Park and Visitor Center
3701 Lockheed Boulevard
Alexandria, VA
(703) 768–2525
www.co.fairfax.va.us/parks/huntley

This 1,425-acre park—the largest operated by FCPA—draws nature lovers of all ages, who love to explore the meadows, forests and ⅔-mile boardwalk trail through the wetlands. Keep your eyes open for wildlife, from butterflies and songbirds to deer, beaver, and waterfowl. Park naturalists conduct hundreds of programs annually at the visitor center, which features exhibits pertaining to the area's natural resources. The park also proves a popular destination for local school and Scout groups, who arrange guided tours by appointment. Visitor center hours vary throughout the year, but generally run from 9:00 A.M. to 5:00 P.M. weekdays except Tuesdays and from noon to 5:00 P.M. Saturdays and Sundays during warm weather.

Lake Accotink Park
7500 Accotink Park Road
Springfield, VA
(703) 569–3464
www.co.fairfax.va.us/parks/accotink

Another popular FCPA park, Lake Accotink features wetlands, streams, and a 55-acre lake with canoe, rowboat, and pedal-boat rentals, along with tour-boat rides. Visitors also can fish, play miniature golf, ride a carousel, and hike trails in this 482-acre park. Special events include an annual cardboard boat race and summer concert series.

Leesylvania State Park
2001 Daniel K. Ludwig Drive
Woodbridge, VA
(703) 670–0372
www.dcr.state.va.us/parks/leesylva.htm
This 508-acre park, off U.S. 1 in Prince
William County, offers precious access to the
Potomac River, upon which visitors enjoy fishing and boating. You'll even find a sandy
beach for strolling and sunbathing—no swimming allowed! Hiking on 6 miles of trails and
picnicking are also popular activities. On the
National Register of Historic Landmarks, Leesylvania sits on land once owned by Revolutionary War hero "Light Horse Harry" Lee
and, later, the Fairfax family. The park holds
frequent educational programs for all ages. A
visitor center, open noon to 4:00 P.M. (weekends only during the winter), houses nature
exhibits and a gift shop. Park admission is
$3.00 per car on weekdays, $4.00 on weekends.

Mason Neck State Park
7301 High Point Road
Lorton, VA
(703) 550–0362
www.dcr.state.va.us/parks/masonnec.htm
This 1,814-acre park adjoins more than 2,000
acres designated as a wildlife refuge. Mason
Neck is a bird-watcher's dream: Bald eagles
nest among the towering pines and hard-
woods, and whistling swans and various varieties of ducks also frequent the park.
Observe the resident birds unseen in blinds
placed along the 3.5 miles of hiking trails.
With wetlands as well as fields and forests,
Mason Neck proves ideal for environmental
study. Visitors also enjoy picnicking, fishing,
canoeing, windsurfing, and primitive camping
for groups (800–933–PARK). A visitor center,
open daily during the summer and on week-

i Take a naturalist-led evening hike to
learn about owls, bats, and other
nighttime creatures. Check your local
parks and recreation authority newsletter
for times.

ends during the spring and fall, offers interpretive exhibits on local plants and wildlife.
The park is open 8:00 A.M. to dusk daily. Parking is $3.00 on weekdays, $4.00 on weekends.

Meadowlark Gardens Regional Park
9750 Meadowlark Gardens Court
Vienna, VA
(703) 255–3631
www.nvrpa.org/meadowlark
One of Northern Virginia's most beautiful
parks, Meadowlark offers more than 2 miles
of pathways through its 95 acres of gardens,
small lakes, and gazebos. The beautiful landscaping showcases native plants and flowers.
Here's a secret: Come here during late March
and early April to see weeping cherry trees in
all their glory around the main lake. It's not
quite as spectacular as the Tidal Basin's
famous display, but you won't have to fight
traffic or hunt in vain for parking.

The regional park also boasts an atrium,
which proves popular for wedding receptions
and other special events. (Couples sometimes
wed in the park's gazebos.) The attractive visitor center houses a snack room, gift shop,
restrooms, and art exhibitions. Call for a
schedule of workshops and programs. Hours
vary seasonally. Admission April through October is $5.00 for visitors ages 18 to 59, $2.50
for those ages 7 to 17 or 60 and older, and
free for children ages 6 and younger. Admission is free November through March. The site
is closed during icy weather and on New
Year's Day, Thanksgiving, and Christmas.

Pohick Bay Regional Park
6501 Pohick Bay Drive
Lorton, VA
(703) 339–6104
www.nvrpa.org/pohickbay
Like neighboring Mason Neck State Park, this
regional park in southeastern Fairfax County
is home to nesting bald eagles. Water is the
park's mainstay. Visitors can bring their own
boats, or rent sailboats or pedal boats. The
park also features an outdoor pool, miniature

and disc golf, picnic areas, and nature trails and bridle paths. You also can camp out here year-round at the family campground. (See our Golf listings for information about the course here.) Nonarea residents must pay an entrance fee of $7.00 per vehicle.

Prince William Forest Park
18100 Park Headquarters Road
Triangle, VA
(703) 221–7181
www.nps.gov/prwi

Part of the Quantico Creek watershed, this national park covers more than 18,500 acres of dense pine and hardwood forests and meandering creeks. More than 30 miles of trails beckon bikers, hikers, and cross-country skiers, on those rare occasions when the region receives more than a dusting of snow. The Pine Grove Visitor Center, open from 8:30 A.M. to 5:00 P.M. daily, features exhibits about the area's resources and, on weekends, naturalist-led programs. The park offers plenty of tent sites for campers and cabins for family camping during the summer and group camping year-round. Admission to the park, valid for three consecutive days, is $5.00 per car or $3.00 for pedestrians. An annual pass is $20.

Upton Hill Regional Park
6060 Wilson Boulevard
Arlington, VA
(703) 534–3437
www.nvrpa.org/uptonhill

This suburban NVRPA park is known for its challenging, lushly landscaped miniature golf course, open, along with batting cages, mid-March through October. Test your skill on hole number 10—at 140 feet in length, it's one of the world's longest miniature golf holes. The large outdoor pool is open Memorial Day weekend through Labor Day.

Suburban Maryland

See this chapter's Dancing section and the Kidstuff and Arts chapters for information about Glen Echo Park.

Black Hill Regional Park
20930 Lake Ridge Drive
Boyds, MD
(301) 972–3476
www.mcparkplanning.org/parks/
nature-centers/blackhill

With more than 1,300 acres, this Maryland-National Capital Park and Planning Commission (M-NCPPC) park attracts trail lovers and fishing and boating enthusiasts. You can rent a canoe or rowboat or ride on a guided pontoon boat, which offers Little Seneca Lake tours on the hour, noon to 6:00 P.M., on summer weekends. Admission is $2.00 per person; children younger than three are admitted free. You may be lucky enough to spot beavers, muskrats, otters, or other resident wildlife. The park attracts lots of waterfowl and other birds. The visitor center, open 11:00 A.M. to 6:00 P.M. daily during the summer and 11:00 A.M. to 5:00 P.M. weekends the rest of the year, houses wildlife exhibits and is surrounded by natural gardens that attract songbirds and butterflies.

Bohrer Park at Summit Hall Farm
506 South Frederick Avenue
Gaithersburg, MD
(301) 258–6445
www.gaithersburgmd.gov

Highlighted by a water park with two long slides, this site of nearly 60 acres also offers outdoor game facilities, a circular path, a miniature golf course, ponds, a playground, a concession stand, and an activity center. It's a popular summer hangout for Gaithersburg residents. Park admission is free, but pool, water park, and miniature golf prices vary, so call ahead.

Cabin John Regional Park
7400 Tuckerman Lane
Rockville, MD
(301) 299–0024
www.mncppc.org

This popular M-NCPPC park features numerous recreational activities, including indoor and outdoor tennis courts, a year-round ice-skating rink (301–365–2246), handball and volleyball courts, playing fields, and trails for bikers and hikers. There's also limited primitive camping space. (See our Kidstuff chapter for more on the park's child-pleasing attractions.)

Great Falls Tavern, Chesapeake and Ohio Canal National Historical Park
11710 MacArthur Boulevard
Potomac, MD
(301) 299–3613
www.nps.gov/choh

The Maryland side of Great Falls and the C&O Canal looks remarkably similar to the way it appeared more than 100 years ago. It's a lovely park in which to bike or walk. You can also take a ride on an 1870s-era canal boat, piloted by two mules. Guides dressed in period costume relate stories of life on the canal and sing songs from the era ($2.00 per person). The park's visitor center, open from 9:00 A.M. to 5:00 P.M. daily except Christmas and New Year's Day, features exhibits and an audiovisual presentation as well as special programs. Park admission is the same as Great Falls Park admission: $5.00 per car or $3.00 per pedestrian, jogger, or bicyclist, valid for three consecutive days and also good for entrance to the park on the other side of the falls (the admission fees are charged intermittently). An annual park pass, good for Great Falls and the C&O Canal, is available for $20. The park is open daily from 7:00 A.M. to dusk, except on Christmas. The gates are locked at dark.

Greenbelt Park
6565 Greenbelt Road
Greenbelt, MD
(301) 344–3944
www.nps.gov/gree

Just off the Beltway in Prince George's County, this 1,100-acre national park defies its highly urban setting with 9 miles of wooded trails and special interpretive nature programs for kids, such as summer Junior Rangers activities. It also offers numerous campsites for tents and vehicles. The camping fee is just $16 per night per site. Make reservations by calling (301) 344–3944 April 1 through October 31.

Little Bennett Regional Park
23701 Frederick Road
Clarksburg, MD
(301) 972–6581
www.mc-mncppc.org/parks/enterprise/park-facilities/little_bennett/index.shtm

This park in upper Montgomery County is a popular site for family camping from spring through fall. Make reservations by calling (301) 972–9222. The remains of historic sites accent the park's expansive network of hiking trails. Visitors also enjoy nature programs, a playground, and an 18-hole, par 72 golf course (301–253–1515).

Louise F. Cosca Regional Park
11000 Thrift Road
Clinton, MD
(301) 868–1397
www.pgparks.com/places/parks/cosca.html

This nearly 700-acre Prince George's County park features a 15-acre lake for fishing and boating. You can rent rowboats and paddle boats. It also boasts indoor and outdoor tennis courts (301–868–6462), trails for hiking and horseback riding, athletic fields, and a family campsite. Visit the Clearwater Nature Center (301–297–4575) for children's activities.

Robert M. Watkins Regional Park
301 Watkins Park Drive
Upper Marlboro, MD
(301) 218–6700
www.pgparks.com/places/parks/watkins.html

Besides the many offerings for children, described in the Kidstuff chapter, this park of more than 400 acres boasts indoor and outdoor tennis courts and playing fields. It's a popular recreational site for Prince George's County residents.

Rock Creek Regional Park
6700 Needwood Road
Rockville, MD
(301) 948–5053
www.mc-mncppc.org/parks/facilities/
regional_parks/rockcreek/index.shtm
Hike through the woods, picnic, visit a nature
center, visit an archery range, or play golf on
an 18-hole course. The park's Lake Needwood offers fishing, tourboat rides, and
rental pedal boats, canoes, and rowboats.
The site also has a snack bar.

Seneca Creek State Park
11950 Clopper Road
Gaithersburg, MD
(301) 924–2127
www.dnr.state.md.us/publiclands/central/
seneca.html
Near Gaithersburg, this park's 7,000 acres
offer outstanding hiking, boating, and fishing
opportunities almost within eyesight of suburban housing developments. A visitor center holds frequent programs year-round.

South Germantown Recreational Park
18041 Central Park Circle
Boyds, MD
(301) 601–4400
www.mc-mncppc.org/parks/facilities/
south_germantown.shtm
You'll never run out of things to do at this
large, bustling park in Montgomery County.
In the summer, visit the unique, accessible,
splash playground, which features a water
maze, tumbling buckets, walk-through fountains, and other soaking mechanisms on a
flat surface. Admission is $3.50 per person.
Adjacent to the playground, two lushly landscaped miniature golf courses, charging
$5.00 per person, boast challenging natural
obstacles. Call for hours of operation, which
vary throughout the season, for these two
activities. Other park highlights include an
accessible adventure playground, driving
range, archery range, walking and biking
trails, and a lake for model boating. See the
Soccer listing for information about the

park's Maryland SoccerPlex and Discovery
Sports Center.

Wheaton Regional Park
2000 Shorefield Road
Wheaton, MD
(301) 680–3803
www.mc-mncppc.org/parks/facilities/
regional_parks/wheaton/index.shtm
This Montgomery County favorite bustles
with activity, particularly on weekends, when
families and large groups flock to the park.
The park boasts numerous attractions and
programs for children (see our Kidstuff chapter for more on those) as well as hiking and
biking trails, a five-acre stocked lake for fishing, an ice-skating rink (301–649–3640), and
sports courts and fields. You can walk or
drive to the peaceful Brookside Gardens,
1800 Glenallen Avenue (301–949–8231),
offering 50 acres of various flowers and other
plants and a new visitor center for educational programs.

RECREATION

We could go on forever listing and describing
the thousands of recreational opportunities
available to residents throughout Metro
Washington. Here's a sampling of popular
resources to get you started in your leisurely
pursuits. If you don't see your favorite activity listed individually here, contact your local
recreation department. You'll find phone
numbers in this chapter. Check our Parks listings in this chapter for camping, trails, and
sports court locations. Look at our Kidstuff
and Senior Scene chapters for additional
ideas for children and senior citizens.

Amusement Parks

Six Flags America
13710 Central Avenue
Largo, MD
(301) 249–1500
www.sixflags.com/america
The closest theme park to Washington, Six
Flags America boasts such crowd-pleasers as

the Joker's Jinx steel coaster and Two Face—the Flip Side, a face-to-face roller coaster. The park features numerous Looney Tunes–themed attractions, including Looney Tunes Movietown, a rides area especially for young children. The 25-acre Paradise Island water park includes such attractions as Crocodile Cal's Outback Beach House and Monsoon Lagoon, a wave pool with waves up to four feet high.

Six Flags America is open weekends during early May and daily from Memorial Day weekend to Labor Day. Admission prices are $49.99 ($39.99 if you purchase online) for adults, $34.99 for children 53 inches and shorter, and free for children younger than age four. Parking costs $10. (See our Kidstuff chapter for a description of children's activities here.) The park reopens during October weekends and Halloween week for Hallowscream, featuring events such as hayrides, costume contests, and a haunted train.

We recommend avoiding Six Flags on weekends, particularly those featuring special events. Our experience on one such Saturday included long lines, malfunctioning rides, surly employees, and overflowing trash cans. Kids who visited the park during midweek camp outings, however, had no complaints.

Ballooning

How about a bird's-eye view of all that gorgeous green space we described earlier? The following FAA-certified pilots offer hot-air balloon excursions, complete with champagne and treats, at sunrise and sunset over the scenic Virginia and Maryland countrysides. Call at least a couple of weeks before the date you wish to book, and be flexible: Bad weather or high winds can whip up before you know it, forcing a postponement. Don't forget your video camera! Your pilot will be happy to recommend a bed-and-breakfast, should you want to extend your getaway.

Balloons Unlimited
2946-O Chain Bridge Road
Oakton, VA
(703) 281–2300
www.balloonsunlimited.com
Owner Bob Thomas has been piloting balloons above Middleburg and the Shenandoah region for 31 years. Flights cost $175 per person and last approximately an hour. Children accompanied by at least one adult are admitted for $100 (ages 12 and younger). You can book your trip for any day of the week, April through mid-November. Thomas also offers ballooning classes and sells balloons of the helium-filled variety at his Oakton store.

Bicycling

Bike the Sites
Old Post Office Pavilion
1100 Pennsylvania Avenue NW
Washington, DC
(202) 842–BIKE
www.bikethesites.com
The best way to see the monuments and memorials is by bike. You can cover a large distance in a short amount of time and get up close and personal with D.C.'s national treasures. Fortunately there's a tour company that recognizes this fact and offers daily guided excursions, as well as rentals for those who prefer touring alone. The three-hour Capital Sites tour, offered both during the day and at night, is priced at $40 for adults and $30 for children.

Virginia Bicycling Federation Inc.
P.O. Box 5621
Arlington, VA 22205
www.vabike.org
This advocacy organization promotes bicycling safety, keeping its members informed about such issues as road and trail improvements, new riding facilities, and legislation pertinent to cyclists. The bimonthly newsletter also includes information about upcoming rides and events sponsored by bicycling organizations throughout the state. Individual

membership is $18 annually, and a family can join for $30 a year.

Washington Area Bicyclist Association
1803 Connecticut Avenue NW, 3rd Floor
Washington, DC
(202) 518–0524
www.waba.org
Metro Washington boasts several bicycling clubs. The best way to find out more about them and discover which ones might be right for you is to contact this advocacy organization, which promotes safe bicycling conditions and greater bicycle use in the Metro Washington area. WABA, with more than 2,000 members, sponsors events like the National Capital Bicycle Tour and puts together newsletters and other publications. Membership is $35 per individual and $45 per family. Call to request a free copy of the *Bicycle Resource Directory,* listing clubs throughout the Washington area.

Bird-Watching

Audubon Naturalist Society of the Central Atlantic States Inc.
8940 Jones Mill Road
Chevy Chase, MD
(301) 652–9188
www.audubonnaturalist.org
Beginning bird walks take place at Woodend, the society's headquarters and 40-acre wildlife sanctuary, at 8:00 A.M. on Saturdays from September through June. Meet at the Audubon Naturalist store entrance. Call for directions and information about other birding events. Call (301) 652–1088 to hear the Voice of the Naturalist describing recent local bird sightings.

Audubon Society of Northern Virginia
4022 Hummer Road
Annandale, VA
(703) 256–6895
www.asnv.org
This organization sponsors frequent bird walks and educational programs, detailed in its *Potomac Flier* newsletter and on its Web site.

Society membership costs $20 annually and includes a subscription to *Audubon* magazine.

Bowling

Bowl America
10641 Balls Ford Road
Manassas, VA
(703) 368–6256

5615 Guinea Road
Burke, VA
(703) 425–9303

4525 Stonecroft Boulevard
Chantilly, VA
(703) 830–2695

46940 Woodson Drive
Sterling, VA
(703) 430–1350

9699 Lee Highway
Fairfax, VA
(703) 273–7700

140 South Maple Avenue
Falls Church, VA
(703) 534–1370

1101 Clopper Road
Gaithersburg, MD
(301) 330–5200

9000 Mathis Avenue
Manassas, VA
(703) 368–2161

6450 Edsall Road
Alexandria, VA
(703) 354–3300
Good, classic family fun abounds at this regional network of bowling alleys. On select evenings the lights go off and the lanes and balls glow in the dark for "Cosmic Bowling." Come during the week and enjoy unlimited bowling privileges from 9:00 P.M. to closing for just $10.99.

i Many bird-watchers enjoy participating in the annual Christmas Bird Count.

Lucky Strike Lanes
701 7th Street NW
Washington, DC
(202) 347–1340
www.bowlluckystrike.com/html_site/
locations/washington/washington.html
This is not your mother's bowling alley. Lucky Strike burst onto the D.C. nightlife scene in late 2005. Unlike the other bowling alleys on this list, there's a dress code here, and you won't find many children bowling after dark. The upscale vibe also translates to higher prices. Depending on when you come, expect to pay $4.95 to $7.95 per person per game and $3.95 for shoe rental. You can also rent lanes by the hour for $55 to $75. If you want to bowl on the weekend, call ahead for reservations.

National Duckpin Bowling Congress
4991 Fairview Avenue
Linthicum, MD
(410) 636–2695
www.ndbc.org
This organization just outside the Washington area can provide information about local lanes featuring duckpin bowling, a unique game featuring smaller, holeless balls (between three and four pounds each) and tiny pins. This variation got its start in Baltimore and continues to be a popular pastime in the Northeast. Young children especially enjoy the game, with its easily handled balls and three tries per frame.

Nation's Capital Area Bowling Association
9315 Largo Drive West, Suite 110
Largo, MD
(301) 499–1693
www.ncaba.org
Are you interested in joining an American Bowling Congress (ABC)–sanctioned league? Call for information about leagues in your community.

Chess

The U.S. Chess Center
1501 M Street NW
Washington, DC
(202) 857–4922
www.chessctr.org
Adults and children can take classes and participate in tournaments at this center in the heart of the city. It's open evenings, starting at 6:00 P.M., Monday through Thursday, and weekends, noon to 6:00 P.M. Chess enthusiasts shouldn't miss the center's free U.S. Chess Hall of Fame and Museum and gift shop.

Climbing

Adventure Schools Rock Climbing
Springfield, VA
(301) 263–0900, (800) 39–CLIMB
www.adventureschool.com
Before you attempt to scale those inviting formations at Great Falls and other local parks, learn from an expert. Expert instructors give lessons for beginners and advanced students, generally taking folks on-site for a day of hands-on education at Carderock Park in Maryland or Great Falls Park in Virginia. They provide all the necessary equipment, too. A one-day, eight-hour course for ages 11 and older is $95; a two-day session is $210. Owner Dave Nugent also leads climbing adventures in places like West Virginia and Looking Glass, North Carolina. Call for a course catalog. The climbing school is based at Potomac Outdoors, Ltd., which also offers merchandise, white-water canoe and kayaking trips, and backcountry skiing and snow camping sessions.

Sportrock Climbing Centers
5308 Eisenhower Avenue
Alexandria, VA

45935 Maries Road
Sterling, VA

14708 Southlawn Lane
Rockville, MD
(703) 212–7625
www.sportrock.com
These indoor climbing facilities feature 30- and 40-foot walls with a multitude of routes. Novices can learn beginning climbing skills, and more experienced climbers can hone their tech-

niques with indoor practice sessions. The centers are open noon to 11:00 P.M. Tuesday through Friday and noon to 8:00 P.M. Saturdays and Sundays. Daily rates are $18.00 for adults and $7.00 for ages 12 and younger. Discount passes and memberships also are available, along with rental gear and special beginners' sessions. (See our Kidstuff chapter for information about children's programs here.)

Dancing

Glen Echo Park
7300 MacArthur Boulevard
Glen Echo, MD
(301) 492–6282
www.glenechopark.org
The 74-year-old Spanish Ballroom at this former amusement park turned national park still possesses the same 7,500-square-foot sprung maple floor upon which dancers swayed to the sounds of big bands led by the likes of the Dorseys and Artie Shaw. In the summer of 2003, the ballroom reopened to oohs and aahs after an extensive renovation, which has the building looking brand-new. Today it's the local hot spot for swing dancing, but you also can take your pick from several other dances offered on a regular basis. Best of all, all events take place in a smoke- and alcohol-free atmosphere.

Friday nights feature traditional country dances like contras, squares, and mixers from 8:30 to 11:30 P.M., usually at $8.00 a person. Two left feet? Show up an hour early, March through October, and you'll get a lesson in beginning contra dancing, included in the admission fee.

"Big Night Out" Saturdays attract as many as 600 people who relish swing dancing. Dances run from 9:00 P.M. to midnight, preceded by a beginners' workshop at 8:00 P.M. Admission is usually $13. The second Saturday of each month generally features Louisiana-style dancing.

Most Sunday afternoons feature ballroom-style dancing from 3:30 to 6:00 P.M. at $8.00 per person, preceded by waltz lessons at 3:00 P.M.

(Check out the Arts and Kidstuff chapters for more of this unique park's features, including an antique carousel, children's shows, a museum, and art studios.)

Northern Virginia Country Western Dance Association
P.O. Box 384
Merrifield, VA 22116
(703) 860–4941
nvcwda.com
Looking for a place to show off your Two Step or learn the latest line dance? This 500-member organization—annual membership is $18—sponsors at least two dances per month at various area community centers. Featuring a nonsmoking, family-oriented atmosphere, the events include free lessons. Admission generally runs $8.00 for members, $10.00 for nonmembers, and $5.00 for young people younger than 20 years.

Golfing

Our region offers numerous attractive and challenging public golf courses, many operated by local park authorities. We can't begin to list them all, but here's a representative sampling. Most offer discounted greens fees for youths and seniors. Be sure to check our Spectator Sports chapter for information about the professional golf scene.

Washington, D.C.

East Potomac Park Golf Course and Driving Range
Hains Point and Ohio Drive SW
Washington, DC
(202) 554–7660
www.golfdc.com
How about a game of golf in the shadow of the Washington Monument? You'll aim right at the towering obelisk on the ninth hole of the recently renovated par 27, Red Course, which has a yardage of 1311. You'll also see the familiar landmark in the background of the ninth hole on the 18-hole regulation, par 72 Blue Course, which has a yardage of 6600

from the blue tees and 6197 from the white tees. The ninth-hole regulation White Course is par 34, with a yardage of 2505. Set on National Park Service land next to the Potomac, the flat course is open year-round, generally from dawn to dusk.

Weekday greens fees are $9 to $22 for 9 holes and $20 for 18 holes; weekends and holidays, fees are $12 to $18 for 9 holes and $27 for 18 holes. Power carts are available for $22 for 18 holes. Rent a pull cart for $3.50 for 9 holes and $4.50 for 18 holes. Rental clubs, available in half-sets, are $9.00 for 9 holes and $12 for 18. A double-deck, 100-station driving range is partially covered and heated during winter. A range token costs $5.50. The course also has a snack bar and grill and a fully stocked pro shop. Hours vary seasonally, but generally run 7:00 A.M. to 10:00 P.M. Thursdays through Tuesdays, 10:00 A.M. to 10:00 P.M. Wednesdays, May through September.

Also on-site, East Potomac Mini Golf dates to the early 1920s and claims to be the nation's longest-running miniature golf operation. With each hole a par 3, it's probably one of the area's most challenging courses. The designs include such features as multiple levels and a spiraling shot. Native stonework and ponds with goldfish, water lilies, and a bridge highlight the landscaping. It's open 11:00 A.M. to 7:00 P.M. on Saturday and Sunday only, with admission priced at $5.00 for adults and $4.00 for children.

Langston Golf Course and Driving Range
26th and Benning Road NE
Washington, DC
(202) 397–8638
www.golfdc.com
This 18-hole, par 72 course features tree-lined fairways and three holes with water. The total yardage is 6340. Look for the "Joe Louis Tree," which the "Brown Bomber" always hit, on hole number 3. The facility includes a pro shop, snack bar, and recently renovated, partially covered driving range. Fees are about the same as those at East Potomac.

Rock Creek Park Golf Course
16th and Rittenhouse Streets NW
Washington, DC
(202) 882–7332
www.golfdc.com
Here's another of Rock Creek Park's many surprises: a hilly, wooded golf course in the middle of the city. The 18-hole, par 65 course has a yardage of 4800. Its signature hole, number 17, features a downhill par 3 to a narrow fairway. The course has a snack bar and pro shop but no driving range. Fees are similar to those at the previously mentioned courses.

Northern Virginia

Burke Lake Golf Center
7315 Ox Road
Fairfax Station, VA
(703) 323–1641
www.co.fairfax.va.us/parks/golf/burkegolf.htm
Adjacent to popular Burke Lake Park, this 18-hole, par 54 course with 2539 yardage boasts a pleasant lakeside setting. It features a putting green and lighted driving range, along with a full-service clubhouse. Tee times for this and six other Fairfax County Park Authority courses can be arranged through an automated phone-in system, with a $26 annual subscription. Burke offers private and group lessons and a Junior Golf Program for youngsters ages 5 to 17. Fees are $14 to $16 for 9 holes, and $20 to $23 for 18 holes, depending on the time you play. Rent clubs for $5.00 to $8.00.

Burke Lake Golf Center is one of six courses operated by the Fairfax County Park Authority throughout Fairfax County.

Pohick Bay Regional Park Golf Course
10301 Gunston Road
Lorton, VA
(703) 339–8585
www.nvrpa.org/pohickbaygolf.html
One of three Northern Virginia Regional Park Authority courses—the others are the 701-yard Algonkian in Sterling and 6764-yard Brambleton in Ashburn—recently renovated Pohick Bay takes pride in being rated by golf

magazines as one of the area's most challenging courses. The hilly, 18-hole, par 72 course with narrow fairways features a 6405 yardage. Reserve tee times by phone or in person at 3:00 P.M. seven days in advance. The course also features a driving range, pro shop, and snack bar. Fees are $20 to $27 for 9 holes and $30.50 to $42.50 for 18 holes, with discounts for play after 2:00 P.M. Power carts cost $9.00 to $14.20 per rider; pull carts, $3.00 or $4.00.

Raspberry Falls Golf & Hunt Club
41601 Raspberry Drive
Leesburg, VA
(703) 779–2555
www.raspberryfalls.com
Gary Player designed this 11-year-old, 18-hole, par 72 course, noted for its challenging play, abundance of bent grass, and stunning views of the surrounding Hunt Country. Yardage is 7191, with a 134 slope. Hole number 3, a challenging par 4, features an elevated tee box with an outstanding view. Fees for 18-hole play range from $78 to $98 and include a rental cart. Call up to eight days in advance to arrange a tee time. You'll find the club off U.S. 15, just 3 miles north of Leesburg. It also houses a pro shop, full grill, and driving range with practice sand bunkers and a chipping green.

Reston National Golf Course
11875 Sunrise Valley Drive
Reston, VA
(703) 620–9333
www.virginiagolf.com/restonnational.html
This 18-hole, par 71 course, noted for its tree-lined fairways, is one of the Metro Washington area's top-ranked public golf courses, according to the *Washington Post* and *Washington Flyer* magazine. Yardage from the middle tee is 6506. The 460-yard, par 4 hole number 10 proves most challenging, with an elevated green guarded by two bunkers. Although not required, tee times preferably are made a week in advance at this bustling course. The course has a driving range and putting and

chipping greens, as well as a snack bar and pro shop. Fees, including carts, run $69 to $89 on weekends, $49 to $55 Monday through Thursday, and $59 to $75 on Fridays. The course also features an enclosed deck for parties and a state-of-the-art irrigation system costing nearly $1 million.

Suburban Maryland

Needwood Golf Course
6724 Needwood Road
Rockville, MD
(301) 948–1075
www.montgomerycountygolf.com
Needwood is a par 71, 18- and 9-hole executive course with a yardage of 6300 from the back tee. The front is flatter than the back, and there's water on the back nine holes. Fees for 18 holes vary from $25 to $56, depending on the day, player's age, and whether or not a cart is required. The course includes a pro shop with snack bar, putting green, driving range, and a resident pro who gives lessons.

Trotters Glen Family Golf Center
16501 Batchellors Forest Road
Olney, MD
(301) 570–4951
www.trottersglengolf.com
On the number 11 hole at this 18-hole, par 72 course, a player must hit a perfect tee shot to avoid a water pond to the right and woods to the left. The course has a 6220 yardage. Amenities include a practice area, putting and chipping greens, pro shop, snack bar, and golf school. Call seven days in advance to make a required tee time. Fees are $31 and under and include a cart. The site also includes a bed-and-breakfast inn.

Hang Gliding

Silver Wings Inc.
6032 North 20th Street
Arlington, VA
(703) 533–1965
silverwingshanggliding.com
If you get the urge to soar like an eagle after

your visit to Mason Neck State Park, consider learning how to hang glide. John Middleton, a U.S. hang gliding certified instructor, runs the area's only hang gliding school. Beginners start at Ground School, a $10, 90-minute class in which Middleton shows videos and describes the sport. He offers flight classes, complete with essential equipment, on Saturdays and Sundays, usually from around 10:00 A.M. to 5:00 P.M. or 6:00 P.M. Students carpool to a training site, where they start on small hills. Classes are $80 each per person. Most folks need five to eight lessons before they get the "hang" of it.

Ice Skating

Equity Office Skating Pavilion
Reston Town Center, 1818 Discovery Street
Reston, VA
(703) 709–6300
www.restontowncenter.com/pavilion.html
At ever-growing Reston Town Center, this elegant, glass-domed, open-sided pavilion is Northern Virginia's answer to Rockefeller Center, complete with a huge Christmas tree across the street. A visit to the rink is one of our favorite winter outings, whether we attempt to skate or just sip hot cocoa and watch those who know what they're doing. Public skating takes place usually from early November until the weather warms up. Hours are from 11:00 A.M. to 11:00 P.M. on Fridays, 10:00 A.M. to 11:00 P.M. on Saturdays, 10:00 A.M. to 7:00 P.M. on Sundays, and 11:00 A.M. to 7:00 or 9:00 P.M. Monday through Thursday. A two-hour session is $8.00 for adults and $7.00 for kids and seniors. Skate rentals are $3.00, and you can borrow free helmets for the little ones. You also can purchase season passes and discount books. Lessons for various skill levels take place before and after public sessions. In the summer the pavilion hosts open-air concerts on Thursday and Saturday nights.

Fairfax Ice Arena
3779 Pickett Road
Fairfax, VA
(703) 323–1132
www.fairfaxicearena.com
U.S. National Champion and World Bronze Medalist Michael Weiss has trained at this popular indoor skating facility. Call for a schedule of public skating, offered daily at varying times. Sessions cost $5.25 to $7.25, and skate rental is $2.50. Open for more than 30 years, the arena offers private and group lessons for all skill levels, holds an annual competition, and occasionally hosts ice shows. Weiss's former coach, Audrey Weisiger, named 1999 Coach of the Year by the United States Figure Skating Association, is a staff member. An in-house adult ice-hockey league plays fall/winter and spring/summer seasons. The Skating Club of Northern Virginia, an organization for competitive skaters, practices here.

The Gardens Ice House
13800 Old Gunpowder Road
Laurel, MD
(301) 953–0100
www.thegardensicehouse.com
The huge indoor facility—the largest of its kind in the region—features three rinks: the 200-by-100-foot Olympic-size Resor Rink and two 200-by-85-foot NHL rinks, the Patrick and the Logsdon. The Patrick seats 700 spectators, while the other two each seat 100. A planned expansion will double the Patrick's seating capacity. The site also houses a Wellness for Life Fitness Center and a cafe. Public skating times vary daily, but Fridays from 8:00 to 10:00 P.M. generally feature a light show and disc jockey, and on the third Sunday of each month, visitors can skate with a costumed mascot from 1:00 to 3:00 P.M. General admission is $5.00 on weekdays, $6.00 Friday night through Sunday. Skate rental is $3.50. The rinks host numerous hockey events. Olympic gold medalist Scott Hamilton's former coach, Donald Laws, directs the figure-

skating program, in which Olympic-caliber athletes like Michael Weiss train.

National Gallery of Art Sculpture Garden Ice-Skating Rink
Constitution Avenue, between 3rd and 9th Streets NW
Washington, DC
(202) 289–3360
www.nga.gov/ginfo/skating.htm
Visit the area's newest outdoor skating rink and enjoy skating with a view. The rink sits amid the Sculpture Garden's intriguing works of art. Open mid-November through mid-March, the rink features two-hour sessions from 10:00 A.M. to 9:00 P.M. Monday through Thursday, 10:00 A.M. to 11:00 P.M. Friday and Saturday, and 11:00 A.M. to 9:00 P.M. Sunday. Admission is $7.00 for adults, $6.00 for children ages 12 and younger, seniors ages 50 and older, and students with IDs. Skate rental is $3.00, and locker rental is 50 cents. The Pavilion Cafe serves light meals and beverages.

Pershing Park Ice Rink
Pennsylvania Avenue and 14th Street NW
Washington, DC
(202) 737–6938
www.pershingparkicerink.com
Skate under the stars at this popular rink, right across the street from the elegant Willard InterContinental hotel and just steps from the city's theater district. For a picture-perfect holiday outing in December, hit the ice after visiting the National Christmas Tree and Pageant of Peace on the Ellipse, only a couple of blocks away. The rink is open early December until the ice starts to melt, usually early March. Two-hour sessions take place from 11:00 A.M. to 9:00 P.M. Monday through Thursday and from 11:00 A.M. to 11:00 P.M. Friday, Saturday, and Sunday. Admission is $6.50 for adults and $5.50 for children; figure-skate rental is $2.50. Parking is scarce, so you're better off taking the Metro to nearby Federal Triangle or Metro Center.

Kites

Maryland Kite Society
10113 Lloyd Road
Potomac, MD
www.mdkites.org
The second-oldest kite club in the United States, this 150-member, American Kitefliers Association–affiliated group began almost 40 years ago to spoof a distinguished poet's society. AKA 1998 Grand National Champion Tanna Haynes, a Pennsylvania resident, belongs to the club. Annual $10 membership includes a subscription to a quarterly newsletter. The club sponsors the Great St. John's Kite Festival, the annual Maryland Kite Retreat kite-making workshop during President's Weekend in February, and a monthly kite fly.

Wings Over Washington (WOW)
www.wowkiteclub.com
An affiliate of AKA, this active local club sponsors monthly kite flies behind the Washington Monument (look for Captain WOW, a huge soccer player) and sometimes holds kite-making workshops. Annual membership, which includes a quarterly newsletter and retailer discounts, is $15 ($10 renewal) per individual, $20 ($15 renewal) per household. Check the Web site for information.

Orienteering

Quantico Orienteering Club
6212 Thomas Drive
Springfield, VA
(703) 528–INFO
qoc.nova.org
This club sponsors map hikes and orienteering events for all ages and skill levels throughout the Metro Washington and Baltimore area. An annual membership costs $20 per individual or $30 per family.

Outdoor Sports

Washington Women Outdoors Inc.
19450 Caravan Drive
Germantown, MD
(301) 864–3070
www.washingtonwomenoutdoors.org
This nonprofit organization offers instruction in outdoor sports, by women and for women. All skill levels are welcome to participate in such outings as hiking and backpacking, bicycling, rock climbing, canoeing, and kayaking. Nonmembers are welcome, but members get discounts, as well as newsletters, use of equipment, and other perks. Basic annual membership is $30.

Running

American Running Association
4405 East–West Highway, Suite 405
Bethesda, MD
(301) 913–9517, (800) 776–2732
www.americanrunning.org
With so many wonderful park trails and pleasant streets at their disposal, many Washingtonians choose running as their favorite way to exercise. This nonprofit, national association promotes the benefits of running and other aerobic exercise for fitness. Membership, $35 annually, includes a monthly newsletter; discounts on books, travel, and programs; free trail maps; and other benefits. Contact the organization for a list of more than 50 running clubs in Metro Washington.

Road Runners Club of America
8965 Guilford Road, Suite 150
Columbia, MD
(410) 290–3890
www.rrca.org
If you're a long-distance runner, you'll be interested in this national association of non-profit running clubs. RRCA educates runners on different facets of the sport, supports legislation that benefits runners, and publishes a quarterly newsletter. Contact the national headquarters for a list of more than 25 member clubs in the Washington/Baltimore area.

Sailing

The Mariner Sailing School
Belle Haven Marina, Inc., P.O. Box 7093
Alexandria, VA 22307
(703) 768–0018
www.saildc.com
You'll find the biggest sailing school in the Metro Washington area just off the George Washington Memorial Parkway. Qualified sailors teach hands-on classes in adult basic sailing; youth (ages 8 to 15) basic and intermediate sailing; windsurfing; cruising; and racing. The facility is an authorized American Red Cross provider, as well as a charter member of U.S. Sailing's Commercial Sailing Program. Call for class schedules and rates.

Washington Sailing Marina
1 Marina Drive
Alexandria, VA
(703) 548–9027
www.washingtonsailingmarina.com
The Washington Sailing Marina, about 1½ miles south of Ronald Reagan Washington National Airport, will rent you a cute little Sunfish sailboat for $10 an hour or a 19-foot Flying Scot for $19 an hour.

Soccer

Northern Virginia

Fairfax Women's Soccer Association
Fairfax County, VA
(703) 550–4107
www.fwsasoccer.org
Players of all skill levels are welcome in this league of 900 women in three age groups: Open for age 18 and older, Master for age 30 and older, Grand Master for age 40 and older, and Great-Grand Master for age 50 and older. Teams play April through June and September through November, usually 10 games per season. Most games take place Saturdays on Fairfax County soccer fields. Registration is $61 for county residents, $81 for out-of-county residents.

Sports Network
8320 Quarry Road
Manassas, VA
(703) 335–1555
www.sports-network.com
This indoor soccer arena holds year-round leagues, mostly for adults, and winter youth leagues and summer camps. Volleyball and lacrosse teams also play here. Call for a schedule.

Virginia's Coed Sports and Recreation Association, Inc.
P.O. Box 3050
Merrifield, VA 22116
www.coedfun.org
Metro Washington's largest coed adult soccer league includes about 500 people on 24 teams that play outdoors March through November. Registration generally costs $1,150 per team for 24 games. Games take place seven nights a week in Burke, Virginia. Registration is available on a first-come, first-served basis. Usually, men's spots fill up more quickly than women's. Affiliated with the U.S. Soccer Federation, the league also sponsors at least two big annual tournaments that draw approximately 45 teams from the area and other states.

Suburban Maryland

Maryland SoccerPlex and Discovery Sports Center
South Germantown Recreational Park
18031 Central Park Circle
Boyds, MD
(301) 528–1480
www.mdsoccerplex.org
Local teams flock to this huge sports complex in west-central Montgomery County. You'll find about 20 outdoor fields, including an 80-by-20-yard championship stadium, at this ever-growing site, a joint venture of the Maryland Soccer Foundation and the Maryland-National Capital Park and Planning Commission. The neighboring Discovery Sports Center, a 66,000-square-foot indoor

i If you like to run, you should try "hashing," a combination of recreational jogging and recreational drinking with roots in Australia and a growing following in several major cities—including Washington. Log on to www.dchashing .com to learn more.

facility, accommodates not only indoor soccer, but also basketball, volleyball, lacrosse, field hockey, baseball, and flag football, as well as special programs, a cafe, and health and wellness activities such as Xtreme Acceleration training. See the South Germantown Recreational Park listing for information about the surrounding park.

Ultimate Frisbee

Washington Area Frisbee Club (WAFC)
1808 North Quantico Street
Arlington, VA 22205
(301) 588–2629
www.wafc.org
Kind of like football played with a flying disc, Ultimate Frisbee boasts quite a following in Metro Washington, judging from WAFC's membership of 2,300. The club sponsors spring, summer (most popular), and fall/winter coed leagues for a range of skill levels. Serious players participate in WAFC's traveling teams, while folks looking for informal play usually can find pickup games on Saturday and Sunday afternoons at the Ellipse in D.C. Most league games take place on the Anacostia Park Fields or on the National Mall. League fees vary, and members can buy their own Frisbees through the club. Call for more information.

Yoga

Mid-Atlantic Yoga Association, Inc.
P.O. Box 30850
Alexandria, VA 22310
(703) 822–9389
www.mayayoga.org
Take a deep breath, relax, and contact MAYA to learn all about this unique way to exercise mind and body. Student membership is $30,

i Keep track of upcoming hikes, runs, and cycling events; recreational club activities; amateur sports leagues; and classes in such areas as diving and kayaking by checking out "On the Move" listings in the *Washington Post's* Weekend section.

while teachers pay an annual fee of $40. Benefits include the nonprofit corporation's quarterly newsletter, discounts on educational events, and opportunities to attend yoga exchanges.

Sun & Moon Yoga Studio
3811 Lee Highway
Arlington, VA

9998 Main Street
Fairfax, VA
(703) 525–YOGA
www.sunandmoonstudio.com
One of the region's most popular yoga studios, Sun & Moon offers a full slate of hatha yoga classes for beginners and experienced students, as well as certification programs for budding teachers. Both the Arlington and Fairfax studios are spacious, quiet, and calming, and the instructors are among the best.

Tranquil Space
2024 P Street NW
Washington, DC
(202) 223–9642
www.tranquilspace.com
Drop in for vinyasa classes in this cozy Dupont Circle studio. It's easy to find a class time that suits you; there are eight classes offered daily Monday through Thursday and Saturday, five classes on the Friday schedule, and six more on Sunday. Owner Kimberly Wilson is more than just a yogini; she also designed a line of comfortable, affordable fashions that are appropriate for yoga class or a day on the town including some that would even work for the office. They're available for sale at the studio. Drop-in classes are $17, and discounts are available if you buy a series of three or more classes.

Youth Sports

Ready to become a soccer mom—or dad? Your best bet for locating a youth sports organization that's just right for your child is to call your local recreation center. (See our list in this chapter.) They frequently sponsor their own leagues and can point you in the direction of groups in the area. Don't overlook smaller neighborhood pools and community centers, most of which offer competitive team sports and instruction.

PARKS AND RECREATION AUTHORITIES

Many of the area's recreational opportunities can be found through national, regional, and state park authorities and through community departments of parks and recreation. Here's a rundown of Metro Washington's major parks and recreation authorities and community centers. All the recreation departments and community centers listed here, unless otherwise stated, offer after-school and seniors' activities, enrichment classes, sports instruction, gymnasiums, pools, exercise programs, leagues for kids and adults, and recreational excursions. Contact them or check their Web sites to receive their latest programming guides.

Washington, D.C.

District of Columbia Department of Parks and Recreation
3149 16th Street NW
Washington, DC
(202) 673–7647
www.dpr.dc.gov
The department oversees more than 70 neighborhood recreation centers, the recently renovated Anacostia Wellness/Fitness Recreation Center, seven indoor swimming pools, 57 tennis courts, three therapeutic recreation centers, and many park spaces.

National Park Service National
Capital Region
1100 Ohio Drive SW
Washington, DC
(202) 619–7111/7256
www.nps.gov/ncro
The National Park Service oversees more
than 6,500 acres of park space in Washington, D.C. and the surrounding area, along
with such landmarks as Ford's Theatre and
Frederick Douglass National Historic Sites;
FDR, Korean War Veterans, Lincoln, Thomas
Jefferson, and Vietnam Veterans Memorials;
the Washington Monument; and the White
House.

Northern Virginia

Alexandria Department of Recreation, Parks
and Cultural Activities
1108 Jefferson Street
Alexandria, VA
(703) 838–4343
alexandriava.gov/recreation
The department has seven neighborhood
recreation centers, including Mount Vernon
Recreation Center and Nannie J. Lee Recreation Center. Chinquapin Park and Recreation
Center boasts a 25-meter indoor pool and
diving well. The department also oversees 12
major parks, the City Marina, seasonal special events, camps, and weekend nature programs at Jerome "Buddie" Ford Nature
Center, 5700 Sanger Avenue, (703) 838–4829
(currently undergoing renovation).

Arlington County Department of Parks,
Recreation and Community Resources
2100 Clarendon Boulevard, Suite 414
Arlington, VA
(703) 228–3323
www.arlingtonva.us/departments/
parksrecreation/parksrecreationmain.aspx
Arlington's department oversees 13 community centers, three year-round swimming
pools, two nature centers, Virginia Cooperative Extension programs, a 68,000-square-
foot fitness facility, and six parks with picnic
pavilions.

i Pontoon-boat tours of several parks'
lakes offer excellent opportunities to
view wildlife such as herons and turtles.

City of Fairfax Parks and Recreation
John C. Wood Complex
3730 Old Lee Highway (U.S. 29)
Fairfax, VA
(703) 385–7858
www.fairfaxva.gov/ParksRec/ParksRec.asp
The department sponsors 21 parks, including
the 48-acre Daniels Run Park and 20-acre Van
Dyck Park; a network of recreational trails for
bikers, walkers, and runners; the City of Fairfax Band and other arts programs, including
free summer concerts and performances at
Old Town Hall, 3999 University Drive; and seasonal celebrations. The city does not have a
swimming pool.

City of Manassas Department of Recreation
and Parks
8957 Center Street
Manassas, VA
(703) 257–8237
www.manassascity.org/index.asp?nid=18
This department sponsors tours, special
events, and classes and oversees community
gym programs at two local schools.

City of Manassas Park Department of Parks
Recreation
99 Adams Street
Manassas Park, VA
(703) 335–8872
www.cityofmanassaspark.us
This department offers special events,
classes, sports leagues, and two pools.

Fairfax County Department of Community
and Recreation Services
12011 Government Center Parkway,
10th Floor
Fairfax, VA
(703) 324–4386
www.fairfaxcounty.gov/living/parks
Not to be confused with the county park

Great Falls Park: Where the Water Falls

There are few sights that compare to the Potomac's Great Falls, located just upstream from Washington, D.C. along the historic C&O Canal. Watching the water roar through Mather Gorge, tumbling over rocks and boulders, you wouldn't know that it's the same gentle river that separates the Nation's Capital from Arlington. At full throttle, 134,000 cubic feet of water pass through the falls each second, dropping 76 feet through a series of rapids-like falls.

Although most people who visit today come here for a vigorous hike or mountain-biking path, there's also a lot of history to discover. In 1784 the Patowmack Company was established to construct a series of five canals—America's first canal system—to bypass the portions of the river that could not be navigated. Backed by several influential investors (including George Washington), the Patowmack Canal received its first shipments in 1802.

For 26 years, the canal transported furs, tobacco, corn, whiskey, and timber up and down the 190-mile canal. It took three days for the canal's 75-foot, mule-drawn barges to travel from the easternmost point in Georgetown to the westernmost point in Cumberland, Maryland. The Patowmack Canal was bought up by the Chesapeake and Ohio Canal Company in 1828. The slow traffic on the canal, however, was no match for the speedy Baltimore & Ohio Railroad, which was under development at the same time.

Although the canal was gradually passed over for the railroad, it made its mark on the banks of the Potomac. Settlers built homes at various points along

authority, Community and Recreation Services offers a wide variety of quarterly hobby and recreational classes—everything from aerobics and art to weight training and yoga—for Fairfax City and County residents. Most activities take place after hours at schools. The program also operates 7 community centers, 9 teen centers, 13 senior centers, therapeutic recreation services, and summer camps. The department shares its quarterly catalog with Fairfax County Public Schools' Office of Adult and Community Education.

Fairfax County Park Authority
12055 Government Center Parkway, Suite 927
Fairfax, VA
(703) 324–8700
www.fairfaxcounty.gov/parks/parks.htm

This massive park authority oversees more than 350 parks on more than 16,000 acres, including 11 multiple-purpose parks and numerous neighborhood and community parks. Eight full-service recreation centers, 12 historical or archaeological sites, 5 golf courses, 3 miniature golf courses, and a countywide farmers' market program also fall under the park authority's jurisdiction.

Falls Church Recreation and Parks
223 Little Falls Street
Falls Church, VA
(703) 248–5077
www.ci.falls-church.va.us/community/
recsandparks.html
Based at the Falls Church Community Center, the department sponsors a variety of classes, an adult gym program, a Saturday farmers'

the route in planned settlements. One such settlement, Mathildaville, grew up at Great Falls and flourished for nearly 30 years. Mathildaville was sponsored by Revolutionary War hero "Light Horse" Harry Lee, a friend of Washington who named the town in honor of his first wife. The town gradually disappeared, but visitors to the Virginia side of Great Falls Park can see its remnants, just downstream from the falls.

Yes, there are two sides of the park: Virginia and Maryland. On the Maryland side, you'll find a great deal of historic interpretation, including a mule-drawn canal barge and living-history reenactments. You'll also find the infamous Billy Goat Trail, a rigorous hiking and rock-scrambling trail known to challenge D.C.'s hardiest weekend warriors.

The views are spectacular from both sides of the river, but some seem to think that Virginia offers a prettier picture. You'll also find a nature center and a full slate of naturalist-led hikes and activities, along with the remains of Mathildaville.

Although swimming and wading are prohibited on both sides of the river, there's no shortage of outdoor recreation opportunities. Bicyclists can tackle the rugged bike paths. Hikers can explore the network of rugged trails. Rock climbers won't be able to resist the fascinating geological formations. For lighter adventures, there's plenty of room for picnicking or a game of Frisbee, and you'll find plenty of birds and wildflowers to admire. You won't believe that the city is so close by.

market, bike trails, nine parks, and numerous seasonal events, many of which take place at the historic Cherry Hill Farmhouse, 312 Park Avenue, (703) 248–5171. The department does not offer swimming. Its events schedule also lists offerings of the Office of Community Education, 7124 Leesburg Pike, (703) 241–7676.

Herndon Parks and Recreation
814 Ferndale Avenue
Herndon, VA
(703) 435–6868
www.herndon-va.gov/parks.html
Headquartered at the Herndon Community Center, this department offers extensive aquatics classes, nature walks at Runnymede Park, a children's performance series, and numerous special interest and fitness activi-

ties. A "bubble" tops the center's tennis courts from the end of October through March.

Loudoun County Department of Parks, Recreation, and Community Services
215 Depot Court SE
Leesburg, VA
(703) 777–0343
www.co.loudoun.va.us/prcs/
The department owns or oversees more than 15 parks and 11 community centers offering a variety of programs. Three developing historic sites also fall under the division's jurisdiction.

Northern Virginia Regional Park Authority
5400 Ox Road
Fairfax Station, VA
(703) 352–5900
www.nvrpa.org
The park authority's vast network includes 17 parks, the Bull Run–Occoquan Trail, historic Carlyle House, 4 regional park swimming pools, 3 golf courses, 6 miniature golf courses, and areas for boating and camping.

Prince William County Park Authority
14420 Bristow Road
Manassas, VA
(703) 792–7060
www.pwcparks.org
The park authority oversees 46 parks, 4 public golf courses, community centers, and the Chinn Aquatics and Fitness Center and Splash Down and Waterworks water park.

Reston Community Center
2310 Colts Neck Road
Reston, VA
(703) 476–4500
www.restoncommunitycenter.com
This center, serving the community in western Fairfax County, includes an indoor pool, art exhibits, and a theater that hosts performances by its resident theatrical troupe and nationally known performers.

Town of Leesburg Department of
Parks and Recreation
50 Ida Lee Drive NW
Leesburg, VA
(703) 777–1368
www.idalee.org/parks
The department's 16 parks include the 138-acre Ida Lee Park, the site of Ida Lee Recreation Center and a diverse aquatics program. The department also sponsors numerous seasonal events. In-line skaters, bikers, and skateboarders frequent the Catoctin Street Skate Park in the center of town.

Town of Vienna Parks and Recreation
Department
120 Cherry Street SE
Vienna, VA
(703) 255–6360
www.viennava.gov/town_departments/
pr3.htm
Most activities take place at the community center, which includes a teen center and boasts an outdoor bocce ball court. The department also oversees four parks, the Vienna Community Band, and numerous special events. Swimming is not available.

Virginia Department of Conservation and
Recreation
203 Governor Street, Suite 302
Richmond, VA
(800) 933–PARK
www.dcr.state.va.us
Contact the department for information about its 44 state parks and natural areas.

Suburban Maryland

City of Laurel Department of Parks
and Recreation
Laurel Municipal Center
8103 Sandy Spring Road
Laurel, MD
(301) 725–7800
www.laurel.md.us/parks.htm
Laurel's department oversees two community centers, a golf and recreation center, an outdoor municipal pool, a senior center, playing fields, and the Granville Gude Park and Lakehouse at 8300 Mulberry Street, Laurel, (301) 490–3530.

City of Rockville Recreation and
Parks Department ·
111 Maryland Avenue
Rockville, MD
(240) 314–8620
www.rockvillemd.gov
This department oversees more than 50 parks, including a new skate park, and several community centers in Montgomery County's large city of Rockville.

Greenbelt Recreation Department
25 Crescent Road
Greenbelt, MD
(301) 397–2200
www.greenbeltmd.gov
Greenbelt's facilities include an aquatics and fitness center, community center, youth center, and recreation center, as well as two parks available for community rentals.

Maryland Department of Natural Resources/State Forest and Park Service
580 Taylor Avenue, E-3
Annapolis, MD
(410) 260–8186
www.dnr.state.md.us/publiclands
Call the department for information about its 280,000 acres of public parks and forests.

Maryland-National Capital Park and Planning Commission
Montgomery County Department of Parks and Planning
8787 Georgia Avenue
Silver Spring, MD
(301) 495–4610
www.mc-mncppc.org

Prince George's County Department of Parks and Recreation
6600 Kenilworth Avenue
Riverdale, MD
(301) 699–2407
www.pgparks.com
This massive department, covering all of Suburban Maryland, includes numerous parks and, in Prince George's County, community centers. You'll also find historic sites, nature centers, and golf courses.

Montgomery Recreation Department
12210 Bushey Drive
Silver Spring, MD
(240) 777–6804
www.montgomerycountymd.gov/rec
Contact this department for information about its nine swimming pools, more than a dozen community centers, and numerous special programs such as summer camps.

Takoma Park Recreation Department
7500 Maple Avenue
Takoma Park, MD
(301) 891–7290
tprecreation.org
Facilities include a community center, municipal gym, four parks, and two playing fields. Swimming is not available.

JEWISH COMMUNITY CENTERS

These full-service community centers require membership, which is open to anyone. Many special events are open to nonmembers for a fee.

Washington, D.C.

District of Columbia Jewish Community Center
1529 16th Street NW
Washington, DC
(202) 518–9400
www.washingtondcjcc.org
Housed in the extensively renovated original JCC building built in the 1920s, the city's modern JCC offers a wide range of programs, including an arts center, children's after-school and camp programs, an early childhood and parenting center, a library, and activities for all ages. Health and fitness features include a pool, gymnasium, racquetball and squash courts, an aerobics and dance studio, steam room, and exercise equipment and training.

Northern Virginia

Jewish Community Center of Northern Virginia
8900 Little River Turnpike
Fairfax, VA
(703) 323–0880
www.jccnv.org
The center boasts an indoor pool, regulation-size gymnasium, fitness room, library, and auditorium for entertainment and community events. The JCC hosts a variety of programs for all ages, including an early childhood pro-

gram, before- and after-school care, and summer camps. Many events are open to non-members.

Suburban Maryland

Jewish Community Center of Greater Washington
6125 Montrose Road
Rockville, MD
(301) 881–0100
www.jccgw.org
The JCC's facilities include a sports and fitness center with indoor and outdoor pools, exercise equipment, a steam room, and courts for handball, racquetball, squash, and basketball. Men's and women's health clubs are available for additional membership fees. JCC programs include preschool and kinder-

garten, summer camps and after-school activities, classes and special events for all ages, a library, and a cultural arts series.

YMCA

YMCA of Metropolitan Washington
1112 16th Street NW, 7th Floor
Washington, DC
(202) 232–6700
www.ymcadc.org
This membership association holds a variety of fitness, recreation, camp, and child-care programs at its area branches, including four in Washington, D.C., five in Northern Virginia, and seven in Suburban Maryland. Call to find the nearest location.

DAY TRIPS AND WEEKEND GETAWAYS

Let's not kid ourselves. Scores—if not hundreds—of books have been written about daytripping and weekend frolicking in and around the Nation's Capital—and for good reason. Few areas in the United States can boast of the inexhaustible array of scenic, cultural, historic, and recreational attractions within an honest day's drive from an urban region as can Washington, D.C.

Our point here is not to rewrite what already has been inked. Instead, we want to take you to some of the most- and lesser-known nearby destinations—places we proudly put on our must-see itinerary for visiting families and relocating friends eager to discover the rich environs and folkways beyond the Beltway.

When we say "beyond the Beltway," what we really mean is away from the Metro area but close enough to more than justify a day's outing or a weekend minivacation. What a palette we have to work with! From the ancient, forest-covered Blue Ridge Mountains to the tranquil majesty of the Chesapeake Bay, the world's largest and most productive estuary, to all those points in between, the story-book quality of the mid-Atlantic countryside and all that it offers is the stuff of inspiration, rejuvenation, and endless repeat visits. It is part of the cultural fabric of being a Washingtonian.

We've begun this chapter at the beginning—our colonial roots in Virginia. From there, we travel to Virginia Hunt Country and the Blue Ridge, from West Virginia to Maryland, south to the Maryland antique mecca of Frederick County. We've touched on a few ski resorts, then, at the opposite end of the meteorological spectrum, the Chesapeake Bay and the Beaches, with special mention of those waterview towns Baltimore and Annapolis.

We've also made special mention of the Civil War sites that you'll find throughout the region, the crossroads of the North and the South. Of course, from time to time we may have meandered beyond our geographic parameters. After all, we couldn't, in good conscience, omit such special places as the Dolly Sods Wilderness of West Virginia or the Victorian charm of Cape May, New Jersey.

We've touched on a few suggestions for overnight stays, and you can assume that rates are per room, per night unless otherwise specified. Also, bed-and-breakfasts include breakfast for two in the room rates, but if other snacks or meals are included, we've noted it. Please remember that rates can and do change with time and also with the seasons.

So let's go, weekend warriors! Put the maps in the glove box, check the fuel gauge, and fasten those seatbelts. It's time to let your imaginations and frontiers soar.

COLONIAL ROOTS

Before there was Washington, there were Williamsburg, Yorktown, and Jamestown, Virginia's historic triangle. Wedged between the James and York Rivers, arguably the Tigris–Euphrates of the South, if not the nation, **Colonial Williamsburg** (800–HISTORY, www.colonialwilliamsburg.com), **Yorktown National,** and **Jamestown Colonial National Historical Park** (757–898–2410, 888–593–4682, www.historyisfun.org, www.nps.gov/colo) represent, quite frankly, the best and worst of Virginia—the worst in the sense that they are obvious tourist traps, and you can't help but feel a bit regretful on seeing a McDonald's or an outlet shop within a stone's throw from some of the most hal-

Monticello, Thomas Jefferson's home in Charlottesville, Virginia, is about a three-hour drive from Washington, D.C. COURTESY JACK HOLLINGSWORTH, VIRGINIA TOURISM CORPORATION

lowed ground in North America; the best in the sense that the actual historical parks are run by altruistic foundations striving for class over commercialism. It's hard not to walk out of these shrines feeling like a patriot, or at least a pioneer, and we highly recommend that you budget a full day for each locale. The drive there takes a bit more than three hours from Metro Washington, an easy shot south on I–95, then east on I–64. Once in the Williamsburg area, the three towns are easily connected by way of the Colonial Parkway, a gorgeous brick road that winds its way through forests and along the banks of the James and York Rivers.

Jamestown Island is the site of North America's first permanent English settlement in 1607, and in Jamestown Settlement you can board replicas of the three ships that carried the settlers to the Virginia shores. Docents demonstrate typical tasks and answer visitors' questions during reenactments in the reconstructed fort and Powhatan Indian village. Kids especially enjoy learning the truth about Pocahontas, in reality a short-haired, sometimes naked young girl rather than Disney's statuesque beauty. Visit the site's attractive museum to watch a film and browse a variety of exhibits. At Jamestown's Colonial National Historical Park, you'll see thousands of items from the 1600s that have been unearthed by archaeologists or preserved from the era. The equally impressive James River plantations, proud residences of three presidents and numerous statesmen, are a 40-minute drive up panoramic Route 5. These 200-year-old beauties rest gracefully on hills overlooking the James River.

It was at Berkeley Plantation, the birthplace of the ninth U.S. president, William Henry Harrison, that in 1619 the first official celebration of Thanksgiving occurred. Sherwood Forest Plantation was the home of John Tyler, the 10th U.S. president, and Tuckahoe Plantation was the boyhood home of Thomas Jefferson. Tuckahoe is considered by architectural historians to be the finest existing early-eighteenth-century plantation in America.

Yorktown, due east from Jamestown on Route 31, is where the Revolutionary War ended. Important battles—including the Boston Tea Party and the British surrender at Yorktown—are depicted for tourists by actors in costume. Wherever you visit in the historic triangle, you're most likely to stay in or near Colonial Williamsburg, the area's prime attraction and the world's largest and most extensively restored eighteenth-century town. There are more than 500 original and reconstructed buildings in the square that comprises Colonial Williamsburg. You've seen the photos of the costumed actors who depict eighteenth-century townspeople and the replicas of old-time taverns, smithies, and apothecaries. It's all great fun, especially for kids, who delight in reenactments of times of yore.

Scads of hotels in the area fit every budget, but the gracious Williamsburg Inn, right in the center of the colonial section at 136 East Francis Street, will transport you to a former era when waiters wore white gloves and afternoon sherry was a daily ritual. Individually designed rooms are furnished in the Regency manner, and the formal public rooms overlook sweeping manicured lawns flanked by a broad terrace. All reservations for accommodations and dining can be made by dialing (800) HISTORY or visiting www.colonial williamsburg.com.

MR. JEFFERSON'S COUNTRY

We move forward in history to the time of Thomas Jefferson, arguably Virginia's favorite son. You won't live in Virginia, or for that matter in Maryland, a week before someone mentions Charlottesville, which is about three hours from Washington: south on I–95, then west on I–64. Charlottesville is popular for good reason: As home to Virginia's and the nation's most-celebrated Renaissance Man— Thomas Jefferson—Charlottesville is one of the most cherished sites in the region. Here you'll find **Monticello** (434–984–9822, www.monticello.org), Jefferson's captivating hilltop home, and the University of Virginia, one of his many intellectual and architectural achievements.

Charlottesville and surrounding Albemarle County are also about dogwood-lined country roads, hillside vineyards, funky bookstores, and sophisticated galleries, museums and restaurants. At the **Boar's Head Inn** (434–296– 2181, www.boarsheadinn.com), on Highway 250 West just outside of town, you can unwind at a full-service spa and spend the night in one of its many guest rooms decorated in cozy, country English style. Room prices are from $210 to $500 or more.

For a more intimate experience, check out the renowned **Clifton–The Country Inn,** 1296 Clifton Inn Drive, Charlottesville, (888) 971–1800, www.cliftoninn.com. Rooms are from $225 to $545. At Clifton there's a fireplace in every room, beds are four-posters or canopies and dressed with line-dried, cotton sheets. The decor consists of Jeffersonian antiques and reproductions, and no wonder: The estate belonged to Thomas Jefferson's daughter Martha. There's a well-regarded, full-service restaurant on the premises, and breakfast, included in the room tariff, is a calorie-busting affair that might include waffles, quiches, omelettes, fruit compote, muffins, and freshly ground coffee.

Fifteen miles east of Charlottesville is the gloriously romantic **Prospect Hill Plantation Inn,** Highway 613 at Zion Crossroads, Trevilians, (800) 277–0844, www.prospecthill.com. Set amidst rolling hills where sheep graze and wildlife wander, Prospect Hill looks like an idyllic painting. Each room is different—some have Jacuzzis and fireplaces, others are set in cabins of their own apart from the main house—so ask for descriptions. Dinners are a leisurely affair of four or five courses preceded by cocktails in the salon. Rooms are $295 to $595, including breakfast and dinner.

Mr. Jefferson's Country is also Mr. Monroe's Country and Mr. Madison's Country. Literally just down the road from Monticello is **Ash Lawn-Highland** (434–293–9539, www.monticello.avenue.org/ashlawn), James Monroe's home, and about 20 miles to the north, in Orange, Virginia, is Montpelier (540–672–2728, www.montpelier.org) the impressive country estate of James Madison.

Jefferson Country is also home to some of Virginia's finest wineries. The former president planted vines on the land surrounding Monticello, where today you'll find **Jefferson Vineyards** (434–977–3042, www.jefferson vineyards.com). Nearby, **Barboursville Vineyards** (540–832–3824, www.barboursville wine.com) produces the state's most decorated vintages.

Farther south, off the Blue Ridge Parkway in neighboring Nelson County, is **Wintergreen Resort** off Highway 664 (800–926–3723, www.wintergreenresort.com; see section on skiing, this chapter). The year-round facility offers a fine golf course, and the moderate climate makes it possible at times to ski in the morning and play a round of golf in the afternoon. Accommodations range from hotel-style rooms to private rental homes with walls of windows overlooking the mountains. Rates range from $126 to over $849 for a seven-bedroom house.

THE GRAY LADY OF THE CONFEDERACY

The capital city of Virginia, and for a time, the South, is a living, breathing memorial to the Commonwealth. History isn't just a fact of life in Richmond, it's a way of life. Getting there is easy—it's 100 miles due south of Washington on I–95.

Monument Avenue, the South's answer to Pennsylvania Avenue, immortalizes the fallen sons of the Old Dominion through huge statues, tasteful gardens, and expansive greens. The newest addition—and a controversial one—is the statue of tennis legend Arthur Ashe Jr., who was the first and only African American man to win Wimbledon. His monument depicts him surrounded by children, holding books and his tennis racket overhead.

Monument Avenue cuts through the heart of "The Fan," one of Richmond's trendiest and most desirable residential areas, a la Georgetown in Washington, D.C. It is said to be the largest intact Victorian neighborhood in the United States, with approximately 2,000 houses, most of them restored.

The White House of the Confederacy (804–649–1861, www.moc.org), and many of the original government buildings of the Confederate States of America, sit within earshot of downtown and the Virginia State Capitol, yet another building designed by Thomas Jefferson. Adjacent to the White House you'll find the **Museum of the Confederacy,** the largest collection of Confederate artifacts. One exhibit features Robert E. Lee's tent as intact as if he'd just left it. Here you will also find the **Edgar Allan Poe Museum** (804–648–5523, www.poemuseum.org), which also happens to be the oldest building in the city.

Richmond is rightfully proud of its premier museum, the **Virginia Museum of Fine Arts** (804–340–1400, www.vmfa.state.va.us), housing one of the world's largest collections of Fabergé eggs as well as a stunning array of Asian antiquities and French impressionist and British sporting art.

Richmonders are also fond of their numerous parks and cemeteries, some of the most elegant in the South. **Hollywood Cemetery** (804–648–8501, www.hollywoodcemetery.org) is the burial place of Presidents Monroe and Tyler, as well as Confederate President Jefferson Davis and more than 18,000 Confederate soldiers.

A premier place to stay in Richmond is the 262-room **Jefferson** at Franklin and Adams Streets (800–424–8014, www.jeffersonhotel.com), a grand hotel in the old style, with marble columns, palace-size Oriental carpets, and a staircase sweeping from the mezzanine to the lounge. It also contains one of Richmond's top restaurants, Lemaire, featuring French and fusion cuisine. Rooms start at $310.

For more intimate quarters, try the **Linden Row Inn,** 100 East Franklin Street (800–348–7424, www.lindenrowinn.com). Built in 1847, the 71-room structure is listed in the National Register of Historic Places and is located in the middle of the historic district. Rooms are $99 to $189.

For hotel reservations and general information, contact the Metro Richmond Convention and Visitors Bureau at (888) RICHMOND; www.richmondva.org.

A HUNT COUNTRY TAPESTRY

Closer to Washington, in fact just 40 miles west of the bustle of Pennsylvania Avenue, is a quiet, rolling green land of thoroughbred horses, country squires, and antebellum stone mansions. This is hunt country, and you'll be hard pressed to find a more beautiful setting than the farms and fields of Loudoun and Fauquier Counties.

Middleburg, the self-proclaimed "Hunt Country Capital," retains its eighteenth-century charm but with new twists like gourmet bakeries, upscale restaurants, and internationally celebrated antiques shops. A popular lodging and dining spot here is the **Red Fox Inn and Tavern,** 2 East Washington Street (800–223–1728, www.redfox.com), housed in a quaint stone building in the center of town. You'll find four-poster beds, fireplaces, and a full-service restaurant serving three meals a day. Room prices start at $175.

To the west of Middleburg lie the lovely hill country hamlets of Upperville and Paris, where warehouse-size stables and horses seem to outnumber people five to one. Just outside Paris, meanwhile, is the public's access to hunt country living, **Sky Meadows State Park** (540–592–3556, www.dcr.state.va.us/parks/skymeadow.htm). Once a working plantation, Sky Meadows' 1,100 acres entice weekend warriors with a maze of hiking trails, including a stretch of the Appalachian Trail. By the way, Stonewall Jackson's troops camped here before leaving for the Battle of First Manassas.

Leesburg, the largest city in the area, is steeped in Virginia history; indeed, it was named after one of the most prominent families in the Old Dominion. During the War of 1812, when the British were on their way to

State Tourism Offices

All begin with (800)

Maryland	634–7386	www.mdisfun.org
Virginia	847–4882	www.virginia.org
West Virginia	225–5982	www.callwva.com
Pennsylvania	847–4872	www.experiencepa.com

burn Washington, the Federal Archives, including the Declaration of Independence and the Constitution, were hauled through town in 22 wagons on their way to safekeeping in an estate outside of town.

As you might expect from a town named for the Lee family, Leesburg is steeped in Civil War history. **Ball's Bluff Regional Park** (703–737–7800, www.nvrpa.org/ballsbluff .html) commemorates the site of a vicious battle won by the South on October 21, 1861. After the Union forces suffered heavy casualties, U.S. Congress established the Joint Committee on the Conduct of the War, an organization charged with reviewing all military procedures and other leadership issues that became politicized through the war.

Today Leesburg and the surrounding villages of Hamilton, Lincoln, Waterford, Hillsboro, and Purcellville are waging another successful battle for preservation, a concept near and dear to the hearts of hunt country residents who consider themselves just a few miles yet "light years" removed from Washington suburbia.

Though Leesburg is less than an hour from downtown D.C., those looking for a quick romantic getaway might reserve a room at the **Norris House,** 108 Loudoun Street (703–777–1806, 800–644–1806, www.norris house.com), a beautifully restored 1806 home. The interior is reminiscent of Colonial Williamsburg, both in the colors used and in the period antiques. This bed-and-breakfast has five rooms, and guests are welcomed with complimentary wine or soft drinks. Breakfast is a spread featuring fresh fruit, baked goods, and a hot entree.

Also less than an hour from Washington, but due south, is Fredericksburg, another popular day trip. This historic town, now a hot spot for antiques, was founded in 1728 as a trade route for the tobacco grown in Virginia.

George Washington's boyhood home, **Ferry Farm,** is just across the Rappahannock River from Fredericksburg, on Highway 3 at Ferry Road in the village of Falmouth, (540) 373–3381 ext. 28, www.kenmore.org. This is where he reportedly cut down the famed cherry tree, but it later became a major artillery base and river crossing point for Revolutionary forces in the Battle of Fredericksburg.

Fifth president James Monroe was also a Fredericksburg resident at one time—he practiced law here—and his office is now the **James Monroe Museum and Library** (540–654–1043, www.umw.edu/jamesmonroe museum). Here you can see the desk on which he signed the Monroe Doctrine in 1823 during his presidency.

A popular pastime in Fredericksburg—aside from shopping—is a 75-minute trolley tour of the historic district (540–898–0737, www.fredericksburgtrolley.com) or, weather permitting, a tour by horse-drawn carriage (540–371–0094). There are also tour packages available, which allow admission to multiple historic sights. For information, contact the Fredericksburg Visitor Center, (800) 654–4118, www.fredericksburgva.com.

THE BLUE RIDGE MOUNTAINS

Named for their pervasive blue haze, the result of a complex photochemical reaction involving trees, light, and moisture, the Blue Ridge Mountains are the nation's easternmost range, running from north Georgia to southern Pennsylvania, with Virginia claiming the largest stretch.

To give you an idea of their proximity to Metro Washington, D.C., residents of western Fairfax County can see the mountains on a clear day while driving along busy Virginia Highway 28. Conversely, Skyline Drive in Shenandoah National Park got its name because in earlier times one could make out the Washington skyline from its eastern overlooks.

It's the Big Kahuna, the Grand Poobah of the Virginia Blue Ridge: Stretching more than 130 miles along the spine of the mountains, from Front Royal south to Waynesboro, **Shenandoah National Park** (540–999–3500, www.nps.gov/shen) is a naturalist's paradise.

Each year nearly two million people make the 90-minute pilgrimage (I–66 West from Washington) to the park and its famed **Skyline Drive** to take in dramatic vistas of the Appalachians and the rolling, fertile farmland of the Shenandoah Valley and the Piedmont. Don't let the number of visitors scare you, though: The park contains more than 195,000 acres, and once you venture off of Skyline, it's possible to hike, fish, and camp for several days without seeing another human. The same can't be said about wildlife, however. Bobcats, deer, foxes, turkeys, and bears, among other critters, are prevalent in these parts; in fact, the density of deer and black bears is among the highest anywhere in the United States, so if you plan to do some backcountry trekking, be sure to check in at the ranger station to get briefed on safeguarding your camp.

For a less-rugged but equally woodsy experience, try one of the park's four drive-in campgrounds—Big Meadows, Lewis Mountain, Loft Mountain, and Matthews Arm—or two lodges, Skyland and Big Meadows. For information on any of these destinations, call (800) 999–4714.

If bed-and-breakfasts are more your style, try **Steeles Tavern Manor** on Highway 11, Steeles Tavern, (800) 743–8666, www.steeles tavernmanor.com. This romantic five-room inn is a sprawling 1916 mansion on 55 acres overlooking the mountains. Coffee is brought to your door each morning prior to the candlelight breakfast served in the dining room. Or you may have breakfast served in the privacy of your room, each of which has a fireplace and Jacuzzi for two. Rooms range from $190 to $220.

Aside from the fabled **Appalachian Trail,** which runs the distance of the Shenandoah National Park, excellent hiking opportunities can be had on dozens of peaks that comprise the highest mountain range between the Catskills and the Smokies. We highly recommend a day-climb on venerable Old Rag Mountain (elevation 3,291 feet). A hike on the less-strenuous but taller Hawksbill Mountain (4,049 feet) is another favorite of daytrippers, especially in late October when the park's thick, deciduous forests turn into a technicolor fantasyland.

Above all, Shenandoah is ripe with wonderful hidden nooks and crannies. Things like abandoned settlers' cabins, cascading waterfalls, and virtually untouched trout streams brimming with native brookies are just some of the treasures awaiting those with a penchant for leaving the beaten path.

A personal favorite is the 5-mile hike to **Camp Hoover,** President Herbert Hoover's "summer White House" and austere fish camp built along the banks of the pristine Rapidan River, one of the best trout-fishing rivers in the Old Dominion. Each year around August 10, Hoover's birthday, the National Park Service hosts a "Hoover Days" weekend in which the public is allowed to visit the camp and learn a bit about the president's leisure habits and the interesting guests who frequented the remote enclave. The event offers you the option of taking a bus ride down the mountain or hoofing it, trips that both begin at the park's Byrd

Visitor Center, Skyline Drive, at milepost 51.

Advance information can be obtained from the Virginia Tourism Corporation at (800) 934–9184, www.virginia.org, or the Shenandoah Valley Travel Association, (800) 847–4878, www.visitshenandoah.org.

Little Washington, the Little Apple, and the Caverns

Blue Ridge Mountain towns move to their own whimsical, unpretentious beat. Folks still wave to strangers, and shopkeepers are gracious even if you're just browsing. Surprises abound here, sometimes bordering on the surreal.

For instance, in tiny Washington, Virginia, on U.S. 211, sits one of the most highly acclaimed restaurants and country inns in the world—the **Inn at Little Washington** (540–675–3800, www.theinnatlittlewashington.com).

Well-heeled guests come from as far away as New York and Atlanta to dine on the restaurant's nouvelle French cuisine and spend a night in one of the 12 lavishly furnished rooms. Indeed, this is often a must-do for European visitors as well. On any given Sunday morning, "Little Washington," the oldest of 28 towns in the United States named for our first president, probably could claim the world's highest concentration of Jaguars and Mercedes-Benzes. Count on dropping at least $300 for dinner at the inn, and $400 to $900 for a room, but the food and accommodations live up to their reputations. The penthouse suites, in particular, feature living areas that look like Arabian nights fantasies—albeit tasteful. They have marble bathrooms with jetted tubs tucked into bay windows, double-headed showers as large as most normal bathrooms, and loft bedrooms with balconies overlooking a panoramic mountain vista.

Just down the road is a lesser-known, but no less delectable stop called the **Blue Rock Inn** (540–987–3190, www.thebluerockinn.com), which offers a bucolic setting overlooking a pond and the inn's own vineyards. The five bedrooms here are homier than at the Inn at Little Washington, but they are charming and about half as expensive. Pets are even allowed in one room. On a summer night there's nothing more romantic than dinner on the terrace as you watch the sun set. You'll enjoy memorable French cuisine with some interesting twists, then drift up to your room for the kind of restful sleep that only country nights provide. Rooms are from $155 to $220.

Other reasonably priced (rooms between $155 and $245), charming bed-and-breakfasts in the Little Washington area include **Heritage House,** 291 Main Street, Washington, VA (888–819–8280, www.heritagehousebb.com), in the heart of town, a country-style abode where all the knickknacks and furnishings in the room are for sale! So if you love the decor, you can take it home with you.

Sycamore Hill House, 110 Menefee Mountain Lane, Washington (540–675–3046), about 1 mile from Little Washington atop Menefee Mountain (1,043 feet), has a more contemporary atmosphere at $100 to $200 a night, with huge picture windows overlooking the Blue Ridge, cathedral ceilings (and fans to go with them), and shining brass beds. The standout here is the 75-foot veranda and patio—a perfect spot to take in the breathtaking scenery.

Down the road from Little Washington and at the base of Shenandoah National Park lies perhaps the busiest hamlet in all of Virginia. **Sperryville,** the self-proclaimed "Little Apple," is an enterprising apple-farming village; it's also a gift shop mecca that almost dares you to drive through without picking up mountain crafts, antiques, or fresh-squeezed cider from places like the Sperryville Emporium or Wolf Mountain Store. For accommodations here, try the **Conyers House,** Slate Mills Road, Sperryville (540– 987–8025, www.conyers house.com), which features a peaceful country locale and lavish breakfasts. The 1770 manor, with rates ranging from $150 to $300, has been beautifully restored and contains such touches as beamed ceilings, Oriental rugs, stone fireplaces, and elegant country-house furnishings.

Also in the area are several vineyards where you can observe winemaking in progress, sample a bit of wine, and even have lunch or dinner. One of the best known is **Piedmont Vineyards** on Route 626, 3 miles south of Middleburg, (540) 687–5528, www .piedmontwines.com. The vineyards and winery are located on a pre-Revolutionary estate called Waverly.

Across the mountain from Sperryville, the Shenandoah Valley town of Luray is home to the much-hyped, but nevertheless fascinating, **Luray Caverns** (540–743–6551, www.luray caverns.com). Take the tour—it's an hour long, and you'll see some of the most colorful and stunning stalactites and stalagmites in the East. Among the attractions is the Great Stalacpipe Organ, an enhanced natural formation that plays haunting music.

In the same complex as the caverns is the Historic Car and Carriage Caravan, an exhibit of antique cars, carriages, and coaches, some dating from the seventeenth century. You can see Rudolph Valentino's 1925 Rolls Royce here.

Of Patsy Cline, Antiques, and Battlefields

If the pressures of the big city start turning you a tad cynical, take a spin out to the northern Shenandoah Valley and rediscover vintage Americana.

For a powerful lesson in Civil War history, take a trip to **Manassas,** 30 miles west of the Nation's Capital. Several square miles of Virginia countryside have been preserved as a memorial to the two landmark battles that took place here, the First and Second Battles of Manassas, or Bull Run (703–361–1339, www.nps.gov/mana). The fighting claimed more than 4,000 lives and left 30,000 wounded. Today outdoors and history enthusiasts can enjoy miles of horse and hiking trails spread over 5,000 acres, plus interpretive roadside tour markers and picnic areas. The town of Manassas's historic district is also worth a trip, lined with quaint shops and restaurants. The **Manassas Museum** (9101

If you want to plan a Virginia wine country getaway, visit www.virginia wines.org to get more information about the wineries, locations, and to plot your course.

Prince William Street, 703–368–1873, www.manassasmuseum.org) interprets the history of the community and the surrounding Northern Virginia Piedmont.

Northwest of Manassas, **Winchester** is home to dozens of historical attractions, including the western frontier command office of young General George Washington and the Civil War headquarters of Thomas "Stonewall" Jackson.

Civil War buffs may remember that Winchester changed hands at least 70 times during the war, far more than any other community in the country. It is also in Winchester that the spirit of native daughter and country music legend Patsy Cline lives on. Cline, who gave us such heartfelt renditions of "I Fall to Pieces" and "Sweet Dreams," died in a plane crash in 1963 at age 30. She's buried at the Shenandoah Memorial Cemetery on Route 522, also known as the Patsy Cline Memorial Highway.

Virtually all the towns of the northern Valley are riddled with antiques stores, but **Strasburg,** at the foot of Massanutten Mountain, takes the cake. Here you can find nearly 100 dealers in the downtown **Strasburg Emporium** (540–465–3711, www.strasburg emporium.com), which houses furniture from every American era, as well as intricate chandeliers, rugs, quilts, lace, old carousel horses, and pottery. Top it off with a gourmet meal at the Victorian-inspired **Hotel Strasburg,** 201 Holliday Street, Strasburg (800–348–8327, www.hotelstrasburg.com), where you can also stay the night ($83 for a regular room and $180 for a three-room suite with a Jacuzzi).

On the Wild Side of Front Royal

Between Strasburg and Front Royal, the heavily trafficked gateway to Shenandoah National Park, lies one of the region's truly undiscovered natural gems, the **Elizabeth Furnace Recreation Area.** Off of twisty Virginia 678, in the heart of the sprawling George Washington National Forest (540–265–5100, www.fs .fed.us/r8/gwj), this rugged gorge country of spiraling limestone outcroppings and the swift-moving Passage Creek is more akin to the wilds of West Virginia than to the gentle Shenandoah Valley. It also was the site of many a clandestine military operation during the Civil War. Creekside campsites are available at the recreation area, and hikers are encouraged to make the enjoyable day-climb to the summit of Signal Knob, with its commanding views of the valley.

The Generals' City

The legacies of Stonewall Jackson and Robert E. Lee pervade their beloved Virginia, but nowhere is their presence felt more than in the scenic Shenandoah Valley town of Lexington in beautiful Rockbridge County.

Here you can tour the only house Jackson ever owned and walk the hallowed grounds of the Virginia Military Institute, where he taught natural philosophy to Confederate cadets. At the **VMI Museum** (540–464–7334, www .vmi.edu/museum), displays include such objects as Jackson's bullet-pierced raincoat and his favorite war horse, Little Sorrel, preserved through taxidermy. The museum recently added an exhibit on Vietnam and a new expansion.

Within earshot of VMI is the impressive **Washington and Lee University and Lee Chapel** (540–458–8768, www.wlu.edu), the still-used shrine to Jackson's confidant and the final resting place of the South's greatest hero. Don't leave Lexington without visiting the office Lee inhabited while assuming the presidency of W&L after his defeat in the Civil War. It's in virtually the same state as he left it in 1870. Buried nearby on campus is Lee's favorite mount, and maybe the most famous war horse in American history, Traveller.

You'll find several luxurious bed-and-breakfasts and inns around Lexington, three of which are owned by a single company known as **Historic Country Inns** (rates from $65 to $170). By dialing a single phone number, (877) 283–9680, or checking its Web site, www .lexingtonhistoricinns.com, you can choose among the **Alexander-Withrow** (3 West Washington Street) or **McCampbell** (11 North Main Street) inns in the center of Lexington's historic district, or **Maple Hall,** set amidst 56 acres of meadow and forest 6 miles north of town.

Maple Hall even has a restaurant serving gourmet dinner fare. The country manor looks like it belongs on the set of *Gone with the Wind,* with its massive white columns and dramatic front staircase. All three properties feature gracious, Southern-style verandas, antiques, and fireplaces.

A Tale of Two Mountain Resorts

Lodging is in no short supply in the Virginia upcountry; however, two of the more interesting spots to rest and recreate are Mountain Lake Hotel, near Blacksburg, and the queen of mountain resorts, the Homestead in Hot Springs. Still best known as the place where the hit movie *Dirty Dancing* was filmed, **Mountain Lake Hotel** (rates from $185, including dinner and breakfast for two) on Highway 700 in Blacksburg (800–346–3334, www.mountainlakehotel.com) sits nearly 4,200 feet up in the Allegheny Mountains of Giles County. Semirustic in nature, although a far cry from earthy, Mountain Lake caters to families in the summer and has developed quite an extensive package of theme weekends during the off-season, including, of course, a "Dirty Dancing Weekend." It is isolated, yes, but once you get there, expect a wealth of indoor and outdoor activities: a full spa, great hiking trails, excellent fishing in the natural spring-fed pond, and plenty of interpretive programs, such as the one on Appalachian folk art.

Up the mountains to the north, the **Homestead,** Main Street, U.S. 220, Hot Springs (866–354–4653, www.thehomestead.com), is consistently rated by international travel writers as one of the world's top resorts. This plush but relaxed setting is a favorite of the corporate-retreat set (as well as of members of Congress and other segments of Washington officialdom) but also is frequented by couples and families looking to pamper themselves in the resort's five-star spa, restaurants, stables, and golf courses. Golf legend Sam Snead, who grew up in the area, considers the Homestead's Cascades course one of the finest in the South. A bit on the pricey side—double occupancy starts at $165 a night per person, with breakfast and dinner—the Homestead nevertheless is something to be experienced, if just once. Our advice is to start saving now.

WILD, WONDERFUL WEST VIRGINIA

The Mountain State just may be the best-kept secret in the nation. Its rugged terrain and inspiring mountain vistas seem to defy its proximity to the Eastern megalopolis. Within a two-hour drive of Metro Washington is a country as remote and beautiful as Montana or Idaho. The state's laid-back tenor and affordability are attracting increasing numbers of tourists, but don't ever worry about being crowded out here. In the **Dolly Sods Wilderness Area** (304–636–1800, www.fs.fed.us/r9/mnf/sp/dolly_sods_wilderness.htm), near Petersburg, you can walk the land of the Seneca Indians, through patches of wild orchids and blueberries and huge granite boulders that afford hikers views in excess of 100 miles.

About 20 miles south of Dolly Sods is **Seneca Rocks** (304–567–2827, www.fs.fedus/r9/mnf/sp/senrcks_txt.html), a gray wall of ancient sandstone that juts 1,000 feet above the floor of the South Branch Valley. For the truly adventurous, take a mountain-climbing lesson through Seneca Rocks Climbing School (800–548–0108, www.seneca-rocks.com); Seneca Rocks Mountain Guides (304–567–2115, www.senecarocks.com); or Blackwater Outdoor Adventures (304– 478–3775, www.blackwateroutdoors.com).

If you'd rather keep your feet firmly on the ground, take a drive up to the Canaan Valley, the highest valley east of the Mississippi River. Spend a night or two in the cozy lodge at **Canaan Valley State Park** (800–622–4121, www.canaanresort.com), a woodsy retreat and conference center that boasts of—and rightly so—the best fall colors in the United States. Lodge rooms start at $99 during ski season and $61 in the summer. Cabins and cottages are also available.

If you love the outdoors but don't like to rough it, head to the superexpensive and superluxurious **Greenbrier Resort,** 300 West Main Street, White Sulphur Springs, West Virginia. The Greenbrier (800–453–4858, www.greenbrier.com) is considered even more upscale than the Homestead ($389 to $710 per couple), so know what you're getting into. If you can afford it, the experience is well worth the cost. It's a taste of the antebellum South, complete with a sprawling veranda, dancing and a black-tie affair at dinner, afternoon tea, and enough activities to keep you occupied every minute of the day: horseback riding, shooting, golf, bowling, hiking, and, of course, taking the waters and all the related spa activities.

Closer to home and easier on the pocketbook is Berkeley Springs, West Virginia, an area that offers something for both body and spirit. As the name implies, the area revolves around the restorative hot springs and spa, and weary Washingtonians often make the two-and-a-half-hour pilgrimage to the **Berkeley Springs Spa and Inn** (304–258–4536, www.berkeleyspringsinn.com) to be pampered by facials, body scrubs, massages, and, of course, soaks in the hot springs.

An attraction of equal allure is the scenery just outside of town. The Panorama Overlook on West Virginia Highway 9, 4 miles west of Berkeley Springs, has been named by *National Geographic* magazine as one of America's most breathtaking vistas.

Coolfont Resort, 3621 Cold Run Valley Road, Berkeley Springs (800–888–8768, www.coolfont.com), near Berkeley Springs, is the spa of choice for many among the Washington stress set (rates $119 to $249 a night). Former drug czar William Bennett kicked his cigarette habit here, and Al Gore has been a loyal customer for years, even once setting off a minipanic by getting lost in the woods with Tipper. The accommodations are modest but comfortable.

A bit farther, and just as scenic, is **Cacapon State Park,** the third-largest in West Virginia (304–258–1022, www.cacaponresort.com). There are almost 30 miles of well-marked hiking trails—a great place to get your fix of fall color. Lodge rooms and cabins rent from just $49 a night. You can also reach the state park and receive loads of helpful information by calling (800) CALLWVA or by visiting www.callwva.com.

A Tale of Two Rivers

The mighty Shenandoah and Potomac Rivers meet in **Harpers Ferry,** West Virginia, site of abolitionist John Brown's raid on the U.S. Arsenal, a spark that helped ignite the Civil War. Now operated by the National Park Service (304–535–6029, www.nps.gov/hafe), this perfectly restored village provides an excellent journey into days past, with influences spanning not only the Civil War but the founding of the nation, including a healthy dose of period architecture and steep, narrow cobblestone streets.

Craft shops abound, as do glorious views of the Blue Ridge and the wild, crystal-clear rivers running below the hilltop city. At just over 400 feet in elevation, Harpers Ferry marks the lowest point in the state of West Virginia.

When the summer steam envelops Washington, head north approximately 65 miles on I–270 to Harpers Ferry for a day of tubing, white-water rafting, or hiking—the Appalachian Trail runs right through the town center. Trips can be arranged through **River & Trail Outfitters** (888–I–GO–PLAY, www.rivertrail.com) in nearby Knoxville, Maryland.

If the hour-plus drive back to town seems much too formidable after an exhausting day shooting rapids, bunk down at one of the town's cozy bed-and-breakfast inns. The circa-1800 **Ranson-Armory** bed-and-breakfast, 690 Washington Street (304–535–2142), has only two guest rooms, but each offers a private bath and a splendid view for $80 to $90 per night, including breakfast.

If you'd like something a bit more formal, head up the road to Shepherdstown, the second-oldest burgh in the state and home to the gracious **Bavarian Inn and Lodge** (304–876– 2551, www.bavarianinnwv.com), just off West Virginia Highway 480 or directly across the bridge (and state line) from Maryland Highway 34. The inn is a stone structure with a knoll-top perch above the Potomac (rates from $105 to $325, no meals). The dining room here features hearty German and game dishes. Several rooms have two-person Jacuzzis and gas fireplaces, and all are furnished with American colonial reproductions, including some four-poster beds.

Shepherdstown has one of the nation's highest concentrations of eighteenth-century buildings, making it an ideal spot to just meander. Be sure to duck into **O'Hurley's General Store** (304–876–6907, www.ohurley.com), known throughout the East for its wonderful crafts, antiques, and curios.

JUST ACROSS THE RIVER: THE MOUNTAINS OF MARYLAND

On the Maryland side of the Potomac from Harpers Ferry lies Washington County, site of the Civil War's Battle of Antietam, the deadliest clash of the war and one of the bloodiest battles in American history. **Antietam National Battlefield Park** (301–432–5124, www.nps.gov/anti) pays tribute to the more than 23,000 soldiers who were killed, wounded, or left missing on September 17, 1862—the single bloodiest day in the four-year conflict. Union General George B. McClellan failed to fully destroy Confederate General Robert E. Lee and his army, but stopped Lee's attempt to enter Maryland and forced his retreat back to Virginia. Though not a decisive victory, the effort inspired Abraham Lincoln to announce his Emancipation Proclamation.

On a more upbeat note, Washington County, the first such jurisdiction named for George, is home to four of Maryland's best state parks. At **Washington Monument State Park** (301–791–4767, www.dnr.state .md/publiclands/western/Washington.html), high atop South Mountain, you can view the first monument built in the president's honor. Originally constructed by the residents of Boonsboro, Maryland, in 1827, the stone tower has been rebuilt twice since. Climb the monument's 34 steps to take in spectacular views of the Cumberland Valley.

If you plan to stay overnight in the area, book a room at **Antietam Overlook Farm** (800–878–4241, www.antietamoverlook.com), off Highway 34 in Keedysville, Maryland. The view from the property encompasses portions of Maryland, Virginia, West Virginia, and Pennsylvania. The inn's most lavish room features a screened porch and sundeck overlooking the vista. The five rooms each cost $165 to $240 a night.

Moving south, following along the mountain, you'll hit **Gathland State Park** (301–791–4767, www.dnr.state.md.us/publiclands/western/gathland.html), which includes the ruins of Gapland, the country home of Civil War and Reconstruction journalist George Alfred Townsend. Near the entrance to the park stands the imposing War Correspondents Arch, a 50-foot structure Townsend built to honor the documentarians of the great war. Joseph Pulitzer and Thomas Edison contributed to the $5,000 building fund.

Just up the road from both Gathland and Washington Monument is **Greenbrier State Park** (301–791–4767, www.dnr.state.md.us/publiclands/western/greenbrier.html) and its sparkling spring-fed Greenbrier Lake, said to be among the clearest in the nation. Camping, fishing, and hiking are popular activities here as well as across the county at **Fort Frederick State Park** (301–842–2155, www.dnr.state .md.us/publiclands/western/fortfrederick.html).

Nestled along the banks of the Potomac and containing a stretch of the Chesapeake &

Ohio Canal, Fort Frederick was originally built as a defense outpost on the western frontier. Still standing, although in a carefully preserved state, the fort survived the French and Indian, Revolutionary, and Civil Wars and is now honored through a series of historical reenactments each spring through fall.

The President's Mountain

Largely overshadowed by Shenandoah National Park, Maryland's **Catoctin Mountain Park** (301–663–9388, www.nps.gov/cato), is an ideal place to beat the crowds, especially during the autumn months when its 10,000-acre forest of beech, hickory, poplar, oak, and maple trees turns to brilliant shades of red, orange, and gold. Catoctin is probably most famous for being home to Camp David, the woodsy presidential retreat. Don't expect the First Family to wave you on in, though. The compound is well hidden, and security, as you can imagine, is intense.

You can, however, spend the night at the park's Owens Creek Campground or in a rustic cabin at Camp Misty Mount. Catoctin's numerous trails and wild trout streams make it a great place for families and novice campers. From the park you're also within a short drive of the history-rich towns of Gettysburg, Pennsylvania, and Frederick, Maryland.

Also, near the park entrance is the quaint railroad town of Thurmont, and immediately to the south is **Cunningham Falls State Park** (301–271–7574, www.dnr.state.md.us/public lands/western/cunninghamfalls.html), with its gorgeous namesake waterfall.

At the northern end of this area, on U.S. 15 just south of the Pennsylvania border, is the town of **Emmitsburg**, whose Main Street is still lit by gas lamps. This picturesque town, aside from its proximity to the aforementioned parks, is also an antiques-lovers mecca, with its Antique Mall featuring 120 shops.

After a day of hiking or shopping, you can settle at the **Stonehurst Inn** (800–497–8458, www.stonehurstinn.com), where the owners pamper you with a lavish breakfast, afternoon tea, hors d'oeuvres, and dessert. You hardly need to go out for dinner! The inn is located in its own little private park, pond included, at 9436 Waynesboro Road in Emmitsburg (rates $75 to $105).

Just south of town on U.S. 15 is the **National Shrine of St. Elizabeth Ann Seton** (301–447–6606, www.setonshrine.org), dedicated to the first American-born saint, who lived from 1774 to 1821 and was beatified in 1963.

Maryland's Heartland

Fifteen miles south of Emmitsburg, and about one hour north of Washington via I–270, in the heart of the Free State, are two of Maryland's most endearing towns, **Frederick** and **New Market**.

Both are nationally renowned antiques meccas, even more so than Emmitsburg, but they're also just great spots to unwind and enjoy the simple pleasures of graceful centuries-old buildings, perfectly manicured gardens, and friendly denizens. Frederick's 33-block historic district, punctuated by towering church spires, is a must for history and architecture buffs.

At the edge of town is the **Children's Museum of Rose Hill Manor Park,** a 1790s mansion and estate that is now a partially hands-on living museum of nineteenth-century life. Costumed guides lead you through an orchard, blacksmith shop, log cabin, and the manor house itself. You'll also see a carriage museum and farm museum where the vehicles on display are explained in depth and related to developments today. Rose Hill Manor is at 1611 North Market Street, Frederick (301–694–1650, www.co.frederick.md.us/parks/RoseHill.htm).

Frederick preserves its Civil War heritage in sites like the **National Museum of Civil War Medicine** (48 East Patrick Street, 301–695–1864, www.civilwarmed.org). The museum, housed in a circa-1832 building used as an embalming station after Antietam, features exhibitions on Civil War surgeons' tents, field hospitals, and nurses. Unusual artifacts include a Civil War ambulance,

wheelchair, and some medical implements. The museum is open Monday through Saturday from 10:00 A.M. to 5:00 P.M. and Sunday from 11:00 A.M. to 5:00 P.M. Admission is $7.00 for adults and $5.00 for children.

Nearby, the **Monocacy National Battlefield Park** (301–662–3515, www.nps.gov/mono) commemorates the battle in which Union General Lew Wallace and his troops stopped the advance of Confederate General Jubal Early to Washington on July 9, 1864.

To learn of more interesting sights in and around Frederick, contact the Tourism Council of Frederick County, 19 East Church Street, Frederick (800–999–3613, www.visitfrederick.org).

New Market comes alive virtually every weekend of the year with a bazaarlike setting of antiques dealers and craftspeople. It is the self-proclaimed "Antiques Capital of Maryland" and is home to more than 40 shops. You'd be able to walk the length of the village in a few minutes if you didn't need to stop so often to explore the wares for sale.

Both these towns are so close to Metro Washington that an overnight stay is unnecessary; however, if you're looking for a romantic getaway, consider the **Cascade Inn** bed-and-breakfast, about 25 minutes north of Frederick on Highway 550 (301–241–4161, www.thecascadeinn.com). Set into the woods like a fairy-tale cottage, the five-room inn is a light, bright home furnished with lace and wicker. Some rooms have fireplaces and Jacuzzis. Rates range from $125 to $150.

Farther south, on Highway 85, is the romantic **Inn at Buckeystown** (800–272–1190, www.innatbuckeystown.com), in the village of the same name ($115 to $275 per couple, depending on meal plan). The eight rooms are furnished in lavish Victorian style, including crystal chandeliers, brocade upholstery, and brass-screened fireplaces. Dinner is equally lavish, with rich continental specialties like creamy bisques, game pâtés, and homemade pastries.

Maryland's Last Frontier

High in the Allegheny Plateau, in the western-most reaches of the Free State, sparkles Maryland's **Deep Creek Lake**. A fishing and boating dreamland (it's possible to catch wall-eye, bass, catfish, and trout in the same day), Deep Creek also affords weekend travelers with a number of lakeside cabin, cottage, and chalet rentals. **Railey Realty** (800–544–2425, www.railey.com) or **Coldwell Banker Deep Creek Realty** (800–252–7335, www.deep creekrealty.com) can arrange for overnight or extended stays.

With 65 miles of shoreline, Deep Creek is best seen from the deck of a sailboat or motorboat. Rentals are available, but escalating insurance costs have made them an expensive option. Our advice is to bring your own boat or make friends with someone who has one. Honestly, though, it's possible to enjoy the plentiful attractions of Garrett County without ever dipping a toe in the lake.

In nearby Oakland you can hop on the **Western Maryland Scenic Railroad** (800–872–4650, TRAIN–50; www.wmsr.com) or arrange for an afternoon of white-water rafting on the **Cheat** and **Youghiogheny** (pronounced YOK-eh-gain-e) Rivers. No trip to Western Maryland would be complete without a stop along the boulder-strewn banks of the aptly named **Savage River,** site of the 1989 World Whitewater Canoe/Kayak Championships and the 1992 U.S. Olympic Trials.

A DOWNHILL RUN

Snow? Around here? Okay, the Appalachians aren't exactly the Rockies, but you can sneak in a couple of days of passable skiing in these parts without taking the time and money for a trip out West.

In Virginia, if you're looking for full-service, hotel-style resorts, you have the option of **Wintergreen** (800–266–2444, www.winter greenresort.com), $126 to $849, depending on size of accommodations, per night, off Highway 664. They also have some very nice condos about which you may want to inquire.

The **Homestead** is another good choice (800–838–1766, www.thehomestead.com), starting at $165 per person, per night, including breakfast and dinner. Both offer all the après-ski amenities you could wish for, and the restaurants are very good. You could easily spend a luxurious few days at either locale, but Wintergreen has been rated by the national ski magazines as one of the best downhill spots in the South. For daytrippers or a self-catering holiday, try the modest hills at Bryce (800–821–1444, www.bryceresort .com) or Massanutten (540–289–4952, www.massre sort.com).

West Virginia's **Snowshoe** (877–441–4FUN, www.snowshoemtn.com)—a sprawling complex off U.S. 250 that spans several miles—and the smaller **Canaan Valley** off West Virginia Highway 32 (800–622–4121, www.canaanresort.com), though farther from Washington (four to five hours), are popular with more experienced skiers—trails are a bit longer and more varied. Snowshoe has the extra attraction of the **Red Fox Inn** (304–572–1111), one of the premier restaurants in the mid-Atlantic region, a surprising find for gourmets who also like to ski. Reserve ahead if you intend to eat here during your stay—all those raves in the national food magazines guarantee a packed house. Snowshoe has an extensive condo and hotel complex with rates from $151; Canaan's rates range from about $80 to $110. Cross-country aficionados head to the White Grass Ski Touring Center in Canaan Valley (304–866–4114, www.white grass.com) for superb trails, friendly instruction, and a cozy lodge for hanging out, sipping cocoa, and enjoying home-cooked chili and other hearty, wholesome fare.

Just 90 minutes from Washington (about 20 miles beyond I–270, right past the Maryland-Pennsylvania border), Pennsylvania's **Ski Liberty** (717–642–8282, www.skiliberty .com) and **Whitetail** (717– 328–9400, www .skiwhitetail.com), are easy day trip destinations. Liberty is an older ski area with a simple lodge, but Whitetail is a spiffy new day resort whose design has won raves from national ski magazines. The trail selection at both places is limited, and even those ranked most difficult would be considered easy runs in Colorado, but they can't be beat for convenience. **Wisp Resort,** 296 Marsh Hill Road, McHenry, Maryland (800–GO2WISP, www.wispresort.com), near Deep Creek Lake, is Maryland's lone downhill ski area (room rates start at $229 on the weekends).

BY THE WATER: BEACHES AND BEYOND THE CHESAPEAKE BAY

Legendary Baltimore journalist and social commentator H. L. Mencken once called the Chesapeake Bay a "great big protein factory" on account of the inordinate amount of fish, crabs, and oysters found in its brackish waters. If Mencken were alive today, he would probably amend his definition to include the number of people who regularly find sanctuary on the fabled body of water. Of course, the bay is a different creature today than it was during Mencken's time—in some ways better, in other ways worse.

Ecologically, the Bay is being tested by humanity's heavy hand. Pollution and urban sprawl have been blamed for historically low populations of oysters and some fish. Chesapeake watermen, for centuries the life and blood of the region, are slowly dying off as competition heats up in the global seafood industry.

To speak of the Bay and its rich traditions in the past tense would be foolish, though. Recent conservation efforts, such as those of the Chesapeake Bay Foundation, have elevated awareness of this vital natural resource. As the Chesapeake, divided nearly equally between Maryland and Virginia, continues to attract record numbers of tourists to its pleasant shores and peaceful waterside villages, one can only hope that we will continue to find the energy and courage to save the Bay.

The Shore

You may have heard it called Delmarva Peninsula. Washingtonians know it as the Eastern Shore. To locals, it's simply "the Shore." For the uninitiated it's the land found on the eastern side of the Chesapeake Bay Bridge.

This fertile coastal-plain peninsula contains much of Delaware, a good chunk of Maryland, and a sliver of Virginia, thus the name Delmarva. Bounded by the Bay and the Atlantic Ocean, the Eastern Shore is the land of proud watermen, of Canada geese and duck blinds, sprawling farms, colonial villages, and what seems more water than land.

To experience the true flavor of the Chesapeake—which inspired James Michener's novel of the same name—it's imperative to "cross the bridge." Maybe you've already seen the bumper stickers proclaiming, "There is No Intelligent Life West of the Chesapeake Bay." It's a bit parochial (and tongue-in-cheek), sure, but once you catch the spirit of the place, you just might start agreeing with the notion.

After crossing the bridge—the Chesapeake Bay Bridge, that is—think about getting off U.S. 50. There's nothing particularly exciting about this highway unless you're into strips of shopping centers, boat yards, and liquor stores. Our advice is to take the slower-moving but scenic Maryland Highway 213 and head north to **Chestertown,** Maryland, on the banks of the Chester River. On the way you'll pass through Centreville, government seat of Queen Anne's County and site of the oldest courthouse, circa 1792, and still in use in Maryland.

Chestertown, with its eighteenth-century waterside Georgian mansions, is best discovered on foot, like during the Candlelight Walking Tour each September. Stroll through the grounds of **Washington College,** the 10th-oldest college in America and the only one to which George Washington personally granted the use of his name. For an overnight stay consider the **White Swan Tavern** at 231 High Street (410–778–2300, www.whiteswan tavern.com), in the heart of the historic district and a stone's throw from the Chester River (rates from $140). Guests are welcomed with a bottle of wine in their room and, in the morning, served a continental breakfast. The inn is small—only six rooms—so it's best to reserve early in summer. You'll enjoy the flower-rimmed patio and the bright antiques-filled rooms.

From Chestertown, backtrack on Highway 213 and connect with U.S. 50 (but just for a short 20 miles) south to **Easton.** Now you're in the heart of Talbot County, undeniably Maryland's most aristocratic jurisdiction. Easton is the site of the massive **Waterfowl Festival** held each November, in which the world's finest wildlife artists, wood-carvers, and sculptors gather to strut their stuff along with tens of thousands of migratory Canada geese.

Easton's fabled **Tidewater Inn,** 101 East Dover Street (800–237–8775, www.tidewater inn.com), accommodates hunters (including their dogs), sailors, antiques hunters, and the occasional diplomat (rates from $109). Nearby, you can visit Third Haven Friends Meeting House, circa 1682, believed to be the oldest frame building dedicated to religious meetings in America.

Heading west, take a spin through **St. Michael's,** a waterfront hamlet that fooled the British Navy one evening during the War of 1812 when citizens placed lamplights in the tops of trees, thus giving the illusion that the village sat on a hill. The British ships fired at the tops of the trees and missed the town altogether.

You won't want to miss an outdoor crabfest at the **Crab Claw** (410–745–2900, www.thecrabclaw.com), overlooking the harbor, or a walk through the **Chesapeake Maritime Museum** (410–745–2916, www.cbmm .org), with its signature "screwpile" lighthouse, more than a century old. The place to stay in St. Michael's—if you want to splurge—is the **Inn at Perry Cabin,** 308 Watkins Lane (410–745–2200, www.perrycabin.com), owned and decorated by the husband of the late Laura Ashley (summer high-season rates from $385 to $770, including full breakfast and afternoon tea). This is a deluxe, English country-house spot overlooking the water—just the getaway for a special occasion.

From St. Michael's, you're just a few minutes' drive from **Tilghman Island,** a working waterman's community, and **Oxford,** arguably the most scenic town in Maryland. Tilghman is crab and oyster docks, colorful watermen, and rusted boats. It's authentic Eastern Shore. The most colorful lodging on the island can be found at **Harrison's Chesapeake House** (410–886–2121, www.chesapeakehouse.com), a traditional Chesapeake fish camp that specializes in regional cuisine and hassle-free fishing trips.

Oxford, on the other hand, is glistening million-dollar sailboats, painstakingly restored Federal-style homes, and charming bed-and-breakfasts, like the circa-1710 **Robert Morris Inn** at the end of Maryland Highway 333 (888–823–4012, www.robertmorrisinn.com, rates from $90). Head into Oxford from the north and cross the placid Tred-Avon River aboard the Oxford-Bellevue Ferry (410–745–9023, www.oxfordbellevueferry.com), the oldest ferry still in use in the United States. The 10-minute trip is well worth the nominal fee, especially if you're into lowering the old blood pressure.

Don't leave the region without a stop down the bay in **Cambridge,** hometown of American hero Harriet Tubman, founder of the Underground Railroad. Tubman was born on a plantation outside of town and single-handedly made her way to freedom in the North. She ventured back into the South at least 20 times to help free hundreds of other slaves during the Civil War era.

Islands in Time

Near the geographic center of the Chesapeake Bay lie two of the most intriguing islands in the area. **Smith Island,** Maryland (800–521–9189, www.smithisland.org), and **Tangier Island,** Virginia (757–787–7911, www.tangierisland-va.com), are indeed places that have defied the encroachment of modern society. Both islands, just a few square miles large, were settled by the first wave of British

Close-up

A Refuge for Solitude-Seekers

Each weekend in summer, thousands of Washingtonians hit the roads and head to Ocean City, Rehoboth, and Virginia Beach. Fun spots all, but crowded with boardwalks, condos, fast-food joints, and . . . well, thousands of Washingtonians. Choose the road less traveled, though, and you'll be rewarded with miles of pristine beach, wide, fluffy dunes that go on forever—and sweet isolation. Too good to be true? Not on Assateague Island National Seashore, a wildlife refuge of breathtaking, unspoiled beauty, half in Virginia, half in Maryland.

Here you'll find the wild ponies made famous in Marguerite Henry's classic children's book, *Misty of Chincoteague*. A bike ride along the narrow asphalt road that borders the wetlands is the best way to glimpse these graceful herds. They are fairly accustomed to tourists and continue to graze as you look on, but don't get too near because they'll kick!

For a truly dramatic spectacle, station yourself in nearby Chincoteague, Virginia, on the last Wednesday of July, when the local fire department rounds up the ponies and swims them across the bay for auction the next day—to the delight of thousands of spectators. When the crowds depart, Assateague is left once more in tranquillity.

On Assateague be prepared to make your own fun. You won't find amusement parks or family-fun centers—the only facilities are a bathhouse and restrooms on the Virginia side and two campgrounds on the Maryland side. What you will find, though, are more than 300 species of birds and 44 species of mammals, such as the endangered Delmarva fox squirrel and the miniature oriental deer. Scan the water and you may be lucky enough to spot a pod of bottlenose dolphins. A stroll along the undeveloped shoreline will bring you face to face with dozens of sandpipers, pelicans, and gulls. No one bothers these creatures, so they aren't overly bothered by humans.

At the southern end of the island is the picturesque red-and-white striped lighthouse, first lighted in 1867 and still in use today. The original light system, however, has been replaced by a modern system, but the original remains on display in the lighthouse. The structure is operated by the U.S. Coast Guard and is accessible via a cleared trail through the woodlands.

You won't find hotels on Assateague, but a short drive to Chincoteague will lead you to some nice inns, as well as a dozen or so budget motels. The closest to

explorers to the Chesapeake Bay in the early seventeenth century (led by Captain John Smith). The descendants of the colonists, folks with names like Bradshaw, Harrison, Smith, and Crosby, still work the water for crabs and oysters. Other islanders make and sell high-quality crafts, such as hand-carved duck decoys.

These islands are insular, as evidenced by the fact that electricity only arrived there in the 1940s. Also, the islanders' speech even today has traces of the area's Elizabethan/Cor-

WIld ponies make for an unusual sight at Assateague Island's sandy beaches. COURTESY WASHINGTON, D.C. CONVENTION AND TOURISM CORPORATION

Assateague—only about 100 yards away, in fact—is **Best Western Chincoteague Island** (800–553–6117, www.bestwestern.com), on Maddox Boulevard, right beside the bridge that connects the preserve to Chincoteague. You'll also find bicycle rentals everywhere you turn, because that is a great way to see the area.

Assateague's two campgrounds are on the Maryland side, which takes about one hour to reach via the mainland—you can't cross over on the island in a vehicle. One campground is run by the National Park Service (410–641–1441), and the other is operated by the state of Maryland (410–641–2120). Visit www.assateague island.com for more visitor's information.

A word of advice: During the months of July and August, be prepared to battle giant mosquitoes and horse flies; however, from April through June and from September through early November, few spots can rival enchanting Assateague.

nish roots. Residents are friendly, and you may notice that those traveling in trucks and cars honk their horns and wave to greet all other vehicles and pedestrians. Visitors are greeted with good cheer to be sure, but leave your motorized vehicles and pets at home—visitors are not allowed to bring them to the islands, and, anyway, bicycles are more fun and can be easily rented. Spring is a particularly lovely time to visit, because you'll find a variety of exotic trees in bloom, including pomegranates, pears, figs, and, later in the year, mimosas.

Religion has always been a very important part of island life, ever since the Methodist Church was established in the Bay islands during the late 1800s, and tourists are welcomed at local church services. If getting as far off the beaten path as possible interests you, both islands are accessible by U.S. mail boats and other small ferries from the city dock at Crisfield, Maryland, along the far southern edge of the Eastern Shore.

Private cruise lines also provide access in season (April to October). Contact Tangier Island Cruises in Crisfield, at (800) 863–2338, www.tangierislandcruises.com. To reach Crisfield from Washington, head east on U.S. 50, south on U.S. 13, and then follow Maryland Highway 413 to Crisfield. Closer to home, you can reach Smith Island from Point Lookout, Maryland. To get there from Washington, follow U.S. 301 south to Maryland Highway 235—it will lead you right to the Point, where cruises to the islands originate aboard the *Capt. Tyler* (410–425–2771).

For more information on charter companies and schedules, contact the Somerset County Tourism Office at (800) 521–9189, www.visitsomerset.com.

The Humble Western Shore

In all fairness, you don't have to cross the bridge to enjoy the bounty of the Bay. Although less rustic and authentic than the land to the east, Maryland's Western Shore, also known as Southern Maryland, is doing a pretty good job of balancing suburban growth while retaining some of its maritime character. If you've got angling in your blood but lack a good, solid boat to grapple the Chesapeake, drive down to Chesapeake Beach's **Rod N Reel Dock** (301–855–8450) and charter a captain for a day or grab a spot on a headboat. Either option will place you with appropriate tackle and bait and a knowledgeable skipper and first mate.

Typically, fishing on the Bay is best in the late spring and fall when bluefish and striped bass are biting. Summer is always good for panfish or redfish. South from Chesapeake

Beach, head down Route 4 to **Solomons** (www.sba.solomons.md.us), the picturesque sailing hamlet that boasts some of the finest seafood dining on the Bay, including **Di Giovanni's Dock of the Bay** (410–394–6400, www.digiovannisrestaurant.com) and **Solomons Pier** (410–326–2424).

Within a short drive you can visit the crucifix-shaped Middleham Chapel, circa 1748; the fossil-lined **Calvert Cliffs State Park** (301–743–7613); and historic St. Marys City, Maryland's seventeenth-century capital (www.dnr.state.md.us/publiclands/southern/calvertcliffs.html).

Drive down to **Point Lookout State Park** (301–872–5688, www.dnr.state.md.us/publiclands/southern/pointlookout.html) on the southernmost tip of Maryland and explore the remains of Fort Lincoln, one of the largest Union-run prisons during the Civil War. The park's Civil War Museum is open weekends May through September.

Charm City

In many ways **Baltimore** is the ultimate Chesapeake city. The Bay's influence is virtually everywhere, from the seafood cuisine (Ralph Waldo Emerson once dubbed the city "the gastronomic center of the universe"); to the thriving Inner Harbor area of shops, museums, and hotels; to Fells Point, the rejuvenated harborfront district with eclectic pubs, galleries, and Federal-style town homes.

From Fells Point, a variety of sailing trips are available through **Schooner Nighthawk Cruises** (410–276–SHIP), including a three-hour buffet moonlight sail, a Sunday champagne brunch sail, a Sunday evening crab cruise, and a two-hour midnight mystery cruise on Saturdays.

If you're not on the water or at an Orioles game at the showplace **Oriole Park** at Camden Yards (www.orioles.mlb.com), the next best place to be in Baltimore is the **National Aquarium** (410–576–3800, www.aqua.org). It offers more than 10,500 specimens and 560 aquatic species and probably the best shark tank in the nation, from nurse sharks to great whites! The Inner Harbor also boasts the **Maryland Science Center** (410–685– 5225, www.mdsci.org), and the **Port Discovery Children's Museum** (410–727–8120, www.portdiscovery.org).

You can go through the **National Historic Seaport of Baltimore** (877–NH–CPORT, www.natlhistoricseaport.org) for a passcard that admits you to 15 of the city's maritime attractions, including the USS *Constellation*, Fort McHenry, and the U.S. submarine *Torsk*.

Wrap up the day with an overnight's stay at the cozy **Admiral Fell Inn,** 888 South Broadway (410–522–7380, www. admiralfell .com), overlooking the harbor in Fells Point, and you'll discover why Baltimore is called "Charm City." Rates start at $169, including continental breakfast.

Chesapeake (Largely) Undiscovered

Maryland may be for crabs, but Virginia is equally tied to the history, traditions, and fortunes of the Bay. There's no better starting place to explore the Old Dominion's maritime mystique than the Northern Neck, the verdant, five-county-long jut of land bounded by the Bay and the Potomac and Rappahannock Rivers.

Less than a three-hour drive from Washington, the tiny Northern Neck village of **Irvington** has been welcoming anglers, boaters, golfers, and antiques collectors for generations. The centerpiece of the town has to be the opulent **Tides,** 480 King Carter Drive, Irvington, Virginia (800–843–3746, www.the tides.com), a combination resort and conference facility that claims perhaps the top golf course in the state, the world-class Golden Eagle. Newly renovated waterfront rooms in the luxurious inn are from $360 per couple, while rooms in the lodge across the creek begin at $169. Overlooking Carter's Creek and the Rappahannock River, the Tides is just a half-day sail from several points along the open Bay, including the equally refined resort area of Windmill Point.

Baltimore's nickname, "Charm City," comes from a 1970s advertising campaign. Visitors were given a charm bracelet and were encouraged to buy souvenir charms at the city's attractions. The name stuck.

Farther north up the Neck lies the sleepy little town of **Reedville,** a popular stay for bed-and-breakfast lodgers, many of whom come from as far away as the Carolinas and New England to soak up the quiet Chesapeake atmosphere. On Reedville's shaded Main Street, visitors can choose from the **Gables** (804–453–5209, www.thegablesbb.com/ reedville.html), a dramatic waterside Victorian mansion, or **Morris House,** a renovated early-nineteenth-century fishing captain's house (804–453–7016). (Rates at both start at less than $100.)

Just south of the Northern Neck is the Middle Peninsula, a region of wide-open spaces and shadowy coves; it's amazingly undiscovered given its proximity to Richmond and the Hampton Roads area. One of the more interesting sites on the peninsula is the Rappahannock River town of **Urbanna,** home to a number of antiques stores and perhaps the world's largest oyster festival, scheduled every fall. The nearby communities of **Gloucester,** with its village green dating back to the early eighteenth century, and **Gwynn,** on postcard-perfect Gwynn's Island, make for interesting side trips through the peninsula's fragrant backroads.

The Urban Bay

Rivaling Baltimore in industrial stature is Hampton Roads, a booming metro area that includes the Virginia cities of Norfolk, Hampton, Newport News, Portsmouth, Chesapeake, Suffolk, and Virginia Beach. It's a region of hyperboles, beginning with the world's biggest natural harbor, Hampton Roads, and the world's largest naval installation, based in Norfolk.

A leisurely Bay cruise is mandatory here, and one of the best is offered by the **Miss Hampton II** (888–757–BOAT, www. miss hamptoncruises.com), in Hampton Harbor. The skipper will bring you up close to some of the nation's most awesome military vessels, including Trident subs and aircraft carriers seemingly the size of Rhode Island. The region is also pocketed with great museums, including the world-class fine-art **Chrysler Museum** (757–664–6200, www .chrysler.org), in Norfolk; the **Mariners Museum** (800–581–SAIL, www.mariner.org), in Newport News; the **Virginia Marine Science Museum** (757–425–FISH, www.vmsm .com), in Virginia Beach; the **Virginia Air & Space Center** (757–727–0900, www.vasc .org), in Hampton; and the **Casemate Museum** (757–788–3391), also in Hampton. Virginia Beach also has an environmentally oriented visitor center, the **Chesapeake Bay Center** (757–412–2320), located in First Landing/Seashore State Park. Here you'll find aquariums, exhibits, a wet lab, and touch tank—all developed by the Virginia Marine Science Center.

Also, be sure to budget time to walk through prestigious Hampton University, one of the nation's first African American colleges and easily one of the most beautiful academic settings in the Commonwealth.

Those Crazy Beaches

A cultural phenomenon strikes Washington every Friday afternoon during the summer. It seems like the whole metro area has gone to the beach, at least judging from the endless snake of traffic along U.S. 50 or down I-95. Beachgoing in these parts isn't a solitary experience, so don't expect the ambience of a deserted tropical island once you get there (the exceptions are Assateague and Chin-

> **i** To appease the kids, or simply get your quota of thrills, make a day trip down to Paramount's King's Dominion theme park in Ashland, Virginia, just north of Richmond.

coteague, the former described in this chapter's Close-up).

The mid-Atlantic, however, does have its share of perfectly fine beaches, each with its own distinctive personality. To beach his own, in other words. **Assateague Island National Seashore** (www.nps.gov/asis), a favorite place in the sun, is 33 miles of pristine, undeveloped beachfront stretching from nearly Ocean City, Maryland, to Chincoteague, Virginia. It is much less visited than any other beach in the region and is sure to revive your spirits, with its vast stretches of pure, primitive shoreline.

Five other beaches in brief: **Ocean City, Maryland**, three hours from Washington, is a nice stretch of beach, but extremely commercial both on and away from the water (tacky boardwalk emporiums, strip malls, honky-tonks, and high-rise condos, etc.). It is, nonetheless, a huge hangout for the young and wild at heart. There are hotels, motels, and rentals galore—too many to name and in every price range—so your best bet is to contact the Ocean City (or O.C.) Visitor Information line at (800) 626–2326, www.ococean.com.

To the north, **Bethany Beach, Delaware** (800–962–SURF, www. bethany-fenwick.org), attracts a much older (late 20s through retirees) crowd than O.C. but is not nearly as developed with high-rises and commercial properties. Parking is a hassle, though; it's very restricted in residential areas, and options are few, so you'll probably end up walking a bit. Still, it's a great weekend destination just for the relaxed setting and comparatively pristine beaches. **Rehoboth Beach, Delaware** (302–856–1818, www.visitsouthern delaware.com), just north of Bethany, is something of a cross between Bethany and Ocean City. Plenty of families and older singles can be found roaming Rehoboth's busy, colorful boardwalk, but there are also some very posh beach homes here, as well as upscale eateries. Sometimes called the nation's summer capital for its popularity with Washingtonians, Rehoboth is the kind of resort town where you can park your car for a week and go everywhere you want to go on foot (except for the

Key Attractions

Assateague Island National Seashore	(410) 641–1441	www.nps.gov/asis
Maryland State Parks & Public Lands	(877) 620–8367	www.dnr.state.md.us/publiclands
National Aquarium in Baltimore	(410) 576–3800	www.aqua.org
U.S. Naval Academy	(410) 263–6933	www.usna.edu
Colonial Williamsburg	(800) HISTORY	www.colonialwilliams burg.org
Monticello	(804) 984–9822	www.monticello.org
Virginia Museum of Fine Arts	(888) 349–7882	www.vmfa.state.va.us
Shenandoah National Park	(540) 999–3500	www.nps.gov/shen/
West Virginia State Parks	(800) CALLWVA	www.callwva.com
Delaware Beaches	(800) 357–1818	www.visitsouthern delaware.com

great outlet malls just outside town).

Just south, **Dewey Beach, Delaware,** is the recognized hip place for the 20- and 30-something weekenders from Metro Washington. This noisy beach has an active nightlife with lots of bustling restaurants and bars (like Mardi Gras in New Orleans, the legendary Bottle and Cork must be experienced at least once).

Finally, we have to mention **Cape May, New Jersey** (800–227–2297, www.thejersey cape.com), on the southernmost tip of the Garden State and a world apart from the urban corridor of the Northeast.

A ferry ride away from the Delaware shore by way of the Cape May-Lewes Ferry (800–643–3779, www.capemaylewesferry .com), Cape May is a seaside dreamscape of Victorian homes, shops, and cottages. At the turn of the twentieth century, it was a gambling mecca for Southern aristocrats zand sea captains, but today it enjoys a robust tourist trade, luring visitors to such bed-and-breakfasts as the elegant **Mainstay Inn** ($165–$345, breakfast and tea included), 635 Columbia Avenue (609–884–8690, www.main stayinn.com), and the gothic-style **Abbey,** Columbia Avenue and Gurney Street (609–884–4506, www.abbeybedandbreakfast .com) (rates $85–$250, breakfast and tea

included). These bed-and-breakfasts, along with many others, require a three-night minimum stay on summer weekends. The entire town is listed on the National Register of Historic Places; it's one of those treasures of the mid-Atlantic that's not to be missed.

It is easy enough to find lodging at all these areas by searching the classified ads (rentals) or travel section of the Washington, D.C. newspapers. You can also contact the Delaware Tourism Office at (866) 284–7483, www.visitdelaware.com.

ANNAPOLIS—BOATING AND BARS

Maryland's state capital is a pretty town of cobbled streets, historical sights, and glorious water views, but thanks to the United States Naval Academy and St. John's College, it's also a party capital extraordinaire. Just 45 minutes from downtown D.C., Annapolis is an easy day trip, and many Washingtonians make the short trek just to browse the antiques shops, walk along the harbor, or dine in one of the myriad restaurants that line the town's main arteries.

Summer or winter, you'll gravitate to the city dock at the foot of town. All roads seem to lead here, and as you might imagine, the

i Dog owners should check out Annapolis's Quiet Waters Dog Park and Dog Beach, where pups can frolic and play with other dogs and even go for a swim in a designated dog beach. For more information and directions, visit www.aacounty.org/RecParks/parks/quiet_ waters_park/dogpark.cfm.

horseshoe-shaped harbor is bordered by shops, bars, and restaurants for every budget and age group. You will, of course, run into plenty of cadets from the Naval Academy, spiffy in their uniforms. A favorite pastime in summer is to hang out at the water's edge, admiring the yachts that moor here. The singles scene can be very active, with fancy boats replacing fancy cars.

For more serious sightseeing, don't miss the **Naval Academy** (410–263–6933, www.usna.edu), a sprawling campus that dominates the town. There's a visitor center in Ricketts Hall near the entrance (Gate 1 at the base of King George Street, just past the intersection with Randall Street, overlooking the water), where you can sign up for one of four daily walking tours. You'll learn that the academy was founded in 1845 and now trains some 4,300 cadets each year. You'll see the world's largest dormitory, Bancroft Hall, and even visit a sample room. Naval hero and Revolutionary War patriot John Paul Jones is buried in the chapel, which features stained-glass windows depicting biblical stories of the sea. Finally, you'll be left free to browse the Academy Museum, filled with model ships and nautical artifacts.

Maryland's State House is also open for tours. It is the oldest in the nation to remain in continuous legislative use, and many historical events have occurred here, such as the ratification of the Treaty of Paris ending the Revolutionary War (1784). It also once served as the nation's capitol, and it is where George Washington resigned as commander-in-chief in 1783. Tours, which begin with a short video,

are free and conducted daily at 11:00 A.M. and 3:00 P.M., (410) 974–3400. The State House is in the center of State Circle, the confluence of Maryland Avenue, Francis Street, East Street, and West Street.

Travel east on Maryland Avenue, then make your first left onto Prince George Street to arrive at **St. John's College** (www.sjca .edu), a small, beautiful liberal arts campus famous for teaching the great classics. Founded in 1696, it is the third-oldest college in the United States. On campus is the Liberty Tree, a tulip poplar estimated to be more than 400 years old.

Another major Annapolis attraction is **William Paca House** (410–267–7619) and adjoining gardens. The grand Georgian mansion was built by Paca, who served as governor of Annapolis from 1782 to 1785; however, you won't see his handiwork if you visit Paca House. The original was torn down in the 1960s, and only through the painstaking work of preservationists and archaeologists was it able to be reconstructed. It is a remarkably accurate work, and many of the original remains have been incorporated into the building. The gardens have been as beautifully restored, and they feature formal parterres, fountains, a Chinese bridge, and a miniature forest. The site can be rented for weddings and other ceremonial occasions.

When you get hungry, there's plenty to choose from in Annapolis. Opposite the city dock is the **Market House** (www.annapolis markethouse.com), a restored historical structure that used to serve as a warehouse. It now is home to all sorts of fast-food eateries. For real local, try **Buddy's Crabs & Ribs** (410–626–1100, www.buddysonline.com) at the center of Market Place near the city dock, at 100 Main Street. This big informal warehouse overlooking the waterfront is a great place for kids. You'll get crabs by the bushel or ribs by the rack and lots of newspapers and napkins so you can plunge in with no worries about the mess.

For special occasions, try the **Treaty of Paris** (410–263–2641, www.annapolisinns

.com) restaurant in the historic Maryland Inn, 16 Church Circle. The menu features Continental and New American cuisine served in a formal setting. You can also stay overnight at the inn. Annapolis has plenty of chain hotels and inns. For more information, contact the Annapolis and Anne Arundel County Conference & Visitors Bureau, 26 West Street, Annapolis (410–280–0445, www.visit-annapolis .org).

INTERNATIONAL WASHINGTON

The original plans for the Nation's Capital were drafted by a Frenchman, Pierre L'Enfant, so it seems only logical that Metro Washington would develop into a vibrant international crossroads. You don't have to look far to find some of the ingredients for this melting pot of people and traditions.

It's Chinatown, where the spirit of cross-cultural friendship is symbolized in the glittering archway that spans the width of a thoroughfare. It's Adams Morgan, where native Latinos, Ethiopians, Nigerians, Jamaicans, and others have forged a neighborhood of extraordinary contrasts, a place where many of the 100 or so restaurants serve global cuisine. It's Embassy Row, where the diplomatic corps—several thousand strong from over 150 nations—embodies the meaning of international communication, cooperation, trade, and goodwill. It's Arlington, where Vietnamese, Laotians, Cambodians, Koreans, Thai, Filipinos, and other Asian groups have prospered as merchants and small-business owners. It's virtually anywhere in the region where you'll find proud people who fled war-torn, famine-ravaged, economically distressed, or brutally oppressive homelands to begin life anew here in professions as disparate as cab driver, banker, store clerk, police officer, computer technician, engineer, maintenance worker, craftsperson, scientist, and artist. It's the presence of institutions such as the World Bank, the International Monetary Fund, and the

Organization of American States that speaks volumes about living and working in a global economy and a drastically shrinking world.

During the 1990s the immigrant population boomed in the Washington area, with most jurisdictions doubling the number of residents born outside of the United States living within their borders. And unlike previous immigrants, who mainly settled inside the city, most have made the suburbs home. In all, nearly 395,000 immigrants arrived in the Washington area in the 1990s. From 1990 through 1999, immigrants took up residence in Montgomery County, Maryland, and Fairfax County, Virginia, at a rate of about 10,000 in each county, each year. Immigrants now account for 26 percent of Montgomery County's population and 23 percent of Fairfax County's residents, according to the *Census 2000 Supplementary Survey,* a national sample of households taken along with the census. These two counties rank near the top nationally for the percentages of households where foreign languages are spoken, from Korean to Farsi. By comparison, immigrants make up only 12 percent of the residents of the District of Columbia.

Patterns of immigration become apparent as you drive around the metro area and simply look out the window. In Annandale, Korean restaurants and shops line the roads. Langley Park in Prince George's County is overwhelmingly Latino. Falls Church's Seven Corners is home to what is reportedly the nation's largest Asian-oriented shopping center, Eden Center, with more than 100 Vietnamese and Chinese stores and restaurants. The largest immigrant population in the area, some 75,000, hails from war-ravaged El Salvador.

This chapter offers a glimpse of Metro Washington's colorful and diverse character. Note that diversions such as ethnic dining are

i International residents and those seeking friends from far-off places can check out the events and networking opportunities available through Euronet International (www.euronetinternational .com). Look for happy hours, black-tie galas, theater outings, and more.

not covered here, so please see the Restaurants chapter for suggestions on gastronomic globetrotting.

RESOURCES FOR INTERNATIONAL VISITORS

International Monetary Fund Center
700 19th Street NW
Washington, DC
(202) 623–7000
www.imf.org
This intergovernmental agency's 184 member nations promote international monetary cooperation and assist in the expansion and balanced growth of global trade. The IMF also oversees the international monetary system and helps member nations overcome short-term financial problems. The visitor center (202–623–6869) has exhibits on the history of the international monetary system and IMF's role, video programs, a bookstore, and a host of educational programs for school groups.

Meridian International Center
1630 Crescent Place NW
Washington, DC
(202) 667–6800, (202) 939–5544
www.meridian.org
This nonprofit educational and cultural institution, located in two splendid mansions, has a number of educational outreach programs, both for international visitors to the United States and for United States citizens interested in other cultures. It offers seminars on international political issues, intercultural briefings for those relocating or visiting a foreign country (including those coming to the United States), educational workshops, and arts programs.

Perhaps most valuable to the non-English speaker is Meridian's language bank, a service open during weekly business hours and providing immediate help for visitors trying to make themselves understood. Washington museums and Metrorail tap into the bank when at a loss for a translation. Meridian then transfers the tourist to a three-way telephone call with a native speaker of his or her language.

Organization of American States (OAS)
17th Street and Constitution Avenue NW
Washington, DC
(202) 458–3000
www.oas.org
Formed in 1890, the OAS is the oldest international regional organization in the world, providing a forum for political, economic, social, and cultural cooperation among the member states of the Western Hemisphere, including nations in North, Central, and South America and the Caribbean. The headquarters are in a magnificent white marble building just opposite the Ellipse. OAS offers free tours of its beautiful grounds and gardens and also maintains a speakers bureau. Latin American art and antiquities are showcased in the OAS Gallery as well as at the Art Museum of the Americas, an OAS annex at 201 18th Street NW, between Constitution Avenue and C Street. The museum offers slide sets, videocassettes, and publications on Latin American art. Admission is free, and tours are available. Call (202) 458–6016 for more information.

Travelers' Aid Society
1612 K Street NW, Suite 206
Washington, DC
(202) 546–1127
www.travelersaid.org
The society maintains information desks at all Washington airports as well as Union Station (Amtrak rail arrivals). Special assistance for U.S. and foreign travelers is available at the airports from 9:00 A.M. to 9:00 P.M. weekdays and 9:00 A.M. to 6:00 P.M. on weekends.

Washington Convention and Tourism Corporation
901 7th Street NW, 4th Floor
Washington, DC
(202) 789–7000
www.washington.org
This association serves as a clearinghouse for all tourist information and can direct you to

ℹ️ Don't overlook the sometimes-forgotten wealth of resources offered by embassies and numerous international organizations in Washington.

useful foreign language resources, tours, and phone numbers, either in their own organization or elsewhere.

Washington Metrorail
600 5th Street NW
Washington, DC
(202) 637–7000
www.wmata.com
Call this number to obtain free subway and bus maps in a variety of languages or go to the Web site for help with trip planning. Routes are clearly marked, as are transfer points—a useful tool for any tourist.

World Bank
1818 H Street NW
Washington, DC
(202) 473–1000
www.worldbank.org
Officially named the International Bank for Reconstruction and Development, the World Bank's main goal is to promote long-term economic growth that reduces poverty in developing nations. A major way of doing this is by providing loans and financing investments that contribute to economic growth. Although it does not provide the community outreach and one-stop shop for resources that the IMF provides, anyone researching international economic issues should contact the bank.

THE ALLURE OF EMBASSY ROW

Few aspects of life here are more strongly identified with international Washington than the diplomatic community. The images—stereotypical but fairly accurate in most cases—are easy to conjure up: elegant residences in fashionable neighborhoods, lavish receptions and other power social functions,

limousine motorcades, large and attentive staffs, instant access to political leaders and other establishment players, and, of course, perhaps the ultimate perk: diplomatic immunity.

Ambassadors and their staffs do enjoy many special privileges, one of which is protection from many of the laws that the rest of us have to obey. This isn't to say that diplomats abuse the system and intentionally break laws knowing that they won't have to make amends, but in the event that things do happen, suffice it to say they receive considerations that go beyond the realm of even preferential treatment. Occasionally you'll read stories of a particular embassy that has amassed, let's say, several thousand dollars, worth of parking tickets and other minor violations and is being asked by the city to fork over the dough. Don't bet the mortgage on how those cases turn out.

It's tough to explain the degree to which diplomatic coddling is taken, so who better than the U.S. State Department to offer a summary explanation. Quoting Article 29 of the *Vienna Convention on Diplomatic Relations,* as found in the official Diplomatic List: "The person of a diplomatic agent shall be inviolable. He/she shall not be liable to any form of arrest or detention. The receiving State shall treat him/her with due respect and shall take all appropriate steps to prevent any attack on his/her person, freedom, or dignity." Make of it what you will.

Approximately 150 "embassies" (by law, the private residences of ambassadors and family) and "chanceries" (offices where all the work gets done) are in D.C., including those representing such geographic mind-benders as Burkina Faso, Cape Verde, Myanmar, Benin, Belarus, Mali, and the former Soviet republic of Kyrgyzstan. Chanceries are often staid and rather industrial looking, while many of the embassies are gracious old mansions, painstakingly restored, complete with manicured lawns and gardens and massive gates. Diplomatic residences are clustered primarily in the historic northwest neighborhood of

Kalorama, located north of Dupont Circle, and along Massachusetts Avenue northwest between Sheridan and Observatory Circles, thus the common reference to the area as Embassy Row. Some embassies, however, are scattered throughout other parts of town. Coats of arms and flags identify each diplomatic mission, though not all are easy to spot from the street.

Although you're unlikely to have much success walking up to an embassy and asking for a peek inside, some swing their doors open to the public a few times a year during organized tours, often as important fundraisers for charitable causes (see the Annual Events chapter). The walking/bus tours are a great way to see some beautiful homes and get a rare up-close look at a unique world.

Embassies are wonderful, often overlooked sources of information on culture, customs, history, and other facets of a nation, as well as on a broad range of travel and tourism topics, and it's all usually free. Many diplomatic missions, particularly some of the larger ones representing Canada, Mexico, Australia, and western European nations, also offer wonderful outreach programs, lectures, art exhibits, and more that are open to the public. In any one month, you might find a series of Aboriginal films at the Australian Embassy, a symposium at the Canadian Embassy on implications of the North American Free Trade Agreement, or a lecture on gourmet cooking at the French Embassy. Embassies can also direct citizens to area social clubs and various ethnic organizations.

HURDLING MONETARY BARRIERS

Besides most major banks and airports, local firms specializing in currency exchange include:

- **Travelex.** This service is a subsidiary of the large British-based travel and currency-exchange company, which recently acquired Thomas Cook's Global and Financial Services division. Aside from the usual posts at the airports, Ronald Reagan Washington National and Washington Dulles International, there are also four offices in Washington, D.C.: Union Station, 50 Massachusetts Avenue NE, Washington, D.C., (202) 371–9219; and 1800 K Street NW, Washington, D.C., (202) 872–1233. For more information, visit the Web site at www.travelex.com/.
- **American Express Travel Service.** There are several locations throughout the metropolitan area. The Washington, D.C. location is at 1501 K Street NW, Washington, D.C., (202) 457–1300. In Virginia, American Express can be found at 1101 South Joyce Street, Pentagon Row—Suite B2, Arlington, Virginia, (703) 415–5400, and at Tysons Galleria, 1801 International Drive, Suite 3203, McLean, Virginia, (703) 893–3550. Check the Web site at www.americanexpress.com/travel for hours.

SPEAKING THE LANGUAGE

If words, not money, are the problem, there are several major translation services available:

- **Berlitz Language Centers,** One Thomas Circle, Suite 105, Washington, D.C., (202) 331–1160; Tysons Corner Center, 2070 Chain Bridge Road, McLean, Virginia, (703) 883–0646; or 11300 Rockville Pike, Rockville, Maryland, (301) 770–7550. The Web site is at www.berlitz.com.
- **Meridian International Center Language Bank,** 1630 Crescent Place NW, Washington, D.C., (202) 667–6800, (202) 939–5544, www.meridian.org.

To learn more about the glorious mansions on Embassy Row, take a walking tour of the neighborhood with Washington Walks. You will hear stories of the famous and infamous residents who made this area their home. Call (202) 484–1565 or visit www.washington walks.com for details.

Embassy Listings

Unfortunately, there's no central telephone number the public can call for general information on embassies and their resources. But you can log onto www.embassy.org to get general information on each embassy. We've listed the chancery addresses, phone numbers, and Web sites of the 25 most prominent diplomatic missions. Public- or cultural-affairs personnel can help with questions and referrals. Because the turnover rate in the diplomatic corps is rather high (the diplomatic list is updated every three months), we didn't include names.

Argentina, 1600 New Hampshire Avenue NW, (202) 238–6400, www.embajadaargentinaeeuu.org

Australia, 1601 Massachusetts Avenue NW, (202) 797–3000, www.austemb.org

Brazil, 3006 Massachusetts Avenue NW, (202) 238–2700, www.brasilemb.org

Canada, 501 Pennsylvania Avenue NW, (202) 682–1740, www.canadianembassy.org

China, 2300 Connecticut Avenue NW, (202) 328–2500, www.china-embassy.org

Egypt, 3521 International Court NW, (202) 895–5400, www.egyptembassy.us

France, 4101 Reservoir Road NW, (202) 944–6000, www.info-france-usa.org

Germany, 4645 Reservoir Road NW, (202) 298–4000, www.germany-info.org

Great Britain, 3100 Massachusetts Avenue NW, (202) 588–7800, www.britain-info.org

Greece, 2221 Massachusetts Avenue NW, (202) 939–1300, www.greekembassy.org

India, 2107 Massachusetts Avenue NW, (202) 939–7000, www.indianembassy.org

Israel, 3514 International Drive NW, (202) 364–5500, www.israelemb.org

Italy, 3000 Whitehaven Street NW, (202) 612–4400, www.italyemb.org

Japan, 2520 Massachusetts Avenue NW, (202) 238–6700, www.embjapan.org

Mexico, 1911 Pennsylvania Avenue NW, (202) 728–1600, www.embassyofmexico.org

Netherlands, 4200 Linnean Avenue NW, (202) 244–5300, www.netherlands-embassy.org

Philippines, 1600 Massachusetts Avenue NW, (202) 467–9300, www.philippinesembassy-usa.org

Russia, 2650 Wisconsin Avenue NW, (202) 298–5700, www.russianembassy.org

Saudi Arabia, 601 New Hampshire Avenue NW, (202) 337–4076, www.saudiembassy.net

South Africa, 3051 Massachusetts Avenue NW, (202) 232–4400, www.saembassy.org

South Korea, 2370 Massachusetts Avenue NW, (202) 939–5600, www.koreaembassyusa.org

Spain, 2375 Pennsylvania NW, (202) 452–0100, www.spainemb.org

Sweden, 2900 K Street NW, (202) 467–2600, www.swedenabroad.se

Switzerland, 2900 Cathedral Avenue NW, (202) 745–7900, www.swissemb.org

Turkey, 2525 Massachusetts Avenue NW, (202) 612–6700, www.turkey.org

ETHNIC NEIGHBORHOODS

Adams Morgan is one of the Washington, D.C. neighborhoods you don't want to miss touring. Its hub is at 18th Street and Columbia Road NW. The area is alive with restaurants, bars, nightclubs, shops, boutiques, and a host of other attractions, many of which revolve around the community's Caribbean, Latin American, and African roots.

Chinatown encompasses 8 blocks bordered by H Street and 6th and 9th Streets NW. It is 3 blocks from the D.C. Convention Center, 7 blocks from Capitol Hill, and sits conveniently atop the Gallery Place station on Metrorail's Red, Green, and Yellow Lines. You will again see restaurants and shops galore.

The social highlight of the year is undoubtedly the Chinese New Year celebration each January and February. Perhaps the neighborhood's most visible symbol, the glittering jewel-tone Friendship Archway spans H Street at 7th. Decorated in the classical art of the Ming and Ch'ing dynasties and featuring four pillars and five roofs, the $1-million project was paid for and built jointly by the D.C. government and Beijing in 1986. The two capital cities pledged in 1984 to create a mutually beneficial relationship emphasizing cultural, economic, educational, and technical exchanges with a goal of making Washington's Chinatown a world-class center for Asian trade and finance.

INTERNATIONAL LANDMARKS

Landmarks, both natural and man-made, are as much a part of Washington's international landscape as its people. Here's a quick look at a few of the monuments and landmarks that have a distinct international flavor. Countries of all sizes are an integral part of the Nation's Capital. Among the most prominent influences:

Japanese cherry trees were a gift from the city of Tokyo in 1909. More than 3,000 of these gorgeous specimens dot the landscape near the Jefferson Memorial, the adjacent Tidal Basin, and nearby Hains Point. Because the original trees were infected by a fungus, the Department of Agriculture had them destroyed. Replacements arrived in 1912 and were officially welcomed by First Lady Helen Taft and the wife of the Japanese ambassador.

Saving the trees was deemed a national priority. You see, each April (with a little cooperation from Mother Nature), in what is surely one of the most welcome harbingers of spring, the trees sprout their brilliant pink-and-white blossoms. Thousands of passersby enjoy seeing the blooming trees during the weeklong National Cherry Blossom Festival, but the dazzling "peak" period lasts only a few days. The weather greatly affects the arrival, brilliance, and longevity of the blossoms, so listen for the National Park Service's blossom forecasts as spring approaches.

The Netherlands Carillon is an often-overlooked landmark that has strong foreign ties. After World War II the Dutch government gave the 49-bell tower to the United States in gratitude. Looming over Arlington near the Marine Corps War Memorial (Iwo Jima statue) and Arlington National Cemetery, it is surrounded by a sea of tulips. It is also the site of numerous summer and holiday concerts.

Even Washington's most famous landmark, the Washington Monument, has global influence. The 555-foot obelisk—the world's largest masonry structure—contains nearly 200 memorial stones in its interior walls. Among the stones are a block of lava from Italy's infamous Mount Vesuvius, a mosaic block from the ruins of Carthage (present-day Tunisia), a stone from the Swiss chapel of William Tell, and a stone praising George Washington in Chinese. There is also a replica of the stone given by Pope Pius IX. The original stone was stolen by a radical anti-Catholic group in 1854 and dumped in the Potomac. The replacement, a gift to the National Park Service in 1982, is Italian marble inscribed in Latin with the phrase *A Roma Americae*, meaning "From Rome to America."

D.C.'s international character shines through with annual events like the D.C. Caribbean Carnival. COURTESY WASHINGTON, D.C. CONVENTION AND TOURISM CORPORATION

HERITAGE FESTIVALS

What better way to honor the diverse heritage of Metro Washingtonians than with parties, parades, festivals, and other such events? Each year literally starts with a bang as the colorful Chinese Lunar New Year parade draws thousands with music, firecrackers, and colorful costumes. In spring several metro-area municipalities celebrate St. Patrick's Day with their own parades. You can binge on traditional green beer and corned beef and cabbage.

Choose any month of the year and you're likely to find an ethnic celebration in Washington. The Greek, British, Hispanic—they're all ready to party in their unique ways. For a great mix of them all, catch the popular Smithsonian Folklife Festival, which highlights our diverse cultural background. The annual festival is held over a 10-day period in late June and early July (always including the 4th). (For more on these and other celebrations, turn to the Annual Events chapter.)

CULTURAL IMMERSION

Almost every nation has an interest group located in Washington, but most of them focus on promoting their agendas to the media and the U.S. government. If you want to delve deeper into the multicultural side of Washington, many organizations provide public outreach. For more information, contact the following:

Washington, D.C.

Alliance Française de Washington
2142 Wyoming Avenue NW
Washington, DC
(202) 234–7911
www.francedc.org
This organization has branches throughout the world and in other major U.S. cities. Native speakers provide French lessons, and cultural and social activities are available, all at a reasonable cost.

Association of American Foreign Service Worldwide
5555 Columbia Pike, Suite 208
Arlington, VA
(703) 820–5420
www.aafsw.org
Foreign service families moving in and out of Washington are often strangers to the city and its international resources. This organization provides a home base for such families and helps them cope with their itinerant lifestyles. As the name implies, it has close ties with the U.S. State Department and can serve as a resource for those stationed in Washington and abroad.

Central American Resource Center
1459 Columbia Road NW
Washington, DC
(202) 328–9799
www.dccarecen.org
This advocacy organization provides direct legal services on immigration issues to the enormous Latino community in the D.C. area.

Goethe Institut
812 7th Street NW
Washington, DC
(202) 289–1200
www.goethe.de/uk/was
This active nonprofit organization's mission is promoting the German language and culture worldwide. It is run with impressive Teutonic efficiency and offers a wide variety of cultural activities, media outreach, and German language classes.

Hispanic Service Center
1805 Belmont Road NW
Washington, DC
(202) 234–3435
Not a tourist organization, nor exactly one for

i If you're in search of a number of international dining options near one another, consider spending an evening in Arlington, Bethesda, Wheaton, Adams Morgan, or Chinatown.

ℹ️ Parking is scarce and traffic can be a hassle, so take Metrorail or some other form of public transportation to downtown monuments like the Lincoln Memorial or to annual festivals such as the Chinese New Year Parade.

cultural exchange, this service center is instead a resource for Spanish speakers in America who need help with government documents, translation, housing, and other daily life issues.

The Hospitality Information Service (THIS)
1630 Crescent Place NW
Washington, DC
(202) 232–3002
www.meridian.org

THIS is like a Welcome Wagon for foreign diplomats stationed in Washington. It serves as a valuable source of information as they settle here, providing lists of schools, stores, hospitals, and other crucial information. THIS also sponsors social and cultural events to help introduce diplomatic community members to one another.

House of Sweden
2900 K Street NW
Washington, DC
www.houseofsweden.com

For 18 months, beginning in the fall of 2006, House of Sweden will develop several programs and topics that highlight the achievements and values of Swedish society. The organization will examine the relationship between Sweden and the United States through exhibitions, performances, seminars, and discussions. The overall themes are broad in nature, with welcome participation and input from partners and program sponsors. The knowledge and background that various industry representatives contribute will generate artistic, innovative, and thought-provoking exhibits and will provide a foundation for additional seminars, conferences, and other program activities.

Islamic Center
2551 Massachusetts Avenue NW
Washington, DC
(202) 332–8343
www.theislamiccenter.com

The Islamic Center's primary mission is managing the Washington mosque, which is in the same building (see the Worship chapter). The center also offers Arabic language classes and periodic cultural events.

Japan-America Society of Washington
1020 19th Street NW, LL40
Washington, DC
(202) 833–2210
www.us-japan.org/dc

Japan is an enigma to most Americans, and the Japan-America Society seeks to bridge the gap of understanding with exchanges of information on business, culture, and the arts. The society promotes several concerts and performances a year at venues throughout Washington, as well as smaller gatherings aimed at those doing business in or touring Japan. It can also direct you to Japanese language classes by native speakers.

Japan Information and Culture Center
1155 21st Street NW
Washington, DC
(202) 238–6949
www.embjapan.org

There is perhaps no diplomatic outlet in Washington quite like the expansive Japan Information and Culture Center, an adjunct of the Japanese Embassy and definitely the top local authority on all things Japanese. The center offers a friendly, helpful staff; permanent exhibit space for showings by a wide range of Japanese artists; and a calendar of events filled with programs about Japan and its people.

Meridian International Center
1630 Crescent Place NW
Washington, DC
(202) 667–6800, (202) 939–5544
www.meridian.org

Please refer to the beginning of this chapter, where we have included a full listing for the Meridian International Center.

National Council for International Visitors
1420 K Street NW
Washington, DC
(202) 842–1414
www.nciv.org
The council is a national network of program agencies and community-based organizations that provide services to participants in international exchange programs. These nonprofit groups design and implement professional programs and internships and provide cultural activities and home hospitality opportunities for foreign officials and international scholars.

Suburban Maryland

Chinese Culture and Community Service Center
16039 Comprint Circle
Gaithersburg, MD
(240) 631–1200
www.ccac-dc.org
This organization provides a variety of language classes in English and Chinese as well as cultural programs for everyone from tots to seniors. It recently reached out to the large community of Washington-area families who have adopted children from China, to offer classes for both children and parents.

Italian Cultural Society of Washington, DC
4848 Battery Lane, Suite 100
Bethesda, MD
(202) 333–2426
www.italianculturalsociety.org
This group provides language lessons and once-a-month social gatherings for Italians or anyone practicing the language.

Muslim Community Center
15200 New Hampshire Avenue
Silver Spring, MD
(301) 384–3454
www.mccmd.org
This is the largest Muslim center in Maryland, providing a wide range of services for the Muslim community. The center operates a full-time school, the Islamic Academy of MCC, and plans to expand its facilities and services even further.

RELOCATION

With its population of highly educated, afflu-ent residents working everywhere from the White House and the Smithsonian to the booming biotech corridor in Montgomery County, the Washington area is a prime desti-nation for many recent graduates and career changers from around the country. The metro area has one of the highest annual household incomes in the nation, $72,799, according to a 2005 study by Claritas. It has the highest rate of residents holding graduate degrees in the United States—19 percent of all adult res-idents.

At the same time, however, Washingtoni-ans pay a price for living in the Nation's Capi-tal. Despite a recent softening in the market, housing prices are among the highest in the nation, with an average housing cost of $424,700 in 2005. And a study released by the Texas Transportation Institute in late 2003 showed that Washington has the third-worst traffic in the country, with drivers spending an average of 34 hours a year delayed in traffic.

Washingtonians have to put up with some pretty mercurial weather, too. In 2003 alone, Washington-area residents had to contend with a 19-inch snowstorm that shut down much of the region for several days, a soggy spring and summer awash in record rainfall, and Hurricane Isabel, which caused record amounts of damage and power outages. In more "average" years, expect hot, humid sum-mers; crisp falls; moderate winters, with a few small storms that bring an average yearly snowfall of about a foot; and spectacular

> **i** To compare the cost of living in Washington, D.C. with the cost of living in your hometown, visit www.best places.net/col for a quick cost-of-living calculator.

springs, with cherry blossoms, daffodils, tulips, and other blooms abounding through-out neighborhoods.

In this chapter we'll take a look at buying a house or renting an apartment in Washing-ton's booming real estate market. Subsequent chapters cover such important information for newcomers as child care, education, health care, senior citizens, worship, and media.

THE RESIDENTIAL REAL ESTATE MARKET

Finding a home—whether it's an apartment, condominium, town home, or a detached house—can be one of the most stressful activ-ities you'll ever engage in. It's tough enough if you're already familiar with the market, but for most newcomers this isn't the case.

The Metro Washington real estate scene is one of the most intimidating anywhere, given the physical expanse of the region, the volatil-ity of the market, and the subtle but important differences (political, social, demographic) that exist among Washington, D.C., Virginia, and Maryland.

Home prices across the metro area escalated madly in the 1980s, a less-than-auspicious rambler jumping in price from $90,000 in 1980 to $130,000 in 1986 and $155,000 just two years later. But in the early to mid-1990s, housing prices cooled consider-ably, as the economy slumped and interest rates rose.

But by the end of the 1990s, the real estate market began to make up for lost time, with multiple contracts being placed on many houses in the tony suburbs close to the city, such as Bethesda and Chevy Chase.

The booming market slowed down consid-erably in 2006 as interest rates began to climb and housing prices reached their peak. Before then, it was common to hear of sellers who listed their home on a Friday only to receive multiple contracts by Monday—often for several thousand dollars more than the asking price. It's now very much a buyer's market, as falling prices have driven many would-be buyers into a "wait and see" mode.

But even with falling prices, the region's housing costs are still extremely high, and don't forget to factor in property taxes. Newcomers, unless they're from San Francisco, New York, or one of the few other cities pricier than D.C., will be in for sticker shock.

The average price of a home here is $424,700. This is a steep number when you consider that the national average price of a house is about $219,000. According to research firm Runzheimer International, living expenses for a family of four, including housing costs, income taxes, goods and services, public transportation, automobile expenses, and other essentials, are about 67 percent higher than average. What $60,000 per year will buy you in most cities will cost you $102,589 in the Washington, D.C. metro area, trailing only Manhattan, San Francisco, Los Angeles, and San Jose.

With that said, the Washington area still commands a high home ownership rate. An estimated 71 percent of householders own their homes, compared with 67 percent nationally. The implication is that while Metro Washington homes are expensive, many people can still afford them.

The corollary to this volatile home-buying market is a tight rental market. Prices are rising as more people move into the area and wait out the market's ups and downs. The fair-market rent for a one-bedroom apartment—if you can find one—is $1,200 to $1,600 if you take the entire metro area into consideration. For two bedrooms expect to pay $1,600 to $2,000, and for three bedrooms $2,000 and up. House rentals can range from $1,200 to $1,400 a month for a town home in the outer suburbs to $4,000 in Bethesda or $6,000 or more for a plush Georgetown dwelling. Why

these astronomical rental prices? It's simply the law of supply and demand. More people are seeking rentals than there are rentals available, and have been for several years.

One thing to keep in mind, whether you're going to buy or rent, is that the pricing rationale here is similar to other large urban areas. In other words, expect to pay a premium to be close to the District and near major commuting links like I-66, the Capital Beltway, and Metrorail stations. Prices drop as you move outward; commute times increase. It's the age-old tradeoff.

For more information on the local real estate market, licensing practices, ethics, and other issues involving buying or renting a home, we suggest you call one or more of the following agencies:

- Greater Capital Area Association of Realtors, (301) 590–2000, www.gcaar.com
- Maryland Association of Realtors, (800) 638–6425, www.mdrealtor.org
- Northern Virginia Association of Realtors, (703) 207–3200, www.nvar.com

NEIGHBORHOODS AND HOMES

Washington, D.C.

People tend to forget that Washington, D.C., beyond the monuments, is a city of neighborhoods—communities with their own dynamics, history, and sense of place. Most of these enclaves are close knit and largely self-contained. The whole effect is something akin to a patchwork of small towns, albeit connected to an urban core.

In a city tagged for its transience, it may come as a surprise that the majority of the District's neighborhoods are home to several generations of families.

As a place to live, the District offers proximity to all major employment centers, including those in Suburban Maryland and Northern Virginia. Virtually no one here commutes longer than 40 minutes to work. Washington's prized Metro mass transit system, famed nightlife and cultural opportunities, miles of parks and forests, stately homes and shaded streets, plus its allure as the Nation's Capital, will always make it a desirable address.

That desirability comes with a price, however. The median price of a home sold in 2006 was $506,100. The median rent is $940, although rents of $1,500 to $3,000 are more the norm in prime neighborhoods.

The vast majority of newcomers who relocate to the District settle in **Northwest,** so we'll begin our neighborhood tour here.

Adams Morgan, which radiates from Columbia Road and 18th Street NW, is Washington's largest and most celebrated ethnic neighborhood. Its global-minded eateries are famous in these parts (see our Restaurants chapter), and it's here you'll find African clothiers next to Spanish bridal shops and Turkish shoe stores. Adams Morgan and neighboring **Mount Pleasant** have attracted a growing number of young professionals, including many tied to the White House and Capitol Hill who live in gentrified town houses and large apartment buildings. A decade ago, Mount Pleasant experienced an unfortunate riot, but the tensions have cooled and the neighborhood seems determined to carry on as one of Washington's most integrated communities.

Immediately to the south of Adams Morgan is **Dupont Circle,** Washington's answer to Greenwich Village. Interspersed among the cafes, art galleries, and boutiques are grand old brownstones and row houses. Many prominent members of the gay community, artists, young progressives, and aging bohemians call Dupont home. Although it can claim many of the same attributes as Adams Morgan, Dupont is decidedly more established and thus housing costs tend to be higher here.

Closer to downtown, and wrapping around the campus of George Washington University, are the highly urbanized neighborhoods of **Foggy Bottom** and the **West End.** Both are apartment and condo dense, with the former consisting mostly of students and professors and the latter primarily single professionals who commute by Metro or walk to nearby offices. The neighborhoods are wedged between Georgetown to the west and downtown to the east, a consolation for the area's overall lack of restaurants and nightlife.

Downtown living is enjoying somewhat of a renaissance thanks to the continued revitalization of the **Pennsylvania Avenue** corridor. Several older buildings, including the historic Lansburgh, have been revamped and now house some of the most exclusive condo units in Washington.

By most measures Washington's toniest address is still **Georgetown,** with its famed M Street/Wisconsin Avenue nightlife, stylish Federal town homes, and secluded estates. The area west of Wisconsin Avenue is dominated by Georgetown University and its students; east of the avenue it's markedly quieter, with bigger homes and well-heeled residents. For those with money—tiny town houses can demand a million dollars or more—and patience to bear the weekend crush of partygoers, there is simply no other close-in neighborhood that can match the charm and convenience of Georgetown.

Immediately to the north, in **Glover Park,** a more down-to-earth atmosphere pervades. Brick town homes and duplexes cluster around small parks and green spaces all within a short stroll of Wisconsin Avenue. Young families, Georgetown University professors, middle-aged empty nesters, and longtime residents live side by side and in harmony in this civic-minded and politically progressive neighborhood.

Moving farther north puts you in the land of milk and honey. The neighborhoods of **Foxhall Road, Spring Valley,** and **Wesley Heights** are the stuff of *Architectural Digest* photo shoots. The neighbors tend to be older than those who reside to the south, politically more conservative, and measurably wealthier. On some streets multimillion-dollar homes are more the rule than the exception.

To the east, in the heart of Northwest, are **Cleveland Park** and **Woodley Park,** a checkerboard of beautiful Victorian homes with wide porches, shady yards, and sprawling square footage. You'll also find along Wiscon-

Capitol Hill, the city's largest residential district, is home to charming sidewalk cafes and interesting shops.

The Washington area is so large and varied that it's not a bad idea to rent for a while before settling on a neighborhood.

sin Avenue numerous older apartment buildings and remodeled town houses. Easy access to Massachusetts, Wisconsin, and Connecticut Avenues, the Metro, and such attractions as the National Zoo give the neighborhoods considerable prestige with up-and-coming professionals.

In the far stretches of upper Northwest, neighborhoods like **Tenleytown, American University Park, Barnaby Woods,** and **Chevy Chase** (not to be confused with neighboring Chevy Chase, Maryland) glow with a sense of small-town America charm, complete with quiet tree-lined streets, beautiful spacious lawns, and kids on bicycles. Along the upper western edges of Rock Creek Park, **Forest Hills** unfolds with palatial homes and tucked-away streets that allow maximum privacy for the rich and powerful.

East of Rock Creek, along upper 16th Street NW, **Shepherd Park, Brightwood Park,** and **Crestwood** move to a relaxed, suburban beat. Homes are substantially more affordable than similar dwellings to the west of the park, and 16th Street provides a mostly hassle-free link to downtown and points south.

Two Northwest neighborhoods that are rebounding from years of neglect are **Shaw**, which straddles 14th Street above downtown, and **LeDroit Park,** just to the south of Howard University. The Metro Green Line stop at Shaw/Howard University comes with the promise of further revitalization of these Victorian neighborhoods, but crime remains an ongoing problem.

In Northeast another neighborhood on the rebound is **Brookland,** which houses an interesting mix of Catholic University students and professors, as well as elderly middle-class residents who live in well-kept row houses and Cape Cods. The university and its rolling, wooded campus dominate much of the neigh-

borhood and bring a sense of respite from the clamor of the inner city.

The most sought-after address in **Northeast** is **Capitol Hill,** which also spreads into Southeast. As you might imagine, Capitol Hill teems with young congressional staffers, lobbyists, and members of Congress. Huge brownstones and smaller town homes are the mainstays, but a few apartment and condo units can be found. As a rule, those areas closest to the Capitol command the highest prices and are considered the safest. The higher the street numbers, however, the likelier you are to encounter crime. Even in the most exclusive sections, crime remains more of a problem than in other Washington neighborhoods of comparable price.

In **Southwest** the neighborhood of choice is the **Waterfront,** located north of the Anacostia River. A haven for federal employees, much of the Southwest Waterfront is within a short walk of Capitol Hill and L'Enfant Plaza, the massive government complex. The area boasts some fine restaurants, theaters, and pricey town homes. Seventies-style, high-rise condo and apartment buildings, however, make up the bulk of housing, which is typically more affordable than similar close-in units found to the north of the National Mall.

Anacostia, on the opposite side of the river, contains the District's largest concentration of public housing. This portion of Southeast continues to battle widespread poverty and violent crime, the worst in D.C.

Northern Virginia

Parts of Northern Virginia, such as Rosslyn, are so close to Washington that you can walk to the city in 10 minutes or, as in the case of portions of Arlington and Alexandria, drive there in five. Other Virginia suburbs are so far flung that you need close to an hour to reach the city.

Close-in suburbs are hardly distinguishable from D.C. itself. They have high-rises, choked traffic, restaurant rows, and lots of businesses. On the other hand, there are some suburbs that seem to typify the centuries-old vision of Virginia: gracious colonial manors, lush greenery, rolling meadows, white fences, and horses. The remarkable thing is, even some of the suburbs within 40 minutes of the city have that Virginia Hunt Country atmosphere. A good real estate agent will help you narrow down your choices and weigh factors in your decision, such as distance, cost, schools, and atmosphere. To help get you started, you may want to contact some agencies prior to your arrival. Later in this chapter, we've listed the largest ones in Metro Washington. Below is an area-by-area overview of Washington's closest Virginia suburbs.

Alexandria

Sharing ranks with Arlington County as Northern Virginia's closest-in suburb, Alexandria has strong historical and cultural ties to the District of Columbia. Make no mistake, though: Although Alexandria may be a suburb of Washington, it's a Virginia city first and foremost.

Alexandria is immersed in an almost overpowering sense of place. How can it not be, with George Washington and Robert E. Lee having called it home? The municipality is also characteristically Virginian in the way it is run—efficiently and pragmatically.

During rush hour no part of Alexandria is more than 40 minutes from Washington. Metrorail has three stations within the city limits. The median price of a home here is $386,000. Most newcomers' impressions of Alexandria are that it's a lot like Georgetown, but without the urban chaos. And they're right. Sort of.

Old Town, the city's most visible neighborhood, could stand double for its northern counterpart on a number of accounts. It's also pricey: town houses start at $500,000, though you're more likely to see them up in the $600,000 to $1 million range, especially as you progress east toward the handsomely restored Potomac waterfront. Because colonial-era homes weren't designed with the automobile in mind, on-street parking is almost always the rule here, and on weekends things can get a little sticky. But Old Town is, well, Old Town, and that's the biggest selling point of all, especially among the young up-and-coming crowd that tends to migrate here.

Though some would be hard pressed to admit it, there's more to Alexandria than Old Town. Not too long ago **Del Ray,** which wraps around U.S. 1 and Potomac Yards (a massive train-switching yard), was solely a blue-collar neighborhood. Gentrification has set in and many bungalows and Cape Cods now command more than $400,000.

Alexandria communities that most resemble suburbia are **Rosemont, Seminary,** and **Beverly Hills.** Mount Vernon, to the south, has a city address of Alexandria, but is actually part of Fairfax County, so we'll cover it in that section. A lot of the homes in suburban Alexandria were built in the early 1960s on large lots; prices run from $300,000 to more than $1 million, with the greatest concentration in the $500,000 range.

Along the western edge of town are the self-contained neighborhoods of **Park Fairfax** and **South Fairlington.** The majority of housing is town homes and apartment buildings, many of which sprang up after World War II to house federal workers. Now they're popular with single professionals and first-time buyers.

Also out in the West End is **Landmark,** an area of high-rise condos, apartment buildings, and shopping centers located off I-395. Condos start at $200,000 for a one-bedroom unit and can run upward to $500,000 for deluxe models.

Arlington County

Arlington looks and acts a lot like a city. Its 26 square miles are a collage of satellite business districts, high-rise apartment complexes, and tucked-away residential neighborhoods. The county has more Metro stations per capita than any other suburb, and its population is decidedly middle-aged.

Arlington is the most urban county in Metro D.C., and it's unique in that there are no incorporated cities or towns within its borders.

Like Alexandria, it was once part of the District of Columbia, and many residents here are closer to downtown D.C. and Capitol Hill than are most Washingtonians. Needless to say, Arlington is a convenient and especially attractive area for single, workaholic professionals who like being less than 15 minutes from most of the area's employment centers.

The county is usually identified with its massive business/residential corridors—**Crystal City, Pentagon City, Clarendon, Ballston,** and **Rosslyn.** Apartments and condos are the most plentiful housing options here, with the former starting at $1,400 a month for one-bedroom units, and the latter commanding $250,000 to over $400,000.

The northern tier of the county is almost exclusively residential neighborhoods, some of the most stately areas in Metro Washington. Single-family homes in communities like **Country Club Hills** run from $500,000 for older brick colonials to $1 million and more for estate homes. The median price of a single-family home in Arlington County in 2005 was $482,000.

Despite its dense nature, Arlington has set aside hundreds of acres of park land, and its riverfront bike path, which affords stunning views of Washington and the Potomac, is a source of intense civic pride.

Fairfax County

Northern Virginia's largest jurisdiction runs the gamut on the types of neighborhoods and living options available to newcomers. In Fairfax County you'll find two-story colonials on quiet cul-de-sacs, modest Cape Cods and ramblers in older neighborhoods, lakefront town homes in new developments, California contemporaries in planned communities, giant estate homes in wooded parklike settings, and turnkey condos in high-rise buildings. If there is a common thread that runs through this massive county, it is that it's overwhelmingly middle class to upper class.

Fairfax is among the top five counties in the nation in median household income, at $94,610 per household (see the Metro Washington Overview chapter), and in the top 15 in median housing values. The median price for a house in 2005 was $522,800. Apartments start at $1,000 a month in the newer complexes. Those are values if you're coming from the urban areas of the Northeast or parts of the West Coast but a shock if you hail from virtually any other part of the nation.

One affordable neighborhood inside the Beltway is **Annandale,** an area that has long been a magnet for federal workers and their families. Annandale's signature redbrick ramblers and comfortable ranch homes are priced in the $400,000 to $550,000 range. The community is one of the oldest suburbs in Northern Virginia and is centrally located next to several busy road arteries and I-495.

To the north, **Falls Church,** an independent municipality, comes with a small-town charm and a mix of older stately Victorians and new town house developments. Single-family homes start at $400,000 and work their way up to $800,000. Route 7 (Leesburg Pike) cuts through the center of the city, offering easy access to Washington and most of Fairfax County. The average commute time to downtown D.C. is 35 minutes.

Great Falls, located in the gorgeous bluffs that tower above the Potomac River in northern Fairfax, extending through rolling countryside all the way to the Loudoun County line, is a community of large houses situated on expansive lots of a half-acre and more. Most of the homes here are colonial in design, and $700,000 to multimillion-dollar price tags are the norm. Great Falls and neighboring **McLean,** a neighborhood closer to Washington, are known for their great schools, country lanes, and serene, wooded surroundings. Horse farms, ponds, and large wildflower meadows are not uncommon here, and you can still escape the sense of overdevelopment rampant in other parts of the metro area. Although only a 20- to 30-minute drive to D.C., the morning commutes along Chain Bridge Road (Route 123), Georgetown Pike, and the George Washington Memorial Parkway can be trying at times.

Moving outside the Beltway, the fast-growing planned community of Burke attracts suburbanites looking for newer houses, plenty of parks for the kids, and proximity to major shopping centers. The typical single-family home starts at approximately $400,000; town houses run from $300,000. For all its pluses, Burke commuters face a challenge each day along Braddock and Old Keene Mill Roads or via the Fairfax County Parkway to always-congested I–66. Expect a 35- to 50-minute commute into the city.

Wedged between Burke and Annandale is **Springfield,** another older community of modest ramblers on large lots mixed with newer and larger homes on small lots. Like Annandale, Springfield is home to thousands of government and military workers. A large stock of detached homes falls into the $350,000 to $500,000 range. Town houses begin at around $300,000 and condominiums start at $250,000. Although only 15 miles south of Washington, Springfield's major link to the District is I–95, one of the region's most congested arteries. In all fairness, however, the Virginia Department of Transportation has done miracles in recent years improving existing roads and constructing convenient new secondary roads such as the Franconia-Springfield Parkway.

The parkway (as well as Franconia Road and ever-lengthening South Van Dorn Street) has become a vital transportation link for the massive yet still-developing **Kingstowne** community and its much smaller and less-exclusive neighbor, **Manchester Lakes**—places that have become especially attractive to single professionals, the newly married, and young families. Located just east of Springfield in the Franconia section of the county (which in many parts carries an Alexandria mailing address), Kingstowne and Manchester Lakes offer a selection of nice apartments, condominiums, town houses, and (in Kingstowne only) single-family homes. Some of the smaller condos in Manchester Lakes start at $225,000. Expect to pay from $300,000 and up, meanwhile, in either community for town houses,

and closer to $600,000 and more for most single-family residences.

Whatever turns the housing market takes, Kingstowne and Manchester Lakes will likely only grow in popularity thanks to their appealing character, accessibility, convenience to the District and Old Town Alexandria (though it can take an hour to get downtown), and prime location some two miles from the shopping mecca of Springfield Mall and the Franconia-Springfield Metro station.

Mount Vernon, in southeastern Fairfax County, retains a sense of exclusivity because of its proximity to George Washington's venerable riverside estate and Old Town Alexandria. Detached homes on large lots are the backbone of this beautiful, verdant neighborhood located between U.S. 1 and George Washington Memorial Parkway. Small side streets and country lanes lead you to manicured estates overlooking the Potomac River—many with private docks. This is a neighborhood for brisk walks on a fall day, thanks to the numerous quiet roads and bicycle paths in the area. Tucked into this affluent area are some amazing bargains—small ramblers and older homes on large lots just waiting for young families to add improvements. Traveling south on the George Washington Memorial Parkway from Old Town Alexandria, turn right on Wellington Road and take any of the side streets. You'll discover neighborhoods where children still play outside, families walk together along sleepy roads where traffic is so infrequent that no sidewalks are necessary, and old, tall trees form shady canopies on even the warmest summer days.

Heading to **Oakton** and **Vienna** in the north-central part of the county (it wasn't long ago that these two were considered Fairfax's far-western suburbs), you'll encounter an area in transition from woodsy to highly developed. Located off I–66, just a couple of miles outside the Beltway, these communities are now right in the heart of the county, a factor that bodes well with commuters, many of whom use the nearby Vienna Metro station. Oakton is mostly a maze of sprawling subdivisions—albeit with larger-than-normal lots—but some parts resemble Great Falls in both topography and opulence. Vienna, an incorporated town settled by the Scots in the early 1800s, has a more established small-town feel. Homes in both Oakton and Vienna range from $300,000 to more than $1 million.

Farther west along I–66, the city of **Fairfax,** another independent municipality, boasts a fine old historic district and an ample supply of moderately priced homes. Single-family homes start at $400,000, while town houses are available from $300,000. Fairfax is at the junction of several busy roads; commutes into Washington range from 40 to 60 minutes.

In the far western reaches of the county, the rapidly growing communities of **Centreville** and **Chantilly** attract first-time homebuyers with a plentiful variety of town homes and condominiums. Move-up buyers can purchase large colonials ($500,000 to $600,000) for 20 to 30 percent less than comparable homes closer in. Town houses begin in the $300,000s. Commuting times into downtown can run 45 to 75 minutes. Nearby, bordered by Route 123 and Route 28, are the pastoral districts of **Clifton** and **Fairfax Station.** The town of Clifton is actually a small village of white picket fences, gingerbread houses, kitchen gardens, gravel roads, and front-porch swings. You can walk through this historic little town in 15 minutes—it is surrounded by estates of five or more acres that blend into the area known as Fairfax Station.

You can hardly tell the difference between the countryside bordering Clifton and Fairfax Station: Both feature colonials of 3,000 to 7,000 square feet on five-acre tracts, private roads, abundant wildlife, unspoiled woods, and tranquil family neighborhoods. The northern end of Fairfax Station culminates at the edge of the aforementioned Burke—a decidedly middle-priced area—and the rolling hills give way to smaller lots and, in some developments, tract mansions. In fact, at the Burke–Fairfax Station border, the subdivisions are no different from elsewhere in suburbia.

The Fairfax Station–Clifton area, farther south, is a version of lavish Great Falls for a cost of 20 to 30 percent less.

Out near Washington Dulles International Airport, **Herndon,** an independent town, and **Reston,** a lake- and tree-rich planned community, are populated by young professionals and their families. Detached single-family homes ($450,000 to $1 million) are the residences of choice, but a sizable number of town house and condo developments offer first-time buyers $200,000-and-up alternatives. Both areas are booming, and it seems that upscale malls and pedestrian shopping and entertainment complexes are added every few months. Hidden away from the traffic are wonderful recreation areas, like Reston's **Lake Anne,** where waterside residents have docks, pontoon boats, and motorized floats. Winding along this beautiful refuge are town houses and single-family dwellings with large windows overlooking a scene right out of a Monet painting—whimsical bridges, flower-lined canals, weeping willows, and at the center of it all, a glass-surfaced lake suitable for swimming, windsurfing, and even fishing. Also at water's edge is a town plaza featuring a crescent of restaurants and outdoor cafes.

You'd never know that these areas are bordered by the Dulles Toll Road—heavily trafficked but nonetheless functional—and just minutes from Washington Dulles International Airport.

Loudoun County

The fortunes of this beautiful county 30 miles northwest of Washington are closely tied to the development of Washington Dulles International Airport. In 2006 Loudoun County was recognized as the fastest-growing county in the nation. Its 2006 population was more than double that in 1996 and more than triple that in 1990. In 2005 the average home sale price was $545,900.

Dulles's renaissance over the last decade has played out nicely for Loudoun, helping bring in new aerospace and international high-tech firms and boosting the population (see our Metro Washington Overview chapter). Most of the county's population lies in and around Leesburg and points east along Route 7. Single-family homes in diverse communities like Sterling, Ashburn, and Sugarland run between $300,000 and $1 million or more. The average town house costs between $250,000 and $400,000.

As one moves west and south of **Leesburg,** the graceful county seat, you enter hunt country, a land of blue bloods and stone fences, breathtaking country estates, Kentucky Derby–winning stables, and rolling vineyards. The most modest of homes in communities like **Middleburg, Upperville,** and **Bluemont** will cost about $300,000, and these are easily eclipsed by the number of multimillion-dollar horse farms that crisscross the pretty countryside.

Prince William County

In a metropolitan area where the term *affordable housing* seems like an oxymoron, Prince William County has become a sanctuary for suburbanites seeking value and space at prices that don't raise blood pressure.

At $428,000, the county's median-price home is lower than those in jurisdictions to the north, explaining why more first-time buyers and homeowners in the move-up market have settled in Prince William over the last decade. Simple demographics partly tell the story of the county's widespread appeal to young families: About 40 percent of Prince William's residents are younger than 25, according to U.S. Census Bureau estimates.

The sprawling bedroom community is one of the fastest-growing areas in the nation. In 1980 less than 150,000 residents were spread across the county's 350 square miles.

Neighborhoods along the I–95 corridor such as Lake Ridge, Woodbridge, and Montclair have been the biggest gainers so far, with most single-family homes selling between $250,000 to the upper $500,000s. Town houses range from the low to mid-$200s, while condos typically start at $180,000. The area experiencing the fastest growth is the

i Getting settled in a new town can be difficult. One way to look for people with similar interests is to sign up at www.meetup.com for social events and gatherings. You'll find chess players, pug owners, Italian speakers, and more.

western part of the county near Manassas and I–66 (the Gainesville area), where large single-family homes in new subdivisions can be purchased for anywhere from about $300,000 to $700,000.

The rapid transformation from a quiet exurb to thriving suburb has come with its share of growing pains. Road congestion, while getting better, is still chronic. Prince William commuters spend more time on the road than anyone else in Metro Washington. The Virginia Railway Express, with several stops in Prince William, has lured some motorists off the road.

Suburban Maryland
Montgomery County

Montgomery County was the first true suburb of Washington, D.C. Virginia, after all, was across the river; to get to Montgomery all you had to do was cross Western Avenue. Man-made borders, as Marylanders will tell you, are easier to cross than physical borders.

Go up to Montgomery County today and real estate agents will be the first to remind you of this. Indeed, getting into Washington is likely to be less of a hassle from the close-in suburbs because of the absence of bridges. That said, be warned that I–270, which runs north to Rockville, Gaithersburg, and Frederick County, can be a commuting nightmare. In the past few years, major improvements, including new lanes and upgraded feeder roads, have resulted in a better stretch of highway, but a look at the daily traffic reports will show that the improvements have barely kept up with demand. I–495, the Beltway into Montgomery County, is hardly better, though both are good, multilaned roads.

Like Fairfax County, Montgomery County

has every type of housing and neighborhood option under the sun. You will find an abundance of quiet, tree-lined residential communities. The county's 28,000 acres of parkland are right next to many of these communities, from the poshest addresses in Chevy Chase to the lower-income neighborhoods along Veirs Mill Road in **Wheaton.** Like its Virginia cousin, however, housing doesn't come cheap in Montgomery County, with $507,400 the median price for a home in 2005.

The quintessential Montgomery County community has got to be **Bethesda,** a residential sanctuary for thousands of government officials and industry leaders. North Bethesda, convenient to the Beltway and Metro, is the denser section of town, chockfull of town house developments and midrise condo units. To the south, in neighborhoods like **Chevy Chase,** you'll find vintage suburbia, with large Victorians and colonials situated on impeccably manicured lots.

Close to the Beltway, single-family homes range between $500,000 for the tiniest Cape Cod or ranch to upwards of $3 million for a new minimansion or renovated Victorian. Commuting time into the city seldom exceeds 30 minutes.

The equestrian set is still holding on in Suburban Maryland, and nowhere is it more evident than in posh **Potomac.** In some areas subdivisions have chopped down once-magnificent farms into gaudy five-acre horse "farmettes," but the overall atmosphere remains largely pastoral. Town houses—the few that are here—start at $500,000, while single-family abodes seldom sell for less than $1 million—and usually much more. This is where many Washington sports, media, and political figures live, and the name "Potomac" in your address is sure to add cachet to your image. River Road, Potomac's lovely link with the outside world, is a winding two-laner that wasn't designed for express commuting, and

i For a helpful resource in planning and making your move, check out *Insiders' Guide to Relocation.*

the moderate crowding at rush hour is testimony to that. Then again, many of the folks who live in Potomac can probably set their own schedules, which probably explains why rush hour isn't worse.

Hovering near the District line east of Rock Creek Park are **Silver Spring** and **Takoma Park,** two established and quite different residential areas. Silver Spring is probably Montgomery's most ethnic community. Of late, its downtown corridor is witnessing a genuine renaissance, with the Discovery Channel's new headquarters here and the American Film Institute renovating a showcase theater. Single-family homes start at $450,000 and go up past $1 million.

Takoma Park, immediately to the south, is Metro Washington's answer to Berkeley, California, or Boulder, Colorado. Almost beyond politically correct (the entire city is designated a Nuclear Free Zone), the town is a flash point of community activism. A mix of young, free spirits; middle-aged bohemians; and elderly longtime residents live in older and mostly modest Cape Cods and Victorians, and the prices pretty much mirror those in Silver Spring, but the setting is more about trees and big yards than in neighboring Silver Spring (the latter has similar enclaves, however).

The town of **Kensington,** 8 miles north of D.C. and 1 mile north of the Beltway, defies its highly suburban location. Fewer than 2,000 people live in this half-square-mile community that is among the oldest suburbs in Metro Washington (incorporated in 1894). Many of the Victorian homes date back to the 1890s, adding a nostalgic air to the place. There are mature trees and rolling hills dotted with houses on spacious lots, as well as more typical suburban streets featuring sidewalks and closely spaced homes. Parts of Kensington border Rock Creek Park's Beach Drive, and the homes along here can be well over $800,000. For the most part, though, houses start at $500,000 and work their way upward to $1 million in the Kensington area.

Most of the people north of the Beltway live in or around the communities of

Wheaton, Rockville, and **Gaithersburg.**
Metrorail and Georgia Avenue connect
Wheaton—a middle- to lower-middle-class,
ethnically mixed neighborhood—with Washington. In Wheaton you'll find reasonably
priced apartments (from $1,300 for a two-
bedroom) and small, modest brick ramblers
and Cape Cods, many under $500,000. The
more affluent Rockville, the county seat, and
Gaithersburg, its fast-growing northern neighbor, were once serene little dairy towns whose
pastures are now dotted with town homes
and single-family developments. Rockville has
most of the detached housing ($450,000 to
$800,000) and is family oriented. Gaithersburg
has a large population of young professionals
and young families who tend to migrate
toward moderately priced town homes
($350,000 and up) in areas like Montgomery
Village, a planned residential community.

Two northern Montgomery County communities in transition are **Germantown** and
Damascus. Germantown is the denser of the
two, with its rolling hills carpeted by new condominiums, town houses, and shopping centers. About 10 miles up Highway 27,
once-sleepy Damascus is evolving into a bedroom community of first-time homeowners
who are just as likely to commute to Baltimore
as to Washington.

Prince George's County

The median price of a home in Prince
George's County was $329,400 in 2005,
almost 40 percent less than a comparable
house next door in Montgomery County.

Why the sizable price difference? Perception. Prince George's could use some good
spin doctors. The county's reputation is as a
blue-collar haven with subpar schools and too
much crime. Yes, it's more working class than
Montgomery and Fairfax, and yes, it's had its
share of crime problems, especially in neighborhoods close to the District border. Prince
George's is also the most racially integrated
county in Metro Washington, and its schools
have made tremendous progress in recent
years.

Progressive communities like **College
Park** teem with college students, artists, writers, and aging activists. **University Park** and
Greenbelt (home of Goddard Space Center)
have high concentrations of academicians, scientists, and engineers, while **Bowie, Mitchellville,** and **Upper Marlboro** attract white-collar
professionals and families. Waterfront living
gives Fort Washington's **Tantallon** neighborhood a distinct panache, and this is where
you're likely to find some of the most expensive real estate in Prince George's, with many
homes hitting the $700,000 mark.

Several major road arteries, including U.S.
50, I–295, Branch Avenue, and Pennsylvania
Avenue, connect the county with nearby
Washington, helping make commuting times
here among the lowest in Metro D.C.

PROPERTY AND INCOME TAXES

In the District of Columbia, Maryland, and Virginia, homes are appraised at 100 percent of
their market value. Homeowners in D.C. also
get an exemption for the first $60,000 of their
property's value.

For a $425,000 home—about the average
price in Metro D.C.—this is roughly what you'd
pay in property taxes in the following jurisdictions in 2006:

Washington, D.C.:	$3,740
Northern Virginia:	
Alexandria	$3,464
Arlington County	$3,477
Fairfax County	$3,528
Loudoun County	$3,783
Prince William County	$3,430
Suburban Maryland:	
Montgomery County	$4,480
Prince George's County	$4,080

Washington, D.C. recently enacted a tax
break for owners/occupants of private residences. Called the Homestead Act, citizens

may apply for a $60,000 deduction on the assessed value, then pay only $0.88 tax per $100 of assessed value, which would reduce the above levy to $3,212.

In Maryland a state transfer and recordation tax is split 50–50 between the buyer and seller, unless otherwise negotiated. That tax is 2.19 percent in Montgomery County and 2.34 percent in Prince George's County. If, however, the purchaser is a first-time homebuyer, the seller is required by law to pay 0.25 percent of the transfer tax.

In addition to the variation in property taxes, note that there is a wide range of income taxes among the various jurisdictions. If you live in the District, expect to pay 7.5 percent on income up to $30,000 and 9 percent on income above that amount. Maryland residents pay 4.75 percent on income above $3,000 and an additional tax for most counties, such as 3.2 percent in Montgomery and Prince George's. Virginians get the best deal with a 5.75 percent tax on income above $17,000.

REAL ESTATE COMPANIES

The scene in Metro Washington is changing daily, with two giants—Long & Foster and Coldwell Banker Stevens—gobbling up most smaller firms or crowding them out of the area market. As of this writing, the following are some of the major real estate brokerage firms doing business in the entire Metro Washington area. You will find agents at each covering Washington, Maryland, and Virginia. Any of these firms can provide you with good service in residential properties because all have various agents who specialize in different types of property, like undeveloped land or condos.

But how to choose one particular agent? Some suggestions include driving through the area you are interested in and seeing whose name appears on the most signs. That agent may be very busy, but he or she is likely a full-time real estate professional and a go-getter who knows your chosen area and is willing to invest time in prospective clients. If you're not sure of the area in which you'd like to live, browse online listing services like realtor.com or check the classifieds of area newspapers to get an idea of pricing and types of houses available. Many real estate agents advertise in these publications, and they'll often tout their honors and awards (such as million-dollar agent, president's club, or number 1 agent in a given area, county, or state).

Another method of finding an agent is to ask neighbors or co-workers for recommendations. Remember, once you've narrowed down your choices, get three references from former clients. Find out if their agent advertised to their satisfaction, gave them the service they required, and, what's most important, sold their home or located a new one in a timely fashion. Ask the agent directly what he or she will do to market your property or help you find a new one. How much do they spend on advertising? Do they hold open houses? How often do they deal with the type of property you are hoping to buy or sell? What is the median price of the homes they deal with? If the agent specializes, for example, in condos and you're looking for a half-million-dollar home in the exurbs, then they're probably not for you.

Finally, be sure your agent is a good source of newcomer information and services, whether you're buying or selling. If you're selling, you'll want them to put together a nice introductory package on your house and neighborhood for prospective buyers. If you're a buyer, you'll want the information yourself.

Coldwell Banker Stevens Realtors
Residential Real Estate
465 Maple Avenue West
Vienna, VA
(703) 281–1400, (877) 225–5673
www.cbstevens.com
One of the most established brokerages in Metro Washington, and indeed the nation, Coldwell Banker is a billion-dollar sales producer, with more than 100 offices and 4,000 licensed agents. The company has its own

referral network service, which can be of value, since the agency was ranked number 1 in U.S. residential sales by both *Real Trends* magazine and *National Relocation and Real Estate* magazine.

Long & Foster Real Estate Inc.
11351 Random Hills Road
Fairfax, VA
(703) 359–1500
www.longandfoster.com
This dominant regional player in both residential and commercial markets handled about $44.6 billion in residential sales in the mid-Atlantic area in 2005, according to the firm. The firm specializes in new-home, high-end sales and relocation. It's also ubiquitous: Some 16,000 licensed agents work out of 237 offices scattered through the region.

RE/MAX
4825 Bethesda Avenue
Bethesda, MD
(301) 652–0400
www.remax.com
From starter homes to mansions, RE/MAX has one of the largest listings in the market. It has dozens of offices throughout Northern Virginia, Washington, and Suburban Maryland and is part of the RE/MAX International Referral Roster System. One point about RE/MAX: Its agents keep 100 percent of their commissions rather than splitting them with the company, as is typical at other companies. In exchange, they receive little administrative or advertising support. Does this make a RE/MAX agent work harder? It's difficult to say, but agents who agree to these terms are bound to be confident go-getters.

Weichert Realty
6410 Rockledge Drive
Bethesda, MD
(301) 718–4111
www.weichert.com
A few years ago, this Maryland-based firm bought out a portion of D.C.'s Shannon and Luchs Co. and Virginia's Mount Vernon Realty

---

i You want to look, but you don't want to hook up with a real estate agent yet? Go to www.realtor.com, type in the zip code or neighborhood you're interested in, and you'll get to view all available listings, including photos.

(absorbing both names) and overnight became one of the largest and most powerful residential brokerage firms in Metro D.C., second behind Long & Foster. The company is particularly noted for its large inventory of luxury homes and estates.

RELOCATION INFORMATION

Following are some services and organizations you may wish to contact for information before you relocate. Often, your agent is the best source for general relocation information, because most real estate firms either have their own relocation department or partner with an outside relocation firm.

- Employee Relocation Council: A national organization headquartered in Washington that serves corporations that are relocating their employees. It serves as a clearinghouse of ideas, options, and services for companies interested in discovering how other companies are handling relocations. The council publishes a related monthly magazine, *Mobility*. Call (202) 857–0857 or visit the Web site at www.erc.org.
- Corporations are the main clients of Runzheimer International, which provides cost of living data on major U.S. markets; however, individuals can also obtain less extensive information for a cost of about $20. Call Runzheimer International at (800) 942–9949 or see the Web site, www.runzheimer.com.

Relocation Guidelines

We're assuming that if you're reading this section, you're either thinking about moving to Washington or are deep into the process. You may have already arrived. The following tips are intended to help you with this transition:

- Keep the family involved in all discussions: Although the biggest decisions already have been made, it is imperative that even the youngest family members continue to feel like they are part of the relocating process, that they have a say as a newcomer.
- Sever the moving ties—unpack: It sounds so simple, but you'd be amazed how many people are still living out of boxes six months, sometimes even a year, after their move. Stories abound of young Capitol Hill staffers who come to Washington, work for two years, and leave without ever unpacking all their belongings. The quicker the boxes are emptied, the sooner your new place actually feels like home.
- Move into the culture: Don't drop long-held interests or traditions just because you've moved. If the kids were in Cub Scouts in St. Louis, get them in Cub Scouts here. If you were a member of a garden club in Boston, join one here. If you were into white-water rafting in Colorado, investigate the opportunities in these parts. At the same time, explore the myriad new possibilities unique to the Washington area.
- Get out and see the city and the region: It's somewhat natural to hibernate after a move, given all the unpacking and home maintenance logistics that loom. Try to budget time, even if it's just for an hour or two on weekends, to play tourist. You'll find that this will do wonders for reducing stress and, at the same time, will likely inspire a sense of pride in your new hometown.
- Drop the guilt trip about uprooting the kids: Although relocating can be traumatic for youngsters and teens, they're much more malleable than we may think. If you haven't made your final decision about when to move, don't feel that you must smooth the way for the kids with a

summer transition. It used to be that parents were advised to wait and move during the summer, so the kids wouldn't have to be uprooted during the school year. Now, conventional wisdom has it that it's better for kids to move during the school year, even if it's just a few weeks before the summer break. They'll have a chance to get acclimated to their school and make friends before summer vacation.

- Stock up on regional and local maps: Coming to grips with Metro Washington's patchwork of roads and highways can be as trying as advanced calculus. Maps are required reading here, and the best in the land can be had through the Alexandria Drafting Company (ADC) of Alexandria, Virginia. You'll see their maps in virtually all the area's bookshops, as well as in most grocery and convenience stores. For more information, call ADC at (703) 750–0510 or visit the Web site: www.adcmap.com.
- Make trial runs to places of work, school, etc.: A little planning here will greatly improve your mental health. Make the trial commutes during normal rush hours or the approximate times you'll be going to these places. Experiment with different routes and always have a contingency plan. We can't stress enough the importance of following this step.
- Subscribe immediately to a community newspaper and the *Washington Post* and/or the *Washington Times,* the region's two largest daily newspapers. We may be biased here, but there's still no better information access to Metro Washington than through the printed word. Tapping into the Fourth Estate is really the first step in becoming part of the community.
- Get involved with state societies, alumni groups, or embassy cultural programs. Homesickness is a natural consequence of relocation. Fortunately, the Washington area has a plethora of remedies. Virtually

every state has a state society—a social and networking group—based in Washington. Chances are your alma mater also has an alumni chapter in Washington. If they don't, you may consider organizing one. Most embassies offer some type of cultural programming, whether it's through open houses, lecture series, or social clubs, for international newcomers. (See related information in the International Washington chapter.)

CHILD CARE

As we have mentioned at least a couple of times by now, Metro Washington is a wonderful place to live and—as many people happily discover—raise children. Few places can match the abundance of stimulating cultural, educational, historical, and recreational outlets for youngsters to pursue. Here's a brief look at child care, an important consideration in an area where many household budgets may only be fulfilled with two incomes.

First, here are a few words about what to expect from this chapter. Like some of the other subjects we've covered, child care is one that could easily be the sole focus of an entire book. Because Washington-area residents can choose from literally thousands of child-care options, to present a complete rundown with descriptions, services, and other information is simply not possible here. Instead, we've tried to provide a primer on the subject, combining sound advice for choosing child-care facilities with a listing of agencies, nonprofit organizations, and referral agencies. The experts there can answer specific questions and help parents make decisions.

Few quality-of-life issues have become as important to families in recent years as the availability of top-notch child care, something that experts agree is crucial to a child's well-being and healthy development. As with any large expenditure, especially one involving a family member, parents should carefully weigh the various options and talk with relatives, friends, neighbors, and co-workers who have experience in this area.

Whether you're in search of a chain-affiliated commercial day-care center, a private in-home operation, a program associated with a school or religious institution, or something tailored to the special needs of groups such as the physically challenged, the learning disabled, and the non-English-speaking, you're sure to find it in the Washington area. A scan through the Yellow Pages, a community directory, an Internet search, or a listing provided by a human services agency will quickly confirm the wealth of choices available.

THE HIGH COST OF CARE

Just as housing, groceries, and other necessities tend to cost more in Metro Washington than in many parts of the nation, the same holds true for child care. Indeed, it can be one of the biggest financial issues for parents with moderate incomes, particularly if they don't have in-home offices, the luxury of subsidized day-care centers at work, or nearby relatives who can help out.

Typically, according to the Fairfax County Office for Children, full-time child care for infants and toddlers costs from $180 to $200 weekly in a private home, and $228 to $247 weekly at a child-care center. Preschool-age child care ranges from $160 to $180 weekly in a private home, and $180 to $195 weekly at a center. Before- and after-school care for school-age children costs $100 to $155 a week. Your best bet is to sign up as early as possible. Before- and after-school programs in particular often start taking first-come, first-served applications in early spring before the next school year. The Fairfax Office notes that it has been giving out these cost estimates for several years, so the actual costs could be higher.

A growing segment of the child-care sector in Metro Washington involves in-home operations, often classified by licensing agencies as family day-care homes. Their popularity is a reflection not only of the region's number-one national ranking in the number of working women, but also of the high cost of living here. Many people opt to set up child-care operations in their homes, providing a much-needed source of income without having to commute to faraway offices. Like other child-care facilities, private homes must be licensed, insured, inspected, and otherwise held to certain standards for safety, health, and sanitation. Also, those caring for more than five children (although the number may vary slightly in different jurisdictions) must obtain special permits and licenses from local and state authorities.

Parents who wish to examine licensing standards may request comprehensive booklets published by the area's licensing agencies: the D.C. Department of Consumer and Regulatory Affairs in Washington, the Virginia Department of Social Services in Virginia, or the Maryland Department of Human Resources in Maryland. (State guidelines are available through local government offices listed later in this chapter.) Regulations vary slightly among the three jurisdictions, but to receive licenses, child-care centers and homes generally must meet requirements adhering to staff-to-children ratios (as small as one caregiver to four children younger than age two in centers, and one caregiver to two children in family day-care settings), providing developmentally appropriate activities, following safety precautions with furnishings and equipment, administering authorized health procedures, keeping records for each child, and maintaining a sanitary, smoke-free, drug-free environment.

FINDING THE RIGHT OPTION

Remember that just because a child-care facility is licensed after meeting the minimum requirements, it doesn't necessarily guarantee your child a stimulating, high-quality educational experience. When considering a facility, observe the staff, the other children, and the indoor and outdoor spaces. Ask about the daily routine, nutrition, exercise, learning activities and materials, fees and payment schedules, child/staff ratio, extent of

i If you're looking for a nanny share or if you'd like to pose a question about nanny salaries, playgroups, and playgrounds to other moms and dads in the area, check out www.dcurbanmom .com.

parental involvement, and other factors that are important to you.

Other types of child care include day-care centers, where group care is provided for children typically of ages six weeks to five years. These centers are open for full days all year, and some provide transportation. Nursery schools and preschools offer group care for the preschool-age child but may not be open full days or all year. Extended day-care programs, meanwhile, offer supervised settings for school-age children when school is not in session. Besides providing before- and after-school care, the programs—much to the delight of parents—often cover snow days and holidays, and some have full-day summer programs.

Nannies—private, full-time, and sometimes live-in—offer another option, although it is more expensive. Local child-care agencies often have lists of individual nannies or nanny services, or at least can put you in touch with sources that do. Weekly salaries for full-time nannies range from $450 to $650, with live-out nannies earning up to $40,000 per year. If choosing a nanny through a placement agency, parents can expect to pay a registration/application fee of $200 or more and, on hiring, a placement fee of $2,500 or more.

Parents seeking a nanny should pay attention to the type of screening—such as criminal, background, and Social Security checks—required by an agency. Consider the person's experience, age, whether he or she smokes, whether the nanny has a valid driver's license, and whether he or she can speak English. Families planning to hire a live-in nanny should be prepared to provide a private room and bath, preferably on a separate level; a private phone line; and use of a car.

The au pair (French for "as an equal") program is perhaps the most unusual and interesting child-care option, and one that probably will continue to increase in popularity as the global society becomes further pronounced. It's little wonder that au pairs are popular in Metro Washington, with the region's strong multiethnic character and well-traveled populace. Au pair is an international youth exchange program organized to create cross-cultural understanding and cooperation between American families and Western European young adults. Sanctioned by the United States Information Agency (USIA), the program provides a great opportunity for young people from overseas to learn about American culture and family life while living in the United States, and it also serves as a wonderful learning experience for the hosts. The program typically involves au pairs between the ages of 18 and 25 who come to the United States for a year and care for the host family's children. Reciprocal programs allow American youths to perform these services in Europe.

Although most au pair experiences are positive for both young people and host families, it's not something for a family to enter into lightly. Veteran host families, as well as the organizations listed later in this chapter, can help steer prospective hosts in the right direction. Besides what can be a rewarding, memorable, cross-cultural experience, the au pair program can also mean cost savings for a family, compared with other types of in-home child care. Stipends average about $150 per week for 45 hours of child care, but bear in mind that host families must also be prepared to pay $250 for the application, $500 for tuition, and $3,000 to $4,000 for program fees that cover airfare, insurance, and child safety instruction.

All of these choices may seem mind-boggling, but the following resources can help you narrow down your options and zero in on the best situation for your family.

LOCAL GOVERNMENT-BASED CHILD-CARE RESOURCES

For listings of the child-care centers in your area, tips on what to look for, guidelines, requirements, financial assistance, and other information on any facet of child care, contact the appropriate agencies in your jurisdiction.

Washington, D.C.

Department of Health—Licensing, Regulation, and Administration
825 North Capitol Street NE, 2nd Floor
Washington, DC
(202) 442–5888
www.dchealth.dc.gov
This department licenses and monitors child development facilities, home- and center-based day care, and foster homes.

Washington Child Development Council
1400 16th Street NW, Suite 715
Washington, DC
(202) 387–0002
www.wcdconline.org
Contact the council for referrals and other child-care resources.

Northern Virginia
City of Alexandria

Child Care Information Services
2525 Mount Vernon Avenue
Alexandria, VA
(703) 838–0750
www.ci.alexandria.va.us/dhs/children_and_youth_services/childcare_info_svc.html
This service of the Office for Early Childhood Development in the city's Department of Human Services registers and trains child-care providers and provides lists of licensed centers, nurseries and preschools, in-home day care, before- and after-school programs, and summer camps.

Arlington County

Child and Family Services
1801 North George Mason Drive
Arlington, VA
(703) 228–1685
www.arlingtonva.us/departments/human
services/services/family/humanservices
servicesfamilychildrenfamily.aspx
The county's child-care office licenses family
day care, preschools, and centers and offers
free referral lists.

Public Schools Extended Day Program
2801 Clarendon Boulevard, Suite 312
Arlington, VA
(703) 228–6069
www.arlington.k12.va.us/finance/xday
Contact this division for details about the
supervised before- and after-school recreational program offered in elementary and
middle schools.

Fairfax County

Department of Family Services
12011 Government Center Parkway
Fairfax, VA
(703) 324–8100
www.fairfaxcounty.gov/ofc
This early childhood education agency
includes several programs, each of which has
its own phone number. We've included the
most relevant topics. You can also search for
child care online.

Child Care Assistance and Referral
9th Floor
(703) 449–8484
Parents can contact this office for lists of
child-care providers throughout the county.

Child Care Training Programs
8th Floor
(703) 324–8000
Child-care providers can contact this office to
enroll in training courses.

Check the classified ads in community weeklies and parenting publications for numerous child-care
possibilities.

Head Start Programs
9th Floor
(703) 324–8290
This national program offers early childhood
and parent education classes to low-income
families.

Permits and Regulation
8th Floor
(703) 324–8000
This division inspects and issues permits for
family child-care homes.

School-Age Child Care Program
9th Floor
(703) 449–8989
SACC provides before- and after-school and
summer programs at county elementary
schools. A program called Club 78 provides
recreational activities and homework help for
middle-school students.

City of Fairfax

Human Services Coordinator
10455 Armstrong Street
Fairfax, VA
(703) 385–7894
www.fairfaxva.gov/humanservices/human
services.asp
This office provides a list of licensed child-
care providers within the city.

City of Falls Church

Housing and Human Services
300 Park Avenue
Falls Church, VA
(703) 248–5001
This office provides a directory of day-care
homes, preschools, and child-care centers
and also provides one-on-one guidance to
both parents and caregivers.

Office of Community Education—Extended Day Care Office
7124 Leesburg Pike
Falls Church, VA
(703) 248–5683
www.fccps.k12.va.us/html/daycareinfo/daycare.htm
Contact this office for information about the before- and after-school child-care program.

Loudoun County

Department of Family Services
102 Heritage Way NE
Leesburg, VA
(703) 777–0353
www.co.loudoun.va.us/services/childcare/index.htm
This department provides a list of day-care providers, both facilities and individuals.

Prince William County

Department of Social Services/
Child Care Options
15941 Cardinal Drive
Woodbridge, VA
(703) 792–7500
www.co.prine-william.va.us
The office handles research and referrals of licensed day-care providers. It also provides certification and training and operates the USDA food program.

Suburban Maryland

Montgomery County

The Arc of Montgomery County
Family, Infant, and Child-Care Center
1600 Nebel Street
Rockville, MD
(301) 984–5777
www.arcmontmd.org
This specialized center offers care for children between the ages of six weeks and five years who have chronic medical conditions.

Locate: Childcare
(301) 279–1773
This division of the Department of Health and Human Services offers the county's only approved child-care referral for licensed providers. It also trains prospective child-care providers.

Montgomery County Child Care Resource and Referral Center
332 West Edmonston Drive, Room D4
Rockville, MD
(301) 279–1260
www.montgomerycountymd.gov/early childhoodservices
This building houses a variety of child-care-oriented programs, including the following:

Montgomery County Infants and Toddlers Program
401 Fleet Street, Lower Level
Rockville, MD
(240) 777–3997
Parents with developmentally delayed young children can find services through this collaborative program of the Department of Health and Human Services and public schools. Special education and speech and language therapy are among the types of services available to county residents. Your tax dollars at work!

Parenting Resource Center
332 West Edmonston Drive
Rockville, MD
(301) 279–8497
hocmc.org/parentcenters/parentcenters.htm
The Parenting Resource Center is sponsored by the Housing Opportunities Commission of Montgomery County. It provides resources to parents and caregivers and it offers parenting and other types of enrichment classes at three different locations.

Wintergreen Child Development Center
Room B-1
332 West Edmonston Drive
Rockville, MD
(301) 424–7522
www.rockvilledaycare.org
Part of the Rockville Day Care Association, this nonprofit center offers a year-round program to more than 100 children.

Prince George's County

Child Resource Center, Locate Child Care
9475 Lottsford Road, Suite 202
Largo, MD
(301) 772–8420
www.childresource.org
As part of the Prince George's Child Resource Center, which offers child-care information and training to parents and providers, Locate Child Care provides referrals to licensed child-care programs in the county. Information can be obtained by phone or online. The office is open 9:30 A.M. to 3:30 P.M. Monday through Friday. The Web site also offers a searchable database of child-care providers.

HELPFUL ORGANIZATIONS

Metropolitan Washington Council of Governments (COG)
777 North Capitol Street NE, Suite 300
Washington, DC
(202) 962–3200
www.mwcog.org
COG, as it's often called, is an excellent source for child-care information and virtually anything else you can think of in which local governments play some sort of role. COG provides such resources as reports on the status of child care, guidelines for seeking quality child care, and scholarship coordination for child-care providers. As a vast information clearinghouse, COG also refers residents to other organizations, many of which are headquartered in Metro Washington.

National Association for the Education of Young Children (NAEYC)
1313 L Street NW, Suite 500
Washington, DC
(202) 232–8777, (800) 424–2460
www.naeyc.org
Founded in 1926, NAEYC is the country's largest professional organization focused on promoting quality education for children ages eight and younger. Membership includes more than 300 local, state, and regional affiliated organizations. Among many other services,

the association offers educational literature and videos and a national voluntary accreditation program for early childhood centers.

National Black Child Development Institute
1101 15th Street NW, Suite 900
Washington, DC
(202) 833–2220
www.nbcdi.org
This nonprofit organization, founded in 1970, strives to improve the quality of life for African American children. It provides child-care resources to parents and professionals and offers leadership training in child care and education.

Parent Encouragement Program (PEP)
10100 Connecticut Avenue
Kensington, MD
(301) 929–8824
www.parentencouragement.org
PEP is a community-based program that offers in-depth classes and workshops for parents and professionals who want to deal more effectively with children. Its mission is the development of stronger, more encouraging families through step-by-step education, skill training, and support. Students rave about the classes, which are taught by parents who've gone through years of intensive PEP training.

NANNIES

These agencies place part-time, full-time, live-in, and live-out nannies throughout the Washington metropolitan area. Unless otherwise indicated, they also provide short-term and, with at least four hours' notice, emergency or sitter referrals. For long-term placement, try to call at least a month in advance.

A Choice Nanny
2429 26th Road South
Arlington, VA
(703) 685–2229
www.achoicenanny.com/arlington
This highly rated agency interviews all candi-

dates in person and offers basic training to nannies. It has a full range of services, including weekend and evening babysitters, temporary nannies, and after-school "tutorcare" nannies who also do chores.

Mothers' Aides Inc.
5618 Ox Road
Fairfax Station, VA
(703) 250–0700, (800) 526–2669
www.mothersaides.com
Founded in 1979, this agency is a member of NAEYC, an organization described in the Helpful Organizations section. It provides permanent, temporary, and on-call nannies.

Nannies, Inc.
3031 Borge Street, Suite 107
Oakton, VA
(301) 718–0100 (Bethesda)
(703) 255–5312 (Oakton)
(410) 267–0610 (Annapolis)
www.nanniesinc.net
Washington Families newspaper voted this 18-year-old agency, founded by a single dad, the Best Nanny Service in the Washington metropolitan area. The agency places only long-term, full-service nannies.

Potomac Nannies, Ltd.
7315 Wisconsin Avenue, Suite 1300-W
Bethesda, MD
(301) 986–0048
This agency, which opened in 1985, places both live-in and live-out nannies.

TeacherCare
1701 East Woodland Road, #700
Schaumburg, IL 60173
(888) TEACH–07
www.teachercare.com
All nannies in this program are educated in early childhood education, Montessori, gifted, special needs, psychology, or related specialties. TeacherCare has an office in Arlington,

but most communication goes through its national headquarters in Illinois.

White House Nannies
7200 Wisconsin Avenue
Bethesda, MD
(301) 654–1242 (for permanent)
(301) 652–8088 (for temporary)
www.whitehousenannies.com
This 22-year-old agency began when the owner experienced frustration during her own nanny search.

AU PAIRS

For more information about au pairs, contact one of the following organizations, which are sanctioned by the United States Information Agency (USIA) to recruit European participants and unite them with American families.

- **Au Pair in America,** 9 West Broad Street, Stamford, CT 06902; (203) 399–5000, (800) 928–7247, www.aupairinamerica.com
- **AuPairCare,** 600 California Street, 10th Floor, San Francisco, CA 94104; (415) 434–8788, (800) 428–7247, www.aupaircare.com
- **Go Au Pair,** 151 East 6100 South, Suite 200, Murray, UT 84107; (888) 287–2471, www.goaupair.com
- **Cultural Care Au Pair,** EF Center Boston, 1 Education Street, Cambridge, MA 02141; (800) 333–6056, www.culturalcare.com
- **EurAupair,** 3091-A East Shadowlawn Avenue, Atlanta, GA 30305; (800) 618–2002, www.euraupair.com
- **AuPair U.S.A. InterExchange,** 161 6th Avenue, 13th Floor, New York, NY 10013; (212) 924–0446, (800) 287–2477, www.aupairusa.org

HEALTH CARE

The adult population of the Washington metropolitan area is healthier than the nation as a whole, according to a 2001 study by the Metropolitan Washington Council of Governments. For 19 of 27 health indicators, the Washington region is doing as well as or better than the national average: And for coronary heart disease deaths and mammography rates, this region already more than meets national targets for 2010. A 2003 study by Centrum and Sperling's Best Places named Washington, D.C. America's second-healthiest city. On some measures, however, the region appears less healthy than the nation. These include AIDS, sexually transmitted infections, binge drinking, firearms-related deaths, and low-birth-weight babies.

So it's good to know that anyone seeking medical care in the Metro Washington area can take comfort in knowing help is literally right around the corner. In D.C. proper, you can't travel more than a few blocks without encountering a hospital, medical clinic, or a building full of doctors' offices.

The Nation's Capital area is home to some of the world's finest medical researchers and health care professionals, and four area hospitals are consistently ranked among the 100 best in America by *U.S. News and World Report*. Three of the four are Georgetown University Medical Center, Inova Fairfax Hospital, and Children's National Medical Center. The one with the most stellar reputation, however, is Johns Hopkins University Hospital, about an hour away in Baltimore, Maryland. Though it may be a little farther, if you're struck with a serious illness, it's worth the drive. In many specialties, Hopkins is ranked number one by *U.S. News and World Report* surveys and is invariably in the top five.

Looking beyond Metro Washington and Maryland for a moment, there are two other acclaimed medical institutions: the University of Virginia Medical Center in Charlottesville and the Medical College of Virginia in Richmond.

This chapter, however, sticks closer to home and offers an overview of approximately 50 major hospitals and other medical facilities in Metro Washington, including the teaching and research hospitals affiliated with university medical schools that play a vital role in the training of future doctors, nurses, and other health care professionals. We've also included some mental health facilities and touched on the popular walk-in medical centers where minor illnesses and injuries can be quickly treated (see the Emergency Numbers listed toward the end of this chapter). One caveat: By the time you read this, some of the names may have changed because takeovers by large managed-care organizations are ongoing.

We have intentionally omitted a list of hospices, because physicians or hospitals generally refer patients after initial medical treatment. There are, however, more than a dozen in the Washington metro area, and they are easily found in the Yellow Pages or through physician referrals. Also, an excellent clearinghouse for information on hospices and their services is the National Hospice and Palliative Care Organization, 1700 Diagonal Road, Suite 625, Alexandria, VA, (703) 837–1500, www.nhpco.org. Don't forget that all local governments offer community health clinics and other local treatment facilities, included in the government listings in the phone book.

FINDING THE RIGHT DOCTOR: PHYSICIAN REFERRALS

Although finding a hospital may be easy, the same doesn't always apply to finding the right doctor. So before delving too deeply into the hospital world, we've compiled a listing of some free dental and physician referral services—some of which are affiliated with area hospitals and some of which are financed by subscribing doctors. Aside from those listed here, almost every hospital we've named in this chapter has a referral service listed in the phone book along with the hospital's other departments. In most cases the referral services can provide access to hundreds of medical professionals in a wide range of fields and specialties. Caution: Because these services are often financed by those who stand to benefit, you may wish to check with the licensing board for credentials.

In Maryland, the state licensing board is at 4201 Patterson Avenue, Baltimore, MD 21215; (410) 764–4777, www.mbp.state.md.us/index.html. In Washington, D.C., write to 825 North Capitol Street NE, Washington, D.C. 20002, (202) 442–5888, www.dchealth.dc.gov; and in Virginia, 6603 West Broad Street, 5th Floor, Richmond, VA 23230; (804) 662–9900, www.dht.state.va.us/medicine.

To get started, here is a short list of some of the area's most popular referral services. It is by no means comprehensive, but it touches on most counties in Metro Washington:

- Inova HealthSource, (703) 204–3366, connect.inova.com/physician/mddb.welcome.welcomepage
- Montgomery General Hospital Physician Referral Service, (888) 376–8881, www.montgomerygeneral.com/find_a_physician/default.asp
- Physician Match, (301) 896–3939, www.suburbanhospital.org/suburban/directory.cfm

State hospital associations—smaller versions of the American Hospital Association—can be a valuable resource for information on medical facilities in Maryland, Virginia, and Washington, D.C. Just contact the public relations office at the appropriate organization: Maryland Hospital Association, 6820 Deerpath Road, Elkridge, MD 21075, (410) 379–6200, www.mdhospitals.org; Virginia Hospital and Healthcare Association, 4200 Innslake Drive, Glen Allen, VA 23060, (804) 965–1215, (804) 747–8600, www.vhha.com; District of Columbia Hospital Association, 1250 Eye Street NW, Suite 700, Washington, D.C. 20005, (202) 682–1581, www.dcha.org.

Most hospitals featured in this chapter offer community outreach health and education programs (CPR, smoking cessation, weight reduction, family planning and child birth, stress management, etc.), as well as speakers bureaus, outpatient testing, surgery and treatment programs, and other services beyond the usual realm of a hospital's everyday role. Many services are free, but call the individual facilities to find out more.

With one exception, we have not included any of the military or veterans' hospitals because they don't serve the general public. If you are a newcomer seeking information on veterans' hospitals, contact the Veterans' Affairs Medical Center at (202) 745–8000 or visit www.washingtondc.va.gov.

HOSPITALS

Washington, D.C.

Children's National Medical Center
111 Michigan Avenue NW
Washington, DC
(202) 884–5000
www.cnmc.org
When children are seriously ill or hurt, this is one of the top places they can go for treatment—and the patients aren't from just Metro Washington. Children's National Medical Center, often referred to as Children's Hospital, is recognized as one of the preeminent medical-care providers to infants, children, and youths in the entire mid-Atlantic region. Some 75 percent of pediatricians in Metro Washington have trained here.

No one enjoys being hospitalized, particularly kids. Children's recognizes the trauma of hospitalization for children; since 1910 there has been a "rooming in" program for parents. Founded in 1870—although the present 279-bed facility opened in 1977—Children's is a private, nonprofit hospital with two comprehensive-care branch clinics in Washington, D.C. and several clinics in Maryland and Virginia.

Emergency trauma care is perhaps Children's best-known service, but the hospital's expertise extends well into other areas, including cardiology, sports medicine, genetics, plastic and reconstructive surgery, infectious diseases, neonatology, psychiatry, and physical therapy. Naturally, Children's is very active in the research field, with special emphasis on AIDS, sickle cell anemia, and autism.

The George Washington University Medical Center
2300 "Eye" Street NW
Washington, DC
(202) 715–4000
www.gwumc.edu/

One of the area's most comprehensive health care and education centers, the George Washington University Medical Center was founded in 1824 at the former Washington Infirmary on 16th Street NW. It moved to its present location in the Foggy Bottom neighborhood in 1947. Private and nonprofit, it is composed of three entities: the University Hospital; Medical Faculty Associates, a full-time physician group practice; and the School of Public Health and Health Services.

In 2002 the George Washington University Hospital moved all services from its old building directly across the street to a brand-new $96-million, 371-bed facility, which includes $45 million worth of new state-of-the-art medical equipment.

A major teaching and research facility, "GW" is involved in research projects costing in the tens of millions annually (see the Education chapter also). The Medical Center has three research institutes: the Institute for Bio-

Each year *Washingtonian* magazine publishes a rating of area doctors according to specialty. It's a good reference that is freely available in local libraries. It's also posted online at www.washingtonian.com.

medical Sciences, the Institute for Clinical Research and Clinical Trials, and the Institute for Health Policy and Human Values. As could be expected from such a comprehensive health care facility, a broad range of services is offered, including women's health, alternative medicine, OB-GYN, orthopedics, infertility treatment, surgery, psychiatric services, internal medicine, sports medicine, speech pathology, and audiology. In addition, the hospital is a level I trauma center with a busy 24-hour emergency room.

Georgetown University Hospital
3800 Reservoir Road NW
Washington, DC
(202) 444–2000
www.georgetownuniversityhospital.org

Probably the city's most prestigious teaching hospital, Georgetown University Hospital was founded in 1898 and went on to break new ground by offering such conveniences as a special entrance for horse-drawn ambulances—modern indeed for its time. Today's 609-bed facility, which opened in 1948, is located in tony upper Northwest on a residential street lined with gracious mansions and diplomatic residences. The hospital, like its namesake university (see the Education chapter), is highly regarded internationally, and a top-flight team of doctors, nurses, and other personnel have access to the most advanced technology in every clinical discipline.

The hospital has distinguished itself as a medical research hub and is known as an ultra-modern teaching facility. Pioneering efforts at Georgetown led to later successes with heart-valve implants, while work today continues in disciplines such as cancer research, magnetic resonance imaging (MRI), and specialized perinatal and neonatal care. The Lombardi Cancer

Center, founded in 1970, is one of only 50 comprehensive cancer centers in the U.S. that receive such a designation from the National Cancer Institute. The full range of services at the Medical Center includes OB-GYN, pediatrics, neurology, orthopedics, emergency medicine, internal medicine, and radiology.

Greater Southeast Community Hospital
1310 Southern Avenue SE
Washington, DC
(202) 574–6000
www.greatersouthest.org
Greater Southeast Community Hospital, founded in 1966, is a 450-bed facility that serves over 400,000 city residents annually. Despite the fact that it's the largest and most comprehensive hospital of its kind in the immediate area, its fate hung in the balance in late 2003. Beset by financial and quality-of-care issues, the hospital lost accreditation by the Joint Commission on Accreditation of Healthcare Organizations.

GSCH offers a fairly broad range of surgical and medical services, including OB-GYN, pediatrics, neurology, orthopedics, emergency and internal medicine, radiology, family practice, ophthalmology, adult psychiatry, cancer screening, a diabetes management unit, geriatric assessment, oncology, neonatal intensive care, pathology, renal dialysis, and cardiology.

The Hospital for Sick Children
1731 Bunker Hill Road NE
Washington, DC
(202) 832–4400
www.hfscsite.org
The Hospital for Sick Children is another of the city's smaller (131 beds) health care centers with a unique role: that of a pediatric "transitional care" facility—the only one of its kind in Metro Washington—that serves as a link between hospital and home. Here, the

i Howard University's medical school opened its doors in 1868, just three years after the Civil War.

young patients are treated for respiratory and chronic illnesses and a host of other disabilities.

Founded in 1883 as a "fresh air" summer home, the present facility opened in 1968. Services focus on a wide range of therapies, including physical, occupational, recreational, nutritional, respiratory, speech, and language.

Howard University Hospital
2041 Georgia Avenue NW
Washington, DC
(202) 865–6100
www.huhosp.org
The second-oldest of Washington, D.C.'s three major university-based teaching and research medical centers, 482-bed Howard University Hospital has come a long way since its founding in 1863 as Freedman's Hospital, a name that in itself speaks of history. The federal government created Freedman's as an emergency facility to treat the thousands of sick, destitute former slaves who poured into Washington after gaining their freedom. The Howard University Hospital of today opened in 1975 and remains synonymous with African American advancement (some of the nation's top black medical professionals, beginning with Dr. Charles Drew, a pioneer in blood plasma preservation, have been trained here). The school itself, meanwhile, ranks as one of the nation's leading, historically African American universities (see the Education chapter).

Howard is the third-largest private hospital and one of the busiest hospitals in Metro Washington, with annual inpatient admissions of around 13,000 and emergency room visits topping 48,000. Special services for the community include screening and counseling for sickle cell anemia, cancer screening, drug and alcohol addiction treatment, and renal dialysis.

Underscoring its role as a major health care provider, the hospital's vast range of services includes OB-GYN; pediatrics; neurology; orthopedics; internal medicine; radiology; family practice; ophthalmology; oncology; dentistry; dermatology; plastic and reconstructive surgery; neurosurgery; radiotherapy; psychiatric services for children, adolescents, and adults; physical and occupational therapy; sports medicine; and areas dealing with infectious disease.

National Rehabilitation Hospital
102 Irving Street NW
Washington, DC
(202) 877–1000
www.nrhrehab.org

National Rehabilitation Hospital is a godsend for those severely disabled through accident or illness. It is the first and only freestanding facility in Metro Washington dedicated solely to thorough medical rehabilitation, with the aim of helping patients on to active and satisfying lives. The 160-bed hospital offers a host of inpatient and outpatient medical rehabilitation services, including driver evaluation and training, social work, neuropsychology, nutrition, physical therapy, speech and language pathology, and therapeutic recreation.

The hospital is particularly designed for those who are physically disabled by spinal cord and brain injuries, stroke, arthritis, postpolio syndrome, amputation, and other orthopedic and neurological conditions; a 40-bed unit is reserved solely for brain-injury patients. Besides its role as a rehabilitation center, NRH serves as a strong advocacy voice for the disabled.

Providence Hospital
1150 Varnum Street NE
Washington, DC
(202) 269–7000
www.provhosp.org

Providence is yet another District hospital with intriguing Civil War roots. Established in 1861 by four Catholic nuns in a renovated mansion, its original role was to care for the civilian population as the fighting between North and South raged. As luck would have it, Providence was the city's only medical facility not taken over by the military during the war. It is the only private hospital in Washington that has remained in continuous operation since.

Established at its present site in 1954, today's 382-bed Providence Hospital specializes in obstetrics and women's health care, geriatrics, and a full range of acute and emergency services. It also has a 240-bed nursing and rehabilitation center. Other programs include orthopedics, internal medicine, family practice, ophthalmology, infertility treatment, cardiology, psychiatric services for adults, substance abuse diagnosis, and physical and occupational therapy.

Sibley Memorial Hospital
5255 Loughboro Road NW
Washington, DC
(202) 537–4000
www.sibley.org

Sibley is yet another example of a truly "community" hospital, occupying a wooded parcel on a quiet residential street in upper Northwest. The 328-bed facility is also another example of a District medical center with a nineteenth-century heritage; it was founded in 1890 as a nurse-training school for deaconesses and missionaries. The hospital itself came later and was named in honor of William J. Sibley, an early supporter of the school's work, who donated $10,000 for the construction of the medical center in memory of his wife. The current building and site, however, date only to 1961. An extensive renovation and modernization program was completed in 1990.

Sibley has made its mark primarily as a surgical center, both inpatient and out. Specialties include eye and plastic surgeries, a wide range of programs for the elderly, and a sleep disorders center. Services include emergency medicine, family practice, internal medicine, neurology, OB-GYN, oncology, occupational and physical therapy, ophthalmology, orthopedics, radiology, and psychiatry for adults. It also has a residential Alzheimer's unit and an assisted living residence. Unlike the teaching hospitals or publicly founded ones, Sibley is noted for more personalized attention to patients—maybe the word should be *pampering*. So if you're having elective surgery, you might want to treat yourself to one of the private hotel-like "suites" that Sibley offers. After all, what better time to coddle yourself than when you're in the hospital?

The Washington Hospital Center
110 Irving Street NW
Washington, DC
(202) 877–7000
www.whcenter.org
Medlantic Healthcare Group and Helix Health merged in 1998 to form MedStar Health, one of the largest not-for-profit health systems in the East. The flagship hospital in the system, Washington Hospital Center, is the largest private teaching hospital in Washington, D.C. and a hub for research and education. Founded in 1958, the 900-bed facility has developed into one of Metro Washington's top medical centers, with special emphasis on emergency shock-trauma care for the critically ill and injured, many of whom arrive via MedSTAR, the acclaimed air ambulance service. It serves more than 200,000 patients annually.

Washington Hospital Center's expansive list of facilities and services includes a comprehensive burn center and cardiology unit, organ transplantation, high-risk maternal-fetal care, neurology, OB-GYN, orthopedics, radiology, oral surgery, neurosurgery, and treatment for diabetes, cancer, and eye disorders.

Northern Virginia

City of Alexandria

The Inova Alexandria Hospital
4320 Seminary Road
Alexandria, VA
(703) 504–3000
www.inova.com
The Inova Alexandria Hospital is the primary provider of medical services for city residents. It's also a primary provider of jobs, ranking as Alexandria's largest private employer with 1,600 workers and more than 700 physicians. Established in 1872, the hospital occupied five sites before the present 339-bed, nonprofit facility opened in 1962.

The hospital has one of the top cardiac surgery units in the area, with advanced cardiac care, including preventative medicine, chest pain emergency service, and cardiopulmonary rehabilitation. Emergency medicine is also a specialty, and for good reason: Alexandria was the first hospital in the nation to staff its emergency department with full-time emergency physicians, a standard practice today at most major medical facilities. For minor emergencies when a private physician isn't available, the hospital offers an Express Care Center in the hospital's emergency department. There, you might be seen by a nurse or a nurse practitioner, although physicians are also on staff.

Cancer treatment is also a specialty at Alexandria Hospital, which houses the Northern Virginia Cancer Center. Other services include a birthing center, a neonatal intensive care unit, dialysis, a blood donor center, respiratory therapy, and a same-day surgery center for outpatients. The hospital is in the midst of a massive $70-million expansion and reconfiguration project that will include an expanded emergency room and surgical facilities, an enlarged Cardiovascular and Interventional Radiology Department, and a renovated Neonatal Intensive Care Unit.

Inova Mount Vernon Hospital
2501 Parkers Lane
Alexandria, VA
(703) 664–7000
www.inova.com
Alexandria's other major medical facility, Mount Vernon Hospital, is a 232-bed nonprofit community hospital that opened in 1976. Like Inova Alexandria, it's a member of the Inova Health System, a nonprofit, community-based organization that also includes Inova Fair Oaks, Inova Fairfax, and Inova Loudoun Hospitals (see subsequent entries). The system also offers home health care, long-term care, and behavioral services.

Located near its historic namesake, the hospital provides a full range of medical and surgical services, primarily to residents of

Alexandria and southeastern Fairfax County. Services include 24-hour emergency medicine, a psychiatric unit for adolescents and adults, and a range of programs relating to cardiology, cancer, physical medicine, and rehabilitation. Its 350 physicians represent a wide spectrum of the health care field. Diagnostic services offered include magnetic resonance imaging, digital angiography, ultrasound, echocardiogram, cardiac catheterization, stress tests, and mammography.

Perhaps Mount Vernon's broadest special service is the Inova Rehabilitation Center, where patients receive comprehensive care and therapy for stroke, orthopedic injuries, head and spinal cord injuries, amputation, multiple sclerosis, arthritis, workplace injuries, and other neuromuscular disorders. The center includes an inpatient acute-care unit. The Inova Joint Replacement Center received a Mercury Award for its top-rate program from the American Health Network.

Arlington County

Virginia Hospital Center, Arlington
1701 North George Mason Drive
Arlington, VA
(703) 558–5000
www.virginiahospitalcenter.net
Arlington County's largest and most comprehensive health care facility is Virginia Hospital Center, a 334-bed, nonprofit teaching hospital affiliated with Georgetown University's School of Medicine and several nursing schools. Open since 1944, it's well known locally not only for fine medical and surgical services but also as the hospital of the Washington Redskins, because the team's medical staff has privileges here.

With more than 700 physicians, Arlington Hospital offers a wide range of services, including a 24-hour emergency department, treatment for adult alcoholism and other drug addictions, OB-GYN, high-risk nursery, open-heart surgery, outpatient clinics, physical medicine and rehabilitation, psychiatric treatment, and numerous diagnostic and therapeutic serv-

ices, such as nuclear medicine, radiation therapy, and respiratory therapy. A $150-million expansion project completed in 2004 doubled the size of the emergency room and converted all semiprivate rooms to private rooms. In 2003 a new lung cancer center opened at the hospital.

Fairfax County

Columbia-Dominion Hospital
2960 Sleepy Hollow Road
Falls Church, VA
(703) 536–2872
www.dominionhospital.com
Columbia-Dominion, owned by the Columbia Healthcare giant, is one of Northern Virginia's leading mental-health care centers for children, adolescents, and adults. "First Step," a free, confidential mental-health information, assessment, and referral service, offers assistance in various crisis situations, including suicide attempts and threats, substance abuse and other addictive illnesses, eating disorders, serious and prolonged depression, acute stress reactions, uncontrollable fears, behavioral problems in children and adolescents, sexual abuse, childhood trauma, and sleep disorders.

Columbia-Fairfax Surgical Center
10730 Main Street
Fairfax City, VA
(703) 691–0670
For outpatient surgical services without having to go to an actual hospital, many people opt for a facility such as Columbia-Fairfax Surgical Center, part of a national network. Offering what it calls "efficient, personal care in a pleasant atmosphere," the center charges a single fee that covers basic medical history, equipment and most supplies, routine drugs and anesthetics, recovery room services, and operating room time. Be aware, though, that the price does not include the professional services of the surgeon or assistants, the anesthesiologist, radiologist, pathologist, physician consultants, and pharmacist.

i Most community hospitals in the metro area offer deluxe hotel-style wings suitable for those having elective surgery, or who simply wish for added comfort and better cuisine. Count on spending an extra $150 to $250 or more per day.

Inova Fair Oaks Hospital
3600 Joseph Siewick Drive
Fairfax, VA
(703) 391–3600
www.inova.com

Inova Fair Oaks Hospital was one of two hospitals built in Fairfax County in the 1980s—in this case, 1987. The other was Reston Hospital Center (see subsequent entry). Its newness is underscored in such design features as bed-mounted telephones and nurse call buttons, wall-to-wall carpeting in patients' rooms, private televisions with in-room movies, solariums, gourmet meals, and rooms with deluxe amenities. The 160-bed, 1,200-employee facility is part of the Inova Health System that includes Alexandria, Mount Vernon, and Fairfax Hospitals. A western Fairfax location—just off U.S. 50 at I–66—makes Fair Oaks Hospital convenient to many county residents beyond its core service area of Chantilly, Reston, and Fairfax.

More than 1,000 physicians covering dozens of specialties have privileges at Fair Oaks, which can handle emergency, medical, surgical, critical-care, cardiac, orthopedic, obstetric, and pediatric patients. The 24-hour emergency department offers a helipad located just outside the doors. Two additions focus on the care and treatment of young patients: a maternal and infant health center (which opened in 1988), emphasizing a family-centered approach to the birth process, and a children's unit (1990) specially equipped for infants and children through age 18. In-house pediatricians are available 24 hours a day.

Inova Fair Oaks also offers comprehensive sleep evaluations for patients suffering from sleep apnea, insomnia, chronic fatigue, and other problems related to sleep disorders.

Inova Fairfax Hospital
3300 Gallows Road
Fairfax, VA
(703) 698–1110
www.inova.com

This 833-bed, nonprofit regional medical center, the flagship hospital of the Inova Health System, is Northern Virginia's only level I emergency and trauma center, meaning it can handle the most critical illnesses and accidents. The emergency room opened a new expansion in 2005 and can handle up to 80,000 patients per year. Fairfax has Northern Virginia's only pediatric intensive-care unit with 24-hour care. Helicopters are a familiar sight here.

Opened in 1961, Fairfax Hospital has seen tremendous growth over the years during its emergence as one of Metro Washington's premier medical facilities. In fact, a major construction project added 177 beds and a new heart center in the spring of 2004. It's home to the nationally recognized Inova Heart Center, where the region's first heart transplant was performed in 1986. The hospital was also the site of the area's first lung transplant (1991) and first heart-kidney combination transplant (1992). An amazingly busy obstetrics wing (actually its own building) has earned Fairfax its local nickname, "The Baby Factory." A total of 11,013 babies entered the world here in 2002, a figure that's the second highest in the nation. Indeed, babies are a specialty at Fairfax; there's even a unit for high-risk pregnancies, along with a neonatal intensive-care unit. The hospital offers the full range of other medical-surgical services and state-of-the-art technology, but it's also a major teaching hospital, affiliated with Georgetown and George Washington medical schools, the Medical College of Virginia, and nursing schools at George Mason and Marymount Universities and Northern Virginia Community College.

Inova Fairfax Hospital for Children
3300 Gallows Road
Fairfax, VA
(703) 776–4002
www.inova.com

Inova Fairfax Hospital for Children is a comprehensive, highly specialized facility with more than 400 doctors dedicated to caring for children through a full spectrum of pediatric services. The hospital provides everything from simple allergy relief to complex cardiac surgery. As a member of the national Children's Oncology Group, the hospital adheres to state-of-the-art protocols developed to treat childhood cancers. Its helicopter and ground transports, staffed by pediatric and neonatal nurse specialists, are designed especially for critically ill or injured children and infants.

Reston Hospital Center
1850 Town Center Parkway
Reston, VA
(703) 689–9000
www.restonhospital.com

With the opening of Reston Hospital Center in 1986, many residents of western Fairfax County, particularly those in Reston, Herndon, Great Falls, and parts of greater Vienna, realized the luxury of not having to travel across the county to Fairfax Hospital for comprehensive medical care. Residents of booming Eastern Loudoun County also visit this facility. To meet the growing area's needs, an expansion project has added 60 beds, and made all of the hospital's rooms private. Its services are numerous and include most surgical and medical procedures as well as a new 24-hour emergency department, opened in 2003. Of particular note is its maternity center, pediatric center, and a new radiation oncology program opened in 2004. Now patients can receive complete cancer care, including surgery, chemotherapy, and radiation, at Reston Hospital Center.

The same-day surgery department has seen significant growth in recent years, reflecting a national trend toward outpatient services. Reston Hospital Center is the "official" hospital of Washington Dulles International Airport due to its proximity, easy access (just a couple of minutes off the Dulles Toll Road and parallel Airport Access Road), and wide range of services.

Loudoun County

Loudoun Hospital Inova
44045 Riverside Parkway
Leesburg, VA
(703) 858–6000
www.loudounhospital.org

The county's primary medical facility is this 155-room hospital, formerly known as Loudoun Hospital Center. Founded in 1912 as a six-room rural hospital, Inova Loudoun is a recent acquisition by the Inova Health System. Inova Loudoun offers most major medical and surgical services, including 24-hour emergency medicine. Special features include an intensive care unit; an outpatient surgery department; comprehensive diagnostic imaging services; a birthing inn; a behavioral services unit; physical, occupational, and speech therapy; a pain management center; and business health management services. Its cardiopulmonary health center was one of Northern Virginia's first.

The hospital extends its community-outreach efforts to a new level with Lifeline, an electronic alert system that gives elderly residents or the severely disabled a direct connection to assistance (and no doubt provides family and friends with peace of mind).

Affiliated services include the Countryside Ambulatory Surgery Center (703–444–6060), in Sterling; the Loudoun Cancer Care Center (703–444–4460), also in the Countryside community, offering chemotherapy and radiation therapy; the Loudoun Nursing and Rehabilitation Center (703–771–2841), which provides nursing care and assistance with day-to-day activities; the Leesburg Emergency Department (703–737–7520), for urgent medical issues; Mary Elizabeth Miller Radiation Oncology Center, providing radiation treatment for cancer patients (703–858–8850); Physical Medicine & Rehabilitation Center (540–338–1000), offering physical and occupational therapy, as well as other rehabilitation programs; and the Sterling-Dulles Imaging & MRI Center (703–444–5800), for the diagnosis and treatment of a wide variety of disorders and diseases.

Prince William County

Potomac Hospital (affiliate of Inova Health System)
2300 Opitz Boulevard
Woodbridge, VA
(703) 670–1313
www.potomachospital.com
Potomac Hospital, established in 1972 with 29 beds, has grown into a 183-bed comprehensive health care facility with more than 1,000 staff members. The hospital features a fully equipped pediatric unit, maternity unit, and neonatology program; 24-hour emergency medicine, magnetic-resonance imaging, and radiation therapy; and cardiac catheterization and angiography. The hospital offers services in the areas of allergy and immunology, dermatology, family practice, internal medicine, neurology, OB-GYN, pediatrics, psychiatry, radiation oncology, general surgery, neurosurgery, ophthalmology, oral surgery, orthopedics, plastic surgery, thoracic and vascular surgery, urology, anesthesiology, pathology, physical medicine rehabilitation, and radiology and nuclear medicine, plus a newly renovated emergency-care center. In March 2006 Potomac opened a new, four-story, 180,000-square-foot patient care building. The $71-million facility brings 30 additional beds in private rooms equipped with Internet access, a sitting area with a couch or sleep chair, flat-screen televisions, and phone lines.

Prince William Hospital
8700 Sudley Road
Manassas, VA
(703) 369–8000
www.pwhs.org
The county's largest medical facility is 170-bed Prince William Hospital, a private, non-profit community facility established in 1964. In April 2006 Prince William announced its plan to merge with—you guessed it—Inova, the dominant force in the region's hospital system. The hospital features comprehensive medical and surgical services and includes a critical-care unit, inpatient and outpatient surgery, oncology, pediatrics, a 24-hour emergency department, a helipad, OB-GYN, cardiology, nuclear medicine, radiology and other diagnostic services, dialysis treatment, and physical, speech, and occupational therapies.

Spotsylvania County

Mary Washington Hospital
1001 Sam Perry Boulevard
Fredericksburg, VA
(540) 741–1100
www.medicorp.org/mwh
Although located just outside the primary focus area of this book, Mary Washington Hospital merits inclusion for its size, services, branch facilities, and accessibility to many residents of Metro Washington, particularly those in parts of southeastern Prince William County. The 412-bed hospital is part of the regional Medicorp Health System. It offers private rooms, intensive care units (including neonatal ICU), neurosurgery, open-heart surgery, and a 24-hour emergency department. The hospital also offers special birthing suites for labor, delivery, and recovery for new mothers and their babies.

Affiliated facilities include Snowden at Fredericksburg, a psychiatric and addiction treatment center for adolescents and adults; the Family Health Center at North Stafford, a freestanding outpatient facility; Carriage Hill Nursing Home, a provider of professional long-term care; Chancellor's Village of Fredericksburg, a retirement community; and Common wealth Assisted Living Center, a modestly priced home for adults.

Suburban Maryland

Anne Arundel County

Anne Arundel Medical Center
2001 Medical Parkway
Annapolis, MD
(443) 481–1000
www.askaamc.org
Established as Annapolis Emergency Hospital in 1902, AAMC has evolved into a regional medical center serving a population area of more than 600,000. The center went through a major revamping in 2001, including the

addition of its $65-million acute care pavilion, serving critically ill patients. The medical center also includes a women's and children's center that welcomed more than 5,000 babies in 2005, an outpatient surgery center averaging 1,200 procedures a month, a radiation oncology center, a diabetes center, and a breast care center. The hospital has 265 beds, and the medical center's staff numbers more than 2,000.

Baltimore Washington Medical Center
301 Hospital Drive
Glen Burnie, MD
(410) 787–4000
bwmc.umms.org/index.html
This 286-bed nonprofit hospital focuses on short-term acute care and features a 24-hour emergency room with an immediate-care center for minor injuries and illnesses, and a center for severe trauma and injuries. Part of the University of Maryland Medical System, the hospital offers numerous outpatient support programs and services at various locations. The hospital opened the comprehensive Tate Cancer Center and Maryland Vascular Center in 2003.

Montgomery County

Holy Cross Hospital of Silver Spring
1500 Forest Glen Road
Silver Spring, MD
(301) 754–7000
www.holycrosshealth.org
One of Montgomery County's primary medical facilities, Holy Cross is a 425-bed nonprofit hospital founded in 1963 by Catholic nuns. Not only is this the largest acute-care facility in the county, it is also the only teaching hospital and boasts the largest medical staff in Montgomery, with some 1,400 physicians enjoying privileges—a good thing, because the hospital's chief service area of southern Montgomery County and northern and western Prince George's County is home to some 600,000 residents.

Holy Cross Hospital is a recognized teaching center through affiliations with George

> Teaching hospitals may offer cutting-edge technology, but care will often be less personal than at community hospitals. If your procedure is simple, consider the latter.

Washington University's graduate medical education programs in obstetrics, gynecology, medicine, and surgery. More babies—8,239—were delivered here in 2005 than in any other hospital in Maryland or Washington, D.C. The hospital works with GW and Children's National Medical Center in sponsoring a pediatric teaching program. Specialties include critical-care services, emergency medicine, OB-GYN, home care/hospice, pediatrics, psychiatry, and a range of surgical procedures. An expansion completed in 2005 added more private rooms, a new neonatal intensive care unit, and a larger ER.

Montgomery General Hospital
18101 Prince Philip Drive
Olney, MD
(301) 774–8882
www.montgomerygeneral.com
Founded in 1918, this 191-bed nonprofit community hospital is in the northern Montgomery County community of Olney, but it serves many residents of Howard and Prince George's Counties as well. Montgomery General has a full range of inpatient and outpatient medical and surgical services and programs, including obstetrics, pediatrics, 24-hour emergency and cardiac care, and cancer care. The hospital offers psychiatric and addiction treatment along with the latest medical imaging and diagnostic services, health education, and screening programs. More than 500 physicians are on staff.

The National Institutes of Health
9000 Rockville Pike
Bethesda, MD
(301) 496–4000
www.nih.gov
Along with the Centers for Disease Control (CDC) in Atlanta, the National Institutes of

Health is probably the best known and most widely recognized of the medical field's distinguished "alphabet" agencies. Still, there's more to NIH than most people probably realize. Internationally renowned for its work, NIH is one of the largest biomedical research centers in the world and the principal medical research arm of the U.S. Department of Health and Human Services. Some 75 buildings, including the 500-bed hospital and lab complex known as the Warren Grant Magnuson Clinical Center and the new, 242-bed Mark O. Hatfield Clinical Research Center, are scattered about the 300-acre Bethesda campus just 12 miles from downtown Washington. NIH even has its own Metro stop. However, as mentioned in this chapter's introduction, not just anyone can obtain care at this hospital. You have to be referred by a physician, and even then you must qualify for a clinical trial that the center is funding.

Seeing the facility today, you'll be surprised to learn that NIH started out as a one-room hygiene lab in 1887. It now consists of 27 separate research institutes, centers, and divisions. Special components include the National Library of Medicine (the world's largest reference center devoted to a single subject), more than 1,400 labs with some of the best science equipment ever developed, and the Fogarty International Center, which houses foreign scholars-in-residence.

NIH focuses much of its efforts on combating the major life-threatening and crippling diseases prevalent in the United States today. These diseases include heart disease, cancer, arthritis, Alzheimer's, diabetes, AIDS, neurological diseases, vision and mental disorders, infectious diseases, and dental diseases. Other work involves studying the human development and aging processes and exploring the relationship between the environment and human health.

National Naval Medical Center
8901 Rockville Pike
Bethesda, MD
(301) 295–4611
www.bethesda.med.navy.mil

Another of Bethesda's health care icons, the National Naval Medical Center provides care and treatment to active-duty military personnel and is not open to the general public. It does warrant a mention because this is where the president usually goes for annual physicals, routine examinations, and surgery. Not surprisingly, this hospital offers all medical and surgical services and the latest in equipment and technology.

The hospital was founded in 1802 but has been at the present location only since 1942. The site was personally selected by President Franklin Roosevelt, who actually sketched the design and grounds plans that the architect used as a guide. The National Naval Medical Center is among the 10 largest medical facilities in the nation and ranks as perhaps the best military hospital. Nearly 8,000 patients are admitted annually, while its clinic sees a whopping 500,000.

Shady Grove Adventist Hospital
9901 Medical Center Drive
Rockville, MD
(301) 279–6000
www.adventisthealthcare.com/SGAH

This full-service hospital serves a huge swath of Montgomery County, seeing 148,000 patients in its ER annually. Open since 1979, the 943-bed hospital delivers the second-highest number of babies in the state each year. A full range of other inpatient and outpatient medical and surgical services are also offered, including a level III neonatal intensive care unit and a coronary-care unit. The Shady Grove Adventist Hospital for Children operates as the county's only emergency room especially for kids, and the Pediatric Same-Day Surgery center is specially designed to accommodate young patients for basic procedures.

Suburban Hospital
8600 Old Georgetown Road
Bethesda, MD
(301) 896–3100
www.suburbanhospital.org

Another of Montgomery County's comprehensive community hospitals, 228-bed, non-profit Suburban Hospital opened in 1943 but has seen some dramatic changes. An extensive renovation completed during the 1980s included the addition of a luxury wing, the emergency and shock/trauma center, a pharmacy, a cafeteria and restaurant, and an addiction treatment center. Two additions completed in the '90s house radiology facilities, a medical library, the main entrance and admitting area, a 260-seat auditorium for medical and community education, and an elevated helipad.

The more than 900 physicians on staff at Suburban are trained in programs and services as diverse as orthopedics, cardiology, oncology (Suburban was the county's first comprehensive community cancer center and has a comprehensive breast cancer center as well), mental health, dermatology, gastroenterology, infectious diseases, and microvascular and thoracic surgery.

Washington Adventist Hospital
7600 Carroll Avenue
Takoma Park, MD
(301) 891–7600
www.adventisthealthcare.com/WAH
Located in what is nearly a trijurisdictional city—Takoma Park is actually in Montgomery County but is very near the Prince George's and District borders—this 292-bed, acute-care, church-affiliated facility has been in operation since 1907. Offering the most complete cardiology services in the county, Washington Adventist has been nationally recognized for innovative treatments in heart catheterization. The hospital's open-heart surgery center performs more than 700 such procedures annually.

Other services include inpatient and outpatient surgery, maternity, radiation oncology, emergency medicine, rehabilitation medicine, and pulmonary medicine. Mental health services are available on an inpatient or outpatient basis and include substance abuse programs.

i Looking for a little extra cash and don't mind a little physical risk taking? Opportunities abound in the metro area to take part in research trials for everything from asthma to infertility treatments at some of the nation's leading research facilities, including NIH.

Prince George's County

Doctors Community Hospital
8118 Good Luck Road
Lanham, MD
(301) 552–8118
www.dchweb.org
Doctors Community Hospital serves a large portion of central Prince George's County, offering all major medical and surgical services except psychiatry and obstetrics. Open since 1975, the 186-bed adult, acute-care hospital underwent a major change in 1990, going from a national, chain-owned facility to a nonprofit community hospital.

This hospital is renowned for its comprehensive emergency department, which sees some 30,000 patients a year and is the only unit in the county certified to handle victims of hazardous-materials incidents. The hospital also specializes in general and same-day surgery, ophthalmology, cardiology, and physical and occupational therapy and offers complete radiological and laboratory diagnostic services. The Home Care Program is available to many patients upon discharge, helping them adapt to being back home and recuperating successfully.

Laurel Regional Hospital
7300 Van Dusen Road
Laurel, MD
(301) 725–4300
www.dimensionshealth.org/website/c/lrh
Laurel Regional Hospital (formerly Greater Laurel Beltsville Hospital) is a private, nonprofit, 146-bed facility located in the heart of the Baltimore-Washington corridor, close to the Washington, D.C. line, the Capital Beltway, and the Baltimore-Washington Parkway. Open

since 1978, the hospital offers the full spectrum of medical, surgical, and testing services, a 24-hour emergency room that sees some 34,000 patients annually, intensive care and coronary-care units, substance-abuse treatment programs, a maternal and child-health unit, a mental-health unit, and a comprehensive rehabilitation program. Because it is so conveniently located, the hospital is able to serve residents of Prince George's, Montgomery, Anne Arundel, and Howard Counties.

Prince George's Hospital Center
3001 Hospital Drive
Cheverly, MD
(301) 618–2000
www.dimensionshealth.org/website/c/pghc
Prince George's Hospital Center, with 290 beds, is the country's largest medical facility—and one of its most comprehensive. Private and nonprofit, PGHC is recognized nationwide for its outstanding 24-hour emergency care and is the designated regional trauma-care center for all of southern Maryland. Its level I shock-trauma unit boasts a 97 percent save rate for patients, one of the highest in the nation. PGHC also specializes in cardiac care and is the only hospital in the county with an open-heart surgery program.

A wide range of obstetric services enables the hospital to handle high-risk pregnancies and difficult deliveries and to care for premature babies. A specialized unit called the Birth-place allows labor, delivery, and recovery to take place in one area. For outpatient services the hospital offers a newly redesigned short-stay center. Other services at PGHC include family practice, gastroenterology, neurology, oro-facial plastic surgery, podiatry, psychiatry, sports medicine, and urology. A recently built ambulatory surgical wing features 10 operating rooms.

PSYCHIATRIC HOSPITALS

Washington's psychiatric facilities have none of the celebrity cachet of places like the Betty Ford Clinic. They are serious facilities for the seriously ill, and those famous figures who have problems usually opt to go to places outside Metro Washington for treatment.

In the metro area, facilities range from those treating substance addiction to those housing the criminally insane. No matter what the case, rarely does one become a patient in such an institution without a referral by a mental-health care provider—or a judge. The list below is meant to serve as an overview of metro area psychiatric facilities, not a guide from which to choose, as that is a decision best left to the patient (if possible), the mental-health care provider, and the family. As in the case of other long-term care facilities, a personal visit before checking in is a must except in emergency situations. You'll note that our list is in alphabetical order, not subdivided by regions. The reason is simple: If you need a psychiatric facility, you will likely base your decision on what kind of care the hospital offers rather than where it is.

Graydon Manor
801 Children's Center Road SW
Leesburg, VA
(703) 777–3485
www.graydonmanor.org/
Parents of children with psychiatric and other mental difficulties worked together to found Graydon Manor in 1957. A private, 61-bed, nonprofit residential treatment center, Graydon Manor treats children and adolescents (boys ages 7 to 17, girls 13 to 17) diagnosed with severe emotional or psychiatric disorders. Although it does not treat those whose primary diagnoses are substance abuse, it does serve adolescents with secondary diagnoses of chemical dependency. Lengths of stay on the 100-plus-acre campus range from six to eight months, depending on need.

Also known as the National Children's Rehabilitation Center, Graydon offers outpatient services for adults and families in the community. It operates a therapeutic day school in Sterling for students in grades 1 through 12 who are learning disabled or emotionally disturbed. Its on-site school at Graydon Manor is accredited by the Virginia and Maryland departments of education.

Piedmont Behavioral Health Center
42009 Victory Lane
Leesburg, VA
(703) 777–0800

Piedmont Behavioral Health Center, formerly known as Springwood Psychiatric Institute, offers comprehensive mental health treatment for adults, adolescents, and children on either an inpatient or outpatient basis. The hospital specializes in the treatment of depression, substance abuse, codependency, suicidal tendencies, school failure, domestic problems, and stress and anxiety. Special services include 24-hour admissions, free evaluations, and extensive aftercare programs for patients and their families.

The Psychiatric Institute of Washington, D.C.
4228 Wisconsin Avenue NW
Washington, DC
(202) 885–5600
www.psychinstitute.com

The first private psychiatric hospital in Washington, D.C., the 201-bed Psychiatric Institute of Washington was founded in 1967 and moved to its present location in 1973. The facility treats children, adolescents, and adults suffering from emotional and addictive illnesses and even offers an intensive care unit for especially serious cases. The hospital is acknowledged by the nation's psychiatric community as an education and professional development center for mental-health specialists.

Saint Elizabeth's Hospital
2700 Martin Luther King Jr. Avenue SE
Washington, DC
(202) 562–4000
dmh.dc.gov

For more than 150 years "Saint E's" has been perhaps the best known of the District's mental-health facilities. Its reputation may have something to do with criminally insane patients, such as poet Ezra Pound and would-be presidential assassin John Hinckley Jr., who at this writing remains in residence. Still in the same place since its founding in 1855, the massive (1,500-bed) hospital actually sits on the grounds of D.C. General Hospital, but you wouldn't know it just by comparing addresses.

Formerly run by the federal government, Saint Elizabeth's is operated by the city under the purview of the Department of Human Services. In 2002 it was named one of America's 11 most endangered historic places by the National Trust for Historic Preservation because many of the structures are vacant and crumbling.

Psychiatric services for children, adolescents, and adults are offered in the form of acute care, long-term care, nursing care, and residential care. The hospital also deals in forensic medicine. Services are being expanded for children and youth, in-home clients, and multicultural and immigrant populations.

Saint Luke Institute
8901 New Hampshire Avenue
Silver Spring, MD
(301) 445–7970
www.sli.org

This 35-bed, nonprofit psychiatric facility was founded by a minister/doctor and serves priests and other religious men and women active in church ministry. Initially treating only chemical dependency, St. Luke has broadened its focus to include mood disorders, compulsive eating or compulsive sexual behaviors, and reactive or chronic depression. The major areas of service are in evaluation, inpatient treatment, aftercare, residential living, outpatient therapy, and outreach.

NURSING HOMES

Nursing homes here vary widely in terms of atmosphere and services offered. A look in the Metro Washington phone book will lead you to two pages of listings, and, indeed, you'll see many in your travels throughout the area—they are springing up everywhere to keep up with the graying of America. Some homes are actually luxury high-rises managed by hotel companies like Hyatt and Marriott, providing many of the same amenities. Others have the flavor of retirement communities in the degree of independence and the number of activities that patients enjoy. Some even look like summer resorts, complete with lush landscaping, wraparound verandas, and cheerful color schemes.

A nursing home is ultimately a place for long-term care, and choosing one is a highly individual decision. Prospective patients—or their families—must base their decisions on the degree of attention they need, amenities and specialized medical care offered, location, and atmosphere. Choosing a nursing home requires careful investigation, personal visits, and, as in the case of hospices, physician referral. A referral service based in Metro Washington provides information and referrals expressly for nursing homes—they are a starting point, but ultimately the decision is too important to leave to a third party. For more information, contact the American Healthcare Association, 1201 L Street NW, Washington, D.C. 20005, (202) 842–4444, www.ahca.org.

ALTERNATIVE HEALTH CARE

Traditionally, Washington, D.C. is a conventional, conservative town of blue pinstriped suits, pumps, and pearls. People try to fit in rather than stand out, and their approach to medical care reflects this. With a few exceptions in funky neighborhoods like Takoma Park, you generally won't find the locals comparing the latest medical trends, or even such commonplace alternative practitioners as herbalists, nutritionists, or chiropractors.

Washington's upwardly mobile prefer to expend energy on their careers. Meals are an excuse for networking, and workaholics live on hors d'oeuvres, fast food, and liquor. Fortunately, the city's ample parks, trails, and omnipresent fitness facilities help Washingtonians strike a balance if they tend to overindulge. Yoga and pilates studios are also becoming increasingly commonplace—and a welcome addition to the fast pace of life in the Nation's Capital.

The subtle influences of alternative medicine shouldn't be terribly surprising. After all, Washington is much too cosmopolitan and diverse to have completely avoided trends in holistic medicine and nutrition.

Delve a little further into people's backgrounds and they may even admit to popping daily multiple vitamins, though independent health food stores in Metro Washington—the few that exist—are mostly dusty little nooks with the hushed, abandoned atmospheres of the library on Tuesday morning. On the other hand, every Washington-area mall has a GNC vitamin store, and gourmet groceries specializing in organic fare are cropping up all over. To top it off, the world-famous National Institutes of Health, a U.S. government agency, has established a specific office to investigate the value of vitamins, nutrition, biofeedback, acupuncture, and more.

So where to go if you want to try something more holistic than a shot or a prescription? For vitamins and herbs, the aforementioned groceries and GNC stores are numerous and well stocked, or you can search the Internet for independent health food stores. Massage therapists, unless you are working with a doctor-referred physical therapist, are most often found in Washington beauty salons and day spas, as they are still largely considered a frivolity—to be indulged in on rare occasions—rather than a necessity. If you're looking in the phone book, search under beauty salons rather than massage (unless you're really looking for a so-called escort service).

There are quite a few acupuncturists in Washington, but your first selection criterion should be that they use disposable needles. Most do. Second, a look in the Yellow Pages will reveal that some acupuncturists are actually board-certified medical doctors as well, and you may feel safer there. Finally, acupuncturists are licensed, so ensure that your practitioner's credentials are in order with the state licensing boards listed at the beginning of this chapter. If you choose carefully and get the proper clearances, you may even find that your treatments are covered by medical insurance. Indeed, acupuncture is a practice that the American Medical Association and many of its mainstream member physicians acknowledge as useful, so don't be embarrassed to ask your doctor, counselor, or physical therapist for a referral.

Many nutritionists and holistic practitioners now work on medical teams as adjunct therapy advisers, so check with your doctor about that, too; and, don't forget that the Washington area is the home base for several organizations that can serve as useful resources for those seeking alternative medical care:

- American College of Preventive Medicine, 1307 New York Avenue NW, (202) 466–2044, www.acpm.org
- International Massage Association, P.O. Box 421, 25 South 4th Street, Warrenton, VA 20188, (540) 351–0800, www.ima group.com
- National Center for Complementary and Alternative Medicine, Clearinghouse, P.O. Box 7923, Gaithersburg, MD 20898, (888) 644–6226, www.nccam.nih.gov

WALK-IN CLINICS

If you have a medical problem that is urgent, though not life-threatening, a walk-in medical clinic may be a good bet. Most walk-in clinics are found in Virginia-area shopping centers and other high-traffic areas. There is one clinic in the Maryland section of Metro Washington, and, as of this writing, there is no such chain in Washington proper. Area hospitals, however—D.C. included—have jumped on the band-

wagon and, to compete with the freestanding facilities, have in many cases opened their own walk-in centers right in their emergency rooms.

This chapter's section on hospitals makes mention of walk-in centers where they existed at press time, but please remember that these minor-care emergency rooms are a growing trend, and more are opening every day. Freestanding walk-in clinics are typically open seven days a week and into the evening, though hours vary from location to location. Call first to ensure that the office you want to visit is open.

No appointments are necessary, but waits can be long, as in hospital emergency rooms. With a small staff of doctors and nurses, the centers can perform some lab tests, blood work, sports physicals, and other services not requiring the traditional hospital's resources or facilities; however, if you suspect a serious illness, it's probably best to go to a hospital.

Northern Virginia

Inova Urgent Medical Care Locations
6201 Centreville Road
Centreville, VA
(703) 830–5600

100 Maple Avenue East
Vienna, VA
(703) 938–5300
www.inova.com
The Inova health care system includes several respected hospitals in Virginia, including Fairfax Hospital, so if it turns out you need more critical care, you'll be sent on quickly, perhaps by ambulance.

Inova Emergency Care of Fairfax
4315 Chain Bridge Road
Fairfax City, VA
(703) 591–9322

Inova Emergency Care Center of Leesburg
224 Cornwall Street
Leesburg, VA
(703) 737–7520

Emergency Numbers

In most areas of the country, people have been trained to call 911 in the event of a dire emergency, and the Washington Metro area is no exception. Still, other types of health emergencies may require more specific help. Here's a list of numbers for specific mental and physical health crises. (You may want to post a copy near your telephone, in case of emergency.)

Ambulance, Fire Department, Police, 911
AIDS Counseling and Testing Hotline, (800) 590–2437
Alcoholics Anonymous Area Headquarters, (202) 966–9115
Battered Women's Shelter Hotline, (202) 529–5991
Domestic Violence Hotline, (202) 347–2777
Gay and Lesbian Help Line, (301) 439–3524
Narcotics Anonymous Hotline, (202) 399–5316
National Organization for Victim Assistance, (202) 232–6682
Poison Center, (800) 222–1222
Rape Crisis Hotline, (202) 333–7273

For general mental-health crises, including suicide counseling, there are hotlines in Washington, D.C., (202) 223–2255; Virginia, (703) 527–4077; and Maryland, (301) 738–2255.

Inova Emergency Care of Reston/Herndon
11901 Baron Cameron Avenue
Reston, VA
(703) 471–0175

Inova HealthPlex Franconia/Springfield
6355 Walker Lane
Alexandria, VA
(703) 797–6800
These are fully equipped hospital emergency rooms without the hospital. What these convenient and very efficient 24-hour facilities offer is a level of care somewhere between the walk-in shopping center facilities and regular hospitals. Part of the Inova Health System, these outlets also perform on-site lab and X-ray work and will arrange to transport you to a hospital if necessary.

Suburban Maryland

Nighttime Pediatrics
12220 Rockville Pike
Rockville, MD
(301) 468–NITE
www.nighttimepediatrics.com
Here's a place to take your child when she develops an ear infection on a Sunday or comes down with a 104-degree fever at bedtime. Don't let the name fool you—adults are welcome, too. Although affiliated with Suburban Hospital, Nighttime Pediatrics is located in a strip mall several miles away. The center is staffed by pediatricians and pediatric nurses, with an on-site laboratory, pharmacy, and radiological services. It's open Monday through Friday from 5:00 P.M. to midnight, Saturday from noon to midnight, and Sunday and holidays from 11:00 A.M. to midnight.

Secure Medical Care Center
803 Russell Avenue
Gaithersburg, MD
(301) 869–0700

10452 Baltimore Avenue
Beltsville, MD
(301) 441–3355
www.securemedicalcare.com
Secure Medical Care Center is a convenient, cost-effective alternative to the hospital, best for treatment of minor illnesses and injuries.

The centers are staffed by a small team of doctors and nurses and are open seven days a week. Hours are 8:00 A.M. to 8:00 P.M. weekdays and 10:00 A.M. to 6:00 P.M. on the weekend and on holidays. They can also perform a limited amount of lab work and diagnostic tests, physical examinations, and other services.

EDUCATION

The Metro Washington area owes much of its well-respected business, political development, and economic development to a single driving force: education.

People here wax proud when they speak of our outstanding educational infrastructure, and with good reason: Few metro areas can hold a candle to our high-quality and diverse public and private schools, not to mention the concentration of internationally renowned colleges, universities, and research institutions.

This chapter highlights the educational opportunities found throughout the area, beginning with the public school systems and a selection of private institutions. The final section briefly describes the area's major colleges and universities, nearly all of which offer programs for working adults.

PUBLIC SCHOOLS

The common theme here, especially in the suburbs, is intense parental interest in quality public education. Whether they're tutoring beginning readers, assisting in computer labs, or working at PTA fundraisers, parent volunteers are helping schools create new and better programs for students. At the same time teachers and administrators are implementing strategies to improve reading skills and test scores. Maryland third, fifth, and eighth graders must participate in the Maryland School Performance Assessment Program (MSPAP), while Virginia third, fifth, and eighth graders and high school students must pass a comprehensive Standards of Learning (SOL) exam. The state and local jurisdictions continue to fine-tune the test-taking and evaluation guidelines, which include compliance with the federally mandated "No Child Left Behind" initiative.

Washington, D.C.

District of Columbia Public Schools
825 North Capitol Street NE
Washington, DC
(202) 724–4222
www.k12.dc.us/dcps/home.html
Like many of America's inner-city public school systems suffering from budget cutbacks, violence, and chronic absenteeism, the District's seems always to suffer through tough times. D.C.'s new mayor, Adrian Fenty, however, has openly made public school improvement and reform a defining goal of his administration. Superintendent Clifford B. Janey has a long way to go; in 2006, D.C. students posted the lowest SAT scores in the metro region, with an average score of 1518 (out of a possible 2400).

D.C. public schools include 101 elementaries, 11 middle schools, 9 junior high schools, and 20 high schools. Among the system's bright spots are its citywide magnet schools, which have always held their ground for students with special skills or artistic talents. The Ellington School of the Arts, named for esteemed native son Duke Ellington, has some of the finest dance, theater, and music departments in the metro area. Senior High Academies let students specialize in such areas as culinary arts, international studies, teaching, and travel and tourism. Eligible high school students can take advanced placement courses.

D.C. schools enroll more than 56,000 students in traditional schools and 20,000 in charter schools. Testaments to the city's international character, students represent more than 130 nations and speak at least 90 languages. Bilingual programs in Spanish and Chinese have earned the District kudos from educators around the country. Smaller groups of international students are taught English by itinerant teams of language teachers. There's even a school that teaches foreign adults English and prepares them for U.S. citizenship.

Like everything else in Washington, D.C., the public schools are constantly under the national microscope, especially in terms of funding and performance. All education programs, after being approved by an elected school board and the city government, must pass the financial scrutiny of Congress and the White House. Needless to say, not all plans win approval. Budgets and, unfortunately, politics often get in the way of much-needed resources. Student/teacher ratios average about 14 to 1.

Problems aside, the D.C. school system has the unlimited enviable educational resources of Washington in its backyard.

Northern Virginia

Alexandria Public Schools
2000 North Beauregard Street
Alexandria, VA
(703) 824–6600
www.acps.k12.va.us
This small (about 10,000 students) school system boasts a large emphasis on computers in education: The $3.5-million, five-year Technology Initiative works toward implementing such goals as having a multimedia computer workstation in each classroom, school-wide Internet access, laptops available for student loan, video production facilities, and faculty training. The program, funded through the school budget and private partnerships, brings five schools online annually.

The district includes 13 elementary schools, 2 middle schools, 1 ninth-grade school, and 1 senior high school. Special programs include all-day kindergarten, a gifted and talented curriculum, instruction for homebound students, and comprehensive special education services for handicapped students ages 2 to 21. The diverse student population includes children from 86 countries speaking 65 different languages. More than 2,000 students receive English as a Second Language

i Registering your child for public school? Make sure you have the youngster's birth certificate, proof of residency, Social Security number, transfer records from previous schools, a record of a recent medical exam, and current immunization records.

education, and pupils in grades one through eight may participate in a Spanish immersion program. Volunteer tutoring services are available during and after school.

The city's lone high school, T. C. Williams, offers advanced placement and honors courses, a vocational education program with postsecondary degree credit, an award-winning JROTC program, and 17 varsity sports programs for boys and girls. In 2006, T. C. students averaged 1,530 (out of a possible 2,400) on the SAT. Two students in 2006 were National Merit Scholarship semifinalists. About 86 percent of Alexandria's graduates continue to some form of higher education.

Average class sizes are 19 in elementary grades, 16 in middle school, and 18 in secondary grades. Alexandria's per-pupil expenditure of $18,232 is the highest in the metro area. Teachers, 73 percent of whom have advanced degrees, receive starting salaries of $42,040 and average salaries of $58,759.

The system's Adult and Community Education Office provides adult basic education classes along with job skills and training, GED and high school diploma programs, and special interest classes. A nine-member school board meets the first and third Thursdays of the month.

Arlington County Public Schools
1426 North Quincy Street
Arlington, VA
(703) 228–6000
www.arlington.k12.va.us
Arlingtonians care deeply about education: 60 percent of residents age 25 and older are college graduates, and 31 percent have graduate or professional degrees.

Diversity defines Arlington County Public

Schools, where many of the 19,000 students hail from around the world and speak more than 90 languages, from Spanish and Vietnamese to Arabic and Farsi. Although the county is Virginia's smallest geographically, it boasts the 15th largest of the state's 144 school divisions. With 30 schools and several special programs, the district caters to all segments of its varied student population. Parents may choose to send their children to a neighborhood school or to an "alternative" school offering a unique learning environment. Some examples include the Claremont Early Childhood Center for grades kindergarten through second grade; Drew Model School, the county's only public Montessori program for ages six to nine; Science Focus School, at which kindergartners through fifth graders incorporate science into all areas of learning; Kenmore Middle School, where arts and communications technology take center stage; and H-B Woodlawn Secondary Program, in which sixth through twelfth graders control much of their educational experience.

Other special programs include instruction for gifted students, English for speakers of other languages/high-intensity language training, extended day care, outreach for teenage parents, a Spanish partial-immersion program at all grade levels, high school advanced placement and International Baccalaureate courses, summer school, special education, and athletics and other extracurricular activities. Technology proves a high priority: All schools have Internet access, and the district boasts four "electronic classrooms." Kindergartners attend school all day.

The county's comprehensive Adult Education Program offers high school equivalency studies, senior citizens' activities, and an array of multicultural programs.

Arlington spends nearly $17,958 per pupil, and the average class size is 21 students. The investment is paying off: The graduation rate exceeds 90 percent, and most graduates go on to college. The average 2006 SAT score was 1,630, higher than both the state (1,525) and national (1,518) averages. In 2006, 12

Arlington students were named National Merit Scholarship semifinalists. The five-member school board meets two Thursdays a month, and meetings are shown live on Cable TV Arlington Channel 30.

Fairfax County Public Schools
8115 Gatehouse Road
Falls Church, VA
(571) 423–1000
www.fcps.k12.va.us

Fairfax County Public Schools, with more than 164,000 students and more than 20,000 teachers, is the 13th-largest school district in the United States and the largest in Virginia. Growing every year, the district now boasts 137 elementary schools, 22 middle schools, 4 secondary (grades 7–12) schools, 21 high schools, 12 special-services centers, and 38 alternative schools.

These tremendous numbers do not equate to mediocrity or impersonalization in the classroom. Fairfax County high schools are frequently named in *Newsweek*'s list of the Best High Schools in America. Four ranked in the top 100 in 2006. National Merit Scholarship Exam semifinalists from Fairfax County Public Schools numbered 200 in 2006. Students averaged 1,643 on the 2006 SAT—one of the highest average scores in the region.

The system, with a per-pupil cost of $12,917, features countywide programs for students who are gifted and talented, for students with learning disabilities, and for international students who speak English as a second language. Several elementary and middle schools provide partial-immersion programs in French, German, Japanese, and Spanish. Two elementary magnet schools feature arts and sciences curricula, and more than 50 elementaries are designated Model Technology Schools.

At the high school level, 93 percent of graduates go on to some form of higher education. The county's prized magnet school in Alexandria, Thomas Jefferson High School for Science and Technology, consistently boasts the country's largest concentration of National

Merit Scholars (167 semifinalists in 2006). Admission is competitive and open to ninth and tenth graders in the county and other participating Northern Virginia school districts. Eight schools offer the academically demanding International Baccalaureate Program, which includes college-level courses. Extracurricular high school activities include award-winning music programs and interscholastic team sports for boys and girls.

Vocational programs feature studies in business education, home economics, industrial arts, and horticulture. On-site technical studies programs take place at a shopping mall, airport, hotel, construction site, and car dealership. More than 100 elementary schools offer extended day care through the Fairfax County Office for Children. Fees are based on a sliding scale. A Head Start early childhood program is available for eligible three- to five-year-olds. The school system also sponsors adult education, alternative high school programs, a school-to-work transition academy, and a variety of enrichment classes for children and adults.

Administratively, the district is divided into eight clusters, each of which is represented by a director and an office staff. A 12-member elected school board holds meetings the second and fourth Thursdays at 7:30 P.M., broadcast live on Cable Channel 21. Parental involvement in the schools is high, with an average of more than 50,000 logging more than 1 million hours of service during a school year. Parents, teachers, administrators, and students regularly voice their opinions at school board meetings and have great influence over budgets, curriculum, and the establishment of new facilities and programs. Superintendent Jack Dale took office in 2005.

The county also contains two separate municipal school districts: one serving the city of Fairfax and one serving Falls Church. Fairfax city's system, City Hall, 10455 Armstrong Street, Fairfax, Virginia, (703) 385–7855, www.fairfaxva.gov/school/school.asp, includes two elementaries, one middle school, and one high school. The system operates under a

partnership with the county and has its own superintendent and school board. Falls Church City Public Schools, 803 West Broad Street, Falls Church, Virginia, (703) 248–5600, www.fccps.k12.va.us, enrolls more than 1,800 students in its system, widely considered one of the best in the region. The district includes only four schools: Mt. Daniel for kindergarten through first grade, Thomas Jefferson for second through fourth grades, Mary Ellen Henderson Middle School for sixth through eighth grades, and George Mason High School for eighth through twelfth grades. Highlights include the International Baccalaureate Program, special education instruction, gifted and talented services, ESL courses, extended day care, and through the Office of Community Education and the Recreation and Parks Department, adult education and enrichment classes.

Loudoun County Public Schools
21000 Education Court
Ashburn, VA
(571) 252–1000
www.loudoun.k12.va.us

The rapidly growing, 50,740-student Loudoun County public school system is among the best in exurban Metro Washington. The average elementary class size is 22 students, and the per-pupil expenditure is approximately $12,467. The system has 68 schools, including five new buildings that opened for the 2005–06 school year. A technology center serves vocational and adult education students, and an alternative education program helps middle school and high school students who have trouble fitting into traditional programs.

Courses are available for gifted and special education students, and several advanced placement courses are available at the high school level. Each school offers computer education, emphasizing state-of-the-art technology, and has Internet access. The graduation rate is among the best in the state and the nation, and 87 percent of county graduates continue their formal education. SAT scores averaged 1,582 in 2006. Monthly meetings of the nine-member school board, held the second and fourth Tuesdays of most months, are shown live on Cablevision of Loudoun's Channel 59.

Prince William County Public Schools
14800 Joplin Road
Manassas, VA
(703) 791–7200
www.pwcs.edu

The tremendous—and often overwhelming—growth that transformed Prince William over the past 15 or so years never shortchanged the county's public school system, now the second largest in the state. If anything, it improved it. Eighty percent of the county's high school graduates go on to college, and the average SAT score keeps rising. Educational staff, 71 percent of whom hold advanced degrees, have earned numerous awards in recent years, including, in 2001, the Milken Educator Award and Virginia Outstanding Career and Technical Educator of the Year. *Time* magazine recognized Stonewall Jackson High School as High School of the Year. The district maintains several health- and education-related partnerships and continues to upgrade its school-wide computer technology.

In all, more than 70,000 students attend 85 public schools, where the per-pupil cost is $10,496. Prince William's curriculum earmarks specific learning objectives by grade level for each subject. The schools also offer extensive programs for gifted students in all grades and rigorous advanced placement and International Baccalaureate courses for high school students. Other special programs target pupils with disabilities, students who want to pursue vocational studies, those who speak English as a second language, and adults interested in continuing education. Several elementary schools offer before- and after-school care.

> **i** Watch teams from local high schools compete for scholarships on *It's Academic,* a Giant Food–sponsored program that airs on NBC-TV, channel 4, on Saturday mornings.

Public school policy is set by the county school board of eight members elected to four-year terms. Widely attended public meetings of the school board take place the first, second, and fourth Wednesdays of each month.

Both independent cities within the county—Manassas City Public Schools, 9000 Tudor Lane, Manassas, Virginia, (703) 257–8800, www.manassas.k12.va.us, and Manassas Park City Schools, One Park Center Court, Suite A, Manassas, Virginia, (703) 335–8850, www.mpark.net—have their own school systems. Academically, they tend to mirror the county.

Suburban Maryland

Montgomery County Public Schools
850 Hungerford Drive
Rockville, MD
(301) 309–6277
www.mcps.k12.md.us

One of the best public school systems in Metro Washington, Montgomery County boasts a 2006 average SAT score of 1,634, one of the highest in the state. About 70 percent of high school students take honors courses, and 91 percent of county graduates go on to higher education. In 2006, 58 students were named National Merit Scholarship finalists. Schools, staff, and students frequently receive honors at national, state, and local levels.

Like Fairfax, Montgomery has a gigantic system. More than 145,000 students attend 199 public schools, including 25 senior high schools, 38 middle schools, and 129 elementary schools, along with centers specializing in magnet programs, gifted and talented instruction, technology and research, visual arts, and foreign language immersion. The diverse student body includes international pupils, who hail from more than 163 countries.

The county also offers some all-day kindergarten, extended elementary programs, ESOL, instruction for disabled students, adult education, and on-the-job training in business and industry. The schools' Global Access initiative is integrating up-to-the-minute technology into classrooms. The per-pupil cost is approximately $12,422.

A seven-member elected school board, which sets the district's policies, recently hired Jerry D. Weast as superintendent. Volunteers also play a big part in the system, with some 55,000 logging 4 million hours of service annually.

Prince George's County Public Schools
Sasscer Administration Building
14201 School Lane
Upper Marlboro, MD
(301) 952–6000
www.pgcps.pg.k12.md.us
Approximately 134,200 students attend Prince George's 202 schools, making the school system the 18th largest in the country. Per-pupil expenditure for fiscal year 2005 was $8,612, and the average teacher salary was $52,855.

SAT scores are among the region's lowest, averaging 1,295 in 2006. Graduation requirements for high school students emphasize math and social studies over electives. The University High School magnet program offers rigorous college-prep courses like the International Baccalaureate Program. The Visual and Performing Arts High School houses a TV and recording studio, 1,000-seat auditorium, and dance studio. Through a special partnership, some dancers appear at the Kennedy Center for the Performing Arts. The county has innovative, comprehensive reading initiatives, ESL instruction, classes for gifted students, a K–12 French Immersion Program, schools for the learning and physically disabled, evening schools for adults, and even an educational project geared toward the needs of Native American children.

The nine-member elected school board meets two Thursdays a month. The school system recently hired a new superintendent, Dr. John Deasy.

PRIVATE SCHOOLS

Private schools in the region range from traditional liberal arts institutions to alternative programs for gifted or learning-disabled students. Of course, the benefits of such highly personalized and specialized study come with a price tag. Generally speaking, tuition fees here can range from $5,400 to $26,000 at day schools, and from $20,450 to $38,000 or more at boarding schools. A good clearinghouse for additional information on private schools in the area, the Association of Independent Schools of Greater Washington can be reached at P.O. Box 9956, Washington, D.C. 20016, (202) 625–9223, www.aisgw.org.

Washington, D.C.
Archbishop Carroll High School
4300 Harewood Road NE
Washington, DC
(202) 529–0900
www.archbishopcarroll.com
On a small campus near Catholic University, Archbishop Carroll is one of the city's leading Catholic high schools. The coed school, founded in 1951, has an enrollment of more than 600 students in grades 9 through 12 and is known for its rigorous academic standards, dedicated faculty, and strong athletic and activities programs. Its state-of-the-art computer lab includes Internet access. All students must participate in service projects, such as volunteering at a local soup kitchen. Ninety-eight percent of the school's graduates go on to Catholic, Georgetown, the University of Virginia, the University of Maryland, and other nationally competitive colleges.

Capitol Hill Day School
210 South Carolina Avenue SE
Washington, DC
(202) 547–2244
www.chds.org
Founded in 1968, this independent, coed school for 230 children in prekindergarten through eighth grade offers an integrated curriculum with a hands-on emphasis. Students

ℹ️ All students in Montgomery County and Fairfax County public schools are screened in second grade to identify the highly gifted and talented. About 40 percent of Montgomery students and 36 percent of Fairfax County students received that distinction in 2006.

study such specialty subjects as Spanish, French, art, and music. The school encourages both self-reliance and care for others.

Georgetown Visitation Preparatory School
1524 35th Street NW
Washington, DC
(202) 337–3350
www.visi.org

Visitation has been grooming young women for higher education since 1799. About 450 students in grades 9 through 12 attend the prestigious day school, which is affiliated with the Roman Catholic Church and located on a 27-acre campus next door to Georgetown University. The school boasts honors and advanced placement courses in English, foreign language, history, mathematics, and science. A bridge program with the neighboring university enables some seniors to take college-level courses. The school's athletic program features a variety of team sports, and students can choose from more than 30 cocurricular activities, featuring such subjects as computers, Great Books, music, and Christian service. Students must complete 80 hours of community service before graduating. Visitation grads go on to a wide variety of colleges, including some of the top schools on the East Coast.

Gonzaga College High School
19 I Street NW
Washington, DC
(202) 336–7100
www.gonzaga.org

Founded in 1821, this Jesuit-sponsored boys' academy is one of the city's oldest schools. About 930 students in ninth through twelfth grade attend the day school, which offers a college preparatory curriculum, including advanced placement courses. Ninety-nine percent of the school's seniors go on to college. Gonzaga also is known for its sports program. The Gonzaga Eagles soccer team claimed conference titles in 2000, 2001, 2002, and 2006. The campus, situated in the heart of the city, proves easily accessible by bus and Metrorail.

The Lab School of Washington
4759 Reservoir Road NW
Washington, DC
(202) 965–6600
www.labschool.org

The Lab School is designed for intelligent students with learning disabilities, who benefit from the school's average class size of six students. Situated in a quiet residential area of upper Georgetown, the 40-year-old, coed day school boasts more than 100 teachers for its 310 students in grades kindergarten through 12. The school twice received the U.S. Department of Education's National Blue Ribbon School of Excellence designation. The ungraded elementary curriculum equally emphasizes academic skills and a variety of arts. Students study history by participating in Academic Clubs with themes such as Knights and Ladies and Industrialists. They also have the opportunity to dig for and study ancient artifacts buried on the school grounds. Grades 7 through 12 follow a more traditional college preparatory curriculum, supplemented by arts and humanities classes in junior high. High school students apprentice off campus in such places as museums and radio stations and perform community outreach like giving birthday parties at a homeless shelter. More than 90 percent of the school's graduating seniors go on to college.

Competitive team sports include basketball, soccer, and softball. An $8.7-million theater/art complex opened in 1999. The Lab School also offers career and college counseling, tutoring, clinical services, and night classes for adults with learning disabilities.

Nannie Helen Burroughs School Inc.
601 50th Street NE
Washington, DC
(202) 398–5266
www.nhburroughs.org

This private, coed Christian day school, affiliated with the Progressive National Baptist Convention, enrolls approximately 200 students in grades prekindergarten through sixth. Burroughs founded the school in 1909. Her influence continues with the school's guiding "Four M's" philosophy: to serve as a Model to African American Christians with a Mission to reach out to all members of the community, to be a Magnet attracting students from around the world, and to spark a Movement of like-minded educational facilities in other parts of the world. Among the curriculum's prominent features are cultural enrichment, hands-on math and science, formal Bible instruction, values education, Spanish, and computer literacy. The students take many field trips. Pupils can participate in both before- and after-school care.

Sheridan School
4400 36th Street NW
Washington, DC
(202) 362–7900
www.sheridanschool.org

Founded in 1927, this small, coed elementary school (kindergarten through eighth grade) follows traditional liberal arts instruction in a familylike, values-oriented atmosphere. The 215 students, divided into one class per grade in kindergarten through fourth, learn through a "central subject" approach, in which a single topic such as anthropology is used to integrate the curriculum. Two teachers instruct each class. Program highlights include the annual science fair, visits to the school's 130-acre Mountain Campus next to Shenandoah National Park, a French trip for seventh and eighth graders, and an extended-day program loaded with extracurricular activities. The Sheridan campus is in North Cleveland Park, a residential neighborhood not far from the Tenleytown Metro station.

Sidwell Friends School
3825 Wisconsin Avenue NW
Washington, DC
(202) 537–8100
www.sidwell.edu

Sidwell Friends, affiliated with the Society of Friends, was founded in 1883 and has since become one of the preeminent college-prep schools in D.C. The coed day school enrolls 1,100 students on its two campuses, a Bethesda location for prekindergarten through fourth graders and a fourteen-acre District site for grades 5 through 12. The school follows a demanding liberal arts curriculum, including required studies in fine arts, foreign languages, math, and science. Extracurricular activities, such as interscholastic sports, also play an important role in student life. Personalized community service programs are required of all graduates. First Daughter Chelsea Clinton graduated from Sidwell Friends in 1997.

St. Anselm's Abbey School
4501 South Dakota Avenue NE
Washington, DC
(202) 269–2350
www.saintanselms.org/school

Part of the sprawling academic complex that radiates from Catholic University, St. Anselm's is a college-prep school for sixth- through twelfth-grade boys of all faiths. About 265 students attend the school, founded in 1942 and operated by the Benedictine monks of St. Anselm's Abbey. The small average student/teacher ratio of 8 to 1 pays off. In 2004 about two-thirds of St. Anselm's seniors were National Merit Scholar finalists and semifinalists, and the average combined SAT score (reading and math only) topped 1,400. Since the school's founding, every graduate has earned acceptance into a four-year college or university. The curriculum includes challenging programs in music, drama, visual arts, publications, and athletics. The Brookland/ CUA Metro is nearby.

St. John's College High School
2607 Military Road NW
Washington, DC
(202) 363–2316
www.stjohns-chs.org

Run by the De La Salle Christian Brothers, the religious order which founded the school in 1851, St. John's enrolls approximately 1,100 students. The Catholic, coed college-prep high school is known for balancing academics with comprehensive extracurricular activities, such as an Army JROTC program and competitive league team sports. St. John's takes pride in its computer center, and the school boasts a new gym and a renovated arts center. The 27-acre campus borders scenic Rock Creek Park.

St. Patrick's Episcopal Day School
4700 Whitehaven Parkway NW
Washington, DC
(202) 342–2805
www.stpatsdc.org

This Episcopal day school, founded in 1956, touts traditional elementary school programs in the arts, music, and science, along with reinforcement of spiritual values. With 487 students in nursery school through eighth grade, the school is the city's largest independent elementary. The average class size is 15, and the school boasts a 1-to-7 teacher/student ratio. Special features include three science labs, three music rooms, three computer labs, three libraries, a video technology center, art center, and several outdoor playing areas. The school is near Georgetown, between Foxhall Road and MacArthur Boulevard.

Washington International School
Grades 6–12
3100 Macomb Street NW
Washington, DC
(202) 243–1800

Grades pre-kindergarten–5
1690 36th Street NW
Washington, DC
(202) 243–1700
www.wis.edu

It's only fitting that an international city claims a bold international college-prep school. The coed academy enrolls more than 800 students, from prekindergarten through twelfth grade, and promotes diversity. The students and their families represent more than 90 countries. A globalized curriculum, including bilingual studies, is the bread and butter of this independent day school. Nearly all eleventh- and twelfth-grade students follow the challenging International Baccalaureate curriculum, and most graduates continue their education. The teacher/student ratio is 1:8.2.

Northern Virginia

Burgundy Farm Country Day School
3700 Burgundy Road
Alexandria, VA
(703) 960–3431
www.burgundyfarm.org

Burgundy Farm, founded in 1946 and situated on a 25-acre rural campus, offers an interdisciplinary approach to its 250 coed students in prekindergarten through eighth grade. Two instructors teach all classes, with strong emphasis on the liberal arts. Parents are actively involved as volunteers. Extended-day programs feature a variety of enrichment activities. The school sponsors a summer day camp and a residential camp at its Burgundy Center for Wildlife Studies in the Appalachians in West Virginia.

The Congressional Schools of Virginia
3229 Sleepy Hollow Road
Falls Church, VA
(703) 533–9711
www.congressionalschools.org

These coeducational schools—which enroll 60 infants and toddlers, 120 preschoolers and kindergartners, and around 300 students from first through eighth grades—promote traditional education and values. The curriculum emphasizes language arts and accelerated math, and also includes hands-on learning in recently upgraded computer and science labs. The student/teacher ratio averages about 10 to 1. Graduates usually continue their education at the area's most prestigious college prep schools. Physical education, art, and music round out the curriculum, with many activities both during and after school taking place in a fairly new gym and auditorium. Founded in 1939, the schools are nestled on a 40-acre campus with nature trails, playgrounds, swimming pools, and an outdoor education ropes course. During the summer, the campus hosts day camps for children ages 3 to 14.

Episcopal High School in Virginia
1200 North Quaker Lane
Alexandria, VA
(703) 933–3000
www.episcopalhighschool.org/

One of Virginia's most celebrated prep schools, Episcopal is small, personal, and highly demanding of its 435 students. Founded in 1839 and mere minutes from the Nation's Capital, this coed boarding school for ninth through twelfth graders follows a tradition-rich Honor System that has created an environment of openness among students and teachers. Students follow a challenging liberal arts–based curriculum rich with advanced placement courses. Technology plays a big role, through such features as two computer labs, dormitories wired for Internet access, and a requirement that all ninth and tenth graders have their own laptops. The school takes advantage of the myriad resources of the neighboring District through field trips and internships at political and cultural institutions. Many students also spend time studying abroad. The school boasts numerous athletic facilities, including a 2,800-seat stadium, seven playing fields, and a six-lane, 400-meter outdoor track. Spirituality plays an important role in campus life, with students regularly attending chapel and volunteering for community service. The 130-acre, wooded campus resembles a small college, complete with historic buildings.

i Call the National Library of Education at (800) 424–1616 for information about such topics as reading incentive programs and national education initiatives.

Fairfax Christian School
1624 Hunter Mill Road
Vienna, VA
(703) 759–5100
www.fairfaxchristianschool.com

This coed school for kindergartners through twelfth graders, founded in 1961, stresses a traditional liberal arts curriculum in a nondenominational Christian setting. Enrollment numbers around 250 students. Most four-year-olds in the school's kindergarten learn how to read using a phonetic approach. The school offers extended care and provides transportation for most Northern Virginia students. The 28-acre, rural campus is conveniently situated between Vienna and Reston, close to the Dulles Toll Road.

Flint Hill School
East Campus, 10409 Academic Drive
West Campus, 3320 Jermantown Road
Oakton, VA
(703) 584–2300
www.flinthill.org

Flint Hill is a nondenominational, coed college prep school of about 1,061 students. The school boasts a new campus, opened in 2001, for the upper grades. It is known for its lofty academic and competitive athletic programs. The student/faculty ratio is 14 to 1. Founded in 1956, the school also stresses community service: Graduation requirements include 60 hours of service to be completed by the end of the first senior semester. Pupils can take a variety of honors and advanced placement courses, and all seniors design and complete three-week independent study projects. (Senior projects in recent years have included such eclectic themes as living at a Buddhist monastery, working at a hospital in Uruguay, and designing costumes and sets for the Shakespeare Theatre.) The campuses are a stone's throw from I–66, in the upper-middle-class residential community of Oakton.

Foxcroft School
22407 Foxhound Lane
Middleburg, VA
(540) 687–5555, (800) 858–2364
www.foxcroft.org

Founded in 1914, this small, residential prep school strives to foster self-esteem and strong moral character in ninth- through twelfth-grade girls. Around 190 students attend Foxcroft, nationally recognized for its academic and athletic programs. About half the senior class receives merit scholarships. The student/faculty ratio is 7 to 1 and the average class numbers 10 students. Educational highlights include an interim term, featuring nontraditional course offerings, guest lecturers, and field trips; three-week, career-oriented senior projects; a fellowship program that brings to the school such notable visitors as Maya Angelou and Richard Leakey; an ESL program for international students; and an annual poetry festival. The beautiful 500-acre campus is slightly more than an hour away from Washington, in the heart of Virginia's Hunt Country; consequently, riding is a popular extracurricular activity here.

Gesher Jewish Day School of Northern Virginia
8900 Little River Turnpike
Fairfax, VA
(703) 978–9789

3939 Prince William Drive
Fairfax, VA
(703) 323–7274
www.gesher-jds.org

The only Northern Virginia Jewish day school for kindergarten through middle school, Gesher is conveniently situated in the bustling Jewish Community Center of Northern Virginia and Congregation Ahavat Israel just down the street. A new, 28-acre, $12.5-million campus a few miles away is currently under construction. Founded in 1982 by several community families, the school combines Jewish studies and general studies for its 200 students. The student/faculty ratio is 9 to 1. Curriculum highlights include all-day kindergarten, gifted instruction, accelerated reading, Hebrew study, computers, a science lab, and an art studio. The school also uses the community center's full-size gymnasium, indoor swimming pool, and performing arts auditorium, and students can participate in the center's extended-day program. Bus service is available.

Green Hedges School
415 Windover Avenue NW
Vienna, VA
(703) 938–8323
www.greenhedges.org

Founded in 1942, this coed, nonsectarian school emphasizes a classical education for its 190 students in preschool through eighth grade. The student/teacher ratio is 7 to 1. Children ages three to six attend a Montessori Early School, where French is introduced. Phonics-based reading and a hands-on science lab highlight the curriculum for first through fifth grades. Middle-school students complete Algebra I by eighth grade, participate in an environmental observation project via the Internet, perform community service, and take field trips. All fifth- through eighth-grade students study Latin and Spanish or French. The school is in residential, centrally located Vienna. Green Hedges places a major emphasis on fine arts and promotes a relaxed, happy atmosphere for the socially and culturally diverse student body.

The Langley School
1411 Balls Hill Road
McLean, VA
(703) 356–1920
www.langleyschool.org

The state's largest independent elementary, this coed day school for preschool through eighth-grade students prides itself on its personalized and accelerated instruction. The student/teacher ratio is 7 to 1. A 27,000-square-foot middle school building features a greenhouse, and every classroom has 18 computer terminals. The school offers all-day kindergarten, a structured extended-day program, and summer school and day camps. Founded in 1942, Langley is set on a 10-acre campus in one of Northern Virginia's most exclusive neighborhoods.

Loudoun Country Day School
237 Fairview Street NW
Leesburg, VA
(703) 777–3841
www.lcds.org

The mission of Loudoun Country Day, founded in 1953, is advanced instruction, including accelerated programs in foreign languages and the arts for 267 students in prekindergarten through eighth grade. The student/teacher ratio is 9 to 1. Sports also play a major role at the school, located in quaint, historic Leesburg, the county seat. A new 69-acre campus is currently under development and is scheduled for completion in 2008.

The Madeira School
8328 Georgetown Pike
McLean, VA
(703) 556–8200
www.madeira.org

Founded in 1906, Madeira offers its 300-plus young women, grades 9 through 12, a challenging academic environment that includes advanced placement courses. The average student/faculty ratio is 8 to 1, and the average class size is 10 to 12. The school's unique Wednesday Co-Curriculum is a required full-day program that fosters independence and leadership skills through such activities as public speaking, outdoor education, community service, and congressional and career-oriented internships. The boarding/day school's lovely 376-acre campus, one of the largest in Metro Washington, overlooks the Potomac River and houses such facilities as a 32,000-square-foot sports center, a riding ring and stables, and an indoor, competition-size swimming pool. The school is set in McLean, close to most points in the metro area.

Nysmith School for the Gifted
13625 EDS Drive
Herndon, VA
(703) 713–3332
www.nysmith.com

As the name implies, accelerated academics are the rule here. Nysmith's more than 600 students, preschool to eighth grade, receive daily instruction in such subjects as computers, French, hands-on science, and individualized math. Student/teacher ratios range from 7 to 1 for preschoolers to 10 to 1 for grade-school children. Students frequently go on field trips around the Washington area and to such places as Colonial Williamsburg and the United Nations. Extended-day and summer programs are available, as is van transportation. The school is in the northwest Fairfax County community of Herndon, convenient to the Dulles Toll Road and Washington Dulles International Airport.

The Potomac School
1301 Potomac School Road
McLean, VA
(703) 356–4101
www.potomacschool.org

This prestigious, independent, coed day school places a premium on competitive academics and extensive community service. Its 875 pupils, kindergarten through twelfth grade, benefit from a student/teacher ratio of about 8 to 1 and average class size of 16. The school takes pride in its interscholastic sports, and its teams include some of the area's top athletes. Founded in Washington in 1904, the school moved in 1951 to its current location, an 83-acre campus in a residential section of McLean. A new, state-of-the-art upper school opened in 2006. Bus transportation is available.

St. Stephen's & St. Agnes School
Grades JK–5
400 Fontaine Street
Alexandria, VA
(703) 212–2736

Grades 6–8
4401 West Braddock Road
Alexandria, VA
(703) 212–2741

Grades 9–12
1000 St. Stephen's Road
Alexandria, VA
(703) 751–2700
www.sssas.org

The emphasis behind this coed, 1,155-student Episcopal day school is balancing challenging academics with community service and other types of extracurricular activities. Courses in religion are required, as are 40 hours of community service and adherence to an honor code.

Middle-school students take single-gender math and science courses. Some students participate in foreign or specialized summer programs. All graduates continue their studies in college. Interscholastic sports are a vital part of campus life. The school became established in 1991 through a merger of St. Stephen's, founded in 1944, and St. Agnes, founded in 1924. After-school and extended-day programs are available. The 15-acre lower school, 7-acre middle school, and 35-acre upper school campuses are minutes apart and easily reached via U.S. 395.

Suburban Maryland

The Bullis School
10601 Falls Road
Potomac, MD
(301) 299–8500
www.bullis.org

Students are immersed in a range of academic and extracurricular programs at Bullis, founded in 1930. The 608-student coed school, with students in grades 3 through 12, boasts a curriculum that includes traditional subjects and a heavy emphasis on the fine and performing arts, as well as many advanced placement courses. The average student/teacher ratio is 8 to 1. The school also takes pride in its extensive athletic program, in which a large percentage of the stu-

dent body becomes involved. The Marriott Family Library, which includes a technology center, opened in October 1998. The Bullis Athletic Center houses a 1,000-seat gym, while the school's 2,000-seat stadium holds a football field and eight-lane track. The 80-acre, pastoral campus is nestled in the midst of Potomac, an attractive, wealthy community a short drive from Washington.

Capitol Christian Academy
610 Largo Road
Upper Marlboro, MD
(301) 336–2200
www.ccacad.org

Capitol Christian Academy, founded in 1961, offers both traditional and alternative academic programs for coed grades kindergarten through 12. Sponsored by Capitol Baptist Church, the school boasts an enrollment of 340 students. Of special note here are the intimate tutoring and counseling programs for special-needs children.

Charles E. Smith Jewish Day School
1901 East Jefferson Street
Rockville, MD
(301) 881–1400

11710 Hunters Lane
Rockville, MD
(301) 881–1404
www.cesjds.org

With more than 1,500 students in kindergarten through twelfth grade and both lower- and upper-school campuses, Charles E. Smith is the largest Jewish community day school in the country. This coed, Conservative school, founded in 1966, blends a liberal arts curriculum with traditional Jewish studies programs. The campuses are conveniently situated in downtown Rockville, near the Montgomery County administrative complex.

DeMatha Catholic High School
4313 Madison Street
Hyattsville, MD
(240) 764–2200
www.dematha.org

One of the region's true academic and athletic powerhouses, 61-year-old DeMatha twice has been recognized by the U.S. Department of Education as a National School of Excellence. The all-male prep school, with 1,000 students in grades 9 through 12, is in Hyattsville, convenient to the District and most points in Suburban Maryland.

Georgetown Preparatory School
10900 Rockville Pike
Rockville, MD
(301) 493–5000
www.gprep.org

Founded in 1789 by the Jesuits, Georgetown Prep is one of the metro area's oldest private schools and is the country's oldest Jesuit school. The 435 ninth- through twelfth-grade students who attend the all-male boarding school follow a curriculum steeped in academic and religious tradition. Honors and advanced placement courses are plentiful. Seniors are required to perform 40 hours of community service and participate in an ethics class. The 90-acre, collegelike campus is just a mile from the Capital Beltway.

Holton-Arms School
7303 River Road
Bethesda, MD
(301) 365–5300
www.holton-arms.edu

The 106-year-old Holton-Arms is an all-girls' college prep school that has a long-held reputation for its excellent liberal arts instruction. Subjects like computer science and African American history add a contemporary edge to the traditional curriculum. The Bethesda-based day school, with 659 students in grades 3 through 12, excels in athletics, fine and performing arts, and other extracurricular programs. Along with their traditional academic requirements for graduation, students must complete 50 hours of community service and pass a swimming competency test. Seniors participate in off-site senior projects and independent study options. After-school programs are available for all ages. The

school holds a coed summer camp for ages 3 through 13 at its 58-acre wooded campus.

Landon School
6101 Wilson Lane
Bethesda, MD
(301) 320–3200
www.landon.net

An independent, nonsectarian college prep school for boys, Landon is structured around rigorous academics and a variety of out-of-classroom opportunities in music, drama, and art. Founded in 1929, the day school has 675 students in grades 3 through 12. The average class size is 15. The rigorous curriculum includes many advanced placement courses. Volunteer work and community service are valued traditions here, as is an honor code among middle- and upper-school students. Off-campus learning opportunities include a semester spent on a working farm in Vermont and a summer language program in Spain and several French-speaking nations. The lush 72-acre campus is in Bethesda, not far from the National Institutes of Health.

Riverdale Baptist School
1133 Largo Road
Upper Marlboro, MD
(301) 249–7000
www.rbschool.org

Riverdale Baptist, with 900 students in pre-kindergarten through twelfth grade, is one of Maryland's largest Christian schools. An outreach of Riverdale Baptist Church, the coed school offers academic and extracurricular programs that revolve around the Bible and fundamentalist Christian beliefs. Honors and advanced placement courses are available for academically qualified high school students. The school's athletics department boasts 14 competitive varsity teams, including a highly ranked boys' baseball team and girls' basketball program. A newly refurbished gymnasium offers seating for 700. The band, chorus, and yearbook also garner honors on a regular basis. Riverdale offers extended-day care options and bus transportation for county students.

COLLEGES AND UNIVERSITIES

Metro Washington colleges and universities attract students and faculty from all 50 states and more than 125 countries. About a dozen of the region's leading schools are linked by the Consortium of Universities (202–331–8080, www.consortium.org), a network that allows for extensive cross-study programs and sharing of resources such as libraries and faculty. Consortium members include the University of the District of Columbia and the University of Maryland, College Park; American, Catholic, Gallaudet, George Mason, George Washington, Georgetown, Howard, Marymount, National Defense, Trinity, and Southeastern Universities; Joint Military Intelligence and Corcoran College of Art and Design. Of course, many residents of Northern Virginia and Suburban Maryland choose to attend schools in their states, but outside the metro area. The State Council of Higher Education for Virginia, 9th Floor, 101 North 14th Street, Richmond, Virginia 23219, (804) 225–2600, www.schev.edu, offers pamphlets with general information about the state's public and private colleges and universities. Virginia boasts 15 state-supported, four-year colleges and universities, including the highly respected College of William & Mary (757–221–4000, www.wm.edu), in Williamsburg; James Madison University (540–568–6211, www.jmu.edu), in Harrisonburg; and University of Virginia (434–924–0311, www.virginia.edu), in Charlottesville. Interested in Maryland schools? Obtain a copy of the Student Guide to Higher Education in Maryland through the Maryland Higher Education Commission, 839 Bestgate Road, Suite 400, Annapolis, Maryland 21401-1781, (410) 260–4500, www.mhec.state.md.us. The guide describes more than 50 colleges and universities in the state, including such popular, nearby choices as Hood College (800–922–1599, www.hood.edu), in Frederick; Mount Saint Mary's College and Seminary (301–447–6122, www.msmarys.edu), in Emmitsburg; and St. John's College (410–263–2371, www.stjohnscollege.edu), in Annapolis. The booklet also includes information about all five U.S military academies, including the United States Naval Academy (410–293–1000, www.usna.edu), in Annapolis, and private career schools offering training in fields from allied health to truck driving.

Washington, D.C.

American University
4400 Massachusetts Avenue NW
Washington, DC
(202) 885–6000
www.american.edu
"AU," as it's commonly known in these parts, attracts many who aspire to be diplomats and journalists. The independent, coed school, chartered in 1893 by an act of Congress, offers competitive programs in arts and sciences, business administration, communications, international service, and public affairs. It features extensive study-abroad programs in Europe and Latin America. The campus also makes good use of its city as a learning lab: AU interns in the Washington Semester Program are almost as ubiquitous to D.C. as lawyers and lobbyists. The school takes pride in its university and law libraries, which contain hundreds of thousands of volumes and up-to-date technical support.

Student life is surprisingly close knit, with nearly 3,900 of the 11,000 students housed on the 84-acre campus, which is in a beautiful residential section of Northwest. Graduate students number about 3,200, and various programs accommodate almost 1,600 working professionals. The university's athletic programs are gaining popularity, spurred by the fairly new on-campus gymnasium. Students also can choose from more than 180 co-curricular activities, 11 fraternities, and 11 sororities.

i Meet representatives from colleges and universities at college information nights, held during the fall at local shopping malls.

The Catholic University of America
620 Michigan Avenue NE
Washington, DC
(202) 319–5000
www.cua.edu
The Catholic Church's national university, founded in 1887, draws strength from the diversity of its students, who hail from all 50 states and 95 countries. Programs are offered through the schools of religious studies, philosophy, law, arts and sciences, engineering, social service, nursing, music, library and information science, and architecture and planning, and include 41 doctoral, 90 master's, and 83 bachelor's programs. The university's 3,077 graduate students outnumber the 3,053 undergrads. The school's drama department is considered one of the nation's best, having produced the likes of Susan Sarandon, Jon Voight, and other stage and screen stars.

Housing on the 144-acre campus, adjacent to the stunning Basilica of the National Shrine of the Immaculate Conception, is guaranteed for freshmen and sophomores. Day care and kindergarten are available for young children of students and staff. Working adults can enroll in a bachelor of arts program through the Metropolitan College. Call (202) 319–5256 or visit metr.cua.edu for more information. Many students commute to the Northeast campus from the suburbs and other parts of the District. Catholic's highly acclaimed library contains 1.5 million volumes and is often frequented by students from other schools in the metro area. The Center for Planning and Information Technology offers a sophisticated array of computer equipment for use by students and faculty.

Corcoran College of Art and Design
17th Street and New York Avenue NW
Washington, DC
(202) 639–1801
www.corcoran.edu
The city's sole professional college of art and design, founded in 1890, offers fully accredited undergraduate programs for visual artists, photographers, and designers.

i The football huddle originated at Gallaudet in 1894, when players noticed that the opposing team was trying to read sign language to guess their next plays.

Approximately 330 full-time students receive lots of personal attention: The student/faculty ratio is 4 to 1. More than 3,000 people annually register for the Division of Continuing Education's Open Program, filled with all kinds of nifty classes for children and adults. The school is affiliated with the venerable Corcoran Gallery of Art, near the White House and the National Mall. There's a second campus in Georgetown (1801 35th Street NW, 202–298–2541).

Gallaudet University
800 Florida Avenue NE
Washington, DC
(202) 651–5000
www.gallaudet.edu
Gallaudet, which grew from a small school founded in 1856, is the nation's only university dedicated exclusively to hearing-impaired students. The private liberal arts college awards bachelor's and master's degrees in more than 50 areas, such as business, biology, communications, the arts, computer science, education, engineering, and environmental design.

The 2,000-strong student body is active in campus and community life. Fraternities and sororities, student societies and intercollegiate athletics are all vital components of the college. Gallaudet also operates model elementary, secondary, and college prep schools for hearing-impaired students. The visitor center conducts, by reservation, tours of the school.

Georgetown University
37th and O Streets NW
Washington, DC
(202) 687–0100
www.georgetown.edu
Georgetown is undoubtedly one of Washington's—and one of the nation's—most visible

> **i** Hoya, the name used for George-town University's bulldog mascot, comes from a Greek and Latin phrase, *hoya saxa*, which means something like "what rocks"! Nobody's quite sure whether the term refers to the school's stone walls or is a cheer for the school's Stonewalls baseball club.

and highly regarded universities. The 218-year-old school, the oldest Catholic college in America, has outstanding programs in the arts and sciences, business, engineering, the health professions, and foreign service. The enrollment of more than 14,000 is almost evenly split between undergrads and graduate students, who are drawn to Georgetown's fine law, business, and medical schools, the last of which includes a teaching hospital. The university also has one of the area's most comprehensive continuing education programs, including dozens of interesting non-credit courses open to all adults.

Some may argue that the university's raison d'être is its government department, which each year pumps out scores of budding lawmakers, policy analysts, advisors, researchers, and diplomats. (The alumni list includes former president Bill Clinton.) And when it comes to sports, men's basketball is among the country's finest, producing such stars as former coach John Thompson, Patrick Ewing, Alonso Mourning, and Allen Iverson.

Students come here from all 50 states and from more than 130 countries, giving the beautiful 104-acre campus an unmistakably cosmopolitan air. As you can imagine, campus life is rich and intense. Undergrads tend to be the fashion- and trendsetters for Washington's 20-something set. The school also promotes spirituality and community service.

The George Washington University
2121 I Street NW
Washington, DC
(202) 994–1000
www.gwu.edu
George Washington is a private, independent

institution with more than 9,600 undergraduates and almost the same number of graduate students. Students hail from all 50 states and more than 130 countries. Graduate programs for working professionals prove a growing commodity at GW. Bachelor degree sequences, meanwhile, span the liberal arts and technical spectrum, with international affairs, psychology, political science, business administration, finance, and electrical engineering also proving popular. The international MBA program is one of the best anywhere, and the university's highly acclaimed medical center bolsters the health professions school. The school offers 80 doctoral and 180 master's degree programs.

Washington's biggest school of higher education, GW started in 1821 via an act of Congress. Despite an urban setting, in the oddly named Foggy Bottom, the 43-acre campus maintains a distinctive collegiate atmosphere. Fraternities and sororities prove popular here, as do the more than 250 active student organizations, ranging from international and political societies to literary and theater groups. GW athletics are a growing attraction, especially the men's and women's basketball teams. Freshmen are guaranteed on-campus housing, which also is available to upperclass students who prefer to live here. Many students choose to commute.

The school recently added a 26-acre Mount Vernon campus, formerly Mount Vernon College, at 2100 Foxhall Road NW, Washington, D.C. It specializes in programs for women and is situated in the prestigious Foxhall neighborhood just 3 miles from the main campus. GW also has a Virginia campus (see the listing later in this chapter).

Howard University
2400 6th Street NW
Washington, DC
(202) 806–6100
www.howard.edu
Howard is the nation's largest predominantly African American university—and one of the most respected. The school's list of distin-

guished alumni includes Thurgood Marshall, Andrew Young, Douglas Wilder, Jessye Norman, Roberta Flack, and Vernon Jordan, to name a few. Twelve schools and colleges, supported by 26 research centers, institutes, and special programs, accommodate around 11,000 students. Medicine, law, and engineering are among the top draws. Founded in 1867, the school has grown to include numerous resources, such as a hospital, radio and television stations, and press specializing in African American–oriented topics. The school's athletic program includes acclaimed football and women's basketball teams among its 26 Division I sports.

Howard students (80 percent African American) come from nearly every state and more than 100 countries. More than a third live in student housing, while most of the rest live in the neighboring LeDroit Park section of Northwest D.C. The 89-acre campus is just a couple of miles north of the Capitol.

Southeastern University
501 I Street SW
Washington, DC
(202) 265–5343
www.seu.edu
Founded in 1879, this business school offers flexible class schedules as a convenience to its 1,000 students, most of whom are working adults who take classes part-time. Programs of study include such fields as accounting, business management and marketing, and computer science. Close to two Metro stops, the school is convenient for commuters.

Strayer University
1133 15th Street NW, Suite 200
Washington, DC
(202) 408–2400, (888) 4–STRAYER
www.strayer.edu
Strayer is a private, independent business university with campuses in the District (including Takoma Park), Maryland (Germantown, Owings Mills, and Suitland), and Virginia (Alexandria, Arlington, Ashburn, Fredericksburg, Manassas, and Woodbridge). The com-

muter school, originating in 1892, offers associate, bachelor's and master's degree programs. Many of the more than 16,700 students are working adults, most of whom take classes in the evenings and on weekends. Classes now are offered online too.

Trinity University
125 Michigan Avenue NE
Washington, DC
(202) 884–9000
www.trinitydc.edu
Founded in 1897 by the Sisters of Notre Dame, Trinity is one of the first Roman Catholic women's colleges. The school boasts a personalized, liberal arts–oriented learning atmosphere and enrollment of around 1,600. Business administration, political science, and information studies are the most popular degrees. Some of the school's graduate programs are coed. A large athletic center opened in 2002.

About 95 percent of Trinity's day students live on the 26-acre campus just across the street from the Basilica of the National Shrine of the Immaculate Conception. About 650 students take courses through the Weekend College, founded in 1984 to meet the needs of working women hoping to complete their bachelor's degrees.

University of the District of Columbia
4200 Connecticut Avenue NW
Washington, DC
(202) 274–5000
www.udc.edu
UDC is the only publicly funded college in the District and therefore its mission is a bit different than that of its neighbors. Many of its 5,400-plus students enrolled in credit courses are D.C. high school graduates. UDC offers two-year, bachelor's, and master's degrees through its College of Arts and Sciences, Col-

GW's famous alumni include Jacqueline Kennedy Onassis, Kenneth Starr, Alec Baldwin, and a host of congressmen and senators.

lege of Professional Studies, a graduate studies program, and the Division of Continuing Education.

This is exclusively a commuter school, having no on-campus housing. In addition, the university is spread across several locations. Features include a media center, 1,000-seat auditorium, and athletics facility.

Northern Virginia

George Mason University
4400 University Drive
Fairfax, VA
(703) 993–1000
www.gmu.edu
Fast-growing George Mason is now the second-largest university in the Commonwealth. Since its founding in 1957, the college has undergone the transformation from a fledgling regional institution into a powerful national public university. The school grabbed national attention when its men's basketball team reached the NCAA Final Four tournament in 2006. Mason draws on a diverse and impressive faculty, many of whom come from the public policy, business, and political ranks of Washington. Undergraduate programs include studies in the arts and sciences, education, information technology, engineering, fine arts, business, and nursing. The graduate school accounts for about 40 percent of the student body and contains rapidly expanding programs in business and international studies, public policy, and biotechnology, among others.

The vast majority of Mason's more than 29,000 students attend classes on the 677-acre main campus just outside Fairfax City. The compact Arlington campus houses the international commerce and policy program and the law school. The school opened a campus in Prince William County in August of 1997.

i Area campuses offer great entertainment bargains for all ages. Call for information about film series, concerts, and art exhibitions.

About 87 percent of GMU students are commuters, and nearly the same percentage hail from Virginia. The school can, however, accommodate 4,000 people in university housing. Campus life is what you'd expect from a commuting school: sparse. However, the fine arts center and Patriot Center arena (see our Arts chapter for further details) bring a growing slate of nationally renowned entertainment to the campus. Completed in 1996, the George W. Johnson Center, with eight acres of floor space, houses restaurants and a food/study court in addition to a library and media center. The campus also boasts an aquatics and fitness center, featuring a 50-meter Olympic pool and whirlpool sauna. The school's sports program boasts 330 student athletes.

The George Washington University Virginia Campus
20101 Academic Way
Ashburn, VA
(703) 726–8200
www.gwvirginia.gwu.edu/index.html
This satellite campus of GWU (see listing under Washington, D.C. in this chapter) is an innovative venture between industry and education. The school offers 13 master's and doctoral degree programs in areas such as engineering, business, information systems, and human resources. The center also conducts a number of nondegree professional development workshops. The National Crash Analysis Center, which crash tests automobiles, is one of several research facilities here. The school is located in the sprawling University Center, a corporate and research park that sits in the middle of eastern Loudoun County's rapidly growing Route 7 corridor, convenient to Washington Dulles International Airport.

Marymount University
2807 North Glebe Road
Arlington, VA
(703) 522–5600
www.marymount.edu

Marymount began as a private Catholic college for women. In 1986 it went coed, and today it continues to expand, with a branch campus in Loudoun County and a school of business in a separate location in Arlington. The mission remains the same, though: to provide an intimate and accelerated atmosphere to grow and learn. The university offers undergraduate and graduate programs in such areas as nursing, business, education, human resource development, psychology, and liberal studies, and the region's only bachelor's degree in fashion design and fashion merchandising. Day and evening classes are available for working professionals. The school's enrollment of around 3,600 features a few more undergraduate than graduate students.

University of Mary Washington
1301 College Avenue
Fredericksburg, VA
(540) 654–1000
www.mwc.edu
Thanks to the Virginia Railway Express and a large stock of affordable housing, Fredericksburg has become an exurb of Metro Washington. That being the case, we thought it only appropriate to include in this list the city's academic pride and joy: the University of Mary Washington (named for George's mother). This publicly funded coed college is consistently rated among the nation's top regional liberal arts schools and one of the best buys in higher education. Undergrads number approximately 4,000. Students seem to migrate to the school's psychology, business, and English departments. Bachelor's and master's degree programs in liberal studies are offered to working professionals. MWC's lush, tree-lined 176-acre campus is a recruiting tool in itself.

Virginia Tech/University of Virginia
Northern Virginia Center
7054 Haycock Road
Falls Church, VA
(703) 538–8324 (Virginia Tech)
(703) 536–1100 (UVA)
www.nvgc.vt.edu

This jointly run, 105,000-square-foot center in Falls Church links Northern Virginia with two of the Commonwealth's largest and arguably most influential universities. The main campus of the University of Virginia is in Charlottesville, in central Virginia, while Tech is in Blacksburg, in the southwestern part of the state.

The Northern Virginia center offers adult students an array of graduate and continuing education liberal arts and technical courses. Graduate degree programs are offered in such fields as urban planning, education, and engineering. More than 1,500 students attend each school each semester.

Suburban Maryland

Bowie State University
14000 Jericho Park Road
Bowie, MD
(301) 860–4000
www.bowiestate.edu
Part of the University of Maryland system, Bowie State is a regional liberal arts institution that boasts strong undergraduate programs in business, education, and computer science. The majority of the circa-1865 school's 5,400-plus students are African Americans, but Bowie's enrollment is multicultural and international. About a quarter of all students are enrolled in the graduate school. The 500-acre campus includes such features as a learning-resource center, art gallery, radio and TV station, and the Adler-Dreikurs Institute of Human Relations. The school also boasts a strong athletic program, including the NCAA Division II Bulldogs. Close proximity to the MARC commuter rail makes the school easily accessible.

Capitol College
11301 Springfield Road
Laurel, MD
(301) 369–2800, (800) 950–1992
www.capitol-college.edu
This college opened in 1927 as a correspondence school called the Capitol Radio Engineering Institute. Today, the private college champions "teaching tomorrow's technology,"

ⓘ Attending a University of Maryland football game? For entertainment value, you can't beat the school's wildly energetic marching band, which performs halftime shows built around music such as cartoon theme songs. While you're on campus, stop by the statue of Kermit the Frog and his creator, alumnus Jim Henson. You'll find the tribute, dedicated in September of 2003, on the grounds of the Adele Stamp Student Union at Campus Drive and Union Lane.

and awards bachelor's and associate's degrees in communications and engineering, including programs in telecommunications management, computer engineering, optoelectronics, and engineering technology. The college is among only 2 percent to receive the National Security Agency's designation as a Center of Excellence in Information Assurance Education. The majority of students are professionals. The school takes pride in the fact that 98 percent of graduates receive job offers in their chosen fields within 90 days after graduation. Capitol is situated on a 52-acre campus in Laurel, a Prince George's County community between Washington and Baltimore.

Columbia Union College
7600 Flower Avenue
Takoma Park, MD
(301) 891–4000, (800) 835–4212
www.cuc.edu

Tiny Columbia Union (enrollment about 1,100) is a private liberal arts college founded in 1904 and affiliated with the Seventh-Day Adventist Church. It's on a pretty, 19-acre campus in Takoma Park, a city known for its grassroots activism and progressive politics. Business and nursing prove popular among the school's more than 50 majors. Students also can choose from 8 associate degrees and 27 minors. (There are no graduate programs.) Spiritual life and community service play active parts in extracurricular activities, which include several outreach projects. The school

also takes pride in its music and sports programs. Most students commute to campus.

University of Maryland
U.S. 1
College Park, MD
(301) 405–1000
www.umcp.umd.edu

With more than 35,000 students in its 13 undergraduate and graduate schools, the University of Maryland may be large, but with its size come almost unlimited opportunities for academic and social life. Seventy percent of the students here are undergraduates, and they flock to the university's strong programs in engineering, computer science, physics, education, and business management. Graduate programs in the physical sciences and engineering are bolstered by expanding research facilities on and off campus. *U.S. News and World Report* in 2006 listed the Robert H. Smith School of Business as 18th in the nation. The National Research Council gives top-20 rankings to the school's programs in agricultural economics, art history, astronomy, business, computer science, criminology, economics, education, engineering, journalism, mathematics, oceanography, physics, and others.

The University of Maryland's innovative University College was established in 1947 as one of the nation's pioneering adult education programs. Today, it is one of the metro area's most popular continuing-ed programs, offering bachelor's and master's degrees in business, biology, communications, the arts, engineering, and health professions, among others.

Campus life at Maryland tends to be pretty traditional. About 10 percent of the students are members of Greek societies, and those groups are joined by more than 400 social and professional clubs. The new Clarice Smith Performing Arts Center hosts numerous classical and jazz concerts as well as plays. Terrapins have always been bullish on their 24 Division I NCAA sports teams, particularly the men's and women's basketball teams who won the 2002 and 2006 national championships, respectively (see our Spectator Sports chapter).

COMMUNITY COLLEGES
Northern Virginia
Northern Virginia Community College
4001 Wakefield Chapel Road
Annandale, VA
(703) 323–3000
www.nv.cc.va.us
Northern Virginia Community College, or "NOVA" in the local vernacular, awards two-year associate degrees in more than 130 occupational, technical, and college transfer programs. The 60,000-plus-student school, the largest college in Virginia and the second-largest multicampus community college in the country, has additional campuses in Alexandria, Loudoun County, Manassas, and Woodbridge. The Extended Learning Institute provides credit and noncredit courses for study at home. Continuing education programs abound on all five campuses and community facilities throughout Northern Virginia, with more than 200,000 students enrolled in noncredit courses.

Suburban Maryland
Maryland College of Art and Design
10500 Georgia Avenue
Silver Spring, MD
(301) 649–4454
www.mcadmd.org
This small school, with about 85 students, has a two-year professional program culminating in an Associate of Fine Art degree. Students concentrate in fine art studies or visual communication areas like graphic design. Class sizes are small, and students spend a lot of time doing studio work.

Montgomery College
51 Mannakee Street
Rockville, MD
(301) 279–5000

20200 Observation Drive
Germantown, MD
(301) 353–7700

7600 Takoma Avenue
Takoma Park, MD
(301) 650–1300

Gaithersburg Business Training Center
12 South Summit Avenue
Gaithersburg, MD
(240) 683–1863

Westfield South Center
11102 Veirs Mill Road, Suite 306
Wheaton, MD
(301) 279–5188
www.mc.cc.md.us
This community college, with 22,000 credit students and 15,000 continuing education students per semester, is spread across three campuses in Maryland's largest county and is the state's oldest and largest community college. The Rockville campus, by far the largest with nearly 14,000 students, offers numerous technical and liberal arts transfer programs. The Takoma Park campus, with more than 4,500 students, specializes in health studies and professional programs. The Germantown campus offers specialized career programs plus the gamut of arts and science courses to its 4,000 students. In addition to more than 100 degree and certificate programs with regular, for-credit courses, noncredit programs are taught at campuses and community sites across the county, including a business training center in Gaithersburg. These popular

i Check out local community centers and recreation centers for a diverse selection of enrichment classes, from dog obedience to pottery workshops. (See our Parks and Recreation chapter for phone numbers.)

classes, ranging from auto maintenance to canoeing, enroll more than 17,000 students a year.

Prince George's Community College
301 Largo Road
Largo, MD
(301) 336–6000
pgweb.pg.cc.md.us
Another one of Maryland's fine community colleges, Prince George's, founded in 1958, has an open admissions policy and a menu of more than 50 areas of study, including accounting, health sciences, education, and law enforcement. Students, numbering more than 38,000, are as diverse as the curriculum, and class enrollment may include a mix of recent high school graduates, midcareer adults, and senior citizens. Summer programs, contract training arrangements, and extension and telecredit courses are all available here. More than half of all credit students transfer to four-year colleges and universities, with the University of Maryland among the top destinations.

SENIOR SCENE

Metro Washington doesn't exactly top the list of the country's most popular retirement destinations. Certainly it's no Boca Raton, Florida, or Phoenix, Arizona. Pervasive national lifestyle trends are working in favor of dynamic urban areas like ours, however. Urban retirement is gaining steam today as more seniors look to metropolitan areas for their health care, transportation, recreation, and education needs. According to the 2000 Census, Virginia's population of older adults increased 28 percent between 1995 and 2000. The trend is continuing in this decade as more of America's nearly 80 million baby boomers retire, and for good reason. The Capital region enjoys a moderate climate, much of the population-dense East Coast is within a day's drive, and there are real estate values to be found when you venture outside of D.C. and its immediate surroundings.

The implications of urban retirement are especially profound in the Nation's Capital, a region that's saturated with the types of diversions and opportunities so craved by active seniors. Whether you're just visiting or considering the area as a permanent home, you may be pleasantly surprised by the variety of resources for people ages 60 and older. Housing options include luxury apartments and lush campus developments, geared toward both independent residents and those requiring varied degrees of assistance. Hundreds of senior and community centers offer classes, exercise programs, and field trips, and numerous organizations and businesses feature volunteer and employment options. Meals on Wheels and Friendly Visitor programs provide nourishment and companionship to homebound seniors. Families facing difficult decisions regarding medical care, legal aid, and financial management can find assistance through local agencies.

In this chapter we offer an overview of helpful resources, as well as a sampling of retirement communities. See our Health Care chapter for information about hospitals and urgent-care facilities, and for suggestions on finding nursing homes and hospice care.

AREA AGENCIES ON AGING

Are you trying to locate a senior center to meet your recreational needs? Confused about housing options? Looking for home health care? Help is close at hand, through the nearest Area Agency (or Office) on Aging. Mandated by the Older Americans Act of 1965, these offices oversee federally and locally funded grants for programs serving citizens ages 60 and older. The agencies either directly provide or put seniors in touch with such services as Meals on Wheels, senior centers, adult day care, home health visits, long-term care concerns, transportation, discounts, volunteer programs, job banks, emergency aid, financial planning, moving assistance, and numerous other resources.

What follows is a list of Metro Washington's offices on aging and some of their programs.

Washington, D.C.

District of Columbia Office on Aging
One Judiciary Square, 441 4th Street NW, Suite 900 South
Washington, DC
(202) 724–5622 (main office),
(202) 724–5626 (info and assistance)
www.dcoa.dc.gov
The office's Senior Service Network features 30 agencies that run more than 40 programs, a 262-bed nursing home, adult day care, and meal delivery. It also publishes a monthly newsletter, *Spotlight on Aging*. The office's six

i Washington Metropolitan Area Transit Authority (METRO) (202–637–7000, www.wmata.com) offers priority seating for seniors and disabled passengers. Area residents and visitors ages 65 and older can buy discounted fare cards by showing a Metro ID card, available free at public libraries and Metro sales offices.

lead agencies, listed here, coordinate many nutrition, social, and health programs, along with senior transportation for residents in the city's eight divisions, known as wards.

Anacostia Community Services Center
1649 Good Hope Road SE
Washington, DC
(202) 610–0466
This center serves residents of Ward 6.

Barney Neighborhood House Senior Citizen Satellite Center
504 Kennedy Street NW
Washington, DC
(202) 939–9020
This agency serves residents in Wards 1 and 4.

Greater Washington Urban League, Aging Division
2900 Newton Street NE, 1st Floor
Washington, DC
(202) 529–8701

2041 Martin Luther King Jr. Avenue SE, Suite 401
Washington, DC
(202) 610–6103
The Newton Street location serves residents in Wards 2 and 5. The Martin Luther King Jr. Avenue location serves Ward 8.

IONA Senior Services
4125 Albemarle Street NW
Washington, DC
(202) 966–1055
IONA serves residents of the Kalorama Heights section of Ward 1, the Foggy Bottom and Dupont Circle areas of Ward 2, and all of Ward 3.

United Planning Organization/ Project KEEN—Comprehensive Senior Services
4025 Minnesota Avenue NE
Washington, DC
(202) 388–4280
This agency serves residents of Ward 7.

United Planning Organization Senior Services
1508 East Capitol Street NE
Washington, DC
(202) 547–0569
This agency serves residents of Ward 6, east of the Anacostia River.

Northern Virginia

Alexandria Office of Aging and Adult Services
2525 Mt. Vernon Avenue, Unit 5 ·
Alexandria, VA
(703) 838–0920
ci.alexandria.va.us/dhs/community_partners/
Besides providing information and referrals, the agency operates a 10-bed assisted living facility and an adult day-care program, oversees two multiservice senior centers, and runs an in-home respite program for Alzheimer's patients and their families. It also offers job training and counseling for low-income seniors, operates a bus service, and publishes a quarterly newsletter. The city council–appointed, 21-member Commission on Aging studies and makes recommendations regarding issues and programs for the elderly.

Arlington Agency on Aging
3033 Wilson Boulevard, Suite 700-A
Arlington, VA
(703) 228–1700
www.arlingtonva.us/DEPARTMENTS/Human Services/services/aging/aaa/Human ServicesServicesAgingAaaAgencyonAging .aspx
This information and referral agency also trains volunteers to provide more in-depth assistance to seniors. The agency offers

details on such programs as Meals on Wheels, adult day health care, and housing concerns.

Fairfax County Area Agency on Aging
12011 Government Center Parkway,
Suite 708
Fairfax, VA
(703) 324–1186, (703) 449–1186 TTY
www.fairfaxcounty.gov/aaa
A division of the Department of Family Services, this agency serves elderly residents of Fairfax County and the cities of Fairfax and Falls Church. It offers such services as job training for people ages 55 and older, volunteer visits to and assistance for homebound elderly residents, Meals on Wheels, the Seniors in Action volunteer program, resources for finding home health care, and medical claims assistance. The agency also publishes a monthly newspaper, the *Golden Gazette,* featuring senior center program schedules and articles about topics and local events of interest to seniors.

Loudoun County Area Agency on Aging
215 Depot Court SE
Leesburg, VA
(703) 777–0257
www.loudoun.gov/services/senior.htm
The agency's Elder Choices program provides information and referrals. Other services include a licensed respite center for Alzheimer's patients, home-delivered meals, four senior centers for ages 60 and older, a Retired Senior Volunteer Program for ages 55 and older, a discount program that includes some medical care, and a free taxi service to and from medical appointments. The Commission on Aging serves as a citizens advisory board to the agency and the county's board of supervisors.

Prince William Area Agency on Aging
7987 Ashton Avenue, Suite 231
Manassas, VA
(703) 792–6400
www.co.prince-william.va.us/aoa

Among the agency's services are home-delivered meals, a senior center, two adult day-care centers, home-care assistance, chore and personal-care services for financially eligible seniors, and a popular tour bus program for day and overnight trips, including an annual "mystery trip." The agency serves Prince William County and the cities of Manassas and Manassas Park.

Virginia Department for the Aging
Preston Building
1600 Forest Avenue
Suite 102
Richmond, VA
(800) 552–3402
www.aging.state.va.us
This agency directs state and federal funds to local programs. Call the toll-free number to voice concerns or receive information about local services, finances, scams, and long-term care, or visit the Web site.

Suburban Maryland

Maryland Department of Aging
State Office Building, Room 1007
301 West Preston Street
Baltimore, MD
(410) 767–1100, (800) 243–3425
www.mdoa.state.md.us
This office oversees the network of 19 local agencies throughout the state. It offers a wealth of information in such areas as senior employment, grandparenting, local events, and wellness. It also includes a report card evaluating Maryland nursing homes.

i Call Eldercare Locator, (800) 677–1116, 9:00 A.M. to 8:00 P.M. Eastern Standard Time, Monday through Friday, to find community services for seniors anywhere in the country, or visit www.eldercare.gov to conduct an online search.

Montgomery County Department of Health and Human Services Aging and Disability Services
401 Hungerford Drive, 3rd Floor
Rockville, MD
(240) 777–3000
www.montgomerycountymd.gov/hhs
This agency offers information, assistance, assessments, and referrals to elderly residents and their families. The Commission on Aging (240–777–1120) researches pertinent issues and offers recommendations to local government.

Prince George's County Department of Family Services
Aging Services Division
5012 Rhode Island Avenue
Hyattsville, MD
(301) 699–2696
www.goprincegeorgescounty.com/Government/AgencyIndex/FamilyServices/aging.asp
Besides offering an information and referral service, the agency provides such services as senior centers, a foster grandparents program, a Retired Senior Volunteer Program, and assistance with housing issues.

PUBLICATIONS

Guide to Retirement Living
1919 Gallows Road, 2nd Floor
Vienna, VA
(800) 394–9990
www.retirement-living.com
This twice-yearly magazine and extensive Web site features a comprehensive guide to senior housing options, lifestyle articles, and information about helpful organizations. Call for a free copy or check the Web site for more information.

Senior Beacon Newspaper
P.O. Box 2227
Silver Spring, MD 20915
(301) 949–9766
www.seniorbeacon.com

Published monthly, this Mature Media award-winning newspaper focuses on national and local news and feature stories for the over-50 crowd. The *Senior Beacon* covers health, finance, travel, arts, and volunteer topics. Each year, it publishes three special sections on senior housing options in the area. The paper also sponsors several annual expos that include speakers and exhibitors on a range of topics of interest to seniors. Every other year it publishes the *Montgomery County Seniors' Resource Guide,* a comprehensive, one-hundred-plus-page directory for local housing, health care, government, and services. The paper is available free of charge at libraries, places of worship, banks, drugstores, bookstores, and restaurants.

OTHER HELPFUL RESOURCES
Washington, D.C.

AARP
601 E Street NW
Washington DC
(202) 434–2277
www.aarp.org
This national nonprofit, nonpartisan membership organization, headquartered in Washington, offers many benefits for people ages 50 and older, retired or not, which is why it changed its name from American Association of Retired Persons to just AARP. Members receive discounts on lodgings and car rentals and are eligible for insurance, prescription, and credit card programs. AARP's almost 4,000 local chapters provide tax and legal assistance, 55 Alive driving classes, and social and volunteer opportunities. The $12.50 annual membership includes a subscription to *AARP: The Magazine* and the monthly AARP Bulletin, special rates for online services, and free publications on topics of interest to seniors.

The organization boasts more than 37 million members nationwide, more than 80,000 in Washington, D.C., and more than 940,000 in Virginia and 770,000 in Maryland. For local chapters call (202) 434–7701 in Washington,

D.C., (410) 837–4300 in Maryland, and (703) 739–9220 in Virginia.

Family and Child Services of Washington D.C. Inc.
929 L Street NW
Washington, DC
(202) 289–1510
www.familyandchildservices.org
This agency, founded in 1969, offers a variety of services, including a Retired and Senior Volunteer Program with more than 500 participants, respite opportunities for Alzheimer's patients, help for homebound patients, and recreational and social activities.

IONA Senior Services
Isabella Breckinridge Center
4125 Albemarle Street NW
Washington, DC
(202) 966–1055
www.iona.org
This 32-year-old nonprofit community organization, largely supported by local churches and synagogues and volunteers, offers a large network of programs for residents ages 60 and older. Some of IONA's many services include an information and assistance specialist (202–895–9448); Healthy Aging Programs such as exercise programs, trips, classes, and lunch clubs; a volunteer network featuring such activities as telephone calls and visits to homebound elderly, meal deliveries, help with medical claims, and cleanup; transportation; a long-term-care ombudsman; an adult daycare program; and a resource guide and Web site jam-packed with information.

National Association of Retired Federal Employees (NARFE)
606 North Washington Street
Alexandria, VA
(703) 838–7760
www.narfe.org
Founded in 1921 by 14 federal employees, this membership organization promotes legislation benefiting retired civil servants. NARFE boasts about a half-million members nationwide. Contact the headquarters for information about local chapters.

National Caucus and Center on Black Aged (NCBA)
1220 L Street NW, Suite 800
Washington, DC
(202) 637–8400
www.ncba-aged.org
Health, housing, and other issues of concern to low-income and minority elderly receive this organization's focus. Membership is open to anyone.

National Council on the Aging Inc. (NCOA)
1901 L Street NW, 4th Floor
Washington, DC
(202) 479–1200
www.ncoa.org
NCOA produces programs and publications that educate seniors and those who work with the aging on such topics as retirement planning, job training, and health care standards. Annual dues vary, but cost $47.50 for retirees.

Northern Virginia

All the Right Moves
3284 Laneview Place
Herndon, VA
(703) 758–2577
Moving is stressful at any age, but the experience can prove extra unsettling for seniors preparing to relocate to a smaller home or retirement community. This company specializes in making the process go smoothly through such services as decluttering a household; holding moving or estate sales; locating real estate agents, moving services, and contractors; coordinating moving arrangements; designing floor plans; and unpacking and putting away items in your new home. The initial consultation is free.

 Local department stores offer discount shopping days for seniors.

Elder Crafters of Alexandria Inc.
405 Cameron Street
Alexandria, VA
(703) 683–4338
You'll find such handcrafted goodies as quilts, cloth dolls, stuffed animals, carved wooden miniatures, woven baskets, pottery, and stitched, smocked, knitted, and crocheted babies' and children's outfits at this nonprofit consignment shop, just across the street from historic Gadsby's Tavern in Old Town. It showcases an array of items created by area craftspersons ages 55 and older. Hours are 10:00 A.M. to 5:00 P.M. Tuesday through Saturday, and 1:00 to 5:00 P.M. Sunday; the shop is closed on Monday.

Pam Newton & Company
11153 Lake Chapel Lane
Reston, VA
(703) 262–7929
www.pamnewtonandcompany.com
This interior design company specializes in working with seniors who are downsizing their residences. The firm helps clients choose furnishings to move and select colors and accessories for decorating their new home. The business also oversees the move, organizes household goods, and unpacks and puts away items in the new residence.

Retired and Senior Volunteer Program (RSVP)/The Campagna Center
418 South Washington Street
Alexandria, VA
(703) 549–1607
www.campagnacenter.org/RSVP.htm
If you're 55 or older and seeking an interesting volunteer opportunity, contact this organization for information about a variety of options in the Alexandria community.

The Seniors Coalition
4401 Fair Lakes Court, Suite 210
Fairfax, VA
(800) 325–9891
www.senior.org

This conservative lobbying organization, with 4 million members nationwide, focuses on such issues as Social Security, health care reform, and the Global Climate Treaty. Annual membership is $13.50 per couple and includes a subscription to the *Seniors Advocate,* an online magazine.

Suburban Maryland

Jewish Council for the Aging of Greater Washington
11820 Parklawn Drive, Suite 200
Rockville, MD
(301) 881–8782
www.jcagw.org
This organization's Senior HelpLine, (301) 255–4200 in Washington and Maryland and (703) 425–0999 in Virginia, fields a wide array of inquiries regarding elderly concerns. The 34-year-old nonprofit organization offers several other programs, including transportation, adult day care, in-home help with chores and personal care, aerobics programs, computer training, employment services, and estate planning. All programs are open to people of all faiths.

Jewish Social Service Agency
6123 Montrose Road
Rockville, MD
(301) 881–3700
www.jssa.org
Kosher home-delivered meals, home health and hospice care, counseling, and long-term care planning are among the services this agency provides for elderly adults, their caregivers, and families of all faiths.

Older Adult Service and Information System (OASIS)
Macy's Home Store
Westfield Montgomery Mall
7101 Democracy Boulevard
Bethesda, MD
(301) 469–6800
www.oasisnet.org
This educational program for seniors ages 55

and older features classes, lectures, and discussions on topics related to health, fitness, the arts, travel, history, and other areas of interest. Most classes are inexpensive, and a few are free, but registration requires a $15 semester fee.

Over-60 Counseling and Employment Service
4700 Norwood Drive
Chevy Chase, MD
(301) 652–8072
www.oversixty.org
The Montgomery County Federation of Women's Clubs, Inc., sponsors this employment counseling and referral service for seniors ages 55 and older.

Pam Newton & Company
11153 Lake Chapel Lane
Reston, VA
(703) 262–7929
www.pamnewtonandcompany.com
This interior design company specializes in working with seniors who are downsizing their residences. The firm helps clients choose furnishings to move and select colors and accessories for decorating their new home. The business also oversees the move, organizes household goods, and unpacks and puts away items in the new residence.

Senior's Interfaith Resource Center, Inc. (SIRC)
3950 Ferrara Drive
Wheaton, MD
(301) 962–0820
This nonprofit, volunteer-run organization offers information and assistance to elderly residents of Bethesda, Chevy Chase, and Kensington. SIRC's Hands of Shared Time (HOST) program trains volunteers ages 15 and older willing to provide two hours of weekly service to frail or lonely seniors. Office hours are 9:00 A.M. to 3:00 P.M. Monday through Friday.

COMMUNITY AND SENIOR CENTERS

You'll find many senior centers by contacting the area agencies on aging listed earlier in this chapter. The following centers and recreation departments also offer numerous seniors' activities.

Washington, D.C.

Body Wise
University of the District of Columbia
Institute of Gerontology
4340 Connecticut Avenue NW, 2nd Floor
Washington, DC
(202) 274–6651
www.udcfirebirds.com/community
programs/communityprograms.asp
This free exercise program for D.C. residents age 60 and older features water exercise, stretch, walk, movement, and chair exercise in eight locations around the city. Each participant must complete an application form and submit an annual signed medical release form.

District of Columbia Department of Parks and Recreation
3149 16th Street NW
Washington, DC
(202) 673–7647
www.dpr.dc.gov
The department's 16 locations, including 14 senior centers, feature daily fitness classes, lunch programs, and special interest activities like creative design classes and drama from 10:30 A.M. to 7:00 P.M. on weekdays. The department also sponsors special activities throughout the year, such as a seasonal farm and garden project, day trips, concerts, parties, and dances. Check the online programs listing for details.

District of Columbia Jewish Community Center
1529 16th Street NW
Washington, DC
(202) 518–9400
www.washingtondcjcc.org

The center sponsors the Behrend-Adas Senior Fellowship Program from 10:00 A.M. to 2:00 P.M. Monday through Friday at Adas Israel Congregation, 2850 Quebec Street NW. Open to every D.C. senior age 60 and older, the program features a hot kosher lunch ($2.50 donation suggested) along with exercise and nutrition classes, musical performances, bridge, special interest clubs, and at a nominal fee, bus outings. Call (202) 363–7530 to make reservations at least two days in advance. Senior programs, open to all faiths, also take place at the JCC. Senior memberships are $859 annually, including nonpeak fitness hours, $156 annually without fitness privileges. Nonmembers can attend most events for an additional fee. Seniors can earn a month's membership by volunteering 18 hours of time at the center.

YMCA of Metropolitan Washington
1112 16th Street NW, Suite 720
Washington, DC
(800) 473–YMCA
www.ymcawashdc.org
Seven YMCA membership facilities in the District, Arlington, Alexandria, Bethesda, Montgomery Village, and Silver Spring offer reduced rates for seniors age 65 and older. Each location schedules a free senior swim session. Members also can choose from a variety of fitness classes. Both full-privilege and program memberships are available; rates vary at each site.

Northern Virginia

Alexandria Department of Recreation, Parks and Cultural Activities
1108 Jefferson Street
Alexandria, VA
(703) 838–4831
www.ci.alexandria.va.us/recreation/seniors/seniors.html

i Before dining out, call ahead to find out if the restaurant offers early-bird or other specials for seniors.

Four centers serve Alexandria seniors: Nannie J. Lee Recreation Center, 1108 Jefferson Street, (703) 838–4845; Mt. Vernon Recreation Center, 2701 Commonwealth Avenue, (703) 838–4825; Charles Houston Senior Center, 901 Wythe Street, (703) 838–4832; and St. Martin de Porres Senior Center, 4650 Taney Avenue, (703) 751–2766. They all offer a mix of activities, including art, tai chi, bridge classes, walking clubs, wellness lectures, bingo, and trips. In addition, the de Porres Senior Center offers citizenship and English classes to Alexandria's growing Hispanic senior population.

Arlington County Department of Parks, Recreation and Community Resources
300 North Park Drive
Arlington, VA
(703) 228–4744
www.arlingtonva.us/Departments/Parks Recreation/ParksRecreationMain.asp
Contact the Office of Senior Adult Programs for a newsletter describing activities at nine senior centers and several activity sites. Membership cards cost $10 annually. Health and fitness classes feature several types of dance, strength training, tai chi, aqua exercise for arthritis, chair exercise, and more. Other popular programs include walking clubs, a bowling league, performing arts groups, arts and crafts classes, film screenings, special-interest clubs featuring such topics as genealogy and books, and cards and games, including duplicate bridge. The travel program features numerous trips each month.

City of Fairfax Senior Center
4401 Sideburn Road
Fairfax, VA
(703) 359–2487
www.fairfaxva.gov/seniorcenter/seniorcenter.asp
Residents ages 55 and older can visit weekdays and Saturdays for drop-in and scheduled activities, such as lectures, arts and crafts classes, games, and trips.

Fairfax County Community and Recreation Services
12011 Government Center Parkway, Suite 1050
Fairfax, VA
(703) 324–5532
www.fairfaxcounty.gov/rec/senior_ctr/senior_main_pg.htm

The department's 13 senior centers, most of which are open 9:00 A.M. to 4:00 P.M. Monday through Friday, offer classes, games, discussion groups, outings, and fellowship. Call a day in advance to reserve a hot lunch. Four other sites offer adult meals. Call for locations. Some centers feature choral, drama, and tap-dancing performing groups. Fairfax County and City seniors age 55 and older pay half the registration fee for recreation classes, held at senior centers and schools throughout the county.

Fairfax County Park Authority
12055 Government Center Parkway, Suite 927
Fairfax, VA
(703) 324–8702
www.fairfaxcounty.gov/parks/parks.htm

The park authority's eight full-service recreation centers offer several exercise classes for seniors ages 60 and older. Call for the latest *Parktakes* magazine, which lists detailed information about classes and events. Residents of Fairfax County and the city of Fairfax age 60 and older can register for most events and classes at half off the regular cost.

Falls Church Recreation and Parks
223 Little Falls Street
Falls Church, VA
(703) 248–5077
www.ci.falls-church.va.us/community/recsandparks/recsandparks.html

Seniors' activities take place at the community center at the address listed and at the adjacent Falls Church Senior Center, 401 West Great Falls Street, (703) 248–5020, and Winter Hill Senior Center, 330-B South Virginia Avenue, (703) 237–4750. Popular programs include fitness classes like line dancing, aerobics, chair exercise, and P.A.C.E.; weekly conversation groups in Italian, Spanish, French, German, and Russian; games such as bridge and mah-jongg; twice-monthly duckpin bowling; Thursday walking trips; and movies on the second and fourth Friday. Special entertainment takes place once a month at the community center. Day trips include recreational outings and grocery shopping.

Herndon Parks and Recreation
814 Ferndale Avenue
Herndon, VA
(703) 435–6868
www.herndon-va.gov/parks

Senior programming highlights include art classes, movies, and fitness programs such as indoor walking in the gym, with mileage rewards for those seniors who pile up the most distance.

Ida Lee Recreation Center
50 Ida Lee Drive NW
Leesburg, VA
(703) 777–1368
www.idalee.org

This facility of the Leesburg Department of Parks and Recreation offers several fitness classes at half price to seniors ages 60 and older.

Jewish Community Center of Northern Virginia
8900 Little River Turnpike
Fairfax, VA
(703) 323–0880
www.jccnv.org

Ongoing clubs meet weekly on Mondays or Thursdays for lectures and seminars on Judaic issues and other topics. Other programs of interest to seniors include bridge, canasta, mah-jongg, chess, discussion groups, Yiddish conversation hours, aquatic exercise classes, and events for singles ages 55 and older. Full senior membership, including use of fitness facilities, is $185 per single, $325 per couple. Activities are open to all faiths, and most are available to members and nonmembers, with discounts for members.

Loudoun County Department of Parks, Recreation, and Community Services
215 Depot Circle SE
Leesburg, VA
(703) 777–0343
www.loudoun.gov/prcs/home.htm
The department's 10 community centers offer a variety of fitness programs and leisure classes for seniors. Contact the Loudoun County Department of Parks and Recreation office for a schedule.

Prince William County Park Authority
14420 Bristow Road
Manassas, VA
(703) 792–7060
www.pwcparks.org
Two Prince William County Park Authority facilities offer aqua exercise programs for seniors and reduced admission and membership fees for people ages 60 and older: Chinn Aquatics and Fitness Center, 13025 Chinn Park Drive, Prince William, Virginia, (703) 730–1051; and Sharon Baucom–Dale City Recreation Center, 14300 Minnieville Road, Dale City, Virginia, (703) 670–7112.

Town of Vienna Parks and Recreation
Vienna Community Center
120 Cherry Street SE
Vienna, VA
(703) 255–6360
www.viennava.gov/Town_Departments/pr3.htm
The center hosts numerous senior activities, including pickleball, bocce ball, mah-jongg, fitness classes, blood-pressure checks, craft instruction, travel lectures, financial classes, and meetings of clubs and organizations such as AARP and NARFE.

Suburban Maryland

Bethesda Senior Source
8580 Second Avenue
Bethesda, MD
(301) 754–3404
www.holycrosshealth.org/svc_senior_source.htm
This health and wellness center, a partnership between Holy Cross Hospital and Montgomery County Government features tai chi, stretching, aerobics, and other exercise classes, as well as films, crafts, lectures, and very popular computer courses for seniors age 50 and older.

Greenbelt Recreation Department
Greenbelt Community Center
15 Crescent Road
Greenbelt, MD
(301) 397–2208
www.greenbeltmd.gov/recreational facilities/community-center.htm
A senior game room and lounge are open during regular hours. Other seniors' activities include hot lunches on weekdays, available by reservation at least a day in advance; a weekly Golden Age Club; monthly movies; craft and continuing education classes; and a weekly intergenerational program with nursery school and kindergarten students. Call for the latest program guide.

Jewish Community Center of Greater Washington
6125 Montrose Road
Rockville, MD
(301) 881–0100, ext. 3751
www.jccgw.org
The Senior Adult Division offers activities and hot kosher lunches Tuesdays, Thursdays, and Fridays. Among senior-oriented programs are seminars, craft lessons, a chess club, cards and games, Yiddish, a choral group, a quarterly magazine, Elderhostel classes, trips, water aerobics, and arthritis exercise. Special Sunday for Seniors features a performance or lecture and social time at 1:00 P.M. the first

Sunday of the month. Activities are open to all faiths, and most are open to nonmembers for a small fee. Membership for seniors age 65 and older is $495 per single or $770 per couple for full rights, including sports and fitness. A social membership, which allows participation in classes, is $150.

Laurel Department of Parks and Recreation
Laurel Municipal Center
8103 Sandy Spring Road
Laurel, MD
(301) 725–7800
www.laurel.md.us/parks.htm
Senior programming and meetings of senior-oriented organizations like AARP and the Retired Senior Volunteer Program take place at the Phelps Senior Citizens Center, 701 Montgomery Street, (301) 776–6168. Other sites around the city also host classes, workshops, exercise programs, and day trips for seniors.

Maryland-National Capital Park and
Planning Commission
Prince George's County Park and Recreation
Administration Building
6611 Kenilworth Avenue
Riverdale, MD
(301) 699–2407
www.pgparks.com
For information about seniors' activities at the county's 40 community centers, contact the above number or these area administrative offices: Central at (301) 218–6700, Northern at (301) 445–4500, and Southern at (301) 203–6000.

Montgomery County Department of
Recreation
12210 Bushey Drive
Silver Spring, MD
(301) 468–4540
www.montgomerycountymd.gov
Seniors' activities take place at five senior centers and 12 community recreation centers. Especially popular are the 1:00 P.M. programs at Holiday Park Multiservice Senior Center,

3950 Ferrara Drive, Wheaton, (301) 468–4448, featuring such activities as tea dances, concerts, travel lectures, and bingo. Other center offerings include hula and folk dance classes, photography, duplicate bridge, ceramics, painting, woodshop, and several exercise choices. Senior Outdoor Adventures in Recreation (SOAR) offers trips involving walking tours, boating, and other trips.

The four other county-supported senior centers are: Damascus Senior Center, 9701 Main Street, Damascus, (240) 777–6995; Gaithersburg Upcounty Senior Center, 80A Bureau Drive, Gaithersburg, (301) 258–6380; Long Branch Senior Center, 8700 Piney Branch Road, Silver Spring, (301) 431–5708; and Margaret Schweinhaut Senior Center, 1000 Forest Glen Road, Silver Spring, (301) 681–1255.

Rockville Senior Center
1150 Carnation Drive
Rockville, MD
(240) 314–8800
www.rockvillemd.gov/seniorcenter
Serving city residents 60 and over, this center in a former elementary school offers such programming as low-impact aerobic exercise classes, a fitness room, a computer lab, and bridge. The Carnation Players write and perform two skits a year. Special social activities include the Carnation Supper Club, featuring dinner and entertainment on Tuesday nights; the annual May Gala dinner dance; and a prom with high school students. The center also sponsors about 40 day trips, four to five overnighters, and a cruise each year through the Trips and Tours program. Registration is by lottery. Center membership is $25 annually for city residents, $125 for nonresidents.

RETIREMENT COMMUNITIES

These independent-living sites include 24-hour security and safety features such as medical alert systems. Some also offer assisted living options for residents who require some degree of medical or personal care.

Washington, D.C.

Friendship Terrace
4201 Butterworth Place NW
Washington, DC
(202) 244–7400
www.esm.org/ft
Convenient to IONA Senior Services, this apartment complex includes a daily meal, health and fitness programs, and cultural and religious activities in the $899 to $1,800 monthly rent. Features include a library, garden, sundecks, laundry, and hair salon. Residents may have pets.

Methodist Home of the District of Columbia
4901 Connecticut Avenue NW
Washington, DC
(202) 966–7623
www.methodisthomeofdc.org
This nonsectarian apartment community offers independent and assisted living options, with sizes ranging from efficiency to four-bedroom. Rent starts at $3,900 and includes such amenities as three daily meals, housekeeping service, activities, transportation, a hair salon, library, and chapel.

Northern Virginia

Caton Merchant House
9201 Portner Avenue
Manassas, VA
(703) 335–8402
www.pwhs.org/services/assistedliving
Affiliated with Prince William Hospital and Annaburg Manor Nursing Home, this facility offers four levels of care, from independent to intensive assisted living. Residents can choose from three floor plans among the site's 77 apartments. On-site amenities include laundry and hairstyling facilities, a library, and activity and lounge areas. A certified recreation therapist leads optional educational and social programs. Nursing care is available 24 hours a day, and residents receive three meals daily. The facility does not require an admission fee. Single-occupancy monthly costs range from $1,700 for a studio to $3,250 for a one-

bedroom apartment. Care fees range from no extra charge for independent living to $1,000 per month or more for intensive assisted living.

First Centrum Senior Communities
Forest Glen at Sully Station
14401 Woodmere Court
Centreville, VA
(703) 802–9501

River Run at Prince William Commons
13910 Hedgewood Drive
Woodbridge, VA
(703) 878–4618

Park Place
9659 Manassas Drive
Manassas, VA
(703) 257–3455
www.firstcentrumcommunities.com
These one- and two-bedroom apartments for active seniors range from $650 to $1,125 and feature such amenities as optional meal programs, hair salons, libraries, lounges, and activities. All three communities are located in bustling suburbs with lots of shopping and community services. First Centrum also has apartments in Maryland (see Suburban Maryland).

Greenspring Village
7440 Spring Village Drive
Springfield, VA
(800) 788–0811
www.ericksoncommunities.com/gsv
This Senior Campus Living property features both independent and assisted living options, as well as nursing care. The complex targets active retirees with such activities as health and wellness programs, classes, cultural events, special interest clubs, and gardening. On-site services include banking and beauty shops. Refundable apartment entrance deposits begin at $99,000. Residents have easy access to both I–95 and public transportation. Senior Campus Living also built Riderwood Village, a similar housing complex in Silver Spring, Maryland, that opened in 2000 (see Suburban Maryland).

The Jefferson
900 North Taylor Street
Arlington, VA
(703) 351–0011
www.sunriseseniorliving.com
Just a block's walk from the Ballston Common
Metro station and shopping mall, this Sunrise
Senior Living condominium complex offers
such services as daily meals, a weekly linen
and housekeeping service, a hair salon, and
activities planned by a full-time coordinator.
Residents can take advantage of a creative
arts center, library, game room, exercise
room, heated pool and Jacuzzi, lounge area,
and private dining room for parties. Choose
from 10 floor plans, subject to availability, for
one- and two-bedroom residences for rent or
purchase. Monthly service fees start at
$3,955, and condo fees start at $95. The complex also offers assisted living and Alzheimer's
care, and an on-site home health agency and
nursing care.

Retirement Unlimited Inc.
2917 Penn Forest Boulevard, Suite 110
Roanoke, VA
(800) 776–2320
www.rui.net
This company owns and operates three retirement communities for adults age 62 and
older in Northern Virginia: Heatherwood,
9642 Burke Lake Road, Burke, (703)
425–1698; Paul Spring, 7116 Fort Hunt Road,
Alexandria, (703) 768–0234; and Aarondale in
Springfield, 6929 Matthew Place, Springfield,
(703) 813–1800. Monthly rates include one
daily meal, weekly housekeeping, a linen service, special activities, a wellness program, and
scheduled transportation to medical appointments and shopping. Rates, per single occu-
pant, range from $1,850 for a studio to
$3,700 for a two-bedroom apartment at Paul
Spring; $2,675 to $3,785 at Heatherwood;
$3,760 to $5,375 at Aarondale. Residents do
not have to pay an entrance fee. Additional
options include more comprehensive meal
plans and assisted living care. The Retirement
Unlimited sites also offer such amenities as

walking trails, individual gardening sites, picnic areas, hair salons, chapels, and private
dining rooms.

Sommerset Retirement Community
22355 Providence Village Drive
Sterling, VA
(703) 450–6411
Set in eastern Loudoun County, about 45 minutes from D.C., this rental community includes
in its monthly rental fees a daily meal, weekly
housekeeping and linen services, and scheduled transportation. Residents have access to
hairstyling, a community store, a dining area,
lounge areas featuring a fireplace and solar-
ium, an arts and crafts studio, games and billiards, programs, and free laundries. Monthly
rent ranges from $2,465 for a one-bedroom
apartment to $3,145 for a two-bedroom with
two baths. Double occupancy adds $500 per
month.

The Virginian
9229 Arlington Boulevard
Fairfax, VA
(703) 385–0555
www.thevirginian.org
This apartment complex, set on 32 landscaped acres, includes such services as two
daily meals and housekeeping twice a month
and such special features as a wellness center, chapel, library, arts and crafts and woodworking areas, hair salon, convenience store,
and hospitality suites. Rent runs from $2,406
for a one-bedroom apartment to $4,170 for a
two-bedroom, two-bath design, single occupancy. The Virginian also offers assisted living
options, including a recently built Alzheimer's
care facility.

Suburban Maryland

Classic Residence by Hyatt
8100 Connecticut Avenue
Chevy Chase, MD
(301) 907–8895
www.hyattclassic.com
Daily breakfast and dinner, weekly housekeeping and linen services, scheduled transporta-

i Looking for a rewarding volunteer opportunity? Your neighborhood elementary school welcomes older adults who can help students practice reading, assist teachers with projects, and share talents with classes.

tion, and utilities are included in the monthly rent, ranging from $3,090 for a one-bedroom model to $5,630 for an apartment with two bedrooms and two baths. Pets are permitted. Residents of the posh rental complex, which is right next door to a country club golf course, have access to a fitness center, indoor swimming pool, wellness center, hair salon, planned activities, transportation, and on-site home health care and physical therapy.

Collington Episcopal Life Care Community Inc.
10450 Lottsford Road
Mitchellville, MD
(301) 925–9610
www.collington.com

This 128-acre campus community in Prince George's County features garden apartments and cottages for independent seniors, as well as assisted living options and nursing care. Highlights include private balconies and patios, weekly linen service, housekeeping every two weeks, and washers and dryers in the cottages. The Community Center houses a convenience store, hair salon, bank, an interfaith chapel, library, creative art room, woodworking shop, exercise facilities, and a heated pool and Jacuzzi. Residents have access to recreational programs and scheduled transportation. Entrance fees range from $78,500 to $654,200. Monthly fees, including three daily meals, range from around $2,400 to $3,950.

First Centrum Senior Communities
Bay Forest
930 Bay Forest Court
Annapolis, MD
(410) 295–7557

Charter House
1316 Fenwick Lane
Silver Spring, MD
(301) 495–1600

Glen Forest
7975 Crain Highway South
Glen Burnie, MD
(410) 969–2000
See Northern Virginia listing for description.

Leisure World of Maryland
14901 Pennfield Circle
Silver Spring, MD
(301) 598–2500
www.idigroup.com/Maryland.html

Geared toward active adults ages 50 and older, this huge IDI Group Companies retirement community—founded in 1966 by Ross Cortese—houses more than 7,000 residents in 19 condominiums and two cooperatives on a 620-acre site. The latest development, Turnberry Courts, includes three low-rise condominium buildings next to an 18-hole golf course. Prices start in the $300,000s, with monthly amenities fees averaging less than $400. The recreation-oriented Leisure World community includes two clubhouses with features like dining, bowling, swimming, tennis, fitness rooms, spas, and chapels. Residents can choose from more than 80 clubs and numerous activities. Nearby Leisureworld Plaza offers a supermarket, restaurants, specialty shops, services, and medical offices. If you'd prefer to live on the other side of the Potomac, check out the sister community, Leisure World of Virginia, 19400 Leisure Boulevard, Leesburg, Virginia, (703) 581–1711, where condominiums start in the $350,000s.

Maplewood Park Place
9707 Old Georgetown Road
Bethesda, MD
(301) 530–0500
www.sunriseseniorliving.com

Managed by Marriott, a corporation known for its posh hotels, this cooperative in bustling

Bethesda takes pride in its many features designed to make senior living worry-free. Homes cost $375,000 to more than $700,000. A monthly fee of $2,054 for a one-bedroom, one-bath model to $4,202 for a two-bedroom with a den pays for taxes, utilities, and such services as 27 dining-room meals, weekly linens and housekeeping, a heated pool and Jacuzzi, a fitness center, activities, a library and other club rooms, and scheduled transportation. Residents have access to a hair salon, bank, and general store. Pets are permitted. Maplewood also offers assisted-living and nursing care as needed.

Riderwood Village
3140 Gracefield Road
Silver Spring, MD
(301) 495–5700
www.ericksoncommunities.com/rwv
Riderwood Village opened in 2000 and offers independent living, assisted living, and nursing care. The 500 apartments range from efficiencies to two-bedroom/two-bath plus sunroom. Entrance fees for independent living range from $109,000 to $455,000, with monthly charges running from $1,125 to $1,834. Residents enjoy a fitness center, arts and crafts and woodworking rooms, an indoor pool, and hot tub. Other amenities include a bank, hair salon, on-site convenience store, and a medical center with a doctor who practices only at Riderwood Village, transportation, and 24-hour security.

WORSHIP

While Washington's unseemly and—sometimes intertwined—political facets receive endless public scrutiny, the city's spiritual side often maintains a low profile. Nevertheless, behind the city's power struggles and political machinations, a religious current runs deep here.

Virtually every denomination under the sun worships in Metro Washington. A quick scan through the Yellow Pages reveals everything from the mainstream to the obscure to the fringe: African Methodist Episcopal, Armenian Apostolic, Baptist, Catholic, Charismatic, Christian Science, Christian (Disciples of Christ), Episcopal, Foursquare Gospel, Jewish, Lutheran, Metaphysical, Moravian, Swedenborgian, and Unitarian, to name but a few.

The Washington area's international character also is reflected in the way its citizenry worships. Throughout the region you'll find Korean Baptist and Greek Orthodox churches; Islamic mosques; Buddhist, Hindu, and Sikh temples, including, in Lanham, Maryland, Sri Siva Vishnu Temple, one of North America's largest Hindu temples; and less-formal congregations representing religious practices from every corner of the globe.

WASPs—British Anglicans, to be exact—founded Metro Washington, and the Protestant influence still dominates, especially in Northern Virginia. Newcomers should be aware of some interesting dynamics, however. Maryland, a state founded as a haven for persecuted Catholics, continues to boast a strong Catholic heritage. (The first Catholic chapel founded by English settlers sprouted in nearby St. Mary's County in 1635.) Washington, D.C. and suburban Maryland boast a large concentration of African American Roman Catholics, numbering 100,000 out of 570,000 members of the denomination. Another 200,000 are His-

panics. In addition, Jewish families traditionally have migrated to the Maryland suburbs. These factors partly explain why Maryland and Washington historically have been more ethnically diverse than Virginia, but all that is changing as immigrant enclaves alter the face of even the most homogenous sections of the metro area. Drive through Annandale, Virginia, for example, and you'll see many traditional churches bearing signs in Asian characters. Korean, Vietnamese, Indian, and Hispanic settlers all have established their own religious communities in the area. The Jewish community is now a significant presence in Northern Virginia as well, particularly in Fairfax County, home of the busy Jewish Community Center of Northern Virginia and the ultra-Orthodox Chabad Lubavitch organization.

In this brief chapter, we'll introduce you to some of Metro Washington's most colorful and historic houses of worship. We won't recommend or list churches and temples to attend. We'll leave that to clergy and the Yellow Pages. At the end of the chapter, however, we list phone numbers of several religious umbrella groups and associations that might help you get started in finding a specific church, meeting house, temple, or synagogue that suits you.

WASHINGTON'S SPIRITUAL LEGACY

Washington, D.C.'s most prominent spiritual icon is also one of the city's newest churches, completed in 1990 after 83 years in the making! The awe-inspiring **Washington National Cathedral,** at Wisconsin and Massachusetts Avenues NW (202–537–6200, www.cathedral .org), said to be the world's sixth-largest cathedral, is widely revered as "the last of the great cathedrals," a church built in the Old World fashion—stone by stone. Worship services, concerts, and recitals have been conducted here since Theodore Roosevelt's presidency.

The fourteenth-century Gothic-style structure sits atop Mount Saint Alban, the highest point in the District of Columbia. Despite its recent vintage, the cathedral's soaring towers and huge stained-glass rosettes lend it the same grandeur—and the same graceful patina—as its centuries-old counterparts in Europe. The cathedral's commanding perch above Washington's skyline not only affords great views from its ornate bell towers, but also makes the massive structure a distinct presence, viewable for miles even beyond the city. On a clear day, one can discern the 200-yard-long cathedral from as far away as Fort Washington, Maryland, some 15 miles to the south.

Although officially known as the Cathedral Church of St. Peter and St. Paul, affiliated with the Episcopal Church, the National Cathedral truly serves as an interdenominational place of worship, hosting an array of Protestant, Catholic, and Jewish services. Tours take place several times daily, focusing on such highlights as the building's diverse gargoyles and grotesques, more than 200 stained-glass windows, some 1,500 needlepoint pieces, and interments of such well-known Americans as President Woodrow Wilson, Admiral George Dewey, Helen Keller, and her teacher, Anne Sullivan Macy. (For tour and event information, see the Attractions and Kidstuff chapters.)

With its vibrantly decorated blue dome, lofty bell tower, and ornately carved, arching entryway, the **Basilica of the National Shrine of the Immaculate Conception** takes your breath away even before you enter the Byzantine-Romanesque stone structure, at 400 Michigan Avenue NE, (202) 526–8300, www.nationalshrine.com. The largest Roman Catholic Church in the Western Hemisphere, the shrine sits adjacent to Catholic University, a fascinating destination itself. The National Shrine's bell tower, reminiscent of St. Mark's in

> **i** The Brookland neighborhood of Northeast, where you find the Basilica and Catholic University, is nicknamed "Little Rome" because of its concentration of Catholic sites.

Venice, contains a 56-bell carillon that chimes concerts on Sundays. Guided tours, available daily, feature the church's amazing artwork, including many elaborate mosaics and more than 50 decorated chapels dedicated to Mary, the mother of Jesus. (For tour and concert information, see the Attractions chapter.)

The **New York Avenue Presbyterian Church,** at 1313 New York Avenue NW, (202) 393–3700, www.nyapc.org, is not as well known as the previously mentioned churches, but it's every bit as rooted in Washington history. The Scottish stonemasons who built the White House organized the church in 1803. In contrast, the building itself is of modern vintage, completed in 1951. It contains 19 stained-glass windows, more contemporary than traditional in design. Both Abraham Lincoln and John Quincy Adams were members of the congregation. Visitors can thrill to the sight of Lincoln's original manuscript proposing the abolition of slavery, as well as other historical artifacts described during docent-led tours that begin at the Lincoln pew after Sunday worship services.

At one time or another it seems that just about every church in Washington has been honored by the presence of an important politician, statesman, or celebrity. Teddy Roosevelt was a regular at **Grace Reformed Church,** at 1405 15th Street NW, (202) 387–3131, at which he laid the foundation stone in 1903. On Sunday mornings he walked from the White House so quickly his bodyguards couldn't keep up with him, and the single time he was late, he apologized to the head usher and promised never to be tardy again. Roosevelt's wife and family often attended services at **St. John's Episcopal Church,** right across the street from the White House at Lafayette Square, at 16th and H Streets NW, (202) 347–8766, www.stjohnsdc.org. Known as the "Church of the Presidents," because every president since Madison has at some time attended services there, St. John's is where President George H. W. Bush regularly worshiped. Benjamin Latrobe, the architect who restored the Capitol and White House after fire damage during the War of 1812, designed the building. St. John's houses an extensive collection of Roosevelt memorabilia and to this day remains the church most visited by presidents.

President Lyndon B. Johnson attended the neoclassical **National City Christian Church** at Thomas Circle, Massachusetts Avenue and 14th Street NW, (202) 232–0323, www.national citycc.org, designed by John Russell Pope, also responsible for the National Gallery of Art and the Jefferson Memorial. Tours take place after Sunday worship services. **National Presbyterian Church and Center,** 4101 Nebraska Avenue NW, (202) 537–0800, www.natpresch .org, houses the Chapel of the Presidents, a tribute to President Dwight D. Eisenhower, who was baptized at the church's previous location and laid the cornerstone for its current site in 1967. Guided tours following Sunday worship services also include the contemporary Gothic sanctuary's 42 windows, depicting such themes as the Confessions of Faith.

President John F. Kennedy attended services at **St. Matthew's Cathedral** (Catholic), downtown at 1725 Rhode Island Avenue NW, (202) 347–3215, www.stmatthewscathedral .org, also the familiar site of the president's funeral mass. This Renaissance-style structure, which recently completed a four-year restoration, also has an exotic hint of Asia, thanks to the altar and baptismal font, gifts from India. Guided tours take place by appointment. Herbert Hoover, a devout Quaker, worshiped at the quaint stone **Friends Meeting House,** 2111 Florida Avenue NW, (202) 483–3310, www.quaker.org/fmw.

Striking Gothic architecture and a rich history give the **Metropolitan African Methodist Episcopal Church,** 1518 M Street NW, (202) 331–1426, www.metropolitan amec.org, its distinctive nickname, "The

National Cathedral of African Methodism." The church traces its roots to Israel Bethel, a congregation formed in 1821 by African Americans who had become unhappy with segregated seating arrangements at Ebenezer Methodist Episcopal Church. One of the early congregations, at 17th and M Streets, served as a stop on the Underground Railroad. Visitors can sit in pews dedicated to famous people associated with Metropolitan, including abolitionist Frederick Douglass, who often attended services; poet Paul Laurence Dunbar, a frequent guest speaker; and historian Charles H. Wesley, who once directed the church choir. Douglass's funeral took place at the church in 1895.

President Grant attended the dedication in 1876 of **Adas Israel,** the first synagogue built in Washington. The building nearly fell victim to the wrecking ball before being moved to its present location at 3rd and G Streets NW, now the **Lillian and Albert Small Jewish Museum,** (202) 789–0900, www.jhsgw.org, where the sanctuary is restored to its original appearance. The Conservative congregation now worships in a synagogue at 2850 Quebec Street NW, (202) 362–4433, www.adasisrael .org, where you'll also find the city's first Holocaust Memorial, featuring a sculptured tribute and Holocaust artifacts. The stunning **Sixth & I Historic Synagogue,** located at the corner of 6th and I Streets in Chinatown, (202) 408–3100, www.sixthandi.org, was dedicated in 1908 and rededicated in 2004 following a major renovation. The synagogue now serves a downtown audience with classes, concerts, and other programs.

Another Jewish landmark, the **District of Columbia Jewish Community Center** at 16th and Q Streets, is an 88-year-old limestone structure built in the classical style. A local Jewish group in 1990 purchased the building from longtime owner University of the District of Columbia and returned it to its original use. (See the Parks and Recreation chapter for more information.)

The oldest church in Washington is **St. Paul's** (Episcopal), established in 1712. It's in the middle of Rock Creek Cemetery, at Rock Creek Road and Webster Street NW, (202) 726–2080, www.rockcreekparish.org. (Despite the street and cemetery name, the church sits several blocks from Rock Creek Park.) On the grounds you'll see one of the most artful and poignant sculptures in Washington: Augustus Saint-Gaudens' bronze statue of a young woman. Henry Adams commissioned the memorial in 1890 in honor of his wife, who had committed suicide. Noted critic Alexander Wolcot called it "the most beautiful thing ever fashioned by the hand of a man on this continent."

The greatest concentration of houses of worship in Washington can be found along 16th Street (a.k.a. the "Street of Churches") in Northwest—one of the city's widest, most stately north-south boulevards. Among the eye-catchers here is **First Baptist Church,** at 16th and O Streets, (202) 387–2206, www.firstbaptistdc.org, built in 1955 in a pseudo-Gothic style. Presidents Harry Truman and Jimmy Carter, while in office, frequented First Baptist. Stained-glass window tours follow Sunday worship services.

At the southeast corner of 16th and Corcoran Streets is the **Church of the Holy City** (National Swedenborgian Church), an 1896 English-Country, Gothic-influenced building distinguished by a tower, fanciful gargoyles, and numerous stained-glass windows, including one by Tiffany and another by the Lamb studios. For more information, call (202) 462–6734 or go to www.holycitydc.org.

The **Scottish Rite Temple,** at 1733 16th Street, (202) 232–3579, www.scottishrite.org, designed by John Russell Pope, largely resembles the Mausoleum of Halicarnassus in Greece. The temple serves as the headquarters of the Supreme Council of the Southern Jurisdiction of the Thirty-Third Degree of the Ancient and Accepted Scottish Rite of Freemasonry. The building is open for tours Monday through Friday from 8:00 A.M. to 3:00 P.M.

Also not to be overlooked on 16th Street at Harvard Street is **All Souls Unitarian Church,** (202) 332–5266, www.all-souls.org.

The church, whose parishioners include some of the leading African American powerbrokers in Washington, was built in 1924 as a reproduction of London's St. Martin's-in-the-Fields.

Nearby, at 16th Street and Columbia Road, stands the **Unification Church of Washington** (202–462–5700), a denomination started by the eccentric South Korean Rev. Sun Myung Moon, who also founded the *Washington Times* newspaper (see our Media chapter). Up until 1975, however, the church housed the Mormon Washington Chapel, designed in the 1930s by Don Carlos Young, the grandson of Brigham Young.

One of the most intriguing facades in Washington is that of the **Islamic Center of Washington, D.C.,** 2551 Massachusetts Avenue NW, (202) 332–8343, www.theislamiccenter.com. Located in the thick of Embassy Row, the long white building and its 160-foot-high minaret are the religious and cultural focal points of the Washington area's Islamic community. With its elaborate arches, mysterious courtyard, and decorative tile work, the structure looks as though it belongs in a Middle Eastern oasis. Outside, worshipers—many clad in the traditional snowy white garments—can be seen leaving and entering the building. Inside, you'll find a library and a changing exhibit on Islamic culture and religion. Visitors are welcome, but proper attire is the rule here—arms and legs (and, yes, women's heads) must be covered.

VIRGINIA'S COLONIAL CHURCHES

Across the river in Northern Virginia, one can peek into the world of colonial worship at **Christ Church** and the **Old Presbyterian Meeting House** in Old Town Alexandria. Built in 1773 by city founder John Carlyle, Christ Church was the regular place of worship for George Washington and, later, Robert E. Lee. Signature-engraved plaques mark Washington's pew, and across the aisle, the pew rented by Lee, who was 46 years old when confirmed at the church in 1853.

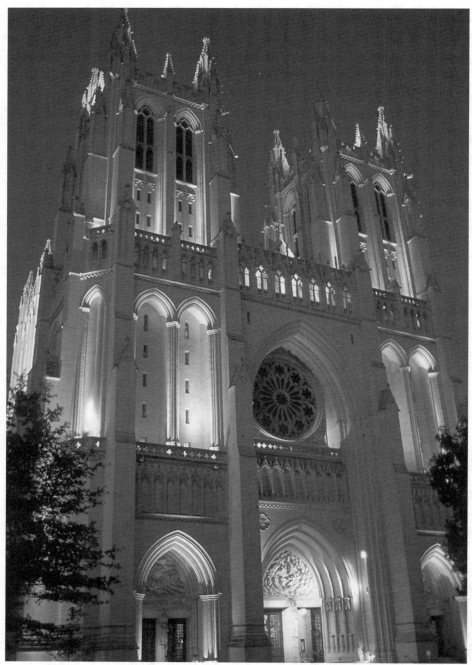

The Washington National Cathedral sits on top of the highest point in the District of Columbia. COURTESY WASHINGTON, D.C. CONVENTION AND TOURISM CORPORATION

Close-up

An Enlightening Experience

A dazzling holiday spectacle little known to Washington visitors is the Festival of Lights, held each Christmas season at the Washington Temple of the Church of Jesus Christ of Latter-day Saints. This seasonal extravaganza of lights, music, and theater is sure to appeal to anyone, regardless of religious affiliation.

The Mormon Temple, as it's commonly known in the metro area, is just a 30-minute drive from downtown Washington—an Oz-like beacon high above the Capital Beltway in Kensington, Maryland. From early December until early January, the temple displays 300,000 multicolored lights topped off by the illuminated spires of the temple itself. So laborious is the illumination that stringing and testing must begin in September of each year to ensure completion in time for the holidays.

Besides the lights, visitors can enjoy the traditional life-size nativity, which features a live Mary and Joseph. The narration of the biblical Christmas story takes place each evening (check at the on-site visitor center for the time and exact location).

Inside the visitor center, you'll discover a display of tall Christmas trees decorated in scriptural themes and adorned with thousands of lights and ornaments such as international and handmade dolls.

Artists from Europe, South America, Africa, and Asia contribute to an international collection of nativity sets, also on display in the visitor center. The sets, or crèches, reflect a colorful blend of the traditional nativity scene and the cultural perspective of each artist.

In addition to the displays, nightly concerts feature choirs and instrumental groups from schools and area churches of many denominations. On Christmas Day a local theater group presents a special family show. The center's five theaters screen Christmas and holiday films.

All events are open to the public. Lights come on at dusk each evening. The center is at 9900 Stoneybrook Drive, Kensington, Maryland. For directions and visitor center hours, call (301) 588–0650 or visit the Web site at www.washington lds.org.

The English Country–style church sits in the center of Old Town, at 118 North Washington Street (also known as the George Washington Memorial Parkway), (703) 549–1450, www.historicchristchurch.org. The courtyard's centuries-old poplar and oak trees provide natural shelter for the graves of several Confederate soldiers who died in Alexandria hospitals. Just about every president has attended services at this historic Episcopal church. (See the Attractions chapter for tour information.)

i George Washington purchased pew number 60 at Christ Church in Alexandria, Virginia, for 36 pounds and 10 shillings when the church opened in 1773.

Alexandria's Scottish forefathers also built the **Old Presbyterian Meeting House** at 316 South Royal Street, (703) 549–6670, www.opmh.org. George Washington's funeral services, originally scheduled for Christ Church, were held here because icy roads made the trip to the center of town impossible. Buried in the cemetery behind the meeting house is the Unknown Soldier of the American Revolution.

In nearby Lorton, Washington, George Mason and George William Fairfax were among the prominent citizens who attended the Georgian-style **Pohick Church,** listed on the National Register of Historic Places. Visitors' tours follow Sunday services. The church is at 9301 Richmond Highway, Lorton, (703) 339–6572, www.pohick.org.

The **Falls Church** (Episcopal), 115 East Fairfax Street, Falls Church, (703) 532–7600, dates to 1734. George Washington was a vestryman here. Read more about the church and its history at www.thefallschurch.org.

LATTER-DAY SAINTS AND A LITERARY LANDMARK

Suburban Maryland has its share of spiritual landmarks, but none is more imposing than the **Washington Temple of the Church of Jesus Christ of Latter-day Saints** (9900 Stoneybrook Drive, Kensington, MD, 301–588–0650, www.washingtonlds.org), which towers above the Capital Beltway in Montgomery County like a vision of Dorothy's Emerald City. The $15-million white marble temple, complete with gold spires, is a sight to behold, especially when dramatically lit after dark. The outside is all that most people will ever see of this imposing structure because it's off-limits to non-Mormons (although public tours were given for a short time after construction was completed). However, during the winter holiday season, everyone is invited to the temple's Festival of Lights, a not-to-be-missed spectacle. (See the Close-up in this chapter.) In addition, the visitor center features tours, films, and literature.

Literary buffs may want to venture up to Rockville, the Montgomery County seat about 30 minutes from downtown Washington, to view the grave sites of F. Scott Fitzgerald and his wife, Zelda, at the cemetery at **St. Mary's Catholic Church,** at Veirs Mill Road and Rockville Pike, (301) 424–5550, www.stmarys rockville.org. Their remains were moved here in 1975 from their original graves in Rockville Cemetery.

We have not yet even begun to scratch the surface of Metro Washington's fascinating spiritual landmarks. Should you venture into the Washington exurbs, you'll find additional interesting religious sites, but we'll save that for another chapter (see the Day Trips and Weekend Getaways chapter).

WORSHIP RESOURCES

Interdenominational

Interfaith Conference of
Metropolitan Washington
1426 Ninth Street NW, 2nd Floor
Washington, DC
(202) 234–6300
www.ifcmw.org
The unique alliance of nine faiths—Baha'i, Hindu-Jain, Islamic, Jewish, Latter-day Saints, Protestant, Roman Catholic, Sikh, and Zoroastrian—sponsors a fall concert, winter Martin Luther King Jr. prayer day, spring public dialogue led by youth, and summer pilgrimage to places of worship. Call for a schedule of events.

Protestant

African Methodist Episcopal/
Second Episcopal District Headquarters
1134 11th Street NW
Washington, DC
(202) 842–3788
Bishop Adam J. Richardson's office oversees more than 360 congregations in Baltimore, Washington, D.C., Northern Virginia, and North Carolina.

Baltimore Yearly Meeting of the Religious Society of Friends (Quakers)
17100 Quaker Lane
Sandy Spring, MD
(301) 774–7663, (800) 962–4766
www.bym-rsf.org
Based in the Washington area's largest traditional Quaker community, this office can locate area meeting houses.

Christian Church Capital Area (Disciples of Christ)
11501 Georgia Avenue, Suite 400
Wheaton, MD
(301) 942–8266
www.cccadisciples.org
This regional office oversees about 50 congregations in the Washington area, Delaware, and West Virginia.

Church of the Brethren, Mid-Atlantic District
500 Main Street
New Windsor, MD
(410) 635–8790
www.madcob.com
Sixty-four congregations in the Washington area, Pennsylvania, Delaware, and West Virginia fall under the jurisdiction of this regional office.

D.C. Baptist Convention
1628 16th Street NW
Washington, DC
(202) 265–1526
www.dcbaptist.org
This organization coordinates more than 125 Southern, American, and Progressive congregations in Washington, D.C., Northern Virginia, and Suburban Maryland.

Episcopal Diocese of Washington
Episcopal Church House,
Washington National Cathedral grounds,
Mount Saint Alban,
Wisconsin and Massachusetts Avenues NW
Washington, DC
(202) 537–6555
www.edow.org

The office oversees more than 100 Episcopalian churches in Washington, D.C., Southern Maryland, and Montgomery County.

Metropolitan Washington, D.C. Synod of the Evangelical Lutheran Church of America
1025 Connecticut Avenue NW, Suite 904
Washington, DC
(202) 822–1901
www.metrodcelca.org
Seventy-five congregations in Washington, D.C., Maryland, and Northern Virginia fall under the office's jurisdiction.

National Capital Presbytery
8401 Connecticut Avenue, Suite 805
Chevy Chase, MD
(240) 482–1566
thepresbytery.org
The regional office oversees 119 congregations of the Presbyterian Church (U.S.A.) in the Washington area.

Southeastern District, Lutheran Church—Missouri Synod
6315 Grovedale Drive
Alexandria, VA
(703) 971–9371
www.se.lcms.org
The district oversees 215 congregations and missions in the D.C. area, Maryland, Virginia, Delaware, North and South Carolina, and Pennsylvania.

United Church of Christ, Central Atlantic Conference, Potomac Association
916 South Rolling Road
Baltimore, MD
(410) 788–4190
www.cacucc.org
The conference's Potomac Association includes more than 30 congregations in the Washington vicinity.

United Methodist General Board of Church and Society
100 Maryland Avenue NE
Washington, DC
(800) 967–0880
www.umc-gbcs.org
This board deals with United Methodist Ministry programs.

Roman Catholic

Archdiocese of Washington
5001 Eastern Avenue
Hyattsville, MD
(301) 853–4500
www.adw.org
This governing body oversees more than 140 parishes in the capital and in several Maryland counties.

Catholic Diocese of Arlington
200 North Glebe Road, Suite 914
Arlington, VA
(703) 841–2500
www.arlingtondiocese.org
The diocese's bishop, the Most Rev. Paul S. Loverde, oversees more than 60 parishes in 21 counties and seven independent cities in Virginia.

Jewish

Jewish Information and Referral Service of Greater Washington
6101 Montrose Road
Rockville, MD

8900 Little River Turnpike
Fairfax, VA
(301) 770–4848, (703) 978–3910
www.jirs.org
Part of the Jewish Federation of Greater Washington, this office helps people find synagogues and other Jewish organizations in the Washington area.

MEDIA

It's been said that information is a fundamental component of power. If so, residents of Metro Washington could be considered some of the most powerful people in the world. Indeed, many are just that, with number 1 on the list living at 1600 Pennsylvania Avenue NW.

This chapter isn't about the political players, however, but rather the awesome presence of the information players. There are few places beyond Washington where the incoming and outgoing stream of information—specifically the written and spoken products of the print and electronic media—is as intense. There are also few places beyond Washington where citizens have as much interaction with and exposure to the conveyors of that information: literally thousands of reporters, editors, correspondents, broadcasters, freelance writers, and others of the same ilk from around the globe who practice their trade here. It's no wonder that some of the Internet's most prolific bloggers make their homes inside the Beltway.

Washington has the highest concentration of journalists anywhere in the world, a staggering testament to the sphere of influence of the so-called fourth estate, the term used to denote the public press (traditionally, the first three estates, each with its own influence in government, are nobility, clergy, and townspeople). It's also a downright scary thought to many people (at least until they count the lawyers!) that there are all those nosy journalists running around—not to mention the amateurs blogging from their home computers. It's to be expected, however, since Washington plays the dual role of capital of the nation and capital of the free world.

WHEN LOCAL MEANS NATIONAL

Living in Metro Washington, you soon get used to much of the "local" news also being national and international. Call it a blessing or a curse—it's reality. It's what happens when reporters have beats that include not only city hall, the county courthouse, and the school board, but also the White House, Capitol Hill, the Supreme Court, the Pentagon, and other focal points of the federal establishment.

Beyond the newspapers, magazines, radio and TV stations, and other media based in Metro Washington, nearly all major (and some minor) news outlets in the world have a presence here, whether they're full-blown bureaus with dozens of staffers and a complement of high-tech machinery or lone correspondents holding court at the National Press Building with little more than a desk, telephone, and laptop computer.

Metro Washington is home to such media giants as the Washington Post Company, publisher of one of the world's most influential newspapers; Gannett Co. Inc., proud parent of "The Nation's Newspaper," *USA Today*, and a large stable of other print and broadcast properties; America Online, the popular computer network, with more than 35 million subscribers worldwide; United Press International, a Pulitzer Prize–winning news service; XM Satellite Radio, a powerful player in the world of news radio; and the National Geographic Society, an American publishing institution that produces not only great magazines, but also maps, globes, books, and TV specials. Numerous trade associations based here also represent the press in one form or another.

The winds of change are forever blowing in our fair city, and even prominent media are not immune to their gusts. Some longtime residents still mourn the loss of the popular afternoon daily, the *Washington Star*. The *Washington Times* has strived mightily since 1982 to fill the void, but it just hasn't been the same. The *Washington Post* has long been, and remains, the undisputed king of the local media hill. To help cope with the problems of declining subscriptions and advertising revenues, the *Post* launched *Express*, a free tabloid-sized newspaper, distributed Monday through Friday at Metro stations. The *Post* has also built a solid online community with www.washingtonpost.com, where readers can chat with reporters and community experts on topics of interest, from dining out and going out to gardening.

Although some once-popular magazines have stopped their presses, new titles have emerged to take their place. Glossy lifestyle publications like *Capitol File* and Modern Luxury's *DC* magazine cater to a hip local clientele.

IT'S ALL WITHIN YOUR REACH

Whether scanning the radio or TV dial, or flipping through a newspaper or magazine, you quickly realize Washington media are diverse, to say the least. The region's global influence is evident in the availability of foreign and domestic publications at neighborhood convenience stores, bookshops, libraries, and sidewalk newsstands. News junkies, students, academicians, and homesick transplants will be relieved to know they can find numerous foreign and domestic reads at such publication sources as Newsroom, 1753 Connecticut Avenue NW, (202) 332–1489, which carries scholarly journals and bilingual directories, and many large chain bookstores in the metropolitan area.

Several major newspapers based elsewhere, such as the *New York Times* and the *Wall Street Journal*, offer same-day delivery to most areas of Metro Washington. Virginians wanting to keep close tabs on events in their

state capital can pick up a current copy of the *Richmond Times-Dispatch*—one of the South's oldest and most respected newspapers—at some area newsstands; the paper also maintains a Washington bureau. Maryland residents keep up with statewide news by reading the *Baltimore Sun* and the *Capital*, a daily out of Annapolis.

As with other topics covered in this book, this chapter is intended as an overview, not an encyclopedic compilation. We've avoided, for the most part, mentioning any personalities and other details that could become outdated quickly. Although we've tried to be as current as possible, bear in mind that publication titles, radio and TV formats, and the ownership of such entities can and do change with little warning.

NEWSPAPERS

Although TV and radio have come a long way since their inception in delivering the news with unprecedented speed and, in the case of television, amazing visual impact, the newspaper still provides expansive coverage and an overriding sense of permanence.

Dailies

The Washington, DC *Examiner*
1015 15th Street NW, Suite 500
Washington, DC
(202) 903–2000
www.examiner.com
The Denver-based *Examiner* is best known for its well-established daily newspaper in San Francisco. The *Examiner* made its East Coast debut in 2005 after taking over a regional daily, *The Journal*, copying the free-circulation model and tabloid format followed by the *Washington Post's Express*. You'll find it at Metro stations and in newsstands throughout the metro area. The *Examiner* does a respectable job of covering news, sports, and features, plus local culture, restaurants, and nightlife.

The *Washington Post*
1150 15th Street NW
Washington, DC
(202) 334–6000
www.washingtonpost.com

Scan virtually any list of the most influential newspapers in the nation, even the world, and the *Washington Post* is sure to be there with domestic powerhouses such as the *New York Times*, the *Wall Street Journal,* and the *Los Angeles Times*. It boasts an average daily circulation of 656,000 and 931,000 on Sundays.

Like many publications, the *Post* is making changes to evolve with its customers' and advertisers' changing tastes and habits. In 2003 the *Post* launched *Express*, a free daily tabloid distributed primarily to commuters at Metro stations, with a daily circulation topping 180,000. With stories taken largely from wire services, the publication has generated a new stream of advertising revenues. The *Post's* aggressive online counterpart constantly introduces new services, from comprehensive restaurant reviews to neighborhood overviews.

No matter what you think of its liberal editorial-page bent, you'll find the *Post* to be a top-notch major newspaper, with its wealth of resources, its worldwide presence, and an immense staff replete with Pulitzer Prize–winning reporters, editors, and photographers. After all, this is the paper that broke the Watergate scandal, propelling two formerly obscure reporters, Bob Woodward and Carl Bernstein, to international notoriety and forever changing investigative journalism.

Living in Metro Washington and reading the *Post* day in and day out, you come to expect what readers of many other papers do not: in-depth analysis and commentary, from both sides of the political fence, on a broad range of topics; reprints of the entire text of presidential speeches and news conferences; a Sunday magazine; stories and photos from the farthest reaches of the world provided by *Post* staffers, not wire services; heavy coverage of national and international news to complement local happenings; in-depth special series; and stimulating editorial and op-ed

i Metro Washingtonians seeking an inexpensive form of amusement like to compare same-day editions of the *Washington Post* and the *Washington Times* to see how their disparate political leanings influence the placement of major stories and the photos and headlines that accompany them.

pages. The paper also boasts lively lifestyle pages; weekly food, health, business, and community sections; and Friday's weekend section, a comprehensive guide to upcoming events. Because of its heavy national and international news bent, local news has sometimes taken the backseat. But recently beefed-up zoned weekly sections have helped remedy that. The *Post* is also trying to appeal more to younger readers. In 2003 a new section called "Sunday Source" debuted, with tips on everything from throwing a party to adopting a pet. Still, it's easy to get spoiled; just a few days out of town can cause acute information withdrawal—but that's where washingtonpost .com comes in.

The *Washington Times*
3600 New York Avenue NE
Washington, DC
(202) 636–3000
www.washtimes.com

If nothing else, the *Washington Times* gives conservatives a loud, colorful voice. Plucky and aggressive, the *Times* (which also publishes a weekly news magazine, *Insight*) has only been a seven-day-a-week paper since 1991, but you wouldn't know it from the way it challenges the *Post* everywhere in its marketing strategies and daily news coverage.

The *Times* distinguishes itself not only with its strong right-wing tilt, but by its ownership: the Rev. Sun Myung Moon's Unification Church. The *Times* has earned praise for its visual appeal, outstanding sports and business sections, hard-hitting investigative instincts, and for hustle, gumption, and chutzpah in the face of a David and Goliath sort of rivalry with the *Post*.

The *Times* publishes its weekend section on Thursdays as a service to those who like to have Saturday and Sunday planned by the time Friday rolls around—a novel idea indeed. The *Times*, like the *Post*, can be perused online.

As long as the money doesn't run out, the *Times* will continue to be the proverbial fly in the *Post*'s ointment and the darling of the conservative establishment. The battle is good old-fashioned newspaper competition at its finest.

USA Today
7950 Jones Branch Drive
McLean, VA
(703) 854–3400
www.usatoday.com

With its extensive use of color and digest-style news coverage, "The Nation's Newspaper" originated the look that's become the trend in print journalism. The locally head-quartered paper, which published its first edition in 1982, is sold Monday through Friday in newsboxes almost everywhere. It boasts an average circulation of 2.2 million readers. *USA Today* is also online.

Community Newspapers

Residents of Metro Washington have dozens of community news outlets. The weekly chains in particular are vast, with virtually every enclave in Washington, D.C., Northern Virginia, and Suburban Maryland having some sort of newspaper to call its own.

Many publications are free and distributed either by mail or to the doorstep based on zip code.

Washington, D.C.

The Current Newspapers
5185 MacArthur Boulevard NW, Suite 102
Washington, DC
(202) 244–7223
www.currentnewspapers.com

The *Northwest Current, Dupont Current, Foggy Bottom Current*, and *Georgetown Current* newspapers print news and features in neighborhoods from Chevy Chase to Foggy Bottom. The free papers are distributed every Wednesday via bulk drop and home delivery. A yearly subscription for home delivery is $52.

The Georgetowner Newspaper
1054 Potomac Street NW
Washington, DC
(202) 338–4833
www.georgetowner.com

This free paper, founded in 1954, is devoted exclusively to Georgetown, featuring community news and features, historical lore, book reviews, and an events calendar. Published every other week, it's circulated throughout Georgetown and surrounding areas.

Hill Rag
224 7th Street SE
Washington, DC
(202) 543–8300
www.hillrag.com

These monthly magazine-style newspapers, founded in 1976, feature neighborhood news, film and book reviews, and editorials geared toward readers who live or work on Capitol Hill, Southeast, and Northeast. Distributed the first weekend of each month, the free papers are widely available at restaurants, bars, and in news boxes.

Washington City Paper
2390 Champlain Street NW
Washington, DC
(202) 332–2100
www.washingtoncitypaper.com

This hip weekly attracts predominantly young, single professionals, who are drawn to its extensive coverage of culture, the arts, music, and nightlife. It gives a comprehensive run-down of upcoming events, covers controversial and newsworthy issues through in-depth features, and runs personal ads like you don't usually see in mainstream publications. This free tabloid is published on Thursdays and is typically available at book and music stores in the metropolitan area.

The Washington Sun Newspaper
830 Kennedy Street NW
Washington, DC
(202) 882–1021
This weekly targets the entire Metro Washington area, with a mixture of local and world news and information about community events. Published on Thursdays and distributed throughout the area.

Northern Virginia

Connection Publishing, Inc.
7913 Westpark Drive
McLean, VA
(703) 821–5050
www.connectionnewspapers.com
The area's largest local newspaper publisher has numerous weeklies throughout Northern Virginia. The *Alexandria Gazette Packet* features news of the city of Alexandria, while the county's southern end receives coverage in the *Mount Vernon Gazette*. The bustling western Fairfax communities of Centreville and Chantilly receive coverage in *Centre View*. The Connection weekly tabloids cover news and features in Arlington, Burke, Fairfax, Fairfax Station, Springfield, Reston, Herndon, McLean, Great Falls, Loudoun, and Vienna/Oakton.

Falls Church News-Press
929 West Broad Street
Falls Church, VA
(703) 532–3267
www.fcnp.com
The city's free "Independent, Locally Owned Newspaper of Record" is published every Thursday and distributed throughout the city and neighboring areas. It is accessible online.

The Metro Herald
901 North Washington Street, Suite 603
Alexandria, VA
(703) 548–8891
www.metroherald.com
This weekly, published on Fridays, actually covers the entire Metro Washington area through regional news, commentary, business

i Check *Washingtonian* magazine and the weekend sections of the *Washington Post* and the *Washington Times* for helpful guides to local dining, shopping, nightlife, and assorted recreational diversions.

and sports updates, events listings, and lifestyle and entertainment features. A single copy costs 75 cents, and a subscription is $75 annually.

Old Town Crier
112 South Patrick Street
Alexandria, VA
(703) 836–0132
www.oldtowncrier.com
Another Alexandria-based periodical, this one prints lifestyle features, entertainment and restaurant news, business briefs, and events listings, "From the Bay to the Blue Ridge." This monthly paper is available at the Alexandria Visitors Center and at local businesses in Alexandria, Fairfax, Fredericksburg, and the Blue Ridge area of Virginia; Annapolis, Maryland; and Georgetown in Washington, D.C. The company launched the monthly *Georgetown Crier* in 1999. Both publications are also online.

Sun Gazette
6408 Edsall Road
Alexandria, VA
(703) 738–2520
www.sungazette.net
The Sun Gazette chain consists of four weekly newspapers: the *Sun Gazette* (serving McLean, Vienna, Oakton, and Great Falls), the *Arlington Sun Gazette,* the *Fairfax/Fairfax Station Sun Gazette,* and *Gaceta del Sol,* a Spanish-language newspaper.

Times Community Newspapers
13873 Park Center Road, Suite 301
Herndon, VA
(703) 478–6666
www.timescommunity.com
ARCOM Publishing owns this massive, ever-

growing newspaper group, featuring 14 community weekly newspapers, including the flagship *Loudoun Times Mirror* in Leesburg. Other links in this vast chain include the *Eastern Loudoun Times* and the Times Community newspapers in the Fairfax County communities of Burke, Centreville, Chantilly, Fairfax, Fairfax Station, Great Falls, Herndon, McLean, Reston, Springfield, and Vienna. A bit more removed from the Metro Washington area are the *Fauquier Times Democrat,* the *Clarke Courier,* and the *Rappahannock News.*

Suburban Maryland

Almanac Newspapers
10220 River Road
Potomac, MD
(301) 983–3350
www.connectionnewspapers.com
Owned by Connection Publishing, Inc., a major force in Northern Virginia community news, the *Almanac* carries local news about Bethesda and Chevy Chase and the Potomac vicinity. The paper has earned numerous awards from the Maryland Delaware D.C. Press Association. Distribution is free.

Bowie-Blade News
Crofton News Crier
6000 Laurel-Bowie Road, Suite 101
Bowie, MD
(301) 262–3700
www.capitalonline.com
Owned by Capital Gazette Communications Inc., which also publishes the *Capital* daily newspaper in Annapolis and *Maryland Gazette,* a weekly in Glen Burnie, these suburban weeklies carry news and features from their respective communities. Published on Thursdays, they're available at newsstands and by carrier delivery ($1.47 for four weeks) or subscription by mail ($13 for six months).

The Enquirer-Gazette
14801 Pratt Street
Upper Marlboro, MD
(301) 627–2833
www.gazette.net

This weekly covering Prince George's County and parts of nearby Charles, St. Mary's, and Calvert Counties was founded in 1851. Distributed on Thursdays by mail and at local newsstands, it costs 25 cents a copy or $46 for an annual subscription. The parent company, Chesapeake Publishing, also owns weeklies in the three nearby counties previously mentioned.

Gazette Newspapers
1200 Quince Orchard Boulevard
Gaithersburg, MD
(301) 948–3120
www.gazette.net
They seem to be everywhere: The Gazette Newspapers publish news and features in the communities of Aspen Hill, Bethesda, Burtonsville, Chevy Chase, Damascus, Frederick, Gaithersburg, Germantown, Kensington, Mt. Airy, Olney, Poolesville, Potomac, Prince George's County, Rockville, Silver Spring, Takoma Park, and Wheaton. The papers are published Wednesdays and distributed free to homeowners. The company also publishes the monthly *Montgomery Business Gazette* and *Tech Gazette.* You can find Gazette newspapers online.

Montgomery County Sentinel
30 Courthouse Square, Suite 405
Rockville, MD
(301) 838–0788
www.thesentinel.com
Covering community news, the *Sentinel* is the county's oldest weekly newspaper. It's published on Thursdays.

Prince George's Sentinel
9458 Lanham-Severn Road
Seabrook, MD
(301) 306–9500
www.thesentinel.com
This weekly features community news about Prince George's County. This one's also published on Thursdays.

African American Newspapers

The African Shopper
P.O. Box 2540
Washington, DC 20003
(202) 882–8840
This free monthly newspaper includes international news briefs, columns on business and legal issues, a guide to African currency, and assorted features. It's available locally and nationally at libraries, the African embassies, universities, and various stores.

The Prince George's Post
15207 Marlboro Pike
Upper Marlboro, MD
(301) 627–0900
www.pgpost.com
Founded in 1932, this weekly newspaper serves the African American community in Prince George's County. Distributed on Thursdays, free copies are available at county libraries, but most papers are circulated through subscriptions, which cost $15 annually, and are half-price for senior citizens and students.

Washington Afro-American Newspaper
1612 14th Street NW
Washington, DC
(202) 332–0080
www.afro.com
Founded in 1892, the *Washington Afro-American* is one of the oldest newspapers in the city. It's published every Thursday and contains news and features aimed at Metro Washington's black community. It is widely distributed and costs 50 cents per issue, or $28 for a yearly subscription. This paper is also online.

The Washington Informer Newspaper
3117 Martin Luther King Jr. Avenue SE
Washington, DC
(202) 561–4100
www.washingtoninformer.com
This weekly newspaper, founded in 1965, features positive news aimed at the metro area's African American residents. Active in the community, the paper sponsors the annual citywide spelling bee. It's available for 25 cents per copy, or $21 for a one-year subscription.

Business and Real Estate

Montgomery Business Gazette
1200 Quince Orchard Boulevard
Gaithersburg, MD
(301) 670–2690
www.gazette.net/business
Published weekly by the Gazette newspaper chain, this aggressive publication aims to be a must-read for Montgomery County's business community.

Mortgage Banking
1919 Pennsylvania Avenue NW
Washington, DC
(202) 557–2853
www.mortgagebankingmagazine.com
Published monthly by the Mortgage Bankers Association of America, covering the field of real-estate finance, this magazine features topical articles and provides regular departments focusing on areas like training, technology, breaking news, and noteworthy people in the field. A subscription costs $60 annually.

Washington Business Journal
1555 Wilson Boulevard, Suite 400
Arlington, VA
(703) 875–2200
www.washington.bizjournals.com/washington/
Published on Fridays, this weekly examines the local business scene with news and features and regular columns on subjects like advertising and marketing, banking and finance, health care, international business, real estate and tourism, and hospitality. It costs $2.00 per copy, or $98.00 per year.

Foreign

Asian Fortune
P.O. Box 578
Haymarket, VA 20168
(703) 753–8295
www.asianfortune.com
Written in English, this monthly newspaper adheres to the motto "Where East Meets West," targeting Asian Americans throughout the Metro Washington area. It is free and can be found at libraries, bookstores, Asian markets, and restaurants. It's also available by subscription for $30.

El Tiempo Latino
2200 Wilson Boulevard, Suite 201
Arlington, VA
(703) 527–7860
www.eltiempolatino.com
This weekly for Hispanic residents in the Washington area covers local and international news, entertainment, sports, and features in Spanish. Published on Fridays, it's free at libraries, universities, restaurants, and ethnic businesses. A yearly subscription is $40.

Lifestyles

Capitol File
1660 L Street NW, Suite 316
Washington, DC
(202) 293–8025
www.capitolfile-magazine.com
This glossy upscale magazine, a sister to New York's *Gotham*, is delivered to the mailboxes of Washington's elite. For those who dare to dream, it's also available on the newsstand. In each issue, you'll find gorgeous photo spreads of the city's most beautiful people, plus celebrity and fashion information. The magazine has profiled the city's most eligible bachelors, theater moguls, athletes, and other public figures. Ample attention is paid to the local dining, nightlife, and entertainment scene as well. An annual subscription is $34.

DC Modern Luxury
927 15th Street, 7th Floor
Washington, DC
(202) 408–5665
www.modernluxury.com
DC launched just weeks before *Capitol File,* leaving many Washingtonians wondering if both upscale glossies would survive in the marketplace. Although they use a similar formula, they've managed to survive their first two years. This publication aims to differentiate itself by focusing more on arts and culture than its competitor. Just the same, you'll find lots of society photos and artistic ads inside.

Pathways Magazine
2321-C Stewart Avenue
Silver Spring, MD
(240) 247–0393
www.pathwaysmag.com
Published quarterly, this unique journal focuses on New Age topics such as metaphysical sciences, holistic health, vegetarian cuisine, and spiritual awareness. Besides in-depth features on subjects like herbal health and becoming your own guru, the magazine features an exhaustive listing of resources and lots of intriguing advertising. It's circulated via direct mail ($10 for a two-year subscription) and is free of charge at libraries and local businesses. It is accessible online.

The Washington Blade
1408 U Street NW, 2nd Floor
Washington, DC
(202) 797–7000
www.washingtonblade.com
This free weekly for the gay and lesbian community offers comprehensive coverage of hard news and features, as well as entertainment reviews, commentaries, events calendars, and a large classified and personal ads section. The paper, now in its third decade, is distributed widely at bookstores, libraries, and businesses throughout the metropolitan area. Check it out online.

Washington Woman
4701 Sangamore Road
Bethesda, MD
(301) 229–0247
www.washingtonwoman.com
This free newspaper covers a variety of topics generally aimed at women in the 35- to 55-year-old age bracket. Regular features focus on unique events and businesses, arts programs, places to go with friends, and expert advice on topics such as fitness and home decorating. An extensive regional calendar lists scores of upcoming lectures, concerts, shows, and other activities. Published monthly, the paper is widely distributed at area libraries, bookstores, medical centers, and supermarkets.

Political

The Hill
1625 K Street NW, Suite 900
Washington, DC
(202) 628–8500
www.hillnews.com
Specializing in behind-the-scenes coverage of Congress, it's distributed free to congressional offices and is available at newsstands for $2.50 per issue or by annual subscription for $100. It is available online.

Legal Times
1730 M Street NW
Washington, DC
(202) 457–0686
www.legaltimes.biz
This weekly paper focuses on "Law and Lobbying in the Nation's Capital," and its target readership naturally consists of lawyers, lobbyists, the Supreme Court, and members of Congress. A single copy, available at newsstands, is $7.00. Annual subscriptions are $399.

The New Republic
1331 H Street NW, Suite 700
Washington, DC
(202) 508–4444
www.tnr.com
Founded in 1914, the *New Republic* is one of

the most highly respected periodicals of its type. It features an impressive array of political commentary, poetry, art news, and reviews of films and books. It's available for $3.50 an issue, and $39.95 for a yearly print subscription. The magazine's online version is $19.95 a year.

Roll Call
50 F Street NW, Suite 700
Washington, DC
(202) 824–6800
www.rollcall.com
This biweekly (published Mondays and Thursdays), founded in 1955, covers Capitol Hill in depth and is distributed to all House and Senate offices. A print subscription costs $435 annually. It is available online for $275.

Washington Monthly
1611 Connecticut Avenue NW
Washington, DC
(202) 462–0128
www.washingtonmonthly.com
Featuring commentary on current affairs, this magazine presents a monthly award honoring media stories "that demonstrate a commitment to the public interest" by chronicling such issues as successful or failing government programs. It costs $4.50 per issue, or $29.95 for a one-year subscription.

NATIONAL MEMBERSHIP MAGAZINES

Air and Space Magazine
750 9th Street NW, Suite 7100
Washington, DC
(202) 275–1230
www.airspacemag.com
Produced by the Smithsonian Institution's National Air and Space Museum, this magazine is just the ticket for flight enthusiasts. Published six times a year, *Air and Space* fea-

i Popular local blogs like www.dcist.com allow residents to chime in on local and national issues.

You don't have to be a member of the press to visit the National Press Club. If you want to rub shoulders with the national media, meet a friend for lunch at the Fourth Estate, the club's on-site fine dining restaurant. Call (202) 662–7170 or www.press.org/restaurants/fourthestatecfm.

tures news about upcoming special exhibits, a calendar of museum events, and assorted features on both historical and current topics, with many photographic illustrations. An Air and Space membership, which includes the subscription, costs $24 annually. (See the Attractions and Kidstuff chapters for museum information.)

National Geographic Magazine
1145 17th Street NW
Washington, DC
(202) 857–7000
www.nationalgeographic.com
With its incredible accounts and photography of people and places all over the world, not to mention those great maps, *National Geographic* is one of the country's oldest and most treasured periodicals. Published by the National Geographic Society, which was founded in 1888, the magazine is included in a 12-month society membership for $34. The society also publishes magazines for children, books, and maps. (See the Attractions and Kidstuff chapters for more about things to see and do at the headquarters.)

Smithsonian Magazine
750 9th Street NW, Suite 7100
Washington, DC
(202) 275–2000
www.smithsonianmag.si.edu
For Smithsonian Institution members, reading this magazine is like making an armchair visit to the museums. Each monthly issue contains a variety of features, vivid photographs, intriguing profiles of Smithsonian exhibits, and listings of upcoming events. (See the Arts, Attractions, and Kidstuff chapters for

museum information.) The subscription cost is $29 yearly.

Regional Publications

Washington Flyer Magazine
1707 L Street NW, Suite 800
Washington, DC
(202) 331–9393
www.fly2dc.com
This glossy bimonthly owned by the Metropolitan Washington Airport Authority covers a range of business and travel topics pertinent to air travelers—locals and visitors alike. With complimentary distribution at Ronald Reagan National and Washington Dulles International Airports, the magazine occupies a unique market niche with impressive demographics and a high pass-along rate.

Washingtonian
1828 L Street NW
Washington, DC
(202) 296–3600
www.washingtonian.com
The area's true city magazine—although its readership is predominantly suburban—is a slick, thick monthly known for its "best of" lists, dining/shopping guides, maps of stars' homes, interesting features and personality profiles, and the occasional hard-hitting investigative piece. High paid-circulation numbers, a well-heeled readership, and a large staff have helped *Washingtonian* maintain its enviable position in the local magazine market. A one-year subscription is $29.95.

Washington Jewish Week
1500 East Jefferson Street
Rockville, MD
(301) 230–2222
www.washingtonjewishweek.com
Washington Jewish Week, founded in 1965, is chock-full of local, national, and international news and features aimed at Metro Washington's ever-growing Jewish community. Published on Thursdays, each issue features an extensive calendar of events scheduled by area synagogues, Jewish community centers,

museums, and organizations and regular departments devoted to sports, seniors, singles, food, travel, real estate, and social announcements. In July the paper publishes the *Guide to Jewish Life in Washington,* a comprehensive sourcebook of more than 200 pages. Other special editions focus on such topics as weddings, bar and bat mitzvahs, and party planning. The paper costs $1.00 per copy or $44.00 per yearly subscription.

RADIO

Of course, like any major city, Washington, D.C. also has its share of local radio stations that broadcast in a range of formats. Turn on your car radio and push the "scan" button. In a matter of seconds you will lock on one of these stations.

National Public Radio
635 Massachusetts Avenue NW
Washington, DC
(202) 513–2000
www.npr.org
Washington, D.C.'s role as a media capital extends beyond print media. The District is also home base for public radio giant NPR, a membership organization of U.S. public radio stations. As such, it's here that many of your favorite NPR programs are developed and recorded, then distributed to its member networks. In 2005 a Harris poll revealed that NPR was the nation's most trusted news source.

Voice of America Radio Network
330 Independence Avenue SW
Washington, DC
(202) 203–4959
www.voanews.com
News leaves the District and travels to all corners of the world through the Voice of America (VOA), the federal government's official international radio and television broadcasting service. You can tour the VOA's headquarters and watch as content is developed and disseminated in dozens of languages to sta-

i Tune in to the *D.C. Politics Program* with Mark Plotkin for a lively radio call-in show that covers the latest scandals and issues facing our nation's capital. It's broadcast on Washington Post Radio at 1500 AM and 107.7 FM every Friday from 10:00 to 11:00 A.M.

tions around the globe. Visit the Web site for details.

XM Satellite Radio
1500 Eckington Place NE
Washington, DC
(202) 380–4000
www.xmradio.com
One of two vying satellite radio platforms, XM was founded in 1988 and is headquartered in Northeast D.C. Subscribers purchase radio receivers and pay a $12.95 monthly fee for commercial-free access to 73 different music channels, 39 news and talk channels, 21 regional traffic and weather channels, and 23 sports channels. Most of the network's stations are also broadcast through the Internet, and Web-only subscriptions are also available.

Adult Contemporary/Soft Adult Contemporary Stations
WASH 97.1 FM
WRQX 107.3 FM

Classical
WETA 90.9 FM (also information/National Public Radio)

Country Stations
WFRE 99.9 FM
WMZQ 98.7 FM
WKIK 1560 AM

Jazz Stations
WJZW 105.9 FM
WPFW 89.3 FM (also Pacifica radio)

News/Talk/Sports/Information Stations
WAMU 88.5 FM (National Public Radio; also, folk and bluegrass music)
WCSP 90.1 FM (C-SPAN)
WFMD 930 AM
WJFK 106.7 FM
WMAL 630 AM
WMET 1160 AM
WTEM 980 AM
WTNT 570 AM (all talk)
WTOP 103.5 FM, 103.9 FM
WTWP 1500 AM, 107.7 FM, 820 AM
WWRC 1260 AM

Oldies and Classic Rock Stations
WARW 94.7 FM
WBIG 100.3 FM

Religious/Inspirational/Gospel Stations
WAVA 780 AM and 105.1 FM
WCTN 950 AM
WFAX 1220 AM
WGTS 91.9 FM
WPGC 1580 AM
WYCB 1340 AM
WWGB 1030 AM

Rock Stations
WWDC 101.1 FM

Soul/Talk Station
WOL 1450 AM

Top 40/Contemporary Hits Stations
WIHT 99.5 FM

Urban Adult Contemporary Stations
WHUR 96.3 FM
WKYS 93.9 FM
WMMJ 102.3 FM
WPGC 95.5 FM

Foreign Language/Ethnic Stations
WDCT 1310 AM (Korean)
WILC 900 AM (Spanish)
WKDV 1460 AM (Spanish)
WPWC 1480 AM (Spanish)
WUST 1120 AM (multicultural)
WZHF 1390 AM (Spanish)

TELEVISION

As you'd expect in this high-profile city, news coverage is a big deal at the major networks' local affiliates. The stations are highly competitive, whether trying to be first to break a story or attempting to put together the most comprehensive "team coverage" of an event. You'll find newscasts first thing in the morning, at noon, late afternoon, and twice in the evening—and around-the-clock on cable's News Channel 8.

Virtually anything a television viewer wants is available in Metro Washington. Along with all the major networks, numerous independent stations and literally hundreds of cable channels are at your fingertips.

Local TV Stations
Following are Washington's major local TV stations and their network affiliates:

WRC Channel 4 (NBC)
WTTG Channel 5 (Fox)
WJLA Channel 7 (ABC)
WUSA Channel 9 (CBS)
WDCA Channel 20 (UPN)
WMPT Channel 22 (PBS)
WETA Channel 26 (PBS)
WHMM Channel 32 (PBS)
WBDC Channel 50 (CW)

Others
WNVT Channel 53 (PBS)
WNVC Channel 56 (PBS)

Baltimore and Hagerstown TV
These stations are available to many residents of Metro Washington:

WMAR Channel 2 (ABC)
WBAL Channel 11 (NBC)
WJZ Channel 13 (CBS)
WHAG Channel 25 (NBC)
WBFF Channel 45 (Fox)
WNUV Channel 54 (CW)
WMPB Channel 67 (PBS)

Cable TV

Comcast is the Washington area's largest provider of cable services, but its prices and offerings differ slightly depending on which jurisdiction you live in. The most basic service costs about $20 a month; regular cable with about 65 channels is about $48 a month; and digital cable, with 150 or so channels, is around $65.

Cox Communications is the rare exception, serving Fairfax County's more than 250,000 cable subscribers.

Cable offerings for local residents run the gamut, from local public access channels that offer community and civic information to the major players such as premium movie channels (HBO, Showtime, Disney, etc.), the locally owned Black Entertainment Television (BET), CNN, Discovery, MTV, ESPN, TNT, USA Network, and Chicago and New York "super stations." Let's not forget C-SPAN (Cable-Satellite Public Affairs Network) and C-SPAN II, which offer live coverage of the U.S. House of Representatives and U.S. Senate, respectively, and related political programming; for some strange reason these channels seem especially popular around here.

The following companies provide cable TV service to residents of Metro Washington.

Washington, D.C.

Comcast
900 Michigan Avenue NE
Washington, DC
(202) 832–2001
www.comcast.com

Comcast is the dominant cable TV company in the Washington region. Over the last few years, it has gobbled up many smaller providers. It also offers Internet and phone services in some areas. However, there is no one main Comcast office for the region; each area has its own lineup of channels and costs. In general, basic service, with just the networks and several municipal channels, is about $20, including tax. Add $30 if you want such channels as Bravo, the Weather Channel, MTV, and about 30 others. Digital cable offers even more choices, like Toon Disney and Women's Entertainment.

Northern Virginia

Comcast
2707 Wilson Boulevard
Arlington, VA
(703) 841–7700

508D South Van Dorn Street
Alexandria, VA
(703) 823–3000

4391 Dale Boulevard
Woodbridge, VA
(703) 730–2225
www.comcast.com
See listing under Washington, D.C.

Cox Communications
14650 Old Lee Road
Chantilly, VA
(703) 378–8422
www.cox.com

The company has the capacity for more than 100 channels, and basic full service starts at approximately $45. Digital rates vary depending on package selected, from $65 to more than $100.

RCN
196 Van Buren Street, Suite 300
Herndon, VA
(800) RING–RCN
www.rcn.com

Formerly known as Starpower, this smaller player in the cable market has made a run at Comcast by offering premium cable at a lower cost. Rates are generally $5.00 to $20.00 less a month, but the service area is limited. Like its competitors, RCN offers greater discounts when cable, Internet, and phone services are bundled together.

ℹ️ Check out your cable TV's public access station for an eclectic array of programming produced by and starring local citizens.

Suburban Maryland

Comcast
20 West Gude Drive
Rockville, MD
(301) 424–4400

9609 Annapolis Road
Lanham, MD
(301) 731–4260
www.comcast.com
See listing under Washington, D.C.

RCN
10000 Derekwood Lane
Lanham, MD
(800) RING–RCN
See listing under Northern Virginia.

INDEX

A

Aangan Indian Restaurant, 120
AARP, 420–21
Abbey, 339
Abraham Lincoln *Emancipation Group
    Statue,* 210
Abraham Lincoln's Birthday, 169
Acadiana, 77
Acajutla Mexican Restaurant, 121
accommodations, 50–75
    bed and breakfasts, 72–75
    budget accommodations, 69–71
    extended-stay hotels and inns, 51–57
    full-service hotels, 57–69
    hostels/university inns, 71–72
Adam's Inn, 72
Adams Morgan, 354
Adams Morgan Day, 180
Adas Israel, 434
ADC Map & Travel Center, 150
Admiral Fell Inn, 337
adult contemporary/soft adult contemporary
    radio, 451
Adventure Schools Rock Climbing, 302
Adventure Theatre, 270
African American Civil War Memorial, 210
African American newspapers, 447
African Methodist Episcopal/Second Episcopal
    District Headquarters, 438
African restaurants, 85, 87
African Shopper, The, 447
AIDS Counseling and Testing Hotline, 392
Air and Space Magazine, 449–50
airports, 45–49
Aladdin's Lamp Children's Books & Other
    Treasures, 264
Alcoholics Anonymous Area Headquarters,
    392
Alexander-Withrow, 326
Alexandria, Virginia
    area overview, 11–13

budget accommodations, 70
child care, 370
extended-stay hotels and inns, 55
full-service hotels, 66–67
hospitals, 380–81
neighborhoods and homes, 357
Alexandria Antiques Show, 184
Alexandria Black History Museum, 211
Alexandria Colonial Tours, 219
Alexandria Convention & Visitors
    Association, 17
Alexandria Department of Recreation, Parks
    and Cultural Activities, 311, 424
Alexandria Economic Development Partner-
    ship Inc., 19
Alexandria Office of Aging and Adult
    Services, 418
Alexandria Public Schools, 395
Alexandria Scottish Christmas Walk, 186
Alexandria Transit Company's DASH, 42
Algonkian Regional Park, 293
All Fired Up, 265–66
Alliance Française de Washington, 349
Allie's Bethesda Marriott, 137
All Souls Unitarian Church, 435
All the Right Moves, 421
Almanac Newspapers, 446
alternative health care, 390–91
Al Tiramisu, 94
AMC Loews Shirlington 7, 246
AMC Loews Uptown Theatre, 245
American/Continental restaurants
    Northern Virginia, 96–101
    Suburban Maryland, 111–14
    Washington, D.C., 76–85
American Express Travel Service, 345
American Film Institute Silver Theatre and
    Cultural Center, 246–47
American Inn of Bethesda, 71
American Running Association, 308
American University, 280–81, 408

American University Park, 356

Amphora Restaurant, 96

Amphora's Diner Deluxe, 96

Amtrak, 43–44

amusement parks, 299–300

amusements, 267–69

Anacostia, 356

Anacostia Community Museum, 202

Anacostia Community Services Center, 418

Andalucia, 121

Andre Chreky, 161

Andrews Air Force Base Open House, 174

Anecdotal History Tours, 219

Anita's, 106–7

Annandale, Virginia, 358

Annapolis, Maryland, 339–41

Annapolis and Anne Arundel County Conference and Visitors Bureau, 17

Anne Arundel County, Maryland
  area overview, 16
  hospitals, 384–85

Anne Arundel County Office of Economic Development, 19

Anne Arundel Medical Center, 384–85

annual events, 167–87
  Northern Virginia, 169–70, 171, 172–73, 174, 175–77, 178, 179, 180–81, 183–84, 186–87
  Suburban Maryland, 169, 171, 174, 179, 181–82, 184, 187
  Washington, D.C., 167–69, 170–71, 172, 173–74, 174–75, 178, 180, 182–83, 186

Annual Lombardi Gala, 182–83

Annual Quilt Show, 171

Annual Soap Box Derby, 178

Antietam National Battlefield Park, 328

Antietam Overlook Farm, 329

Antique Car Show, 175

antiques districts, 149–50

Apartment Zero, 154

Apex, 123

Appalachian Trail, 323

Archbishop Carroll High School, 399

Archdiocese of Washington, 440

Arc of Montgomery County Family, Infant, and Child-Care Center, The, 372

area agencies on aging, 417–20

area overview, 3–19
  contacts, 18–19
  convention and tourist bureaus, 17
  crime, 10
  economic development authorities, 18–19
  jobs, 9–10
  Northern Virginia, 11–14
  readings and resources, 18–19
  September 11 impact, 8–9
  statistics, 4–5
  Suburban Maryland, 14–18
  today, 10–11
  work force, 7–9

Arena Stage, 230

Arlington, Virginia
  budget accommodations, 70
  extended-stay hotels and inns, 55

Arlington Agency on Aging, 418–19

Arlington Arts Center, 243

Arlington Cinema 'n' Drafthouse, 246

Arlington Convention and Visitors Service, 17

Arlington County, Virginia
  area overview, 11–13
  child care, 371
  full-service hotels, 67–68
  hospitals, 381
  neighborhoods and homes, 357–58

Arlington County Commuter Assistance Program, 44

Arlington County Department of Parks, Recreation and Community Resources, 311, 424

Arlington County Economic Development, 19

Arlington County Fair, 179

Arlington County Public Schools, 395–96

Arlington National Cemetery, 211–12

Aroma, 129

Arthur M. Sackler Gallery, 198, 234, 249–50

Artie's, 96–97

Artisans, The, 163

arts, 221–47
  cinema, 245–47
  galleries, 242–45
  literary arts, 247
  major galleries and museums, 234–42
  outdoor stages, 228–30
  performing arts venues, 221–28

theater, 230–34
tickets, 247
Arts and Industries Building, 198
Arundel Mills, 148
Ash Lawn-Highland, 320
Asian Fortune, 448
Asia Nora, 87–88
Asian restaurants
Northern Virginia, 101–4
Suburban Maryland, 114–17
Washington, D.C., 87–89
Assateague Island National Seashore,
334–35, 338
Association of American Foreign Service
Worldwide, 349
attractions, 189–220
Northern Virginia, 211–16
Suburban Maryland, 216–18
tour operators, 218–20
Washington, D.C., 189–211
Audubon Naturalist Society of the Central
Atlantic States Inc., 301
Audubon Society of Northern Virginia, 301
AuPairCare, 374
Au Pair in America, 374
au pairs, 374
AuPair U.S.A. InterExchange, 374
Austin Grill Springfield, 107–8
Avalon Theatre, 245

B

B. J. Pumpernickel's New York Style Deli &
Diner, 261
Bacchus, 120–21
Backstage Inc.: The Performing Arts Store, 163
Bailiwick Inn, 73–74
ballooning, 300
Balloons Unlimited, 300
Ball's Bluff Regional Park, 322
Ballston, Virginia, 358
Ballston Common Mall, 144
Baltimore, Maryland
day trips and weekend getaways, 336–37
television stations, 452
Baltimore Orioles, 277–78
Baltimore/Washington International Thurgood
Marshall Airport, 46

Baltimore Washington Medical Center, 385
Baltimore Yearly Meeting of the Religious
Society of Friends (Quakers), 439
Bangkok 54, 101
Bang Salon and Spa, 162
BAPA's Imagination Stage, 270–71
Barboursville Vineyards, 320
Barnaby Woods, 356
Barney Neighborhood House Senior Citizen
Satellite Center, 418
baseball, 277–80
major league, 277–78
minor leagues, 279–80
Basilica of the National Shrine of the Immacu-
late Conception, 133, 209
Basin St. Lounge, 132
basketball, 280–81, 283
collegiate, 280–81, 283
professional, 280
Battered Women's Shelter Hotline, 392
Bavarian Inn and Lodge, 328
Beacon Hotel and Corporate Quarters, 51
Beall-Dawson House and the Stonestreet
Museum of 19th-Century Medicine, 216
beauty spas, 161–62
bed and breakfasts, 72–75
Northern Virginia, 73–74
Suburban Maryland, 74–75
Washington, D.C., 72–73
Bed & Breakfast Accommodations, Ltd., 72
Bed & Breakfast Association of Virginia, 73
Bee-won Secret Garden, 102
Beltway (I-495), 34–36
Beltway Plaza Mall, 146–47
Benjarong, 114–15
Ben's Chili Bowl, 77
Berkeley Springs Spa and Inn, 327
Berlitz Language Centers, 345
Bertucci's Brick Oven Pizzeria, 261
Best Western Chincoteague Island, 335
Best Western Georgetown Hotel and
Suites, 51
Bethany Beach, Delaware, 338
Bethesda, Maryland
budget accommodations, 71
neighborhoods and homes, 362
Bethesda Crab House, 111
Bethesda Marriott, 68

Bethesda Senior Source, 426
Beverly Hills, 357
bicycling, 300–301
Bike the Sites Inc., 219, 300
Birchmere, The, 132
bird watching, 301
Birreria Paradiso, 126
Bistrot du Coin, 90
Black Cat, 123
Black Family Reunion, 180
Black Hill Regional Park, 297
Black's Bar & Kitchen, 111
Blair Mansion Restaurant, 139
Blue Duck Tavern, 77
Bluemont, Virginia, 361
Blue Ridge Mountains, 323–27
Blue Rock Inn, 324
Blues Alley, 123
B'nai B'rith Klutznick National Jewish
    Museum, 203
Boar's Head Inn, 320
Body Wise, 423
Bohrer Park at Summit Hall Farm, 297
Bombay Bistro, 110, 121
Bombay Club, 93
Book Nook, 153
bookstores, 150–53, 263–65
Borders Books & Music, 263–64
Bourbon, 129–30
Bowie, Maryland, 362
Bowie Baysox, 279
Bowie-Blade News, 446
Bowie State University, 413
Bowl America, 301
bowling, 301–2
Brassene Les Halles Bastille Day, 178
Brass Knob, The, 164
Brickskeller, The, 126
bridges, 35–36
Bridge Street Books, 150–51
Brightwood Park, 356
Brookland, 356
Buddy's Crabs & Ribs, 340
budget accommodations, 69–71
Buffalo Billiards, 129
Bukom Cafe, 123–24
Bullis School, The, 406
Bull Run Regional Park, 293–94

Bureau of Engraving and Printing, 157, 193
Burgundy Farm Country Day School, 402
Burke Lake Golf Center, 304
Burke Lake Park, 272, 294
Bus, The, 43
Busara, 102
Busboys and Poets, 130
business and real estate newspapers, 447
bus systems, 41–43
Butlers Orchard, 262–63

C

C. J. Ferrari's, 119
Cabin John Regional Park, 274, 297–98
cable TV, 453–54
Cacapon State Park, 328
Cactus Cantina, 91–92
Cafe Atlantico, 92
Cafe Berlin, 91
Cafe Saint-Ex, 77, 126
California Tortilla, 92
Calvert Cliffs State Park, 336
Cambridge, Maryland, 333
Cameron Run Regional Park, 294
Campagna Center, The, 422
Camp Hoover, 323
Canaan Valley, 331
Canaan Valley State Park, 327
Cape May, New Jersey, 339
Capital Beltway (I-495), 34–36
Capital Grille, 79
Capital Hilton Hotel, 57
Capitals, 286–87
Capitol Christian Academy, 406
Capitol College, 413–14
Capitol File, 448
Capitol Hill, 356
Capitol Hill Day School, 399–400
Capitol Hill Suites, 51–52
Capitol River Cruises, 219
Carlyle Grand Cafe, 97
Carlyle House, 212
Carlyle Suites Hotel, 52
Carter Barron Amphitheatre in Rock Creek
    Park, 228
Cascade Cafe/Espresso Bar, 259
Cascade Inn, 330

Casemate Museum, 338
Cashion's Eat Place, 79
Castle, The, 198
Cathedral Medieval Workshop, 266
Catholic Diocese of Arlington, 440
Catholic University of America, The, 409
Catholic worship resources, 440
Catoctin Mountain Park, 329
Caton Merchant House, 428
Ceiba, 92
Celadon Spa, 161
Celebrate Fairfax! Festival, 175–76
Central American Resource Center, 349
Centreville, Virginia, 360
Centreville Mini Golf & Games, 267
Cesco, 118
Chadwicks, 79–80, 134
Channel Inn Hotel, 57
Chantilly, Virginia, 360
Chapters: A Literary Bookstore, 151
Charles County, Maryland, 16–18
Charles E. Smith Jewish Day School, 406
Charter House, 430
Cheat River, 331
Chesapeake Bay Bridge-Tunnel, 217
Chesapeake Bay Center, 338
Chesapeake Maritime Museum, 333
Chesapeake & Ohio Canal National Historical
    Park, 289
chess, 302
Chestertown, Maryland, 332
Chevy Chase, Maryland, 362
Chevy Chase neighborhood (Washington,
    D.C.), 356
Chi-Cha Lounge, 130
Chick Hall's Surf Club, 137
Chief Ike's Mambo Room, 124
Child and Family Services, 371
child care, 368–74
    au pairs, 374
    cost, 368–69
    nannies, 373–74
    Northern Virginia, 370–72
    options, 369–70
    organizations, 373
    Suburban Maryland, 372–73
    aWashington, D.C., 370
Child Care Assistance and Referral, 371

Child Care Information Services, 370
Child Care Training Programs, 371
children. See kidstuff
Children's Museum of Rose Hill Manor
    Park, 330
Children's National Medical Center, 376–77
Child Resource Center, Locate Child Care, 373
China Bistro/Mama's Dumplings, 115
Chinese Culture and Community Service
    Center, 351
Chinese New Year Parade, 167
Ching Ching Cha, 88
Chloe Restaurant Lounge, 124
Chocolate Moose, 164
Choice Nanny, A, 373–74
Christ Church, 212, 435
Christian Church Capital Area (Disciples of
    Christ), 439
Christmas Attic, The, 164
Christmas Lights Parade, 187
Chrysler Museum, 338
Churchill Hotel, The, 57
Church of the Brethren, Mid-Atlantic
    District, 439
Church of the Holy City, 435
Chutzpah Deli, 97
cigar bars, 130–31
cinema, 245–47
Cinema Arts Theatre, 246
Circulator, 41
City of Fairfax CUE Bus Service, 42
City of Fairfax Parks and Recreation, 311
City of Fairfax Senior Center, 424
City of Laurel Department of Parks and Recre-
    ation, 314
City of Manassas Department of Recreation
    and Parks, 311
City of Manassas Park Department of Parks
    Recreation, 311
City of Rockville Recreation and Parks Depart-
    ment, 314
CityZen, 80
civil rights, 27
Civil War
    history, 23–25
    sites, 210–11
Civil War Camp Day, 176
Clarendon, Virginia, 358

Clarendon Ballroom, 132
classical radio, 451
Classic Residence by Hyatt, 429–30
classic rock radio, 452
Classika Theatre, 269–70
Claude Moore Colonial Farm at Turkey Run, The, 256
Clay Cafe Studios, 266
Cleveland Park, 354
Clifton, Virginia, 360
Clifton-The Country Inn, 320
climbing, 302–3
clothing, 159–60
Clyde's, 97, 134, 262
Clyde's of Chevy Chase, 111
Clyde's of Georgetown, 80
Coldwell Banker Deep Creek Realty, 331
Coldwell Banker Stevens Realtors, 364–65
Collection at Chevy Chase, The, 147
College Park, Maryland, 362
College Park Airport, 49
College Park Aviation Museum, 217
colleges and universities, 408–15
    basketball, 280–81, 283
    Northern Virginia, 412–13
    Suburban Maryland, 413–15
    Washington, D.C., 408–12
Collington Episcopal Life Care Community Inc., 430
colonial churches, 435, 437–38
colonial roots day trips and weekend getaways, 317–19
Colonial Williamsburg, 317
Columbia-Dominion Hospital, 381
Columbia-Fairfax Surgical Center, 381–82
Columbia Union College, 414
Colvin Run Mill Historic Site, 212, 272–73
Comcast, 453, 454
comedy clubs, 131, 136
ComedySportz, 270
Comedy Spot, The, 136
Comfort Inn and Suites College Park, 56–57
"Commandant's Own, The," 173, 174
community and senior centers, 423–27
    Northern Virginia, 424–26
    Suburban Maryland, 426–27
    Washington, D.C., 423–24
community colleges, 415–16

community newspapers, 444–46
Commuter Connections, 45
Congressional Cemetery, 193
Congressional Schools of Virginia, The, 402–3
Connection Publishing, Inc., 445
Consignment Galleries, 160
contemporary hits radio, 452
Continental, 134
convention and tourist bureaus, 17
Conyers House, 324
Coolfont Resort, 327–28
Corcoran College of Art and Design, 409
Corcoran Gallery of Art, 235, 252
Cordell Collection, The, 160
Country Club Hills, Virginia, 358
Country Curtains Retail Shop, 154
country radio, 451
Courtyard by Marriott Silver Spring, 68
Cox Communications, 453
Cox Farms, 257, 262
Crab Claw, 333
crafts, 265–67
Creative Partners Gallery, 244
Crestwood, 356
crime, 10
Crisfield Seafood Restaurant, 112
Crofton News Crier, 446
Crystal City, Virginia, 358
Crystal City Shops, The, 144
Cultural Care Au Pair, 374
Cunningham Falls State Park, 329
currency exchange, 345
Current Newspapers, The, 444

D

daily newspapers, 442–44
Damascus, Maryland, 362
dancing, 303. See also music and dancing, live
Daniel's Salon, 162
Danker Furniture, 154
DAR Constitution Hall, 222
DAR Museum, 203, 252
DASH, 42
Dave & Buster's, 137–38
David Craig, 112
Days Inn Connecticut Avenue, 69
Days Inn Silver Spring, 71

day trips and weekend getaways, 317–41
    Maryland, 328–41
    Virginia, 317–27
    West Virginia, 327–28
D.C. Arts Center, 242
D.C. Baptist Convention, 439
D.C. Caribbean Carnival, 174–75
D.C. Digs, 52
D.C. Ducks, 219
D.C. GuestHouse, 72–73
D.C. Modern Luxury, 448
D.C. Office of the Deputy Mayor for Planning
    and Economic Development, 18
D.C. Spring Antiques Fair, 170
D.C. United, 287
Dean & DeLuca Cafe, 80
Decatur House Museum, 203
Deep Creek Lake, 331
Degrees, 130
Del Ray, 357
DeMatha Catholic High School, 406–7
Department of Family Services, 371, 372
Department of Health-Licensing, Regulation,
    and Administration, 370
Department of Social Services/Child Care
    Options, 372
Department of State, 193–94
Dewey Beach, Delaware, 339
Di Giovanni's Dock of the Bay, 336
dinner theaters, 136, 139
Discovery Creek Children's Museum of
    Washington, 255
Discovery Theater, 269
Distinctive Bookbinding, 164
District of Columbia Department of Parks and
    Recreation, 310, 423
District of Columbia Department of Trans-
    portation, 38
District of Columbia Jewish Community Center,
    315, 423–24
District of Columbia Office on Aging, 417–18
District of Columbia Public Schools, 394–95
Doctors Community Hospital, 387
Dolly Sods Wilderness Area, 327
Domestic Violence Hotline, 392
Donald W. Reynolds Center for American Art
    and Portraiture, 157, 202
Doubletree Bethesda, 68

Dr. Dremo's Taphouse, 134–35
Dubliner Pub, 124
Duke Ellington Jazz Festival, 183
Dukem Ethiopian Market, 85, 87
Dulles Greenway, 37
Dulles Toll Road, 36–37
Dulles Town Center, 144
Dumbarton Oaks, 203–4
Dupont at The Circle, The, 73
Dupont Circle, 354
Dupont Current, 444
Dupont-Kalorama Museum Walk Day, 175

E

Easter Sunrise Service, 172–73
Easton, Maryland, 333
East Potomac Park Golf Course and Driving
    Range, 303–4
Econo Lodge Metro, 70
economic development authorities, 18–19
Edgar Allan Poe Museum, 321
education, 394–416
    colleges and universities, 408–15
    community colleges, 415–16
    private schools, 399–407
    public schools, 394–99
Eighteenth Street Lounge, 127
Eldercare Locator, 419
Elder Crafters of Alexandria Inc., 422
El Guajillo, 107
Elizabeth Arden Red Door Salon & Spa, 161
Elizabeth Furnace Recreation Area, 326
El Pollo Rico, 107
El Tiempo Latino, 448
embassies, 208, 344–45, 346
Embassy Suites Hotel Downtown, 52
Embassy Suites/Tysons Corner, 56
emergency numbers, 392
Emmitsburg, Maryland, 329
Encore Resale Dress Shop, 159
Enquirer-Gazette, The, 446
Episcopal Diocese of Washington, 439
Episcopal High School in Virginia, 403
Equity Office Skating Pavilion, 306
Etete, 87
ethnic neighborhoods, 347
ethnic radio, 452

EurAupair, 374
Europa Lounge, 138
Evening Star Café, 97–98
Executive Club Suites, The, 55

F

Fahrney's Pens Inc., 164
Fairfax, Virginia
    child care, 371
    neighborhoods and homes, 360
Fairfax Christian School, 403
Fairfax Connector, 42
Fairfax County, Virginia
    area overview, 11
    bed and breakfasts, 73–74
    child care, 371
    extended-stay hotels and inns, 56
    full-service hotels, 64–66
    hospitals, 381–83
    neighborhoods and homes, 358–60
Fairfax County Area Agency on Aging, 419
Fairfax County Community and Recreation
    Services, 311–12, 425
Fairfax County Economic Development Author-
    ity, 19
Fairfax County Park Authority, 312, 425
Fairfax County Parkway, 37
Fairfax County Public Schools, 396–97
Fairfax County Tourism & Convention Bureau,
    17
Fairfax CUE Bus Service, 42
Fairfax Hunt, The, 285
Fairfax Ice Arena, 306
Fairfax Parks and Recreation, 311
Fairfax Senior Center, 424
Fairfax Station, Virginia, 360
Fairfax Women's Soccer Association, 308
Fairmont Washington, The, 57
Fair Oaks Mall, 144–45
Fall for the Book, 180–81
Falls Church, Virginia
    budget accommodations, 70
    child care, 371–72
    neighborhoods and homes, 358
Falls Church (Episcopal church), 438
Falls Church News-Press, 445

Falls Church Recreation and Parks,
    312–13, 425
Family and Child Services of Washington
    D.C. Inc., 421
Fanatics, 129
farms, 255–57, 262–63
Fashion Centre at Pentagon City, 145
Fast Eddie's Billiards Cafe, 135
Fat Tuesday's, 132
Fauquier County, Virginia, 13–14
Federal Bureau of Investigation, 194
federal sites, 193–97
Felix and the Spy Lounge, 127
Ferry Farm, 322
Festival of Lights, 187, 437
film, 245–47
Filmfest D.C., 172, 246
Fireplace, The, 124
First Baptist Church, 435
First Centrum Senior Communities, 428
First Centrum Senior Communities Bay
    Forest, 430
First Friday Gallery, 243
Fish Market, 98, 132
Five, 127
Flanagan's Harp & Fiddle, 137
Flashpoint, 242
Fleet Feet, 164–65
Flint Hill School, 403–4
Fly Lounge, 127
Foggy Bottom, 354
Foggy Bottom Current, 444
Folger Shakespeare Library, The, 230–31
football, 283–84
Ford's Theatre, 210–11, 222, 224–25
foreign-language/ethnic radio, 452
foreign newspapers, 448
Forest Hills, 356
Fort Frederick State Park, 329
Fort Ward Museum and Historic Site, 212–13
Foundry Gallery, 242
Four Seasons Hotel, 57–58
Foxcroft School, 404
Foxhall Road, 354
Franciscan Monastery, 209–10
Franklin Delano Roosevelt Memorial, 189–90
Franklins, 261
Franz Bader Bookstore, 151

Frederick, Maryland, 330
Frederick County, Maryland, 16–18
Frederick Douglass National Historic Site, 211
Frederick Keys, 279–80
Frederick's 4th—An Independence Day
    Celebration!, 179
Freer Gallery of Art, 198, 235, 249–50
French restaurants
    Northern Virginia, 104–6
    Suburban Maryland, 117–18
    Washington, D.C., 90–91
Friendship Terrace, 428
Friends Meeting House, 434
Fuddruckers, 262
Full Kee, 88
furniture and home decorating, 153–57, 160

G

Gables, 337
Gadsby's Tavern Museum, 213
Gaithersburg, Maryland
    budget accommodations, 71
    neighborhoods and homes, 362
GALA Hispanic Theatre, 231
Galaxy Hut, 132–33
Galileo, 94
Gallaudet University, 409
galleries, 242–45
    Northern Virginia, 243–44
    Suburban Maryland, 244–45
    Washington, D.C., 234–43
Gardens Ice House, The, 306–7
Gathland State Park, 329
Gay and Lesbian Help Line, 392
Gazette Newspapers, 446
Generous George's Positive Pizza and
    Pasta, 108
George Mason University, 281, 412
George Mason University Bookstore, 153
George Mason University Center for the
    Arts, 227
Georgetown, 208–9, 354
Georgetown Current, 444
Georgetowner Newspaper, The, 444
Georgetown Garden Day, 173
Georgetown Inn, The, 58
Georgetown Preparatory School, 407

Georgetown Suites, 52
Georgetown University, 281, 409–10
Georgetown University Conference Center, 71
Georgetown University Hospital, 377–78
Georgetown Visitation Preparatory
    School, 400
Georgette Klinger, 161–62
George Washington Masonic National Memo-
    rial, 213–14
George Washington Memorial Parkway, 37
George Washington Memorial Parkway Turkey
    Run Park, 294
George Washington's Birthday Parade, 169–70
George Washington's Grist Mill, 294
George Washington University, The, 281,
    283, 410
George Washington University Inn, 71
George Washington University Medical Center,
    The, 377
George Washington University's Lisner
    Auditorium, 222–23
George Washington University Virginia
    Campus, The, 412
Georgia Brown's, 80
Geppetto's, 119
German restaurants, 91
Germantown, Maryland, 362
Gesher Jewish Day School of Northern
    Virginia, 404
Glass Gallery, The, 244
Glen Echo Park, 245, 274, 303
Glen Echo Spanish Ballroom, 138
Glen Forest, 430
Gloucester, Virginia, 337
Glover Books & Music, 151
Glover Park, 354
GMC Capital Home & Garden Show, 170
Go Au Pair, 374
Goddard Space Flight Center, 217
Goethe Institut, 349
golf, 303–5
Go Mama Go!, 154
Gonzaga College High School, 400
gospel radio, 452
Grace Reformed Church, 133
Grand Hyatt Washington, The, 58
Graydon Manor, 388–89
Gray Line Worldwide, 219

Greater Reston Arts Center, The (GRACE), 243
Greater Southeast Community Hospital, 378
Greater Washington Board of Trade Office
    of Research, Policy, and Transportation,
    The, 18
Greater Washington Urban League, Aging
    Division, 418
Great Falls, Virginia, 358
Great Falls Park, 288, 295, 312–13
Great Falls Tavern, 298
Greenbelt, Maryland, 362
Greenbelt Marriott Hotel, 69
Greenbelt Park, 298
Greenbelt Recreation Department, 315, 426
Greenbrier Resort, 327
Greenbrier State Park, 329
Green Hedges School, 404
Green Papaya, 115
Green Spring Gardens Park, 295
Greenspring Village, 428
Greyhound Bus Lines, 42
Gua-Rapo, 135
Guide to Retirement Living, 420
Gunston Hall Plantation, 214
Gwynn, Virginia, 337

H

Haad Thai, 88
Hagerstown Speedway, 287
Hagerstown Suns, The, 280
Hagerstown television stations, 452
hair salons, 162–63
Hampton Roads, Virginia, 337–38
Hangar Club, The, 138
hang gliding, 305–6
Hard Rock Cafe, 259
Hard Times Cafe, 98, 112
Hardwood Artisans, The, 154–55
Harpers Ferry, West Virginia, 328
Harrison's Chesapeake House, 333
Hawthorn Suites Alexandria, 70
Hay-Adams Hotel, The, 58
Head Start Programs, 371
health care, 375–93
    alternative health care, 390–91
    emergency numbers, 392
    hospitals, 376–89

    nursing homes, 390
    physician referrals, 376
    psychiatric hospitals, 388–89
    walk-in clinics, 391–93
Heart in Hand, 98
Hee Been, 102–3
Helix Lounge, 127–28
Hemphill Fine Arts, 242–43
Henley Park Hotel, The, 58
heritage festivals, 349
Heritage House, 324
Hermitage Inn, 105
Herndon, Virginia, 360
Herndon Parks and Recreation, 313, 425
Hill, The, 449
Hill Rag, 444
Hillwood Museum and Gardens, 157, 204
Hilton Alexandria Old Town, 66
Hilton McLean at Tysons Corner, 64–65
Hilton Washington Embassy Row, 58
Hirshhorn Museum and Sculpture Garden,
    157, 198, 235–36, 250
Hispanic/Caribbean/Tex-Mex restaurants
Northern Virginia, 106–8
    Suburban Maryland, 121
    Washington, D.C., 91–93
    Hispanic Service Center, 349–50
Historic Annapolis Antiques Show, 169
Historic Country Inns, 326
Historic Garden Week in Virginia, 173
Historic Savage Mill, 163
history, 20–30
Holiday Inn Capitol at the Smithsonian, 59
Holiday Inn National Airport, 67
Hollywood Cemetery, 321
Hollywood Contemporary Ballroom, 138
Holton-Arms School, 407
Holy Cross Hospital of Silver Spring, 385
Home Rule, 155
Homestead Resort, 326–27, 331
horse events, 284–86
Hospital for Sick Children, The, 378
Hospitality Information Service,
    The (THIS), 350
hospitals, 376–89
    Alexandria, 380–81
    Anne Arundel County, 384–85
    Arlington County, 381

Fairfax County, 381–83
Loudoun County, 383
Montgomery County, 385–87
Northern Virginia, 380–84
Prince George's County, 387–88
Prince William County, 384
psychiatric, 388–89
Spotsylvania County, 384
Suburban Maryland, 384–88
Washington, D.C., 376–80
hostels/university inns, 71–72
Hotel George, 59–60
Hotel Harrington, 69
Hotel Helix, 60
Hotel Lombardy, 60
Hotel Monaco, 60
Hotel Monaco, Alexandria, 66–67
Hotel Rouge, 60
hotels, extended-stay, 51–57
Alexandria, 55
Arlington, 55
Fairfax County, 56
Montgomery County, 57
Northern Virginia, 55–56
Prince George's County, 56–57
Suburban Maryland, 56–57
Washington, D.C., 51–55
hotels, full-service, 57–69
Alexandria, 66–67
Arlington County, 67–68
Fairfax County, 64–66
Loudoun County, 68
Montgomery County, 68–69
Northern Virginia, 64–68
Prince George's County, 69
Suburban Maryland, 68–69
Washington, D.C., 57–64
Hotel Strasburg, 325
Hotel Washington, 61
hot lines, mental-health crisis, 392
House in the Country, 164
House of Sweden, 350
Housing and Human Services, 371
HOV restrictions, 37–38
Howard County, Maryland, 16–18
Howard University, 283, 410–11
Howard University Hospital, 378–79
H Street Martini Lounge, 127

Human Services Coordinator, 371
hunt country, 321–22
Huntley Meadows Park and Visitor Center, 295
Hyatt Regency Bethesda, 68–69
Hyatt Regency Crystal City, 67
Hyatt Regency Washington on Capitol Hill, 61

I

I-495 (Capital Beltway), 34–36
ice hockey, 286–87
ice skating, 306–7
Ida Lee Recreation Center, 425
IKEA Washington, 260
Il Pizzico, 119
Il Radicchio, 108–9
Imagination Station, 264
Improv, The, 131
income taxes, 364
IndeBleu, 93
Indian restaurants, 93
Inga's Once Is Not Enough, 159
Inn at Buckeystown, 330
Inn at Little Washington, 324
Inn at Perry Cabin, 333
inns, extended-stay. See hotels, extended-stay
Inova Alexandria Hospital, The, 380
Inova Emergency Care of Fairfax, 391–92
Inova Emergency Care of Leesburg, 391–92
Inova Emergency Care of Reston/Herndon, 392
Inova Fairfax Hospital, 382
Inova Fairfax Hospital for Children, 382–83
Inova Fair Oaks Hospital, 382
Inova HealthPlex Franconia/Springfield, 392
Inova Mount Vernon Hospital, 380–81
Inova Urgent Medical Care, 391
inspirational radio, 452
interdenominational worship resources, 438
interest groups, national, 349–51
Interfaith Conference of Metropolitan
    Washington, 438
Interior Museum, The, 194
International Children's Festival, 181
International Gold Cup Races, The, 285
International Guest House, The, 69
International Language Centre, 151
International Monetary Fund Center, 343
International Spy Museum, 204, 252

international Washington, 342–51
  currency exchange, 345
  embassies, 344–45, 346
  ethnic neighborhoods, 347
  heritage festivals, 349
  international landmarks, 347
  national interest groups, 349–51
  resources for international visitors,
    343–44
  translation services, 345
IONA Senior Services, 418, 421
IOTA, 133
Ireland's Own, 133
i Ricchi, 94
Irish Times, 124
Irvington, Virginia, 337
Islamic Center of Washington, D.C., 350, 435
Italian Cultural Society of Washington,
  D.C., 351
Italian restaurants
  Northern Virginia, 108–10
  Suburban Maryland, 118–20
  Washington, D.C., 93–95
Italian Store, 109

J

J. R.'s Stockyards Inn, 98–99
Jack's Boathouse, 288
Jaleo, 96
James Monroe Museum and Library, 322
Jamestown Colonial National Historical
  Park, 317
Janet Annenberg Hooker Hall of Geology,
  Gems, and Minerals, 200–201
Japan-America Society of Washington, 350
Japan Information and Culture Center, 350
Jaxx, 133
jazz radio, 451
Jean-Michel, 117
Jeepers, 267
Jefferson, The, 429
Jefferson Hotel, 321
Jefferson Vineyards, 320
Jewish Community Center of Greater
  Washington, 315–16, 426–27
Jewish Community Center of Northern
  Virginia, 425–26

Jewish community centers, 315–16
Jewish Council for the Aging of Greater
  Washington, 422
Jewish Information and Referral Service of
  Greater Washington, 440
Jewish Social Service Agency, 422
Jewish worship resources, 440
jobs, 9–10
Joe Theismann's, 135
John F. Kennedy Center for the Performing
  Arts, 157, 223, 226, 269
Jokes On Us Comedy Club, 138–39
Jurys Normandy Inn, 61
Jurys Washington Hotel, 61
JW Marriott, 61

K

Kalorama Guest House at Kalorama Park, 73
Kalorama House and Embassy Tour, 180
Kaz Sushi Bistro, 88
Kenilworth Park and Aquatic Gardens, 291
Kennedy Center Open House, 180
Kensington, Maryland, 362
Kensington Labor Day Parade, 181–82
Key Bridge Marriott, 67
kidstuff, 249–75
  amusements, 267–69
  books and toys, 263–65
  crafts, 265–67
  farms, 255–57, 262–63
  museums, 249–55
  parks, 271–75
  pottery painting, 265–66
  restaurants, 258–62
  theater, 269–71
  Kidwell Farm at Frying Pan Park, 256
Kilroy's, 99
Kingstowne, Virginia, 359
Kinkead's, 80–81, 130
kites, 307
Komi, 81
Korean War Veterans Memorial, 190
Kramerbooks & afterwords Cafe & Grill, 124,
  126, 151
Kreeger Museum, The, 236
Kunta Kinte Heritage Commemoration and
  Festival, 182

L

La Bergerie, 105
Labor Day Weekend Concert, 180
Lab School of Washington, The, 400
La Chaumiére, 90
La Cote d'Or Cafe, 105
La Ferme, 118
La Fourchette, 90
Lake Accotink Park, 273, 295
Lake Anne, Virginia, 360
Lake Fairfax Park, 273
Lakeforest Mall, 147
La Miche, 118
Landmark, 357
Landmark E Street Cinema, 245–46
Landmark Mall, 145
Landon School, 407
Langley School, The, 404–5
Langston Golf Course and Driving Range, 304
Lansburgh, The, 52–53
Lansdowne Resort, 68
Latter-day Saints, 438
L'Auberge Chez François, 105–6
Laurel Department of Parks and Recreation, 314, 427
Laurel Park, 285–86
Lavandou, 90
Layalina, 110
Lazy Susan Dinner Theater, 136
Lebanese Taverna Restaurant, 95
LeDroit Park, 356
Lee Chapel, 326
Lee-Fendall House Museum and Garden, 214
Leesburg, Virginia, 361
Leesburg Corner Premium Outlets, 148
Leesburg Department of Parks and Recreation, 314
Leesburg Municipal Airport, 48
Leesylvania State Park, 296
Legal Times, 449
Le Gaulois, 106
Legg Mason Tennis Classic, 287–88
Leisure World of Maryland, 430
L'Enfant Plaza Hotel, 62
Le Paradou, 90–91
Le Refuge, 106
Le Vieux Logis, 118

Lexington, Virginia, 326
Library of Congress, 194–95
Library of Congress National Book Festival, 183
lifestyle newspapers, 448–49
Likely Story, A, 264–65
Lillian and Albert Small Jewish Museum, 434
Lillian Laurence Ltd., 162
Lincoln Memorial, 190
Linden Row Inn, 321
literary arts, 247
literary landmark, 438
Little Bennett Regional Park, 298
Lobby Lounge, 133
Locate: Childcare, 372
Long & Foster Real Estate Inc., 365
Longwood Manor Bed and Breakfast, 74
Loudoun Country Day School, 405
Loudoun County, Virginia
    area overview, 13–14
    bed and breakfasts, 74
    child care, 372
    full-service hotels, 68
    hospitals, 383
    neighborhoods and homes, 360–61
Loudoun County Area Agency on Aging, 419
Loudoun County Convention and Visitors Association, 17
Loudoun County Department of Parks, Recreation, and Community Services, 313, 426
Loudoun County Public Schools, 397–98
Loudoun Hospital Inova, 383
Louise F. Cosca Regional Park, 298
Louisiana Express Company, 112
LOVE, 128
Lucky Strike Lanes, 302
Luray Caverns, 325
Lyceum, The, 214

M

Madam's Organ, 126
Madeira School, The, 405
Madison, The, 62
Maestro, 109
Mainstay Inn, 339
Major League Baseball, 277–78
Makato, 88–89

malls and prime shopping districts, 140–47
    Northern Virginia, 143–46
    Suburban Maryland, 146–47
    Washington, D.C., 140–43
Mama Ayesha's, 95
Mama Wok and Teriyaki, 115
Manassas, Virginia, 325
Manassas Department of Recreation and
    Parks, 311
Manassas Museum, 325
Manassas Park Department of Parks
    Recreation, 311
Manassas Regional Airport, 48–49
Manchester Lakes, Virginia, 359
Mandarin Oriental, Washington, DC, 62
Maple Hall Inn, 326
Maplewood Park Place, 430–31
Marcel's, 91
Marine Corps Marathon, 183, 287
Mariner Sailing School, The, 308
Mariners Museum, 338
Market House, 340
Mark Keshishian & Sons Inc. Oriental
    Rugs, 165
Marlo Furniture Warehouse & Showroom, 155
Marrakesh, 95
Marriott Residence Inn Herndon/Reston, 56
Marriott Suites Bethesda, 56
Marriott Suites/Washington Dulles, 56
Marriott Wardman Park, 62
Martin Luther King Jr.'s Birthday
    Observance, 167
Maryland. See also Suburban Maryland
    day trips and weekend getaways, 328–41
    tourism offices, 17, 322
Maryland Book Exchange, 153
Maryland College of Art and Design, 415
Maryland Commuter Rail Service (MARC), 44
Maryland Department of Aging, 419
Maryland Department of Business and
    Economic Development, 18
Maryland Department of Natural
    Resources/State Forest and Parks
    Service, 315
Maryland Kite Society, 307
Maryland-National Capital Park and Planning
    Commission, 315, 427
Maryland Office of Tourist Development, 17

Maryland Renaissance Festival, 179
Maryland Science Center, 337
Maryland Seafood Festival, 182
Maryland SoccerPlex and Discovery Sports
    Center, 309
Maryland State House, 217, 340
Maryland Transportation Authority, 38
Marymount University, 412–13
Mary Washington Hospital, 384
Mason Neck State Park, 296
Matchbox, 81
Matuba, 103, 115
Mazza Gallerie, 140
McCampbell Inn, 326
McLean, Virginia, 358
McLean Project for the Arts, 243
Meadowlark Gardens Regional Park, 273, 296
media, 441–54
    national membership magazines, 449–51
    newspapers, 442–49
    radio, 451–52
    regional publications, 450–51
    television, 452–54
Medlin Art Ltd., 243
Meeps & Aunt Neensie's Fashionette, 159
meet and greet nightlife
    Northern Virginia, 134–36
    Suburban Maryland, 137–39
Melrose Hotel, The, 62–63
Memorial Day Ceremonies, 173, 174
Memorial Day Weekend Concert, 173
mental-health crisis hot lines, 392
Meridian International Center, 343, 350–51
Meridian International Center Language
    Bank, 345
Merriweather Post Pavilion, 230
Meskerem, 87
Methodist Home of the District of
    Columbia, 428
Metro, 39–41
Metro Herald, The, 445
Metropolitan African Methodist Episcopal
    Church, 434
Metropolitan Washington, D.C. Synod of
    the Evangelical Lutheran Church of
    America, 439
Metropolitan Washington Council of
    Governments (COG), 18, 373

Mid-Atlantic Yoga Association, Inc., 309–10
Middleburg, Virginia, 361
Middle Eastern/Indian/Afghan/Mediterranean
   restaurants
      Northern Virginia, 110–11
      Suburban Maryland, 120–21
      Washington, D.C., 95–96
Military Band Concerts, 175
minor league baseball, 279–80
Mi Rancho, 121
Miss Hampton II, 338
Mitchellville, Maryland, 362
Modern, 128
Monocacy National Battlefield Park, 330
Montgomery Business Gazette, 447
Montgomery College, 415–16
Montgomery County, Maryland
area overview, 14–15
   child care, 372
   extended-stay hotels and inns, 57
   full-service hotels, 68–69
   hospitals, 385–87
   neighborhoods and homes, 361–63
Montgomery County Agricultural Fair, 179
Montgomery County Child Care Resource and
   Referral Center, 372
Montgomery County Conference and Visitors
   Bureau, 17
Montgomery County Department of Economic
   Development, 18
Montgomery County Department of Health
   and Human Services Aging and Disability
   Services, 420
Montgomery County Department of Recre-
   ation, 315, 427
Montgomery County Infants and Toddlers
   Program, 372
Montgomery County Public Schools, 398–99
Montgomery County Sentinel, 446
Montgomery General Hospital, 385
Monticello, 319–20
Montmartre, 91
monuments, 189–93
Morris House, 337
Morrison-Clark Inn, The, 63
Morrison House, 67
Mortgage Banking, 447
Morton's of Chicago, 99

Morven Park International Equestrian
   Center, 285
Motel 6 Gaithersburg, 71
Mothers' Aides Inc., 374
Mountain Lake Hotel, 326
mountain resorts, 326–27
Mount Pleasant, 354
Mount Vernon, 214–15, 256
Mount Vernon, Virginia, 359
Mount Vernon Inn Gift Shop, 157–58
Mount Vernon Open House, 170
movies, 245–47
Mr. Smith's of Georgetown, 81, 130
Muleh, 155
Murphy's of Alexandria, 133
Museum of the Confederacy, 321
museums
   kidstuff, 249–55
   Northern Virginia, 211–16, 254
   Suburban Maryland, 216–18, 255
   Washington, D.C., 198–208, 234–42,
      249–54
museum shops, 157–59
music and dancing, live
   Northern Virginia, 132–34
   Suburban Maryland, 137
   Washington, D.C., 123–26
Music Box Center, 165
Muslim Community Center, 351
Muvico Egyptian 24 Theatres, 247

N

Nam Viet, 103
Nannie Helen Burroughs School Inc., 401
nannies, 373–74
Nannies, Inc., 374
Narcotics Anonymous Hotline, 392
NASA Goddard Space Flight Center Visitor
   Center, 255
National Air and Space Museum, 158,
   198–99, 250
National Aquarium, 195, 252–53, 336–37
National Archives Building, 195
National Archives Museum Store, 158
National Association for the Education of
   Young Children (NAEYC), 373

National Association of Retired Federal
Employees (NARFE), 421
National Black Child Development
Institute, 373
National Building Museum, 158, 204–5, 253
National Capital Presbytery, 439
National Caucus and Center on Black Aged
(NCBA), 421
National Cherry Blossom Festival, 170
National Children's Museum, 205, 251
National Christmas Tree Lighting/Pageant of
Peace, 186
National City Christian Church, 434
National Colonial Farm of the Accokeek
Foundation, 257
National Council for International Visitors, 351
National Council on the Aging Inc. (NCOA), 421
National Duckpin Bowling Congress, 302
National Gallery of Art, 158, 205, 236–38,
253–54, 259
National Gallery of Art Sculpture Garden
Ice-Skating Rink, 307
National Geographic Magazine, 450
National Geographic Society, 158, 206
National Geographic Society's Explorers
Hall, 254
National Historic Seaport of Baltimore, 337
National Independence Day Celebration, 178
National Institutes of Health, 217–18, 385–86
national interest groups, 349–51
National Law Enforcement Officers Memorial,
The, 190
National Mall and Memorial Parks, 198–202,
291–92
national membership magazines, 449–51
National Museum of African Art, 158, 199,
238, 250
National Museum of American History,
199, 250
National Museum of Civil War Medicine, 330
National Museum of Natural History,
199–201, 251
National Museum of the American Indian, 158,
199, 251
National Museum of Women in the Arts, 158,
206, 238–39, 254
National Naval Medical Center, 386

National Organization for Victim
Assistance, 392
National Park Service National Capital
Region, 311
National Postal Museum, 202, 251
National Presbyterian Church and Center, 434
National Public Radio, 451
National Rehabilitation Hospital, 379
National Shrine of St. Elizabeth Ann Seton, 330
National Theatre, The, 226–27
National Wildlife Visitor Center, 219, 255
National World War II Memorial, 190–91
National Zoological Park, 202–3, 272
Nation's Capital Area Bowling Association, 302
Naval Academy, 340
Navy Museum, The, 206, 254
Needwood Golf Course, 305
neighborhoods and homes, 353–63
Alexandria, 357
Arlington County, 357–58
ethnic neighborhoods, 347
Fairfax County, 358–60
Loudoun County, 360–61
Montgomery County, 361–63
Northern Virginia, 356–61
Prince George's County, 363
Prince William County, 360–61
Suburban Maryland, 361–63
Washington, D.C., 208–9, 353–56
New Deal, 26–27
New Market, Maryland, 330
New Republic, The, 449
Newseum, 206
newspapers, 442–49
African American, 447
business and real estate, 447
community, 444–46
dailies, 442–44
foreign, 448
lifestyles, 448–49
political, 449
senior scene, 420
Newsroom, The, 151
newsstands, 150–53
news/talk/sports/information radio, 451–52
News World, 151
New York Avenue Presbyterian Church, 133
nightclubs, 126–29

nightlife, 122–39
    Northern Virginia, 131–36
    Suburban Maryland, 136–39
    Washington, D.C., 123–31
Nighttime Pediatrics, 392
9:30 Club, 126
94th Aero Squadron, 139
Nissan Pavilion at Stone Ridge, 229
Nizam's, 110
Norris House, 322
Norris House Inn, The, 74
Northeast neighborhoods, 356
Northern Virginia. *See* also Northern Virginia
    restaurants
      airports, 48–49
      amusements, 267
      annual events, 169–70, 171, 172–73, 174,
        175–77, 178, 179, 180–81, 183–84,
        186–87
      area agencies on aging, 417–19
      area overview, 11–14
      attractions, 211–16
      bed and breakfasts, 73–74
      bookstores, newsstands and toys, 153,
        264–65
      budget accommodations, 70
      bus systems, 42–43
      cable TV, 453
      child care, 370–72
      cinema, 246
      colleges and universities, 412–13
      community and senior centers, 424–26
      community colleges, 415
      community newspapers, 445–46
      convention and tourist bureaus, 17
      extended-stay hotels and inns, 55–56
      farms, 256–57, 262
      full-service hotels, 64–68
      galleries, 243–44
      golf, 304–5
      horse events, 285
      hospitals, 380–84
      Jewish community centers, 315–16
      kidstuff, 254, 256–57, 262, 269–70,
        272–74
      malls and prime shopping districts,
        143–46
      minor league baseball, 279
      museums, 254
      neighborhoods and homes, 356–61
      nightlife, 131–36
      outdoor stages, 229–30
      parks, 272–74, 293–97
      parks and recreation authorities, 311–14
      performing arts venues, 227–28
      private schools, 402–6
      public schools, 395–98
      retirement communities, 428–29
      senior resources, 421–22
      soccer, 308–9
      theater, 233–34, 269–70
      walk-in clinics, 391–92
      watersports, 288
Northern Virginia Christmas Craft Market,
    186–87
Northern Virginia Community College, 415
Northern Virginia Country Western Dance
    Association, 303
Northern Virginia Regional Park Authority, 314
Northern Virginia restaurants, 96–111
    American/Continental, 96–101
    Asian, 101–4
    French, 104–6
    Hispanic/Caribbean/Tex-Mex, 106–8
    Italian, 108–10
    kid-friendly, 260–61
    Middle Eastern/Indian/Afghan, 110–11
Northwest Current, 444
Northwest neighborhood, 354
Now This! Kids!, 271
nursing homes, 390
Nysmith School for the Gifted, 405

O

Oakton, Virginia, 359–60
Oakwood, 55
Oatlands Plantation, 215
Obelisk, 94–95
O'Brien's Pit Barbecue, 112
Occoquan Fall Craft Show, 181
Ocean City, Maryland, 338
Octagon, The, 206–7
Odyssey Cruises, 219
Office of Community Education—Extended
    Day Care Office, 372

Off the Record, 130–31
O'Hurley's General Store, 328
Oktoberfest, 181
Okyo Beauty Salon, 162
Old Angler's Inn, 112–13
Old Dominion Speedway and Dragstrip, 287
Old Ebbitt Grill, 81–82
Older Adult Service and Information System
    (OASIS), 422–23
Old Europe, 91
Old Glory, 82
oldies and classic rock radio, 452
Old Post Office Pavilion, The, 140–41, 195
Old Presbyterian Meeting House, 435,
    437, 438
Old Town, 357
Old Town Crier, 445
Old Town News, 153
Old Town Trolley Tours, 219
Olney Ale House, 113
Olney Theatre Center for the Arts, 234
Olsson's Books & Records, 152, 153
OmniRide, 42–43
Once Upon a Time, 265
One Washington Circle, 53
Organization of American States (OAS),
    195–96, 343
orienteering, 307
Oriole Park, 336
outdoor stages, 228–30
outlet malls, 148–49
Over-60 Counseling and Employment
    Service, 423
Oxford, Maryland, 333
Oxon Hill Farm, 257
Ozio Restaurant & Lounge, 131

P

P. J. Skidoos, 135
Paint Your Own Pottery, 266
Pam Newton & Company, 422, 423
Paolo's Ristorante, 109
Paradiso Ristorante, 260
Parent Encouragement Program (PEP), 373
Parenting Resource Center, 372
Park Fairfax, 357
Park Hyatt Washington, 63

Park Place, 165, 428
parks, 289–99, 312–13. See also recreation
    kidstuff, 271–75
    Northern Virginia, 272–74, 293–97
    Suburban Maryland, 274–75, 297–99
    Washington, D.C., 272, 289–92
parkways, 37
Pasha Cafe, 110–11
Pathways Magazine, 448
Patricia's Skin Care Center, 162
Patriot Center at George Mason University,
    227–28
Peking Gourmet Inn, 103
Pennsylvania Avenue, 354
Pennsylvania tourism office, 322
Pentagon, The, 215
Pentagon City, Virginia, 358
performing arts venues, 221–28
    Northern Virginia, 227–28
    Suburban Maryland, 228
    Washington, D.C., 221–27
Permits and Regulation (family child-care
    homes), 371
Perry's, 89
Pershing Park Ice Rink, 307
Persimmon, 113
Phillips Collection, The, 207, 239
Pho 75, 103, 115
Phoenix Park Hotel, 63
physician referrals, 376
piano music, 129–30
Piedmont Behavioral Health Center, 389
Piedmont Vineyards, 325
Pimlico Race Course, 286
Pines of Rome, 119
Play Wise Kids, 255
Pleasant Springs Farm, 74
Pohick Bay Regional Park, 296–97
Pohick Bay Regional Park Golf Course, 304–5
Pohick Church, 438
Point Lookout State Park, 336
Poison Center, 392
political newspapers, 449
Politics & Prose Bookstore & Coffeehouse, 152
Polly's Café, 82
Polly Sue's Vintage Shop, 159–60
Pope-Leighey House, 216
Port Discovery Children's Museum, 337

Potomac, Maryland, 362
Potomac Gallery, The, 244
Potomac Hospital, 384
Potomac Mills, 148
Potomac Nannies, Ltd., 374
Potomac Nationals, 279
Potomac Party Cruises, Inc., 220
Potomac Riverboat Company, 220
Potomac School, The, 405
pottery painting, 265–66
Pouillon, Nora, 82–83, 84–85
Prime Outlets Hagerstown, 149
Prime Rib, 82
Prince George's Community College, 416
Prince George's Community College Blue Bird
    Blues Festival, 182
Prince George's County, Maryland
    area overview, 15–16
    child care, 373
    extended-stay hotels and inns, 56–57
    full-service hotels, 69
    hospitals, 387–88
    neighborhoods and homes, 363
Prince George's County Conference and
    Visitors Bureau, 17
Prince George's County Department of Family
    Services, Aging Services Division, 420
Prince George's County Department of Parks
    and Recreation, 315
Prince George's County Economic Develop-
    ment Corp., 18
Prince George's County Fair, 182
Prince George's County Public Schools, 399
Prince George's Hospital Center, 388
Prince George's Post, The, 447
Prince George's Publick Playhouse for the Per-
    forming Arts, 228
Prince George's Sentinel, 446
Prince William Area Agency on Aging, 419
Prince William County, Virginia
    area overview, 13
    child care, 372
    hospitals, 384
    neighborhoods and homes, 360–61
Prince William County/Manassas Conference
    and Visitors Bureau, 17
Prince William County Office of Economic
    Development, 19

Prince William County Park Authority, 314, 426
Prince William County Public Schools, 398
Prince William Forest Park, 297
Prince William Hospital, 384
property taxes, 363–64
Prospect Hill Plantation Inn, 320
Protestant worship resources, 438–40
Providence Hospital, 379
psychiatric hospitals, 388–89
Psychiatric Institute of Washington, D.C., 389
Public Schools Extended Day Program, 371
Pulp, 165
Puppet Co. Playhouse, The, 271

Q

Quality Inn Iwo Jima, 70
Quantico Orienteering Club, 307
Quincy, The, 53

R

radio, 451–52
Railey Realty, 331
Rainforest Cafe, 260–61
Ramsay House Visitors Center, 215
Ranson-Armory, 328
Rape Crisis Hotline, 392
Rasika, 93
Raspberry Falls Golf & Hunt Club, 305
Ray's the Classics, 114
Ray's the Steaks, 99
RCN, 453, 454
real estate companies, 364–65
recreation, 299–316. See also parks
    amusement parks, 299–300
    ballooning, 300
    bicycling, 300–301
    bird watching, 301
    bowling, 301–2
    chess, 302
    climbing, 302–3
    dancing, 303
    golf, 303–5
    hang gliding, 305–6
    ice skating, 306–7
    Jewish community centers, 315–16
    kites, 307

orienteering, 307
outdoor sports, 308
running, 308
sailing, 308
soccer, 308–9
Ultimate Frisbee, 309
YMCA, 316
yoga, 309–10
youth sports, 310
Red, Hot & Blue, 99–100, 113
Red Cross Waterfront Festival, 177
Red Fox Inn, 331
Red Fox Inn and Tavern, 321
Red Roof Inn Downtown D.C., 69–70
Reedville, Virginia, 337
Reef, The, 128–29
regional publications, 450–51
Rehoboth Beach, Delaware, 338–39
Reincarnations, 155
Reiter's, 152
religious/inspirational/gospel radio, 452
religious sites, 209–10
relocation, 352–67
    guidelines, 365–67
    information, 365–67
    neighborhoods and homes, 353–63
    property and income taxes, 363–64
    real estate companies, 364–65
    residential real estate market, 352–53
RE/MAX, 365
Renaissance Mayflower, 63
Renaissance Washington, D.C. Hotel, 63
Renwick Gallery, 203, 239
Reprint Bookshop, 152
residential real estate market, 352–53
Restaurant Eve, 100
Restaurant Nora, 82–83, 84–85
restaurants, 76–121
    African, 85, 87
    American/Continental, 76–85, 96–101,
        111–14
    Asian, 87–89, 101–4, 114–17
    French, 90–91, 104–6, 117–18
    German, 91
    Hispanic/Caribbean/Tex-Mex, 91–93,
        106–8, 121
    Indian, 93
    Italian, 93–95, 108–10, 118–20
    kid-friendly, 258–62
    Middle Eastern/Indian/Afghan/Mediter-
        ranean, 95–96, 110–11, 120–21
    Northern Virginia, 96–111
    Spanish, 96, 121
    Suburban Maryland, 111–21
    Washington, D.C., 76–96
Reston, Virginia, 360
Reston Community Center, 314
Reston Hospital Center, 383
Reston National Golf Course, 305
Reston Storefront Museum & Shop, 266–67
Retired and Senior Volunteer Program
    (RSVP)/The Campagna Center, 422
retirement communities, 427–31
    Northern Virginia, 428–29
    Suburban Maryland, 429–31
    Washington, D.C., 428
Retirement Unlimited Inc., 429
Reynolds of Derwood Bed and Breakfast,
    The, 74–75
RFK Stadium, 228–29
Richmond, Virginia, 320–21
Ride-On, 43
Riderwood Village, 431
Rio Grande Cafe, 107–8, 121
Ritz-Carlton, Pentagon City, 67
Ritz-Carlton Tysons Corner, 65
Riverdale Baptist School, 407
River Farm, 273
River Inn, The, 53
River Run at Prince William Commons, 428
River & Trail Outfitters, 328
Road Runners Club of America, 308
roadways, 34–39
Robert M. Watkins Regional Park, 274, 298
Robert Morris Inn, 333
Roche Salon, 163
Rock Creek Park, 272, 292
Rock Creek Park Day, 180
Rock Creek Park Golf Course, 304
Rock Creek Regional Park, 299
rock radio, 452
Rockville, Maryland, 362
Rockville Recreation and Parks
    Department, 314
Rockville Senior Center, 427
Rod N Reel Dock, 336

Roll Call, 449
Roman Catholic worship resources, 440
Romano's Macaroni Grill, 262
Ronald Reagan Washington National Airport,
    46–47
Rosa Mexicano, 92
Rosecroft Raceway, 286
Rosemont, 357
Rosslyn, Virginia, 358
Rotary Crab Feast, 179
Round House Theatre, 234
Royal Mile Pub, The, 137
running
    recreation, 308
    spectator sports, 287

S

S. Dillon Ripley Center (The Smithsonian
    International Gallery), 202
Saah Unfinished Furniture, 156
Sabang, 116
sailing, 308
Saint Elizabeth's Hospital, 389
Saint Luke Institute, 389
Salon Jean Paul, 163
Sam Woo, 116
Savage River, 331
Savoy Suites Georgetown, 53
Scandal Tours of Washington, 220
School-Age Child Care Program, 371
schools, private, 399–407
    Northern Virginia, 402–6
    Suburban Maryland, 406–7
    Washington, D.C., 399–402
schools, public, 394–99
    Northern Virginia, 395–98
    Suburban Maryland, 398–99
    Washington, D.C., 394–95
Schooner Nighthawk Cruises, 336
Science Club, 128
Scottish Rite Temple, 435
secondhand stores, 159–60
Secondi, 160
Second Story Books Inc., 152, 153
Secure Medical Care Center, 393
Seminary, 357

Seneca Creek State Park, 299
Seneca Rocks, 327
Senior Beacon InfoExpo, 182
Senior Beacon newspaper, 420
senior scene, 417–31
    area agencies on aging, 417–20
    community and senior centers, 423–27
    publications, 420
    retirement communities, 427–31
    senior resources, 420–23
Seniors Coalition, The, 422
Senior's Interfaith Resource Center,
    Inc. (SIRC), 423
September 11, 2001 attacks, 8–9
Sergio's Ristorante Italiano, 119–20
Seven Seas Chinese Restaurant, 116
1789 Restaurant, 83
7300 Van Dusen Road, 387–88
Sewall-Belmont House, 207
Shady Grove Adventist Hospital, 386
Shakespeare's Birthday Celebration, 172
Shakespeare Theatre, The, 231, 233
Shakespeare Theatre Company Free-for-All,
    The, 175
Shark Club, The, 133–34
Shaw, 356
Shenandoah National Park, 323
Shepherd Park, 356
Sheraton Premiere at Tysons Corner, 66
Sheraton Suites Old Town Alexandria, 55
Sheridan School, 401
Shoney's, 262
shopping, 140–66
    antiques districts, 149–50
    bookstores and newsstands, 150–53
    furniture and home decorating,
        153–57, 160
    malls and prime shopping districts,
        140–47
    museum shops, 157–59
    outlet malls, 148–49
    secondhand stores, 159–60
    spas and salons, 160–63
    unique stores, 163–66
Shops at Chevy Chase Pavilion, The, 141
Shops at Georgetown Park, The, 141
Shops at National Place, The, 141
Showbar Presents the Palace of Wonders, 128

Show Place Arena, The, 286
Sibley Memorial Hospital, 379–80
Sidwell Friends School, 401
Signature Theatre, 233–34
Silent Drill Platoon Sunset Parades, 176–77
Silver Diner, 100, 113–14, 262
Silver Spring, Maryland
    budget accommodations, 71
    neighborhoods and homes, 362
Silver Wings Inc., 305–6
Six Flags America, 267, 269, 299–300
Sixth & I Historic Synagogue, 434
skiing, 331–32
Ski Liberty, 331
Skyline Drive, 323
Sky Meadows State Park, 321
Smith Island, Maryland, 333–34
Smithsonian American Art Museum and
    National Portrait Gallery, 157, 202,
    239–41
    arts, 240–41
Smithsonian Craft Show, 172
Smithsonian Folklife Festival, 175
Smithsonian Information Center, The, 249
Smithsonian Institution
    kidstuff, 249–51
    on the National Mall, 198–202
    off the National Mall, 202–3
Smithsonian International Gallery, The, 202
Smithsonian Kite Festival, 171
Smithsonian Magazine, 450
Snowshoe, 331
soccer
    recreation, 308–9
    spectator sports, 287
Solomons, Maryland, 336
Solomons Pier, 336
Sommerset Retirement Community, 429
soul/talk radio, 452
South Austin Grill, 107–8
Southeastern District, Lutheran Church—
    Missouri Synod, 439
Southeastern University, 411
South Fairlington, 357
South Germantown Recreational Park, 299
Southside 815, 100–101
Southwest neighborhoods, 356
Spanish restaurants, 96, 121

spas and salons, 160–63
spectator sports, 276–88
Sperryville, Virginia, 324
Spices Asian Restaurant & Sushi Bar, 89
Spirit Cruises, 220
SplashDown Waterpark, 273–74
Sportrock Climbing Centers, 267, 302–3
sports, outdoor, 308
sports, spectator, 276–88
    baseball, 277–80
    basketball, 280–81, 283
    football, 283–84
    horse events, 284–86
    ice hockey, 286–87
    running, 287
    soccer, 287
    stock car racing, 287
    tennis, 287–88
    watersports, 288
sports bars, 129
Sports Network, 309
Spotsylvania County hospitals, 384
Springfield, Virginia, 359
Springfield Mall Regional Shopping Center, 145
Spring Valley, 354
St. Anselm's Abbey School, 401
St. John's College, 340
St. John's College High School, 402
St. John's Episcopal Church, 133–34
St. Mary's Catholic Church, 438
St. Matthew's Cathedral, 434
St. Michael's, Maryland, 333
St. Patrick's Day Parade, 170–71, 171
St. Patrick's Episcopal Day School, 402
St. Paul's, 434–35
St. Regis Washington, D.C., The, 63–64
St. Stephen's & St. Agnes School, 405–6
Stabler-Leadbeater Apothecary Shop, 215
Stafford County, Virginia, 13–14
stages, outdoor, 228–30
Stained Glass Pub Too, 261
Starland Cafe, 83
State Plaza Hotel, The, 53, 55
state tourism offices, 322
Steeles Tavern Manor, 323
Stephen Decatur House Museum, The, 159
Steven F. Udvar-Hazy Center, 254
stock car racing, 287

Stonehurst Inn, 329–30
Stonestreet Museum of 19th-Century Medicine, 216
Strasburg, Virginia, 325
Strasburg Emporium, 325
Strathmore Hall Arts Center, 228
Strayer University, 411
Studio Theatre, The, 233
Suburban Hospital, 386–87
Suburban Maryland. *See also* Suburban Maryland restaurants
   airports, 49
   amusements, 267, 269
   annual events, 169, 171, 174, 179, 181–82, 184, 187
   area agencies on aging, 417–20
   area overview, 14–18
   attractions, 216–18
   bed and breakfasts, 74–75
   bookstores, newsstands and toys, 153, 265
   budget accommodations, 71
   bus systems, 42–43
   cable TV, 454
   child care, 372–73
   cinema, 246–47
   colleges and universities, 413–15
   community and senior centers, 426–27
   community colleges, 415–16
   community newspapers, 446
   convention and tourist bureaus, 17
   extended-stay hotels and inns, 56–57
   farms, 257, 262–63
   full-service hotels, 68–69
   galleries, 244–45
   golf, 305
   horse events, 285–86
   hospitals, 384–88
   Jewish community centers, 316
   kidstuff, 255, 257, 262–63, 270–71, 274–75
   literary arts, 247
   malls and prime shopping districts, 146–47
   minor league baseball, 279–80
   museums, 255
   national interest groups, 351
   neighborhoods and homes, 361–63
   nightlife, 136–39
   outdoor stages, 230
   parks, 274–75, 297–99
   parks and recreation authorities, 314–15
   performing arts venues, 228
   private schools, 406–7
   public schools, 398–99
   retirement communities, 429–31
   senior resources, 422–23
   soccer, 309
   theater, 234, 270–71
   walk-in clinics, 392–93
   watersports, 288
Suburban Maryland restaurants, 111–21
   American/Continental, 111–14
   Asian, 114–17
   French, 117–18
   Italian, 118–20
   kid-friendly, 261
   Middle Eastern/Indian, 120–21
   Spanish, 121
   Tex-Mex/Hispanic, 121
Sugar House Day Spa & Salon, 162
Sugarloaf's Autumn Crafts Festival, 184
suicide counseling, 392
Sully Historic Site, 257
Summers Grill and Sports Pub, 135
Sunflower Vegetarian Restaurant, 103–4
Sun Gazette, 445
Sun & Moon Yoga Studio, 310
Suporn's, 116
Supreme Court of the United States, 196
Surrey, The, 165
Sushi-Ko, 89
Swann House Historic Dupont Circle Inn, 73
Sweetwater Tavern, 108, 136
Sycamore Hill House, 324
Sylvan Theatre, 229

T

Taberna del Alabardero, 96
Tachibana, 104
Tako Grill, 116–17
Takoma Park, Maryland, 362
Takoma Park Recreation Department, 315
Tangier Island, Virginia, 333–36
Tantallon, Maryland, 362

Taqueriz Distrito Federal, 93
Tara Thai, 104, 117
Taste of Bethesda, 184
Taste of Saigon, 117
taxes, property and income, 363–64
taxicabs, 44
TeacherCare, 374
Teaism Tea Shop, 165–66
television, 452–54
Tenleytown, 356
tennis, 287–88
Tennis Factory, 166
Textile Museum, The, 207, 242
That's Amore, 120
theater, 230–34
    kidstuff, 269–71
    Northern Virginia, 233–34, 269–70
    Suburban Maryland, 234, 270–71
    Washington, D.C., 230–33, 269
Theodore Roosevelt Memorial, 216
Theodore Roosevelt's Birthday
   Celebration, 183
Theodore's, 156–57
Third Edition, 129
Thomas Jefferson Memorial, 191–92
Thyme Square Cafe, 114
Tides Resort, 337
Tidewater Inn, 333
Tiffany Tavern, 134
Tilghman Island, Maryland, 333
Times Community Newspapers, 445–46
Tiny Jewel Box, 166
Tivoli Restaurant, 109–10
toll roads, 36–37
Tony Cheng's Mongolian Barbecue, 89
top 40/contemporary hits radio, 452
Torpedo Factory Art Center, 244
Tortilla Factory, 108
Touchstone Gallery, 243
tourist bureaus, 17, 322
Tourmobile Sightseeing, 220
tour operators, 218–20
Tower Oaks Lodge, 114
TownePlace Suites by Marriott, 56
Town of Leesburg Department of Parks and
   Recreation, 314
Town of Vienna Parks and Recreation Depart-
   ment, 314, 426

toys, 265
Tragara, 120
train service, 43–44
Tranquil Space, 310
translation services, 345
transportation, 31–49
    airports, 45–49
    bus systems, 41–43
    commuter aids, 44–45
    Metro, 39–41
    roadways, 34–39
    taxicabs, 44
    train service, 43–44
Travelers' Aid Society, 343
Travelex, 345
Treaty of Paris, 340–41
Trinity University, 411
Trotters Glen Family Golf Center, 305
Trover Shop, 152–53
Tuscarora Mill, 101
2941 Restaurant, 101
Twins Jazz, 126
Tysons Corner Center, 145–46
Tysons Galleria, 146

U

Ultimate Frisbee, 309
Unification Church of Washington, 435
Union Station, 141, 143, 259–60
Union Street Public House, 101, 136
United Church of Christ, Central Atlantic Con-
   ference, Potomac Association, 439
United Methodist General Board of Church
   and Society, 440
United Planning Organization/Project KEEN—
   Comprehensive Senior Services, 418
United States Botanic Garden
   Conservatory, 196
United States Capitol, 196–97
United States Chess Center, The, 302
United States Department of Agriculture, 197
United States Holocaust Memorial Museum,
   207–8
United States Information Agency, 197
United States Marine Corps Memorial, 216
United States National Arboretum, The, 208
United States Naval Academy, 219

United States Navy Memorial and Naval Heritage Center, 192
United States Powerboat Show, 184, 288
United States Sailboat Show, 184, 288
universities. *See* colleges and universities
university inns/hostels, 71–72
University of Maryland, 283, 414–15
University of Mary Washington, 413
University of the District of Columbia, 411–12
University Park, Maryland, 362
Upper Marlboro, Maryland, 362
Upperville, Virginia, 361
Upscale Resale, 160
Upton Hill Regional Park, 297
urban adult contemporary radio, 452
Urban Country Designs Ltd., 157
Urbanna, 337
USA Today, 444

V

Vegetable Garden, 117
Verizon Center, 227
Veterans Day Ceremonies, 184
Vidalia, 83
Vienna, Virginia, 359–60
Vienna Fall Carnival, 181
Vienna Halloween Parade, 183
Vienna Parks and Recreation Department, 314, 426
Vienna's Fourth of July Celebration, 178
Vietnam-Georgetown, 89
Vietnam Veterans Memorial, 192
Virginia. *See also* Northern Virginia
    colonial churches, 435, 437–38
    day trips and weekend getaways, 317–27
    tourism offices, 17, 322
Virginia Air & Space Center, 338
Virginia Bicycling Federation Inc., 300–301
Virginia Department for the Aging, 419
Virginia Department of Conservation and Recreation, 314
Virginia Department of Transportation, 38
Virginia Economic Development Partnership, 18
Virginia Gold Cup Races, The, 174, 285
Virginia Hospital Center, Arlington, 381
Virginia Marine Science Museum, 338

Virginia Museum of Fine Arts, 321
Virginian, The, 429
Virginian Suites, 55
Virginia Railway Express (VRE), 44
Virginia Regional Transportation Association, 43
Virginia's Coed Sports and Recreation Association, Inc., 309
Virginia Scottish Games, 181
Virginia Tech/University of Virginia Northern Virginia Center, 413
Virginia Tourism Corporation, 17
Visitor Information Center, 17
VMI Museum, 326
Voice of America Radio Network, 451

W

walk-in clinics, 391–93
Walkingtown, DC, 172
Warehouse Bar and Grill, 101
Warner Theatre, 227
War of 1812, 22
Washington, D.C. *See also* Washington, D.C. restaurants
    annual events, 167–69, 170–71, 172, 173–74, 174–75, 178, 180, 182–83, 186
    area agencies on aging, 417–18
    attractions, 189–211
    bed and breakfasts, 72–73
    bookstores and newsstands, 150–53
    budget accommodations, 69–70
    bus systems, 41–42
    cable TV, 453
    child care, 370
    cinema, 245–46
    colleges and universities, 408–12
    community and senior centers, 423–24
    community newspapers, 444–45
    convention and tourist bureaus, 17
    extended-stay hotels and inns, 51–55
    federal sites, 193–97
    full-service hotels, 57–64
    galleries, 234–43
    golf, 303–4
    hospitals, 376–80
    Jewish community centers, 315
    kidstuff, 249–54, 269, 272

malls and prime shopping districts, 140–43

museums, 198–208, 234–42, 249–54

national interest groups, 349–51

neighborhoods and homes, 208–9, 353–56

nightlife, 123–31

outdoor stages, 228–29

parks, 272, 289–92

parks and recreation authorities, 310–11

performing arts venues, 221–27

piano music, 129–30

private schools, 399–402

public schools, 394–95

retirement communities, 428

senior resources, 420–21

sports bars, 129

statistics, 4–5

theater, 230–33, 269

tourism offices, 17, 322

watersports, 288

worship, 432–35

Washington, D.C. Convention & Tourism Corporation, 17, 343–44

Washington, D.C. Economic Partnership, 18

Washington, D.C. *Examiner, The,* 442

Washington, D.C. restaurants, 76–96

   African, 85, 87

   American/Continental, 76–85

   Asian, 87–89

   French, 90–91

   German, 91

   Hispanic/Caribbean/Tex-Mex, 91–93

   Indian, 93

   Italian, 93–95

   kid-friendly, 258–62

   Middle Eastern/Mediterranean, 95–96

   Spanish, 96

Washington, D.C. Restaurant Week, 167, 169

Washington Adventist Hospital, 387

Washington Afro-American Newspaper, 447

Washington and Lee University, 326

Washington Area Bicyclist Association, 301

Washington Area Frisbee Club (WAFC), 309

Washington Auto Show, 186

Washington Blade, The, 448

Washington Boat Show, 169

Washington Business Journal, 447

Washington Child Development Council, 370

Washington City Paper, 444

Washington College, 332

Washington Dulles Airport Marriott, 66

Washington Dulles International Airport, 47–48

Washington Flyer Magazine, 450

Washington Home & Garden Show, 171

Washington Hospital Center, The, 380

Washingtonian, 450

Washington Informer Newspaper, The, 447

Washington International American Youth Hostel, 71–72

Washington International Film Festival (Filmfest D.C.), 172, 246

Washington International Horse Show, 183, 286

Washington International School, 402

Washington Jewish Week, 450–51

Washington Metropolitan Area Transit Authority (Metro), 39–41

Washington Metrorail, 344

Washington Monthly, 449

Washington Monument, 192–93

Washington Monument State Park, 329

Washington Mystics, 280

Washington National Cathedral, 159, 210, 432–33

Washington National Cathedral Christmas Celebration and Services, 186

Washington National Cathedral Flower Mart, 174

Washington Nationals, 277

Washington Photo Safari, 220

Washington Post, The, 443

Washington Redskins, 283–84

Washington Sailing Marina, 308

Washington Sun Newspaper, The, 445

Washington Temple of the Church of Jesus Christ of Latter-day Saints, 438

Washington Times, The, 443–44

Washington Walks, 220

Washington Wizards, The, 280

Washington Woman, 449

Washington Women Outdoors Inc., 308

Waterford Homes Tour and Crafts Exhibit, 184

Waterfowl Festival, 333

Waterfront, 356

Watergate era, 27–28
Waterlily Festival, 178
Water Park at Bohrer Park at Summit Hall
    Farm, 274–75
watersports, 288
weekend getaways. See day trips and week-
    end getaways
Weichert Realty, 365
Wesley Heights, 354
West End, 354
Western Maryland Scenic Railroad, 331
Westfield Shoppingtown Wheaton Plaza Shop-
    ping Center, 147
Westfields Marriott, 66
Westin Arlington Gateway, The, 67–68
Westin Embassy Row, 64
West Virginia
    day trips and weekend getaways, 327–28
    state tourism office, 322
Wheaton, Maryland, 362
Wheaton Regional Park, 275, 299
Whirligigs & Whimsies, 265
White Flint Mall, 147
White House, The, 197
White House Easter Egg Roll, 172
White House Nannies, 374
White House of the Confederacy, The, 321
White House Spring Garden and House
    Tours, 172
White Swan Tavern, 332–33
Whitetail, 331–32
White Tiger, The, 93
Whitlow's on Wilson, 136
Why Not?, 265
Willard InterContinental, The, 64
Willard Room, 83–84
William Paca House, 340
Winchester, Virginia, 325
Windsor Inn, 70
Windsor Park Hotel, 70
Wings Over Washington (WOW), 307
Wintergreen Child Development Center, 372
Wintergreen Resort, 320, 331
Wisp Resort, 332
Wolf Trap National Park for the Performing
    Arts, 229–30, 270
Woodlawn Plantation and Frank Lloyd Wright's
    Pope-Leighey House, 216

Woodlawn Plantation Annual Needlework
    Exhibition, 171
Woodley Park, 354
Woo Lae Oak, 104
Woolly Mammoth Theatre Company, 233
work force, 7–9
World Bank, 344
worship, 432–40
    colonial churches, 435, 437–38
    interdenominational, 438
    Jewish, 440
    Latter-day Saints, 438
    literary landmark, 438
    Protestant, 438–40
    religious sites, 209–10
    resources, 438–40
    Roman Catholic, 440
    spiritual legacy, 432–35
Writer's Center, The, 247
Wyndham Washington, D.C., 64

X

XM Satellite Radio, 451

Y

Yes Organic Market, 166
YMCA of Metropolitan Washington, 316, 424
yoga, 309–10
Yorktown National, 317
Youghiogheny River, 331
youth sports, 310

Z

Zaytinya, 95–96
Zed's Ethiopian Cuisine, 87
Zola, 84–85
ZYZYX Inc., 166

ABOUT THE AUTHORS

Mary Jane Solomon

A native of Dayton, Ohio, Mary Jane Hoak Solomon left the Buckeye State for the Old Dominion 20 years ago. She is well acquainted with Metro Washington, having lived in Washington, D.C., Rosslyn, Old Town Alexandria, Leesburg, and Reston before settling with her family in Annandale, Virginia, nine years ago.

As a lifestyle editor and feature writer at the *Alexandria Gazette* and the *Loudoun Times-Mirror*, Mary Jane received nine Virginia Press Association awards, including a first-place honor for an article about the effects of Alzheimer's disease on families. She also served as the *Times-Mirror*'s deputy editor, helping the paper earn the National Newspaper Association's top award for general excellence.

After a job producing special sections and the company newsletter for Arundel Communications Inc., Mary Jane decided to freelance so she could stay home with her then-infant daughter. Her articles appear regularly in the *Washington Post*'s "Weekend" section. She worked as entertainment editor for *Northern Virginia Parent*, which folded in April of 2004. She also has written for such publications as *Newsday, Where Washington Magazine, Sesame Street Parents*, and *The Journal*.

Mary Jane and her husband, Steve, live with daughters Rachel and Anna and cat Macaroon in the heart of Fairfax County. She enjoys exploring area attractions with her family, playing in the women's basketball league at the Jewish Community Center of Northern Virginia, and volunteering at her daughters' schools.

Barbara Ruben

Barbara Ruben has lived in the Washington

area for 22 years, since graduating from Miami University in Oxford, Ohio, and taking an internship with *National Geographic*. She has served as editor of a national environmental magazine and an international health magazine, and has written freelance articles for numerous publications, including the *Washington Post, Interactive Week*, and *Physician's Financial News*.

Barbara is currently managing editor of the *Senior Beacon*, a newspaper that reaches more than 300,000 Washington and Baltimore-area senior citizens, where she has won first-place awards for feature and news writing from the North American Mature Press Association and the Mature Market Resource Center. She is also a freelance reporter for the *Washington Post* and regularly writes about local restaurants, real estate, schools, and senior citizens.

Barbara lives in Kensington, Maryland, with her daughter, Sarah.